Joomla!™
Programming

Joomla! Press

Addison-Wesley

Visit **informit.com/joomlapress** for a complete list of available publications.

The mission of Joomla! Press is to enhance the Joomla! experience by providing useful, well-written, and engaging publications for all segments of the Joomla! Community from beginning users to platform developers. Titles in **Joomla! Press** are authored by the leading experts and contributors in the community.

Make sure to connect with us!
informit.com/socialconnect

Joomla!™
Programming

Mark Dexter
Louis Landry

♦♦Addison-Wesley

Upper Saddle River, NJ • Boston • Indianapolis • San Francisco
New York • Toronto • Montreal • London • Munich • Paris • Madrid
Capetown • Sydney • Tokyo • Singapore • Mexico City

Library of Congress Cataloging-in-Publication Data
Dexter, Mark, 1954–
    Joomla! programming / Mark Dexter, Louis Landry.
        p.   cm.
    Includes index.
    ISBN 978-0-13-278081-0 (pbk. : alk. paper) 1. Joomla! (Computer file) 2. Web sites—Authoring programs. 3. Web site development. I. Landry, Louis, 1980- II. Title.
    TK5105.8885.J86D492 2012
    006.7'6—dc23   2011052204

ISBN-13: 978-0-13-278081-0
ISBN-10:   0-13-278081-X

Text printed in the United States on recycled paper at at RR Donnelly in Crawfordsville, Indiana.
First printing, March 2012

Editor-in-Chief
Mark L. Taub

Executive Editor
Debra Williams Cauley

Development Editor
Sheri Cain

Managing Editor
John Fuller

Full-Service Production Manager
Julie B. Nahil

Copy Editor
Scribe Inc.

Indexer
Scribe Inc.

Proofreader
Scribe Inc.

Technical Reviewer
Andrea Tarr

Publishing Coordinator
Kim Boedigheimer

Compositor
Scribe Inc.

This book is dedicated to the many hardworking volunteers in the Joomla! community whose cheerful dedication renews on a daily basis the authors' faith in humankind.

Contents

Preface

Joomla! development encompasses a wide variety of tasks. One project might be to create a single override file to change the way one page is presented. Another project might be to create an extension with multiple components, plugins, and modules.

Although no book can be all things to all people, this book provides helpful information for a variety of people, from beginners with no Joomla development experience to experienced Joomla developers who need a quick start on version 2.5.

Experienced Joomla User Who's New to Programming

You have probably run into situations where adjusting parameters isn't quite enough to get your site just the way you want it. Or perhaps you need an extension that isn't quite like anything you have found in the Joomla Extensions Directory (JED). If so, this book will help you get started customizing Joomla by writing PHP code. You absolutely do NOT need to be an expert programmer to do basic Joomla development. Remember, just as Joomla was designed to let you create websites without knowing anything about PHP or MySQL, it is also designed to let you do a lot of customizing with a very modest amount of development knowledge. You will be pleasantly surprised at how much you can do with just a small amount of code and how quickly you can learn what you need to expand the flexibility and functionality of Joomla.

This book assumes that you know nothing whatsoever about PHP or MySQL programming. Everything we do is explained from the ground up. We also provide references to free resources to help you learn more about these subjects.

Experienced Web Programmer Who's New to Joomla

In this case, you already have the basic technical knowledge to jump in; you just need to know how Joomla works. This book is organized to let you find this information quickly. Although we provide some basic PHP and MySQL information, the book is organized to make it easy for you to skip sections that you already know so you can focus on the specific information about Joomla. We also explain the design choices that were made in the overall Joomla architecture so you can understand why the program was built this way.

Need a Quick Start on Version 2.5 Development

Joomla version 1.6 was a significant change from version 1.5, especially from a developer's point of view. Joomla versions 1.7 and 2.5 were incremental changes from 1.6. This book is based entirely on the 1.6/1.7/2.5 versions of Joomla. Where applicable, changes from version 1.5 are highlighted.

Need to Learn More about How Joomla Works and Developing Extensions

This book will provide a number of insider insights into not only how Joomla works, but also why it was designed as it was. In any large, complex package like Joomla, there are a number of design decisions that were made that have important implications for the developer. Understanding how it works and what the best practices are for Joomla development will allow you to write extensions that take full advantage of the Joomla framework and architecture and will be easy to modify and maintain going forward.

What This Book Is Not About

This book does not cover Joomla templates and design issues in general. Also, this book does not cover how to use Joomla. There are separate books that do a great job of covering these topics.

Joomla developers use a variety of tools, including PHP, SQL, XHTML, CSS, and JavaScript. Most of what we cover in this book involves writing PHP code. We do not assume that the reader already knows a lot of PHP or SQL, and we explain the code used in this book as we go along. However, this book does not try to teach the reader PHP or SQL in depth. Where appropriate, we point the reader to additional resources to supplement the information presented.

How This Book Is Organized

This book is organized from the simple to the complex. If you are an experienced Joomla developer, you can skim the first two chapters and start with Chapter 3. If you are less experienced, you will find it best to work through each chapter in order, although you may want to skip some of the sidebar information where we discuss more advanced design considerations.

This book is also designed to make it easy to use as a reference. If your initial project is a plugin, you can go straight to Chapter 5 and then fill in from prior chapters as needed, based on your experience.

This book contains a number of sidebars with supplemental information, including discussions of why Joomla works the way it does, background information on security or other important issues, and other topics that are not strictly needed to continue the flow of the book. These sidebars allow you to read or skip topics depending on your level of interest. They also make it easy to come back to something later.

Each major type of development includes a step-by-step tutorial. The authors strongly believe that the best way to understand how something works is to create a working example. Each step in the tutorial is explained so that you will understand what you are doing and why you are doing it.

The Challenge of Web Development: Too Many Things to Know!

One challenging aspect of web development—especially for newcomers—is the number of topics with which we need to be at least somewhat familiar. For example, in a typical Joomla development project, we will almost certainly work with PHP and probably with SQL queries. Working with HTML and XML is very common, and sometimes you need to be familiar with CSS and JavaScript. To set up your working environment on your PC, you will need to install and configure a web server such as Apache or Microsoft Internet Information Services (IIS) and get PHP and MySQL installed, configured, and working as well.

That's a lot of things to know about, and we haven't even started with Joomla yet! Each of these topics is large enough for an entire book, and no one could possibly hope to be an expert in all of them.

Fortunately, to develop programs for Joomla you do *not* need to be an expert in any of these topics. However, you do need to understand how they fit together and enough about each to do the job at hand.

This book does not assume that you have in-depth knowledge of any of these topics. Everything you need to know about each topic is explained as we go along. To keep this book to a manageable length, we provide the information you need to understand the material presented and then list resources that provide greater depth for a given subject.

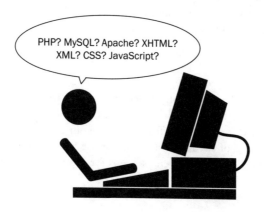

What's New in Joomla Version 2.5?

Joomla version 1.6 was released in January 2011. It included a number of major changes from version 1.5. Starting with version 1.6, the Joomla project committed to releasing a new version every six months and a new long-term-support (LTS) release every 18 months. As a result, version 1.7 was released in July 2011 and version 2.5 in January 2012.

Why did the number skip from 1.7 to 2.5? This was done so that all LTS releases would be numbered as X.5, where X is the major release. Version 1.5 was an LTS release. Version 2.5 is the LTS release for the 1.6/1.7/2.5 series. Version 3.5 (due in July 2013) will be the next LTS release, after versions 3.0 (July 2012) and 3.1 (January 2013).

This book covers Joomla version 2.5. Since a major goal of this book is to help developers with the transition from version 1.5, we highlight areas where things are done differently for version 2.5.

Version 1.6 was a major upgrade that incorporated a number of significant changes. Version 1.7 contained some smaller new features, and 2.5 more additional features. The most important of these are listed here.

Access Control List System

Version 1.6 added a new access control list (ACL) system that allows site administrators to fine-tune what different groups of users are allowed to do in the front and back end of Joomla. This system is extremely powerful and flexible, and it is easy for third-party developers to hook into. We explain how the system works and what you need to know to take full advantage of it in your projects.

User-Defined Category Levels (and No More Sections!)

Prior Joomla versions had two fixed levels for articles called *section* and *category*. In version 1.6, sections are eliminated. Instead, you can create your own category structure. For example, you can have a simple category structure with just one level, or you can have categories, subcategories, sub-subcategories, and so on—up to any (reasonable) depth. This allows for simpler and more complex structures than were available before.

This feature is designed to make it easy for developers to add this same feature to their own extensions.

JForm

In version 1.5, you could easily create screens for setting parameters using the JParameter class. In version 1.6, this is replaced with a new class called JForm, which makes it easier to create powerful forms for your applications. JForm gives you a great combination of flexibility and ease of use when you need to create data entry forms in Joomla. All the back-end screens for Joomla were rewritten for version 1.6 using JForm.

One impact of this change is that the format for XML files for extensions has changed. This is discussed in each of the chapters about writing extensions.

JTableNested

JTableNested is a new base class for the Category, Menu, and other tables that allow for nested levels of items. It provides an API to make it easy for developers to create tables based on nested sets in our code.

JDatabaseQuery

JDatabaseQuery is a new class that makes it easier to write complex SQL queries in Joomla. It gives you an application programming interface (API) to build SQL queries in a logical manner, based on the logical structure of the query. This makes it much easier to write and maintain complex SQL queries. You don't have to use this new class in your SQL queries, but we hope you will agree that it is a better way to work with SQL queries in Joomla.

PHP Version 5.2

Joomla version 1.5 had to be compatible with PHP version 4. This limited the extent to which Joomla could take advantage of the object-oriented programming (OOP) improvements made to PHP in version 5.0 and 5.2.

Starting with Joomla version 1.6, PHP version 5.2 or higher is required. This allows version 1.6 to use static and abstract classes. In addition, in PHP 5.2, all objects are passed by reference by default, which means that the &= (assigned by reference) operator is no longer needed in most cases.

The newer PHP also allows Joomla to use the native SimpleXML class for parsing XML files and to use the native DateTime class. So JXMLElement and JDate have been modified and simplified accordingly.

MySQL Version 5.0.4

Joomla 1.6 requires MySQL version 5.0.4 or higher. This version of MySQL provides a number of enhancements, including stored procedures, triggers, views, and a number of performance improvements. It also allows for large columns of type varchar.

Language File Format

Joomla version 1.6 introduces a major change to the language file format. Previously, Joomla used a proprietary format. Starting in version 1.6, that was changed to the standard PHP .ini file format. This allows Joomla to use the standard PHP parse_ini_file command, which is much faster and simpler than the old proprietary method.

This does, however, require that language files be reformatted to the new standard.

One-Click Update

Version 2.5 allows your Joomla website to be updated automatically. The site administrator is notified whenever an update is available either for the core Joomla files or for any extension used on the site (as long as the extension developer supports this feature). The site can be updated simply by clicking on the Update button. Instructions for setting up this capability for extensions is discussed in the companion website, http://joomlaprogrammingbook.com.

Improved MVC

The model-view-controller (MVC) design pattern was improved for version 1.6. This included using the pattern more consistently in the back end and improving code reuse by moving code to standard library classes where possible. We discuss Joomla's MVC implementation in detail in Chapters 7–10.

Support of Other Databases

Version 2.5 introduced support for other databases (besides MySQL), starting with Microsoft SQL Server. Support for PostgreSQL is also under development and is expected to be added soon.

Improved Search

Version 2.5 introduced Smart Search. This is a completely new search engine that greatly improves the quality and accuracy of full-text searching of the content in a Joomla website.

Companion Website

The authors have set up a website at http://joomlaprogrammingbook.com where we have additional information about Joomla programming. We also have zip archive files with the code from the book, organized by chapter.

This website will be kept up to date with new information about Joomla versions and will list any corrections to the print version of the book.

Welcome to Joomla Development

Joomla developers come from all backgrounds and have varied amounts of experience in software development. Many started with HTML websites and have learned more about web programming as they worked with Joomla. Some have degrees in computer science; some come from a background in web design. Others just learned by using Joomla, reading, and working with others.

The Joomla development community strives to be open and welcoming to new people, including those with little or no programming experience or formal technical education. A number of resources are available for reading about various topics and asking questions. Two of the most important ones are as follows:

- `http://developer.joomla.org` is the Joomla site exclusively devoted to Joomla development. This website includes information about the current state of the project and the latest development news. It also includes links to the Google groups where Joomla development issues are discussed.

- `http://docs.joomla.org/Developers` is the entry point for all developer-related, online documentation in the Joomla wiki site. Note that this site is a wiki that is maintained by the community. Anyone can register and update or add information to the wiki.

The authors hope this book makes it easier for people to learn to develop programs for Joomla, regardless of their prior level of experience.

Acknowledgments

The Joomla! development community is friendly, and experienced developers routinely take time to help newcomers. This book would not have been possible without the help of many people in that community who answered questions and helped to fill in the numerous gaps in my knowledge. I want to especially thank the people who read chapters and provided invaluable feedback: Andrea Tarr, Elin Waring, Omar Ramos, and Sam Moffatt. Finally, I want to thank my wife, Deb, whose support and encouragement (and occasional homemade fudge) kept me going.

—*Mark Dexter*

About the Authors

Mark Dexter has been writing software since the 1970s. He cofounded and ran a commercial software company for 28 years before retiring to do volunteer work in open-source software. Mark first started using Joomla! in 2008 and joined the Production Leadership Team in 2009. He has worked extensively in different areas of the project, including the user forums, Google Summer of Code, documentation and help screens, and the Bug Squad. Mark has actively participated in the Joomla development process since 2009, including fixing bugs, adding features, and coordinating the release of new Joomla versions. Mark lives in Seattle, Washington.

Louis Landry wrote a large part of the Joomla framework for versions 1.5 and 1.6, and he has been a major design architect for Joomla for over five years. His first experience with computers was playing on a 286 with Basic at his father's office. Louis has programmed in many languages, ranging from low level x86 assembly to managed languages like Java and scripting languages like PHP. He was a founding member of his university's robotics team. Louis is a car nut, and enjoys working on them in his spare time. He lives in Silicon Valley in California.

1

What Is Joomla! Development?

This chapter outlines the different ways you can extend and customize the functionality of Joomla!. In order to understand this, we need to first describe the various software programs that are used to build and run Joomla.

Developing for Joomla Is Not Difficult!

If you are new to Joomla and web development, you can feel overwhelmed by acronyms, jargon, and new concepts. However, with a little help and perseverance, you can succeed in writing code for Joomla to make it work just the way you want it to. Joomla is designed from the ground up to be modified and extended, and many people with limited technical knowledge have successfully learned to write programs for Joomla.

This book explains every new concept and topic as we proceed. We will not assume that you already know anything about Joomla or web development. As needed, we will point out more in-depth resources you can use to fill in gaps or explore topics in greater detail.

The Joomla Technical Environment

Newcomers to dynamic website development face a bewildering array of acronyms and jargon. Joomla uses web servers like Apache or Microsoft Internet Information Services (IIS); the PHP programming language; the MySQL database; the JavaScript programming language; HTML, XHTML, and XML document types; and CSS.

Let's start with the server. The server is the computer where the Joomla program files reside and where most (but not all) Joomla programming code gets run. To run a Joomla website, a server must run the following three programs:

- A web server (Apache or Microsoft IIS)
- The PHP programming language
- A database (usually MySQL)

The web server is the software that actually allows the server to interact with the browser. It is the bridge between the external world and the local folders on the server.

When a browser requests a URL, the web server knows which file directory on the server maps to that URL and finds the file to execute (for example, "index.php").

PHP is the primary programming language that Joomla is written in. PHP is by far the world's most popular program for writing dynamic websites. It interacts with the web server software and creates XHTML pages dynamically. For most Joomla development tasks, the coding will be done in PHP.

Server as a Concept versus Server as a Machine

When we refer to the *server* in the context of web development, we refer to the software that "serves" the HTML code to the browser. In a production website, this will typically run on a remote computer at a web hosting company. However, when we run Joomla locally (which we often do for development and testing), we still have a server. In that case, it is the server software (Apache or IIS) running on our PC.

From a technical standpoint, both environments work the same way. The server and the browser always communicate via TCP/IP. The only difference is that, with a remote server, the TCP/IP packets that carry the information back and forth travel a lot farther.

MySQL is the database that most Joomla sites use. It is by far the most popular database for web applications. In a Joomla website, the database holds almost all the information about the site. For example, every time you add an article or a menu or module, this gets saved in the database.

When you are using Joomla (or any other website), what you actually see in your browser is XHTML. This stands for extensible hypertext markup language and is the updated version of HTML. Most Joomla developers need to have a basic working knowledge of XHTML. The end result of all the processing that a Joomla program does is the display of XHTML in the browser. Note that in this book we will use the term HTML to refer to both HTML and XHTML.

CSS stands for cascading style sheets. CSS code is used to "style" the XHTML code so that it displays the way we want in the browser. For example, CSS controls the font size, type, color, the text spacing, and all other aspects of the way the information is formatted inside the browser.

All the information for how the site will be displayed—including the CSS and the way the content is laid out on the page—is contained in the Joomla template. This design allows us to completely separate the content of a site from the site's appearance. That is why you can completely change the appearance of a Joomla website dynamically just by changing the template.

JavaScript is a program that runs inside your browser and is the J in the acronym AJAX (asynchronous JavaScript and XML). JavaScript allows us to make websites feel more like desktop programs. For example, in Joomla, JavaScript allows things to pop up automatically when you hover the mouse over a field and to highlight a field in a form when it is not valid. Since JavaScript runs on the client, it can respond to events without having to interact with the web server, so things change instantly in the browser, without the user having to press a Submit button.

Joomla Programming: What Do You Need to Know?

Most Joomla programming involves writing PHP code. Since the information for a Joomla website is in the database, some of this PHP code interacts with the database. This is normally in the form of SQL queries. Database queries are used to store data to the database and to pull data from the database. So Joomla developers need to know how to write SQL database queries to interact with the database.

Some Joomla programming involves working with XML or HTML. For example, parameters for forms are typically stored in XML files. The parts of the program that actually output the information to the browser (called views or layouts) typically contain a mixture of PHP and HTML code. So Joomla developers need to be somewhat familiar with HTML.

Some Joomla developers are heavily involved with the way a site is laid out and the way it looks. These people need to be very good at working with HTML and CSS. Most of this work is done during the development of the template. As indicated earlier, this book does not cover template development.

Other Joomla developers are mostly concerned with getting the correct information on the page. In this case, you do not need to be an expert on HTML or CSS, although a general familiarity is still very helpful.

JavaScript is in a special category. It interacts with the PHP programs as well as the HTML and CSS. At this time, most Joomla development does not require a lot of JavaScript programming or knowledge. We will discuss the role of JavaScript in Joomla in greater detail in Chapter 12.

As developers, we don't have to know much about the web server (Apache or IIS). When you deploy a site to the web, the security of the site is a high priority. Much of the security of a site depends on the host you use and the way they have configured the web server and database software. But this does not normally affect the way we write our Joomla programs.

To sum up, a Joomla website uses a number of programs and file types to do its work. Most Joomla development involves writing PHP code, and that is the main focus of this book. Some of this code will include queries to the database. We discuss database issues in detail in Chapter 11. Some of our code will output HTML to the browser. We will explain how PHP works elegantly with HTML when creating the final output.

Unless you are working on templates, you don't need an extensive knowledge of HTML and CSS, so we won't discuss much about CSS.

We can do a lot of Joomla development without knowing JavaScript. However, it is an important topic and we cover JavaScript topics in Chapter 13.

Extending Joomla: Let Me Count the Ways

We said earlier that Joomla was designed to be extended. What does that mean in practice? Extending Joomla means making it do what you want it to do. This can be in the form of changing the way something works or adding entirely new functionality. This section will outline all the different ways that Joomla can be extended.

Open Source Means You Have Control

Joomla is free and open-source software (FOSS). As such, the programming source code is part of the normal package download. Anyone who creates a Joomla website can, if they wish, edit any of the source code files and alter the working of the program.

Let's define two terms you will see when people discuss modifying Joomla programs:

- *Core* code is source code that is distributed as part of the set of files you get when you download and install Joomla (for example, in a zip archive file).
- A *hack* or *core hack* is making a change directly to one of the core source code files.

Because Joomla is FOSS, you are completely within your legal rights to hack any file in the system. However, this is generally considered inadvisable.

Why? Hacking the core files is not recommended for two simple reasons. First, if you change these files, you can no longer rely on the integrity of the system. If you encounter a problem in your system, you won't know for sure whether it is a bug in Joomla or a result of something you changed. To make matters worse, it will make getting updates for your site much more difficult. Normally, the Joomla project releases maintenance updates on a regular basis. For example, when you initially load your site, you might be on Joomla version 2.5.1 and then version 2.5.2 will be released.

The 2.5.2 archive file will contain a full copy of every file that was changed since the last version, and when you do the upgrade, your old files will be replaced. If you have modified some of these programs, you have a problem. If you do the upgrade, you will lose your modifications. If you don't upgrade those files, you will not get the bug fixes or other changes. The only solution is to either redo your changes on the new version of the files or identify what was changed between Joomla versions and make the same changes to your modified files.

If you have a small number of minor hacks, this could be manageable. However, it complicates the process of keeping your site updated.

The good news here is that hacking core files is almost never needed to make Joomla work your way. The next sections discuss all the different ways you can modify Joomla without changing any core files.

Overrides Let You Change What Shows on the Page

One of the most common changes that people want to make to a site is to modify what is shown on the page. If you are familiar with using Joomla, you know that most components, modules, and plugins provide parameters that let you control different aspects of how these extensions will operate. For example, when you show an article on a page, you can decide with a parameter whether you wish to show the author or the date it was created. Those types of changes require no programming at all to implement.

However, the different ways that people might choose to show information on a page is almost limitless, and it is not practical to try to have a parameter setting for every possibility. Let's consider a simple example. The standard article list layout in Joomla looks like what's shown in Figure 1.1.

Suppose we prefer to show the author in the first column and the title in the second column. There is no parameter that controls the order of display. So what do we do?

By simply copying one file and cutting and pasting a few lines of code, we can change the output to what's shown in Figure 1.2.

Because this is done as an override, we are not hacking any core files. So we don't have to worry about our files getting overwritten during a version upgrade.

Display # 5 ▾

Title	Author	Hits
Beginners	Written by Joomla!	1
Getting Help	Written by Joomla!	16
Getting Started	Written by Joomla!	6
Joomla!	Written by Joomla!	0
Parameters	Written by Joomla!	1

Figure 1.1   Standard layout for articles in a single category

Display # 5 ▾

Author	Title	Hits
Written by Joomla!	Beginners	1
Written by Joomla!	Getting Help	16
Written by Joomla!	Getting Started	6
Written by Joomla!	Joomla!	0
Written by Joomla!	Parameters	1

Figure 1.2   Modified layout using template override file

Starting with version 1.6, the use of override files has been greatly expanded. Template overrides are still supported. But now language files, menu items, and modules can all have overrides independent of the template in use.

Overrides will be discussed in detail in Chapter 4.

Extensions

Extensions are the most visible aspect of any Joomla website. The word *extension* is commonly used to mean two different things with respect to Joomla. The most common usage is as an add-on software program that works with Joomla to add functionality to a website. The Joomla project maintains a website called the Joomla Extensions Directory or JED (`http://extensions.joomla.org`) that lists many of the extensions available from developers in the community.

From a programming point of view, the word *extension* has a slightly different meaning. In this sense of the word, an extension is any component, module, plugin, language, or template. Extensions that are included with the standard Joomla download are called *core extensions*. Extensions from other sources, such as the JED, are called *third-party extensions*.

A key point to understand is that, when Joomla is running, it doesn't see any difference between core extensions and third-party extensions. That is why third-party extensions appear to be completely integrated into the package. They are treated exactly like core extensions.

If you are using a Joomla website that incorporates well-written third-party extensions, it can often be difficult to tell where the core package leaves off and an extension begins. This is by design.

Plugins

Plugins are perhaps the best-kept secret in the Joomla development world. Many times, plugins provide a simple way to do something that would otherwise be difficult or impossible. But since they are a bit difficult to visualize, it is easy to overlook them as a solution to a problem.

One way to understand plugins is to visualize the program flow as a conveyor belt or assembly line. At different points in the process, we define events. Figure 1.3 shows the program flow for saving an article to the database.

In the first box, the user has entered in the article and presses the Save button. In the second box, Joomla checks to make sure the article has valid data. If so, in the next step the article is saved to the database. The last step shows we are done with this activity.

With Joomla's event system, the process actually is a bit more complex but much more powerful. This is shown in Figure 1.4.

The steps going down the left are the same as in the first example. However, we now introduce two events. The first event, called onBeforeSave, takes place after the article's data is validated but before the article is saved to the database. The second event, called onAfterSave, happens just after a successful save to the database but

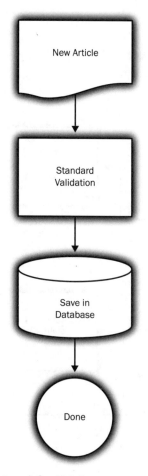

Figure 1.3 Simple save process

before we finish the process. These events break into the normal program flow and allow us to do some special processing. Once the special processing is completed, the normal program flow continues.

In Figure 1.4, Joomla found two plugin programs with onBeforeSave and onAfterSave methods. This just happens to be the case in this example. It is important to understand that, depending on your Joomla implementation, there might be no plugins to run for an event or there could be ten. Each time an article is saved, Joomla checks for any methods that need to be executed and runs them one at a time.

This is best illustrated by an example. Suppose we want to examine every article on the site and make sure it has appropriate keywords defined in the metadata. Let's say we have already written a program that looks for certain words in each article and adds them as keywords.

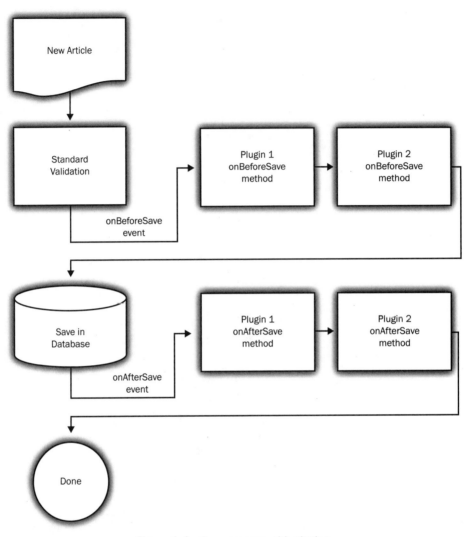

Figure 1.4   Save process with plugins

Using the onBeforeSave event, it is very easy to implement this feature as a custom plugin. We simply create a plugin with an onBeforeSave method and run our program. In this case, our plugin method has the article as a parameter, so we can easily examine the contents of the article and update the keywords column before the article is saved to the database. We don't change any core files. We just add our new code in the right place and Joomla finds it and runs it at just the right time.

The cool thing about events is that they are always there but they don't get in your way. Joomla very quickly can check to see whether there are any methods that need to be run for a given event. An event is said to be fired when the program checks for methods tied to that event and executes them if found. You can fire events from your own code and even create custom events if needed.

Chapter 5 discusses plugins and events in detail and walks you through how to use them to great advantage to extend Joomla.

Modules

In Joomla, modules are extensions that render on a page typically as small "boxes" that show around the main content of the page (which is normally a component). For example, Figure 1.5 shows the sample data home page for version 2.5. The modules are the small areas outlined in black. One page can show multiple modules.

Modules typically are simple extensions. A module can be linked to a component. For example, the Related Items module is linked to the Single Article view of the Articles component and shows a list of articles that have keywords that match the keywords for the article in view. In other cases, a module will show the same information regardless of the component on the page.

All menus in Joomla are modules and there are many other types of modules included with the Joomla core. We will discuss the core modules in Chapter 3.

We would typically choose to use a module when we want to show information on multiple pages and when that information won't be the central focus of that page.

We will discuss developing modules in Chapter 6.

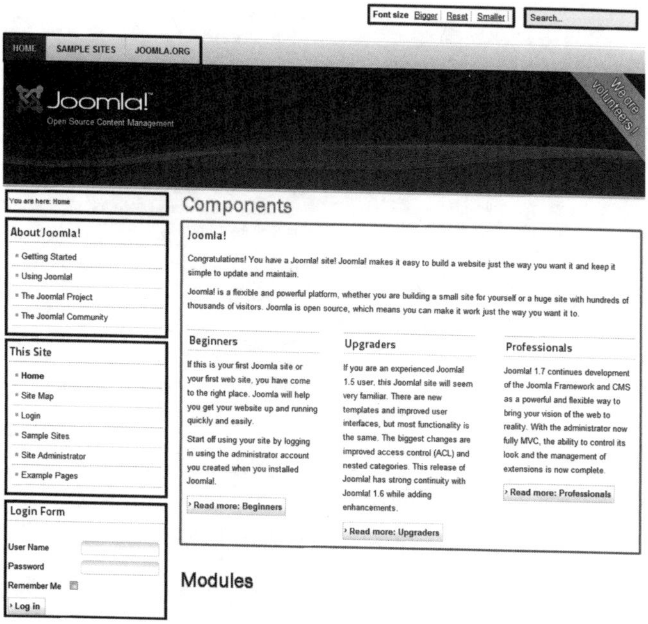

Figure 1.5   Example home page component and modules

Components

The component, in most cases, provides the central focus of a page. In the previous example, the content outlined in gray shows the Featured Articles Blog menu item, which is one of the menu items included with the articles component. Components include one or more menu item types that you choose when you create or edit a menu item. Each menu item type corresponds to a view for the component. For example, the articles component provides seven possible menu types or views: Archived Articles, Single Article, List All Categories, Category Blog, Category List, Featured Articles, and Create Article.

Examples of Joomla's core components include articles (also known as content or com_content), banners (com_banners), and contacts (com_contact). We will discuss all the core components in Chapter 3. Figure 1.6 shows all the Menu Item Types available for the core components.

Components in Joomla are written using the model-view-controller (MVC) design pattern. This makes it easier to maintain the programs over time and allows for separation between the different tasks associated with preparing and displaying a Joomla

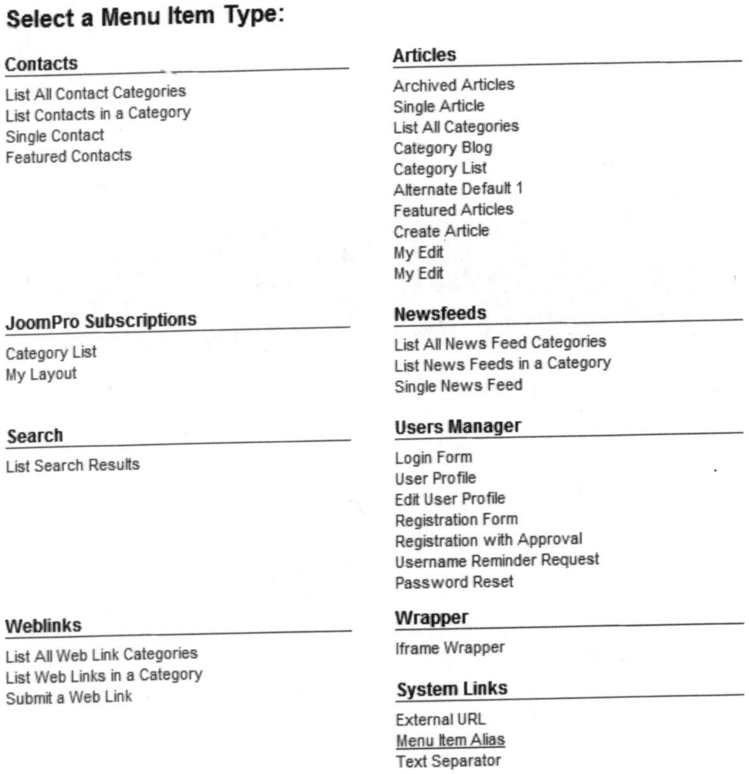

Select a Menu Item Type:

Contacts
List All Contact Categories
List Contacts in a Category
Single Contact
Featured Contacts

Articles
Archived Articles
Single Article
List All Categories
Category Blog
Category List
Alternate Default 1
Featured Articles
Create Article
My Edit
My Edit

JoomPro Subscriptions
Category List
My Layout

Newsfeeds
List All News Feed Categories
List News Feeds in a Category
Single News Feed

Search
List Search Results

Users Manager
Login Form
User Profile
Edit User Profile
Registration Form
Registration with Approval
Username Reminder Request
Password Reset

Weblinks
List All Web Link Categories
List Web Links in a Category
Submit a Web Link

Wrapper
Iframe Wrapper

System Links
External URL
Menu Item Alias
Text Separator

Figure 1.6   Core menu item types for Joomla 2.5

web page. Use of this pattern also makes it much easier for developers who are already familiar with object-oriented programming (OOP) and design patterns to understand how Joomla components work.

Components are typically the most complicated type of extension. We will discuss writing components in Chapters 7–10.

Languages

One of Joomla's strengths is its very high degree of internationalization. Joomla is currently translated into over 68 languages. This allows people to work with the entire Joomla program in their own language.

Language translation is implemented by way of language extensions. A language extension is a set of special files (with the extension ".ini") that include all the words and phrases that are displayed as part of the Joomla user interface. This makes it possible to translate the user interface into any language. Let's look at how this is done.

In PHP, we use the echo command to display text on a page in the browser. Let's look for example at the administrator login screen for Joomla, shown in Figure 1.7.

Looking at the screen in Figure 2.5, you might reasonably expect that, somewhere in the Joomla PHP code, there is an echo command, something like echo 'Joomla! Administration Login'. However, if we search for that code inside a PHP file, we will not find it.

In Joomla, we don't "hard-code" text that is part of the user interface. If we did, we would have to change the program code for each different language. Instead, we hard-code the language file keys and read the actual text at runtime.

If we search for the string Joomla! Administration Login in a language .ini file, we will find that it is in a file called administrator/language/en-GB/en-GB.com_login.ini, as shown in Figure 1.8.

The part on the left, COM_LOGIN_JOOMLA_ADMINISTRATION_LOGIN, is called the language key (or tag). The part in double quotes on the right is the actual text that Joomla will display when the language is set to en-GB.

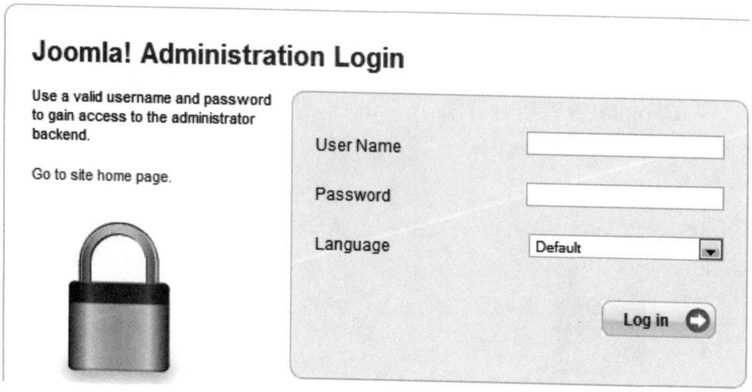

Figure 1.7   Administrator login screen

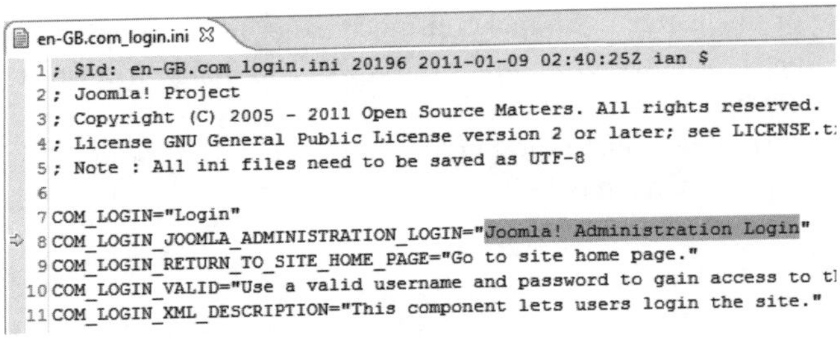

```
en-GB.com_login.ini ⊠
1 ; $Id: en-GB.com_login.ini 20196 2011-01-09 02:40:25Z ian $
2 ; Joomla! Project
3 ; Copyright (C) 2005 - 2011 Open Source Matters. All rights reserved.
4 ; License GNU General Public License version 2 or later; see LICENSE.t
5 ; Note : All ini files need to be saved as UTF-8
6
7 COM_LOGIN="Login"
8 COM_LOGIN_JOOMLA_ADMINISTRATION_LOGIN="Joomla! Administration Login"
9 COM_LOGIN_RETURN_TO_SITE_HOME_PAGE="Go to site home page."
10 COM_LOGIN_VALID="Use a valid username and password to gain access to t
11 COM_LOGIN_XML_DESCRIPTION="This component lets users login the site."
```

Figure 1.8   Search results for text in ".ini" files

We can see this in action if we search for that tag in the PHP files. We find this tag appears twice, in the files `administrator/templates/bluestork/login.php` and `administrator/templates/hathor/login.php`. Here is the line of code:

```
<h1><?php echo JText::_('COM_LOGIN_JOOMLA_ADMINISTRATION_LOGIN') ?></h1>
```

Instead of using `echo` with the English text, we echo the output of the method `JText::_()`. The argument for that method is the language key from the `.ini` file. The `JText::_()` method looks up the key in the `.ini` file for our language and returns the matching text. If for some reason the key is not found, it just returns the key instead.

If we had a different language extension (also called language pack) installed and had that selected, we would see the text in that language. Figure 1.9 shows the login screen with a Chinese language pack installed.

Language extensions are created by making new files for each core `.ini` file with all the tags translated into the target language. As you can imagine, this is a big job and it is not surprising that the Joomla Translation Team is the largest team in the project, with 68 languages and counting.

If you create an extension for the Joomla community, it is strongly advised that you create language `.ini` files for the extension and use the `JText` class methods to output the text. That way, it is easy for someone to provide a translation for your extension. We will show an example of how you do this in Chapter 5 when we add a language file to a plugin extension.

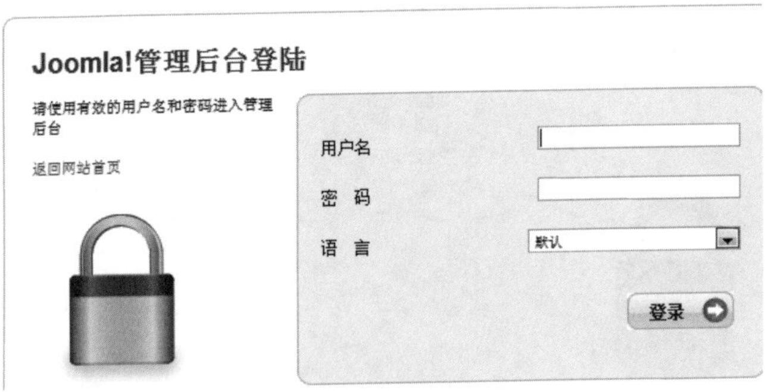

Figure 1.9   Login screen in simplified Chinese

Templates

The last type of extension in Joomla is a template. The template controls the way all the information is shown on each page of the website. A basic principal of Joomla (and other content management software) is to separate the content of the site from the presentation of that content. This is accomplished by separating the preparation of each page into different steps. In Joomla, the entire document for each page is created and then, as the last step in the process, this document is passed to the template where it is actually converted (or rendered) by the template into the final HTML that will get passed to the browser.

You can see the result of this separation of content and presentation in dramatic fashion by changing the default template. If we navigate to the front end of the site with the default Beez2 template, we see the home page, shown in Figure 1.10.

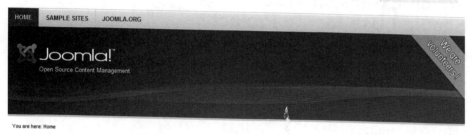

Figure 1.10   Home page with Beez2 template

If we navigate to the Template Manager, and change the default template to "Beez5 – Default – Fruit Shop," the same home page now appears, as shown in Figure 1.11.

It is the exact same content, but the display is different. This separation allows site designers to work on the layout and presentation of the site and site developers to work on getting the right information shown on each page. To a site administrator, it means that the presentation of the site can be changed easily without changing anything about the way the site is built.

Because this book is targeted to developers and not designers, we will not go into details about how to build templates. However, there are some aspects of template structure that we will need to understand to do our development tasks. These include the folder structure for template override files—which we discuss in Chapter 4—and the way that module positions are created in a template, which we discuss in Chapter 6.

Which Extension Type Should I Use for My Project?

We have seen that we have four options for extending the functionality of Joomla: layout overrides, plugins, modules, and components. How do we decide which one to use for a given project?

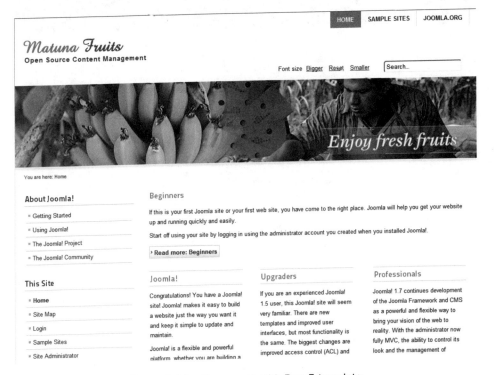

Figure 1.11   Home page with Beez5 template

In many cases, once we understand how each extension type works, it becomes obvious which one to use. It is also important to realize that some projects will require a combination of different extension types to do the job.

If your project will result in something similar to how a core extension works, then that will often tell you the best extension type to use.

One way to think about this is to try to use the simplest approach to solve the problem at hand. As a general rule, layouts and plugins are the simplest extension types. Modules come next. Components are the most complicated and difficult to write. So if you can do the job with a simpler extension, that is usually the best approach.

Using Joomla as a Platform or Framework

Joomla is a content management system (CMS) built using a set of reusable library classes mostly contained in the folder `libraries/joomla`. These library classes do many low-level tasks that a CMS or any other web application might need to do, including the following:

- Allow users to log in with different sets of permissions, interacting with the database.
- Keep track of the current browser session.
- Cache output to improve performance.
- Process events for plugins.
- Filter user input to prevent malicious security attacks.
- Process error conditions in a consistent and user-friendly manner.

Suppose we want to create a new web application for tracking the inventory for an online business. The application is not going to have users submitting or displaying articles, contacts, or banners. In fact, our application may not even display web pages at all. Perhaps we will just check inventory and return the information to another application.

In this example, we would not need or want to install the entire Joomla CMS. However, we might still need to check that a user has correct permissions for the actions. We would definitely be interacting with a database. We would want to filter requests to improve the application's security. We might need to handle error conditions.

In other words, we wouldn't need the CMS part of Joomla, but we could use the Joomla libraries to save ourselves a lot of work by reusing code that is already written and that works well.

With Joomla versions 1.5 and 1.6, you could handle this scenario by installing Joomla and then stripping out the parts you don't need in your application. However, this involves extra work and should not be necessary.

For this reason, the functionality contained in the Joomla libraries has been broken out into a separate project, as of July 2011. Known as the Joomla Plaform Project, this allows developers who want to use the Joomla platform without the CMS to have an easy way to get what they need.

It also allows the platform to operate as a separate project from the CMS, with its own release schedule, code base, and developers.

Chapter 13 discusses using the Joomla platform in greater detail and creates an example application using only the platform.

Summary

In this chapter, we learned that the Joomla developer must be at least a little familiar with web servers, PHP, SQL, XHTML, XML, CSS, and Javascript. This can seem daunting to a newcomer, but Joomla actually makes doing web development easier than we might imagine.

We then discussed the different types of development we can do in Joomla: layout overrides, plugins, modules, and components.

We then learned how Joomla works with multiple languages and how that affects the way we output text to the browser. We briefly showed how templates can dramatically change the way a site looks, while presenting the exact same content.

We discussed how you can choose which approach is the best for a given project.

Finally, we discussed how Joomla can be used as a platform for building entirely new applications outside the scope of a CMS.

2

Getting Your Workstation Ready for Joomla! Development

When we are developing programs for Joomla!, we normally run Joomla on our local workstation. So we need to install the web server software required to run Joomla on our local machine. In addition, we need to have some way to edit the PHP files and other files that compose a Joomla application.

Fortunately, all this software is freely available for download and can be set up on all the common operating systems, including Windows, Mac OS X, and Linux. Also, we will see that there are many free options for editing our Joomla program files.

In this chapter, we will show you how to get your workstation set up to run Joomla and to edit and create the files you will need to write your programs.

If you already have your workstation set up to run Joomla and to do Joomla development, you can skip the "Requirements to Run Joomla" section. If you are already using an integrated development environment (IDE) such as Eclipse or NetBeans, you can skip the "Tools of the Trade" section.

Requirements to Run Joomla

As discussed in Chapter 1, Joomla requires a web server (Apache or Microsoft Internet Information Services [IIS]), PHP, and a database (normally MySQL) in order to run. Each of these programs can be downloaded and installed separately from their respective websites. However, it is normally easier to install Apache, PHP, and MySQL as part of a combined package. On Mac OS X and Linux, these programs may already be installed by default.

It is important to understand that whether you install them individually or as a combined package, the end result is the same—to have Apache, PHP, and MySQL installed on your workstation. The only difference is the way they are installed and the specifics of each bundle. For example, the specific versions of each package will differ somewhat with each bundle, as well as the folder names and some of the specific default configuration settings.

Important Note about Security

This chapter assumes that we are creating a local environment for development work and testing. It also assumes that the test websites we work with here are not connected to the World Wide Web. Accordingly, we are not concerned with securing our server the way we would be if we were hosting an actual web application. Of course, we are still concerned with making sure that our Joomla programs are written to be safe from outside attacks.

If you are working on a remote site that is visible to the World Wide Web, be sure to protect the site, even during development. There are a number of ways you can do this, including using Apache's .htaccess file to require a password to access the URL. You may want to consult with someone familiar with web and Joomla security in this case.

Apache DocumentRoot Folder

There is an important detail to know about any of these environments. As discussed earlier, the Apache web server is the program that provides the link between the browser and the website. When you install Apache locally, the URL `http://localhost` is mapped to a folder on your local workstation. When you type this URL into your browser, Apache will look for a file called either `index.php` or `index.html` in your DocumentRoot folder, which is a folder on your local computer.

For XAMPP installations, the DocumentRoot is normally `C:\xampp\htdocs`. For WampServer installations, it defaults to `C:\Program Files\wamp\www`.

You can change the DocumentRoot folder to another folder by editing the file `httpd.conf` in your `apache/conf` folder. For example, in XAMPP this file is in `c:\xampp\apache\conf`. For WampServer, you can edit the `httpd.conf` file inside the application by selecting Config Files → `httpd.conf`.

Once you have your DocumentRoot folder identified, you can decide where to install your Joomla files. Any URL you enter in the browser that starts with `http://localhost` will start at the DocumentRoot folder and work down the folder tree from that point.

For example, if your document root is `c:\xampp\htdocs`, you could install Joomla in a folder called `c:\xampp\htdocs\joomla_development\joomla_25`. In this case, the URL you would type to access the back end of this installation would be `http://localhost/joomla_development/joomla_25/administrator`. Apache will look for a file called `index.php` in the folder `joomla_development/joomla_25/administrator` under the `DocumentRoot` folder.

You could install Joomla directly in the `DocumentRoot` folder, but then you would be limited in what else you might install there. Using something similar to the example above makes it easy to have multiple projects going at one time, each in its own subfolder under `DocumentRoot`.

With this in mind, we are ready to discuss the different options for installing the required software on different platforms.

Getting Up-To-Date Instructions

The programs and bundles discussed here are constantly being updated with newer versions. Newer versions of Windows, Linux, and OS X are also introduced over time.

The information presented here is accurate (to the best of the authors' knowledge) as of the time of writing, but this information may become out of date or incomplete because of changes to the web server or platform software.

For this reason, the website links presented here are the safest way to get up-to-date instructions. In addition to the links presented for each of the bundles, there is an article on the Joomla documentation website with detailed instructions here: `http://docs.joomla.org/Setting_up_your_workstation_for_Joomla!_development`. This article is kept up to date with changes as things change over time.

Windows Platforms

On the various Windows platforms (Windows 7, Windows Vista, and Windows XP), Apache, PHP, and MySQL are not installed by default. The two most popular bundled packages for setting up a dynamic web environment on Windows are XAMPP and WAMPP.

XAMPP (`http://www.apachefriends.org/en/xampp.html`) is probably the most popular package for Windows. It is easy to install and has good documentation. It also is available on Linux and Mac OS X. Detailed instructions for installing XAMPP on Windows is available at `http://www.apachefriends.org/en/xampp-windows.html`.

WampServer is another bundled package for Windows. It has the advantage of making it very easy to toggle between different versions of Apache, PHP, and MySQL. This is a great advantage if you need to test a program across different versions of PHP, for example. WampServer can be found at `http://www.wampserver.com/en`. It has an easy Windows installation process that is documented on the site.

Note About Microsoft IIS and SQL Server

Joomla can run on either the Apache web server or the Microsoft IIS web server. Because Apache has been supported the longest, and because the majority of Joomla production websites are run on Apache, most people use Apache for their development environment. If you are reading this chapter, you probably do not have a lot of experience setting up Joomla. In that case, we recommend using Apache for your development server.

Starting with Joomla version 2.5, the Microsoft SQL Server database is also supported. However, for basic Joomla development, it is recommended to use MySQL in your development environment.

Mac OS X Plaform

As previously mentioned, a version of XAMPP is available for Mac OS X. You can download it at `http://www.apachefriends.org/en/xampp-macosx.html`. With XAMPP, the default `DocumentRoot` folder is `/Applications/XAMPP/htdocs/`.

There is also a package called MAMP that is exclusively for Mac. You can download it at `http://www.mamp.info/en/mamp/index.html`. With MAMP, the default DocumentRoot folder is `Applications/MAMP/htdocs`.

Another option for both Mac OS X and Linux is to use the versions of Apache, MySQL, and PHP that are distributed as part of the native operating system. Because OS X is a derivative of Linux, these applications run natively on OS X.

If you are new to these programs, it is probably easier to use one of the existing bundles than to use the native versions. Also, the XAMPP and MAMP bundles normally contain more current versions of Apache, MySQL, and PHP than the versions that come bundled with the OS X operating system.

Important Note

Apache may be installed by default on your OS X system. If so, it identifies a port on the computer as the "listening" port. If you then install a second version of Apache from XAMPP or MAMP, it will also try to use this same port and will not be able to operate correctly.

To fix this, you need to change one of the ports. Probably the simplest thing is to change the XAMPP or MAMP port to something like 8080.

In XAMPP, this is done by editing the file `\Applications\XAMPP\xamppfiles\etc\httpd.conf` and changing the line `Listen 80` to `Listen 8080`.

In MAMP, you can change the port using the MAMP application Preferences Panel (which in turn edits the `httpd.conf` file). Again, you want to change the `Listen` port to 8080.

Linux Platforms

The considerations for Linux platforms are similar to those for OS X platforms. You have the option of using XAMPP or using native versions of Apache, MySQL, and PHP. For beginners, XAMPP is normally easier. The download information for XAMPP's Linux version is at `http://www.apachefriends.org/en/xampp-linux.html`.

By default, the DocumentRoot folder will be located at `/opt/lampp/htdocs/`. As discussed earlier for Mac OS X, you may need to change the default "Listen" port if another instance of Apache is already running on your system. For XAMPP, the file you need to edit is `/opt/lampp/etc/httpd.conf`. Again, you need to change the line that says `Listen 80` to something like `Listen 8080`.

Default Owner for Files and Folders

Default file and folder permissions on Linux and Mac OS X can cause problems when trying to install Joomla or edit Joomla files. You need to make sure that your Linux user is able to write to the folder where you install Joomla and to the Joomla files themselves.

The owner of all files created by Apache is set with the User and Group options in the `httpd.conf` file. By default, these are set to "daemon." This means that you may not have write permission for the Joomla files and folders.

If this is a local site to be used only for testing and development, you can change the User and Group to be your login user. That way, you will have permission to create, edit, and delete the Joomla files and folders.

Tools of the Trade

Joomla developers can choose from a number of different tools for creating and editing the Joomla program files.

If you want a sure-fire way to start an impassioned discussion, ask a group of software developers what programs they like to use for writing their code. You will almost always get a variety of opinions about why this or that program is good or terrible.

Different people have very different views on this subject, and different Joomla developers use different development tools. There is no program that is the best for every person or every situation.

The following section attempts to discuss the pros and cons of the different options in a reasonably objective manner.

IDE versus Text Editor

When you install Joomla, all the source code for the program is loaded on your system in plain text files. The main file types included in the core installation are PHP (".php"), XML (".xml"), JavaScript (".js"), CSS (".css"), and SQL (".sql"). All these file types are plain text files, which means that they can be edited with any text editor. So you can edit existing Joomla files and create new ones without any special software at all.

Given that, why would you want to go to the trouble of installing and learning a new software program just for Joomla development?

The answer, at least for many developers, is productivity.

IDE stands for integrated development environment. The goal of an IDE is to make developers more productive. For example, an IDE (like Eclipse or NetBeans discussed later in this chapter) provides the following functionality to make writing PHP programs easier:

- Identifies syntax errors in code as you type
- Automatically completes portions of code based on the known language syntax
- Automatically shows method and field information about a class being edited
- Allows you to compare two versions of a file (or two different files) to see the exact differences
- Makes it easy to search and replace across the entire code base
- Allows you to "look inside" your PHP programs with a debugger

You don't always need an IDE to accomplish these things. However, an IDE provides one tool that does all of them.

Another advantage of an IDE is that it can bring different development tasks under one application. For example, many Joomla developers use version control software, such as Git or Subversion. These programs have plugins that work with IDEs so that you can use the version control software from inside the IDE. Automated builder software, like Phing or Ant, is another example. You can run these programs from inside the IDE. For many developers, this makes life easier and less confusing.

To some, using an IDE comes at a high price—namely, learning how to use it. Also, with an IDE you are more likely to encounter bugs in the development tool itself, since it is a more complex software program than an editor. Some people find this frustration is not worth the potential productivity gains.

To others, learning a new piece of software and tolerating the possibility of bugs is a small price to pay for the advantages offered by the IDE.

If you are planning to do a lot of Joomla development, it is probably worth your time to at least try an IDE to see how it works for you. If you don't want to spend time learning how to use a new program and just want to jump into writing code, then perhaps using an IDE isn't for you.

Open-Source IDE Choices

The two most popular IDEs for Joomla development are Eclipse and Netbeans. Both of them do a great job of helping the developer be more productive. Each is discussed in the following sections.

Eclipse

Although Eclipse has been the most popular IDE for Java development for years, its use for PHP development is more recent. In 2007, PDT (PHP Development Tools) was released for PHP developers. This is a set of plugins for Eclipse that adapt Eclipse to work with PHP.

At the present time, PDT version 3.0 is the latest release. The Eclipse project releases a new version every year in June, and a new PDT version is normally released at the same time. Eclipse can be downloaded from the Eclipse website at `http://eclipse.org/downloads`. Joomla developers would normally want the "Eclipse for PHP Developers" package.

Detailed instructions for setting up Eclipse for Joomla development are available on the Joomla documentation site at `http://docs.joomla.org/Setting_up_your_workstation_for_Joomla!_development`.

Eclipse is written in Java and runs on Windows, Linux, and Mac OS X platforms. It is free and open-source software. Although there is no formal data about which IDEs Joomla developers prefer, Eclipse is probably the most popular IDE among experienced Joomla developers, if for no other reason than that it was the first free IDE for PHP development.

Let's take a closer look at how Eclipse can help with Joomla development. The first thing to understand about an IDE like Eclipse or NetBeans is the concept of a project.

In most text editors, you edit one file at a time and the editor doesn't know or care about other related files.

In an IDE, you create a project that holds a group of related files. If we are working on Joomla, for example, the entire Joomla application would be one project. This can be confusing at first but makes a lot of sense for Joomla development, since we are always working with groups of related files.

When you create a PHP project in Eclipse, you get a view called the PHP Explorer that allows you to browse the entire project and open any file for editing. Figure 2.1 shows the PHP Explorer view on the left, with one file open for editing in the upper right.

Now let's look at examples of the IDE features we discussed earlier. We'll start with syntax highlighting. Figure 2.2 shows a PHP program open for editing in Eclipse. Different types of code are shown in different colors, making it easier to read the code.

Now let's look at what happens if we make a mistake. In Figure 2.3, we left out the parentheses after the `if` statement.

We see the red X symbol on the left and red underlines in two places. This immediately tells us that something is wrong with this code. Hovering the mouse on the red X shows the pop-up text in Figure 2.4. This pop-up text gives us information about what is wrong and how we might fix it.

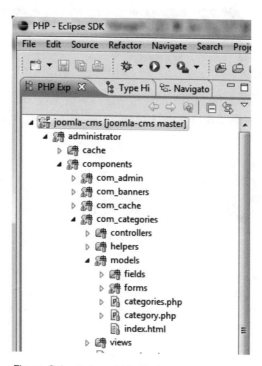

Figure 2.1   Eclipse PHP Explorer view example

```php
/**
 * Class constructor.
 *
 * @param   array  $config  A configuration arra
 *                          session_name, client
 *
 * @since   11.1
 */
public function __construct($config = array())
{
    jimport('joomla.utilities.utility');
    jimport('joomla.error.profiler');

    // Set the view name.
    $this->_name = $this->getName();

    // Only set the clientId if available.
    if (isset($config['clientId'])) {
        $this->_clientId = $config['clientId'];
    }

    // Enable sessions by default.
    if (!isset($config['session'])) {
        $config['session'] = true;
    }
```

Figure 2.2   Eclipse PHP editor syntax highlighting

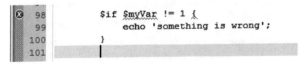

```php
98      $if $myVar != 1 {
99          echo 'something is wrong';
100     }
101
```

Figure 2.3   Eclipse PHP editor showing syntax error

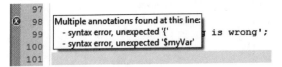

```
97
98      Multiple annotations found at this line:
99      - syntax error, unexpected '{'         is wrong';
100     - syntax error, unexpected '$myVar'
101
```

Figure 2.4   Pop-up error text

Another important feature is automatic code completion. This comes in several forms. The simplest form is giving you some characters in pairs. For example, in PHP when you type a left-parenthesis, you will almost always want a right-parenthesis as well. So the editor gives you both. This is also true for curly braces, quotes, and HTML elements.

Another form of code completion occurs when you want to type the name of a method. In Figure 2.5, we typed in `$x = $this->` and then pressed Ctrl+Space.

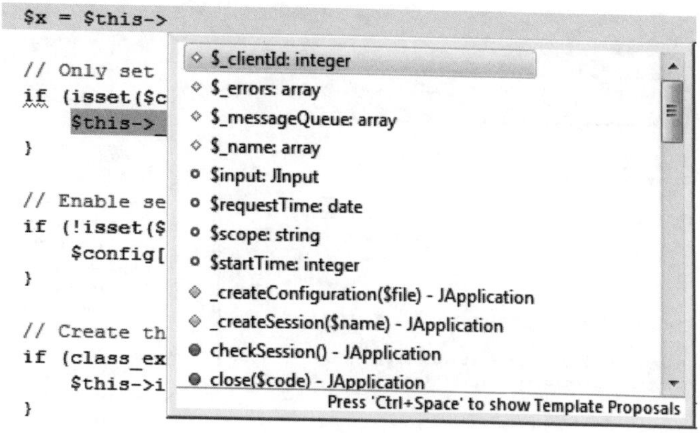

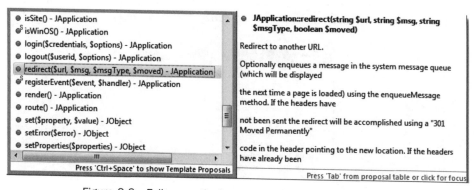

Figure 2.5   Eclipse PHP method selection

The editor knows that `$this` is an object of type `JApplication`, so it shows us all the fields and methods that are available for that class. We can choose one by clicking with the mouse or using the arrow keys. When we choose one, it will automatically insert the method or field name for us. This saves typing and reduces the chance of misspelling. Note that if we start typing a method name, the search window is updated to show only the names that match what we have typed.

It also can tell us about each of the methods. In Figure 2.6, we highlighted the `redirect()` method. On the right, it shows us the parameters and the documentation block for that method.

This is a handy way to help us find the method that we need and is quicker than hunting through a separate file or window.

When we are editing a file, Eclipse can show us the list of fields and methods for that file in a separate view. In Figure 2.7, we see the edit area on the left and the Outline view on the right.

Figure 2.6   Eclipse method parameter list and documentation

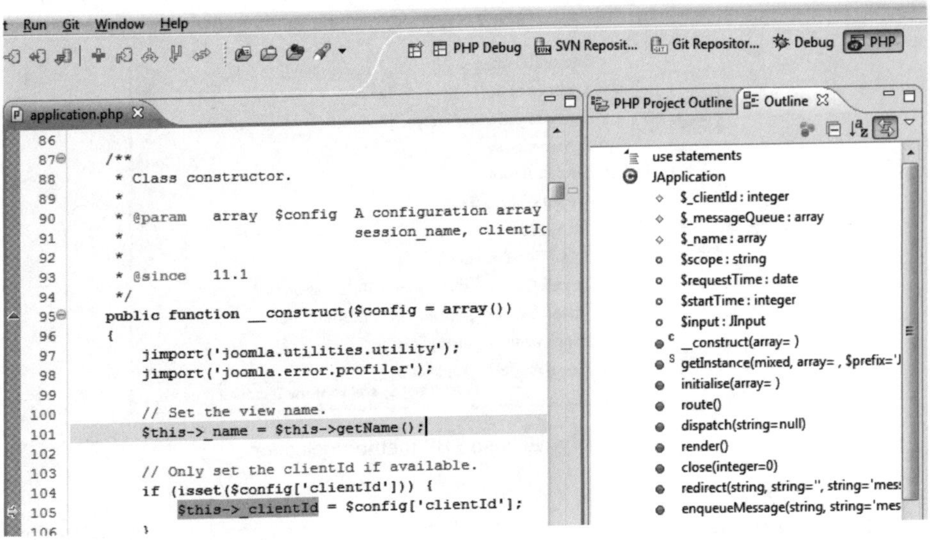

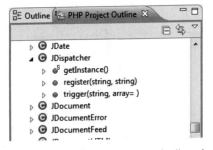

Figure 2.7   Eclipse Editor and Class Outline view

The Outline view shows us the fields and methods for the class being edited. We can also see an outline of the entire project in the PHP Project Outline view, as shown in Figure 2.8. In this view, we can look up any class in Joomla and see all its fields and methods.

Another handy feature of an IDE like Eclipse is the ability to quickly compare two versions of a file to see exactly what has changed. Figure 2.9 shows a comparison of the current version of a file with a version before some recent edits were made.

You can use the compare feature to compare different versions of the same file. This could be from local history (which Eclipse keeps for you automatically) or, if you are using version control software, from other versions in the repository.

When writing code, we often need to search across a group of programs, or the entire project, to see where a variable was used or where some other text appears. Eclipse provides a simple but powerful search capability. In Figure 2.10, we searched the project for occurrences of the phrase `JFactory::getSession()`.

Figure 2.8   Eclipse PHP Project Outline view

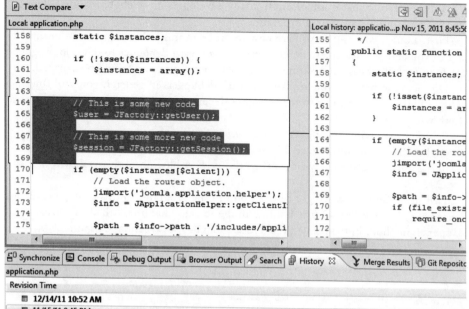

Figure 2.9   Eclipse file compare example

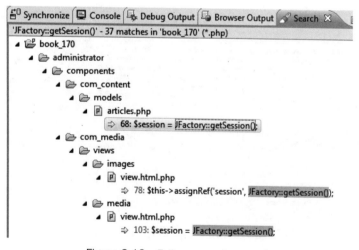

Figure 2.10   Eclipse search example

As a convenience, the search results are linked with the editor. For example, if we double-click on one of the lines in the search results, the target file is opened in the editor with the cursor placed at the line number where the text was found. We can also search and replace from this view.

Another feature that is important to many developers is the ability to use a debugger to "look inside" a running program.

First, a quick warning. If you are new to programming, this might seem intimidating to you and you absolutely do not need to ever use a debugger to develop programs for Joomla. In that case, just skim over the next few figures and don't be alarmed.

On the other hand, if you are familiar with debuggers in general, you will find the Eclipse PHP debugger to be similar to other debuggers and relatively easy to learn and work with.

Eclipse works with a debugger called *Xdebug* to allow you to suspend and step through a PHP program. Figure 2.11 shows a Joomla program suspended.

In the upper left, we see what is called the *stack*. A blowup of this is shown in Figure 2.12.

This stack shows how we got to this point in the program. In this example, we started at index.php line 43 (the last line in the stack). That line, called the `JSite->dispatch` method, in turn called the `JComponentHelper::renderComponent`

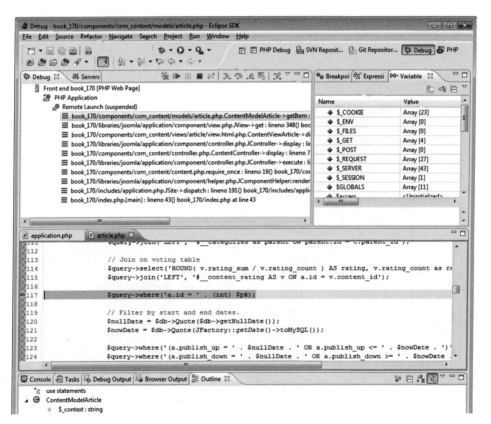

Figure 2.11   Eclipse debugger

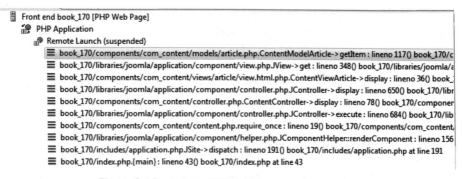

Figure 2.12   Eclipse PHP debugger stack example

method and so on, until we get to the top of the stack, where we have called the `ContentModelArticle->getItem` method.

Important Note

Don't worry if you don't understand the stack. We discuss this in more detail in Chapter 3.

The Variables view, shown in Figure 2.13, displays the value of every variable in scope at this point in the program.

Name	Value
$_COOKIE	Array [23]
$_ENV	Array [0]
$_FILES	Array [0]
$_GET	Array [4]
$_POST	Array [0]
$_REQUEST	Array [27]
$_SERVER	Array [43]
$_SESSION	Array [1]
$GLOBALS	Array [11]
$access	<Uninitialized>
$archived	<Uninitialized>
$asset	<Uninitialized>
$data	<Uninitialized>
$db	JDatabaseMySQLi
$e	<Uninitialized>
$error	<Uninitialized>
$groups	<Uninitialized>

Figure 2.13   Eclipse debugger Variables view

Many other handy features in Eclipse help make Joomla development more efficient. The built-in Eclipse Help that is installed with the program has detailed information about the various features available.

One weakness of Eclipse for PHP developers is the relative lack of tutorials and user documentation, although the Joomla documentation site has some useful Eclipse articles.

PHPEclipse

PHPEclipse (http://www.phpeclipse.com) is another open-source PHP IDE with features similar to the Eclipse PDT program. It is supported outside the official Eclipse project family. At this time, PHPEclipse no longer appears to be actively developed, although it is still available for download.

NetBeans

The other major free and open-source IDE for PHP development is called NetBeans and is available for download at http://netbeans.org/downloads/index.html. Like Eclipse, NetBeans was originally developed for Java and is now available for a number of different programming languages.

One advantage of NetBeans is that it has excellent documentation available for PHP development, including video tutorials. For this reason, NetBeans is a good option for people who are new to using an IDE.

NetBeans has a similar feature set to Eclipse, including syntax highlighting, code completion, file compare, global search, and a debugger.

Like Eclipse and other IDEs, NetBeans organizes your work based on projects and allows you to easily explore the project to find the file you need. Figure 2.14 shows the Project view in NetBeans.

NetBeans for PHP supports syntax highlighting, error reporting, and code completion. Figure 2.15 shows the syntax highlighting in NetBeans.

Figure 2.16 shows NetBeans's display of a PHP syntax error.

If we hover on the error marker, it shows us more information about the error, as shown in Figure 2.17.

NetBeans has code completion that's similar to Eclipse. For example, the JApplication code completion is shown in Figure 2.18, which was displayed by typing $x = $this-> and pressing Ctrl+Space. As with Eclipse, if we type the first part of the desired method, the list narrows to methods that match the typed letters.

And we can see the parameters and documentation block for a method by highlighting that method, as shown in Figure 2.19.

NetBeans displays an outline of the class being edited that shows the methods and fields of the class. An example is shown in Figure 2.20.

NetBeans includes a file compare feature, either for local history or for version control history. Figure 2.21 shows a comparison with an earlier version of the file.

NetBeans allows you to search a project. An example is shown in Figure 2.22.

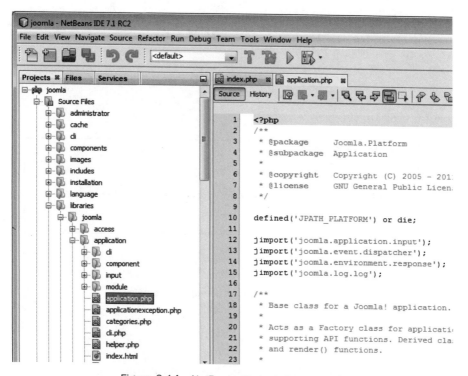

Figure 2.14   NetBeans Project view example

```php
/**
 * Class constructor.
 *
 * @param   array  $config  A configuration array
 *                          session_name, clientId
 *
 * @since   11.1
 */
public function __construct($config = array())
{
    jimport('joomla.utilities.utility');
    jimport('joomla.error.profiler');

    // Set the view name.
    $this->_name = $this->getName();

    // Only set the clientId if available.
    if (isset($config['clientId'])) {
        $this->_clientId = $config['clientId'];
    }

    // Enable sessions by default.
    if (!isset($config['session'])) {
        $config['session'] = true;
    }
```

Figure 2.15   NetBeans syntax highlighting

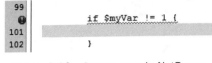

Figure 2.16   Syntax error in NetBeans

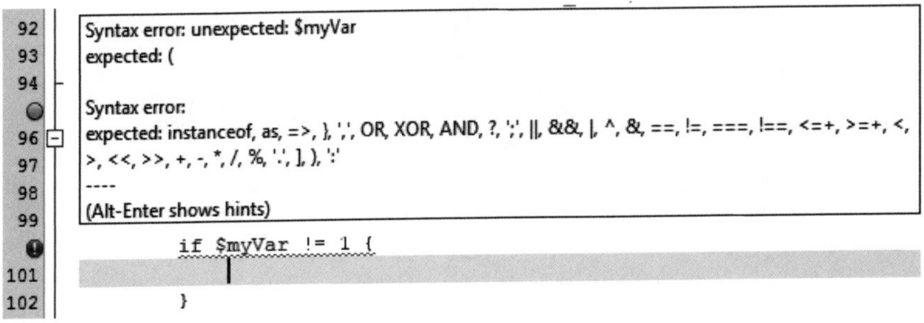

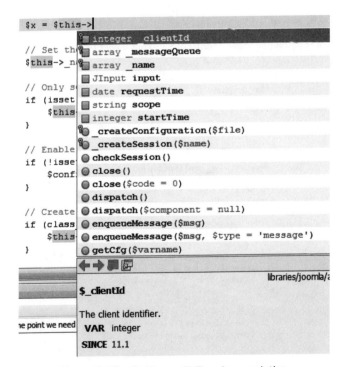

Figure 2.17   NetBeans pop-up error display

Figure 2.18   NetBeans PHP code completion

```
⊙ logout($userid = null, $options = array())
● redirect($url)
⊙ redirect($url, $msg = '')
⊙ redirect($url, $msg = '', $msgType = 'message')
⊙ redirect($url, $msg = '', $msgType = 'message', $moved = false)
⊕ registerEvent($event, $handler)
⊙ render()
⊙ route()
⊙ setUserState($key, $value)
```

←→▣⬚

libraries/joomla/application/application.php

redirect($url, $msg =", $msgType ='message', $moved =false)

Redirect to another URL.

Optionally enqueues a message in the system message queue (which will be displayed the next time a page is loaded) using the enqueueMessage method. If the headers have not been sent the redirect will be accomplished using a "301 Moved Permanently" code in the header pointing to the new location. If the headers have already been sent this will be accomplished using a JavaScript statement.

Parameters:

string	**$url**	The URL to redirect to. Can only be http/https URL
string	**$msg**	An optional message to display on redirect.
string	**$msgType**	An optional message type. Defaults to message.

Figure 2.19   NetBeans code completion method documentation

Projects ✖ Files   Services

```
□ php joomla
  └ ⬚ Source Files
      ├ ⬚ administrator
      ├ ⬚ cache
      ├ ⬚ di
      ├ ⬚ components
      └ ⬚ images
```

index.php ✖   application.php ✖

Source   History   🗗 🗒 ▾ 🗒 ▾ 🔍 🗗 🗗

application.php - Navigator ✖

```
□ JApplication::JObject
  ◆ __construct(array $config)
  ⊙ __toString():string
  🔖 _createConfiguration(string $file):object
  🔖 _createSession(string $name):\JSession
  ⊙ checkSession():\void
  ⊙ close(integer $code):\void
  ⊙ dispatch(string $component):\void
  ⊙ enqueueMessage(string $msg, string $type):\void
  ⊙ getCfg($varname, $default):mixed
  ⊙ getClientId():integer
  ⊕ getHash(string $seed):string
  ⊕ getInstance(mixed $client, array $config, $prefix)
  ⊙ getMenu(string $name, array $options):\JMenu
  ⊙ getMessageQueue():array
  ⊙ getName():string
```

```
87 ┌   /**
88 │     * Class constructor.
89 │     *
90 │     * @param   array  $c
91 │     *
92 │     *
93 │     * @since   11.1
94 │     */
     ⊙  public function __con
96 ┌   {
97 │       jimport('joomla.u
98 │       jimport('joomla.e
99 │
100│       // Set the view n
101│       $this->_name = $t
102│
103│       // Only set the c
104│       if (isset($config
105│           $this->_clien
106│       }
107│
108│       // Enable session
109│       if (!isset($confi
```

Figure 2.20   NetBeans navigator showing class methods

Version	Label
⊟ 📋 Today	
Dec 14, 2011 3:14:48 PM	
⊟ 📋 Older than 6 days ago	
Nov 7, 2011 12:10:50 PM	

application.php Nov 7, 2011 12:10:50 PM		1/1		Current File
`*`	153	⇨	159	
`* @since   11.1`	154		160	`if (!isset($instances)) {`
`*/`	155		161	`    $instances = array();`
`public static function getIn`	156		162	`}`
`{`	157		163	
`    static $instances;`	158		164 ✖	`// This is some new code`
	159		165	`$user = JFactory::getUser();`
`    if (!isset($instances))`	160		166	
`        $instances = array()`	161		167	`// This is more new code`
`    }`	162		168	`$session = JFactory::getSession();`
	163		169	
`    if (empty($instances[$cl`	164		170	`if (empty($instances[$client])) {`

Figure 2.21   Compare editor in NetBeans

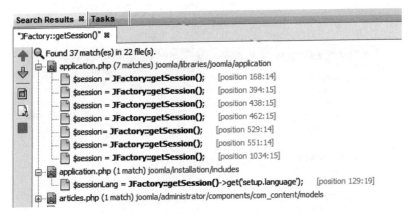

Figure 2.22   NetBeans search example

As with Eclipse, the search is linked to the editor, so you can double-click any line in the search results view and open that file for editing, with the cursor placed at that location.

NetBeans also includes an integrated debugger, again using the Xdebug program. Figure 2.23 shows a program suspended during a debug session.

The NetBeans Variables view shows the values of all variables in scope at the point the program was suspended, as shown in Figure 2.24.

The NetBeans Call Stack view shows the call stack, as shown in Figure 2.25.

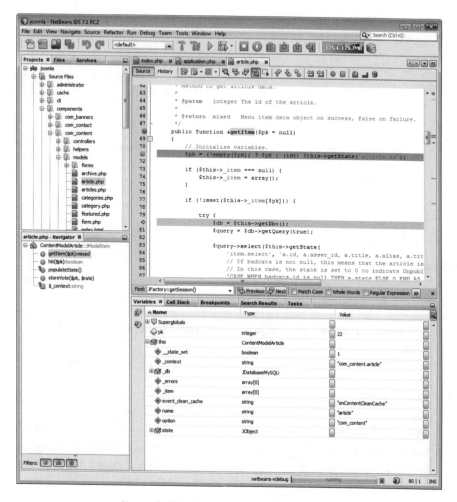

Figure 2.23   NetBeans debug example

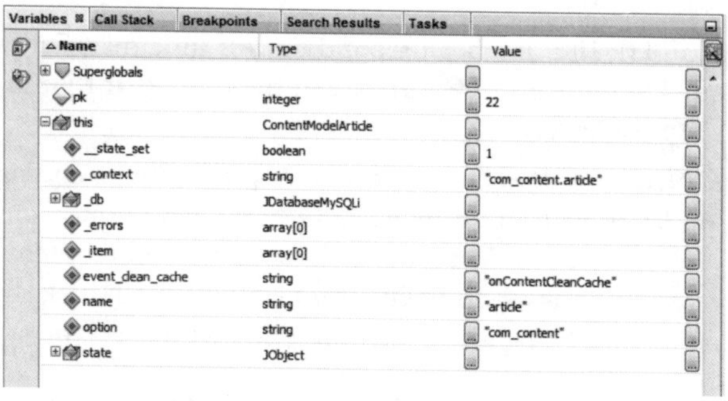

Figure 2.24   NetBeans debug Variables view

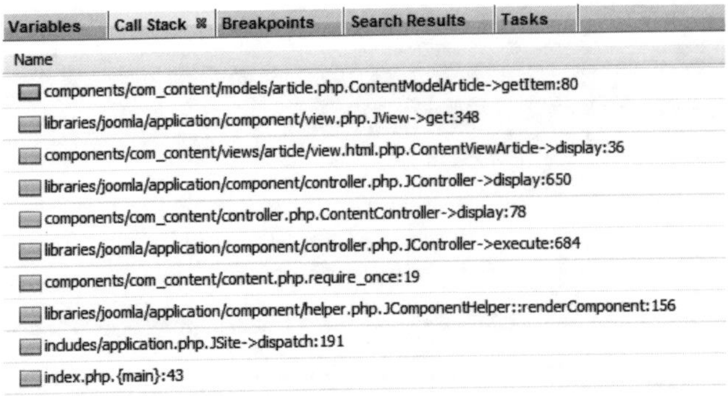

Figure 2.25   NetBeans debug Call Stack view

As with Eclipse, this lists all the method calls that brought us to this point in the program.

Eclipse or NetBeans?

Both NetBeans and Eclipse are full-featured IDEs that provide a number of useful functions for the Joomla developer. If either one of these were available for free, we would be fortunate. To have both of them available for free is that much better. If you plan to do more than a little PHP or Joomla development, it may be a good investment of time to give one of them a try.

So which one should you try? That's a difficult call, but here are a few things to consider when making the decision:

- For PHP development, NetBeans has better documentation for beginners. It is also easier to configure and use the debugger. Some people think NetBeans is also simpler and easier to learn than Eclipse (although perhaps less configurable).

- Eclipse uses user-interface widgets that are native to each operating system, so Eclipse looks and feels like a native application on each platform. On Windows, it looks like other Windows applications and on Mac or Linux it looks like other Mac or Linux applications. NetBeans uses the Java SWING set of user-interface widgets and looks the same on all platforms. So it doesn't look as much like a native application. For some people, this is an advantage of Eclipse.

- NetBeans as a PHP IDE has been around for less time than Eclipse, but it has caught up quickly in terms of feature set to the point that they are comparable, at least for the basic tasks.

- At this time, NetBeans does not support cross-platform line endings. If you are developing on Windows, for example, and need to have Linux line endings on your files, you will need to do a bit of extra work to put the Linux line endings on files you create in Windows. In Eclipse (or many other editors), this is just a simple configuration option. Hopefully, NetBeans will add this feature at some point.

If you are still undecided about which one to try, another option is to try out both and see which one works the best for you.

Commercial IDEs

Many commercially marketed IDEs work well for developing PHP programs:

- ZendStudio (`http://www.zend.com/en/products/studio`) is a popular commercial PHP IDE, based on Eclipse.

- Aptana Studio Pro (`http://www.aptana.com`) is another commercial PHP IDE that is highly recommended by some users. It is also based on Eclipse.

- Komodo IDE (`http://www.activestate.com/komodo-ide`) is another commercial IDE for PHP developers.

- Nusphere's PhpED (`http://www.nusphere.com/products/phped.htm`) provides an integrated debugger and profiler as well as deployment functionality.

Text Editor Choices

If the previous section didn't convince you to try an IDE, here are some simpler options.

Notepad++

Notepad++ is a simple-to-use but powerful open-source editor for Windows platforms that includes syntax highlighting and some code completion for a number of programming languages, including PHP. You can download it at `http://notepad-plus-plus.org`.

Figure 2.26 shows a Joomla PHP file open in Notepad++. As shown in the example, there is no error highlighting available.

```
application.php
193      */
194      public static function getInstance($client, $config = array(), $pr
195      {
196          if (empty(self::$instances[$client]))
197          {
198              // Load the router object.
199              $info = JApplicationHelper::getClientInfo($client, true);
200
201              $path = $info->path . '/includes/application.php';
202              if (file_exists($path))
203              {
204                  include_once $path;
205
206                  // Create a JRouter object.
207                  $classname = $prefix . ucfirst($client);
208                  $instance = new $classname($config);
209              }
210              else
211              {
212                  $error = JError::raiseError(500, JText::sprintf('JLIB_
213                  return $error;
```

Figure 2.26   Notepad++ Editor

For Mac OS X users, Smultron (`http://www.apple.com/downloads/macosx/development_tools/smultron.html`) provides PHP syntax highlighting for PHP.

For Linux users, the standard system editor gedit provides PHP syntax highlighting.

It is also possible to use a standard text editor such as Notepad or vi that does not include PHP syntax highlighting. Any editor that can edit plain text will work fine to edit all the Joomla files. Obviously, the farther you move away from an IDE, the harder it will be to visually check if your code is correct and free of typographical errors.

It is also important to understand that you can use different programs on the same set of Joomla files. If a file is inside a defined project for an IDE, for example, it is still accessible from the file system and can be edited outside the IDE. So you can use different programs for different tasks if you like.

Other Tools

Other software tools can be helpful when doing Joomla development. Some of these are now discussed briefly.

Version Control Software

Version control software is considered essential for most software projects, including Joomla. Version control software tracks every change to the code base and allows a group of developers to make changes to the code base in an organized fashion. If a problem is encountered with a change made to the code, the change can be undone to fix the problem. Even if you are the only developer on a project, version control software can be enormously helpful. When you find a problem, you can "turn back the clock" to see where the problem was introduced. This often helps you narrow down the source of the problem.

The Joomla content management system (CMS) and platform projects use a program called Git (`http://git-scm.com`) and are hosted at Github (`https://github.com/joomla`). Other popular version control programs include Subversion (`http://subversion.apache.org`) and Mercurial (`http://mercurial.selenic.com`).

If you use an IDE, typically the version control software is included in the IDE. For example, Eclipse and NetBeans both support GIT, Subversion, and Mercurial.

Automatic Builder Software (Ant and Phing)

PHP files are run as scripts, directly from the text files. So there is no compile step for PHP programs as there is for Java or C programs.

Developers writing in languages that require compiling or building often use programs to automate this process. Two such programs are Phing and Ant. Ant was originally developed for working with C and Java programs. Phing is a PHP program for doing batch build operations in PHP projects.

Given that we don't have to build PHP programs, why would we want a program like Ant or Phing? The answer is that sometimes it is handy to be able to automate repetitive batch jobs.

For example, if you are building a Joomla extension, one way to organize your work is to have two projects in the IDE. One project contains only your extension code and might be tied to a version control repository. The other project is a Joomla installation with the extension installed. This project allows you to test the extension inside a Joomla installation.

In this example, you will be testing the extension in the test project but tracking the code changes in the extension project. It might be convenient to be able to make code changes in the files inside the test project and then, once they work properly, to copy the files from the test project to the extension project. With Phing or Ant, you can automate the process of copying files from one project to another. You can also automate the process of creating zip archives for packaging your extensions.

A tutorial that discusses using Phing for this purpose is available in the Joomla documentation site at `http://docs.joomla.org/Setting_up_your_workstation_for _extension_development`.

Automated Test Programs

There is a strong trend in software development toward automated testing of software. Automated tests can be written once and then run frequently to detect errors that have been introduced into the code base as changes are made.

The Joomla project currently uses two types of automated testing: unit testing and system testing. Unit testing is used to test the Joomla platform. Unit tests use a PHP program called `PHPUnit`. This allows us to write tests that feed data directly to a PHP method and compare the actual results to the results we expect. If they are different, an error report is generated.

System testing tests the operation of the CMS from a user's perspective by running a browser session under control of the test program. The browser does a sequence of data-entry commands, including mouse clicks and keyboard entries, simulating a user using the software. The document in the browser can be checked automatically inside the system test to make sure that certain information shows in the page. An error is reported if the expected information does not show on the page. Joomla uses a program called Selenium to create and run the system tests.

These automated tests are an important part of the Joomla development process. When changes are made, either in the form of bug fixes or in the form of enhancements, the automated tests can be run to help check that nothing was broken as a result of the changes.

Summary

In this chapter, we discussed how to get your workstation ready to start writing programs for Joomla. We discussed the options for installing the web server software on different platforms, including specific bundles for different operating systems. Then we discussed the two open-source IDEs for PHP, Eclipse, and NetBeans, and showed some examples of how they can help make you more productive with Joomla development.

We also briefly discussed editor options for people who don't want to use an IDE.

Finally, we presented a quick description of version control software, such as Subversion or Mercurial; automatic builder software, such as Phing and Ant; and automated testing software.

At this point, we have our workstation set up and are ready to dive into the Joomla program itself.

3

How Joomla! Works

Are you one of those people who likes to take things apart to see exactly how they work? Are you new to web programming and want to understand how it is different from other types of programming? Do you want to know how Joomla! is organized and why? If you answered yes to any of these, this chapter is for you!

On the other hand, if you just want to learn how to write a Joomla override or extension and you don't need or want to know the inner workings of Joomla, you can just skim or skip this chapter for now and come back to it later, if needed.

In this chapter, we look inside Joomla to understand how it works and why it works that way. We explore the files and folders that make up a Joomla installation and discuss what they do.

Then we look in detail at a Joomla session and understand what is happening behind the scenes when you fill out forms and click the buttons or links.

We discuss places where you can—or need to—use special names for folders or files for your programs in order to have Joomla find them and run them at the right time in the program. We show you how to access frequently needed objects inside your Joomla programs. Finally, we take you on a brief tour of the Joomla database tables.

Tour of Joomla Folders

When you install Joomla, it installs the folders and files shown in Figure 3.1.

After you install Joomla, a file called `configuration.php` will be created in the root folder. In a production version, the `installation` folder would normally be deleted, because keeping it around presents a security vulnerability. If you download Joomla using the Github or SVN repository, you will get a folder called tests that contains the automated unit and system test files, a folder called docs that includes information for creating documentation in PDF format, and a folder called build that includes the program for building the Joomla archive files. These are removed when Joomla is packaged for normal installation.

Name	Date modified	Type
administrator	10/28/2011 7:58 AM	File Folder
cache	10/28/2011 7:58 AM	File Folder
cli	10/28/2011 7:58 AM	File Folder
components	10/28/2011 7:58 AM	File Folder
images	10/28/2011 7:58 AM	File Folder
includes	10/28/2011 7:58 AM	File Folder
installation	10/28/2011 7:58 AM	File Folder
language	10/28/2011 7:58 AM	File Folder
libraries	10/28/2011 7:58 AM	File Folder
logs	10/28/2011 7:58 AM	File Folder
media	10/28/2011 7:58 AM	File Folder
modules	10/28/2011 7:58 AM	File Folder
plugins	10/28/2011 7:58 AM	File Folder
templates	10/28/2011 7:58 AM	File Folder
tmp	10/28/2011 7:58 AM	File Folder
htaccess.txt	4/7/2011 8:47 AM	Text Document
index.php	2/21/2011 11:45 AM	PHP File
joomla.xml	10/17/2011 7:59 AM	XML File
LICENSE.txt	12/12/2009 7:44 AM	Text Document
README.txt	9/25/2011 12:00 PM	Text Document
robots.txt	9/20/2011 6:37 AM	Text Document
web.config.txt	4/7/2011 8:30 AM	Text Document

Figure 3.1   Joomla version 2.5 folders and files

Front End versus Back End

If you have used Joomla, you are familiar with the concept of the front end and back end (sometimes called the administrative back end). We can think of these as completely separate applications that happen to share some common libraries.

If you look at the subfolders of the administrator folder, you will see many of the same folders that you see in the top-level folder. These include cache, components, includes, language, modules, and templates.

The administrator folder also has its own version of index.php. So when you enter the URL http://mywebsite.org/administrator it loads this file (administrator/index.php), which starts the administrator application. When you enter the URL http://mywebsite.org, it loads the index.php file from the top-level folder, which starts the front-end application.

Each of these folders is briefly discussed next. Since the administrator folder is similar in structure to the top level, we will discuss it last.

Cache

The cache folder is very easy to understand. This is just where we store our cached files. In a dynamic website, the system does a lot of work to pull together the information to display a page. For example, if the page is displaying a blog layout, the system has to access the database to get the articles for the blog, lay out the articles on the page, and load the desired modules for the page.

In many real-life websites, the information for a page might stay the same for hours or days. If you have 50 users requesting the same page per hour, and the information is only changing once per day, you would be getting the exact same information from the database about 1,200 times (50 × 24) before the information actually changed.

With caching enabled, we try to reduce the number of times we access the database to get exactly the same information. In our previous example, if we cache the page, we save a copy of the page in the `cache` folder for a specified period of time—perhaps 15 minutes. When the first user requests the page, it is compiled from the database in the normal manner, and a copy of the entire page is saved in the `cache` folder.

If a second user requests exactly the same information, the system first checks to see if there is a cached copy of the page that has not yet expired (less than 15 minutes old, in our example). If so, the page is read from the cached copy and we don't have to access the database or assemble the page. This allows the page to load much faster and also reduces the amount of work the server must do.

On a busy website where the frequency of viewing is greater than the frequency of database changes, caching can improve overall system performance dramatically.

The files in this folder are deleted when you select Site → Maintenance → Clear Cache or Site → Maintenance → Purge Expired Cache. If you run a large production site, you may also run a system-level job to remove unneeded cache files from this folder.

CLI

The `cli` folder was added as a standard location for storing command-line-interface (CLI) applications. One of the great features of the Joomla platform is the ability to easily create CLI applications that interact with a Joomla website. CLI applications are well suited to running on a schedule—for example, using the Linux cron program. We demonstrate an example of this in Chapter 13.

Components

A component is normally the main thing on a given page and usually corresponds to a menu item. When you select an item from a menu, the page that loads contains the component defined by that menu item.

If we look at the subfolders for components, we see each of the core components for Joomla: `com_banners`, `com_contact`, `com_content` (for articles), `com_finder` (for Smart Search), `com_mailto`, `com_media`, `com_newsfeeds`, `com_search`, `com_users`, `com_weblinks`, and `com_wrappers`. As you have probably figured out by now, the component folders all start with the letters `com_` followed by the component name. This is one example of strong naming conventions that are used throughout Joomla. We discuss these later in this chapter.

If we look at the options when you are creating a new menu item for the core components, we have the options shown in Figure 3.2.

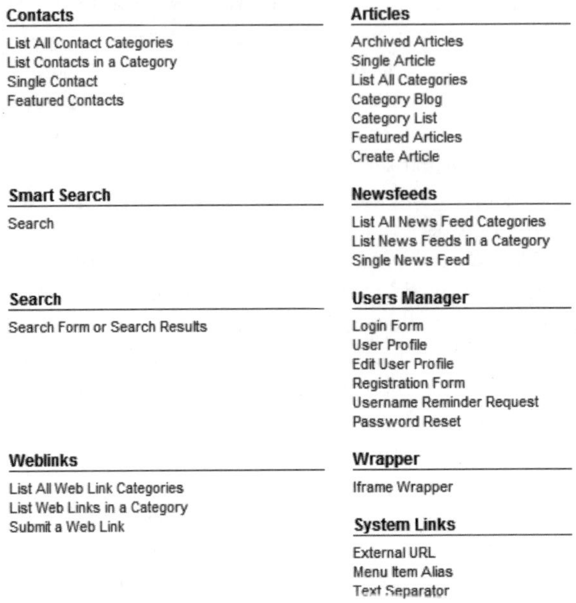

Contacts

List All Contact Categories
List Contacts in a Category
Single Contact
Featured Contacts

Articles

Archived Articles
Single Article
List All Categories
Category Blog
Category List
Featured Articles
Create Article

Smart Search

Search

Newsfeeds

List All News Feed Categories
List News Feeds in a Category
Single News Feed

Search

Search Form or Search Results

Users Manager

Login Form
User Profile
Edit User Profile
Registration Form
Username Reminder Request
Password Reset

Weblinks

List All Web Link Categories
List Web Links in a Category
Submit a Web Link

Wrapper

Iframe Wrapper

System Links

External URL
Menu Item Alias
Text Separator

Figure 3.2   Front-end core menu types

Most of these menu item types match up exactly to one of the folders. These include contacts, articles (which uses the com_content folder), news feeds, search, users, weblinks, and wrapper.

The components com_banners, com_mailto, and com_media do not correspond to menu item types. Banners are components but they get inserted into pages inside modules. When you click on the E-mail icon to e-mail an article to someone, the component com_mailto is called. The com_media component is called when you edit an article in the front end and you press the Image button to load the Media Manager.

These components do not display as the main thing on a page and therefore don't fit the simple definition of a component. This brings us to the more detailed and technical definition of a component, which is this: A component is an extension that has to take some action other than displaying something. For example, when you click on a banner, it has to write to the database to record the click and then perhaps redirect you to another URL. Similarly, when you click the E-mail icon, it has to offer you a form to fill out and then send the e-mail. When you want to insert an image into an article, you are again taking actions, such as uploading an image to the web server.

So in all these cases, we need a component to handle these actions, even though these components will never be the central content of a page on our site.

Images

The `images` folder is one place where image files for the site can be stored. For example, in the core distribution, we have subfolders called `banners` and `sampledata`. As you would expect, the `banners` folder stores images for the example banners that are included in the core distribution. The `sampledata` folder stores images that are used in the sample data that you can install (optionally) when you install Joomla.

Important Note about Index.html Files

You will notice that every subfolder in the Joomla distribution (except administrator and installation, which contain `index.php` files) contains a file called `index.html`. If you open this file in an editor, you will see the following content:

```
<!DOCTYPE html><title></title>
```

This is an HTML file with an <html> element and an empty <title> element. This file has no content and when displayed in a browser will show an empty page.

Why do we have these files everywhere? The answer is for security. If a user tries to browse to a folder, the web server looks for a file called `index.php` or `index.html` to load. If it can't find either of these files, the browser instead shows a list of files and subfolders in that folder.

You can see an example of this by temporarily renaming the `images/index.html` to `images/index1.html`. Then if you browse to the URL "<your Joomla! root>/images", you will see something similar to Figure 3.3.

If you rename the file back to `index.html`, you will just see a blank page with this same URL.

Allowing an unauthorized user to see information about the files and folders on your server is considered a security risk. Someone who wants to hack your website can use this information to try to get more information and to probe the site for possible

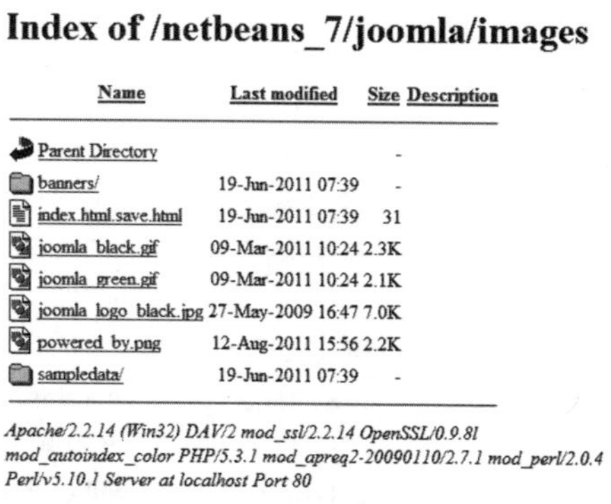

Index of /netbeans_7/joomla/images

Name	Last modified	Size	Description
Parent Directory		-	
banners/	19-Jun-2011 07:39	-	
index.html.save.html	19-Jun-2011 07:39	31	
joomla_black.gif	09-Mar-2011 10:24	2.3K	
joomla_green.gif	09-Mar-2011 10:24	2.1K	
joomla_logo_black.jpg	27-May-2009 16:47	7.0K	
powered_by.png	12-Aug-2011 15:56	2.2K	
sampledata/	19-Jun-2011 07:39	-	

*Apache/2.2.14 (Win32) DAV/2 mod_ssl/2.2.14 OpenSSL/0.9.81
mod_autoindex_color PHP/5.3.1 mod_apreq2-20090110/2.7.1 mod_perl/2.0.4
Perl/v5.10.1 Server at localhost Port 80*

Figure 3.3   Browser window of images folder without index.html file

vulnerabilities. That is why every subfolder in the system should contain a blank `index.html` file.

The `installation` and `administrator` folders are the only ones that do not contain an `index.html` file. This is because they contain an `index.php` file that serves as the entry point for the installation process and the administrative back end. In this case, the `index.html` would prevent the `index.php` file from loading.

Includes

We mentioned earlier that the `administrator` folder, which controls the back end of the site, can be thought of as an entirely separate application from the front end of the site. For this reason, when we start a front-end or back-end session, we need to load different classes and constants into memory.

The `includes` folder contains the programs that are specific to either the front- or back-end application. So the top-level `includes` folder loads the files that we need to get a front-end session started, whereas the `administrator/includes` folder has files we need to load to get a back-end session started.

The `includes` folder contains the files shown in Table 3.1.

Installation

The `installation` folder is an entirely separate miniapplication that does one thing: the initial Joomla installation. When you initially start either a front- or back-end session, the system checks for the presence of a file called `configuration.php` in the root folder. If it doesn't find this file, it assumes you need to run the installation and it loads the installation miniapplication.

Since this is a self-contained miniapplication, it has its own `includes` folder as well as other folders needed to run the installation process. One of the great things about Joomla is how easy it is to install. Everything is done for you, including creating the database. This cool stuff is done in the installation miniapplication.

Table 3.1 **Files in Root includes Folder**

File	Action
`application.php`	Creates the `JSite` class
`defines.php`	Defines constants for paths to files
`framework.php`	Loads commonly used portions of the Joomla framework (also known as the platform)
`menu.php`	Loads the entire site menu into memory
`pathway.php`	Creates the `JPathwaySite` class, which is used in the `mod_breadcrumbs` module to show the path to the current menu item
`router.php`	Loads the `JRouterSite` class; we will discuss the router in more detail later in this chapter

Language

Joomla is designed to be run natively in any of 68 (and counting) languages. As discussed in Chapter 2, virtually all text in Joomla is translated before it is shown in the browser. This is done by way of language packs, which install a set of language files. The `languages` subfolder is where these language packs get installed.

With a standard English installation, we get two subfolders: `en-GB` and `overrides`. The first folder holds all the language files needed to translate the front end of the site into English. (The GB stands for Great Britain. The official English for Joomla is British English.)

The second folder is related to a new feature in version 1.6: language overrides. Language overrides allow you to change the value of any text string without having to replace the entire language file. We will show an example of this in Chapter 4.

Note that there are often two language files per extension, one ending in `.sys.ini` and one ending in just `.ini`. The `.sys.ini` files are loaded to get the name and description of the extension—for example, for showing in the Module Manager. We load the `.ini` file when we are actually working with the extension to show all the text used by this extension.

Libraries

A software library is a set of programs that are designed to be reused in different contexts. A library normally performs a specific task or set of related tasks. These software libraries are stored in subfolders of the libraries folder.

In version 1.5, Joomla used 14 libraries. Of these, 13 were external libraries from third-party developers and one was the Joomla library.

In version 2.5, this has been reduced to four. The three external libraries are `phpmailer`, used for sending e-mail; `phputf8`, used for some operations on UTF-8 text; and `simplepie`, used for RSS feeds.

The library folder we are most interested in is the `joomla` folder. This folder contains the Joomla platform classes. We will discuss this in detail later in this chapter. Starting with version 2.5, we have a folder called `cms`. This folder contains library files used for the Joomla content management system (CMS) but not applicable to the platform.

Logs

This folder is used to store log files generated by Joomla. Events are logged based on certain conditions. For example, any error condition will be logged in a file called `error.log`. In addition, turning on debug mode will cause some events to be logged.

Media

The `media` folder holds CSS, Javascript, and image files for some of the components, modules, and editors. The system subfolder contains, among other things, the

MooTools JavaScript framework, which is used in Joomla to supply certain JavaScript functionality. We discuss JavaScript and MooTools in more detail in Chapter 12.

Modules

The `modules` folder contains a subfolder for each front-end module available. Figure 3.4 shows the subfolders on the left and a list of the Module Types you see when you create a new module in the Module Manager on the right.

Each module type has its own subfolder. Table 3.2 shows which module names correspond with which subfolder names.

When you install module extensions, they get added as subfolders to the `modules` folder and become completely integrated into your Joomla application. We will discuss modules in detail in Chapter 6.

Plugins

The plugins folder holds the plugins extensions. In version 2.5, there are ten types of plugins, each with its own subfolder, as indicated in Table 3.3. Each plugin type deals with a specific type of activity on the site and responds to events that are triggered during these activities.

We will discuss plugins in more detail in Chapter 5.

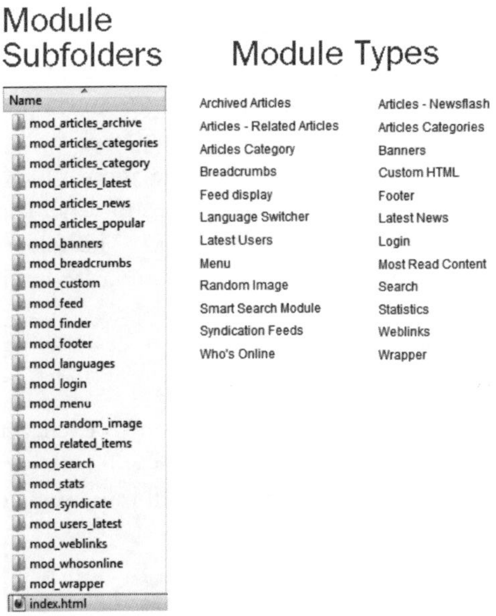

Figure 3.4   Module subfolders and module types

Table 3.2 **Module Subfolders and Corresponding Types**

Subfolder Name	Module Type Name	Comment
`mod_articles_archive`	Archived Articles	Called `mod_archive` in version 1.5.
`mod_articles_categories`	Articles Categories	Added in version 1.6.
`mod_articles_category`	Articles Category	Added in version 1.6. Replaces `mod_sections`.
`mod_articles_latest`	Latest News	Called `mod_latestnews` in version 1.5.
`mod_articles_news`	Articles–Newsflash	Called `mod_newsflash` in version 1.5.
`mod_articles_popular`	Most Read Content	Called `mod_mostread` in version 1.5.
`mod_banners`	Banners	
`mod_breadcrumbs`	Breadcrumbs	
`mod_custom`	Custom HTML	
`mod_feed`	Feed Display	
`mod_finder`	Smart Search	Added in version 2.5.
`mod_footer`	Footer	
`mod_languages`	Language Switcher	Added in version 1.6.
`mod_login`	Login	
`mod_menu`	Menu	Called `mod_mainmenu` in version 1.5.
`mod_random_image`	Random Image	
`mod_related_items`	Articles–Related Articles	
`mod_search`	Search	
`mod_stats`	Statistics	
`mod_syndicate`	Syndication Feeds	
`mod_users_latest`	Latest Users	Added in version 1.6.
`mod_weblinks`	Weblinks	Added in version 1.6.
`mod_whosonline`	Who's Online	
`mod_wrapper`	Wrapper	

Templates

In Joomla, the content of each web page is separated as much as possible from the way the page is presented on the screen. The presentation is controlled by extensions called templates.

The `templates` folder contains a subfolder for each front-end template that is installed on the system. In the default installation, this includes `atomic`, `beez_20`, and `beez5`. This folder also contains a `system` folder. The system template has some layout

Table 3.3 **Table of Plugin Types**

Folder Name	Where Used
`authentication`	During login to check user name and password
`captcha`	When processing a captcha screen
`content`	During content creation and editing
`editors`	When loading standard editors (for example, TinyMCE)
`editors-xtd`	Creates edit buttons (Article, Image, Page Break, Read More) when loading editors
`extension`	When installing, updating, or uninstalling extensions
`finder`	When Smart Searches are performed
`search`	When searches are performed
`system`	At various points during the command execution cycle, including initializing the session, routing the request, dispatching, and rendering; we discuss this in more detail later in the section called "Anatomy of a Joomla Command Cycle"
`user`	When creating, editing, or deleting users and when users are logging in or out

information that is shared by all the other templates and also is used by the system as a fallback in case a CSS class or file can't be found in the named template.

We discuss the `templates` folders in more detail in Chapter 4.

Tmp

The `tmp` folder, as you might guess, is a place for the system to store files on a temporary basis. One of the most frequent uses of this folder is when extensions are installed. When a new extension is installed, a copy of the extension's archive file is copied into the `tmp` folder and then is unpacked into the correct Joomla folders.

Administrator

As discussed earlier, Joomla can be thought of as two separate applications that share some of the same underlying code. These applications are the front end of the site and the administrative back end of the site.

This is evident when you look at the subfolders under the `administrator` folder. The `administrator` folder contains many of the same subfolders as the top-level folder, including `cache`, `components`, `help`, `includes`, `language`, `modules`, `templates`, and the file `index.php` (see Figure 3.5).

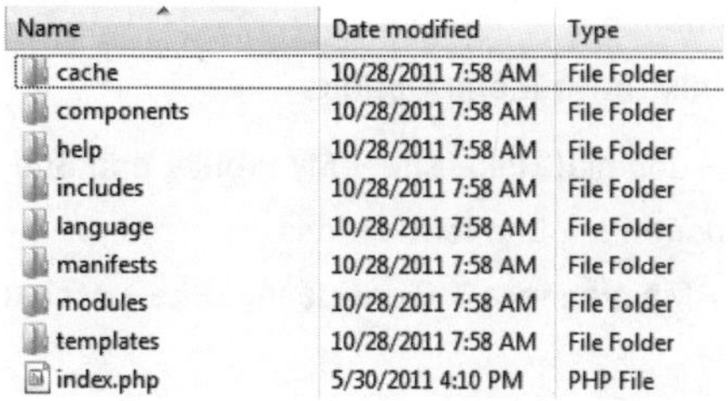

Name	Date modified	Type
cache	10/28/2011 7:58 AM	File Folder
components	10/28/2011 7:58 AM	File Folder
help	10/28/2011 7:58 AM	File Folder
includes	10/28/2011 7:58 AM	File Folder
language	10/28/2011 7:58 AM	File Folder
manifests	10/28/2011 7:58 AM	File Folder
modules	10/28/2011 7:58 AM	File Folder
templates	10/28/2011 7:58 AM	File Folder
index.php	5/30/2011 4:10 PM	PHP File

Figure 3.5 Contents of administrator folder

Adminstrator/Cache

This folder holds the cache files for the back end of the site. When back-end pages are cached, the temporary cache files are stored in this folder.

Administrator/Components

This folder contains all the components that are available in the back end of the website. Every menu choice in the back end is provided by one of these components. Table 3.4 lists each component and the back-end menu options that it provides.

Administrator/Help

This folder contains a file called `helpsites.xml`. This file contains the list of available online help sites. Normally, when you press the Help button, you are linked to the online help at `docs.joomla.org`.

There is also a folder called `en-GB` that contains an HTML file for each help topic. This allows for the option of having the help file on the local server. As shipped, the files in this folder simply redirect the user to the online help. But they can be overridden if desired to provide the help files locally.

Administrator/Includes

This folder serves the same purpose as the top-level `includes` folder discussed earlier. This folder holds the files we need to get a back-end session started, as shown in Table 3.5.

Administrator/Language

This is exactly the same as the top-level `language` folder, except that it is for the translation of the back end of the site. Each component, module, plugin, and template has its own language files.

Note that, like the front-end language files, we normally have a `.sys.ini` file and an `.ini` file for each extension. As discussed earlier, the `.sys.ini` file typically includes just the name and description of the extension for displaying in a list of extensions. The `.ini` file translates all the text strings used by the extension.

Table 3.4 **Front-End Components**

Folder Name	Administrative Menu Options
com_admin	Help → Joomla! Help, Site → My Profile, and Site → System Information
com_banners	Components → Banners options
com_cache	Site → Maintenance → Clear Cache, Site → Maintenance → Purge Expired Cache
com_categories	Content → Category Manager, Components → Banners → Categories, Components → Contacts → Categories, Components → Newsfeeds Categories, Components → Weblinks → Categories
com_checkin	Site → Maintenance → Global Check-in
com_config	Site → Global Configuration
com_contact	Components → Contacts options
com_content	Content → Article Manager, Content → Featured Articles
com_cpanel	Site → Control Panel
com_finder	Components → Smart Search*
com_installer	Extension → Extension Manager
com_languages	Extensions → Language Manager
com_login	Administrative Login screen, Site → Logout
com_media	Content → Media Manager
com_menus	Menus → Menu Manager, Menus menu (this lists a menu option for each front-end menu defined for the site)
com_messages	Components → Messaging
com_modules	Extensions → Module Manager
com_newsfeeds	Components → Newsfeeds Options
com_plugins	Extensions → Plugin Manager
com_redirect	Components → Redirect**
com_search	Components → Search
com_templates	Extensions → Template Manager
com_users	Users menu options (User Manager, Groups, Access Levels, Mass Mail Users)
com_weblinks	Components → Weblinks

* Added in version 2.5
** Added in version 1.6

Table 3.5 **Administrator includes Files**

File	Action
`application.php`	Creates the `JAdministrator` class
`defines.php`	Defines constants for paths to files
`framework.php`	Loads commonly used portions of the Joomla framework (also known as platform)
`helper.php`	Checks if you are already logged in and sends you to the desired component option
`menu.php`	Loads the entire administrator menu into memory
`router.php`	Loads the `JRouterSite` class. We will discuss the router in more detail in later in this chapter
`toolbar.php`	Provides methods for loading the back-end toolbars

Administrator/Manifests

This is a new folder for version 1.6 to support the new one-click update feature. It contains three subfolders (`files`, `libraries`, and `packages`):

- The `files` folder contains a file called `joomla.xml` that lists all the top-level folders and files in a standard Joomla installation. It also contains a list of update servers (URLs) where the program can look for updated versions of these files. This XML file tell the updater which files to update for this application.

- The `libraries` folder contains an XML file for each library used in Joomla. These XML files list all the folders and subfolders in the library and, again, a URL where the program can check for updates to the library.

- The `packages` folder also contains a file called `joomla.xml`. This supports a method of updating the Joomla installation as a package instead of a set of files. This feature is not implemented for version 2.5 but may be added in a future version. It will support dependency relationships between extensions. For example, if you request to update or install extension A and that extension requires extensions B and C, these will automatically be included in the installation or update.

See the website (`http://joomlaprogrammingbook.com`) for more information on setting up one-click updates.

Administrator/Modules

This folder serves the same purpose for the back end as the top-level `modules` folder serves for the front end. In contains one subfolder for each back-end module. These are shown in Figure 3.6. Each module type has its own subfolder. Table 3.6 shows which module names correspond with which subfolder names.

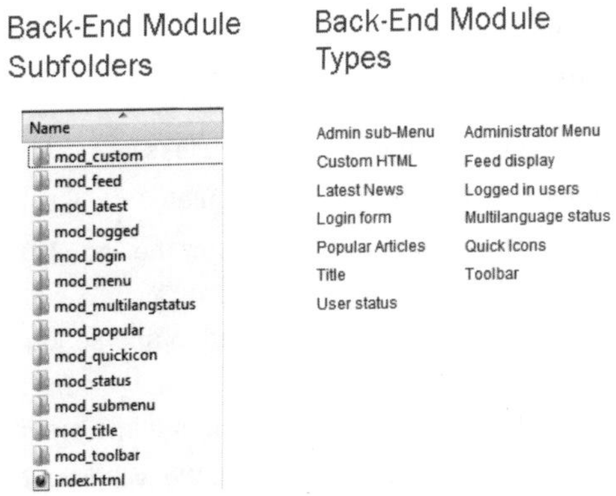

Back-End Module
Subfolders

Back-End Module
Types

Name
mod_custom
mod_feed
mod_latest
mod_logged
mod_login
mod_menu
mod_multilangstatus
mod_popular
mod_quickicon
mod_status
mod_submenu
mod_title
mod_toolbar
index.html

Admin sub-Menu	Administrator Menu
Custom HTML	Feed display
Latest News	Logged in users
Login form	Multilanguage status
Popular Articles	Quick Icons
Title	Toolbar
User status	

Figure 3.6   Back-end modules

Table 3.6 **Back-End Modules**

Subfolder Name	Module Type Name
mod_custom	Custom HTML
mod_feed	Feed display
mod_latest	Latest News
mod_logged	Logged-In Users
mod_login	Login Form
mod_menu	Administrator Menu
mod_multilangstatus	Multilanguage status
mod_popular	Popular Articles
mod_quickicon	Quick Icons
mod_status	User Status
mod_submenu	Admin Submenu
mod_title	Title
mod_toolbar	Toolbar

Administrator/Templates

This folder holds the templates used to display the back-end pages. Two templates are included with the standard implementation: Bluestork and Hathor. Bluestork is the default template; Hathor is a template designed especially for accessibility. For example, Hathor is designed to work well with screen readers (used by people with visual impairments), without using the mouse (for those who might have difficulty using a mouse).

As with the front end, we also include a system template that is used for common displays and as a fallback if the assigned template is missing.

Administrator/index.php

This file is loaded automatically by the web server when your browser points to the `administrator` folder. It is the entry point for the back end of Joomla. It controls the back-end command cycle in the same way that the top-level `index.php` file controls the front-end command cycle. Note that because we want the system to load this file, we don't have an `index.html` file here.

Files

The files shown in Table 3.7 are found in the top-level Joomla folder. The table describes their purpose.

Table 3.7 **Top-Level Files and Descriptions**

File	Function
configuration.php	This is created after a successful installation and contains settings that are specific to the site, such as the database connection information, and other settings. Most, but not all, of these settings can be edited in the Global Configuration screen in the back end.
htaccess.txt	This is a file that can be renamed to .htaccess and used with the mod_rewrite feature of the Apache web server. When used, it removes the index.php from all Joomla URLs and provides some additional security.
index.php	This is the file that starts all front-end page loads for the Joomla site. It is loaded automatically by the web server when you load any URL that points to the front end of the site (in other words, that does not point to the administrator folder).
joomla.xml	This is a copy of the file administrator/manifests/files/joomla.xml and is used during installation and then deleted from the root folder after installation.
LICENSE.txt	This contains the text of the Joomla license agreement. Joomla is licensed under the GNU GENERAL PUBLIC LICENSE, Version 2, dated June 1991.
README.txt	Contains some general information about Joomla
robots.txt	Web robots is a term for programs that automatically traverse the web and gather information about websites. Search engines, like Google and others, use robots to keep their indexes updated. Spammers and other bad guys use robots to gather e-mail addresses and for other malicious purposes. The robots.txt file included keeps the robots from accessing the subfolders of your site.
web.config.txt	This file is similar to the .htaccess file except that it is used for web servers running Microsoft IIS.

Joomla Platform

We can think of the Joomla CMS as a platform for building applications. We can also view the Joomla CMS as an application that sits on top of something even more fundamental, something that forms the foundation on which everything in Joomla is built. That something is the Joomla platform. It has been previously called "the Joomla framework," "the Joomla libraries," and probably many other things. What we are talking about, though, are the programs inside the `libraries` folder of the Joomla distribution.

Prior to version 1.5 of Joomla, the foundational classes and functions that made Joomla run were all jumbled up in a handful of files within the `includes` folder. For Joomla 1.5, it was decided to create a cleaner, more maintainable way of keeping the foundation code organized. We wanted things to look and feel familiar to someone coming from a professional development background where frameworks are relied upon to provide foundational logic. For example, we wanted Joomla development to be more comfortable for people coming from a Java or .NET background. Because of this, we set out to build what is now known as the Joomla platform.

When you first look in the `libraries` folder, you see five folders and four PHP files (along with the obligatory HTML file). Within the `loader.php` file there is an important class and two very important functions. The class is called `JLoader` and this is the class that handles including platform programs so that you can use them in your projects. The two functions are `jexit()` and `jimport()`.

The `jexit()` function is a wrapper around the PHP `exit` function (actually a language construct). It exists to make unit testing easier and you should always use it in your scripts instead of using `exit()` directly. The `jimport()` function is a shorthand way of calling `JLoader::import()` and is intended to provide a similar syntax to the `import` statement in Java or the `using` statement in C#. The general idea is that you give the `jimport()` method a dot-separated path to the library you want to use and then the platform makes sure it is available to you when you use it.

The folders are `joomla`, `cms`, `phpmailer`, `phputf8`, and `simplepie`. The three that are not Joomla are third-party library packages that the Joomla CMS uses to provide various functionalities:

- `phpmailer` is a package for handling complex e-mail sending written in PHP.

- `phputf8` is a package for making PHP more UTF8 friendly and is used to augment the native PHP functionality for dealing with UTF-8 strings.

- `simplepie` is a package to handle parsing XML feeds such as ATOM and RSS. The `joomla` folder contains all the libraries that compose the Joomla platform.

The `cms` folder was added in version 2.5. It holds Joomla library classes needed by the Joomla CMS but not applicable to the Joomla platform.

There are two PHP files directly in the `libraries/joomla` folder.

- `factory.php` contains a static class called `JFactory` and provides an easy way to get various system objects from a common interface.

- `methods.php` contains some static helper classes for interacting with URLs and translating text.

The folders found inside `libraries/joomla` are known as library packages and are grouped logically around the type of functionality they provide (see Table 3.8).

Table 3.8 **Joomla Platform Packages**

Library Package	Description
access	Functionality for the access control list (ACL) system, which allows you to control what actions different users can take on different objects in the website
application	Functionality for extensions as well as the main application class
base	Very low-level classes that are generally very abstract and implement some sort of design pattern or data structure
cache	Classes that handle data caching of various types and storage mechanisms
client	Client classes to connect to various servers such as FTP or LDAP
database	Classes used to connect to and interact with databases
document	Classes for building and manipulating the document that is eventually sent to the browser
environment	Classes to interact with the request (GET, POST, COOKIE values) and the response headers
error	Classes that help with error handling
event	Classes that constitute our event system so that we can listen to and fire events
filesystem	Classes used to interact with the file system
filter	Classes to sanitize and filter input and output values
form	Classes to help build, manipulate, and process web forms
github	Classes to interact with the platform's version control system repository on http://github.com
html	Helper methods to generate HTML markup and easily load CSS or Javascript
http	Classes to work with different types of http requests
image	Classes to work with image files
installer	Classes to install and upgrade application extensions
language	Classes to translate strings into different languages
log	Classes to implement the platform logging functionality
mail	Helper methods to send e-mail
plugin	Classes related to the plugin system
registry	Classes to work with complex data objects—for example, to import and export to INI, JSON, and XML formats
session	Classes to create, manipulate, and store the session
string	Classes to work with strings
updater	Classes to support auto-updating extensions
user	Classes to manipulate or interact with user objects
utilities	Helper classes that don't otherwise fit into a separate package

Web Programming versus "Normal" Programming

Two important factors distinguish dynamic web programming, like what we see in Joomla, from what we'll call "normal" programming—for example, a typical desktop application such as a spreadsheet program. These have to do with how the state of the program is maintained and what type of command validation is required.

Maintaining the State of the Program

The first difference is how the state of the program is maintained during the execution of the program. By state, we mean what the program knows about itself and its environment as stored in the working memory of the computer. We can think of state as a software program's version of consciousness: its awareness of who it is and what has been going on. Let's compare how a desktop spreadsheet program works with how Joomla works with respect to how it maintains state.

Let's illustrate this by thinking of our software programs as Aladdin with his magic lamp. Imagine that when we issue a software command, inside the computer Aladdin is actually getting a software genie to do the work. The spreadsheet genie is happy to grant as many wishes as we like. By contrast, the Joomla genie only grants one wish each time.

With our spreadsheet program, the first thing we do is load the software by clicking on a desktop icon. Aladdin sees this and rubs the lamp to make the genie appear. The genie comes out of the lamp and Aladdin commands, "Display the spreadsheet software on the user's screen!" The genie does this and awaits Aladdin's next command.

Next, we tell the software to open the "budget" file. Aladdin transmits this command to the genie and the file is opened. This process continues until we close the program. At this time, Aladdin tells the genie, "You are no longer needed. Go back into the lamp!" and the spreadsheet genie disappears back into the lamp.

Now let's see how this works with Aladdin and the Joomla genie. We start the process by loading the URL for our home page into our browser. Aladdin sees this and rubs the lamp. The Joomla genie appears and Aladdin commands, "Display the URL!" The genie does his magic and our home page shows in the browser. However, since the Joomla genie only does one command at a time, he immediately disappears back into the bottle!

Now we click a menu item in the home page to display the Parks article. Aladdin has to rub the lamp again, and again the genie appears. Aladdin commands, "Load the Parks article!" The genie loads the new page into the browser and then immediately disappears back in the lamp.

This process continues until eventually we close down the browser or navigate out of the Joomla site. At that time, *Aladdin doesn't have to do anything, since the genie is already back in the lamp.* This is very important. With web programming, we can't rely on the user to nicely close down the program. Fortunately, we don't need to.

Tables 3.9 and 3.10 show these examples step by step.

With a web program like Joomla, each time you click a link or a form submit button, you are starting what we call a new request or command cycle. The URL, any

Table 3.9 **Command Sequence with Spreadsheet Genie**

User	Aladdin	Spreadsheet Genie
Clicks spreadsheet icon	Rubs lamp and says, "Open the spreadsheet program!"	Comes out of the lamp, opens the spreadsheet program, and awaits next command
Selects the "budget-1" file to open	Tells genie, "Open the 'budget-1' file!"	Opens the file and waits
Issues more commands	Transmits commands to genie	Executes each command and waits
Selects the exit command	"Close the program and return to the lamp!"	Closes the program and disappears back into the lamp

Table 3.10 **Command Sequence with Joomla Genie**

User	Aladdin	Joomla Genie
Enters home page URL into browser	Rubs lamp and tells genie, "Load the home page URL!"	Comes out of the lamp, displays the URL in the browser, and disappears back into the lamp
Clicks on the Parks article link	Rubs the lamp and tells genie, "Open the Parks article!"	Comes out of the lamp, opens the file, and goes back into the lamp
Issues more commands	Rubs lamp and transmits each command to genie	Comes out of the lamp, executes each command, and goes back into the lamp
Closes the browser	No action needed	No action needed

form data, and other information related to the request is packaged up by the browser and sent to the web server.

With Joomla (or any other web program), nothing is remembered in the computer's working memory between request cycles. Each cycle has to start over to create all the program objects. The Joomla genie starts from scratch each time.

Given this, how does the Joomla genie "remember" important information from one request cycle to the next? For example, the genie needs to know who the user is so he can check what actions the user is allowed to do. If the genie's mind is a complete blank at the start of each cycle, how can he do this?

We have several ways to store data across cycles. The most common one is the session variable. This is maintained on the server and is specific to the user for this session. It is stored on the server's disk and is available to Joomla. Normally, the session file is automatically deleted or disabled after a period of inactivity (for example, 15 minutes). From the session, for example, the Joomla genie can identify the current user without requiring that the user log in each time. It can also "remember" where the user was in the last command cycle and what options the user might have entered (for example, how a column was sorted in a screen).

The database is another way to save information from one command cycle to the next. It is updated as we make changes to the site—for example, by adding articles or other component items, or by changing our user profile. When we access the database in future cycles, we will see the updated information.

Using the session and the database allows Joomla to find information from previous command cycles. This allows the user to experience the different command cycles as a continuous program flow. However, it is important to keep in mind that each request cycle has to stand alone. We will see as we go along that this has important consequences for how things are done in the code.

Controlling and Checking the Commands

There is another difference between these two types of programming that has important consequences for security. With a self-contained desktop program, all the possible commands are typically predefined in the program. Commands are typically entered via a mouse click from a list. Even if commands can be typed in directly, they are normally validated against a fixed list of possible commands and an error shows if the command is not valid.

With a web program like Joomla, we have two challenges that a desktop program normally doesn't have. First of all, we are exposing our site to the entire online world, which unfortunately includes people with bad intentions. We have to expect that someone will try to hack our website. This could include someone trying to steal our administrative password, to deface the site (perhaps by putting in their own file for one of ours), or to try to bring the site down by altering the database. We need to practice defensive programming to guard against this.

The second challenge is that we cannot control or limit the commands that come in as part of the request. Normally, the command will be a combination of a URL and possibly some field values from an HTML form. Most users will enter commands simply by clicking a link or a form submit button and will therefore always enter valid commands.

It is possible, however, that a user has deliberately entered a command to try to do something that they shouldn't do—for example, by manually typing in a URL or altering the HTML form inside their browser. Unfortunately, there is no way for the web server to tell whether a user has clicked a link or manually entered in a URL. Likewise, there is no across-the-board way to tell whether a user has simply filled out the form and pressed submit or whether they have modified the form to submit some malicious data.

To be safe, we must always assume that commands coming in with the request could be designed to attack or hack the site and we must examine them accordingly before we execute them.

We will talk more about security and defensive programming as we go along. However, the subject is important enough to warrant an example now to illustrate the point.

Let's say we have a simple comments system where users can enter comments about articles. We let anyone submit a comment, but we only allow authorized users to approve comments. A comment is not shown on the site unless it is approved, so we protect against inappropriate comments being shown on the site.

For this example, we have two fields: the comment and whether or not it is approved. We might implement this as follows. When we display the form, we check if a user is authorized or not. If they are, we show the form as it appears in Figure 3.7.

Before we show the form, we check whether the current user is authorized to approve the comments. If they are not authorized, we simply omit the Approved field on the form and only show the Comment field. So unauthorized users will never see the Approved field and therefore won't be able to check the box.

Now we might think with this design we have prevented unauthorized users from approving comments. But we have not. Someone with knowledge about how the application works could very easily use a program like Firebug or Web Developer to edit the HTML on the page to include the missing Approved field and set its value to Approved. Then, when the form is submitted, it would be approved as if the user were authorized. The web server doesn't know whether the form was altered before the submit button was pressed. It just sees the form data in the request information.

So this design has a serious security hole. How can we fix it?

One way would be to add a check before the database is updated. Even though normally an unauthorized user would not submit the form with the approved field set to yes, we would nevertheless check this again before posting the comment to the database. In this example, before we update the database we would test that the user is authorized. If not, we would always set the approved field to no and then save the data. That way, even if an unauthorized user adds the approved field to the form, the invalid data won't get saved in the database, so no harm will be done.

We will discuss other examples of security issues and how to fix them as we go along.

Anatomy of a Joomla Execution Cycle

Now let's look at a typical Joomla execution cycle in more detail.

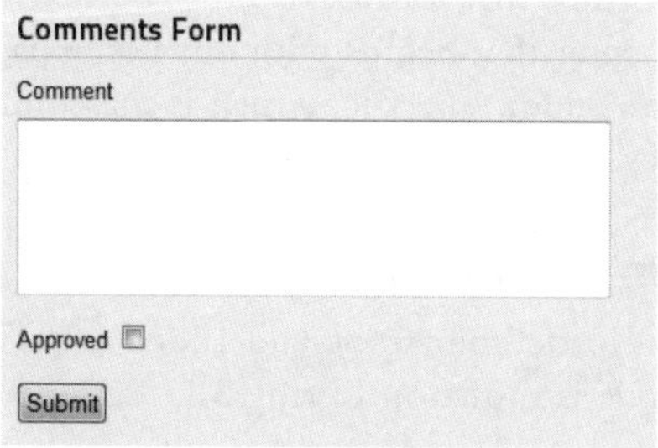

Figure 3.7   Example comments form

Important Note

You do NOT need to understand all of this in order to write Joomla programs. However, this section will give you an insider's view of how Joomla works and help you better understand the various parts of the core code base. In this section, we will be looking at specific blocks of code. If you are not familiar with PHP and object-oriented programming (OOP), you have the following options:

- Read along and not worry about the specifics of the code for now. We will introduce specific PHP and OOP topics as needed in the following chapters.

- Refer to Appendix A, "Crash Course on PHP and OOP," as you look at the code blocks to help you figure out what each line of code is doing.

- Skip this section for now and come back to it once you are more familiar with PHP code.

Load the Index.php File

Let's start our session by typing a URL that points to an article in the front page of our site, something like `http://myjoomlasite.org/index.php/my-article-name`.

The first thing that happens depends on the web server (Apache or IIS), not Joomla. The web server doesn't know that we are pointing to a dynamic Joomla website. It first tries to find a file or folder called `my-article-name` in a folder called `index.php`. Failing that, it goes up to the next segment of the URL and tries to find a file called `index.php`. Since that file exists, that file is executed. Since all URLs for the front end will start the same way, every front-end command cycle starts with the web server loading the `index.php` file.

If we have our site configured to use Apache's `mod_rewrite` module, we can leave out the `index.php` in the URL and it still takes us to that same file. In this case, Apache still executes the front-end `index.php` file for any URL starting with our base URL (in this case, `http://myjoomlasite.org`).

The same process applies to the back-end URLs, except that these point to the `index.php` file in the `administrator` folder. Any URL that starts with `http://myjoomlasite.org/administrator` will execute the back-end `index.php` file, since that will be the first file it finds that it can execute.

In short, any URL we enter that begins with our home page URL will cause the web server to load the site's `index.php` file, which is the common starting point for any front-end command cycle.

Check the Execution Environment

So now the web server has loaded our front-end `index.php` file. Let's look at this file. The first section of this code is shown in Listing 3.1.

Listing 3.1   **Start of Front-End index.php File**

```
<?php
/**
 * @package        Joomla.Site
 * @copyright      Copyright (C) 2005 - 2012 Open Source Matters, Inc. All
➥rights reserved.
 * @license        GNU General Public License version 2 or later; see
➥LICENSE.txt
 */

// Set flag that this is a parent file.
define('_JEXEC', 1);
```

The first comment section is called the **doc block**. These lines are (or should be!) present in every core PHP file in Joomla. The @package is the name of the file package. The package is normally Joomla.Site for front-end files and Joomla.Administrator for back-end files. The @copyright and @license lines are the same for every file.

The next line, define('_JEXEC', 1);, is important. This line defines a constant called '_JEXEC'. Every other PHP file in the system (except for the administrator index.php file) contains a line at the beginning like this: defined('_JEXEC') or die;. This checks that the _JEXEC constant is defined, which means that we entered the application from the index.php file.

If someone tries to run a PHP file directly, outside the application, the '_JEXEC' constant won't be defined and the file will not be executed. If you include a PHP file in the application that does not have the **defined** line at the start, someone could enter the path to the file directly in the browser. In many cases, if you execute a Joomla PHP file outside the CMS, you will get a PHP error (for example, because a constant or class is not defined). In the PHP error message, the full path to the PHP file will show. This is considered a security risk, because it gives a would-be attacker information about your server and folders.

To see an example, remove the 'defined('_JEXEC') or die;' from the file components/com_banners/banners.php. Then enter this URL into your browser: http:<your-joomla-site>/components/com_banners/banners.php. You should get an error message similar to what's shown in Figure 3.8.

Notice that in the error message it shows the full path to our Joomla installation. If we restore the "defined" line to that file and try it again, we just get a blank screen that doesn't reveal any information about our site.

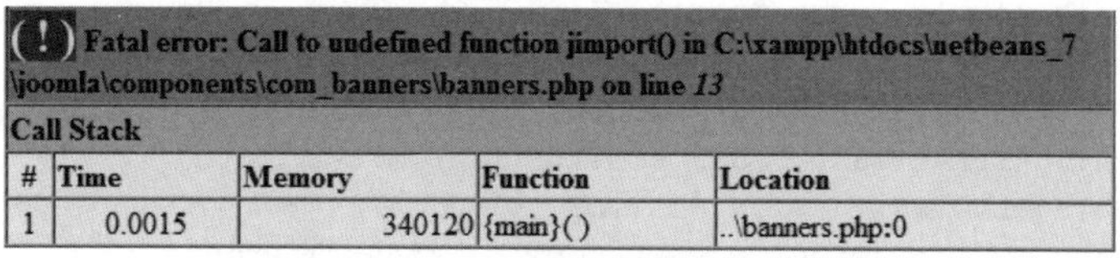

#	Time	Memory	Function	Location
1	0.0015	340120	{main}()	..\banners.php:0

Fatal error: Call to undefined function jimport() in C:\xampp\htdocs\netbeans_7\joomla\components\com_banners\banners.php on line *13*

Call Stack

Figure 3.8   Full path disclosure example

Define the File Locations

The next section of the index.php file, as shown in Listing 3.2, defines a number of constants that we need to find our way around.

Listing 3.2 **Loading of defines.php File**

```
define('DS', DIRECTORY_SEPARATOR);

if (file_exists(dirname(__FILE__) . '/defines.php')) {
  include_once dirname(__FILE__) . '/defines.php';
}

if (!defined('_JDEFINES')) {
  define('JPATH_BASE', dirname(__FILE__));
  include_once JPATH_BASE.DS.'includes'.DS.'defines.php';
}
```

First we define the DS constant. This is actually being phased out, since it is no longer needed. It defines the directory separator character, which is the forward slash ("/") for Linux and Mac systems and the back slash ("\") for Windows systems. However, since PHP for Windows can now work correctly with the forward slash, the DS constant will be removed.

The next two if code blocks give us two possible ways to define a set of constants. Joomla includes a standard file called includes/defines.php. In the index.php file, the first if block looks for a defines.php file in the top-level folder. In a standard installation, there is no such file. So the first if block is not executed and, since the constant 'JPATH_BASE' is not yet defined, the standard includes/defines.php file is executed using the PHP include_once command.

The includes/defines.php file defines the constants shown in Listing 3.3.

Listing 3.3 **Standard defines.php File**

```
//Global definitions.
//Joomla! framework path definitions.
$parts = explode(DS, JPATH_BASE);

//Defines.
define('JPATH_ROOT', implode(DS, $parts));

define('JPATH_SITE', JPATH_ROOT);
define('JPATH_CONFIGURATION', JPATH_ROOT);
define('JPATH_ADMINISTRATOR', JPATH_ROOT.DS.'administrator');
define('JPATH_LIBRARIES', JPATH_ROOT.DS.'libraries');
define('JPATH_PLUGINS', JPATH_ROOT.DS.'plugins'  );
define('JPATH_INSTALLATION', JPATH_ROOT.DS.'installation');
define('JPATH_THEMES', JPATH_BASE.DS.'templates');
```

```
define('JPATH_CACHE', JPATH_BASE.DS.'cache');
define('JPATH_MANIFESTS', JPATH_ADMINISTRATOR.DS.'manifests');
```

Each constant is used to find the folder where the various types of core Joomla files can be found. If you want to override the standard defines.php, you can simply create a file called defines.php at the top level and make sure it defines the required constants. If this file is executed and defines the JPATH_BASE constant, then the standard includes/defines.php file won't be executed.

This is our first example where Joomla gives you a simple way to override the standard setup. If you wanted to move the files to different folders in your installation, you could easily do that and just create your own custom defines.php file to point to the new folders.

The use of PHP constants allows us to define each of these locations once for the entire application. When we need to find these files in other parts of the application, we can refer to the constant and be confident that it will point to the correct location for our setup.

Let's Ask Louis: Including PHP Files

Mark: Louis, I am confused about the way in which other PHP files get executed or included. I mean, we start with our one index.php file, and the next thing you know, we are running a whole bunch of other files. What's the deal?

Louis: The ability to include other files is a really cool feature of PHP. It lets us keep our files relatively small and focused on one task and then put them together as needed. I mean, we could have the entire Joomla application be one giant script file, but how easy would that be to read?

Mark: OK, you have me there. I guess a bunch of small files makes things easier to understand and maintain. But I still don't understand something about the way this is done. If you look at the code, we use at least four different commands to include files. I've seen include_once, require_once, jimport, and require. Don't they all basically do the same thing and just execute the PHP file?

Louis: Yes and no. I mean, they all execute the named PHP file. But they have important differences.

For example, include_once will not halt the execution of the program if the file is not found, whereas require_once will. jimport is used when the files being included use our Joomla library naming conventions. This command does some other cool Joomla-specific stuff along the way, like checking for helper class names. So there are generally good reasons to use the different commands.

The include_once and require_once commands don't load the same file twice. This is really important if your file contains a class declaration and might already have been included. If you try to run a class declaration a second time, you will get a PHP error. On the other hand, with these commands, PHP has to check to see if the file has already been included. On some systems—especially large servers that use storage array networks (SANs)—this can really slow down the performance of Joomla.

Mark: So when I'm writing my own extensions, how do I know which command to use?

Louis: I'm really glad you asked. We really should not be using `require_once` or `include_once` anywhere in Joomla, since they are slow on some platforms. It turns out that it is much faster if we just keep track of the classes that are loaded in the application instead of asking PHP to keep track of the files that have been loaded.

Most of the time when we are including other files, we are actually loading classes. And we already have a great method for including class files in the file `libraries/loader.php`, called `JLoader::register`. The cool thing about this method is that it uses the PHP autoloader feature to load classes into memory only when they are needed. So this method just adds the `class` file to the list of files that PHP can load automatically if they are called. However, if it turns out we don't need that file, it doesn't get loaded into memory.

This method for loading classes is much faster than using `require_once`, at least on some hardware platforms.

Mark: OK, big shot. A lot of the Joomla PHP files are just class declarations and don't actually do anything when you do a `jimport`, `require_once`, or `include_once` command. What's that all about?

Louis: As you know, with PHP you can write procedural scripts or you can write files that create classes. If a file only contains a class declaration (meaning it declares a class with fields and methods), then no code is actually executed when that file is included. The code is only executed when you create an object of that type or execute one of the methods of the class.

That's why the `JLoader::register()` method is great. Because, with that method, it doesn't even use memory to include a class file unless you actually need to execute one of its methods. If we really wanted to, we could even automatically register every class in Joomla with this method during the initialization routine and then all the core classes would be available without any further work. The only reason not to do this is that it uses some computer memory to store all the class and file names.

Mark: OK, that makes sense, I guess. What about the autoload feature that was added in Joomla version 2.5? What is an autoloader?

Louis: The autoloader is another step toward making life as easy as possible for the Joomla developer. The basic idea is very simple. If you try to use a standard Platform or CMS class that isn't already loaded into memory, the autoloader automatically loads the class and the developer doesn't have to use `jimport` or `JLoader`. So, for most Platform classes, you don't have to deal with any of these include or load commands.

Load the Joomla Framework

The next line of code loads the Joomla framework via the `includes/framework.php` file:

```
require_once JPATH_BASE.DS.'includes'.DS.'framework.php';
```

The `framework.php` file does some important tasks. It loads the file `libraries/joomla/import.php`, which in turn loads some important classes, including `JFactory` (`libraries/joomla/factory.php`).

It makes sure we have a `configuration.php` file. If we don't have one, it forces us to the `installation` application to try to install Joomla. If the installation files cannot be found, it shows an error message and quits.

Finally, it imports the framework classes. This is done in the lines of code shown in Listing 3.4.

Listing 3.4 **Importing the Joomla Framework Classes**

```
//
// Joomla! library imports.
//

jimport('joomla.application.menu');
jimport('joomla.environment.uri');
jimport('joomla.utilities.utility');
jimport('joomla.event.dispatcher');
jimport('joomla.utilities.arrayhelper');
```

Note that the `libraries/joomla/import` file was already executed earlier in the `framework.php` file. This script loaded the `JLoader` class, which in turn provides the `jimport` method. So we can then use the `jimport` method to import the other framework classes.

Recall from the earlier discussion about command cycles that each command cycle has to entirely stand alone. That is why we have to load all these classes into memory for each cycle.

Whew! At this point, we have done a lot, but we are still just getting started. The real Joomla work can start now that we have the framework loaded.

Start or Continue the Session

If we return to `index.php`, the next lines we see are shown in Listing 3.5.

Listing 3.5 **Index.php getApplication() and initialise()**

```
// Mark afterLoad in the profiler.
JDEBUG ? $_PROFILER->mark('afterLoad') : null;

// Instantiate the application.
$app = JFactory::getApplication('site');

// Initialise the application.
$app->initialise();

// Mark afterIntialise in the profiler.
JDEBUG ? $_PROFILER->mark('afterInitialise') : null;
```

We can ignore the two `JDEBUG` statements. In normal operation, these are skipped. They are used to help evaluate the performance of different parts of the code.

So the two things we do in this section are create the application object ($app) and then execute its initialise() method. (Note the British spelling for the word "initialise," since that is the official language of Joomla.)

When we create the application object, we end up loading the JSite class from the file includes/application.php. This class extends the JApplication class. A similar JAdministrator class in administrator/includes/application.php is used when you create a back-end application object.

At this point, we get our session. We either load the existing session or create a new one if one isn't found. Recall that Joomla doesn't know anything about what has happened in prior command cycles except for what has been saved in the session or the database. So finding the existing session is critical to carrying over information from one cycle to the next.

At this point, we also load the configuration.php file, which gives us access to the Joomla database and other settings for this specific website.

Another small but helpful thing that happens here is to create a field called requestTime. This is a time stamp field in the JApplication class that contains the date and time in GMT that the request cycle was started. If you need a current time stamp field, this is a simple way to get it ($app->requestTime or JFactory::getApplication()->requestTime). Unlike using the now() method, this value will stay constant during this entire command cycle.

Next, we run the initialise() method for the application. Since we are in the JSite class, we are running the method from the includes/application.php file. The most important thing this method does is to figure out which language the user needs and loads this language object so that the text strings can be translated correctly. Near the end of the method, it also calls the parent's initialise() method (parent::initialise($options);). This calls the initialise() method from the JApplication class in the file libraries/joomla/application/application.php, which figures out which editor is the right one for this user.

Route the URL

The next section of code in the index.php file is shown in Listing 3.6.

Listing 3.6 **Application route() Method**

```
// Route the application.
$app->route();

// Mark afterRoute in the profiler.
JDEBUG ? $_PROFILER->mark('afterRoute') : null;
```

In Joomla jargon, a router is a class that translates between a URL and an array of commands. A router has two public methods, parse() and build(). The parse() method takes a JURI object as input and returns an array of commands. The build() method reverses the process and takes an array of commands and turns it into a JURI object.

Let's see how this works in more detail. Recall that $app is a JSite object. Looking at the route() method for JSite (includes/application.app), we see what's shown in Listing 3.7.

Listing 3.7   **JSite route() Method**

```
public function route()
{
  parent::route();

  $Itemid = JRequest::getInt('Itemid');
  $this->authorise($Itemid);
}
```

Recall that JSite extends JApplication (libraries/joomla/application/application.php). JApplication also has a route() method. So the route() method in JSite overrides the one in JApplication.

The first thing this does is call the route() method of the parent (JApplication), with the command parent::route(). If we look at the route() method in JApplication, we see the code shown in Listing 3.8.

Listing 3.8   **JApplication route() Method**

```
public function route()
{
  // Get the full request URI.
  $uri  = clone JURI::getInstance();

  $router = $this->getRouter();
  $result = $router->parse($uri);

  JRequest::set($result, 'get', false);

  // Trigger the onAfterRoute event.
  JPluginHelper::importPlugin('system');
  $this->triggerEvent('onAfterRoute');
}
```

This code gets the current JURI object. The clone command tells the system to make a copy of the JURI object instead of using the original one. This is done because we don't want to inadvertently modify the actual request URI when we are working with the JURI object. By making a clone of it, we can work with the clone, and perhaps modify it, without changing the original.

That gives us the URL we need to parse. The next line gets the actual router class. In this case, we are in the front end, also known as the site, so when we execute the command $this->getRouter(), we get a JRouterSite object (includes/router.php).

Then we execute the `parse()` method of the router, which gives us an associative array of commands. In our example, the `JURI` object would contain the URL information for the article menu item (`http://myjoomlasite.org/index.php/my-article -name`) and turn it into a command array as follows:

- Itemid: 123 (id of the menu item)
- option: `com_content` (name of the component)
- view: article (name of the view)
- id: 234 (id of the article)

Then we put this information back into the PHP `$_GET` variable using the `JRequest::set()` method. Finally, we trigger the `onAfterRoute` system event so that we can execute any system plugins for this event. We talk more about events and plugins in Chapter 5.

At this point, we have finished with the parent's `route()` method and return to the `route()` method of `JSite`. Here, we get the `Itemid`, which is the `id` column in the database for the menu item we are going to display. Then we check whether or not the current user is authorized to view this menu item, with the `$this->authorise()` method.

Last, we return to the `index.php` file and run a `DEBUG` command to mark the end of the routing process.

Execute the Component

Now we know what we are supposed to do. The URL entered by the user (for example, by clicking on a menu item link) has been checked and translated into an array of commands and saved in the PHP `$_GET` variable. We are now ready to execute the component.

Returning to `index.php`, we see the next section of code, as shown in Listing 3.9.

Listing 3.9   Dispatch() Method

```
// Dispatch the application.
$app->dispatch();

// Mark afterDispatch in the profiler.
JDEBUG ? $_PROFILER->mark('afterDispatch') : null;
```

The `dispatch()` method actually executes the component. Let's look at how this works. Listing 3.10 shows the code for the `dispatch()` method.

Listing 3.10   JSite dispatch() Method

```
public function dispatch($component = null)
{
  try
```

```php
{
  // Get the component if not set.
  if (!$component) {
    $component = JRequest::getCmd('option');
  }

  $document  = JFactory::getDocument();
  $user      = JFactory::getUser();
  $router    = $this->getRouter();
  $params    = $this->getParams();

  switch($document->getType())
  {
    case 'html':
      // Get language
      $lang_code = JFactory::getLanguage()->getTag();
      $languages = JLanguageHelper::getLanguages('lang_code');

      // Set metadata
      if (isset($languages[$lang_code]) && $languages[$lang_code]->metakey) {
        $document->setMetaData('keywords', $languages[$lang_code]->metakey);
      } else {
        $document->setMetaData('keywords', $this->getCfg('MetaKeys'));
      }
      $document->setMetaData('rights', $this->getCfg('MetaRights'));
      if ($router->getMode() == JROUTER_MODE_SEF) {
        $document->setBase(htmlspecialchars(JURI::current()));
      }
      break;

    case 'feed':
      $document->setBase(htmlspecialchars(JURI::current()));
      break;
  }

  $document->setTitle($params->get('page_title'));
  $document->setDescription($params->get('page_description'));
  $contents = JComponentHelper::renderComponent($component);
  $document->setBuffer($contents, 'component');

  // Trigger the onAfterDispatch event.
  JPluginHelper::importPlugin('system');
  $this->triggerEvent('onAfterDispatch');
}
// Mop up any uncaught exceptions.
catch (Exception $e)
{
```

```
    $code = $e->getCode();
    JError::raiseError($code ? $code : 500, $e->getMessage());
  }
}
```

First, note that this entire method is done inside what is called a try/catch block. This means that the code executes as follows:

- The code inside the curly braces after the try statement (called the try block) is executed as normal.

- If any statement in the try block generates an error, program control transfers to the first line of the catch block at the end of the method.

We discuss try/catch blocks more in Chapter 8.

Inside the try block, we get the component name from the `option` command that we got when we parsed the URL. Then we create a new document. The `$document` object will be used to store everything about the page that will eventually be sent back to the browser.

There are a couple of important things to understand about the document. First of all, since it is an object in memory, we don't have to build it sequentially. We can insert portions of the document in any order we find convenient. We take advantage of this and build the document in a nonsequential order. For example, we will add the component first and then later insert the modules.

A second important point about the document is that Joomla supports different document types. When we are browsing a site, the type is normally `html`. For this type, we do some special processing. We get the language for the page, set the meta-data, and set the base if we are using SEF URLs. If the document is a news feed (`type = "feed"`), we skip most of this and just set the document base. If the document is any other type, we skip all this special processing.

After setting the page title and description, we get to the heart of the matter with this line of code:

```
$contents = JComponentHelper::renderComponent($component);
```

This executes our component and places the output into the `$contents` variable. Let's see how this works.

Here we are running a static method called `renderComponent()` from the `JComponentHelper` class (`libraries/joomla/application/component/helper.php`). Listing 3.11 shows the first part of this code.

Listing 3.11 **JComponentHelper render() Method Part I**

```
public static function renderComponent($option, $params = array())
{
  // Initialise variables.
```

```php
$app   = JFactory::getApplication();

// Load template language files.
$template  = $app->getTemplate(true)->template;
$lang = JFactory::getLanguage();
  $lang->load('tpl_'.$template, JPATH_BASE, null, false, false)
|| $lang->load('tpl_'.$template, JPATH_THEMES."/$template", null,
false, false)
|| $lang->load('tpl_'.$template, JPATH_BASE, $lang->getDefault(),
false, false)
|| $lang->load('tpl_'.$template, JPATH_THEMES."/$template",
$lang->getDefault(), false, false);

if (empty($option)) {
  // Throw 404 if no component
  JError::raiseError(404,
JText::_('JLIB_APPLICATION_ERROR_COMPONENT_NOT_FOUND'));
  return;
}

 // Record the scope
$scope = $app->scope;
// Set scope to component name
$app->scope = $option;

// Build the component path.
$option = preg_replace('/[^A-Z0-9_\.-]/i', '', $option);
$file   = substr($option, 4);

// Define component path.
define('JPATH_COMPONENT',       JPATH_BASE . '/components/' . $option);
define('JPATH_COMPONENT_SITE',     JPATH_SITE . '/components/' . $option);
define('JPATH_COMPONENT_ADMINISTRATOR',  JPATH_ADMINISTRATOR .
'/components/' . $option);

// Get component path
if ($app->isAdmin() && file_exists(JPATH_COMPONENT . '/admin.'.$file.'
.php')) {
   $path = JPATH_COMPONENT . '/admin.'.$file.'.php';
} else {
   $path = JPATH_COMPONENT . '/' . $file.'.php';
}

// If component is disabled throw error
if (!self::isEnabled($option) || !file_exists($path)) {
   JError::raiseError(404,
JText::_('JLIB_APPLICATION_ERROR_COMPONENT_NOT_FOUND'));
```

```
    }

    $task = JRequest::getString('task');

    // Load common and local language files.
        $lang->load($option, JPATH_BASE, null, false, false)
     || $lang->load($option, JPATH_COMPONENT, null, false, false)
     || $lang->load($option, JPATH_BASE, $lang->getDefault(), false, false)
     || $lang->load($option, JPATH_COMPONENT, $lang->getDefault(), false,
➥false);
```

Here we are loading the template and the template language. Then we save the component name in a field of the JSite object called scope ($app->scope = $option). This is a handy field. It means that, at any point in the cycle, we can check this field to see what component is being run. We might, for example, make use of this when running a plugin that should only run for selected components.

The line with the preg_replace command just makes sure that the $option variable only has letters, numbers, and underscores. It replaces any other characters with dashes. That way we know that there are no characters that will cause problems inside a file name. The next line says "use the part of the $option name after position 4 as the file name." This is the naming convention for components. In our example, the component is called com_content, so the file we will execute is called content.php. We'll see more about other naming conventions in the next section.

We are almost ready to actually execute our component! The next section of code defines the path to the component's front-end and back-end files and we set the $path variable based on whether this component is a front-end (site) or back-end (administrator) component.

Then we make sure the component is enabled. Finally we use the or trick again to load the language from one of the four possible file locations.

Tricky Code Alert!

Notice we have some tricky code in the four lines with $lang->load near the beginning of Listing 3.10 and again in the last four lines. These lines load the language using the boolean or operator (||). We frequently use this inside an "if" statement when we want to check if more than one condition is true. However, this operator does something interesting: It stops processing as soon as it hits an expression that evaluates to the boolean true.

The load() method of the JLanguage class returns a boolean true if the load is successful and a boolean false otherwise. So this is a quick (and tricky) way to say, "try loading the language file starting with the JPATH_BASE, then JPATH_THEMES, and so on. And, by the way, stop as soon as one of the loads is successful."

The next section of code actually loads our component file, as shown in Listing 3.12.

Listing 3.12   **JComponentHelper render() Method Part II**

```
// Handle template preview outlining.
$contents = null;

// Execute the component.
$contents = self::executeComponent($path);
```

This code block clears out anything that might have been in the `$contents` variable. Then we call the `executeComponent()` method. Note that we use the key word "self" when calling this method. That is because `executeComponent()` is a static method of our current class. See Appendix A for more information about the "self" key word.

The code for the `executeComponent()` is as follows:

```
protected static function executeComponent($path)
{
    ob_start();
    require_once $path;
    $contents = ob_get_contents();
    ob_end_clean();
    return $contents;
}
```

The `ob_start()` command tells PHP to turn on output buffering. So everything the component outputs will be saved in memory. Then we load the component file with `require_once $path`. In our example, it loads the file `components/content.php`.

We will cover components and the Joomla model-view-controller (MVC) design pattern in Chapters 7 and 10. The important thing here to understand is that the only thing that Joomla actually does to execute the component is to load this one file (the file in the `$path` variable). The rest is up to the component.

This means, for example, that a component does not have to follow the MVC pattern or even use classes and objects. It could be a single script, as long as it follows the naming convention. Having said that, there are very good reasons for following the MVC pattern for components we discuss when we build our component.

You can do a quick experiment to prove to yourself how this works by creating your own `com_test` component according to the instructions on the Joomla documentation site here: `http://docs.joomla.org/Testing_Checklists#Testing_Code _Snippets`. By entering in `?option=com_test` in your URL, it executes the `test.php` file in your `components/com_test` folder.

Once the component has finished executing, we store the buffer contents of the buffer back into the `$clean` variable using the `ob_get_contents()` method. Finally, we clean out the buffer with the `ob_end_clean()` method.

At this point, our component has been executed and its output is in the `$contents` variable. The last part of the `JComponentHelper` `render()` method is shown in Listing 3.13.

Listing 3.13   JComponentHelper render() Method Part III

```
// Build the component toolbar
jimport('joomla.application.helper');

if (($path = JApplicationHelper::getPath('toolbar')) && $app->isAdmin()) {
    // Get the task again, in case it has changed
    $task = JRequest::getString('task');

    // Make the toolbar
    include_once $path;
}

// Revert the scope
$app->scope = $scope;

return $contents;
}
```

It checks to see if we need to show a toolbar and shows it if needed. Then it sets the `$app->scope` variable back to its previous value. Finally, we return the `$contents` variable to the calling method, which was the `dispatch()` method in `JSite`.

The next line in the `dispatch()` method of `JSite` is as follows:

```
$document->setBuffer($contents, 'component');
```

This loads the `$contents` into the `component` part of the document. Finally, we trigger the `onAfterDispatch` event for system plugins and, if we are debugging, we mark the `afterDispatch` point. Now we have the output of the component in the document and are ready to put in the other pieces of the page.

Render the Page

The next part of the `index.php` file is as follows:

```
// Render the application.
$app->render();
```

At this point, we have the output from the component, but we don't have any formatting and we don't have other page content, such as modules or messages.

Listing 3.14 shows what the `$app->render()` method looks like.

Listing 3.14   **JSite render() Method**

```php
public function render()
{
  $document  = JFactory::getDocument();
  $user      = JFactory::getUser();

  // get the format to render
  $format = $document->getType();

  switch ($format)
  {
    case 'feed':
      $params = array();
      break;

      case 'html':
      default:
        $template     = $this->getTemplate(true);
        $file       = JRequest::getCmd('tmpl', 'index');

        if (!$this->getCfg('offline') && ($file == 'offline')) {
           $file = 'index';
        }

        if ($this->getCfg('offline') && !$user->authorise('core.admin')) {
            $uri      = JFactory::getURI();
            $return     = (string)$uri;
            $this->setUserState('users.login.form.data',
array( 'return' => $return));
            $file = 'offline';
            JResponse::setHeader('Status', '503 Service Temporarily
Unavailable', 'true');
         }
          if (!is_dir(JPATH_THEMES.DS.$template->template)
&& !$this->getCfg('offline')) {
           $file = 'component';
           }
        $params = array(
           'template'     => $template->template,
           'file'     => $file.'.php',
           'directory'     => JPATH_THEMES,
           'params'   => $template->params
      );
      break;
  }

  // Parse the document.
```

```
$document = JFactory::getDocument();
$document->parse($params);

// Trigger the onBeforeRender event.
JPluginHelper::importPlugin('system');
$this->triggerEvent('onBeforeRender');

$caching = false;
if ($this->getCfg('caching') && $this->getCfg('caching',2) == 2
➥&& !$user->get('id')) {
    $caching = true;
}

// Render the document.
JResponse::setBody($document->render($caching, $params));
// Trigger the onAfterRender event.
$this->triggerEvent('onAfterRender');
}
```

Here we start by getting the document, the user, and the document type or format. Based on the format, we do some processing in the switch statement. In our example, our type is html, so we get the template and set the $params array.

After the switch statement, we call the document's `parse()` method, as shown in Listing 3.15. Note that, since the type is html, the document object is of type JDocumentHTML (`libraries/joomla/document/html/html.php`).

Listing 3.15 **JDocumentHTML parse() Method**

```
public function parse($params = array()) {
        return $this->_fetchTemplate($params)->_parseTemplate();
}
```

The first part of the command loads the template and corresponding language file. Because the `_fetchTemplate()` method returns the current object, we can use method chaining to then call the `_parseTemplate()` method. We discuss method chaining in Appendix A. The `_parseTemplate()`, shown in Listing 3.16, examines the template's index.php file and creates an array of all the `jdoc:include` elements.

Listing 3.16 **JDocumentHTML _parseTemplate() Method**

```
  protected function _parseTemplate()
  {
    $matches = array();

    if (preg_match_all('#<jdoc:include\ type="([^"]+)" (.*)\/>#iU',
➥$this->_template, $matches))
      {
```

```
    $template_tags_first = array();
    $template_tags_last = array();

    // Step through the jdocs in reverse order.
    for ($i = count($matches[0]) - 1; $i >= 0; $i--)
    {
      $type = $matches[1][$i];
      $attribs = empty($matches[2][$i]) ? array() :
➥JUtility::parseAttributes($matches[2][$i]);
      $name = isset($attribs['name']) ? $attribs['name'] : null;

      // Separate buffers to be executed first and last
      if ($type == 'module' || $type == 'modules')
      {
        $template_tags_first[$matches[0][$i]] = array('type' => $type,
➥'name' => $name, 'attribs' => $attribs);
      }
      else
      {
        $template_tags_last[$matches[0][$i]] = array('type' => $type,
➥'name' => $name, 'attribs' => $attribs);
      }
    }
    // Reverse the last array so the jdocs are in forward order.
    $template_tags_last = array_reverse($template_tags_last);

    $this->_template_tags = $template_tags_first + $template_tags_last;
  }

  return $this;
}
```

The key to understanding this method is the preg_match_all statement. This is a complex statement to create, but what it does is easy to explain. This statement creates three arrays. The first one is a list of all the jdoc:incude elements in the template file. This is put into $matches[0]. The second is a list of the type attribute for each of these elements. This is put into $matches[1]. The type will normally be head, modules, messages, debug, or component. The third is a list of the other attributes that come after the type attribute in the element. This is stored in $matches[2].

The for loop creates an associative array of type, name, and attribs using this information and stores it into the _template_tags field of the $document as $this->_template_tags.

Now we are ready to actually put the page together, placing each of the parts of the page into the right location on the template.

Returning now to the render() method of the JSite class, we trigger the onBeforeRender system event and then check to see if this page is cached.

Then we execute this line of code:

```
JResponse::setBody($document->render($caching, $params));.
```

Here we set the field of the `JResponse` object using the `render()` method of the `JDocumentHTML` class. That method contains the code shown in Listing 3.17.

Listing 3.17 JDocumentHTML render() Method

```
public function render($caching = false, $params = array())
{
  $this->_caching = $caching;

    if (!empty($this->_template))
    {
      $data = $this->_renderTemplate();
    }
    else
    {
      $this->parse($params);
      $data = $this->_renderTemplate();
    }

  parent::render();
  return $data;
}
```

The key line of code here is the highlighted line of code that calls the `_render Template()` method. This method reads through the array we created earlier in the `$document->_template_tags`, as shown in Listing 3.18.

Listing 3.18 JDocumentHTML _renderTemplate() Method

```
private function _renderTemplate() {
  $replace = array();
  $with = array();

  foreach($this->_template_tags AS $jdoc => $args)
  {
    $replace[] = $jdoc;
    $with[] = $this->getBuffer($args['type'], $args['name'],
➥$args['attribs']);
  }

  return str_replace($replace, $with, $this->_template);
}
```

The key line here is

```
$with[] = $this->getBuffer($args['type'], $args['name'],
➥$args['attribs']);
```

Recall that the `template_tags` field contains an array with the component, modules, head, messages, and debug element information. Each of these is processed in this loop and loaded into the `$with` array.

The component has already been rendered, so it is just copied from the `$contents` field. The `jdoc:include` elements for modules normally are done by position. If so, then each module assigned to that position for that menu item is executed and its output is placed into the `$with` array. Similarly, the `head`, `messages`, and `debug` elements are processed.

Then the last line does a string replace statement to "inject" the actual rendered text output for each module, component, message, head, and debug element into the actual template file. At this point, the elements of the page are formatted inside the template and ready to be sent to the browser.

One important result of the way this is done is that a module is only executed if it is assigned to a position in the template. So there is no performance penalty for modules that are assigned to other positions or menu items.

Now we return to the `render()` method from `JDocumentHTML` above and execute the `render()` method of its parent class, `JDocument` (`libraries/joomla/document/document.php`). This method simply sets the modified date and content type for the document header. Then it returns the `$data` variable, which is the template's `index.php` file with the page contents taking the place of the `jdoc:include` elements.

Recall that we started this part of the program with the following line of code from the `render()` method of the `JSite` class:

```
JResponse::setBody($document->render($caching, $params));
```

At this point, we have completed the `$document->render($caching, $params)` portion of the statement. The last thing to do is to pass the result of this to the `JResponse::setBody()` method. This method is shown in Listing 3.19.

Listing 3.19 **Response setBody() Method**

```
public static function setBody($content)
{
  self::$body = array((string) $content);
}
```

This simply places the resulting text into the `$body` field of this class.

The last thing done by the `render()` method is to fire the `onAfterRender` system event. At that point, we return to our top-level `index.php` file.

Output the Page

The last thing we need to do is actually send the output to the browser. Looking at the end of the index.php file, we see the code shown in Listing 3.20.

Listing 3.20   **End of the index.php File**

```
// Mark afterRender in the profiler.
JDEBUG ? $_PROFILER->mark('afterRender') : null;


// Return the response.
echo $app;
```

The JDEBUG statement, as before, simply marks the afterRender point for profiling the application. The last line, echo $app, has a trick to it. Recall that $app is a JSite object. The PHP echo command is used to send text to the browser. What does it mean to echo an object?

The answer is simple. If an object has a special method called __toString(), this method is executed automatically when you use the echo command with an object. If not, the echo just returns the name of the class.

If we look at the JSite class ('includes/application.php'), we don't find a __toString() method. Not to worry. If we look at the parent class of JSite, which is JApplication (libraries/joomla/application/application.php), we see that it has a __toString() method that JSite inherits, as shown in Listing 3.21.

Listing 3.21   **JApplication __toString() Method**

```
public function __toString()
{
  $compress = $this->getCfg('gzip', false);

  return JResponse::toString($compress);
}
```

This method in turn calls the toString() method of JResponse, which does what's shown in Listing 3.22.

Listing 3.22   **JResponse toString() Method**

```
public static function toString($compress = false)
{
  $data = self::getBody();

  // Don't compress something if the server is going to do it anyway. Waste
➥of time.
  if ($compress && !ini_get('zlib.output_compression')
➥&& ini_get('output_handler')!='ob_gzhandler') {
```

```
    $data = self::compress($data);
  }

  if (self::allowCache() === false) {
    self::setHeader('Cache-Control', 'no-cache', false);
      // HTTP 1.0
    self::setHeader('Pragma', 'no-cache');
  }

  self::sendHeaders();

  return $data;
}
```

This method

1. Puts the body of the page in the $data variable

2. Checks whether to compress the page or not

3. Checks the caching and sets the page header accordingly

4. Sends the page headers

5. Returns the $data containing the entire page

The contents of $data are then fed back to the PHP echo command, which sends it to the browser.

Summary of Joomla Session

Whew! That was a lot of work to display the page. What did we learn?

We saw that the first few steps in the process were just getting the file locations figured out, loading the Joomla framework, and figuring out if we are starting or continuing a session. Then we found and executed the component. Then we ran all the modules and put everything into the template file. Finally, we sent it all to the browser.

Along the way, we triggered events that can work with plugins.

Even though there is a lot of code involved in each step, it is organized into a relatively small number of high-level methods, each of which can drill down to lower-level methods as needed. The high-level methods are set up in a structured way so that, at any given stage in the process, we are working on one task in the process. This process is diagramed in Figure 3.9.

We can also see from this overview how Joomla is designed to easily fit extensions into the framework provided by the CMS. Components, modules, plugins, and the template are executed at well-defined points in the process, and there is absolutely no distinction made between core extensions included in the standard installation, on the one hand, and extensions provided by third-party developers, on the other. All are treated exactly the same way, which allows for the seamless operation of extensions.

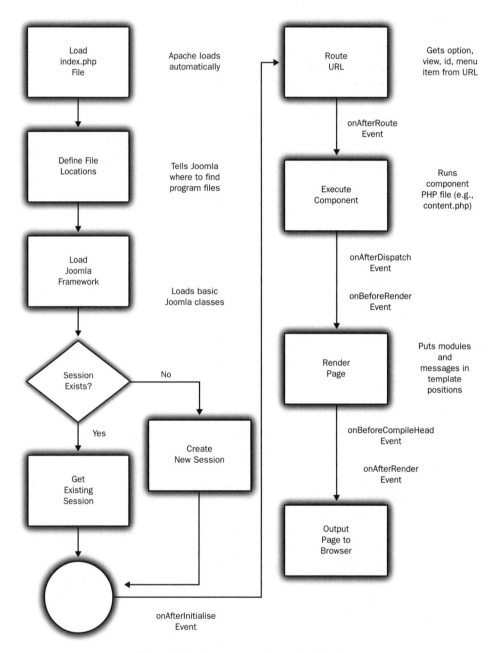

Figure 3.9   Joomla execution cycle flowchart

Naming Conventions (Conventional Wisdom?)

One strategy that makes it easier to read and understand the Joomla code base is to use naming conventions for files and folders. We saw one example in the previous section. Recall that we got the component name from the `route()` method—in our example, `com_content`. Once we knew this, Joomla "knew" to look for a file called `content.php` in the `components` folder. This logic is hard-coded into Joomla. So, for any component, we know the file that gets loaded to start the component's execution.

Once we know about this convention, it is easy to investigate existing components and also to understand how to make a new component. We know to look for a folder called something like `com_mycomponentname` and a file called `mycomponentname.php` in that folder. We also know that when Joomla encounters a URL that routes to an option called `com_mycomponentname`, this file will be executed.

This type of naming convention is used in many places in Joomla. We highlight these as we discuss the various extension types in future chapters.

Global Objects

Some of the objects in Joomla are used in so many places in the code that it makes sense to have them be readily available at all times. The `JFactory` class (`libraries/joomla/factory.php`), as mentioned earlier, is loaded when the `includes/framework.php` script loads the `libraries/joomla/import.php` script.

`JFactory` give us quick access to a number of objects at almost any point in the program. These are listed in Table 3.11.

Except for `JDate`, each of these classes should only have one object for that class. For example, there should only be one application object, `JSite` if you are in the front end and `JAdministrator` if you are in the back end. Similarly, there should only be one `JSession`, `JUser`, `JDatabase`, and so on.

In object-oriented programming, when we have a situation like this, we often use what is called the "singleton" and "factory" design patterns to ensure that we only have one object of a given type in existence at one time. The way it works is actually very simple.

Let's look at an example of how this works using the application object. The `JFactory` class contains a field called `$application` that stores the one application object we want to use for this entire execution cycle. When we need the application object, we use the command `JFactory::getApplication()`.

When we do that command, `JFactory` first checks to see if there is already an object in the `$application` field. If so, it just returns that object. If the `$application` field is empty, it means this is the first time in this cycle that we have tried to access it. In this case, we create the new application object, store it in the `$application` field in the `JFactory` class, and then we return the `$application` field. That way, it is in the `JFactory` class field the next time we need it. So we ensure that we only create one application object and that it is available whenever we need it.

Table 3.11 **Global Objects**

Object Type	Description	Code to Access
JApplication JSite JAdministrator	Application object; JSite when in the front end, JAdministrator when in the back end	`$app = JFactory::getApplication();`
JRegistry	configuration.php file values in form of JRegistry object	`$config = JFactory::getConfig();`
JSession	Current session	`$session = JFactory::getSession();`
JLanguage	Language object	`$language = JFactory::getLanguage();`
JDocument, JDocumentHTML, JDocumentFeed, JDocumentJSON	Current document	`$document = JFactory::getDocument();`
JUser	Current user	`$user = JFactory::getUser();`
JAccess	Current access object (used in access control)	`$access = JFactory::getACL();`
JDatabase	Database object used for running queries	`$dbo = JFactory::getDbo();`
JMail	Mailer object for sending e-mails from the site	`$mail = JFactory::getMailer();`
JXMLElement	XML element	`$xml = JFactory::getXML($pathToXml)`
JEditor	Editor object	`$editor = JFactory::getEditor();`
JURI	URI object	`$uri = JFactory::getUri();`
JDate	Date/time object	`$date = JFactory::getDate();`

Overview of Database Tables

Joomla uses a database (normally run with the MySQL database program) to store all the data for the site. The standard Joomla database for version 2.5 contains 34 tables. In this section, we will give a brief description of each table and its role in the program.

Note about Table Prefixes

When you install Joomla, you can select a prefix for the table names in the database. When you see a table accessed inside the PHP code, you will normally see it with the generic prefix #__. The `query()` method of the `JDatabaseMySQLi` class calls a method called `replacePrefix()` that replaces the generic prefix with the actual one from the `configuration.php` file.

For the purposes of this book, we will use the `#__` prefix for the table names (for example, `#__content`; see Table 3.12). However, the tables that you see for your database will use the prefix that was entered when Joomla was installed.

Some tables have an associated `JTable` class. This is generally done when rows for the table will be edited by a user. By creating a `JTable` class for a table, most of the code for editing table rows is done for us. We see how this works when we create our custom component in Chapter 9.

Table 3.12 **List of Joomla Database Tables**

Table Name / PHP Class	Description
`#__assets` / `JTableAsset`	This is a new table added for ACL in version 1.6. It includes a row for every component and contains a row for every item that has ACL permissions. This includes a "Root Asset" for the global permissions, a row for every component, plus a row for every component category, and finally a row for every article. The "rules" column stores the group permissions in JSON format. This table is used whenever we check if a user is authorized to perform an action.
`#__associations` / none	Used for the native multilanguage feature in Joomla to allow you to associate a given menu item to a menu item in a different language
`#__banners` / none	Contains a row for every banner defined in the site
`#__banner_clients` / none	Contains a row for every banner client defined in the site
`#__banner_tracks` / none	Contains a row for every banner track defined in the site
`#__categories` / `JTableCategory`	Contains a row for every category defined in the site; includes article, banner, contact, news feed, and Weblinks categories
`#__contact_details` / none	Contains a row for every contact defined in the site
`#__content` / `JTableContent`	Contains a row for every article defined in the site
`#__content_frontpage` / none	Contains a row for every article assigned to the featured blog menu item
`#__content_rating` / none	Contains a row for every rated article in the site
`#__core_log_searches` / none	Contains a row for every search term logged by the site
`#__extensions` / `JTableExtension`	Contains a row for every extension installed in the site; includes component, library, module, plugin, template, language, and file extensions

(continued on next page)

Table 3.12 **List of Joomla Database Tables (*continued*)**

Table Name / PHP Class	Description
#__finder_filters / FinderTableFilter	Contains a row for each Search Filter (set up in Smart Search → Manage Search Filters)
#__finder_links / FinderTableLink	Contains a row for each content item indexed by Smart Search
#__finder_links_terms(0-f) / none	Map search terms to links and include a weighting factor. (Note that these 15 tables are actually one logical table. They are divided into separate tables to speed up indexing.)
#__finder_taxonomy / FinderTableMap	Contains one row for each type of item (category, language, region, country, and so on)
#__finder_taxonomy_map / none	Maps links to taxonomy items
#__finder_terms / none	Contains a row for each possible search term indexed in all content items
#__finder_terms_common / none	Contains a row for each common word in a language (to be excluded from the indexes)
#__finder_tokens, #__finder_tokens_aggregate / none	Temporary tables used during indexing
#__finder_types / none	Contains a row for each content type (category, contact, article, news feed, Weblink, and so on)
#__languages / JTableLanguage	Contains a row for every language installed in the site
#__menu / JTableMenu	Contains a row for every front- and back-end menu item defined for the site
#__menu_types / JTableMenuType	Contains a row for every front-end menu defined for the site
#__messages / none	Contains a row for every private message sent in the site
#__messages_cfg / none	Contains a row for every back-end user who sets a configuration in the Components → Messaging → My Settings option
#__modules / JTableModule	Contains a row for every module defined in the system. A client_id column of "0" indicates it is a front-end module; "1" indicates a back-end module.
#__modules_menu / none	This is a mapping table to show which modules are assigned to which menu items. The menuid column indicates which menu items the module is assigned to, as follows: "0" means assigned to all menu items; positive integer means assigned to this one menu item; and negative integer means assigned to all menu items except for this menu item.
#__newsfeeds / none	Contains a row for every news feed created in the site

(continued on next page)

Table 3.12 **List of Joomla Database Tables (*continued*)**

Table Name / PHP Class	Description
`#__redirect_links /` `none`	Contains a row for every redirect created in the site
`#__schemas / none`	Contains a row for each extension that has made database changes during its installation, along with the latest installed version of the extension
`#__session /` `JTableSession`	Contains a row for every active session for the site
`#__template_styles /` `none`	Contains a row for every template style defined for the site
`#__updates / JTableUpdate`	Contains a row for every available package to be installed
`#__update_categories /` `none`	This table is used to categorize the updates. It is maintained automatically by Joomla.
`#__update_sites / none`	This is a list of update sites. This comes from the update XML file for each extension.
`#__update_sites` `_extensions / none`	Mapping table that links `#__extensions` with `#__updates` and contains a row for each combination of extension and update site where that extension can be updated
`#__usergroups /` `JTableUsergroup`	Contains a row for every user group defined for the site
`#__users / JTableUser`	Contains a row for every user defined for the site
`#__user_profiles / none`	Contains a row for every combination of user id and profile field. This table is used if you have the User–Profile plugin enabled
`#__user_usergroup_map` `/ none`	Contains a row for every group that a user is a member of
`#__viewlevels /` `JTableViewlevel`	Contains a row for every View Level defined in the site
`#__weblinks / none`	Contains a row for every Weblink defined in the site

Summary

In this chapter, we learned a lot about the inner workings of Joomla. First, we explored the folder and file structure for the Joomla front and back end. Then we discussed some general concepts that make web programming different from programming a desktop application, including the need for guarding against hackers.

Then we took a detailed look at the code that controls a typical Joomla execution cycle. We also discussed how naming conventions are used in Joomla to make life easier for the developer.

Finally, we discussed how to find a number of useful global objects when writing code and we briefly described the tables that make up a standard Joomla installation.

4

Extending Joomla! with Layout Overrides

Do you want to change the way something is shown on your Joomla! site? Add or remove some information? Do something wild and crazy to make the page look just the way you want it to? If so, then this chapter is for you.

Joomla makes it incredibly easy to change the way your website displays the contents of each page. What's more, you can do this without needing to delve into the details of how the information on the page is put together and, honestly, without understanding much PHP programming.

As we will see, simply by copying and doing some simple editing of one or more files, we can take total control of how our information is shown on the page.

In this chapter, we start with the very basics of templates in Joomla. Then we show how layout overrides work—in other words, the code that makes the magic happen. Then we work through some examples, starting with a simple module and then working through some more advanced examples. These examples will illustrate the different types of layout overrides that are possible.

Finally, we discuss some things other than layouts that you can override in Joomla. These include language files, parameters, and even programming files.

Template Basics

Content is the information that is shown on a web page. Presentation includes everything about how the content is shown, including things like the layout on the page; the choice of fonts and colors; and any graphics, such as boxes, lines, pictures, or logos.

A fundamental goal of Joomla is to allow you to make changes to content and presentation independently. This is accomplished by using templates.

A template is a type of extension that controls every aspect of the presentation for the site. Recall in Chapter 2 that we did a quick demonstration of changing the entire appearance of the site just by changing the default template. In this section, we take a closer look at how that works.

Bear in mind that we do not go into detail about how to write templates for Joomla. That subject is very large and outside the scope of this book. This section is just to help you understand, from a developer point of view, what a template does and how it works.

Template Folders and Files

The default template for the Joomla front end is `beez_20`. If we look at the folder `templates/beez_20`, we see the folders and files shown in Figure 4.1.

The `css` folder, as you would expect, contains the CSS style sheets for the template. Likewise, the `fonts` folder contains any special fonts needed for the template.

The `html` folder is the folder where any layout override files are stored. In the case of `beez_20`, we only have one override file, called `modules.php`. This is a custom module chrome file. Module chrome is a term for PHP functions that provide some optional HTML markup in which the module code is placed. This is often called a wrapper for the module output. We discuss module chrome later in this chapter.

If we look at the folder `templates/beez5/html`, we see folders called `com_contact` and `com_content.` These folders contain override files for the Contacts and Content components.

We discuss how layouts work a bit later in this chapter. For now, the important thing to understand is that you need to put the layout override file in the correct folder inside your template to allow Joomla to find it and use it.

The `images` folder contains the images for the template, such as logos, buttons, icons, and so on.

The `javascript` folder contains any required JavaScript files needed for the template. With `beez_20`, for example, we have two JavaScript files, one that provides general functionality and one that lets the user change the font size.

We manage template options in the back end of Joomla using the Template Manager. This functionality requires language files to allow the text on the screen to be translated. These language files are stored in the `language` folder.

Below the folders we see a list of files. These are described in Table 4.1.

Name	Date modified
css	12/14/2011 3:03 PM
fonts	12/14/2011 3:03 PM
html	12/14/2011 3:03 PM
images	12/14/2011 3:03 PM
javascript	12/14/2011 3:03 PM
language	12/14/2011 3:03 PM
component.php	4/7/2011 8:38 AM
error.php	7/8/2011 5:20 AM
favicon.ico	4/25/2010 6:53 PM
index.html	6/19/2011 6:39 AM
index.php	6/10/2011 2:38 PM
template_preview.png	9/6/2011 12:37 AM
template_thumbnail.png	9/6/2011 12:37 AM
templateDetails.xml	6/10/2011 1:22 AM

Figure 4.1   Beez_20 folders and files

Table 4.1 **Description of Template Files**

File	Description
component.php	Template for printing or e-mailing a component (for example, when you select "Print" or "E-mail" an article)
error.php	Template for displaying error pages (for example, when an invalid URL is entered)
favicon.ico	Icon that shows in the browser, next to the URL
index.html	Empty file to prevent a user from browsing the folder
index.php	Main template file that controls positioning of modules, components, and messages
template_preview.png	Preview graphic with picture of the template
template_thumbnail.png	Thumbnail graphic with picture of the template
templateDetails.xml	XML file that lists all the template folders, files, and positions and also defines any parameters for the template

Template index.php File

By convention, a Joomla template contains an `index.php` file that is literally the template for the pages on the site. (The main template file can be called anything, based on the value of the `tmpl` variable inside the request. The default value is `index.php` if `tmpl` is not specified.) The `index.php` file contains the outline of the page, with the placeholders to be filled in by the actual contents of each page.

In Chapter 3, we discussed how the `render()` method assembles a Joomla page. Specifically, we mentioned that the program makes a list of all the `jdoc:include` elements in the template's `index.php` file and then fills in the blanks with the appropriate content for each element.

Let's take a look at the `index.php` file for the `atomic` template. The `atomic` template is provided as part of the standard Joomla distribution as a very basic template that can be used as a starting point for creating new templates.

If you are unfamiliar with PHP programming, this would be a good time to get familiar with Appendix A, "Crash Course on PHP and Object-Oriented Programming."

The `index.php` file is a great example of how the PHP language makes it very easy to mix PHP code with HTML code. The first part of the file, shown in Listing 4.1, is just a single block of PHP code in a single PHP element.

Listing 4.1   **Opening PHP Element in index.php File**

```php
<?php
/**
 * @package        Joomla.Site
 * @copyright      Copyright (C) 2005 - 2012 Open Source Matters, Inc.
↪All rights reserved.
```

```
*  @license          GNU General Public License version 2 or later; see
↪LICENSE.txt
*/

defined('_JEXEC') or die;

/* The following line loads the MooTools JavaScript Library */
JHTML::_('behavior.framework', true);

/* The following line gets the application object for things like
↪displaying the site name */
$app = JFactory::getApplication();
?>
```

This code ensures we are executing from within Joomla, loads the MooTools JavaS-cript library, and then gets an instance of the JApplicationSite object. We talk more about MooTools and JavaScript in Chapter 12.

The next block of code, shown in Listing 4.2, illustrates some important points about templates.

Listing 4.2   **Second Code Block of Atomic index.php File**

```
<?php echo '<?'; ?>xml version="1.0" encoding="<?php echo $this->_charset
↪?>" ?>
<!DOCTYPE html PUBLIC "-//W3C//DTD XHTML 1.0 Strict//EN"
↪"http://www.w3.org/TR/xhtml1/DTD/xhtml1-strict.dtd">
<html xmlns="http://www.w3.org/1999/xhtml"
↪xml:lang="<?php echo $this->language;?>"
↪lang="<?php echo $this->language; ?>" dir="<?php echo $this->direction;
↪?>" >
  <head>
    <!-- The following JDOC Head tag loads all the header and meta
↪information from your site config and content. -->
    <jdoc:include type="head" />

    <!-- The following five lines load the Blueprint CSS Framework
↪(http://blueprintcss.org). If you don't want to use this framework,
↪delete these lines. -->
    <link rel="stylesheet" href="<?php echo $this->baseurl ?>/templates/
↪<?php echo $this->template ?>/css/blueprint/screen.css" type="text/css"
↪media="screen, projection" />
    <link rel="stylesheet" href="<?php echo $this->baseurl ?>/templates/
↪<?php echo $this->template ?>/css/blueprint/print.css" type="text/css"
↪media="print" />
    <!--[if lt IE 8]><link rel="stylesheet" href="blueprint/ie.css"
↪type="text/css" media="screen, projection"><![endif]-->
```

```
    <link rel="stylesheet" href="<?php echo $this->baseurl ?>/templates/
↪<?php echo $this->template ?>/css/blueprint/plugins/joomla-
↪nav/screen.
css"
↪type="text/css" media="screen" />
↪<?php echo $this->template ?>/css/blueprint/plugins/joomla-nav/
↪screen.css" type="text/css" media="screen" />


    <!-- The following line loads the template CSS file located in the
↪template folder. -->
    <link rel="stylesheet" href="<?php echo $this->baseurl ?>/templates/
↪<?php echo $this->template ?>/css/template.css" type="text/css" />

    <!-- The following four lines load the Blueprint CSS Framework and the
↪template CSS file for right-to-left languages. If you don't want to use
↪these, delete these lines. -->
    <?php if($this->direction == 'rtl') : ?>
    <link rel="stylesheet" href="<?php echo $this->baseurl ?>/templates/
↪<?php echo $this->template ?>/css/blueprint/plugins/rtl/screen.css"
↪type="text/css" />
    <link rel="stylesheet" href="<?php echo $this->baseurl ?>/templates/
↪<?php echo $this->template ?>/css/template_rtl.css" type="text/css" />
    <?php endif; ?>

    <!-- The following line loads the template JavaScript file located in
↪the template folder. It's blank by default. -->
    <script type="text/javascript" src="<?php echo $this->baseurl ?>/
↪templates/<?php echo $this->template ?>/js/template.js"></script>
  </head>
```

First, notice that this file includes the HTML DOCTYPE declaration. The document type is controlled entirely by the template. This makes sense when we consider that the template controls the entire presentation of the site. If you want to see this in action in the Joomla sample data, you can go to the template manager, open the Beez5 — Default template style, and change the parameter called html version from xhtml to html5. Then display the Fruit Shop page and look at the page source code. You will see <!DOCTYPE html> instead of <!DOCTYPE html PUBLIC "-//W3C// DTD XHTML 1.0 Transitional//EN" "http://www.w3.org/TR/xhtml1/DTD/xhtml1 -transitional.dtd">.

Second, notice that the template file contains the HTML head elements meta, title, and script. You can change these elements dynamically in code if you need to. For example, the title element is often changed for each page on the site. However, others can be defined here and can be used on all pages for the site.

The third important point about this file is that it is a normal PHP file. This means that we can execute any PHP commands we like. This opens up the possibility for doing some fun tricks in the template. We discuss one example of this later in this chapter.

Mixing PHP and HTML Elements

One of the reasons PHP is so popular for creating web pages is that you can easily mix PHP and HTML elements together in any .php file. Consider this line from the index.php file:

```
<link rel="stylesheet" href="<?php echo $this->baseurl ?>/templates/
↪<?php echo $this->template ?>/css/blueprint/screen.css"
↪type="text/css" media="screen, projection" />
```

This is just an HTML "link" element, but with a dynamic PHP twist. The href attribute contains two PHP elements. These elements are evaluated by the PHP interpreter and converted to their text values. Then these text values are inserted into the HTML exactly as if they were typed in as text.

So the PHP element "<?php echo $this->baseurl ?>" is converted to the value of the PHP variable "$this->baseurl" and the PHP element "<?php echo $this->template ?>" is converted to the value of the PHP variable "$this->template".

For example, if the value of "$this->baseurl" is "http://myjoomlasite.org" and the value of "$this->template" is "atomic," then the preceding code produces this exact text, just as if you had typed it in manually.

```
<link rel="stylesheet"
href="http://myjoomlasite.org/templates/atomic/css/blueprint/screen.css"
type="text/css" media="screen, projection" />
```

You can see a number of other places in the preceding code where PHP elements are inserted in the middle of HTML elements. See Appendix A for more information about PHP code and syntax.

Positions in Templates

Now let's look at the rest of the index.php file from the atomic template. This is shown in Listing 4.3.

Listing 4.3 **Last Part of Atomic index.php File**

```
<body>
   <div class="container">
     <hr class="space" />
     <div class="joomla-header span-16 append-1">
        <h1><?php echo $app->getCfg('sitename'); ?></h1>
     </div>
     <?php if($this->countModules('atomic-search')) : ?>
```

```
            <div class="joomla-search span-7 last">
             <jdoc:include type="modules" name="atomic-search" style="none"
/>
            </div>
        <?php endif; ?>
    </div>
    <?php if($this->countModules('atomic-topmenu')) : ?>
      <jdoc:include type="modules" name="atomic-topmenu" style="container"
/>
    <?php endif; ?>

    <div class="container">
       <div class="span-16 append-1">
       <?php if($this->countModules('atomic-topquote')) : ?>
          <jdoc:include type="modules" name="atomic-topquote" style="none"
/>
      <?php endif; ?>
      <jdoc:include type="message" />
      <jdoc:include type="component" />
      <hr />
      <?php if($this->countModules('atomic-bottomleft')) : ?>
         <div class="span-7 colborder">
           <jdoc:include type="modules" name="atomic-bottomleft"
              style="bottommodule" />
         </div>
         <?php endif; ?>

         <?php if($this->countModules('atomic-bottommiddle')) : ?>
         <div class="span-7 last">
         <jdoc:include type="modules" name="atomic-bottommiddle"
            style="bottommodule" />
         </div>
       <?php endif; ?>
       </div>
       <?php if($this->countModules('atomic-sidebar')) : ?>
         <div class="span-7 last">
         <jdoc:include type="modules" name="atomic-sidebar" style="sidebar"
/>
         </div>
       <?php endif; ?>

       <div class="joomla-footer span-16 append-1">
         <hr />
         &copy;<?php echo date('Y'); ?> <?php echo $app->getCfg('sitename'); ?>
       </div>
         </div>
</body>
</html>
```

Except for the PHP elements, we read this file just as we would read a static HTML file. We define our `body` element with some `div` elements.

Notice in the fourth line we are doing the same thing we did earlier: We are getting the value of `$app->getCfg('sitename')` and then inserting that inside an `h1` element.

There are two important things to understand about this section of the file. The first thing is that we have a number of `jdoc:include` HTML elements. The `jdoc:include` is not a standard HTML element. It is specific to Joomla. Recall in Chapter 3 we discussed how Joomla uses these elements as placeholders and replaces these elements with the text for the component, for messages, and for modules. The placement of the `jdoc:include` elements controls the placement of the text for each of these parts of the page.

In the middle of the table, we see these two lines of code:

```
<jdoc:include type="message" />
<jdoc:include type="component" />
```

These tell Joomla where to put any messages and where to put the component. Joomla only allows one component per page, so we only have one `jdoc:include` for components. Similarly, messages are displayed in one location, although more than one message can show on a page. A message might be a confirmation that an action was completed, a warning, or an error.

If we look at a `jdoc:include` element for a module, we see two additional attributes, as in the following:

```
<jdoc:include type="modules" name="atomic-search" style="none" />
```

The `name` attribute is the name of the module position. In the Module Manager, when you create a module, you assign it to a position. When Joomla renders the page, it finds and executes all the modules for each position in the template. Then, as with messages and the component, it inserts the output for the modules in place of the `jdoc:include` tag.

We also have an attribute called `style`. This is called the module chrome. Chrome was used to decorate cars in the old days, and the word is used here in the sense of providing a decorative framework on the page. So our chrome tells Joomla how we want to wrap or decorate our module. We discuss this in the section "Module Chrome."

Alternative PHP If/Then/Else Syntax

As discussed earlier, a great feature of PHP is the ability to mix PHP elements in with HTML elements in the same file. To support this, PHP provides an alternative way to write if/then/else statements.

Look at the following code snippet, which was taken from the index.php file for the atomic template.

```
<?php if($this->countModules('atomic-bottomleft')) : ?>
  <div class="span-7 colborder">
    <jdoc:include type="modules" name="atomic-bottomleft"
↵style="bottommodule" />
  </div>
<?php endif; ?>
```

The logic flow here is as follows. We evaluate the expression inside the parentheses after the if—in this case, the following:

```
$this->countModules('atomic-bottomleft')
```

If this evaluates to the boolean true, then the lines between the if element and the endif element are sent to the browser. Otherwise, these lines are ignored.

Since the if statement is a self-contained PHP element, we can use normal HTML elements between the if and endif elements—in this case, a div element that contains a jdoc:include element.

We could have written this code in a single PHP element as follows:

```
<?php if($this->countModules('atomic-bottomleft'))  {
    echo '<div class="span-7 colborder">';
    echo '<jdoc:include type="modules" name="atomic-bottomleft"
↵style="bottommodule" />';
    echo '</div>';
} ?>
```

Both code snippets output exactly the same text. However, the first one is superior. Someone familiar with HTML can easily read the HTML code in the first example. Also, an HTML editor can read and validate these lines.

To make matters even more confusing, there is a third way to write the same code, shown in the following example:

```
<?php if($this->countModules('atomic-bottomleft')) { ?>
  <div class="span-7 colborder">
    <jdoc:include type="modules" name="atomic-bottomleft"
↵style="bottommodule" />
  </div>
<?php } ?>
```

The only difference between this third example and our first one is here we use a left curly brace (instead of the colon) in the opening PHP tag and a right curly brace (instead of endif;) in the closing tag. This syntax also allows us to put HTML elements inside the PHP code block. However, it is not as readable as the first example. The first method is recommended and what is normally used in Joomla.

Similar syntax is available for the other PHP control statements, such as switch and for and foreach loops. They offer the same benefit of being able to enter normal HTML elements inside the PHP control block. See Appendix A for more examples of the alternative syntax.

How do we decide which syntax to use? The answer is simple. In Joomla, most files consist of a single PHP element and contain no HTML at all. This is because they don't directly output any text to the browser. For these files, we always use the normal syntax with the curly braces.

The files that do contain HTML elements are template files and layout files. For these files, we normally use the alternative syntax.

It is important to understand that PHP doesn't care which syntax we use. We choose based on which is easier for people to read. This is true of many choices we make in designing and writing code. It is very important for the code to be readable and understandable to people.

One universal truth about software is that, once implemented, software almost always has a longer life than the developers expected. This means that future programmers might be reading and maintaining your code long after you have moved on to other projects. That is why we always try to write code so that someone unfamiliar with it can easily understand it.

This is doubly important with open-source software like Joomla and most Joomla extensions. We cannot possibly anticipate all the places where our code might end up being used. But we can try to make it as clear, logical, and understandable as possible to help others who might want to use it.

Template Parameters

If we log in to the back end of Joomla and navigate to Extensions → Template Manager and then click `Beez2 — Default` to edit this template style, we see on the right-hand side of the screen the options shown in Figure 4.2.

This is our first of many examples of parameters in Joomla. Let's look at where these come from, how they are used, and how they are stored in the database.

Parameters are defined in XML files. In this case, the file is the `templates/beez_20/templateDetails.xml` file, which also includes other information about the template.

Figure 4.2   Beez_20 template parameters

The portion of the file that contains the parameter information is inside the `config` element. This is shown in Listing 4.4.

Listing 4.4   **Beez_20 Template Parameter Definitions**

```
<config>
    <fields name="params">
      <fieldset name="advanced">
            <field name="wrapperSmall"  class="validate-numeric"
➥type="text" default="53"
          label="TPL_BEEZ2_FIELD_WRAPPERSMALL_LABEL"
          description="TPL_BEEZ2_FIELD_WRAPPERSMALL_DESC"
          filter="int" />

            <field name="wrapperLarge"  class="validate-numeric"
➥type="text"  default="72"
          label="TPL_BEEZ2_FIELD_WRAPPERLARGE_LABEL"
          description="TPL_BEEZ2_FIELD_WRAPPERLARGE_DESC"
          filter="int" />

      <field name="logo" type="media"
         hide_default="1"
         label="TPL_BEEZ2_FIELD_LOGO_LABEL"
➥description="TPL_BEEZ2_FIELD_LOGO_DESC" />

       <field name="sitetitle"  type="text" default=""
          label="TPL_BEEZ2_FIELD_SITETITLE_LABEL"
          description="TPL_BEEZ2_FIELD_SITETITLE_DESC"
           filter="string" />

      <field name="sitedescription"  type="text" default=""
          label="TPL_BEEZ2_FIELD_DESCRIPTION_LABEL"
          description="TPL_BEEZ2_FIELD_DESCRIPTION_DESC"
          filter="string" />

      <field name="navposition" type="list" default="center"
          label="TPL_BEEZ2_FIELD_NAVPOSITION_LABEL"
          description="TPL_BEEZ2_FIELD_NAVPOSITION_DESC"
          filter="word"
        >
          <option value="center">TPL_BEEZ2_OPTION_AFTER_CONTENT</option>
          <option value="left">TPL_BEEZ2_OPTION_BEFORE_CONTENT</option>
      </field>

      <field name="templatecolor" type="list" default="nature"
          label="TPL_BEEZ2_FIELD_TEMPLATECOLOR_LABEL"
          description="TPL_BEEZ2_FIELD_TEMPLATECOLOR_DESC"
```

```
        filter="word"
    >

        <option value="nature">TPL_BEEZ2_OPTION_NATURE</option>
        <option value="personal">TPL_BEEZ2_OPTION_PERSONAL</option>

    </field>

        </fieldset>
    </fields>
</config>
```

If we compare the XML file to the Advanced Options screen, we can see that the following is true:

- Each `slider` group is defined by a `fieldset` element in the XML file.
- Each option field is defined by a "field" element in the XML file.
- The attributes define the behavior of each parameter, as indicated in Table 4.2.

Table 4.2 **Parameter Field Element Attributes**

Attribute	Description
name	This is the name used in the program to retrieve the value of the parameter.
class	This is the CSS class for form field when the form is rendered on the page. For example, the class `validate-numeric` triggers some special JavaScript code to show an error on the page if nonnumeric characters are entered.
type	This is the name of the PHP file and class that will be called to create the parameter. For example, if `type` is set to `text`, then the file `libraries/joomla/form/fields/text.php` is loaded. This file defines the PHP class `JFormFieldText`.
default	This is the default value to show on the form when creating a new template style.
label	This is the label for the field on the form. Note that this is normally translated, so it is normally a tag found in the templates language file. For example, the tag `TPL_BEEZ2_FIELD_WRAPPERSMALL_LABEL` is defined in the file `language/en-GB/en-GB.tpl_beez_20.ini`, where it is translated to Wrapper Small (%). We discuss how translation works in more detail in Chapter 5.
description	This is the description for the field on the form and shows as a pop-up tool tip when you hover the mouse on the field. As with the label, this is normally translated.
filter	This is the filter, if any, to apply to the field input when the form is saved. For example, the `wrapperSmall` field uses the `int` filter. As you might expect, this requires an integer value. When the `filter` attribute is present, the `clean()` method of the class `JFilterInput` (file `libraries/joomla/filter/filterinput.php`) is called. See Appendix B for a list of all standard filter types.

Note that the `fieldset` and `field` elements were added in Joomla version 1.6. They replace the `params` and `param` elements that were used in version 1.5.

Notice that the parameter named `navposition` has a type of `list`. This indicates that the user will select from a list of options in a drop-down list box. Each possible option is defined in a separate `option` element. Each `option` element has an attribute called "value," which is the value passed to the form when this option is selected. The text for the "option" element is the text that will show in the list box. Note that this is normally translated, so it is a tag that will be defined in the language file for the template.

Next, let's look at how parameters are stored in the Joomla database. If we look at the database table called `#__template_styles`, we find a row with the title column of `Beez2 — Default`. If we look at the `params` column for this row, we see the following value:

```
{"wrapperSmall":53,"wrapperLarge":72,"logo":"images\/joomla_black.gif",
"sitetitle":"Joomla!","sitedescription":"Open Source Content
Management","navposition":"left","templatecolor":"personal"}
```

This text is in JSON format, which stands for JavaScript object notation. As of Joomla version 1.6, JSON is the format for saving Joomla parameters in the database.

If we look at Table 4.2, we can easily figure out how it works. The parameter name shows first, in quotes, before the colon. Then we see the parameter value after the quote. Each parameter is separated by a comma, and the whole thing is enclosed in curly braces.

You can see the complete definition of the JSON format at `http://www.json.org`. PHP includes the function `json_decode`, to convert JSON-formatted text to objects or arrays, and the function `json_encode`, to convert PHP arrays or objects to JSON-formatted text.

Note that all the parameters are stored in a single database column called *parameters*. This means that we can add new parameters without adding columns to the database. So, for example, a template style can contain any number of parameters, with whatever parameter names the template designer chooses. This approach of storing multiple parameters in one database column is used throughout Joomla and allows for very flexible parameter creation.

A disadvantage of this approach is that it is not as easy to use parameters in database queries.

Module Chrome

The `jdoc:include` element for modules (`type="module"`) has an optional attribute called `style`. For example, in the `index.php` file for atomic, we see the following line:

```
<jdoc:include type="modules" name="atomic-topmenu" style="container" />
```

The container style tells Joomla to look for a function called `modChrome_container` in one of two files. The standard styles are included in the file `templates/system/html/modules.php`. Additional styles can be defined as functions in a `modules.php` file in your template's HTML folder. For example, the atomic template defines three additional module styles in the file `templates/atomic/html/modules.php` as shown in Table 4.3.

Note that these `modules.php` files do not declare PHP classes. Instead, they only declare functions. This has a subtle advantage when it comes to adding new chrome styles. Since we don't have any class names, we don't need a naming convention for any classes. We just need to find the PHP file and include it.

Let's look at the `modChrome_container` function in the atomic `modules.php` file. This is shown in Listing 4.5.

Listing 4.5   **Container Style from Atomic Template**

```php
function modChrome_container($module, &$params, &$attribs)
{
  if (!empty ($module->content)) : ?>
      <div class="container">
        <?php echo $module->content; ?>
      </div>
  <?php endif;
}
```

This function is passed three arguments. The first, `$module`, is an object that contains the fields shown in Table 4.4.

The second argument is a `JRegistry` object with the parameters for this module. This makes it convenient to check the value of any parameter inside the chrome function.

The third argument is an array of the attributes from the `jdoc:include` element (for example, `name`, `style`, and so on). Note that you can enter in any attributes in the `jdoc:include` tag and these will be available in the `modChrome` function. This can be useful for further customizing the appearance of modules.

Suppose, for example, that your module chrome had a border around it and you wanted to be able to set the border width when you created the position in the template. One way to implement this would be to add an attribute called `border_width` in the `jdoc:include` element and then read this attribute inside the `chrome` function

Table 4.3 **Atomic Template Module Styles**

Style Name	Function Name
container	modChrome_container
bottommodule	modChrome_bottommodule
Sidebar	modChrome_sidebar

Table 4.4 Fields in $module Object Passed to modChrome Functions

Field Name	Description
id	The id number of the module (in the #__modules table)
title	The title of the module entered in the Module Manager (for example, "Login Form")
module	The folder name of the module (for example, mod_login)
position	The position of the module in the template
content	The text content of the module (the HTML text that will be shown on the page, inside the module "chrome" function)
showtitle	Whether or not to show the title
params	The parameters for the module, in JSON format
menuid	The id number of the menu item in which the module is being rendered
user	Not used
name	Name of the module (for example, "login")
style	The module style from the jdoc:include element

to set the width (for example, using a different CSS class based on the border_width value).

Let's look at the rest of the modChrome_container function. The first line checks to see if there is any content for this module. If not, nothing is shown. If there is content, it creates a div element and outputs the module's content inside that element.

To see a more complex example, look at the file for beez_20 (templates/beez_20/html/modules.php).

In all cases, the actual output of the module is contained in the variable $module->content.

Since the modules.php function is supplied as part of your template, you can add as many styles as you like to customize the appearance of the modules on your site.

Copy Template

All layout override files are placed under a folder called templates/<template name>/html. So, for example, if your template is called my_beautiful_template, all the layout override files will be located under a folder called templates/my_beautiful_template/html.

This approach means that your override files are safely stored inside your template's folder. However, this is only "safe" if the template is not a core template.

The core templates that ship with Joomla might be changed when you update to a newer Joomla version. This is fine if you are using the template as is and haven't made any changes to any of its files. However, when we do overrides, we could be changing files and adding new ones.

It is easy to ensure that our customized override files will not be replaced when we upgrade to a newer Joomla version. All we need to do is use a template that is not included in the core distribution. For the purposes of this book, we will use a copy of the `beez_20` template called `beez_20_copy`. There are two ways you can get this template:

- Create your own copy of `beez_20` using the following instructions.
- Download the `beez_20_copy.zip` file from the book website here: `http://joomlaprogrammingbook.com/downloads.html`. Then install it using Extension Manager → Install.

Making a copy of a template is reasonably easy and a useful thing to know. Here are the steps:

1. Copy template folder to a new folder. In this case, we will use our operating system copy folder function to copy the `templates/beez_20` folder (including all its subfolders and files) to a new folder called `templates/beez_20_copy`. Make sure you check that all of the files copied correctly.

2. Change the file names in the `beez_20_copy` XML file. Open the `templates/beez_20_copy/templateDetails.xml` file for editing. We just want to do a global search and replace, replacing `beez_20` with `beez_20_copy`. This should do three replacements: the `name` element and the two language files inside the "language" elements.

3. Rename the language files. In step 2, we changed the name of the language files in the XML file. Now we need to actually rename these files in the file system as follows:
   - `en-GB.tpl_beez_20.ini` to `en-GB.tpl_beez_20_copy.ini`
   - `en-GB.tpl_beez_20.sys.ini` to `en-GB.tpl_beez_20_copy.sys.ini`

4. Copy these two files from `templates/beez_20_copy/language/en-GB/` to `language/en-GB/`, again using your operating system file copy.

5. Discover and install. Joomla version 1.6 introduced a great new feature called Discover. This provides an alternative method for installing new extensions. When an extension is installed, two separate things happen:
   - The files for the extension get copied to the correct folders in your Joomla installation.
   - The Joomla database gets updated with the new extension information.

With Discover, we can manually copy the files into the folders and then tell Joomla to look for new extensions. When a new extension is discovered, we have the option to install it. This creates the correct entries for the extension in the Joomla database.

We'll use this feature to install our new template. If we navigate to Extension Manager → Discover and press the Discover icon in the toolbar, Joomla will find our new template as shown in Figure 4.3.

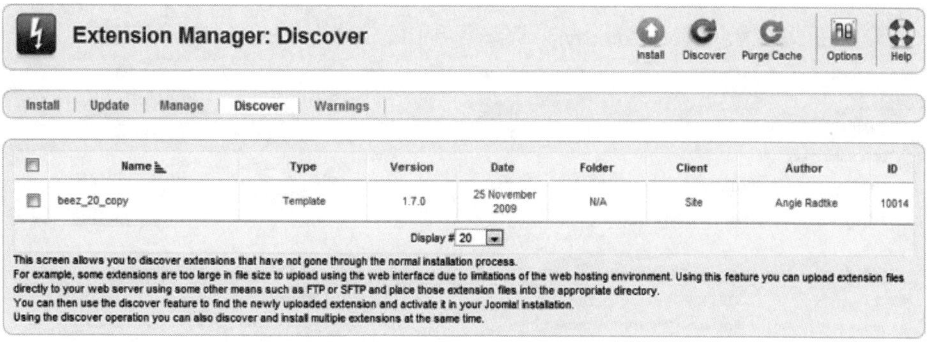

Figure 4.3   Install Discover

Now we can install the template by clicking on the select box and clicking the Install icon in the toolbar. When it has been installed, we will get a message saying "Discover Install Successful."

Next, we want to make our `beez_20_copy` template the default template for the site. Navigate to the Extensions → Template Manager: Styles. Then select the new template and click the Make Default button (see Figure 4.4).

Finally, if we want our new template to look like the original template, we need to change the style parameters for the new template style to match the old style. Click `beez_20_copy` – `Default` to open the Edit Style form, as shown in Figure 4.5.

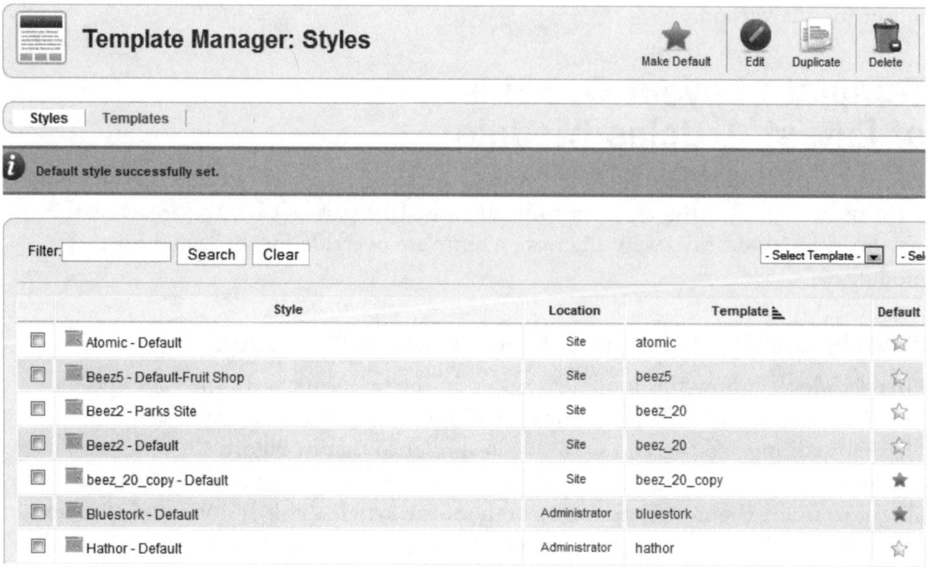

Figure 4.4   New template as default

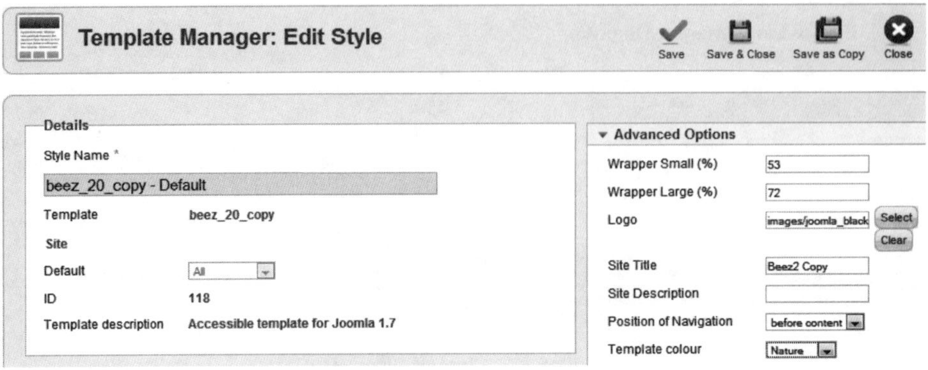

Figure 4.5 Edit style of new template

Set the fields as follows:

Logo: `joomla_black.gif`

Position of navigation: Before content

Template colour: Personal

With these settings, our new template should look exactly like the original `beez_20` template.

At this point, we are ready to start creating layout overrides. Our override files will be stored in our own template, so our changes will not be lost when we update to a newer Joomla version.

Template Layout Override of Latest Articles Module

For our first example, let's say that we want to change the way our Latest News module displays. Specifically, we want to include the first part of each article below the article's title. To do this, we will create a template override for the layout for this module.

Module Configuration in Sample Data: loadposition

First, let's look at how this module is set up in the sample data. In the back end of Joomla, navigate to Content → Article Manager and open the article called Latest News for editing. You should see a screen similar to that in Figure 4.6.

Now this is a bit tricky. This is an article, but we are using the `loadmodule` plugin to insert the module into the body of the article. This is done with the text `{loadmodule articleslatest,Latest News}`. This command tells Joomla to insert the `articles_latest` module called "Latest News" into the body of this article at this point.

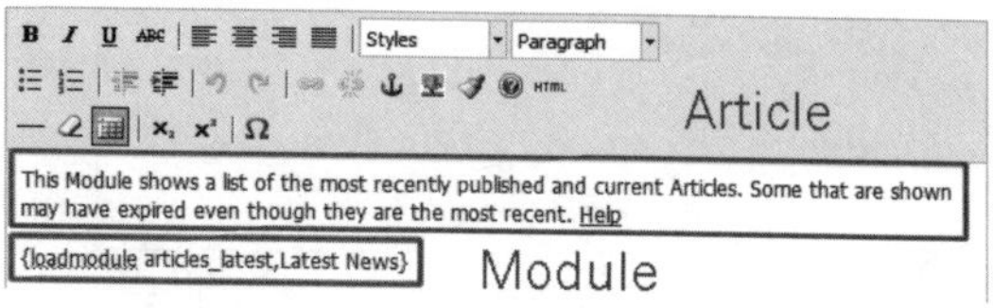

Figure 4.6   Latest Articles module article

Close this and navigate to Extensions → Module Manager and open the Latest News module. You should see a screen similar to the one shown in Figure 4.7.

Now in the front end navigate to Using Joomla! → Using Extensions → Modules → Content Modules → Latest Articles. This will display the article called Latest Articles, as shown in Figure 4.8.

The first part of the screen is the first part of the article, before the {loadmodule} tag. The lower part of the screen is the actual Latest News module. We see that it is a simple list of article titles, where the titles are links to the articles.

Creating the Layout Override File

Now how do we start the process of customizing this layout? The first thing we need to do is find out where the original layout is located. For our example, the answer is in the modules/mod_articles_latest/tmpl folder. How did we know this? Recall

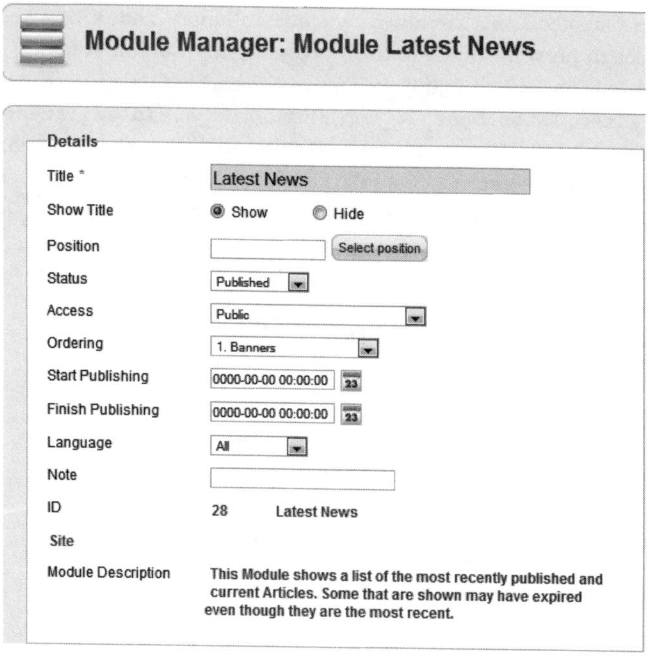

Figure 4.7   Latest News module

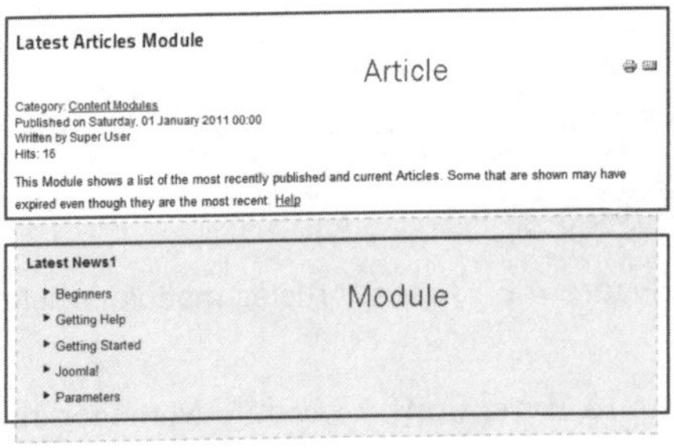

Figure 4.8   Latest Articles module screenshot

in Chapter 3 that we show a table of the subfolder name for each module type name. In there, we can see that `mod_articles_latest` is the subfolder name for the Latest News module type.

The `tmpl` subfolder is where the layout files for modules are stored. In this case, there is just one layout, called `default.php`.

Now that we know where the standard layout is to be found, we need to know where to put our override file. The answer is in the `html` subfolder of our template folder. In our example, the folder is `templates/beez_20_copy/html/mod_articles_latest`. If we create a file in that folder called `default.php`, that file will be loaded instead of the standard `default.php` file for any page that is using the `beez_20_copy` template.

Recall from Chapter 3 that we always include an empty `index.html` file in each Joomla subfolder to prevent someone from browsing that subfolder to see its contents. For this reason, you should also copy an empty `index.html` file into the new templates subfolder (`templates/beez_20_copy/html/mod_articles_latest`).

Now let's give it a try. First, create a new folder called `templates/beez_20_copy/html/mod_articles_latest`. Then copy the file `modules/mod_articles_latest/tmpl/default.php` to `templates/beez_20_copy/html/mod_articles_latest/default.php`.

The contents of this file are shown in Listing 4.6.

Listing 4.6   **Latest News Module Layout File**

```php
<?php
/**
 * @package      Joomla.Site
 * @subpackage   mod_articles_latest
 * @copyright    Copyright (C) 2005 - 2012 Open Source Matters, Inc. All
 ↪rights reserved.
 * @license      GNU General Public License version 2 or later; see
 ↪LICENSE.txt
 */

// no direct access
```

```
defined('_JEXEC') or die;
?>
<ul class="latestnews<?php echo $moduleclass_sfx; ?>">
<?php foreach ($list as $item) :  ?>
  <li>
    <a href="<?php echo $item->link; ?>">
      <?php echo $item->title; ?></a>
  </li>
<?php endforeach; ?>
</ul>
```

Since this is a layout file that is showing HTML elements, we use the alternative PHP syntax for the foreach loop. The file is small and simple. It just loops through a list of articles (the $list variable) and displays each title as a link element. The list is contained in a ul (unordered list) element, with each article's title in an li (list item) element. Again, notice how PHP makes it easy to inject the value of variables inside HTML elements and attributes.

Now we're going to have some fun with this file. First, we want to make sure we are really running the override file and not the standard file. An easy way to do this is to add some text to the override version of the file. Let's add a heading on the line above the opening ul tag so that the first few lines now look like the following:

```
// no direct access
defined('_JEXEC') or die;
?>
<h1>My First Override</h1>
<ul class="latestnews<?php echo $moduleclass_sfx; ?>">
```

Now when we reload the article called Latest Articles Module, the module should display as shown in Figure 4.9.

If you don't see this, check that you have the correct folder names and file name, and make sure you edited the version of the file in the templates/beez_20_copy/ html/mod_articles_latest folder.

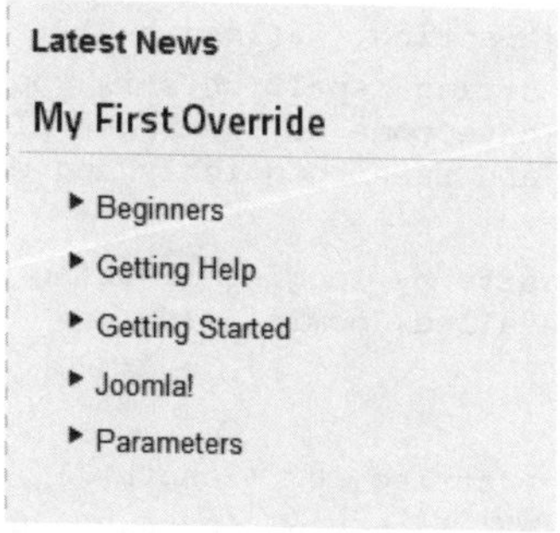

Latest News

My First Override

- ▸ Beginners
- ▸ Getting Help
- ▸ Getting Started
- ▸ Joomla!
- ▸ Parameters

Figure 4.9   Test of layout override

At this point, we know that Joomla is running our override file. Now we can get to work on customizing it to show the first part of each article.

Customizing the Layout

If we look again at the `default.php` file, we see that it is extracting the title and link for the article from a variable called `$item`. The PHP `foreach` command loops through an array, so we know that `$list` is an array of objects and that each object in the array is available in the `$item` variable.

We know that `$item` has at least two fields, `link` and `title`, because these are used in the layout. From this file, however, we don't know what other information is available. Fortunately, there is an easy way to tell. If we add the command `var_dump($item)` to the file, inside the `foreach` loop, PHP will dump out the entire contents of `$item` so we can see what else it contains.

Here is what the modified file looks like:

```php
<?php foreach ($list as $item) :   ?>
  <li>
    <a href="<?php echo $item->link; ?>">
      <?php echo $item->title; ?></a>
      <?php var_dump($item);?>
  </li>
<?php endforeach; ?>
```

Now when we reload the Latest Articles Module article, we see a long display showing us the `var_dump` output. A partial view of this is shown in Listing 4.7.

Listing 4.7   **Output of var_dump Function**

```
Beginners
object(stdClass)[539]
  public 'id' => string '8' (length=1)
  public 'title' => string 'Beginners' (length=9)
  public 'alias' => string 'beginners' (length=9)
  public 'title_alias' => string '' (length=0)
  public 'introtext' => string '<p>If this is your first Joomla! site or
your first website, you have come to the right place. Joomla! will help
you get your website up and running quickly and easily.</p>

<p>Start off using your site by logging in using the administrator account
you created when you installed Joomla!.</p>

' (length=293)
  public 'checked_out' => string '0' (length=1)
  public 'checked_out_time' => string '0000-00-00 00:00:00' (length=19)
  public 'catid' => string '19' (length=2)
```

If you use a PHP debugger, you can get the same information by inserting a break at the point where we added the `var_dump` command and then examining the variables inside the debugger.

This output tells us that `$item` is an object of the type `stdClass`. The `stdClass` object is built into PHP and is similar to an array. You access each field in a `stdClass` object using the notation `<object variable>-><field name>`. So in the standard layout we see the code `$item->title`, which gives us the `title` field inside the object called `$item`. The output also tells us the type of each field (string, integer, and so on), its value, and its length.

In this case, we can see that we have a large number of fields for the article available to us in the layout. For our example, we only need one—the `introtext` field. This field stores all the text for an article up to the Read More break. If there is no Read More break, it stores the entire article text.

Recall that our assignment is to include the first part of each article under the title. Our first idea might be to use the PHP `substr` function, which allows us to find part of a string based on position. Let's say we want the first 50 characters of each article. We could modify the layout as follows:

```
<li>
  <a href="<?php echo $item->link; ?>">
    <?php echo $item->title; ?></a>
    <?php echo substr($item->introtext, 0, 50) . '...'; ?>
</li>
```

The `substr` function takes three arguments, which are inside the parentheses. The first argument is the text we want to use, the second is where to start, and the third is how long we want our new text to be. In this case, we want to start at the beginning (which is 0, not 1), and use the first 50 characters.

If you are new to PHP, the dot (".") operator is called *concatenate*. That is just a fancy word for putting two string or text fields together into one field. So the . '...' just adds three periods to the end of our text. This lets the reader know that there is more text in the article.

Let's reload the page with our revised layout and look at the output, as shown in Figure 4.10.

Fixing a Problem Using the strip_tags Function

At first glance, this looks like what we want. We have the first portion of each article's text under the title, followed by the "..." that we added.

If we take a closer look, however, we see a problem. The third article in the list should be Getting Started, but this is shown under the Getting Help article instead. What happened?

To answer this, let's look at the Getting Help article's text. If we go back to our `var_dump` output and look at the `introtext` for the Getting Help article, we see a long `img` tag, as shown in Listing 4.8.

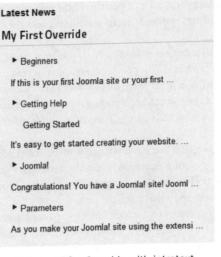

Figure 4.10   Override with introtext

Listing 4.8   **Introtext of Getting Started Article**

```
Getting Help
object(stdClass)[551]
   public 'id' => string '21' (length=2)
   public 'title' => string 'Getting Help' (length=12)
   public 'alias' => string 'getting-help' (length=12)
   public 'title_alias' => string '' (length=0)
   public 'introtext' => string '<p><img class="image-left"
↪src="administrator/templates/hathor/images/header/icon-48-
↪help_header.png" border="0" /> There are lots of places you can get help
↪with Joomla!. In many places in your site administrator you will see the
↪help icon. Click on this for more information about the options and
↪functions of items on your screen. Other places to get help are:</p>

<ul>

<li><a href="http://forum.joomla.org">Support Forums</a></li>

<li><a href="http://docs.joomla.org">Documentation</a></li>

<li><a href="' . . . (length=649)
```

When we took the first 50 characters of the `introtext`, we happened to get just the first part of the `img` tag, including the first part of the `src` attribute. So the HTML text for the Getting Started article was incorrectly placed inside the `img` tag.

Since we don't know what HTML tags an article might have, and how long they might be, we have a bit of a problem. Fortunately, there is an easy solution. We can simply strip out the HTML using the PHP `strip_tags` function. This strips out all HTML tags from the text so we don't have to worry about breaking the string in the middle of an HTML element.

The revised code looks like this:

```
<li>
  <a href="<?php echo $item->link; ?>">
    <?php echo $item->title; ?></a>
    <p>
      <?php echo substr(strip_tags($item->introtext), 0, 50) . '...';
↵?>
    </p>
</li>
```

If you are new to programming, this line of code could be confusing because we are putting the results of one function (`strip_tags`) inside a second function (`substr`). This is telling PHP to strip the tags from `$item->introtext` and then pass the result of that to the `substr` function. Then take the first 50 characters of that result, and add the "...". Finally, echo all of that out to the browser.

Notice that we are putting our preview text inside a `p` element. We do this because the `introtext` won't have any HTML in it. So putting it inside a `p` element will make sure it is valid HTML and formatted as a paragraph.

The output of our revised layout is shown in Figure 4.11.

This fixes our problem with the Getting Started article. Now we have all five of our articles and exactly 50 characters of text for each one.

Figure 4.11   Output of layout with strip_tags function

There is one slight problem, however. Notice that in the second and third articles we are stopping in the middle of a word. It would be more professional to end the preview text at a word boundary.

Using the JHtmlString truncate Method

We could write our own method to fix this problem. For example, we could use the PHP function `strrpos` to find the last space in our preview text and only show the part up to that space.

However, we just happen to have a method already written in Joomla that does exactly this. It is called `truncate()` and is located in the Joomla library in the file `libraries/joomla/html/html/string.php`.

If we look at the code for this method, we see that it uses the method `JString::substr` instead of the standard PHP `substr` command. For example, we see this line of code:

```
$tmp = JString::substr($text, 0, $length);
```

Why do we do this? The answer relates back to the international scope of Joomla. Because we work in all major languages, we need to work correctly with the UTF-8 character set. This is the standard character set that allows us to display any character from any language, including Chinese, Greek, Korean, Arabic, and other languages that use non-Latin characters.

Some PHP string commands do not work correctly with all UTF-8 characters. For this reason, Joomla has its own set of string methods that do work with UTF-8 characters. These are located in the `JString` class (`libraries/joomla/utilities/string.php`). This class includes replacement functions for standard PHP string functions such as `substr`, `strlen`, `str_split`, `strpos`, and others. All the methods in `JString` are designed to work correctly with any UTF-8 characters, so these should be used any time you might be working with non-Latin characters.

Using the `JHtmlString::truncate` method gives us a chance to demonstrate two additional points:

1. A lot of useful methods already exist in the Joomla platform. So when you need a method to solve an issue, check to see if it already exists before writing it yourself.

2. When you want to use a platform class, you need to make that class available to the layout. We'll show some different options for how to do this.

The Joomla library (or platform) contains many useful methods that solve common problems for web developers. The `html` folder in the library contains methods that are especially useful to web designers. A list of handy HTML methods is available in Appendix C. When you run into a problem that requires some programming, it is always a good idea to check to see if there is a solution already programmed in the platform.

It is worth pausing at this point and asking a question: How do we look through the methods available in the Joomla platform to see if there is something we can use?

There are several possible sources of information. In Appendix C we list some of the methods in the platform that are most useful for web designers. We can also go to the Code Summary page of the Joomla developer site at `http://developer.joomla`
`.org/code.html` and click on the API Documentation link. This takes us to `http://`
`api.joomla.org`. This site shows all the classes in the latest version of the Joomla platform. For example, if we select the Joomla-Platform package and then select HTML →
Classes → JHtmlString, we see something similar to Figure 4.12.

Note that this documentation is subject to change, so the screen you see may be different from Figure 4.12. However, it will have the same general information.

If we scroll down to the information about the `truncate()` method, we see the information shown in Figure 4.13.

When you are trying to find out whether a Joomla platform method exists for a specific issue, you can also ask on the various Joomla developer communication channels. The important point is this: When you need a method to do something in Joomla, check to see if it already exists in the platform before writing your own.

The second thing we can demonstrate is how to add a library file to our layout. Notice in Figure 4.12, under Description, there is a line called "Located in." This tells us where this file is located so we know how to include the file in our program. In this case, the file is located in `joomla/html/html/string.php`. Remember that all platform classes are located in the `libraries` folder, so the full path is `libraries/`
`joomla/html/html/string.php`.

We will use the `JLoader::register` method to load the `JHtmlString` class. The `register()` method takes two arguments: the name of the class and the full path to

---

JHtmlString

Description

Description | Methods (details)

HTML helper class for rendering manipulated strings.

- **abstract:**
- **since:** 11.1

Located in /joomla/html/html/string.php (line 19)

> JHtmlString   (Subpackage HTML)

Method Summary

Description | *Methods* (details)

static *string* abridge (*string* **$text**, [*integer* **$length** = 50], [*integer* **$intro** = 30])
static *string* truncate (*string* **$text**, [*integer* **$length** = 0])

Figure 4.12   JHtmlString documentation

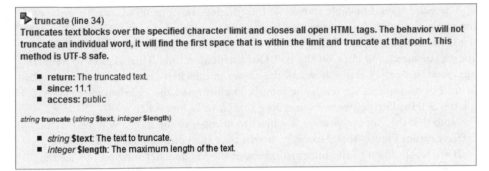

truncate (line 34)
Truncates text blocks over the specified character limit and closes all open HTML tags. The behavior will not truncate an individual word, it will find the first space that is within the limit and truncate at that point. This method is UTF-8 safe.

- **return:** The truncated text.
- **since:** 11.1
- **access:** public

string **truncate** (*string* $text, *integer* $length)

- *string* **$text**: The text to truncate.
- *integer* **$length**: The maximum length of the text.

Figure 4.13   JHtmlString truncate method information

the file. In this case, the class name is `JHtmlString` and the file path is `libraries/joomla/html/html/string.php`. We can use the constant `JPATH_LIBRARIES` to point to the location of the libraries folder, so the actual line of code to load the `JHtmlString` class is as follows:

```
JLoader::register('JHtmlString',
↪JPATH_LIBRARIES.'/joomla/html/html/string.php');
```

Recall from Chapter 3 that Joomla always loads a set of constants, including `JPATH_LIBRARIES`, to tell the system where various folders are located. It also loads some basic classes for the platform, including `JLoader`.

However, other classes need to be loaded as they are needed. The `JHtmlString` class is one of those. To load it, we just add the `register()` method to the beginning of our layout file (normally, just after the `defined` statement).

Now we can use that class in our layout. The code is shown in Listing 4.9.

Listing 4.9 **Layout Using JHtml::**

```php
<?php
/**
* @version        $Id: default.php 20196 2011-01-09 02:40:25Z ian $
* @package        Joomla.Site
* @subpackage     mod_articles_latest
* @copyright      Copyright (C) 2005 - 2011 Open Source Matters, Inc. All
↪rights reserved.
* @license        GNU General Public License version 2 or later; see
↪LICENSE.txt
*/

// no direct access
defined('_JEXEC') or die;
JLoader::register('JHtmlString', JPATH_LIBRARIES.'/joomla/html/html/string.php');
?>
```

```
<h1>My First Override</h1>
<ul class="latestnews<?php echo $moduleclass_sfx; ?>">
<?php foreach ($list as $item) :  ?>
  <li>
    <a href="<?php echo $item->link; ?>">
      <?php echo $item->title; ?></a>
      <p>
        <?php echo JHtmlString::truncate(strip_tags($item->introtext),
↪53); ?>
      </p>
  </li>
<?php endforeach; ?>
</ul>
```

If we tried to use the `JHtmlString` class without the `register()` method, we would get a PHP error saying that the class `JHtmlString` could not be found.

Now that we have access to the methods of `JHtmlString`, we can use its `truncate()` method to break the `introtext` field at a word boundary. The line of code that actually does the work is

```
<?php echo JHtmlString::truncate(strip_tags($item->introtext), 53); ?>
```

This uses the syntax we got from the API documentation, where the first argument is the text to be truncated and the second is the maximum length of the string. We changed it from 50 to 53 and removed the "..." because the `truncate` method adds the periods for us and includes them in the length.

Now let's reload the page and see what we have. Figure 4.14 shows an example.

Latest News

My First Override

▸ Beginners

If this is your first Joomla site or your first...

▸ Getting Help

There are lots of places you can get help with...

▸ Getting Started

It's easy to get started creating your website....

▸ Joomla!

Congratulations! You have a Joomla! site! Joomla!...

▸ Parameters

As you make your Joomla! site using the extension...

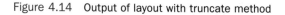
Figure 4.14   Output of layout with truncate method

Notice that now the preview text always breaks on a space instead of the middle of a word.

Using the JHtml::_ Syntax

At this point, we are almost done. However, there is one very nice programming trick we can use to finish this example. If we search the Joomla code base for places where we use the `JHtmlString::truncate` method, we won't find that exact command anywhere. Instead, what we will find is something like this:

```
<?php echo JHTML::_('string.truncate', $item->introtext,
➥$params->get('introtext_limit')); ?>
```

This statement is another way to call the exact same `truncate()` method. This is calling a function in the class `JHTML` called _ (underscore). (Important note: PHP class names are not case sensitive, so `JHTML` and `JHtml` refer to the same class. We should use `JHtml` because that is consistent with our naming convention, but PHP doesn't care.)

The `JHtml::_` method does a very cool thing. It interprets the first argument as follows. The first segment, `string`, is part of the class name. In this case, the full class name is `JHtmlString` (remember, it is not case sensitive). The second segment, `truncate`, is the method we want to call. The rest of the arguments are passed to this method. So, in this example, we pass the text and the maximum length.

Now here is the really great thing about using `JHtml::_()`: *it automatically loads our class for us!* So we don't need to worry about loading the class, and we don't need the `JLoader::register()` line in our layout.

Listing 4.10 shows the final code for the first layout, using the `JHtml::_()` syntax.

Listing 4.10   Final Layout with JHtml::_ Syntax

```php
<?php
/**
 * @version       $Id: default.php 20196 2011-01-09 02:40:25Z ian $
 * @package       Joomla.Site
 * @subpackage    mod_articles_latest
 * @copyright     Copyright (C) 2005 - 2011 Open Source Matters, Inc. All
➥rights reserved.
 * @license       GNU General Public License version 2 or later; see
➥LICENSE.txt
 */

// no direct access
defined('_JEXEC') or die;
?>
<h1>My First Override</h1>
<ul class="latestnews<?php echo $moduleclass_sfx; ?>">
```

```
<?php foreach ($list as $item) :  ?>
  <li>
    <a href="<?php echo $item->link; ?>">
      <?php echo $item->title; ?></a>
      <p>
        <?php echo JHtml::_('string.truncate', strip_tags($item->
↪introtext), 53);?>
      </p>
  </li>
<?php endforeach; ?>
</ul>
```

Notice that we no longer have the `JLoader::register()` line. The output of this version is exactly the same as the prior version.

We covered a lot of topics in this section, but our work can be summarized into two steps:

1. We created the subfolder for our layout override file in our template and copied the standard layout file into this new subfolder.

2. We modified the layout override file to fit our needs. In this case, we just added some preview text from the article.

Now whenever we show this module using the `beez_20_copy` template, it will use our modified file instead of the standard file.

Change the Look of a Component: User Registration

We can override the layouts for components in exactly the same way as we did with modules. Let's say, for example, that we want to change the layout of the front-end user registration to include an agreement that the user has to accept before registering.

Our first task is to find the layout file and put a copy of that file in the appropriate subfolder in the `beez_20_copy` template folder. Front-end user registration is a layout in the `com_users` component. If we look in the folder `components/com_users/views` we see a folder called `registration`. This has a subfolder called `tmpl`, which in turn has four files, as shown in Figure 4.15.

The file `default.php` contains the user registration form. The file `complete.php` contains the layout for the screen that shows after the registration is completed.

The folder structure for component layout overrides is similar to what we did for modules. We need to create a subfolder called `templates/beez_20_copy/html/<component name>/<view name>`. In our example, this will be `templates/beez_20_copy/html/com_users/registration`.

Then we copy the `default.php` file from the `components` folder above to the new folder. When we have done this, the template folder structure should look like Figure 4.16.

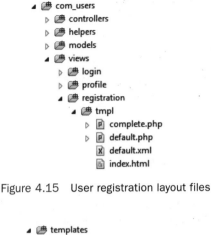

Figure 4.15　User registration layout files

Figure 4.16　Registration layout override folder structure

With modules, we just put the override files in the subfolder with the module name. Components are a bit more complicated. They normally have multiple views, each of which can have its own default layout. Accordingly, we have to create a subfolder for each view under the component folder and then put the layout override files in that subfolder. Note that we have copied empty **index.html** files into the override folders to prevent someone from browsing directly to our folders.

Next, let's make sure that we are running our override file. To do this, we can again add some text to the file and make sure it displays as expected. In Listing 4.11, we've added an h1 element with "My User Registration Override."

Listing 4.11　**New Heading to Check That Override Layout Is Executed**

```
<div class="registration<?php echo $this->pageclass_sfx?>">
<h1>My User Registration Override</h1>
<?php if ($this->params->get('show_page_heading')) : ?>
  <h1><?php echo $this->escape($this->params->get('page_heading'));
```

```
↪?></h1>
<?php endif; ?>
```

When we navigate to Home → Create an Account (with the Joomla sample data installed), we load the user registration form. If we have our `beez_20_copy` template defined as our default template, our modified layout file will show, as in Figure 4.17.

Now we know we have everything set up correctly, so we can customize the file. We said in our example that we wanted the user to accept an agreement before they register. If we look at the layout file, we see that the Register button is at the end of the file. Listing 4.12 shows the code.

Listing 4.12   **End of Layout File**

```
<?php endforeach;?>
  <div>
    <button type="submit" class="validate" ><?php echo
↪JText::_('JREGISTER');?></button>
    <?php echo JText::_('COM_USERS_OR');?>
    <a href="<?php echo JRoute::_('');?>"
↪title="<?php echo JText::_('JCANCEL');?>"><?php echo JText::_('JCANCEL');?></a>
      <input type="hidden" name="option" value="com_users" />
      <input type="hidden" name="task" value="registration.register" />
      <?php echo JHtml::_('form.token');?>
  </div>
</form>
</div>
```

We want to insert the check box for our agreement just before the Register button code (highlighted in Listing 4.12). The modified version of the file is shown in Listing 4.13.

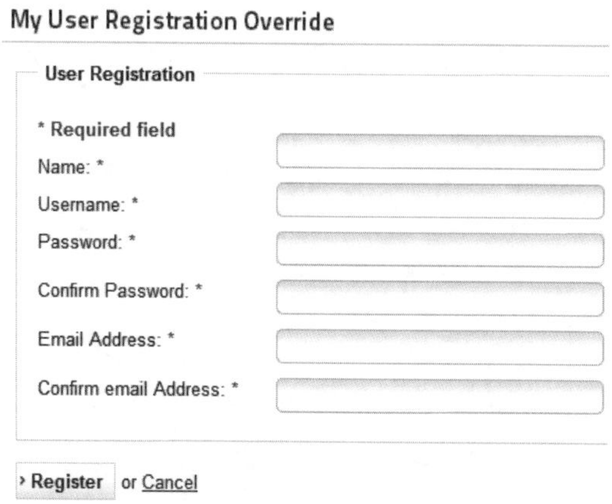

Figure 4.17   User registration override output with heading

Listing 4.13   **Layout with Terms of Service Check Box**

```
<?php endforeach;?>
  <div>
    <fieldset>
      <legend>Terms of Service</legend>
        <p><input type="checkbox" /> I agree to the terms of service for
➥this website.</p>
    </fieldset>
    <button type="submit" class="validate" ><?php echo
➥JText::_('JREGISTER');?></button>
    <?php echo JText::_('COM_USERS_OR');?>
    <a href="<?php echo JRoute::_('');?>"
➥title="<?php echo JText::_('JCANCEL');?>"><?php echo JText::_('JCANCEL');?></a>
      <input type="hidden" name="option" value="com_users" />
      <input type="hidden" name="task" value="registration.register" />
      <?php echo JHtml::_('form.token');?>
  </div>
</form>
</div>
```

We inserted a standard HTML `fieldset` element with a legend and a check box.
The result displays as shown in Figure 4.18.

Notice that there are two limitations to this new form:

- We are not requiring that the user check the box before registering.

- The wording of the check box is hard-coded in English and will not be translated if the site is run in a different language.

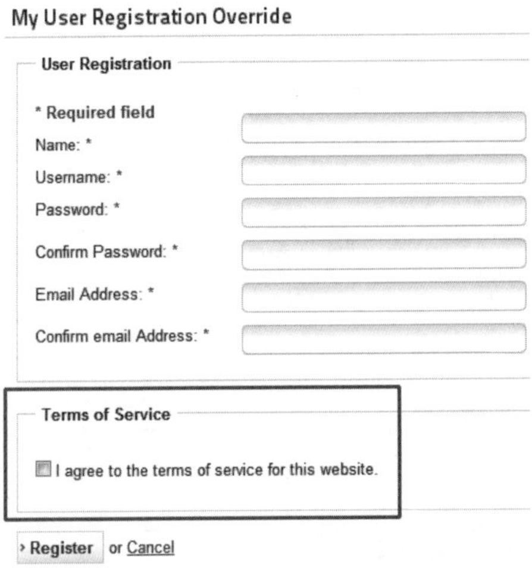

Figure 4.18   Registration form with terms of service

In Chapter 5, we add a plugin that validates that the check box is actually checked. Later in this chapter we add a language file override and modify our form to allow the text to be translated into other languages.

Alternative Layouts

In the two examples so far, the overrides are "hard-coded" for a specific template. If we show any menu item using the `beez_20_copy` template, for example, Joomla will always use the override file for a module or a component view, if one exists in the `beez_20_copy/html` folder.

Joomla version 1.6 introduced a new feature called *alternative layouts*. This is a more flexible way to use overrides. Alternative layouts work almost the same as template overrides, with two differences:

- With template overrides, we want to keep the layout file name the same as the standard (`default.php` in our examples). With an alternative layout, we create the file with a different name.

- With template overrides, the override file is always used. With alternative layouts, we select which file to use when we create the module or the menu item.

Let's demonstrate alternative layouts by renaming our Latest News module layout from `default.php` to `preview.php`. (Recall that it is in the `templates/beez_20_copy/html/mod_articles_latest` folder.) Now when we navigate to the Module Manager and open this module for editing, we can see our alternative layout as an option in the Advanced Options, as shown in Figure 4.19.

We can use this same method to create alternative layouts for articles, contacts, news feeds, web links, category lists, and category blogs. These work the same as template overrides. If you name the alternative layout file something other than the standard layout name, it is treated as an alternative layout. You can set each component or category to use an alternative layout either in the component settings screen (for example, Article Manager → Settings) or for individual items (articles, contacts, news feeds, web links, or categories). You can read more about using alternative layouts on the Joomla documentation wiki (`http://docs.joomla.org/Layout_Overrides_in_Joomla_1.6#Component_Alternative_Layouts`).

There are two major advantages to alternative layouts. First, you can have multiple layouts for the same module, without needing multiple templates. Second, you

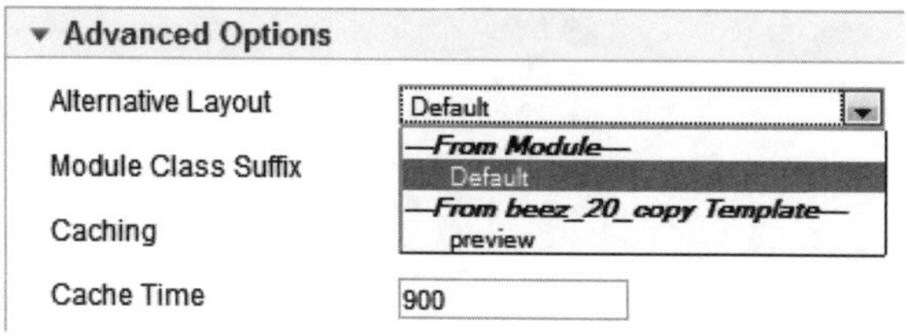

Figure 4.19   Alternative module layout example

can select a layout from a template even if you are not using that template to display the page.

The only requirements for naming an alternative layout are (1) that it is a different name from that of the standard layout and (2) that it doesn't contain an "_" (underscore) in the name. Names with underscores are assumed to be sublayout files.

Adding a New Menu Item Layout

Also starting with Joomla version 1.6, it is possible to create alternative menu items. An alternative menu item includes a layout file and an XML file. Using the XML file, we can override the parameters for the menu item.

Creating an alternative menu layout is similar to creating a template override. Here are the steps:

1. Create a subfolder in the templates folder called `templates/<your template name>/html/<component name>/<view name>/` (same as for template overrides).

2. Create one or more view PHP files and one menu item XML file. The main view file and the XML file must have the same name, and the name must be different from the standard file name.

3. If needed, create sublayout files, again using the same name as in (2) for the first segment of the sublayout file.

We can see how this works by changing our modified User Registration form from a template layout to an alternative menu item layout. To do this, we will follow these steps:

1. Rename `default.php` (in the folder `templates/beez_20_copy/html/com_users/registration`) to `approval.php`.

2. Copy `components/com_users/views/registration/tmpl/default.xml` to `templates/beez_20_copy/html/com_users/registration/approval.xml`.

3. If desired, add or remove any parameters from the XML file. In our example, we will add an optional check box for the user to indicate that he or she is at least 18 years old. We will modify the layout file to show a second check box if this parameter is set.

After we copy the files, our `beez_20_copy` folder should look like Figure 4.20.

Figure 4.20   Alternative menu item files

Parameter Overrides

For each new menu item layout, we are creating a new XML file for our parameters. This gives us the opportunity to customize the parameters for the new menu item layout. We are free to add or remove parameters, and we can access any added parameters inside the layout file.

Let's add a parameter for the second check box in our layout file. The revised XML file code is shown in Listing 4.14.

Listing 4.14   **User Registration Alternative Menu Item XML File**

```xml
<?xml version="1.0" encoding="utf-8"?>
<metadata>
  <layout title="Registration with Approval" option="Approval">
    <help
        key="JHELP_MENUS_MENU_ITEM_USER_REGISTRATION"
    />
    <message>
        <![CDATA[COM_USER_REGISTRATION_VIEW_DEFAULT_DESC]]>
    </message>
  </layout>


  <!-- Add fields to the parameters object for the layout. -->
  <fields name="params">

    <!-- Basic options. -->
    <fieldset name="basic" label="COM_MENUS_BASIC_FIELDSET_LABEL">
      <field
        name="show_age_checkbox"
        type="radio"
        label="Show Age Checkbox"
        description="Show or hide the age checkbox."
        default="0" >
        <option value="0">Hide</option>
        <option value="1">Show</option>
      </field>
    </fieldset>
  </fields>
</metadata>
```

This file is a copy of the `components/com_users/views/registration/tmpl/default.xml` file with some modifications.

We changed the `title` and `option` attributes. The `title` attribute is what will show when you create a new menu item. This should be different from the standard title so you know which menu item type you are creating.

The `help` element provides the key for the help system to know which article to load when the help icon is pressed. Since we don't have a separate help file for our override, we leave this unchanged.

The last change is adding the `field` element for our new parameter. This is called `show_age_checkbox` and is a radio button parameter. It has two options, `Hide` or `Show`, with the default being `Hide`.

When a new menu item is created, this XML file is processed by the `JForm` classes in the Joomla library to render the options for the menu item.

Now let's see what this looks like when we use the new alternative menu item. When we navigate to Menus → Main Menu and press the New icon and then press the Select button for the Menu Item Type field, we see Figure 4.21.

Note that our new Registration with Approval menu item type is now listed. If we select that type, we see the New Menu Item screen. This now displays the Show Age Checkbox option, as shown in Figure 4.22.

Notice that our new option shows inside the Basic Options group.

Now let's use our new parameter to conditionally add a second check box in our layout. The modified code for the revised layout is as follows:

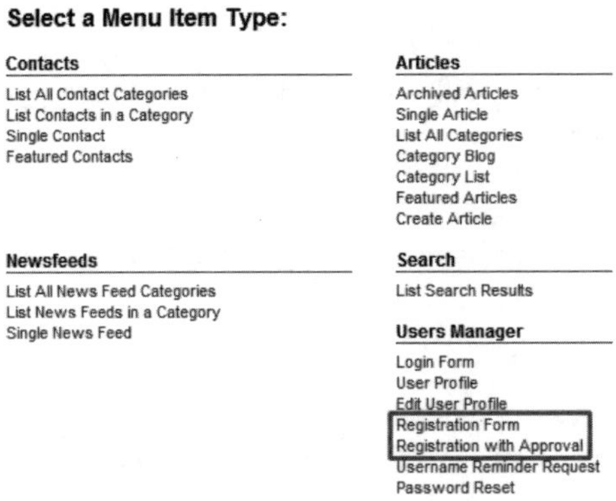

Figure 4.21   Menu item type list with alternative menu item type

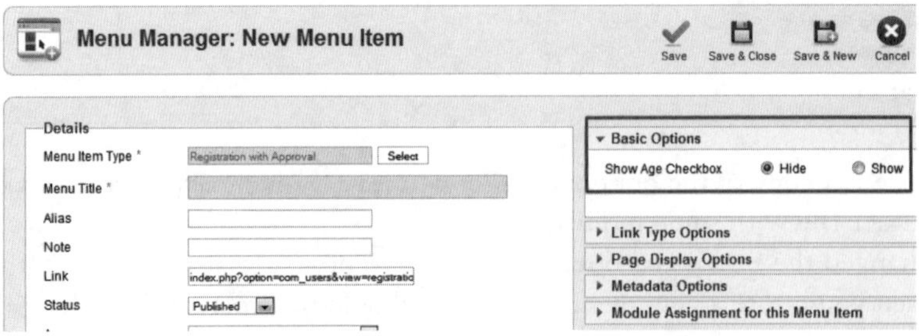

Figure 4.22   Menu item entry screen with custom options

```
<fieldset>
  <legend>Terms of Service</legend>
    <p><input type="checkbox" /> I agree to the terms of service for this
website. </p>
    <?php if ($this->params->get('show_age_checkbox')) : ?>
      <p><input type="checkbox" /> I am at least 18 years old. </p>
    <?php endif; ?>
</fieldset>
```

In this case, we have added code to check the new `show_age_checkbox` parameter. It is automatically made available in the `$this->params` field via the `get()` method. The parameter value is 0 for hide and 1 for show. A 0 in PHP evaluates to a boolean `false` inside the if condition. With this code, the age check box is only rendered if the option is set to Show, which is what we want.

Using our new alternative menu item, create a new menu item called My User Registration. Then try displaying the layout for both option values to make sure it works correctly.

How Do Layout Overrides Work?

The code behind module and component layout overrides is interesting and instructive. However, it makes more sense to do this once we have a more detailed understanding of the normal operation of modules and components. Accordingly, we discuss the code that implements module layouts in Chapter 6 and alternative menu items in Chapter 8.

Nonlayout Overrides

Joomla also allows us to override other aspects of our site. These include the following:

- Module `chrome`, which is the decoration around a module layout
- Language files
- Menu Item Parameter

These are discussed next.

Module Chrome: Add New Module Style

We discussed module chrome and styles earlier in this chapter. To see how this works, let's create a new module style for our customized template.

The steps we need to take are as follows:

1. Create the new `modChrome` function in the `modules.php` file for our customized template.

2. Use the new style in a `jdoc:include` position declaration in our template's `index.php` file.

3. Assign a module to this position.

To save a bit of time, we will copy the existing `modChrome` function called `modChrome_table` from the file `templates/system/html/modules.php` and paste it into the end of the template's `modules.php` file (`templates/beez_20_copy/html/modules.php`). Then we will rename the PHP function `modChrome_beezCopyFramed Table`. The result is that the last part of the file `templates/beez_20_copy/html/modules.php` reads as shown in Listing 4.15.

Listing 4.15   New modChrome_framedTable Function

```php
/*
* Customized module chrome example for beez_20_copy
*/
function modChrome_beez20_copyFramedTable ($module, &$params, &$attribs)
{ ?>
    <table cellpadding="0" cellspacing="0"
➥class="moduletable<?php echo
➥htmlspecialchars($params->get('moduleclass_sfx')); ?>">
    <?php if ($module->showtitle != 0) : ?>
        <tr>
            <th>
                <?php echo $module->title; ?>
            </th>
        </tr>
    <?php endif; ?>
        <tr>
            <td>
                <?php echo $module->content; ?>
            </td>
        </tr>
        </table>
    <?php
}
```

This function is a simple and great example of mixing HTML and PHP in a layout. Notice that the "`} ?>`" in the fourth line closes the PHP tag so we can include HTML elements.

First we create an HTML `table` element. Then we check to see if we are supposed to show the module's title. If so, we create a table heading (`th`) element for the table with the title. Finally, we output the content of the module in a table row (`tr`) and table cell (`td`) element.

There are several things to note about this. As mentioned earlier, this is a PHP function and not a method inside a PHP class. Because of this, this function is the very last thing in the file and is not wrapped inside a closing curly brace (`}`) for a class definition. So make sure you insert this at the very end of the `modules.php` file, after the last curly brace.

Notice also that we have included the template name `beez20_copy` as part of the function name. This is important if we plan to use this template in sites with other templates.

As you would expect, PHP will not allow us to name the same function twice, since it wouldn't know which one to use. When we add a new template to the site, we don't know what `modChrome` functions these templates might add in their `modules.php` files. By including our template name as part of the function name, we can be reasonably confident that it will not be the same as a name from another template (and therefore not cause a PHP error). This technique of adding a unique prefix to the name is sometimes called "namespacing." We use a similar technique when we create keys for language files.

Now let's modify our new style to include a 5-pixel border around the table. We'll change the table element by adding a `border` attribute as follows:

```
function modChrome_beez20_copyFramedTable($module, &$params, &$attribs)
{ ?>
    <table cellpadding="0" cellspacing="0" border="5"
➥class="moduletable<?php echo
➥htmlspecialchars($params->get('moduleclass_sfx')); ?>">
```

Now that we have our new style, we have to modify the template's `index.php` file to create a position that uses this style. So we'll edit the file `templates/beez_20_copy/index.php` and add a new position called `position-7a`. Recall that module positions are added using the `jdoc:include` tag. Here is a segment of the modified file, with the added code highlighted:

```
<div class="left <?php if ($showRightColumn==NULL){ echo 'leftbigger';}
➥?>" id="nav" >

    <jdoc:include type="modules" name="position-7"  style="beezDivision"
➥headerLevel="3" />
    <jdoc:include type="modules" name="position-7a"
➥style="beez20_copyFramedTable" />
    <jdoc:include type="modules" name="position-4" style="beezHide"
➥headerLevel="3" state="0 " />
```

If this were going to be a real position for our template, we would also want to add this new position to the `templateDetails.xml` file. But we don't need to for this example.

The last step is to change the module to use position-7a. We do this by going to the Module Manager and changing the position value, as shown in Figure 4.23.

Because we didn't add the position to the `templateDetails.xml` file, it will not appear in the list of positions. So we must enter it manually. Let's also change the module's Menu Assignment to display On All Pages.

Figure 4.23   Module manager with new position

Now when we display our home page, the Latest News module shows with our new chrome style, as shown in Figure 4.24. (Note that we are again using the standard layout and not the override, because we renamed default.php to preview.php in the folder `templates/beez_20_copy/html/mod_articles_latest`.)

Next let's use the attribute feature of chrome to allow the designer to set the border width inside the `jdoc:include` tag. We'll change the function as follows:

```
{ ?>
  <table cellpadding="0" cellspacing="0"
⮞border="<?php echo $attribs['border'] ?>"
⮞class="moduletable<?php
⮞echo htmlspecialchars($params->get('moduleclass_sfx')); ?>">
```

Here the value for the `border` attribute is being set using the PHP variable `$attribs['border']`. This value will be passed to the function based on attributes in the `jdoc:include` element. To use this, we need to modify the template `index.php` file as follows:

```
<jdoc:include type="modules" name="position-7a"
⮞style="beez20_copyFramedTable"
⮞border="2" headerLevel="3" />
```

In this case, we have set the value of `border` to 2 pixels. We can vary the border width for any position that uses the `beez20_copyFramedTable` style, just by setting the "border" attribute in the `jdoc:include` element.

What happens if we leave the `border` attribute out of the `jdoc:include` element? Before we try that, let's go to Global Configuration → Server in the back end of our site and set the Error Reporting to Maximum, as shown in Figure 4.25. 

Figure 4.24   Output of new style

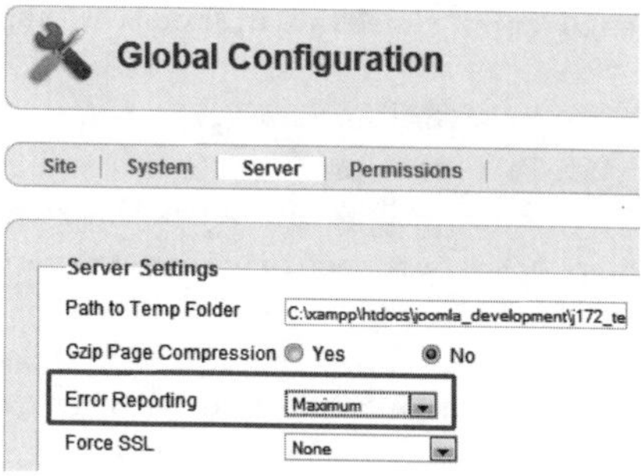

Figure 4.25   Server error reporting setting

It is strongly recommended to use this setting whenever you are writing code for Joomla, and we are about to see why. We'll go back to the template index.php file and remove the border attribute from the jdoc:include element, as shown:

```
<jdoc:include type="modules" name="position-7a"
➥style="beez20_copyFramedTable" />
```

Now when we display our module, we get a PHP Notice message, as shown in Figure 4.26. This is because we are referencing an array element, $attribs['border'] that is not defined. If we had our error reporting set to normal, we wouldn't see this notice. When we are writing code, it is important to make the code as robust or "bulletproof" as possible. One example of this is to always make sure we have a variable defined before we try to use it.

Once we realize our mistake, fixing it is easy. One way is to use the PHP function isset, along with the ternary operator, as follows:

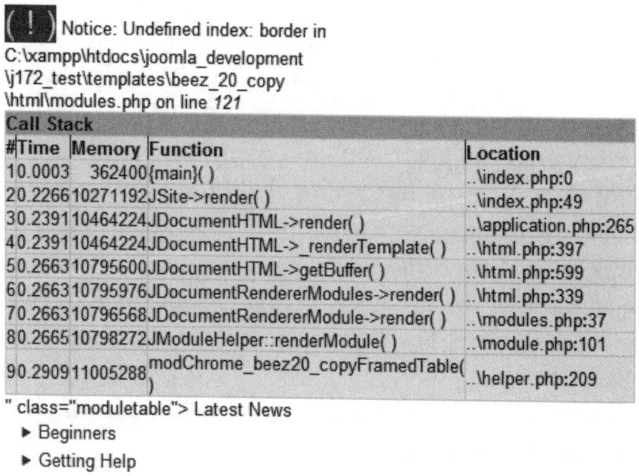

Figure 4.26   PHP notice for undefined array index

```
function modChrome_beez20_copyFramedTable($module, &$params, &$attribs)
{ ?>
  <?php $border = (isset($attribs['border']))
↪? (int) $attribs['border'] : '1'; ?>
  <table cellpadding="0" cellspacing="0" border="<?php echo $border ?>"
↪class="moduletable<?php echo htmlspecialchars($params->
↪get('moduleclass_sfx')); ?>">
```

The PHP ternary operator returns a value based on whether a condition is true or not. It uses the following syntax:

```
<condition> ? <value if condition is true> : <value if condition is false>
```

In our example, we evaluate the expression `isset($attribs['border'])`. If that is true, we set the variable `$border` equal to the integer value of `$attribs['border']`. Otherwise, we set `$border` to the value of 1.

We use the `(int)` function because the value of this attribute should always be an integer. If the user makes a mistake and sets the `border` attribute to a noninteger value, we will always have a valid value for the `border` attribute.

Note that we could have done the exact same thing with an if/then statement. However, the `ternary` operator does the work with one line of code.

Language Overrides: Add Translation to Our Override

Version 1.6 added a handy new feature for customizing the text that shows in Joomla. Two new folders are available for placing optional language override files: `language/overrides` for the front end and `administrator/language/overrides` for the back end.

Let's look at an example. If we look at the language file `administrator/language/en-GB/en-GB.ini`, we see this line of text:

```
JACTION_EDIT="Edit"
```

The language key `JACTION_EDIT` is used in the ACL permissions—for example, in Global Configuration → Permissions to show the `Edit` permission.

We can override any language key value in the back end simply by creating an override file of the proper name and putting any language keys we like in that file. The naming convention for the file is `xx-XX.override.ini`, where `xx-XX` is the desired language identification. For the default Joomla language "en-GB," the file is called `en-GB.override.ini`.

To try it, create a new file called `administrator/language/overrides/en-GB.override.ini` and put the following line in it:

```
JACTION_EDIT="Update"
```

Now when you display the Global Configuration → Permissions screen, you should see Update instead of Edit.

We can also use this same method to fix a problem in our User Registration alternative menu item. Recall that we have the following lines of code in this file:

```
<fieldset>
  <legend>Terms of Service</legend>
    <p><input type="checkbox" />I agree to the terms of service for this
➥website. </p>
    <?php if ($this->params->get('show_age_checkbox')) : ?>
      <p><input type="checkbox" />I am at least 18 years old. </p>
    <?php endif; ?>
</fieldset>
```

In this code block, we have three places where we are displaying English text. This practice is strongly discouraged when developing for Joomla, since so many Joomla users speak languages other than English.

Joomla has a handy feature, called Debug Language, that helps us check that all of our language strings are translated. If we go to Global Configuration → System and look at the Debug Settings group, we see Debug System and Debug Language, as shown in Figure 4.27.

Debug System is useful for troubleshooting database queries, and we demonstrate that in Chapter 11. Debug Language shows us whether literal strings are translated or not. If we set Debug Language to yes and show our alternative menu item for user registration, it looks like Figure 4.28.

All the translated strings have "**" before and after the translated text. Note that the three strings that we added ("Terms of Service," "I Agree . . . ," and "I Am . . .") do not have the "**". This indicates that these strings cannot be translated.

Using language override files, it is easy to make our layout override work with multiple languages. All we do is substitute our literal text with the method JText::_ ('DESIRED_TEXT_KEY'), as shown here:

```
<fieldset>
  <legend><?php echo JText::_('BEEZ_20_COPY_TERMS_OF_SERVICE')?></legend>
    <p><input type="checkbox" /> <?php echo JText::_('BEEZ_20_COPY_AGREE')?>
➥</p>
    <?php if ($this->params->get('show_age_checkbox')) : ?>
      <p><input type="checkbox" /> <?php echo JText::_('BEEZ_20_COPY_AGE')?>
➥</p>
```

Figure 4.27 Debug settings in global configuration

```
<?php endif; ?>
</fieldset>
```

The argument for the `JText::_()` method is called the language key. Joomla will find that key value in one of the loaded language ".ini" files and return the value of that key.

There are two rules for keys. First, they may not contain spaces and may not be equal to a few reserved words (null, yes, no, true, false, on, off, and none). This is because Joomla uses the PHP function `parse_ini_file()` to process language files.

Second, each language key must be unique. Otherwise, we will change some other text value that we didn't mean to change. The simplest way to ensure that we have a unique language key is to include the name of the extension as part of the key. Since we don't have an extension in this example, we have used the name of our template as the first part of the key. That way we only have to make sure the rest of the key is unique within our template. This is another example of using a simple namespace to create a unique name.

The key values must be placed in double quotes. If you need to put double quotes inside a language string, you can use `&quot;` or `_QQ_`. You can find examples of this in the core Joomla language files.

Now let's look at the registration form with our modified layout, as shown in Figure 4.29. Our key values are surrounded by double question marks (??). This indicates that `JText::_()` could not find the keys in a language file. This is what we

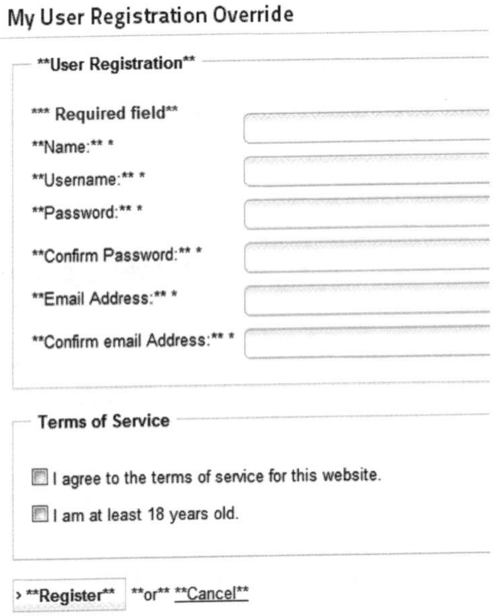

My User Registration Override

```
┌─ **User Registration**─────────────────────────
│
│ *** Required field**
│ **Name:** *                      [                    ]
│ **Username:** *                  [                    ]
│ **Password:** *                  [                    ]
│ **Confirm Password:** *          [                    ]
│ **Email Address:** *             [                    ]
│ **Confirm email Address:** *     [                    ]
│
└───────────────────────────────────────────────

┌─ Terms of Service ─────────────────────────────
│
│  ☐ I agree to the terms of service for this website.
│  ☐ I am at least 18 years old.
│
└───────────────────────────────────────────────

┌──────────────────────────────┐
│ › **Register** │ **or** **Cancel** │
└──────────────────────────────┘
```

Figure 4.28   Override layout with language debug = yes

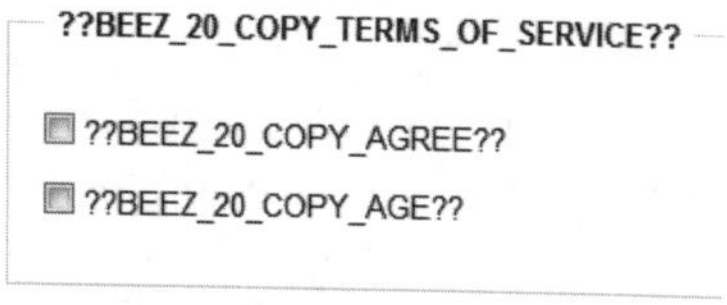

??BEEZ_20_COPY_TERMS_OF_SERVICE??

☐ ??BEEZ_20_COPY_AGREE??

☐ ??BEEZ_20_COPY_AGE??

Figure 4.29   Registration form with missing language keys

want because it indicates that our keys are unique and are not present in any loaded language files.

The last step is to create our override language file with the new keys in it. Since this is a front-end screen, we need to create the front-end override file for the en-GB language. So the full name of the file will be language/overrides/en-GB.override.ini and its contents will be as follows:

```
; Example front-end language override file
; Keys for templates/beez_20_copy/html/com_users/registration/approval.php
layout file
BEEZ_20_COPY_TERMS_OF_SERVICE="Terms of Service"
BEEZ_20_COPY_AGE="I am at least 18 years old."
BEEZ_20_COPY_AGREE="I agree to the terms of service for this site."
```

Now when we display the form, our text is bracketed with the ** characters, indicating that the text is translated from a language file, as shown in Figure 4.30.

Language overrides can be used in two different ways: (1) to change the text for an existing language key and (2) to provide translated text for a layout override. When we create an extension, we will typically create new language files for the extension and not use override files. We discuss language files for plugins, modules, and components in the following chapters.

As of Joomla version 2.5, we can create and edit language overrides using the Overrides tab in Extensions → Language Manager in the administrative back end. This accomplished exactly the same thing as we have done manually.

Table and Model Overrides

Joomla allows us to override the standard PHP classes used for tables (subclasses of the JTable class) and models (subclasses of the JModel class). The most flexible way to do this is using a plugin. This is discussed in Chapter 5.

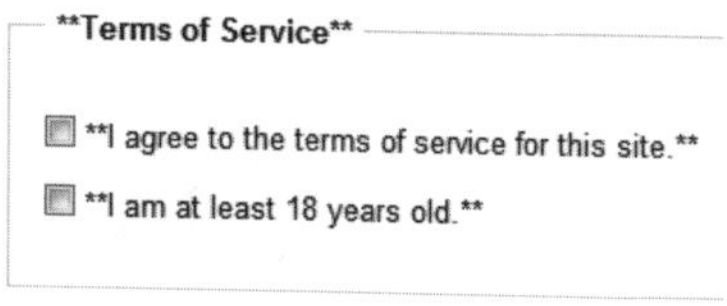

Terms of Service

☐ **I agree to the terms of service for this site.**

☐ **I am at least 18 years old.**

Figure 4.30   Registration form with translated text

Summary

In this chapter, we presented an overview of templates in Joomla and we demonstrated many of the ways that Joomla allows you to override the standard layouts. All of this was done with very little coding and without writing any new extensions.

We can customize a lot of existing core functionality in Joomla in this manner. However, to really see the power of extending Joomla, we need to create our own extensions. We address this in the following chapters.

Extending Joomla! with Plugins

In this chapter, we examine how plugins work and the different types of events that can trigger plugins. We look at some core plugins and then create our own plugin, based on the user registration form we created previously.

Then we create a zip archive that allows any Joomla! website to install and use our plugin extension. Next we add some parameters to the plugin and discuss the `JForm` class that handles parameters. We add a language file to handle translating the text for our plugin.

Finally, we discuss some powerful things that plugins allow us to do, including overriding models, tables, and other standard Joomla classes. We finish by discussing some best practices for developing and using plugins.

What Is a Plugin?

A plugin is simply a PHP program that executes at one or more predefined points in the Joomla execution cycle. These points are called events and are triggered from within Joomla.

A plugin can be very simple—for example, to set a value before saving a field to the database. Or it can be very complex—for example, to convert all the URLs in a document to a different format. Plugins can even be used to override standard core classes.

Plugins are tied to events. To understand plugins, we need to understand the predefined events in Joomla and also how to create our own events.

How Do Plugins Work?

Plugins work in three steps, as follows:

1. One or more plugin files are included into the current script, usually with the `JPluginHelper::importPlugin()` method. Because plugins are normally class declarations, no code is executed at this point.

2. An event is triggered, usually with the `$dispatcher->trigger()` method (where `$dispatcher` is a `JDispatcher` object). Each event has a name, such as `onBeforeInitialise` or `onContentBeforeSave`.

3. The event processing code looks for any enabled plugins that are currently loaded that have a method that matches the event name. If any matching methods are found, they are executed.

Loading and Executing PHP Scripts that Declare Classes

Most plugins in Joomla contain only a class declaration. This means that they declare a class and define the methods for the class, but they don't include any lines of code outside the class declaration.

When this type of file is loaded (for example, with the PHP command `require_once`), a new class is created in working memory, with all its methods. However, none of the methods in the class actually get executed. A method will only get executed when a line of code calls that method.

This is why the `JPluginHelper::importPlugin()` method gets the plugin ready to execute, but it normally doesn't actually execute any code. The plugin methods are only executed when the event is triggered, for example with the `$dispatcher->trigger()` method.

Naming Conventions for Plugins

For plugins to be found by the `JPluginHelper::importPlugin()` method, we need to follow the correct naming conventions for the plugin file and class names.

Plugin folder and file names are created as follows:

```
plugins/<plugin type>/<plugin name>/<plugin name>.php
```

So, for example, the SEF file is `plugins/system/sef/sef.php`. Plugins have an XML file with the same name (for example, `plugins/system/sef/sef.xml`). We discuss the XML file later in the chapter when we talk about packaging a plugin extension.

The class name of the plugin is based on the naming convention

```
"plg" + <plugin type> + <plugin file name>
```

So, for example, the class name of the SEF plugin is `plgSystemSEF`.

Plugin Types: Where Can You Insert a Plugin?

Plugins execute when their events are triggered. Plugin events as defined in Joomla are different from events in event-driven programs. In event-driven programming, the program waits for an event, which is frequently a user action such as a mouse click or keyboard entry. Joomla events can be thought of as checkpoints along the various paths of the execution cycle. Every time the execution cycle reaches an event checkpoint, the event is triggered. The events are fixed, although different events get triggered depending on what type of execution cycle we are in. Let's look briefly at each event type.

Authentication

There is only one event for authentication, called `onUserAuthenticate`. This event is triggered whenever a user attempts to log in to the front or back end of the site.

Captcha

Captcha is a way to prevent spamming by requiring a user to type some text based on a distorted image of the letters. Joomla version 2.5 added the ability to use captcha to validate user registration. This is implemented by means of three events: `onInit`, `onDisplay`, and `onCheckAnswer`.

Content

Content events are triggered when content is displayed or edited. This includes articles, contacts, and other types of content.

Editors

Editors are implemented in Joomla as plugins. However, they don't really fit the pattern of plugins as discussed in this chapter. Adding a new editor in Joomla requires indepth knowledge of JavaScript and is not an easy task. In this book, we do not discuss in detail how to add an editor, but we do show how to use editors in form fields.

Editors-XTD

Editors-XTD plugins are used to create the buttons that show below the editors (for example, Image, Pagebreak, and Read More). There is only one event for these plugins, called `onDisplay`.

Extension

This plugin type was introduced in Joomla version 1.6. Extension events are triggered when extensions are installed, uninstalled or edited and saved in the Module, Plugin, Template, or Language Manager.

Search

Search plugins implement the search functionality in Joomla. The core plugins are categories, contacts, content, news feeds, and Weblinks. The search events are `onContentSearchAreas` and `onContentSearch`. The `onContentSearchAreas` event is used to create an array of content items to search, and the `onContentSearch` event is used to actually execute the search for each of the content types. Extension developers can include search plugins to allow the Joomla search to work with their components.

Smart Search (Finder)

The Smart Search plugins are found in the plugins/finder folder. These plugins are used to index the site's content for use with Smart Search. A plugin is provided for each content type (contacts, content, news feeds, and weblinks) and can be enabled to allow indexing of this type. The events provided are `onFinderAfterDelete`, `onFinderAfterSave`, `onFinderBeforeSave`, `onFinderCategoryChangeState`, and `onFinderChangeState`.

System

System plugins provide events that are triggered during each Joomla execution cycle. These include `onAfterInitialise`, the first event triggered in Joomla, and events tied to the `render()`, `dispatch()`, and `route()` methods. System events should be used for plugins that need to be triggered during every execution cycle, regardless of which task is being performed.

User

User events are triggered during two different tasks. One group of events is tied to editing user information in the User Manager. These include `onUserAfterDelete`, `onUserAfterSave`, `onUserBeforeDelete`, and `onUserBeforeSave`. A second group of events is related to logging on and off the site. These include `onUserLogin` and `onUserLogout`.

Tour of Selected Core Plugins

One confusing thing about plugins is that they vary so much. The only thing they have in common is how they are called. Given this, we will start our discussion with a quick look at a few core plugins. These examples will give you an idea of the variety of tasks you can accomplish with plugins.

System: SEF

Our first example is the SEF plugin. This is a class called `plgSystemSef` in the file `plugins/system/sef/sef.php` and enables Joomla to use search-engine-friendly (SEF) URLs.

Where Is It Triggered?

Let's start with how this plugin gets executed—in other words, the code that includes the plugin class and triggers this plugin's event.

The SEF plugin is a system plugin and it is triggered with the `onAfterRender` event. Before we trigger the event, we need to include the plugin file.

If we are loading a page in the front end of our site, we invoke the `render()` method of the `JSite` class (in the file `includes/application.php`). Near the end of this method, we see the following line of code:

```
JPluginHelper::importPlugin('system');
```

This command loads all the enabled system plugins into working memory. (If a plugin is disabled in the Plugin Manager, it doesn't get loaded.) We only have to do this command once during a given method. After the system plugin classes are loaded into working memory, we can trigger one or more system events.

Because these plugins are class declarations, we haven't executed any code yet. Later in the `render()` method of the `JSite` class we actually trigger the `onAfterRender()` method:

```
// Trigger the onAfterRender event.
$this->triggerEvent('onAfterRender');
```

This triggers the `onAfterRender` event. Let's follow the code to see how it works. The variable `$this` is an object of type `JSite`, so `$this->triggerEvent` calls the `triggerEvent()` method of the `JSite` class with one argument, the string `'OnAfterRender'`.

`JSite` extends the `JApplication` class (`libraries/joomla/application/application.php`). Because `JSite` doesn't have its own `triggerEvent()` method (in other words, it does not override that method inherited from its parent class), it calls the method from `JApplication`.

So the `triggerEvent()` method from `JApplication` gets executed. This code is as follows:

```
function triggerEvent($event, $args=null)
{
        $dispatcher = JDispatcher::getInstance();
        return $dispatcher->trigger($event, $args);
}
```

This code creates an object of type `JDispatcher` and then calls the `trigger()` method for that object. The `$event` argument is set to "onAfterRender" and, because we didn't pass a second argument, the `$args` argument is set to its default value of `null`.

The result is that it executes the `onAfterRender()` method of every enabled plugin that is available in working memory. In this case, the search is limited to system plugins because we specified the type as "system" when we called `importPlugin('system')`, so only system plugins are loaded into our working memory.

Normally, our plugin method names should be consistent with the plugin type. For example, we should only use system event method names in system plugins. If we follow this convention, it doesn't matter if we have other plugin types loaded into memory, since only methods that match the event type will be executed.

Trigger Method Implementation

We will not go into detail about exactly how the `trigger()` method is implemented in Joomla. To create plugins, we just need to know what it does, which is to execute all the methods that match the event name. If you are interested in digging deeper into how this works, you can explore the code. You will find that Joomla uses the "observer" design pattern, where events are "observable" and the plugins are "observers."

What Does It Do?

Now let's look at the SEF plugin code. The code for the first part of the `sef.php` file is as follows:

```
// no direct access
defined ('_JEXEC') or die;

/**
 * Joomla! SEF Plugin
 *
 * @package     Joomla
 * @subpackage  System
 */
class plgSystemSef extends JPlugin
{
        /**
         * Converting the site URL to fit to the HTTP request
         */
        public function onAfterRender()
        {
```

The first line of code (after the documentation block which is not shown) is our standard `defined` command, which ensures that we are running this code inside Joomla. Before version 2.5, we needed a `jimport` statement to import the library file `libraries/joomla/plugin/plugin.php`. Starting with version 2.5, this file is loaded for us automatically by the Joomla platform's autoloader. It contains the class `JPlugin`, which is the parent class for all our plugins. We use it when we declare this class name, `plgSystemSef`, as a subclass of the `JPlugin` class.

In this case, the type is `system` and the file name is `sef`, hence the full name `plg-SystemSef`. Finally, we declare the public function `onAfterRender()`.

Upper and Lower Case in Class and Method Names

PHP doesn't distinguish between uppercase and lowercase in class and method names. However, we normally use "camel case" for class and method names. Camel case is where the first letter in each word is capitalized. Normally, class names start with an uppercase letter and method names start with a lowercase letter, but for plugin class names we start with lowercase. This convention just makes the code easier for people to read.

This plugin scans the HTML document for links and converts those links to search-engine-friendly links. It also replaces relative URLs with full-path URLs for a few other types of links. We aren't going to discuss the onAfterRender() method in detail, but let's look at two of aspects of it.

First, let's look at this code near the beginning of the method:

```
if ($app->getName() != 'site' || $app->getCfg('sef')=='0') {
        return true;
}
```

This is checking two conditions. The first one, $app->getName() != 'site', checks to see if we are *not* in the front end of our website. The second condition, $app->getCfg('sef')=='0', checks whether we have the search-engine-friendly URL's parameter set to zero (off) in our Global Configuration. If either of these conditions is true, then we exit the method immediately with a return value of boolean true.

Why do we do this? We only want to change the URLs when (a) we are in the front end of the site and (b) when the SEF setting is set to yes. However, we need to understand that this plugin is executed *every time* we encounter the onAfterRender event, whether we are in the front end or the administrative back end, and regardless of the SEF setting. That is why we have to put the check inside our plugin to make sure that the conditions for running this apply. We check that the conditions are met and, if not, we just exit the method before we have made any changes to the document object.

The second important point is that the onAfterRender() method does not take any arguments and it returns a boolean value to indicate whether or not it executed successfully. Different plugin types and methods have different method signatures (sets of arguments passed to the method) and return different values, so you have to be aware of these when you create a plugin.

Authentication: joomla Folder

This plugin is run when a user logs in to the site. It checks that the user name and password are valid. It is one of three authentication plugins included in the core Joomla distribution and is the default method for checking Joomla users.

This plugin is in the file plugins/authentication/joomla/joomla.php and its class name is plgAuthenticationJoomla.

How Does It Get Executed?

When a user attempts to log in to a Joomla site, the authenticate() method of the JAuthentication class (libraries/joomla/user/authentication.php) is executed. In that method, we see the expected line of code

```
$plugins = JPluginHelper::getPlugin('authentication');
```

that loads all the enabled authentication plugins into working memory.

Later in that method, we see a `foreach` loop as follows:

```
foreach ($plugins as $plugin)
{
    $className = 'plg'.$plugin->type.$plugin->name;
    if (class_exists($className)) {
        $plugin = new $className($this, (array)$plugin);
    }
    else {
        // bail here if the plugin can't be created
        JError::raiseWarning(50, JText::sprintf(
'JLIB_USER_ERROR_AUTHENTICATION_FAILED_LOAD_PLUGIN', $className));
        continue;
    }

    // Try to authenticate
    $plugin->onUserAuthenticate($credentials, $options, $response);
```

This loops through any enabled authentication plugins and checks that the class name exists. If any enabled authentication plugin does not exist, it fails with an error. If all the classes exist, then it executes the last line, which triggers the `onUserAuthenticate` method for each plugin. Note that three arguments are passed to the plugin: `$credentials`, `$options`, and `$response`. We discuss them in the next section.

What Does It Do?

The code for the `onUserAuthenticate` method is shown in Listing 5.1.

Listing 5.1   onUserAuthenciate Method for Joomla Authentication

```
function onUserAuthenticate($credentials, $options, &$response)
{
    $response->type = 'Joomla';
    // Joomla! does not like blank passwords
    if (empty($credentials['password'])) {
        $response->status = JAUTHENTICATE_STATUS_FAILURE;
        $response->error_message =
Text::_('JGLOBAL_AUTH_EMPTY_PASS_NOT_ALLOWED');
        return false;
    }
    // Initialise variables.
    $conditions = '';

    // Get a database object
    $db     = JFactory::getDbo();
```

```
$query   = $db->getQuery(true);

$query->select('id, password');
$query->from('#__users');
$query->where('username=' . $db->Quote($credentials['username']));

$db->setQuery($query);
$result = $db->loadObject();

if ($result) {
    $parts    = explode(':', $result->password);
    $crypt    = $parts[0];
    $salt     = @$parts[1];
    $testcrypt = JUserHelper::getCryptedPassword(
        $credentials['password'], $salt);

    if ($crypt == $testcrypt) {
        // Bring this in line with the rest of the system
        $user = JUser::getInstance($result->id);
        $response->email = $user->email;
        $response->fullname = $user->name;
        if (JFactory::getApplication()->isAdmin()) {
            $response->language = $user->getParam('admin_language');
        }
        else {
            $response->language = $user->getParam('language');
        }
        $response->status = JAUTHENTICATE_STATUS_SUCCESS;
        $response->error_message = '';
    } else {
        $response->status = JAUTHENTICATE_STATUS_FAILURE;
        $response- >error_message =
JText::_('JGLOBAL_AUTH_INVALID_PASS');
    }
} else {
    $response->status = JAUTHENTICATE_STATUS_FAILURE;
    $response->error_message = JText::_('JGLOBAL_AUTH_NO_USER');
}
}
```

Let's discuss the code for this plugin. The first lines are as follows:

```
function onUserAuthenticate($credentials, $options, &$response)
{
```

The method takes three arguments. The variable $credentials is an associative array with two elements: "password" and "username." This is the password and username the user has typed in to the form. The second argument, $options, is not used in this method.

The third argument, $response, is very important. Notice that there is an ampersand ("&") in front of $response. This tells us that this variable is passed by reference. This means that when we make changes to this object during our method, the calling method will see the changed object. See the sidebar entitled "Assign by Reference and Pass by Reference" for more information on this.

This method returns a boolean **false** if the login does not succeed. If the login does succeed, no value is returned. We do, however, pass data back to the calling method, because we change the $response object and those changes are available to the calling method after this method finishes.

Assign by Reference and Pass by Reference

Joomla version 2.5 requires PHP version 5.2 or higher, whereas Joomla version 1.5 could work with PHP version 4. PHP 5 changed the default behavior when objects are assigned to variables. In PHP 4, when we had an object variable—for example, $myObject—we did the following:

```
$x = $myObject;
```

$x was created as a copy (or clone) of $myObject. So if later on in our code we changed $myObject, $x was not affected. However, if we did the following,

```
$x = &$myObject;
```

the "&" told PHP to create $x as another reference to $myObject. This is called assigning by reference. In this case, $x and $myObject point to the same object. If we later change $myObject, the same change will be reflected in $x (because they are in effect two names for the same object).

The same thing holds for referencing objects in method signatures—an example is the following:

```
function onUserAuthenticate($credentials, $options, &$response)
```

The "&" tells PHP that we are passing a reference of the $response object to this method. So if we change the $response variable during the method, we will be changing the same object that was passed to the method. This means that when we exit the method and return to the calling method, any changes made to $response will be reflected in this same variable in the calling method.

With PHP version 5, we don't need to use the "&" in the first example. When we do

```
$x = $myObject;
```

in PHP version 5, it assigns by reference. So the "&" is no longer needed. If we want to create a new object, we need to use the command

```
$x = clone $myObject;
```

which actually creates a copy or clone of the object.

If you look at the Joomla version 1.5 code, you will see many places where we use the "&" in assignment statements like this to force PHP 4 to assign by reference. However, in Joomla version 2.5, we don't need these and they have been removed.

The situation with "&" in method signatures (passing by reference) is a bit different. It is still recommended that we put the "&" in when we are passing an object by reference to a method. For one thing, this tells the developer that any changes to this object made during the method will be available to the calling method. For another, there are differences between some PHP versions and this way we know we are forcing a pass by reference.

Before version 2.5, we needed to use `jimport` to import the user helper. We need this class later on to encrypt the test password. In version 2.5 and later this class is loaded by the autoloader.

The next line

```
$response->type = 'Joomla';
```

sets the type field of the `$response` object to `'Joomla'`. This field indicates what authentication plugin was used to validate the user.

The next code block is as follows:

```
// Joomla! does not like blank passwords
if (empty($credentials['password'])) {
        $response->status = JAUTHENTICATE_STATUS_FAILURE;
        $response->error_message = JText::_(
'JGLOBAL_AUTH_EMPTY_PASS_NOT_ALLOWED');
        return false;
}
```

This is an if statement that checks that there was a password entered. If not, the authentication fails. To indicate this, we set the **status** and **error_message** fields of the `$response` object and we return a boolean **false**.

The next block of code does a simple database query to get the user ID and password from the Joomla database. This is our first example of a database query, and it uses the **JDatabaseQuery** class that was added in version 1.6. The line

```
$db = JFactory::getDbo();
```

creates a **JDatabase** object. This is normally the first step for any database query. The next line

```
$query = $db->getQuery(true);
```

creates the `JDatabaseQuery` object. The next line

```
$query->select('id, password');
```

adds the database columns id and password to the SELECT part of the query. The next line

```
$query->from('#__users');
```

adds the #__users table to the query. Note that we access the table with the prefix "#__" (pound sign and two underscore characters). Before the query is actually run, this prefix will be replaced with the table prefix selected when Joomla was installed (for example, "jos_").

The next line

```
$query->where('username=' .
$db->Quote($credentials['username']));
```

adds a WHERE clause that restricts the query to rows where the username column is equal to the username element in the $credentials array. Because the username column must be unique within the database, we will only get one row from this query.

 The method $db->quote() is very important for security. It puts quotes around the username value and "escapes" any characters that have special meaning in SQL queries—for example, if single or double quotes could potentially be used to end one SQL statement and start a new statement. To protect against this, they are converted to \\' or \\". This causes the database to ignore the special meaning of these characters and prevents someone from entering in a SQL command in the username field.

Security Alert: Use $db->quote, (int), and (float) to Prevent SQL Injection

In this example, the variable $credentials['username'] is entered by a user of the website. As we have discussed earlier, we have to protect our data against would-be hackers who might try to enter malicious SQL commands by typing them into data fields. This type of attack or exploit is known as SQL injection.

We can prevent SQL injection by following two simple rules:

1. If a value is expected to be an integer (like –1 or 1234) or a floating decimal number (like 12.3456 or –2.3), use PHP to convert (or cast, in programming jargon) the value to the desired type. To do this, use the (int) or (float) command. For example, the line

    ```
    $query->where('id =' . (int) $id);
    ```

uses the `(int)` command to convert `$id` to an integer. This guarantees that nothing but an integer will get into that SQL command. Anything other than numbers and the minus sign will be stripped. This prevents any SQL commands from being entered via the variable.

2. For any variable types other than integer and float (for example, text or dates), use $db->quote to ensure that the values are safe to use inside a query—for example,

```
$query->where('title =' . $db->quote($myTitle);
```

If $myTitle contains quotes or other characters that have special meaning inside SQL commands, they will be escaped. This causes the database to ignore their special meaning and just treat them as normal text.

If you follow these two rules, you help protect your data and prevent hackers from running unauthorized queries.

At this point, we have built our query and are ready to run it against the database. This is done in the following code:

```
$db->setQuery($query);
$result = $db->loadObject();
```

The first line passes the query to the database object, and the second line runs the query against the database and returns the query results to the `$result` variable. If for some reason the query was not successful, `$result` will be empty or the boolean `false`.

The remainder of the method is an if/then/else block that starts as follows:

```
if ($result) {
  $parts     = explode(':', $result->password);
  $crypt     = $parts[0];
  $salt      = @$parts[1];
  $testcrypt = JUserHelper::getCryptedPassword($credentials['password'],
➥$salt);
```

The first line checks that the `$result` variable evaluates to a boolean `true`. If it doesn't, we skip down to the outside else code block as follows:

```
} else {
    $response->status = JAUTHENTICATE_STATUS_FAILURE;
    $response->error_message = JText::_('JGLOBAL_AUTH_NO_USER');
}
```

This gives the user an error message saying the login was not successful.

Using Non-Boolean Values in PHP If Statement Conditions

If you are new to PHP, the way nonboolean variables (variables other than `true` and `false`) are used in if statements can be confusing. For example, in the statement `"if ($result)"`, `$result` doesn't have to be a boolean. If it isn't a boolean, it is converted to a boolean and then evaluated. If it contains any data other than a blank or zero, it will evaluate to `true` and the code block after the if statement will be executed. For example, if `$result` is an object or array, it will be evaluated as `true`, regardless of what data it contains.

In the example `"$result = $db->loadObject()"`, this is OK because the `loadObject()` method either returns an object or a boolean `false`. If it returns an object, the object will always evaluate as `true`, so we know if we got a valid result or an error.

There is a pitfall to watch out for when working with values that can be zero or blank. For example, if a method can return a zero as a valid value and returns a boolean `false` if there is an error, the code `"if (!$result)"` will not work to check for an error. If zero is returned, the variable $result will evaluate as `false`, so the expression `"!$result"` (not $result) will be true. So the code block will process as though there were an error even though we got a valid result.

Similarly, the statement `"if ($result == false)"` will not work. This is less obvious, but it has the same problem as the previous example. If $result is zero, it will evaluate to `false` and therefore `"$result == false"` will be true and again the code block will be executed as though there were an error.

The solution in this case is to use the PHP comparison operator `"==="` (three equal signs), which checks for an identical match. This means that the two values must be the same *type* (boolean, integer, string, and so on) and the same *value*. So the expression `"$result === false"` will be true only if $result is the boolean `false`. Using this method will fix our example, even if $result is an integer zero. If $result is zero, `"$result === false"` will be false.

The operators `"==="` and `"!=="` both check for an exact match of type as well as value and are useful in cases where you may have an integer zero, a string "0," or a blank string as valid results of a method.

If the database query returned a valid result (in $result), then we execute the if code block. The first part is as follows:

```
$parts    = explode(':', $result->password);
$crypt = $parts[0];
$salt  = @$parts[1];
$testcrypt = JUserHelper::getCryptedPassword($credentials['password'],
➥$salt);
```

In the Joomla database, the password is stored as two fields separated by a colon. The first line in the previous code block uses the PHP explode function to put the two parts of the password column into an array called $parts. Then we put the first part of that into a variable called $crypt and the second part into a variable called $salt.

By default, Joomla uses a one-way hash command called md5 to encrypt passwords. By one way, we mean that you can only encrypt a password. You cannot decrypt it. To check that the user has entered the right password, we encrypt the value entered by the user and store in the $testcrypt variable.

Then we do another "if/then/else" code block, based on whether or not the encrypted value of the entered password equals the encrypted value stored in the database. This code block is as follows:

```
if ($crypt == $testcrypt) {
    // Bring this in line with the rest of the system
    $user = JUser::getInstance($result->id);
    $response->email = $user->email;
    $response->fullname = $user->name;
    if (JFactory::getApplication()->isAdmin()) {
        $response->language = $user->getParam('admin_language');
    }
    else {
        $response->language = $user->getParam('language');
    }
    $response->status = JAUTHENTICATE_STATUS_SUCCESS;
    $response->error_message = '';
} else {
    $response->status = JAUTHENTICATE_STATUS_FAILURE;
    $response->error_message = JText::_('JGLOBAL_AUTH_INVALID_PASS');
}
```

In the first part of the code block, our passwords match. So we get the user object and set the email and fullname fields of the $response object based on the user object values. Then we get the correct language object, depending on whether we are in the front or back end of the site. Finally, we set the status field of the $response to a success message.

If the passwords don't equal, we set the status field to indicate a failure and set the error_message field.

Notice that we don't issue a return command when the login is successful. Instead, this method uses a trick to communicate back to the calling method. The trick is that the $response variable is changed inside this method to show field values from the valid user object.

Recall that the plugin's authenticate() method was called in our example from the authenticate() method of the JAuthentication class. If we look at the JAuthentication code after the plugin is called, we see the following:

```
    // If authentication is successful break out of the loop
    if ($response->status === JAUTHENTICATE_STATUS_SUCCESS)
    {
        if (empty($response->type)) {
            $response->type = isset($plugin->_name) ? $plugin->_name :
```

```
                $plugin->name;
        }
        if (empty($response->username)) {
            $response->username = $credentials['username'];
        }

        if (empty($response->fullname)) {
            $response->fullname = $credentials['username'];
        }

        if (empty($response->password)) {
            $response->password = $credentials['password'];
        }
    }
}
return $response;
```

This altered version of the $response object is available to this method and, in fact, is returned by this method. Even though the plugin method doesn't return the $response object, it still passes its results back to the calling method via the updated $response object.

Content: joomla Folder

This plugin is in the file plugins/content/joomla/joomla.php and its class name is plgContentJoomla.

It has two methods. The onContentAfterSave() method is used to send a notification e-mail to users when a new article has been saved. The onContentBefore Delete() method is used to check whether a category has any items assigned to it before deleting it. Let's look at the onContentBeforeDelete()method.

How Does It Get Executed?

When a user deletes categories, articles, contacts, or other items in the administrative back end of Joomla, the onContentBeforeDelete event is triggered. One place this is done is in the JModelAdmin class (libraries/joomla/application/component/modeladmin.php). If we examine the delete() method, we see the following code:

```
// Trigger the onContentBeforeDelete event.
$result = $dispatcher->trigger($this->event_before_delete,
➥array($context, $table));
```

In this class, the field event_before_delete has been set to the string onContent-BeforeDelete in the class's constructor method.

There are two things to note about this code. First, we are expecting a return value, which is stored in the $result variable. Second, we pass two arguments to the trigger() method: the event name and an array with two elements. The trigger()

method unpacks this array and passes each of its elements as arguments to the `onContentBeforeDelete()` method. In this case, the two arguments are `$context` and `$table`. The variable `$context` is designed to tell us something about the context in which this event has been triggered (for example, "com_categories.category"). The variable `$table` is an array of the data that is about to be deleted.

What Does It Do?

The first part of the method is as follows:

```php
public function onContentBeforeDelete($context, $data)
{
    // Skip plugin if we are deleting something other than categories
    if ($context != 'com_categories.category') {
        return true;
    }
```

As discussed earlier, this plugin will be executed any time a user is deleting any type of content. Because this plugin checks whether a category has any items assigned to it, it only makes sense in the context of deleting a category. So the first `if` statement checks to make sure we are trying to delete a category. If not, we exit the plugin, returning a boolean `true`.

As mentioned earlier, every plugin has a PHP file and an XML file. A plugin's XML file does three things. First, it provides descriptive information about the plugin, such as its name, version, date, author, and license. Second, it lists all the files that need to be installed or uninstalled. Finally, it defines any parameters or options that can be set when using the plugin. These options show in the Plugin Manager screen when the plugin is opened for editing.

Parameters in Joomla allow the website administrator to control details about how the site will work without needing to write programming code. In this example, the Content → Joomla! plugin allows the administrator to control whether or not to check that categories are empty before deleting them. This is accomplished with a parameter by the name of `check_categories`. We will discuss parameters in more detail later in this chapter.

The `check_categories` parameter allows the administrator to disable the category check. This is accomplished in the next code block of the method:

```php
// Check if this function is enabled.
if (!$this->params->def('check_categories', 1)) {
    return true;
}
```

The object `$this->params` is a `JRegistry` object that contains the parameters saved in the `#__extensions` database table for this plugin. The `def()` method reads the parameter value, using a default value of 1 if the parameter is not defined. Recall that in PHP, a zero evaluates to a boolean `false`. Here we take advantage of this.

The parameter will be zero if we don't want to check categories and 1 if we do. If the parameter is zero, the condition (using the PHP "!" not operator) will be true, so we will halt the method and return true. If the parameter is not set or 1, we skip the return statement and continue with the method.

The next part of the method follows:

```
$extension = JRequest::getString('extension');
```

Here, we get the `$extension` based on the value in the PHP `$_REQUEST` variable. Notice that we use the Joomla library method `JRequest::getString()`. We could just read the `$_REQUEST` array directly. However, it is strongly recommended always to use the `JRequest` methods to do this, since they provide built-in filtering. In this case, the `getString()` method filters out hex and URL-encoded characters. `JRequest` provides a number of methods for reading request variables (`getString()`, `getInt()`, `getWord()`, and so on), and we always want to use the most restrictive method that we can. In other words, if we know the request value should always be an integer, we should use `getInt`. See Appendix B for all the filter types available.

The next code block is shown here:

```
// Default to true if not a core extension
$result = true;

$tableInfo = array (
    'com_banners' => array('table_name' => '#__banners'),
    'com_contact' => array('table_name' => '#__contact_details'),
    'com_content' => array('table_name' => '#__content'),
    'com_newsfeeds' => array('table_name' => '#__newsfeeds'),
    'com_weblinks' => array('table_name' => '#__weblinks')
);
```

Here, we set our result variable to true as a default value. Then, we build an array of the different table names for the different extension types. This plugin will only work for these five extensions. This array tells us the table name for each extension.

The next section of code is as follows:

```
// Now check to see if this is a known core extension
if (isset($tableInfo[$extension]))
{
    // Get table name for known core extensions
    $table = $tableInfo[$extension]['table_name'];
    // See if this category has any content items
    $count = $this->_countItemsInCategory($table, $data->get('id'));
```

This checks whether our current extension is in the array of the five core extensions. If it is, we execute the code inside the if statement. If the current extension is not one of the five core extensions, we skip to the bottom of the method and just return the $result variable, which we set to true earlier.

Inside the if code block, we set the $table variable to the table name we defined earlier. Then we set the $count variable, using the private method _countItemsIn-Category(). This method runs the database query to see how many items (articles, contacts, and so on) are in this category. Note that we pass as arguments the name of the table ($table) and the value data->get('id'), which gives us the id field for the category from the $data object that was passed in as the second argument.

Variable Names in Methods and Variable Scope

If you are new to programming, there is a potentially confusing point here about the $table variable. Recall that the code that triggered this event passed an array defined as array($context, $table) and that this array was unpacked to become the two arguments for the onContentDelete() method here.

When the second argument was passed, it was called $table. However, the second argument in the function signature for the onContentDelete() method is called $data. Even though these have different names, the $data variable in our current method has the same value as the $table variable was when the event was triggered.

When arguments are passed to functions, the *position* of the argument is what is important, *not the name* of the variable. The first variable from the calling method gets loaded into the first variable in the method signature, and so on. The variable name in the method signature is the name for that variable inside the method.

In programming, this concept is called *scope*. The scope of a variable is the part of the program where that variable has a specific meaning. In PHP, most variables are local in scope. That means they are only defined inside the method or function where they are used. The great thing about local variables is that we don't have to worry about whether we might have used the same variable name somewhere else in the program. We only have to keep track of variable names within a single method.

The variable $table is local to the onContentDelete() method, so it can mean something different in that method from what it might mean somewhere else in the program. Because we don't use the variable name $table in the method signature of onContentDelete(), we are free to use it inside the method to mean anything we like. In this case, the variable $table in this method refers to the table name defined in the $tableInfo array.

The next section of code follows:

```
// Return false if db error
if ($count === false)
{
        $result = false;
}
```

This checks whether we got a valid result from our _countItemsInCategory()
method. This method returns a number or a boolean `false`. Note that we use the
triple === comparison operator to check that $count is a boolean and is false. We have
to do that because zero is a valid return value from our countItemsInCategory()
method. If the method did return false, then for some reason the database query
returned an error. In this case, we set the return value to `false`. If the method did
return a valid result, we enter the `else` block of code that follows.

```
else
  {
  // Show error if items are found in the category
  if ($count > 0) {
      $msg = JText::sprintf('COM_CATEGORIES_DELETE_NOT_ALLOWED',
➥$data->get('title')) .
      JText::plural('COM_CATEGORIES_N_ITEMS_ASSIGNED', $count);
      JError::raiseWarning(403, $msg);
      $result = false;
  }
  // Check for items in any child categories
➥(if it is a leaf, there are no child categories)
  if (!$data->isLeaf()) {
      $count = $this->_countItemsInChildren(
      $table, $data->get('id'), $data);
      if ($count === false)
      {
      $result = false;
      }
      elseif ($count > 0)
      {
         $msg = JText::sprintf('COM_CATEGORIES_DELETE_NOT_ALLOWED',
➥$data->get('title')) .
          JText::plural('COM_CATEGORIES_HAS_SUBCATEGORY_ITEMS', $count);
          JError::raiseWarning(403, $msg);
          $result = false;
    }
  }
}
```

The first `if` statement checks if the count is greater than zero. If so, we produce a
warning message to the user and set the $result variable to false.

An important point here is that, by returning `false`, this plugin will prevent the
user from deleting the category. Another point here is that we don't actually do the
`return` statement until the end of the method. So we continue to execute the code.

The next section of code checks whether there are any items contained in any child
categories, using the _CountItemsInChildren() method. Note that we use a shortcut
to save a little processing time. There is a method in the $data object called isLeaf().

This method returns a true if the current category is a "leaf" in the category "tree," meaning that it doesn't have any child categories. If so, we don't have to check for items in child categories. In this case, we skip the whole code block.

If there are child categories, and if there are any items in these categories, we create another warning message and we set the `$result` variable to false. Note that if both warning conditions are present—meaning we have items in the current category and in child categories—then we issue both warnings. We use the `JError::raisewarning()` to display the warning to the user, and we include the count of items in the warning message.

A cool new method called `plural()` was added to the `JText` class in Joomla version 1.6. This allows Joomla to automatically select the right language tag based on whether the number being shown is 1 or more than 1. We use that to show both of our warning messages. For example, we want it to say "item" if there is one ("1 item") but "items" if there are more than one ("5 items"). The `JText::plural()` method does this for us without requiring an if statement. Also, it handles languages where there are different forms of a word for one, two, or three items.

The end of the method is the code `"return $result;"`, which just returns true if no items were found or false otherwise. As noted previously, this method only does any real work when we are deleting in the `#__categories` table. We could have added this check into the category table class instead of using a plugin. Why use a plugin?

The answer is flexibility. Performing this check in a plugin provides the administrator a number of options. First of all, plugins can be disabled, which allows an administrator to remove the category checking. Second, the parameters in the plugin allow the individual checks to be turned on and off. Third, you can provide your own plugin that either replaces or supplements the functionality of this or any core plugin. Finally, this plugin provides an easy-to-follow model for third-party extension developers to use to provide category checking for their extensions.

This is a great demonstration of the real power of plugins to enhance the flexibility of the system. They can be disabled or replaced without hacking any core files, allowing you to control lots of behind-the-scenes processing in Joomla.

onBeforeCompileHead

Now we are going to have some fun. We're going to write a simple plugin that uses an event called `onBeforeCompileHead`. This event allows us to modify the HTML head element in the page just before it is rendered. So we can use this event to modify any HTML element that goes in the head, including meta, title, link, or script elements.

How Does It Get Executed?

The `onBeforeCompileHead` event is triggered in the `fetchHead()` method of `JDocumentRendererHtml` (libraries/joomla/document/html/renderer/head.php). This method reads the information for the head HTML element from the document object and prints it out to the buffer in HTML text format. The following code triggers the event:

```
// Trigger the onBeforeCompileHead event
$app = JFactory::getApplication();
$app->triggerEvent('onBeforeCompileHead');
```

What Does It Do?

If we look at the HTML page source code for the home page of a site with the sample data installed, we see a series of meta elements inside the head element:

```
<meta name="robots" content="index, follow" />
<meta name="keywords" content="My keywords." />
<meta name="rights" content="My rights." />
<meta name="language" content="en-GB" />
```

Our plugin will be simple. It will add a "revised" attribute to the HTML meta element, based on a parameter that the user enters for the plugin. For example, the output of our plugin might be as follows:

```
<meta name="revised" content="Mark Dexter, 17 March 2012" />
```

where the content attribute is the text typed into the plugin parameter.

To do this, we will need to understand how the JDocumentHTML object stores the data for the HTML head element. Let's do a bit of investigating. In the fetchHead() method of JDocumentRendererHead class where the onBeforeCompileHead is triggered, we see that we have a variable $document in the method signature. This is a JDocumentHTML object, which has a method called getHeadData() that returns the header data for the document or page. If we put the command

```
var_dump($document->getHeadData());
```

in the fetchHead() method of that class (for example, just before the code that triggers the event) and then display the home page on the site, we will see a long dump of the output of the getHeadData(), part of which is shown in the following.

```
array
  'title' => string 'Home' (length=4)
  'description' => string 'My description.' (length=15)
  'link' => string '' (length=0)
  'metaTags' =>
    array
      'http-equiv' =>
        array
          'content-type' => string 'text/html' (length=9)
      'standard' =>
        array
          'robots' => string 'index, follow' (length=13)
          'keywords' => string 'My keywords.' (length=12)
```

```
'rights' => string 'My rights.' (length=10)
  'language' => string 'en-GB' (length=5)
```

If we compare this to the HTML source code shown earlier, we see that the meta elements with `name` attributes are stored in the object as an associative array stored in the `standard` element inside the `metaTags` element. The value of the `name` attribute is the key to the associative array (for example, "robots"), and the value of the `content` attribute is the value of the associative array (for example, "index, follow").

We want our plugin to add a new meta element with the name attribute of "revised" and the value to be the option entered in the Plugin Manager form by the user. We want to keep any existing meta elements and just add this as a new one.

Our code is going to work as follows:

1. Read the existing header data from the document. This will be an array like the one shown earlier.

2. Add an element to the associative array that is stored inside the `standard` element of the array inside the `metaTags` element. The key for this array will be "revised" and the data will be the value entered by the user for the parameter.

3. Write back the modified array to the document object using the `setHeaderData()` (which is the mirror image of the `getHeaderData()` method).

4. Finally, we only want to do this if there is some data in the plugin parameter. If it is empty, don't do anything.

Now we are going to create the plugin. Here are the steps:

1. Create the folder for the plugin. We'll call the plugin "mymeta," so we need to create a folder called `plugins/system/mymeta`.

2. To save typing, we can copy some existing files and just edit them. Copy the files `index.html`, `p3p.php`, and `p3p.xml` from the `plugins/system/p3p` folder to the new `plugins/system/mymeta folder`. Then rename the `p3p.php` and `p3p.xml` to `mymeta.php` and `mymeta.xml`.

3. Edit the `mymeta.xml` file so it appears as shown in Listing 5.2. Here we changed the name, author, creationDate, copyright, description, and filename XML tags.

Listing 5.2   mymeta.xml File

```xml
<?xml version="1.0" encoding="utf-8"?>
<install version="1.6" type="plugin" group="system">
 <name>My Meta Plugin</name>
 <author>Mark Dexter and Louis Landry</author>
 <creationDate>January 2012</creationDate>
 <copyright>Copyright (C) 2012 Mark Dexter and Louis Landry. All rights
↪reserved.</copyright>
 <license>GNU General Public License version 2 or later; see LICENSE.txt
</license>
 <authorEmail>admin@joomla.org</authorEmail>
 <authorUrl>www.joomla.org</authorUrl>
```

```
<version>2.5.0</version>
<description>My Meta Plugin</description>
<files>
   <filename plugin="mymeta">mymeta.php</filename>
   <filename>index.html</filename>
</files>
<config>
   <fields name="params">
    <fieldset name="basic">
       <field name="revised" type="text"
        description="Meta revised text for content attribute"
        label="Revised Content"
        default=""
        size="50"
        />
    </fieldset>
   </fields>
</config>
</install>
```

We also changed the entire field element to add our new parameter. We set the name to "revised"; set the type to "text"; and set the description, label, and size.

4. At this point, we have the code for entering the parameter for our plugin. Next we need to actually write the plugin. Listing 5.3 shows the listing for the mymeta.php file, with the plugin code.

Listing 5.3   **mymeta.php File**

```
<?php
/**
 * @copyright  Copyright (C) 2012 Mark Dexter and Louis Landry.
 * @license    GNU General Public License version 2 or later; see
↪LICENSE.txt
 */
// no direct access
defined('_JEXEC') or die;
jimport('joomla.plugin.plugin');
/**
 * Example System Plugin
 */
class plgSystemMyMeta extends JPlugin
{
    function onBeforeCompileHead()
    {
       if ($this->params->get('revised')) {
          $document = JFactory::getDocument();
```

```
$headData = $document->getHeadData();
$headData['metaTags']['standard']['revised'] =
    $this->params->get('revised');
$document->setHeadData($headData);                    }
    }
}
```

We have renamed the class to `plugSystemMyMeta` and named the function `onBeforeCompileHead`, the same as the event we are using for the plugin. The code is simple, once you understand the array structure of the `getHeadData()` method.

First we check whether there is anything in the "revised" parameter from our plugin. If not, we skip all the processing.

If there is something in this parameter, we proceed. We get the document object and then save the results of `getHeadData()` in `$headData`.

We create a new associative array element called "revised" and set its value to the parameter value. Note that this is an array that is nested inside two other arrays, as we saw when we dumped this value earlier.

5. At this point, our plugin is complete and ready to go. However, our Joomla installation doesn't know about it yet. The files are in the correct folders, but there is no row in the `#__extensions` table for the plugin.

   Recall from Chapter 4 when we copied the beez20 template that we had to use the Discover feature to install the new template. The same thing holds true here.

   So, in the administrative back end, navigate to the Extensions → Extension Manager and select the Discover tab. Then click the Discover icon in the tool-bar. You should see something similar to Figure 5.1.

6. Now click the check box at the left and then click the Install icon in the toolbar. A message should display that indicates the plugin was successfully installed.

   Installing an extension creates a row in the `#__extensions` table that stores information about the plugin. Joomla only "knows about" extensions that are in this table. The Discover process looks for extensions that are in the file system and not in the `#__extensions` table.

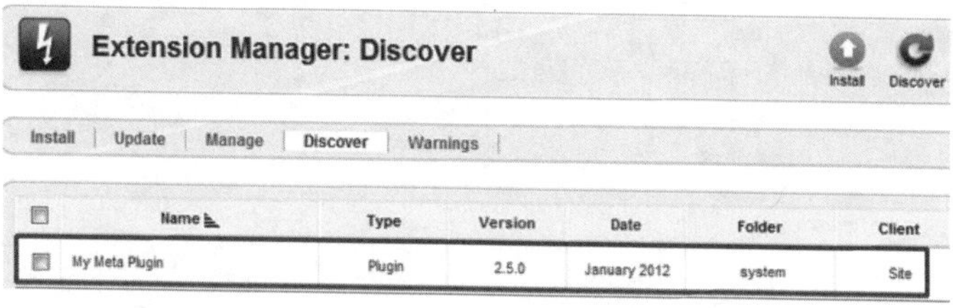

Figure 5.1 Discover screen showing new plugin

The normal way to install an extension is from an archive file created for that purpose. In the next section, we create a plugin and create a zip archive to allow it to be installed.

Now that our plugin is installed, let's test it. Navigate to the Extensions → Plugin Manager and filter on system plugins. You should see the My Meta Plugin listed. Clicking on it should show a screen as shown in Figure 5.2.

Change the plugin to Enabled, enter in something for the Revised Content, and then navigate to the home page of the site. In your browser, select the option to show the HTML source code for the page (for example, in Firefox, select View → Page source). You should see something like the following. The line added by the plugin is highlighted:

```
<meta name="robots" content="index, follow" />
<meta name="keywords" content="My keywords." />
<meta name="rights" content="My rights." />
<meta name="language" content="en-GB" />
<meta name="revised" content="Mark Dexter, 17 March 2011" />
<meta name="description" content="My description." />
```

As a final test, go back to the Plugin Editor and blank out the Revised Content value. Then redisplay the home page and check the source code. Now there should be no meta tag with the `name="revised"`, since there was no content for this tag.

If we step back for a minute, we can appreciate how easy it was for us to make this change. We simply added two new files to the system and edited a few lines of code. With this small amount of work, we were able to change the content of the head element on every page in our site.

User Registration Plugin

For our next example, let's add some validation to the override form we added in the previous chapter.

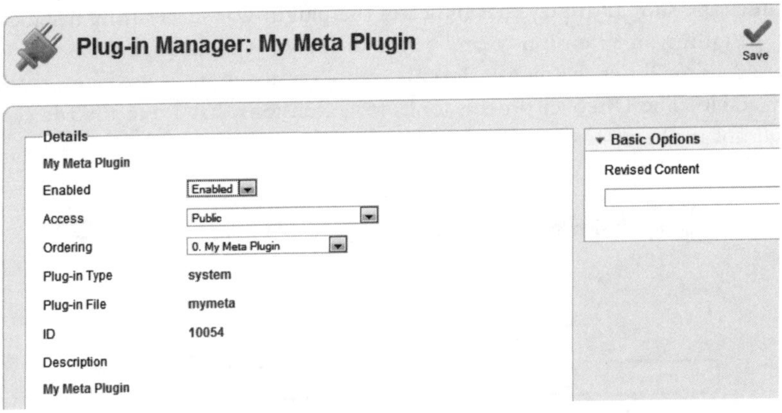

Figure 5.2   Edit screen for My Meta Plugin

Update the Approval Override File

Recall that we added two check boxes to the user registration form, as shown in Figure 5.3.

This was accomplished by adding the following code to the layout override file: `templates/beez_20_copy/html/com_users/registration/approval.php`:

```
<fieldset>
    <legend><?php echo JText::_(
↳'BEEZ_20_COPY_TERMS_OF_SERVICE')?></legend>
    <p><input type="checkbox" />
        <?php echo JText::_()?>  </p>
    <?php if ($this->params->get('show_age_checkbox')) : ?>
        <p><input type="checkbox" />
            <?php echo JText::_('BEEZ_20_COPY_AGE')?> </p>
    <?php endif; ?>
</fieldset>
```

We need to modify this code slightly before we write our plugin. Our plugin will check that both check boxes have been clicked by the user. If not, the plugin will return false, which will stop the registration process.

When we submit a PHP form with the post method, the values for the form are saved in the PHP super global variable called $_REQUEST. The values are saved in an associative array, where the key to the array is the name attribute of each input element. If an input element has no name attribute, it doesn't get saved. Accordingly, we need to add name attributes to both of the check box fields. In the following code, we call the first check box tos_agree and the second one old_enough.

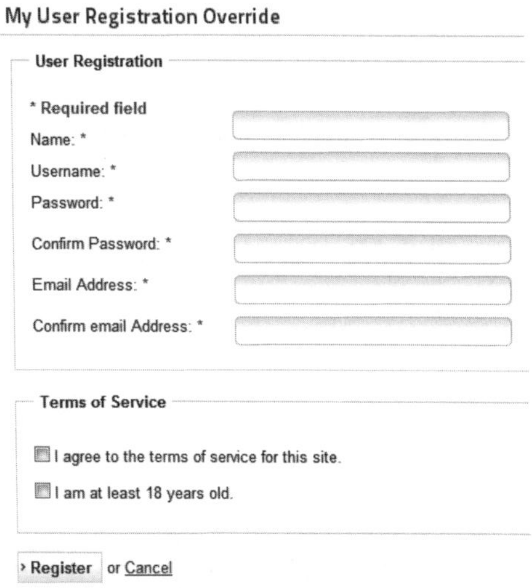

Figure 5.3 Customized registration form

```
<fieldset>
    <legend><?php echo JText::_(
        'BEEZ_20_COPY_TERMS_OF_SERVICE')?></legend>
    <p><input type="checkbox" name="tos_agree" />
        <?php echo JText::_('BEEZ_20_COPY_AGREE')?>  </p>
    <?php if ($this->params->get('show_age_checkbox')) : ?>
        <p><input type="checkbox" name = "old_enough" />
            <?php echo JText::_('BEEZ_20_COPY_AGE')?> </p>
    <?php endif; ?>
</fieldset>
```

Add the XML File

Next, we create the plugin PHP and XML files. The name of the plugin is "myreg-istration," and it is a user plugin. So we will create a folder called `plugins/user/myregistration` and create our two plugin files, `myregistration.xml` and `myregistration.php`, in that folder.

The `myregistraion.xml` file listing is shown in Listing 5.4.

Listing 5.4 **myregistration.xml File**

```
<?xml version="1.0" encoding="utf-8"?>
<extension version="2.5" type="plugin" group="user">
  <name>plg_user_myregistration</name>
  <author>Mark Dexter and Louis Landry</author>
  <creationDate>January 2012</creationDate>
  <copyright>(C) 2012 Mark Dexter and Louis Landry.</copyright>
  <license>GNU General Public License version 2 or later; see
➥LICENSE.txt</license>
  <authorEmail>admin@joomla.org</authorEmail>
  <authorUrl>www.joomla.org</authorUrl>
  <version>2.5.0</version>
  <description>PLG_USER_MYREGISTRATION_XML_DESCRIPTION</description>

  <files>
    <filename plugin="myregistration">myregistration.php</filename>
    <filename>index.html</filename>
    <folder>language</folder>
  </files>

  <config>
  </config>
</extension>
```

This is similar to the earlier example plugin. Note that we are defining a language subfolder for our plugin. We discuss this when we create our zip archive file.

Add the PHP Plugin File

The code for the `myregistration.php` file is shown in Listing 5.5.

Listing 5.5 **myregistration.php File**

```php
<?php
/**
 * @copyright  Copyright (C) 2012 Mark Dexter & Louis Landry. All
➥rights reserved.
 * @license    GNU General Public License version 2 or later; see
➥LICENSE.txt
 */

defined('JPATH_BASE') or die;
jimport('joomla.plugin.plugin');

/**
 * This is our custom registration plugin class.  It verifies that the
➥user
 *  checked the boxes indicating that he/she agrees to the terms of
➥service
 *  and is old enough to use the site.
 */
class plgUserMyRegistration extends JPlugin
{
    /**
     * Method to handle the "onUserBeforeSave" event and determine
     * whether we are happy with the input enough that we will allow
     * the save to happen.  Specifically we are checking to make sure that
     * this is saving a new user (user registration), and that the
     * user has checked the boxes that indicate agreement to the terms of
     * service and that he/she is old enough to use the site.
     *
     * @param   array  $previousData  The currently saved data for the
➥user.
     * @param   bool   $isNew         True if the user to be saved is new.
     * @param   array  $futureData    The new data to save for the user.
     *
     * @return  bool   True to allow the save process to continue,
     *                     false to stop it.
     *
     * @since   1.0
     */

    function onUserBeforeSave($previousData, $isNew, $futureData)
    {
```

```
        // If we aren't saving a "new" user (registration), or if we are
↪not
        // in the front end of the site, then let the
        //    save happen without interruption.
        if (!$isNew || !JFactory::getApplication()->isSite()) {
            return true;
        }

        // Load the language file for the plugin
        $this->loadLanguage();
        $result = true;

        // Verify that the "I agree to the terms of service for this
↪site."
        //    checkbox was checked.
        if (!JRequest::getBool('tos_agree')) {
            JError::raiseWarning(1000,
                JText::_('PLG_USER_MYREGISTRATION_TOS_AGREE_REQUIRED'));
            $result = false;
        }

        // Verify that the "I am at least 18 years old." checkbox was
↪checked.
        if (!JRequest::getBool('old_enough')) {
            JError::raiseWarning(1000,
                JText::_('PLG_USER_MYREGISTRATION_OLD_ENOUGH_REQUIRED'));
            $result = false;
        }

        return $result;
    }
}
```

The first two lines of code should be familiar. First we ensure that we are inside Joomla. Then we import the parent class for this plugin. (Note that, because of the autoloader, this line of code is no longer required as of version 2.5.) The class name follows the required naming convention of "plg" plus the type ("user") plus the plugin name ("myregistration"). The class extends JPlugin.

The class has one method, which is named according to the event that will trigger it. In this case the method is onUserBeforeSave(). This event is triggered when we try to save a new user in the back end or register a new user in the front end.

The first thing we do is to make sure we are creating a new user in the front end. If not, we just return true and skip the rest of the processing.

The next thing we do is to load the language file. This loads the file administrator/language/en-GB/en-GB.plg_user_myregistration.ini, which we discuss a bit later. Then we set our $result variable to true.

The next section is an if block. We use the `JRequest::getBool()` method to get the `tos_agree` element from the PHP `$_REQUEST` variable. This method returns a boolean `true` or `false`. Since this is a check box, we expect it to either have the value "on" or it will not be defined. However, we are also mindful that a hacker can manipulate the `$_REQUEST` variable and put values in there that we don't expect. By using the `JRequestion::getBool()` method, we know that we will always get a `true` or `false` value, no matter what a hacker might put in that field.

If the check box has been checked, the `JRequest::getBool('tos_agree')` will return a value of true and the expression `(!JRequest::getBool('tos_agree'))` will be false (recall that "!" means "not"). In this case, we don't execute the code inside the block.

If the check box has not been checked, we enter the code block. Here we execute two lines of code. The first calls the `JError::raiseWarning()` method. The first argument is the error code, which we don't use in this example (so it can be most anything). The second argument is the error text. Here we are using the `JText::_()` method to make the error text translatable. This means we will need to put the language key `PLG_USER_MYREGISTRATION_TOS_AGREE_REQUIRED` in our language file. The second line in the code block sets the `$result` variable to `false`. This means that the method will return a value of `false`, which will stop the save process.

The second if statement is identical to the first one, except that it checks that the second check box has been clicked and returns a different message to the user.

The last line of code just returns the `$result` variable, which will be true if both if code blocks were skipped. If the user forgot to check both check boxes, they will get both error messages, which is what we want.

Add the Language Files

The last step before we can try our plugin is to add the language files. Recall in our XML file we add the following lines:

```
<files>
    <filename plugin="myregistration">myregistration.php</filename>
    <filename>index.html</filename>
    <folder>language</folder>
</files>
```

The folder element indicates that there will be a subfolder called "language" in the folder for our plugin.

When we create a plugin, we can choose whether to have the language files in the plugins folder or in the `adminstrator/languages` folder. For extensions, it is normally recommended to keep all extension files separate from core files, so putting extension language files in the folder for the extension is normally preferred.

In our example, we will have two language files: `en-GB.plg_user_myregistration .ini` and `en-GB.plg_user_myregistration.sys.ini`. These files will go into the folder `plugins/user/myregistration/language/en-GB/`.

The first file is the primary language file and contains the language keys that will be used when the plugin code is executed and also when the plugin is opened for editing in the Plugin Manager. In this file we put any keys we will need for front-end display or for editing options. Listing 5.5 shows the listing for the main plugin language file.

Listing 5.5   **en-GB.plg_user_myregistration.ini File**

```
; Language file for myregistration plugin


PLG_USER_MYREGISTRATION_TOS_AGREE_REQUIRED="You must agree to the terms of
↪service."
PLG_USER_MYREGISTRATION_OLD_ENOUGH_REQUIRED="You must be at least 18 years
↪old."
```

The second file (with the .sys in the name) is used to translate the name of the plugin when it is listed in the Extension Manager or Plugin Manager. We also put the description of the plugin in the .sys file so that we can translate the description in the message that shows when the plugin has been installed. This convention is used for all extension types. Listing 5.6 shows the listing for the .sys language file.

Listing 5.6   **en-GB.plg_user_myregistration.sys.ini File**

```
; sys language file for myregistration plugin
; The .sys.ini files are used when listing the extensions in the extension
;   manager or plugin manager


PLG_USER_MYREGISTRATION="User - My Registration"
PLG_USER_MYREGISTRATION_XML_DESCRIPTION="Checks that terms and age boxes
↪have been checked."
```

As a last step, copy an `index.html` file from another Joomla folder into the `plugins/user/myregistration` folder and the language and `language/en-GB` sub-folders. As discussed earlier, every folder we create in Joomla should have an `index.html` file to prevent users from browsing the folder directly.

Test the Plugin

At this point, we can test our plugin. Again, we navigate to Extensions → Extension Manager → Discover and click on the Discover icon in the toolbar. Our new plugin extension should be listed using the translated text "User – My Registration" that we used in the .sys language file.

Tip: Using phpMyAdmin to Uninstall the Plugin

When you are testing and debugging a plugin or other extension, you may want to repeat the Discover and Install steps. In this case, you may not want to uninstall the extension, since that will delete the extension files from your Joomla folders.

A simple trick you can do is to delete the row for the extension in the #__extensions table in the database (for example, using phpMyAdmin). This undoes the installation without deleting the extension's files.

If you are unfamiliar with MySQL and phpMyAdmin, we discuss these in Chapter 11.

Again, we click the check box to select the plugin and then click on the Install icon. When we have installed it, note that the plugin description from the .sys language file should show in the Extension Manager: Discover screen, as shown in Figure 5.4.

At this point, we can test the plugin. To test it, first enable it in Plugin Manager. Then try to register a new user with the `approval.php` override file without checking the two check boxes. You should see a message as shown in Figure 5.5.

You should also test the other cases to make sure they work as expected. These include the following:

- Save with one check box checked (should get one error message).
- Save with both check boxes checked (should work correctly).
- Create a user from the administrative back end (Users → User Manager → Add New User should work correctly).

Package the Plugin

So far, we have used the Discover method to install our extensions. This works well during development. However, if we want to be able to install our extension on other Joomla sites, we need to package it in an installation archive file. This is very easy to do. We need a program that allows us to create archives in `zip`, `tar.gz`, or `tar.bz2` format. For Windows, the free program "7-Zip" (`http://www.7-zip.org/download .html`) works well. For Linux and Mac OS X, programs to create a zip archive come installed with the operating system.

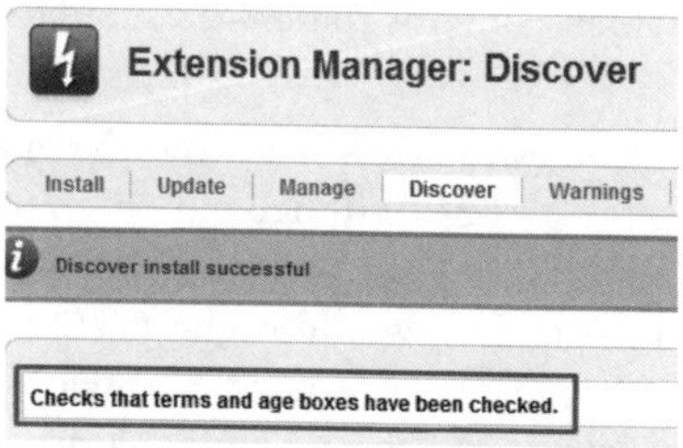

Figure 5.4　Plugin description from .sys language file

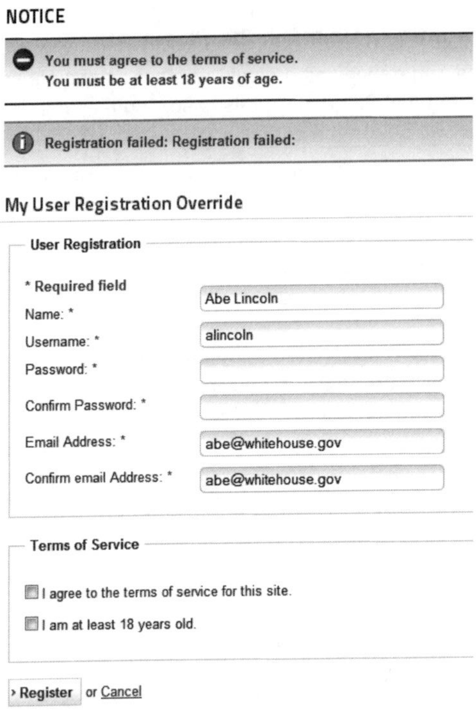

NOTICE

⊖ You must agree to the terms of service.
   You must be at least 18 years of age.

ⓘ Registration failed: Registration failed:

My User Registration Override

┌─ **User Registration** ──────────────────────────────

  * Required field
  Name: *   [Abe Lincoln   ]

  Username: *   [alincoln   ]

  Password: *   [   ]

  Confirm Password: *   [   ]

  Email Address: *   [abe@whitehouse.gov   ]

  Confirm email Address: *   [abe@whitehouse.gov   ]

┌─ **Terms of Service** ───────────────────────────────

  ☐ I agree to the terms of service for this site.

  ☐ I am at least 18 years old.

› **Register** or Cancel

Figure 5.5   User plugin error messages

Note about Slashes ("/" and "\")

If you use Windows, the folders on your file system use the back-slash ("\") character. If you use Mac OS X or Linux, they use the forward-slash ("/") character. For this book, we will use the forward slash. If you use Windows, just use the back slash instead.

The steps to create an installable zip archive are as follows:

1. Create a new folder on your disk system (for example, `temp`) and copy the three plugin files `myregistration.xml`, `myregistration.php`, and `index.html`, and the language folder (which contains the `en-GB` subfolder with the two language files) to this folder.

2. Create a zip file that includes the three files and the language folder. The exact command for creating the archive will depend on your operating system and the software you use.

   For Windows with 7-Zip, you would highlight the three files and language folder in the Windows Explorer, right-click, and select 7-Zip → Add to Archive and then follow the instructions—for example, naming the zip file `plg_user_myregistration.zip`.

For Mac OS X, you would do something very similar, except you would select "Create Archive" from the file menu after highlighting the files.

In Linux, you could go to the command prompt in the temp folder and enter the command

```
$ zip -r plg_user_myregistration.zip *
```

3. After you create the zip archive, open it and check that it has the three files and one folder you expect.

4. Now we want to check that the file installs correctly. Uninstall the plugin by navigating to Extensions → Extension Manager → Manage. Select the plugin and click on the Uninstall icon in the toolbar. You should see the message "Uninstalling plugin was successful." Note that this step will delete the files from your Joomla folders. However, you should already have these files copied to the temp directory created in step 1.

5. Navigate to Extension Manager → Install and click the Browse button. Browse to the zip archive file you created and click the Upload and Install button. You should get the message "Installing plugin was successful."

At this point, we have a fully functioning plugin extension that can be installed on any site that runs Joomla version 1.6 or higher.

Improved User Registration Plugin

In the previous example, we created the `myregistration` plugin to add validation to the alternative user registration menu item we created in Chapter 4. This plugin depends on this alternative menu item. To transfer this functionality to another Joomla website, we would have to install the alternative menu item—including the `beez_20_copy` template—as well as the new `myregistration` plugin. It would be easier to manage if we could do the entire job in the plugin.

Using the new `JForm` class and the form event added in Joomla version 1.6, we can override the registration form inside the plugin, without creating a separate alternative Menu Item file. We can also use `JForm` to do the validation for us, and thereby eliminate the need for the `onBeforeSave()` plugin method. With this approach, we can package all this functionality into one small plugin extension and make it very easy to add this capability to another Joomla website.

We'll call this version of the plugin `myregistration2`. It will contain the following files:

- `forms/form.xml`: File with the `JForm` information for the fields added by the plugin
- `language/en-GB/en-GB.plg_user_myregistration2.ini`: Main language file
- `language/en-GB/en-GB.plg_user_myregistration2.sys.ini`: Sys language file

- `myregistration2.php`: Plugin code file
- `myregistration2.xml`: Plugin XML file

Let's go through the steps to create the plugin.

Create the Plugin XML File

As before, we create the plugin folder (`plugins/user/myregistration2`) and create our main XML file in that folder. The listing for the `myregistration2.xml` file is shown in Listing 5.7.

Listing 5.7 **myregistration2.xml File**

```xml
<?xml version="1.0" encoding="utf-8"?>
<extension version="2.5" type="plugin" group="user" method="upgrade" >
    <name>plg_user_myregistration2</name>
    <author>Mark Dexter and Louis Landry</author>
    <creationDate>January 2012</creationDate>
    <copyright>(C) 2012 Mark Dexter and Louis Landry. All rights reserved.
    </copyright>
    <license>GNU General Public License version 2 or later; see LICENSE.txt
    </license>
    <authorEmail>admin@joomla.org</authorEmail>
    <authorUrl>www.joomla.org</authorUrl>
    <version>2.5.0</version>
    <description>PLG_USER_MYREGISTRATION2_XML_DESCRIPTION</description>

    <files>
        <filename plugin="myregistration2">myregistration2.php</filename>
        <filename>index.html</filename>
        <folder>forms</folder>
        <folder>language</folder>
    </files>

    <config>
    </config>
</extension>
```

This file is similar to the previous example. Note that we change the name of the plugin in the `name` element and twice in the `filename` element. Also, we have added a `folder` element for the `form` folder. We discuss that in the next section.

Create the Form XML File

In this example, we use the `JForm` class to add our two fields to the registration form. With `JForm`, we can add fields to a form using one of two techniques:

- Load the fields from an XML file.
- Load the fields from a string (for example, created inside the plugin PHP file).

The first method is recommended for most cases, since it is generally easier to work with and maintain an XML file. Listing 5.8 shows the code for the `form.xml` file.

Listing 5.8   **form.xml File**

```xml
<?xml version="1.0" encoding="utf-8"?>
<form>
    <fieldset name="tos"
        label="PLG_USER_MYREGISTRATION2_TERMS_OF_SERVICE"
    >
        <field name="tos_agree" type="checkbox"
            default="0"
            filter="bool"
            label="PLG_USER_MYREGISTRATION2_AGREE"
            required="true"
            value="1"
        />

        <field name="old_enough" type="checkbox"
            default="0"
            filter="bool"
            label="PLG_USER_MYREGISTRATION2_AGE"
            required="true"
            value="1"
        />
    </fieldset>
</form>
```

This file defines the two fields we want to add to the user registration form, and it closely mirrors the actual HTML code that will be created by `JForm`. The outer element is called `form` and will create an HTML `form` element. It contains one `fieldset` element. A `fieldset` HTML element is used to group fields together on the form. Inside the `fieldset`, we have our two `field` elements.

Each field element has the following attributes:

- `default`: Default value (if unchecked)
- `filter`: The filter used to check the input from this field
- `label`: The label for this field (note that this will be translated)
- `required`: Flag to tell `JForm` to make this field required
- `value`: The value in the form when the checkbox is checked

The `label` and `value` attributes are standard attributes of the HTML `input` element. The `filter` attribute causes `JForm` to filter the input field using one of the standard `JHtml` filter values. In this case, we are filtering to allow only boolean `true` and `false` values. So even if a user changes the form in their browser to submit some other information (for example, some malicious SQL or JavaScript code), `JForm` will filter this and convert it to a boolean value.

The `default` attribute specifies the value to send if this input is not entered—in this case, if the check box is not checked. We specify a value of "0," which will convert to a boolean `false`.

The `required` attribute causes `JForm` to require this input field to be filled out. In the case of a check box, this requires that the check box is checked. `JForm` will not allow the user to register without checking the box. Because `JForm` handles this validation automatically, we don't need the `onBeforeSave()` method that we used in the `myregistration` plugin.

We see how this file is used in the next section.

Create the Plugin PHP File

Listing 5.9 shows the code for the `myregistration2.php` file.

Listing 5.9   myregistration2.php File

```php
<?php
/**
 * @copyright  Copyright (C) 2012 Mark Dexter and Louis Landry
 * @license  GNU General Public License version 2 or later; see
➥LICENSE.txt
 */

defined('JPATH_BASE') or die;
/**
 * This is our custom registration plugin class.  It verifies that the
➥user checked the boxes
 * indicating that he/she agrees to the terms of service and is old enough
➥to use the site.
 *
 * @package     Joomla.Plugins
 * @subpackage  User.MyRegistration2
 * @since       1.0
 */
class plgUserMyRegistration2 extends JPlugin
{

    /**
     * Method to handle the "onContentPrepareForm" event and alter the
➥user registration form.  We
     * are going to check and make sure that the form being prepared is
➥the user registration form
     * from the com_users component first.  If that is the form we are
➥preparing, then we will
     * load our custom xml file into the form object which adds our custom
➥fields.
     *
```

```
 *  @param    JForm   $form   The form to be altered.
 *  @param    array   $data   The associated data for the form.
 *
 *  @return   bool
 *
 *  @since    1.0
 */
public function onContentPrepareForm($form, $data)
{
    // If we aren't in the registration form ignore the form.
    if ($form->getName() != 'com_users.registration') {
        return;
    }

    // Load the plugin language file
    $this->loadLanguage();

    // Load our custom registration xml into the user registration
form.
    $form->loadFile(dirname(__FILE__).'/forms/form.xml');
}

}
```

The first part is the same as the earlier plugins. We rely on the autoloader to import the JPlugin class, and we extend that class. We name the plugin class according to the plugin naming convention—in this case, plgUserMyRegistration2.

The class has one method, onContentPrepareForm(). The onContentPrepareForm event is triggered at the point where the JForm has been prepared but not yet rendered. We are able to modify the JForm object in working memory just before it is used to create the form. Two arguments are passed to the class. The variable $form holds the JForm object and the variable $data holds a standard object with any data for the form.

Then we make sure we are processing a registration form. If we are not (meaning that we are processing some other form), we just want to quit. So we test the form name. If it is not equal to com_users.registration, we return without doing any processing.

At this point, we know we are processing the user registration form. Next we load the language file so we can translate the language text in our form.

Then the last line does all the work to create the two new fields. It calls the load-File() method of JForm with our form.xml file as the argument. This causes JForm to merge the fields in the form.xml file with the form that is already in working memory from the standard XML file (in this case, components/com_users/models/forms/registration.xml). Since the two fields in our form.xml file are new fields (in other words, they have different names from those of the other fields in the form), the two new fields are added to the form.

That's all there is to it. At this point, the fields in our `form.xml` file have been added to the form and will be included in the output. As mentioned earlier, because we use the required attribute in the fields, we don't need additional code to ensure that these boxes are checked. `JForm` does it for us.

Add the Language Files

As before, we have two language files, located in the folder plugins/user/myregistration2/language/en-GB). The main file is en-GB.plg_user_myregistration2. ini. The .sys file is used for translating the plugin name and description in the plugin manager. These are shown in Listing 5.10 and Listing 5.11.

Listing 5.10   **en-GB.plg_user_myregistration2.ini File**

```
; Language file for myregistration2 plugin

PLG_USER_MYREGISTRATION2_TERMS_OF_SERVICE="Added Fields for Terms of
↪Service Agreement"
PLG_USER_MYREGISTRATION2_AGREE="I agree to the terms."
PLG_USER_MYREGISTRATION2_AGE="I am at least 18 years old."
```

Listing 5.11   **en-GB.plg_user_myregistration2.sys.ini File**

```
; sys language file for myregistration2 plugin
; The .sys.ini files are used when listing the extensions in the extension
↪manager or plugin manager

PLG_USER_MYREGISTRATION2="User - My Registration2"
PLG_USER_MYREGISTRATION2_XML_DESCRIPTION="Demonstration plugin that checks
↪that overrides user registration. Checks that terms and age boxes have
↪been checked."
```

Test the Plugin

Test the plugin as we have done in the previous examples, using the Extension Manager Discover and Install functions.

To test the plugin, you will need to disable the `myregistration` plugin (not the `myregistration2` plugin), enable the `myregistration2` plugin, and make sure that the Registration menu item uses the default menu item type instead of the alternative menu item type (Register With Approval) that we created in Chapter 4.

Once this is set up, when you load the Registration menu item, you should see the form shown in Figure 5.6.

Notice that the two new fields show the asterisk to indicate they are required, just like the other required fields on the form. If you press the Register button without checking the check boxes, you should see the following messages:

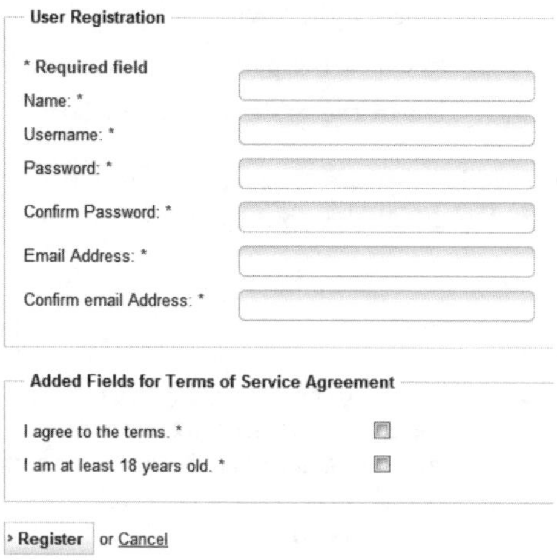

Figure 5.6   Custom registration form from MyRegistration2 plugin

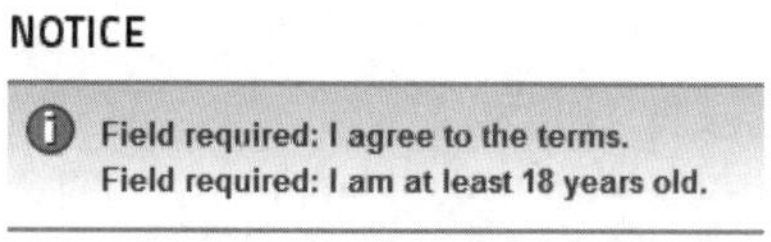

Figure 5.7   JForm required field messages

These are the standard messages that `JForm` shows when the user submits a form that is missing required fields.

Package the Plugin

To package the plugin for installation from an archive file, we follow the same process as described earlier:

1. Copy the files from the `plugins/user/myregistration2` folder to a temporary folder on your computer.

2. Use an archive program to create a zip archive of these files. By convention, the archive would be called `plg_user_myregistration2.zip` (but it can be named anything as long as it contains all the correct files and folders).

Test that the archive file can be installed successfully by uninstalling the existing `myregistration2` plugin and then installing it from the archive file.

Adding Parameters to Our Plugin

Next, let's add a parameter to our plugin. Suppose we want the user to be able to configure whether or not to show the second check box. To do this, we need to do three things:

- Add a parameter field to our plugin XML file.
- Add logic to the plugin to check the parameter and remove the field if desired.
- Add the new language keys to the main language file.

The parameter field is added using a JForm field, similar to what we added in our form.xml file. The revised code for the config element is shown here:

```
<config>
  <fields name="params">
    <fieldset name="basic" >
      <field name="show_age_checkbox" type="radio"
            label="PLG_USER_MYREGISTRATION2_SHOW_AGE"
            description="PLG_USER_MYREGISTRATION2_SHOW_AGE_DESC"
            default="0">
        <option value="0">JHIDE</option>
        <option value="1">JSHOW</option>
      </field>
    </fieldset>
  </fields>
</config>
```

This code is similar to the code for template parameters we saw in Chapter 3. It is used to add the options when we edit this plugin. We create a fields element with the name attribute equal to "params" to hold our fieldset and field elements and put the fields element inside the config element.

We need this fields element with the name attribute in our XML file. Otherwise the options will not show in the plugin edit screen. This is because the layout file used to create the form for editing plugins (administrator/components/com_plugins/ views/plugin/tmpl/edit_options.php) looks for a fields element with a name of "params" and includes the contained fieldset elements as options in the form. If we don't have this fields element, no options will show on the plugin edit screen. This is also true for components, modules, and templates.

Note that we didn't need this fields element when we created our form.xml file. It is only required when we are adding parameters to the installation XML file for an extension.

Inside the fieldset element we define a new field with a type of "radio" with two option elements, "0" for Hide and "1" for Show. Notice that we use the language keys JHIDE and JSHOW. These are standard language keys used throughout Joomla, so we don't have to add them to our plugin language file. Notice also that each option is a separate element. Field types that provide a list of options, like radio or list, use a series of option elements, one for each item in the list.

The next step is to add the two new keys to the language file. We add them to the en-GB.plug_user_myregistration2.ini file (not the .sys.ini file) because these are used when editing the individual plugin in Plugin Manager. The label attribute should be short, since it will be used to label the field. The description attribute can be longer. It will show up in the tool tip that pops up when you hover the mouse on the field.

The new language file lines are as follows:

```
PLG_USER_MYREGISTRATION2_SHOW_AGE="Show Age Checkbox"
PLG_USER_MYREGISTRATION2_SHOW_AGE_DESC="Whether to Hide or Show the Show
↪Age check box. If it is shown, it will be required."
```

Figure 5.8 shows the two new language strings on the Plugin Manager form. Note that we have Debug Language enabled in the Global Configuration → System, so we see the double "**" around the text fields to indicate that they are properly translated.

The last step is to change the plugin code to check the new parameter and act on it. The revised code for the onContentPrepareForm() method is as follows:

```
public function onContentPrepareForm($form, $data)
{
 // If we aren't in the registration form ignore the form.
 if ($form->getName() != 'com_users.registration') {
    return;
 }

 // Load the plugin language file
 $this->loadLanguage();

 // Load our custom registration xml into the user registration form.
 $form->loadFile(dirname(__FILE__).'/forms/form.xml');
 if (!$this->params->get('show_age_checkbox', '1')) {
    $form->removeField('old_enough');
 }
}
```

The only new code is the if statement at the end of the method. This gets the new parameter and uses it as a boolean value inside the if statement condition. If the Show option was selected, the parameter will be true. Since we use a not ("!") in the if statement condition, the statement inside the if code block will not be executed when the parameter is true. So, if we have selected Show, we will skip the if block and the entire form will be shown.

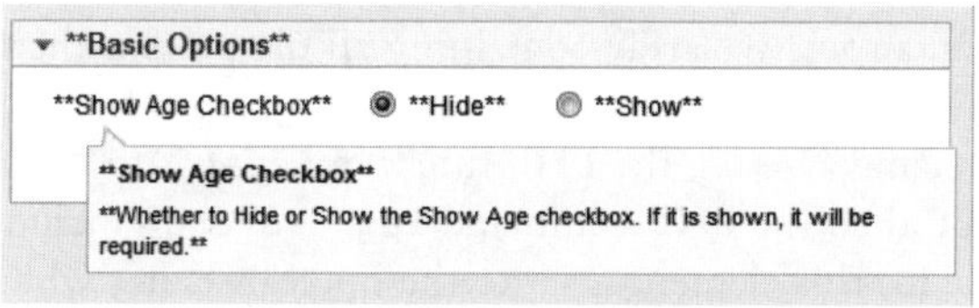

Figure 5.8   New parameter in Plugin Manager

If we have selected Hide, the statement

```
$form->removeField('old_enough');
```

will execute. This uses the `removeField()` method of the `JForm` class to remove the field named "old_enough" from the form. That's all we need to do. After you have made these changes, test that the parameter works as expected.

There are some other useful methods in `JForm` we can use to modify forms in a plugin. One is to change a field attribute. For example, suppose we wanted to have an option to choose whether or not to make a field required. We could use the command

```
$form->setFieldAttribute('old_enough', 'required', 'false');
```

to change the "old_enough" field to no longer be required.

The important thing to remember is this: We can use the `onContentPrepareForm` event to intercept the `JForm` object before the form is shown. Then we can use `JForm` methods to add, remove, or alter fields in the form. This gives us a chance to tailor the form to fit our exact needs.

Using Plugins to Override Core Classes

We can use the existing plugin framework to override most core classes in Joomla. Note: This is an advanced topic and not something that you want to do unless you really need to. However, it is useful to know about in case you need it.

How Plugins Are Imported

We have seen that, to trigger a plugin, you first use the `JPluginHelper::importPlugin()` method to import the plugin. This adds the class and its methods to working memory. If we take a closer look at how this method works, we see that the code that actually does the import is in the private `import()` method of the `JPluginHelper` class (`libraries/joomla/plugin/helper.php`), as follows:

```
if (!isset($paths[$path])) {
   require_once $path;
}
$paths[$path] = true;
```

The first line checks to see if this specific plugin has already been added. The `$paths` variable is an associative array containing all the plugins that have already been imported. The key to the array is the full path to each plugin file and the value of each element is the class name. We use the PHP function `isset()` to check if this element is in the array. If not, then the PHP command `require_once` includes this file.

Finally, the value for this element is set to the boolean `true`, which ensures that the next time through this element will be set in the array, so the `require_once` will not be called again for the same file.

There are two important points to understand about this process:

- As discussed earlier, normally plugin files declare classes, so *no code is executed at that time*. The only thing that happens is that the class and its methods are loaded into memory so that their methods can be called later in the cycle. In that case, no code is actually executed as a result of the `JPluginHelper::importPlugin()` method.

- Nothing in Joomla *requires* a plugin to be a class declaration. A plugin can be a simple PHP script—that is, one that executes as soon as it is included. If we make a plugin this way, it will execute immediately, as soon as the `JPluginHelper::importPlugin` method is executed (instead of when the event is triggered).

This provides a mechanism for loading any PHP script whenever we import plugins.

How Joomla Classes Are Loaded

Next, we need to understand an important point about how Joomla core classes are loaded into working memory. If we look at the `jimport` function that is typically used to load Joomla core classes, we see it is a function in the file `libraries/loader.php.` Note that this is a free-standing function, not a class method. That is why it is invoked just with the function name and no class name. The code for this function is shown here:

```
function jimport($path)
{
    return JLoader::import($path);
}
```

It simply invokes the `JLoader::import()` method. The first lines of code in the `JLoader::import()` method are the following:

```
// Only import the library if not already attempted.
if (!isset(self::$imported[$key]))
```

This is checking to see whether we have already imported this class. The value `self::$imported` is a static associative array with a key (the variable `$key`) equal to the argument passed to `JImport` (for example, "joomla.plugin.plugin") and a value of boolean `true` or `false`. When a class is imported, an element is added to this array, and the value is set to `true` if the import was successful and `false` if it was unsuccessful. So, once a class has been imported, Joomla won't try to import it again.

The `JLoader::load()` and `JLoader::_autoload()` (the Platform "autoloader") methods also check to see if a class has already been loaded before trying to load a class.

So the important point is this: if the class already exists—meaning it is already loaded into working memory—*we skip loading this class.* The method just returns a value of true and exits. None of the Joomla load methods will try to load a class a second time.

This means that we can use a plugin to load a class into working memory, as long as we do it *before* it gets loaded by the Joomla core programs. If we do this, the methods from our class will be used instead of the methods from the core class.

As it happens, system plugins are loaded into working memory very early in the Joomla execution cycle, before most (but not all) Joomla core classes.

Example: Override the JTableNested Class

Let's do a quick example to illustrate this. We will override the core `JTableNested` class. This class is the parent class for all the nested table classes in Joomla (for example, `JTableCategories` for the `#__categories` table). In this example, we will demonstrate how to override this class but we will leave it to the reader to imagine what code and behavior you might want to change.

Here are the steps:

1. Create a new folder called `plugins/system/myclasses` and copy the file `libraries/joomla/database/tablenested.php` to this new folder. This will give you a file called `plugins/system/myclasses/tablenested.php`. (Remember to add `index.html` files to all the new folders we create.)

2. Edit the new file and replace the existing `rebuild()` method with the following code:

```
public function rebuild($parentId = null, $leftId = 0, $level = 0,
↪$path = '')
{
    exit('From myclasses/tabelnested.php file');
}
```

This code will simply prove that we are running our override class in place of the core class. When we press the Rebuild option (for example, in the Category Manager: Articles), if we are running our method, the program should exit with the message just shown.

3. Now we need to add the plugin to load our class in place of the core class. We will call the plugin "myclasses." To do this, create a new file called `myclasses.php` in the `plugins/system/myclasses` folder.

4. In the new file (`plugins/system/myclasses/myclasses.php`), add the code shown in Listing 5.7.

Listing 5.7   **myclasses.php File**

```
<?php
/**
 * Demonstration plugin to replace a core class.
 * This is fired on the first system import (before
 * the onBeforeInitialise event).
 */
// no direct access
```

```
defined('_JEXEC') or die;

// Replace core JTableNested with override version
include_once JPATH_ROOT.'/plugins/system/myclasses/tablenested.php';
```

Notice that this code is not declaring a class. It is simply running a script. This means that it will be executed as soon as the system plugins are imported, before the first system event. This code just includes our new `tablenested.php` file.

5. Create the XML file for this plugin (`plugins/system/myclasses/myclasses.xml`) with the code shown in Listing 5.8.

Listing 5.8   **myclasses.xml File**

```xml
<?xml version="1.0" encoding="utf-8"?>
<extension version="2.5" type="plugin" group="system">
        <name>plg_system_myclasses</name>
        <author>Mark Dexter and Louis Landry</author>
        <creationDate>January 2012</creationDate>
        <copyright>Copyright (C) 2012 Mark Dexter and Louis Landry.</copyright>
        <license>GPL2</license>
        <authorEmail>admin@joomla.org</authorEmail>
        <authorUrl>www.joomla.org</authorUrl>
        <version>1.6.0</version>
        <description>MyClasses plugin demonstration</description>
        <files>
                <filename plugin="myclasses">myclasses.php</filename>
                <filename>index.html</filename>
        </files>
        <config>
        </config>
</extension>
```

6. Navigate to the back end of Joomla and Discover and Install the plugin as we have done before in the previous examples. Remember also to enable the plugin in the Plugin Manager.

7. Navigate to Content → Category Manager in the Joomla back end and click on the Rebuild icon. Joomla should halt and you should see the message "From myclasses/tablenested.php file." This indicates that we have successfully overridden this core class.

This technique can be used to override most Joomla core classes, except for those that are already loaded before the system plugins are imported.

If you override a core class in this manner, you don't need to worry about your class getting overwritten during a Joomla upgrade. So this technique is much better than simply hacking core files. However, a word of caution is in order here. If there are bug fixes for any core classes you have overridden, you will need to check whether these fixes apply to your override classes. If so, you will need to apply the fixes yourself. This will be especially important if the bug fixes correct security issues.

Plugin Best Practices

The most important thing about plugins is to know when to use them. That means understanding the events available in Joomla and what standard behaviors you can override. In many cases, when you are having a difficult time figuring out how to solve a problem with a module or a component, a plugin might make the job a lot easier.

Here are some other tips about plugins:

- Plugins are executed in the order in which they appear in the Ordering column in Plugin Manager. In most cases, the ordering doesn't matter. However, in some cases, where you have more than one plugin triggered from the same event, and where the results of one plugin can affect the processing of a subsequent one, the order can be important. In this case, you can change the order in the Plugin Manager by adjusting the Ordering values to control the execution order.

- Normally, we want to use the naming conventions for plugin class names and method names. Otherwise, the plugins won't get called correctly. The exception is if you want the script to be run when the plugin is imported, in which case only the file and folder name is important (as in the class override example in the previous section).

- Different events require different method signatures. Make sure you are aware of what values are available for each event and what values, if any, your method should return. The Joomla repository includes a folder called `tests/plugins`. This folder contains example plugins for each plugin type. These example files show all the events and the method signatures for each. Also, the plugin events are documented in the Joomla wiki at `http://docs.joomla.org/Plugin/Events`.

- Try to pick the best event for the job at hand. If you need a new event—for example, in a custom component—you can create it just by triggering it at the desired place in the program. If you believe that you need a new event added in a core class, ask about it on one of the development lists. If others agree, the event can be added to the core.

Summary

In this chapter, we learned about plugins. We started by looking in detail at some core plugins. Then we created some plugins of our own, including one that allows us easily to customize the user registration process in Joomla.

Along the way, we saw how plugins allow us to do a lot with a little well-placed code and how they provide the site administrator with a high degree of flexibility. We even saw how we can use plugins, if needed, to override most core classes in Joomla.

In the next chapter, we discuss another important type of Joomla extension: modules.

Extending Joomla! with Modules

In this chapter, we look at how modules work in Joomla!. We start by discussing how modules relate to components. Then we look at a core module to see how it works. Then we create a new module, which includes pulling information from the Joomla database. We add some parameters to the module and package it for easy installation. We end with some recommendations for making the most of modules.

What Is a Module?

A typical page in a Joomla website shows one component and multiple modules. For example, the home page of Joomla version 2.5 with the sample data installed shows the Featured Articles component and five modules (Search, three menus, and Login). Modules typically are small, simple, and "lightweight" (meaning that they don't require a lot of computer time to process). They provide information and navigation options to the user.

Modules versus Components

Modules often rely on components. For example, the Menu module (mod_menu) pulls information from the Menu component (com_menus) and all the article modules (for example, Archived Articles, Articles - Newsflash, and so on) pull information from the Articles component (com_content).

Many modules only display information and perhaps links. Some modules, such as the login and search modules, show simple forms. Modules typically do not allow user interaction, such as navigating to the next or previous page.

There are some nice things about modules in Joomla:

- The same module can be shown on all or selected pages in the site. This is assigned in the Module Manager when you create the module.

- A module can show information based on what is shown in the main component. For example, the Breadcrumbs module shows the menu hierarchy from the home page to the current menu item.

Table 6.1 **Latest Users Files (Excludes index.html Files)**

File Name	Description
tmpl/default.php	Module layout file (prints module output to browser)
helper.php	Contains methods for gathering module data
mod_users_latest.php	Entry point when module is executed
mod_users_latest.xml	XML install file and option field definition

Unlike components, which are executed based on the URL, modules are called as part of the built-in Joomla processing cycle. After the component has been executed and rendered, Joomla finds all modules that are (a) assigned to the current menu item and (b) assigned to a module position that is defined in the template. These modules are executed in turn and the output of each one is injected into the template's **index. php** file at the location of the **jdoc:include** element for each module's position.

Although modules typically require a bit more code to write than plugins, they are generally easy to create and understand.

Tour of a Core Module

To begin our study of modules, let's look at the Latest Users module. This module shows a list of new registered users for the site. Using the module's parameters, you can limit the number of users that show, you can show a link to the user, and you can display information from the user's profile or contact information.

First, let's look at the folders and files for the module. Because this module is a front-end or site module, it is in a subfolder of the **modules** folder. If it were an administrator module, it would be under **administrator/modules**. The Latest Users module internal name is **mod_users_latest**, so that is the name of the folder.

If we look in this folder, we see files shown in Table 6.1 (excluding **index.html** files). Let's look in detail at how this module works.

Module XML File

The module's XML file contains the file and folder information used to install and uninstall a module. It also contains the field definitions for any parameters for the module. The **mod_users_latest.xml** file is very similar to the XML files we saw in Chapter 5, except that the **type** attribute of the **extension** element is "module".

The following code shows the **files** and **languages** elements for the **mod_users_ latest.xml** file:

```
<files>
  <filename
   module="mod_users_latest">mod_users_latest.php</filename>
  <folder>tmpl</folder>
  <filename>helper.php</filename>
  <filename>index.html</filename>
```

```
</files>
<languages>
    <language tag="en-GB">en-GB.mod_users_latest.ini</language>
    <language tag="en-GB">en-GB.mod_users_latest.sys.ini</language>
</languages>
```

This defines each file for the module except for the files in the `tmpl` subfolder.
Note that we do not need to define a filename element for the XML file, but it
doesn't hurt to add that. Note also that this file defines the two language files inside a
languages element. As discussed previously, this means that the two language files will
be installed into the core language folder and not in the extension's language folder.

The next element is as follows:

```
<help key="JHELP_EXTENSIONS_MODULE_MANAGER_LATEST_USERS" />
```

This finds the help article in the Joomla help system that applies to this module.

The rest of the file defines the fields for the module's parameters. In this file, we define
three fields in the "basic" `fieldset` element and five in the "advanced" `fieldset` element. These fields are defined the same way as the fields we have seen in previous
chapters for templates and plugins.

Main Module File

When a module is executed, it loads a PHP file with the same name as the folder. In
this case, this is the file `modules/mod_users_latest/mod_users_latest.php`. The
code for this is shown in Listing 6.1.

Listing 6.1 **mod_users_latest.php File**

```php
<?php
/**
 * @package       Joomla.Site
 * @subpackage    mod_users_latest
 * @copyright     Copyright (C) 2005 - 2012 Open Source Matters, Inc. All
➥rights reserved.
 * @license       GNU General Public License version 2 or later; see
➥LICENSE.txt
 */

// no direct access
defined('_JEXEC') or die;

// Include the latest functions only once
require_once dirname(__FILE__).'/helper.php';
$shownumber = $params->get('shownumber', 5);
$name = moduserslatestHelper::getUsers($params);
$linknames = $params->get('linknames', 0);
$moduleclass_sfx = htmlspecialchars($params->get('moduleclass_sfx'));
```

```
require JModuleHelper::getLayoutPath('mod_users_latest', $params->
↪get('layout', 'default'));
```

The first line after the "defined or die" line includes the module's helper class. Most modules use a helper class that holds the methods needed to render the module. That is where most of the actual processing is done.

The next line calls the `getUsers()` method in the helper and stores the result in a variable called `$linknames`. Notice that we pass a variable called `$params` to this method. This variable is not declared anywhere in this file. Where does it come from?

To answer this, we have to look at where and how the current file is executed. In Chapter 3 we discuss how modules are executed one at a time, based on the template positions they are assigned to. The end result of that process is the following code snippet from the `renderModule()` method of the `JModuleHelper` class (`libraries/joomla/application/module/helper.php`):

```
$content = '';
ob_start();
require $path;
$module->content = ob_get_contents().$content;
```

In the line `require $path`, `$path` is the full name of the entry file of the module. In our example, it is requiring the file **mod_users_latest.php**. The PHP `require` command immediately inserts the required file into the current PHP program. The end result is just like copying and pasting the required file into the current program at that location.

Note that file **mod_users_latest.php** is a normal PHP script and does not declare a class. So the lines in this file get executed as soon as the file is included via the `require` command. Any variables that were in scope when the `require` statement was executed are still in scope during the execution of the required script. This means that, when we are inside the **mod_users_latest.php** program, we have the same variables in scope that we had in the `renderModule()` method of the `JModuleHelper` class where the require statement was executed.

We can see that the `$params` variable is set earlier in the `renderModule()` method, in the following code:

```
// Get module parameters
$params = new JRegistry;
$params->loadJSON($module->params);
```

So this is where `$params` comes from. This variable is a `JRegistry` object that contains the options entered when the module was created in the Module Manager. These options are available to us when we call the module helper method.

Getting back to Listing 6.1, the next line gets the `linknames` option from the parameters and saves it in a variable called `$linknames`. This variable will be used when we execute the layout for the module.

The next line gets the module class suffix option from the $params object. The module class suffix is a text field the site designer can enter when the module is created. It allows you to fine-tune the CSS styling for the module by assigning a unique CSS class to the module's HTML elements. Notice that we use the built-in PHP function htmlspecialchars() to sanitize this value. This function converts characters that have a special meaning in HTML (for example, <, >, single- and double-quotes, and &) to special HTML symbols (for example, \, >, ", and &). This ensures that we don't introduce unintended or malicious HTML code into our module output.

The last line is a require statement:

```
    require JModuleHelper::getLayoutPath('mod_users_latest',
↪$params->get('layout', 'default'));
```

This line does several things. First, it gets the layout option from the module parameters. Recall from Chapter 4 that we can create alternative layouts for modules and select them in the Module Manager when we create a new instance of a module. It then calls the getLayoutPath() method of the JModuleHelper class using the name of the module and the name of the layout. This method returns the full file name of the desired layout. If we haven't specified an alternative layout, this will be the default file modules/mod_users_latest/tmpl/default.php. The layout file again is a normal PHP script (it doesn't declare a class), so it is executed immediately after it is included via the require command. Because of this, all variables in scope at this point in the program are still in scope in the layout script.

This is a bit tricky. We got to the mod_users_lastest.php file because of a require statement in the JModuleHelper class. Now we are in turn using the require statement to bring in the layout file. Although this can be confusing, the advantage of this design is that it allows us to work in smaller programming files and keep different parts of the program in different folders. These advantages outweigh the disadvantage of keeping track of where files are included inside other files.

To summarize, the mod_users_latest.php file

- Loads the helper class into working memory to make its methods available
- Calls the method from the helper class to get the data for the module
- Includes (via the require command) the layout file, which actually displays the module output

In short, it controls the entire process of executing the module.

Including Files versus Calling Methods

In Joomla, we often include files using the PHP commands require, require_once, include, or include_once. As we discuss in the previous chapter, if the included file is a class declaration, the class is loaded into memory but no code is actually executed. If the included file is a "normal" PHP script (that is, a series of statements other than a class or function definition), it is executed immediately and *any variables that are in scope when the file is included are also in scope inside the included file.*

This means that we have to be careful about variable names when we include files. The good news is that we can use variables that are defined earlier in the file that contains the include or require statement (for example, the variable $params in our module file mod_users_latest.php). The bad news is that if we accidentally use the same variable in the included file as in the including file, we can get an unexpected result. For example, we could accidentally change the value of a variable that is used later in the calling program. So we need to be careful about the variables we use inside included files that are not class declarations.

The situation is quite different when we work with classes and methods. Unless otherwise specified, all variables in classes and methods are local to the class or method. So when we call a method, the variables from the calling program are not in scope inside the method. If we need to pass information from the calling program to the method, we normally have to put variables in the method arguments. And if we want to return information from the called method back to the calling program, we normally have the method return this information. However, the benefit of this is that we are free to use any variable name we like inside methods. It doesn't matter if it is the same as used in the calling program, since the scopes of the variables don't overlap.

Module Helper Class

Next let's look at the module helper class. This is where the information for the module is gathered. Listing 6.2 shows the code for the getUsers() method in this class.

Listing 6.2   getUsers() **Method in modUsersLatestHelper Class**

```
// get users sorted by activation date
static function getUsers($params)
{
    $db      = JFactory::getDbo();
    $query   = $db->getQuery(true);
    $query->select('a.id, a.name, a.username, a.registerDate');
    $query->order('a.registerDate DESC');
    $query->from('#__users AS a');
    if (!$user->authorise('core.admin') &&
➡$params->get('filter_groups', 0) == 1)
    {
        $groups = $user->getAuthorisedGroups();
        if (empty($groups))
        {
            return array();
        }
        $query->leftJoin('#__user_usergroup_map AS m
➡ON m.user_id = a.id');
        $query->leftJoin('#__usergroups AS ug ON ug.id = m.group_id');
        $query->where('ug.id in (' . implode(',', $groups) . ')');
```

```
        $query->where('ug.id <> 1');
    }
    $db->setQuery($query,0,$params->get('shownumber'));
    $result = $db->loadObjectList();
    return (array) $result;
}
```

This method is declared as static. As discussed earlier, this means that the method is called using the class name, not an object name. If you are familiar with procedural programming, a static method is just like a subroutine.

The first line creates a JDatabase object called $db. We use JDatabase objects in Joomla any time we need to extract data from the database. The next line creates a new JDatabaseQuery object called $query. Notice that we use our JDatabase object to create the query (with the $db->getQuery(true) method). The boolean true argument tells the JDatabase object to give us a new query (instead of the last query used, if any).

We discuss database queries in more detail in Chapter 11. For now, let's look at how we create and run the query in this example. Databases are organized like a series of spreadsheet files, where each file holds one type of data. The files are organized in rows and columns, just like a spreadsheet. For example, the #__content table holds the data for articles. Each row holds all the data for one article. Each column holds one piece of data for all articles (for example, title or category).

To pull data from a database, we use a SELECT query. This query will return data in row-column format. A simple SELECT query has the following format:

```
SELECT <list of columns>
FROM <table name>
WHERE <where conditions>
ORDER BY <columns to sort the results by>
LIMIT <start at row number>, <number of rows to return>
```

In Joomla version 1.5, we would build a string in our program that contained the exact text for the query and then pass that query to the database. Starting with Joomla version 1.6, we have a class called JDatabaseQuery that makes it easier to build SQL queries in Joomla. This class also handles any differences between databases.

For example, Joomla version 2.5 supports Microsoft SQL Server as well as MySQL, and support for PostgreSQL is expected in the near future. If we use JDatabaseQuery to build all our queries, we can be confident that our code will run correctly on these new databases, since the query class can automatically account for differences in the SQL commands that each database uses.

The methods in JDatabaseQuery closely mirror the format of a SQL statement. Unlike a SQL statement, where the parts of the query must be written in the correct order, with JDatabaseQuery we can construct the commands in any order we like.

The $query->select() method

```
$query->select('a.id, a.name, a.username, a.registerDate');
```

adds columns to the SELECT part of our query. Here we retrieve four columns: id, name, username, and activation. The "a." in front of each column identifies a shortcut name for the table (in case we use more than one table in our query). The shortcut name is defined in the `from()` method.

The `$query->order()` method

```
query->order('a.registerDate DESC');
```

adds the columns that the database will use to sort the query results. In this case, we will sort our query by the register date (`a.registerDate`). Notice that we have the word "DESC" after the column name. This is short for DESCENDING and tells the database to do a reverse sort. Recall that we want our new users ordered by the most recently activated first. Dates are stored as numbers in the database, and recent dates are higher numbers than older dates. So in order to get a list sorted by newest to oldest, we use a reverse sort.

The `$query->from()` method

```
$query->from('#__users AS a');
```

specifies the table to use for the query. In this case, the table is called **#__users** and is followed by **AS a**. When you install a Joomla website, you can pick the letters you want to use as your database prefix. These letters are added to the front of every table name in your database. When we name tables in a SQL query, we don't know what prefix a particular site might use. That is why we always use the prefix **#__** (pound sign followed by two underscore characters). Just before the query is passed to the database, Joomla automatically changes **#__** to the specific prefix for each Joomla website. In this book, we refer to tables using the **#__** prefix, but the prefix for a given Joomla website will be different.

The **AS a** tells the database that the shortcut name for this table will be **a**. So we can use **a.** + <column name> to name any column in the **#__users** table.

After the `$query->from()` line, we get a user object and then start an `if` block. This block implements the feature of being able to filter the users based on the current user's groups. If we have enabled that option (called `filter_groups`) and if the current user is not the "super user" (does not have **core.admin** permissions), then we process the code inside the `if` block.

Inside the `if` block, we first get the array of groups that the current user is a member of, using the `getAuthorisedGroups()` method of the `JUser` class. If this is an empty array, we are done and simply return an empty array. Otherwise, we add two joins, using the `leftJoin()` method, and two WHERE clauses, using the `where()` method. We discuss joins and WHERE clauses in Chapter 11. Here, the joins allow us to see what user groups each user is a member of, and the WHERE clauses limit the query to show only those users where we have at least one user group in common (other than Public, which is group 1).

After the `if` block, the next line in the method is as follows:

```
$db->setQuery($query,0,$params->get('shownumber'));
```

This is where we pass the query to the database and specify the starting row number and maximum row count for the query. The first argument in our example is `$query`, the query object.

If we look at the `setQuery()` method in the JDatabase class (`libraries/joomla/database/database.php`), we see that it expects the first argument to be a string. Recall from Chapter 4 that if we use an object where PHP expects a string, the object's special `__toString()` method is called to convert the object to a string. If we look at the JDatabaseQuery class (`libraries/joomla/database/databasequery.php`), we see it has a `__toString()` method that converts the object to a valid SQL command. Also, because `setQuery()` expects the first argument to be a string, we can just pass a string that contains the exact text of the query if we prefer. However, it is recommended always to use the JDatabaseQuery methods to build queries for Joomla.

The next line is as follows:

```
$result = $db->loadObjectList();
```

This command actually runs the query and returns the results of the query to the `$result` variable. The `loadObjectList()` method returns the list of rows as an array of objects. Each returned row is a standard object with a field for each column in the query. In our example, we will have the fields id, name, username, and register date. The value for each of these fields will be the value from the database for that row. We will have a maximum number of rows equal to the `shownumber` parameter value. Depending on the data, we could have zero rows or any number of rows up to that value.

Default Layout File

The code for the default layout, default.php, is shown in Listing 6.3.

Listing 6.3 **default.php Layout File**

```
<?php
/**
* @package   Joomla.Site
 * @subpackage   mod_users_latest
 * @copyright Copyright (C) 2005 - 2012 Open Source Matters, Inc. All
➥rights reserved.
 * @license   GNU General Public License version 2 or later; see
➥LICENSE.txt
 */
// no direct access
defined('_JEXEC') or die;
?>
```

```
<?php if (!empty($names)) : ?>
   <ul  class="latestusers<?php echo $moduleclass_sfx ?>" >
   <?php foreach($names as $name) : ?>
      <li>
         <?php echo $name->username; ?>
      </li>
   <?php endforeach;   ?>
   </ul>
<?php endif; ?>
```

This simple layout again demonstrates how we can mix PHP and HTML code in the same file.

After the `defined()` statement, we start the layout with an `if` statement. Note that the `if` statement is using the alternative PHP syntax. This is always recommended for layout files that mix HTML and PHP elements. The `if` statement checks that our `$names` array is not empty. We do this to avoid the possibility of showing an empty `ul` element.

Where does the `$names` variable come from? Recall that the current layout file was executed using a `require` command from the `mod_users_latest.php` file. As discussed earlier, because our script is included and is not called as a class method, all variables in scope at the point where it was included are still in scope. It is exactly as though the current layout file was pasted into the file where it was included (`mod_users_latest.php`). So the `$names` variable comes from this line of code in the `mod_users_latest.php` file:

```
$names = moduserslatestHelper::getUsers($params);
```

The next line creates an HTML `ul` element. Here we are inserting the variable `$moduleclass_sfx` as part of the class attribute of the `ul`. This line of code illustrates an important point about spaces in PHP files. Normally, spaces are not important in PHP files. The commands

```
$x = $y + $z;
```

and

```
$x=$y+$z;
```

are exactly equivalent. However, in the following line,

```
<ul class="latestusers<?php echo $moduleclass_sfx ?>" >
```

we are using the `echo` command to insert the variable inside an attribute. In this situation, spaces are important, just as they would be if we were typing in literal text. There are no spaces between the word `latestusers` and the value returned by the

PHP `echo` command. So this value will be appended to `latestusers` *with no space*. For example, if the `$moduleclass_sfx` were `"my_suffix"`, then the output of that line would be

```
<ul class="latestusersmy_suffix" >.
```

For this reason, if we want a module class suffix to create a second CSS class (which we often do), we need to type it into the form with a leading space. That way, the leading space creates a space between the standard class and the suffix. If we typed in `<space>my_suffix` for the class suffix, the element would be rendered as

```
<ul class="latestusers my_suffix" >
```

and you could style this element using the CSS class `my_suffix`.

The next section of code is a `foreach` loop over the `$names` variable. A `foreach` loop is a convenient way to loop through each element in an array. The code block inside the loop is executed once for each element in the array. Inside the code block, the variable `$name` (singular) is the current element in the array. If the array is empty, we skip the entire code block.

Once we are inside the `foreach` block, we create an `li` element. Here we just put the user's name in, without the anchor element. We finish by closing the HTML elements in the same order we opened them. First we close the `li` element, then the `foreach` loop, then the `ul` element, and finally the `if` statement. Notice how the indentation makes the code easier to read, since the indentation indicates which lines are inside other code blocks or elements. Also notice that it is easy to see the structure of the HTML code when we mix PHP elements in with HTML elements.

Show Articles by the Current Author

Next let's apply what we've learned and create our own module. Our module will be similar to the core Articles – Related Articles module. That module shows a list of articles that have one or more keywords in common with the current article shown on the page. Our module will show articles that are written by the same author as the article shown on the page. We will have parameters to allow the administrator to control how many articles show and the ordering of the articles.

When we write extensions that may be used by others, we want to name the extensions in such a way as to make the name unique within the Joomla community. One simple way to do that is to incorporate a company or organization name in the extension name. For example, we might call our company "Joomla Programming Book Examples," or "joompro" for short. Given this, we'll call our module `mod_joompro_articles_author`.

Module Structure

The files we need for our module are shown in Figure 6.1.

Figure 6.1   Files for example module

This is similar to the list of files for the Latest Users module we looked at earlier. However, in this case, we have included our language files inside the module folder instead of in the core language folder.

Logic was added in Joomla version 1.6 to allow extensions to use language files in their own language folders in addition to language files in the core language folders (`language` and `administrator/language`). If a file is not found in the core folder, Joomla will look in the extension folder. This allows us to keep our extension's language files separated from the core language files.

Module XML File

Let's start with the module's XML file. This file does several things. The extension element has attributes for type, version, client (site or administrator), and method. These are used by the Joomla extension installer during the installation process. The files element provides a list of the files and folders (often called a manifest) that tells the Joomla extension installer what files or folders are part of the extension. This allows these files to be copied during installation and deleted if the module is uninstalled.

Inside the extension element we have elements that provide descriptive information for the module, such as name, author, copyright, and so on. Finally, the XML file may contain a `config` element. This element defines any parameters that will show for the module in the Module Manager.

Listing 6.4 shows the first part of our XML file.

Listing 6.4   **mod_joompro_articles_author.xml File Part 1**

```
<?xml version="1.0" encoding="utf-8"?>
<extension
    type="module"
    version="2.5.0"
    client="site"
    method="upgrade">
    <name>mod_joompro_articles_author</name>
    <author>Mark Dexter and Louis Landry</author>
```

```
    <creationDate>January 2012</creationDate>
    <copyright>Copyright (C) 2012 Mark Dexter and Louis Landry. All rights
➥reserved.</copyright>
    <license>GNU General Public License version 2 or later; see
➥LICENSE.txt</license>
    <authorEmail>admin@joomla.org</authorEmail>
    <authorUrl>www.joomla.org</authorUrl>
    <version>2.5.0</version>
    <description>MOD_JOOMPRO_ARTICLES_AUTHOR_DESCRIPTION</description>
    <files>
        <filename module="mod_joompro_articles_author">
➥mod_joompro_articles_author.php</filename>
        <folder>tmpl</folder>
        <filename>helper.php</filename>
        <filename>index.html</filename>
        <filename>mod_joompro_articles_author.xml</filename>
        <folder>language</folder>
    </files>
```

This code is similar to the code for the `mod_users_latest module.xml`, which we discussed earlier. The name is the module folder name and also the name of the main PHP file and XML file. We can optionally have a key in the `.sys.ini` language file to translate this name into something more descriptive when we show the module in the Module Manager. For example,

```
MOD_JOOMPRO_ARTICLES_AUTHOR="Articles by Current Author"
```

We also put a language key in the description element. This will provide a description for the module. We define the description key in both language files.

The `files` element is almost the same as for the `mod_users_latest`. The first file-name element has a module attribute. This defines the name of the module and specifies the file to load when the module is executed. As with `mod_users_latest`, we list the `tmpl` folder, where we will put our layout file for the module. We then list the `helper.php` file, the `index.html` file, and this XML file. Recall that we don't need to list this XML file, but it is good practice to do so.

The one difference from the earlier example is here we have added a folder element for our language folder. This folder will contain a subfolder with the two `.ini` files for each language we include with the module.

The next section of the XML file is shown in Listing 6.5.

Listing 6.5 **mod_joompro_articles_author.xml File Part 2**

```
<config>
  <fields name="params">
   <fieldset name="basic">
    <field
```

```
        name="count"
        type="text"
        default="5"
        label="MOD_JOOMPRO_ARTICLES_AUTHOR_FIELD_NUMBER_LABEL"
        description="MOD_JOOMPRO_ARTICLES_AUTHOR_FIELD_NUMBER_DESC">
    </field>
    field name="article_ordering" type="list"
        validate="options"
        default="a.title"
        label="MOD_JOOMPRO_ARTICLES_AUTHOR_FIELD_ARTICLEORDERING_LABEL"
        description=
➥"MOD_JOOMPRO_ARTICLES_AUTHOR_FIELD_ARTICLEORDERING_DESC"
        >
        <option value="a.title">JGLOBAL_TITLE
        </option>
        <option value="a.hits">MOD_JOOMPRO_ARTICLES_AUTHOR_OPTION_HITS_VALUE
        </option>
        <option value="a.created">
➥MOD_JOOMPRO_ARTICLES_AUTHOR_OPTION_CREATED_VALUE
        </option>
        <option value="a.publish_up">
➥MOD_JOOMPRO_ARTICLES_AUTHOR_OPTION_STARTPUBLISHING_VALUE
        </option>
    </field>
    <field name="article_ordering_direction" type="list"
        validate="options"
        default="ASC"
        label="MOD_ARTICLES_CATEGORY_FIELD_ARTICLEORDERINGDIR_LABEL"
        description="MOD_ARTICLES_CATEGORY_FIELD_ARTICLEORDERINGDIR_DESC"
        >
        <option value="DESC">
➥MOD_JOOMPRO_ARTICLES_AUTHOR_OPTION_DESCENDING_VALUE
        </option>
        <option value="ASC">MOD_JOOMPRO_ARTICLES_AUTHOR_OPTION_
➥ASCENDING_VALUE
        </option>
    </field>
    </fieldset>
```

This section of the XML file defines the custom parameters for our module. We have three parameters. The first one is called count and it is where we can enter in the number of articles we want to show. We default the number to 5, but we let the user enter any number they want. Note that the way we have this set up, we are not requiring the user to enter a valid integer. They could enter text, for example. Later in this chapter, we discuss some approaches for improving the validation for this field.

The next parameter, `article_ordering`, indicates the order for the article list. We have added four options: title, number of hits, date it was created, and the date it was published. Each option element contains a value attribute and text. The value attribute will be the value passed to the form when the option is selected. The text in this case is a language key that will be translated using the value in the language `.ini` file for the module. The language keys are somewhat long because we have included the module name as part of the key. Although a bit awkward, it helps to ensure that we will not have any naming conflicts with other language files that might be loaded at the same time.

In the value attribute we have the exact name of the database column that will be used in the `ORDER BY` clause of the SQL query to sort the list of articles. We also use the `a.` table identifier. We will need to make sure in our query that we create the `FROM` clause with `AS a`—for example,

```
$query->from('#__content AS a');
```

This way, we can use the value of the `article_ordering` directly in our query.

The last parameter in Listing 6.5 defines the `article_ordering_direction` parameter. This allows two values, ASC or DESC. This will be added to the `ORDER BY` clause of the query to determine whether we use a normal low-to-high sort (ASC) or a reverse high-to-low sort (DESC).

 Note that we include the attribute `validate="options"` for both the `article_ordering` and `article_ordering_direction` parameters. This checks that the actual value in the submitted form matches one of the options on the list. This is important to prevent a hacker from submitting invalid data in the form. We discuss this in more detail later in the chapter.

The last section of the XML file is shown in Listing 6.6.

Listing 6.6   **mod_joompro_articles_author.xml Part 3**

```
<fieldset
    name="advanced">
    <field
        name="layout"
        type="modulelayout"
        label="JFIELD_ALT_LAYOUT_LABEL"
        description="JFIELD_ALT_MODULE_LAYOUT_DESC" />

    <field
        name="moduleclass_sfx"
        type="text"
        label="COM_MODULES_FIELD_MODULECLASS_SFX_LABEL"
        description="COM_MODULES_FIELD_MODULECLASS_SFX_DESC" />

    <field
```

```
                name="cache"
                type="list"
                default="1"
                label="COM_MODULES_FIELD_CACHING_LABEL"
                description="COM_MODULES_FIELD_CACHING_DESC">
                <option
                    value="1">JGLOBAL_USE_GLOBAL</option>
                <option
                    value="0">COM_MODULES_FIELD_VALUE_NOCACHING</option>
            </field>
            <field
                name="cache_time"
                type="text"
                default="900"
                label="COM_MODULES_FIELD_CACHE_TIME_LABEL"
                description="COM_MODULES_FIELD_CACHE_TIME_DESC" />
            <field
                name="cachemode"
                type="hidden"
                default="static">
                <option
                    value="static"></option>
            </field>
        </fieldset>
    </fields>
  </config>
</extension>
```

This is an exact copy of the advanced fieldset element from any of the other front-end modules (for example, `mod_articles_archive.xml`). It defines the standard module parameters in the advanced fieldset. These are

- Layout: The name of the optional alternative layout file (as discussed in Chapter 4)
- Module Class Suffix: Optional CSS class suffix to allow styling for individual instances or modules
- Caching: Whether or not to enable caching for this instance of the module
- Cache Time: The number of seconds to use a cached copy of the module

The fourth field, `cachemode`, illustrates an important feature for fields in JForm. This field has `type="hidden"`. This means that the field will be stored just like any other field. However, because it is hidden, the user never sees the field and will not be allowed to alter it. It is rendered as an HTML input element with the attribute type set to hidden.

As discussed earlier, we need to remember that hidden form elements can still be manipulated by hackers—for example, by using a browser add-in like Firebug. So we cannot rely on a hidden field to always have the expected value. We should think of this as a user-interface convenience, but not as a way to ensure the form will always return the expected value. In other words, when we use that value in our code, we should guard against unexpected or malicious values in the field, just as we would for other form fields.

Entry File: mod_joompro_articles_author.php

Listing 6.7 shows the PHP file for our module.

Listing 6.7   **mod_joompro_articles_author.php File**

```php
<?php
/**
 * @copyright   Copyright (C) 2012 Mark Dexter and Louis Landry. All
➞rights reserved.
 * @license     GNU General Public License version 2 or later; see
➞LICENSE.txt
 */

// no direct access
defined('_JEXEC') or die;

// Include the syndicate functions only once
JLoader::register('modJoomProArticlesAuthorHelper',
➞dirname(__FILE__).'/helper.php');

$list = modJoomProArticlesAuthorHelper::getList($params);

// Only show module if there is something to show
if (isset($list[0])) {
    $moduleclass_sfx = htmlspecialchars($params->get('moduleclass_sfx'));
    require JModuleHelper::getLayoutPath('mod_joompro_articles_author',
➞$params->get('layout', 'default'));
}
```

In the first line after the defined statement, we use the `JLoader::register()` method to load the helper class. We could have used `require_once`. Either command works, but the `JLoader::register()` method uses the PHP autoload feature and executes faster than `require_once`. For this reason, whenever possible we should use `JLoader::register()` (or `jimport`, which in turns calls `JLoader::register()`) instead of `require_once`.

The next line calls the helper to get the list of articles. The next line checks to see if we have anything to show. We could have used

```php
if (count($list)) {
```

instead of

```php
if (isset($list[0])) {
```

to check if the $list array has some content. We use the isset command because it is faster. The count function loops through the entire array to get the number of items. In our case, we don't care if the array has 1 or 100 elements; we just care that it has at least one. Since the array is an indexed array (and not an associative array), we know that if it has any elements, it must have a zero element ($list[0]). So this is a quick way to check that it has at least one element.

If we have something to display, we set the module class suffix from the parameter and then include the layout. We use the require command to include the layout because it is not a class. The JLoader::register() method discussed earlier is only for loading classes. Also, we don't need to use require_once, because we know that this is the only place in the code where this layout file is being included. The purpose of require_once is to ensure that we don't try to declare the same class or function twice, which would cause a PHP error. Because require_once has to check whether a file has already been included, it is slower than the require command. So we don't want to use require_once unless we need to.

We use the method JModuleHelper::getLayoutPath() to get the name of the layout file. This allows the user to create and use alternative layouts and template override layouts for the module.

We have made a subtle but important design choice by testing that the $list variable has content before calling the layout. This means that nothing will be output if there are no articles found by the current author. If we wanted the layout to be able to show a message when there are no articles by the author, we would want to call the layout even if the list were empty.

Helper File

Listing 6.8 shows the first part of the helper.php file with the modJoomProArticles-AuthorHelper class.

Listing 6.8 **Helper File Part 1**

```php
<?php
/**
 * @copyright    Copyright (C) 2012 Mark Dexter and Louis Landry. All
➥rights reserved.
 * @license      GNU General Public License version 2 or later; see
➥LICENSE.txt
 */

// no direct access
defined('_JEXEC') or die;

JLoader::register('ContentHelperRoute',
➥JPATH_SITE.'/components/com_content/helpers/route.php');

abstract class modJoomProArticlesAuthorHelper
```

```
{
    public static function getList(&$params)
    {
        // Initialize return variable
        $items = array();

        // Process only if this is a single-article view
        $option = JRequest::getCmd('option');
        $view = JRequest::getCmd('view');
        if ($option == 'com_content' && $view == 'article')
        {
```

This file registers the `ContentHelperRoute` method, which we will use later on. Then it declares the class as abstract. The ability to create abstract classes was added in PHP 5. You cannot create an object for an abstract class. Abstract classes are typically used for one of two purposes:

- To create a class to hold one or more static methods
- To create a class that will be used exclusively as a prototype for subclasses (see, for example, the JDatabase class in `libraries/joomla/database/database.php`)

In this case, this class will just have one static method, called `getList()`. It takes one argument, the `$params` variable that is a `JRegistry` object with the parameters entered for the module.

The next line initializes the `$items` as an empty array. PHP does not require that variables be initialized. However, if you try to use a variable that has never been set, PHP returns a message called a notice. If you have error reporting set to maximum, you will see the PHP notice message. It is strongly recommended to make sure all variables are set before you try to use them. If you always have your development system's error reporting set to maximum, you will see PHP notices and will catch this very common mistake during development.

One frequent cause of PHP notices is setting a variable only inside an if/then block of code. If the block is skipped because the condition is not true, then the variable never gets set. If you use that variable later on, you get a PHP notice. For this reason, it is a good habit to initialize variables used in if/then blocks. This is also true for other code blocks, such as loops, that might be skipped during execution.

The next two lines set two variables from the request. We use the `JRequest::getCmd()` method to get the option and view elements from the request array. The `getCmd()` method filters the request to make sure it only contains letters, numbers, dashes, and underscores. This protects against someone trying to enter in malicious code (such as JavaScript or SQL commands) into the variable.

The next line is very important. Our module shows articles by the same author as the current article shown on the page. However, many pages on our site will not be showing an article. The page may be showing a different component (such as contacts or Weblinks) or it may be showing a list of articles. In this case, our module won't have anything to show. So before we start working on getting our list, we want to make sure we are in a single-article view of the content component, and that is exactly what this line of code does. A single-article view is defined by the option of "com_content" and the view of "article." If you set SEF URLs to no in Global Configuration, you will see these values in the URL of every single article page. In any case, these values are set in the $_REQUEST variable.

Now that we know we are in the right type of menu item, we are ready to start the work of getting our list. Listing 6.9 shows the next portion of the helper file.

Listing 6.9   **Helper File Part 2**

```
// Get the dbo
$db = JFactory::getDbo();
$app = JFactory::getApplication();
$user = JFactory::getUser();
$id = JRequest::getInt('id');

// Get the levels as a comma-separated string
$levels = implode(',', $user->getAuthorisedViewLevels());

// Set the current and empty date fields
$date = JFactory::getDate();
$now = $date->toSql();
$nullDate = $db->getNullDate();

// Initialize the query object
$query = $db->getQuery(true);

// Query the database to get the author info for the current article
$query->select('id, created_by, created_by_alias');
$query->from('#__content');
$query->where('id = ' . (int) $id);
$db->setQuery($query);
$currentArticle = $db->loadObject();
```

The main thing we do in this method is to execute two queries. The first query gets the author for the current article. Then the second query searches the entire articles table for other articles by this same author.

The first three lines get the JDatabase, JApplication, and JUser objects, using the JFactory methods. Then we get the id from the request, using the getInt() method. This method ensures that we get an integer value, thereby filtering out any malicious or unexpected content in the request.

The next line gets a list of the access levels that the current user is allowed to see. It calls the getAuthorisedViewLevels() method, which returns an array of all the access levels for all the groups that this user belongs to. Using the PHP implode function, the array is then turned into a comma-delimited list.

One design decision we have to make is how to handle the case where there are either unpublished articles or articles to which the current user does not have access. The simplest approach is to write the query so that we only see published articles that the current user has access to. Another approach would be to include articles that the user doesn't have access to and, for those articles, provide a link to allow the user to login before viewing the restricted articles. In our example, we will take the simple approach and limit our results to articles we know we can view.

The next section deals with date values that will be used in our queries. In Joomla, articles have a date range during which they are published. We want to include articles where the current date is between the publishing start and stop dates. However, life is a bit more complicated than this, because we also allow an empty date in either of these columns to mean "always start publishing" or "never stop publishing." A final complication is that different databases can have different formats for either the current date or an empty or null date.

The first line in this section just gets the current date-time object from Joomla, again using the **JFactory** class. Then we create a variable $now, which is in the format that the database requires. To do this, we use the **toSql()** method in the **JDate** class. Finally, we create a variable called $nullDate, using the **JDatabase** **getNullDate()** method. Note that this is not really a null value. For example, for MySQL, **getNullDate()** returns a date-time field with all zeros (0000-00-00 00:00:00). The important thing is that we use the same value here as we used when the article was created.

Next, we build our first query, which will get the author information we need from the current article. Here we have another design decision to make. In Joomla, an article has a created_by column, which holds the **id** of the user that created the article. We also have a **created_by_alias** column. This is an optional text field that can be entered when the article is created or edited. Which column should we use to check if another article is by the same author?

There are several ways we could handle this. One way is to use the optional **created _by_alias** if it is present and use the **created_by** otherwise. A simpler way is to just look for a match on either field. Yet another way would be to use a parameter to let the user decide how to do it. For this example we will use the simpler approach and get a list of all articles that match on either column. So we need to get both of these columns for the current article so we can use them in our second query.

Our query is very simple. We create a new query object with the **getQuery()** method. The **true** argument means we will get a new empty query. Then we add our three columns using the **select()** method. We include the id column even though we technically don't need it. It doesn't cost anything to add this, and it makes it easier to debug and check that the query is returning what we expect.

In the **from()** method, we specify the **#__content**. Recall that we always use the **#__** prefix in queries. This gets changed to the actual table prefix before the query is passed to the database. Next we add our **WHERE** clause by using the **where()** method:

```
$query->where('id = ' . (int) $id);
```

In this case, we don't need to cast $id as an integer. We know from earlier that it is an integer, because we used the JRequest::getInt() method to set its value. However, it is a good habit to sanitize variables used in the WHERE clause of SQL queries. For text, you can use the JDatabase quote() method. This places quotes around the text and escapes any special characters (such as quotes) so that they will not allow a hacker to hijack your query. For integers, you can use the cast command, as in this example. See Chapter 11 for more information about protecting against SQL injection attacks.

The next line calls the setQuery() method of the $db object. This sets the query field in the database object but doesn't actually execute the query. The next line,

```
$currentArticle = $db->loadObject();
```

actually executes the query and returns the value as an object.

It is important to understand the different methods we can use to get the results of queries. The most commonly used methods are as follows:

- loadObject() returns the first row of the query as an object, where each column for the row is a field in the object.

- loadObjectList() returns an array of all rows from the query where each array element is an object for that row.

- loadResult() returns the first column from the first row of the query.

Which method we use depends on the type of query we are using. In our current example, we know the query will return at most one row. This is because we are selecting the row where id is one value. Each id in the #__content table is unique, so we can't get more than one row. This is why we use the loadObject() method, which returns the first row from the query.

If we only wanted the first column from the first row, we could use the load-Result() method. If we might get multiple rows from our query, we normally use the loadObjectList() method. There are also methods for loading query results into arrays instead of objects. You can see these in the JDatabase class (libraries/joomla/database/database.php).

At this point, we have the three columns for the current article in the $currentArticle variable. Listing 6.10 shows the next section of the helper file.

Listing 6.10 **Helper File Part 3**

```
// Query the database to get articles that match the current author
$query->clear();
$query->select('a.*');
$query->select('c.access AS cat_access, c.published AS cat_state, c.alias
➥AS cat_alias');
$query->from('#__content AS a');

// We need category information to make the link to the articles and to
➥check access
```

```
$query->leftJoin('#__categories AS c ON c.id = a.catid');

// Only show published articles
$query->where('a.state = 1');
$query->where('c.published = 1');

// Only show where we have access to article and category
$query->where('a.access IN (' . $levels . ')');
$query->where('c.access IN (' . $levels . ')');

// Only show where articles are currently published
$query->where('(a.publish_up = '.$db->Quote($nullDate).' OR
a.publish_up <= '.$db->Quote($now).')');
$query->where('(a.publish_down = '.$db->Quote($nullDate).' OR
a.publish_down >= '.$db->Quote($now).')');

// Check the author of the article
if ($currentArticle->created_by_alias) {
        // If the current article has an author alias, check for matches
in created_by or created_by_alias
        $query->where('(a.created_by =' . (int) $currentArticle->
created_by . ' OR '
            . 'a.created_by_alias =' . $db->quote($currentArticle
->created_by_alias) . ')');
} else {
        // If current article does not have author alias, only check the
created_by column for matches
 $query->where('a.created_by =' . (int) $currentArticle->created_by);
}
```

Here we start to build our main query. First we clear the old query with the clear() method. Then we create our select. The syntax "a.*" tells the database to include all the columns for table "a" in the query. We only need a few columns from the content table for our module: the article's title, id, and category. Recall, however, that we allow users to create alternative layouts for our module. In these layouts, we don't know what information about the article they might want to show.

It doesn't take a significant amount of extra time for the database to retrieve all the columns from the content table, and this gives us maximum flexibility regarding future possible layouts.

In this query, we will also include the columns access, published, and alias from the #__categories table. These will use the table alias "c.". The line of code is

```
$query->select('c.access AS cat_access, c.published AS cat_state, c.alias
AS cat_alias');
```

The same column name is often used in different tables. For example, both the #__content and #__categories table have columns called access and alias. Our query results will be returned to us in an object where the column name is the object's field name. Consequently, when we have a duplicate column name, we need to change the column name for the query. This is done using a column alias (not to be confused with the `alias` column in many Joomla database tables). We do this using "AS," just as we do with table aliases. For example, `c.access AS cat_access` means that the query will return the value of the `access` column for the `#__categories` table with the column name `cat_access`. That way we will know which access column is which (`access` is the article access, `cat_access` is the category access).

The next line names the `#__content` table as the first table in the query, with the table alias of "a". We normally name the main table we are interested in as the first table in the query. In this case, we are mostly interested in information from the `#__content` table.

The next line of code is

```
$query->leftJoin('#__categories AS c ON c.id = a.catid');
```

A join is the way we add information from a second table into our query. In this case, we will add the three columns from the `#__categories` table to every row in the query. How do we know which row from `#__categories` to use? This is specified in the `ON` clause. By saying "`ON c.id = a.catid`", we tell the database to find the row in `#__categories` where the `id` matches the `catid` column in the `#__content` table.

Notice that we use the method called `leftJoin()`. There are different ways to join database tables together in a query. The two that are most frequently used are called left joins and inner joins. They both do the same thing in most cases. The difference is what happens if there is no row in the second table that matches the value in the `ON` clause. With a left join, any columns coming from the second table are set to NULL. With an inner join, the entire row from the first table is excluded from the query results. We discuss this in more detail in Chapter 11.

In our query, this shouldn't make any difference. If our database is not corrupted, we expect to have a valid category for every article. However, if for some reason an article's category got deleted, we are choosing to still show the article in the query. If we wanted to exclude articles where the category was not found, we would use the `innerJoin()` method instead.

Next we have a series of `where()` methods. Here we set the selection criteria for our query. The first two `where()` statements require that both the article and category are published. Note that the article table uses the column name state, whereas the category table uses the name published. These columns mean the same thing, and the value of "1" indicates that it is published.

Why do we care if the category is published? In Joomla, we can think of categories as a container for articles or other types of content, similar to a folder on a computer's disk drive. If we set a category to unpublished, it should also have the effect of setting all the articles in that category to unpublished. We can enforce this by checking both places.

We use similar logic for access levels. If a category has restricted access, this has the effect of restricting the access of all the articles in the category. Recall that we set the variable $levels to be a comma-delimited list of the access levels that the current user has permission to see. The SQL command IN checks if a value is in a comma-delimited list. So the command

```
a.access IN (1,2,3)
```

would check that a.access was equal to 1, 2, or 3. So we build two IN statements: one for the article access and one for the category access.

Notice that we have to be careful about building the string inside the where() method and include the opening and closing parentheses. Perhaps in a future enhancement to the JDatabaseQuery class we could add methods to support different types of comparison operators, such as IN, BETWEEN, LIKE, =, and so on. Perhaps you could then use a command like

```
$query->whereIn('a.access', $levels);
```

This would make it easier to use IN comparisons, and we wouldn't have to worry about adding the parentheses ourselves.

However, such a method doesn't exist at the moment. One of the fun things about software is that we can always think about ways to make it better, and with an open-source project like Joomla, we can actually implement improvements to the package. Alternatively, we could create our own JDatabaseQuery subclass and add our own methods to it.

The next block of code is where we check the article's start and stop publish dates (publish_up and publish_down) to see that our article is published as of the current date and time. This is where we use the $now and $nullDate variables we created earlier. We need to check that either

- The start or stop date is not entered, or
- The current date is between the start and stop dates.

So we add two WHERE clauses: one for the start date and one for the stop date. Inside each, we use the OR operator. Notice that we put the entire value inside a set of parentheses. For example, the result of the first method might look like the following:

```
WHERE (a.published_up = '0000-00-00 00:00:00' OR a.publish_up
       <= '2012-12-31 23:30:00')
```

It is important to understand that, by default, the WHERE clauses created by the where() method are connected with the SQL AND operator. Using AND means that all the WHERE conditions must be true for the row to be selected in the query. By putting these two comparisons inside a single where() method connected with an OR operator, and by putting parentheses around it, this WHERE condition will be true if either of the conditions are true. This is exactly what we want.

Notice also that we use the method `$db->quote()` to put quotes around the `$nullDate` and `$now` variables. Even though we know that these values are valid, we need quotes because these values can contain spaces.

The logic for the stop publishing date is exactly the same, except that we check that the current date is less than the stop publishing date.

The next block of code is where we check that the article's author matches our current author. We decided earlier that we would list all articles that match on either the `created_by` or the `created_by_alias` columns. However, what if the current article doesn't have anything in the `created_by_alias` column? In this case, we don't want to use this column for matching, because we don't want to show all other articles where this column is empty.

The solution is to check the `created_by_alias` column in our current article and then build the `WHERE` clause in one of two ways, based on what we find. If we have something in the `created_by_alias` column, we use it in the `WHERE` clause as follows:

```
$query->where('(a.created_by =' . (int) $currentArticle->created_by
↳. ' OR '
        . 'a.created_by_alias =' . $db->quote($currentArticle
↳->created_by_alias) . ')');
```

Again, we put the entire `WHERE` clause inside a set of parentheses.

The second part of the `if` statement is executed if the `created_by_alias` is empty. In this case, we just do the check for the `created_by`, without checking the `created_by_alias` column, as follows:

```
$query->where('a.created_by =' . (int) $currentArticle->created_by);
```

Notice that we use the `(int)` command to cast the `created_by` column to an integer. It should be an integer, but this is always good practice. It is very important to use the `$db->quote()` method for the `created_by_alias`. This field is entered by the user when an article is created, so it could contain anything, including malicious code. By putting it inside the `$db->quote()`, we make sure it can't inject any harmful code into our query.

The last part of our helper method is shown in Listing 6.11.

Listing 6.11 **Helper File Part 4**

```
// We don't want to show the article we are currently viewing
$query->where('a.id !=' . (int) $currentArticle->id);

// If the language filter is enabled, only show articles that match the
↳current language
    if ($app->getLanguageFilter()) {
        query->where('a.language IN (' . $db->
```

```
➥Quote(JFactory::getLanguage()->getTag()) . ',' . $db->Quote('*') . ')');
    }

    // Set ordering based on parameter
    // We know it is valid because of validate="options" in the form
    $query->order($params->get('article_ordering', 'a.title') . ' ' .
➥$params->get('article_ordering_direction', 'ASC'));
    // Set query limit using count parameter (note that we have no
➥pagination on the module)
    $db->setQuery($query, 0, $params->get('count', 5));

    // Get list of rows
    $items = $db->loadObjectList();

    // Create the link field for each item using the content router class
    foreach ($items as &$item) {
        $item->slug = $item->id.':'.$item->alias;
        $item->catslug = $item->catid.':'.$item->cat_alias;
        $item->link = JRoute::_(ContentHelperRoute::getArticleRoute($item->
➥slug, $item->catslug));
    }
    }

    return $items;
}
```

The first line adds a condition to exclude our current article. We don't want that to show in the list. We know it is by the current author.

The next section of code relates to a feature added in Joomla version 1.6 called the Language Switcher. This feature allows the user to tag articles for a specific language. We only want to add this WHERE clause if the feature is turned on, which we check with the $app->getLanguageFilter() method. If the feature is enabled, then we check that the article's language (a.language) either matches the current language tag or matches the asterisk ("*"), which means match any language. If the Language Switcher feature is not enabled, we skip this code block and don't add the WHERE clause.

The next section uses our ordering parameters to sort the query. The order() method adds an ORDER BY clause to the query. Recall that we designed our parameter values to plug directly into the ORDER BY clause and that we used the validate="options" to ensure that the entered value matches one of the options. Therefore we can use the parameter values directly in the query's order() method as shown.

Note that we provide default values for each parameter. Normally, we will have valid parameter values. However, there are some cases where we might not. For example, say that we create a new version of our module and the new version adds a new parameter. If someone has created a module with the old version and upgrades to the new version, this parameter will not be defined for that instance of the module. If we have specified a valid default value for the new parameter, the module will work correctly even if the parameter isn't defined.

The last thing we do before running the query is to use the count parameter to set the query limit. Most queries we write for Joomla will use the MySQL offset and limit values. These tell MySQL where to start and stop the query. In our case, we want to start at the beginning (row 0) and stop after the number from the count parameter (with a default value of 5). We pass the arguments to the `setQuery()` method.

The next line executes the query and returns the results as an array of objects, using the `loadObjectList()` method that we discussed earlier.

At this point, we have our array of objects, where each object contains the values for one row in our query. We want our list to include a link to each article. So the last thing we need to do (whew!) is create the link to each article.

Creating links in Joomla is easy, as long as we use the correct built-in methods. There are rules that we want to follow when we create links to articles. For example, we normally try to find a menu item in the site that is the "best fit" for this article. If we have a single article menu item for the article, we create the link so that it calls that menu item. If not, then we look for a menu item for the category the article is in. We try to use an existing URL for the article instead of creating a new URL. In this way, if we have links to the same article in multiple places on the site, they will all link to the same URL and page on the site.

How do we do this? Fortunately, we already have methods in Joomla for creating the article links.

Looking at the last block of code, we have a `foreach` loop that loops through the `$items` array. Inside the loop, each object in the array is available in the variable called `$item`.

The first two lines create the article and category `slug` fields. These are just the id, a colon (`:`), and the alias (for example, `23:my-article-alias`). These are needed to create the URL for the article link.

The third line in the `foreach` loop is shown here:

```
$item->link = JRoute::_(ContentHelperRoute::getArticleRoute($item->slug,
➥$item->catslug));
```

This is the line where the actual link to the article gets created. It does two things.

First, it builds the article routing using the `getArticleRoute()` method in the `ContentHelperRoute` class. This takes as its arguments the item and category "slugs" we created in the previous two lines and returns the query we need to build the URL. Recall that we mentioned earlier in this chapter that a module is normally tied to a component. In this case, our module is tied to the `com_content` component. As part of that, we want links to articles that we create inside the module to be consistent with links created in the component itself or in other modules that use `com_content`.

When we create a component, one of the options we have is to create special rules for routing. The `com_content` component does this with its `getArticleRoute()`

method. This method looks for an existing menu item that is the "best fit" for this article. For example, if there is a single-article menu item, a URL pointing to that menu item will be created. If not, then it will look for a menu item that points to the article's category. This is done because we normally want links to a given article to always take us to the same URL.

The key point here is that we want our article links to be the same as those created in the component or in other article modules. So we want to use the same methods to create the links. This ensures that our links will be consistent with other links and it also saves us work. Moreover, if a change is made to the way articles are routed, or if a bug is fixed, our module will pick up that change.

The output of `getArticleRoute()` is fairly simple—for example,

```
index.php?option=com_content&view=article&id=1:administrator-
↪components&catid=21:components&Itemid=273
```

The first part will always be the same: `index.php?option=com_content&view=article`. The next two parts are the article and category slugs we created. So far, the `getArticleRoute()` hasn't done much for us. The last part `&Itemid=xxx` is the important piece. This is the menu item that is the best fit for this article, based on the rules for this component, and this is what the `getArticleRoute()` provides.

Once we have the results of `getArticleRoute()`, we then need to turn it into a full URL. This is done by the `JRoute::_()` method. This method in turn calls the route function, if any, that is provided by the component. In this case, that is the function `ContentBuildRoute()` in the file `components/com_content/router.php`. If the Global Configuration option for SEF URLs is set to `Yes`, the URL is then converted to the SEF version, and the query is replaced with the aliases from the menu item and, in some cases, the category. In the previous example, the full SEF URL would be

```
<Joomla! root path>/index.php/using-joomla/extensions/components/
↪administrator-components
```

This would then be converted by the SEF system plugin to the full URL, adding the host (for example, "http://www.mydomain") to the start of the URL.

After we have processed each object in the `$items` array, we are done with the method. We exit out of the `foreach` loop and exit out of the "if/then" code block. Finally, we return the `$items` array.

Layout File: default.php

The next file in the process is the default.php layout. If we do not create and specify an alternative layout for the module, this is the file name that will be returned by the `JModuleHelper::getLayoutPath()` method we called in our module PHP file. Listing 6.12 shows the code for this file.

Listing 6.12   **default.php Layout File**

```php
<?php
/**
 * @copyright Copyright (C) 2012 Mark Dexter and Louis Landry. All rights reserved.
 * @license GNU General Public License version 2 or later; see LICENSE.txt
 */

// no direct access
defined('_JEXEC') or die;

// Output as a list of links in a ul element
?>
<ul class="joompro<?php echo $moduleclass_sfx; ?>">
<?php foreach ($list as $item) :  ?>
    <li>
        <a href="<?php echo $item->link; ?>">
            <?php echo $item->title; ?></a>
    </li>
<?php endforeach; ?>
</ul>
```

This simple layout creates an unordered HTML element (`ul`) and then does a `foreach` loop over the `$list` array. Recall that the `$list` variable received the array returned by the helper method in this line from the `mod_joompro_articles_author.php` file:

```
$list = modJoomProArticlesAuthorHelper::getList($params);
```

The variables in scope at the point where our layout was included (via the `require` command) are still in scope inside the layout. The layout just executes PHP commands; it does not declare a class or function. So it is executed immediately. The effect is exactly as if the layout were part of the program file that included it.

Inside the `foreach` loop, we create an HTML `li` element that includes the article's link and its title. After we end the `foreach` loop, we close the file with the closing `ul` tag.

Notice that, as before, we use the alternative PHP syntax that allows us to easily mix HTML tags and PHP commands.

Language Files

We have two language files for our module. Listing 6.13 shows the `.sys.ini` file.

Listing 6.13   **en-GB.mod_joompro_articles_author.sys.ini File**

```
; sys language file for mod_joompro_articles_author module
; The .sys.ini files are used when listing the extensions in the extension
```

```
↪manager or module manager

MOD_JOOMPRO_ARTICLES_AUTHOR="Articles by Current Author (sys file)"
MOD_JOOMPRO_ARTICLES_AUTHOR_DESCRIPTION="This module shows articles by the
↪same author as the article in view. (sys file)"
```

As discussed earlier, this file is used to translate the name and description of the module when we are showing it in a list but don't have the module open for edit. Two examples are when the module is installed and in the Module Manager list. We have added "(sys file)" to the text for illustration, to show us which language file is being used.

Listing 6.14 shows the `.ini` file for the module.

Listing 6.14   en-GB.mod_joompro_articles_author.ini File

```
; Language file for mod_joompro_articles_author

MOD_JOOMPRO_ARTICLES_AUTHOR="Articles by Current Author"
MOD_JOOMPRO_ARTICLES_AUTHOR_DESCRIPTION="This module shows articles by the
↪same author as the article in view. (ini file)"
MOD_JOOMPRO_ARTICLES_AUTHOR_FIELD_NUMBER_LABEL="Number of Articles to
↪Show"
MOD_JOOMPRO_ARTICLES_AUTHOR_FIELD_NUMBER_DESC="Enter the maximum number of
↪articles to show in the module."
MOD_JOOMPRO_ARTICLES_AUTHOR_FIELD_ARTICLEORDERING_LABEL="Article Ordering"
MOD_JOOMPRO_ARTICLES_AUTHOR_FIELD_ARTICLEORDERING_DESC="Select the column
↪that will be used to order the articles."
MOD_JOOMPRO_ARTICLES_AUTHOR_OPTION_HITS_VALUE="Hits"
MOD_JOOMPRO_ARTICLES_AUTHOR_OPTION_CREATED_VALUE="Date Created"
MOD_JOOMPRO_ARTICLES_AUTHOR_OPTION_STARTPUBLISHING_VALUE="Date Published"
MOD_ARTICLES_CATEGORY_FIELD_ARTICLEORDERINGDIR_LABEL="Ordering Direction"
MOD_ARTICLES_CATEGORY_FIELD_ARTICLEORDERINGDIR_DESC="Enter Low to High for
↪normal alphabetical sort. Enter High to Low to order by most recent or
↪most hits."
MOD_JOOMPRO_ARTICLES_AUTHOR_OPTION_DESCENDING_VALUE="High to Low"
MOD_JOOMPRO_ARTICLES_AUTHOR_OPTION_ASCENDING_VALUE="Low to High"
```

Note that we have the module name and description in this file as well. These keys are used to display the name and description when we are editing an instance of the module. We have added the text "(ini file)" for illustration purposes. All these keys come from the module's XML file. This is because we are not displaying any text in the output of the actual module. If we were, this file would also include the language keys for that text.

Validating Parameters in JForm

The `JForm` class introduced in Joomla version 1.6 provides us with some great ways to validate the parameters entered in by users. Let's look at two examples.

Check Values in Helper

Let's return to the count field in our XML file, where we specify the maximum number of articles to show in the module. It currently has the following code:

```
<field
    name="count"
    type="text"
    default="5"
    label="MOD_JOOMPRO_ARTICLES_AUTHOR_FIELD_NUMBER_LABEL"
    description="MOD_JOOMPRO_ARTICLES_AUTHOR_FIELD_NUMBER_DESC">
</field>
```

To be valid, this should be a positive integer. However, with the current code, the user can put in text, a negative number, or zero. If the user puts in anything other than a positive integer, the end result will be that there will be no limit when the query is executed. In this case, all articles with this author will be listed. On a large site, this could be dozens, hundreds, or more and would cause display problems and perhaps performance problems.

We have several options to improve our code to prevent this possibility. One option would be to check the value in our helper method and change it to a default value if it is outside the range. For example, we could add something like the following:

```
$count = (int) $params->get('count', 5);
$count = ($count <= 0 || $count > 10) ? 5 : $count;
$db->setQuery($query, 0, $count);
```

This way we know that the count will always be an integer between 1 and 10.

Integer Type in JForm

A limitation of this approach is that we don't prevent the user from entering an invalid entry and we don't alert them if they do. Using `JForm`, we have several options for improving the validation during data entry.

One option is to use the integer type. This limits the entry possibilities to a list of integers. Here is an example of how we might change the field definition in the XML file:

```
<field
 name="count"
 type="integer"
 first="1"
 last="10"
 step="1"
 default="5"
```

```
label="MOD_JOOMPRO_ARTICLES_AUTHOR_FIELD_NUMBER_LABEL"
description="MOD_JOOMPRO_ARTICLES_AUTHOR_FIELD_NUMBER_DESC">
</field>
```

Here we have changed the type from "text" to "integer." When we load the module edit form, the field is presented as a list box, as shown in Figure 6.2.

This has the advantage that it limits the user input to only valid entries. However, it does limit the user to a predefined range. In our example, that is not too limiting. However, we might have a case where any integer from 1–1,000 was valid. We wouldn't want a list box with 1,000 lines.

One option in this scenario would be to use the step attribute to create a larger step, say 50 or 100. This would reduce the number of options and might be a good solution in some situations.

Using `type="integer"` also has the limitation that it does not prevent a hacker from entering an invalid number using a tool like Firebug. It makes life convenient for the user, but it doesn't protect us from hackers.

Integer Filter in JForm

Another option we have with JForm is to use the filter attribute. This uses the predefined filters in Joomla to filter the form input when the module is saved. If we change the type back to text and add a filter attribute, the code looks like the following:

```
<field
 name="count"
 type="text"
 filter="integer"
 default="5"
 label="MOD_JOOMPRO_ARTICLES_AUTHOR_FIELD_NUMBER_LABEL"
 description="MOD_JOOMPRO_ARTICLES_AUTHOR_FIELD_NUMBER_DESC">
</field>
```

This method will automatically convert any noninteger entry in the field to zero. In our example, this doesn't help us much, because we get this result without the filter. However, this is a useful method to know about.

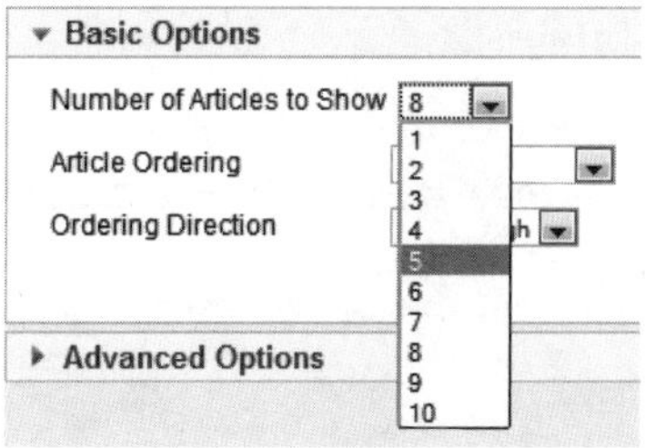

Figure 6.2   Integer field example

One advantage of using the filter attribute is that it is secure. Because this processing happens during the save process, it cannot be tampered with by manipulating the HTML form in the browser. Possible values for filter include all the standard filter types in JFilterInput. These include integer, float, double, boolean, word, cmd, base64, string, html, array, path, and username. In addition, some new filter types were added for JForm. These include rules, unset, raw, int_array, safehtml, server_utc, and user_ utc. See Appendix B for information about filtering options.

Custom JFormRule Class

Another option is to create a custom rule for the field. We access rules using the validate attribute. Joomla includes a number of standard rules, including boolean, email, equals, options, tel, url, and username. These correspond to classes in the folder `libraries/joomla/form/rules`.

If one of these predefined rules doesn't do what we need, we can create our own customized rules with exactly the code we want.

To do this, we would modify the XML file as follows:

```
<fieldset name="basic" addrulepath="modules/mod_joompro_articles_author">
 <field
    name="count"
    type="text"
    validate="countinteger"
    filter="integer"
    default="5"
    label="MOD_JOOMPRO_ARTICLES_AUTHOR_FIELD_NUMBER_LABEL"
    description="MOD_JOOMPRO_ARTICLES_AUTHOR_FIELD_NUMBER_DESC">
 </field>
```

In the fieldset, we include an addrulepath attribute with the path to our custom rule folder. We will just put it in the top-level folder of our module. Then, in the field, we put the name of the rule file in the validate attribute. In our example, this is called countinteger. We add the filter="integer" to force the system to save the input value as an integer. For example, if someone entered something like 15.5, we want the value to be saved as 15.

Then we add a file called countinteger.php in our module folder, with the following code:

```php
<?php
/**
 * @copyright Copyright (C) 2012 Mark Dexter & Louis Landry. All rights
⮡reserved.
 * @license GNU General Public License version 2 or later; see
⮡LICENSE.txt
 */

defined('_JEXEC') or die;
```

```
jimport('joomla.form.formrule');

class JFormRuleCountInteger extends JFormRule
{
 public function test(& $element, $value, $group = null, & $input = null,
↪& $form = null)
 {
    return ((int) $value > 0 && (int) $value <= 30);
 }
}
```

The class is called `JFormRuleCountInteger` and it extends the `JFormRule` class. We only need one method, called `test()`. This method should have the arguments shown in the example. The variable called `$value` will contain the input from the form.

In this example, we are testing that the value is an integer between 1 and 30. Otherwise, we will get an error message saying "Invalid field: Number of Articles to Show" and the form will not save.

Notice that we have the minimum and maximum values hard-coded to 1 and 30. We could make the `JFormRuleCountInteger` class a lot more flexible if we allowed the minimum and maximum values to be set in the XML form field element. To do that, we add attributes called `minimum` and `maximum` to the XML file as follows:

```
<field
    name="count"
    type="text"
    validate="countinteger"
    minimum="1"
    maximum="10"
    filter="integer"
    default="5"
    label="MOD_JOOMPRO_ARTICLES_AUTHOR_FIELD_NUMBER_LABEL"
    description="MOD_JOOMPRO_ARTICLES_AUTHOR_FIELD_NUMBER_DESC">
</field>
```

Then we modify the `test()` method of JFormRuleCountInteger to use the new attributes, as follows:

```
public function test(& $element, $value, $group = null, &
↪$input = null, & $form = null)
    {
        $max = (int) $element->getAttribute('maximum') ?
↪$element->getAttribute('maximum') : 30;
        $min = (int) $element->getAttribute('minimum') ?
↪$element->getAttribute('minimum') : 1;
        return ((int) $value >= $min && (int) $value <= $max);
    }
```

Here we use the PHP ternary operator to set the value of $max and $min. We want the method to work even if the maximum and minimum attributes have not been set correctly. So we check to see if they are set to a positive integer value. If so, we use that value. Otherwise, we use the default values of 30 and 1.

With this code, we can change the range of allowed values simply by setting the minimum and maximum attributes in the XML file, so our custom rule is much more flexible and more likely to be useful for other situations.

Validation Error Message

As we saw earlier, when the user enters an invalid value in the count parameter, the message "Invalid field: Number of Articles to Show" is displayed. This message tells the user that there is something wrong with the field, but it doesn't say what is wrong. This is the default error message that displays if we don't define one explicitly. However, we have two options for defining a different message.

One option is to add an attribute called message to the field element. For example, we could add the following line to the count field element in the XML file:

```
message="MOD_JOOMPRO_ARTICLES_AUTHOR_COUNTINTEGER_MESSAGE"
```

Then we could add a line in the language .ini file as follows:

```
MOD_JOOMPRO_ARTICLES_AUTHOR_COUNTINTEGER_MESSAGE="Article count must be
⇥between 1 and 10."
```

Now if we try to enter in a value outside the range, we get this error message from the language file, which gives the user more useful information.

The other option we have is to return a JException object with a message from the rule's test() method when the value is invalid. We can do this as follows.

First, we remove the message attribute from the XML file. Then we modify the test() method as follows:

```
    public function test(& $element, $value, $group = null, & $input =
⇥null, & $form = null)
    {
        $max = (int) $element->getAttribute('maximum') ?
⇥$element->getAttribute('maximum') : 30;
        $min = (int) $element->getAttribute('minimum') ?
⇥$element->getAttribute('minimum') : 1;
        $result = ((int) $value >= $min && (int) $value <= $max);

        // Build JException object
        if ($result === false) {
            $result = new JException(JText::sprintf(
⇥'MOD_JOOMPRO_ARTICLES_AUTHOR_COUNTINTEGER_MESSAGE', $min, $max));
        }

        return $result;
```

We set `$max` and `$min` as before. Then we save the boolean `true` or `false` value in a variable called `$result`. If this is `false`, we set `$result` equal to a new `JException` object with our error message. Note that we use the `JText::sprintf()` method so we can show the values `$min` and `$max` in the message.

Then we return `$result`, which will either be a boolean `true`, if the field is valid, or the `JException` object with our message.

Finally, we need to change the `.ini` language file as follows:

```
MOD_JOOMPRO_ARTICLES_AUTHOR_COUNTINTEGER_MESSAGE="Article count must be
➥between %1$d and %2$d."
```

We use the values `%1$d` and `%2$d` to hold the places of the `$min` and `$max` values. These will be inserted into the message by the `JText::sprintf()` method. In this case, the error message to the user will be the same as the previous example. However, if we change the minimum or maximum attributes in the XML file, the message will change automatically.

🔒 List Validation

Recall in our module's XML file we included the attribute `validate="options"` for the `article_ordering` and `article_ordering_direction` parameters. This was to make sure that a hacker did not bypass the form validation and enter in some malicious SQL code. Let's look at how this validation works.

As in the previous example, when we define a validate attribute in a `JForm` field, a `JFormRule` class will be called when the `JForm` is saved, inside the form's `validate()` method. The value of the attribute must match the name of the class and file. In our case, the name of the attribute is "options," so the name of the file is `options.php` and the name of the class is `JFormRuleOptions`. The core rule classes are stored in the folder `libraries/joomla/form/rules`. Because this is a core rule, we don't have to include this path in the XML file with the `addrulepath` attribute.

Listing 6.15 shows the code for this file.

Listing 6.15   **libraries/joomla/form/rule/options.php File**

```php
<?php
/**
 * @package     Joomla.Platform
 * @subpackage  Form
 * @copyright   Copyright (C) 2005 - 2012 Open Source Matters, Inc. All
➥rights reserved.
 * @license     GNU General Public License version 2 or later; see
➥LICENSE.txt
 */

defined('_JEXEC') or die;

jimport('joomla.form.formrule');
/**
```

```
 * Form Rule class for the Joomla! Platform.
 * Requires the value entered be one of the options in a field of
↪type="list"
 *
 * @package    Joomla.Platform
 * @subpackage Form
 * @since      11.1
 */
class JFormRuleOptions extends JFormRule
{
    /**
     * Method to test the value.
     *
     * @param   object  $element  The JXMLElement object representing the
↪<field /> tag for the
     *                            form field object.
     * @param   mixed   $value    The form field value to validate.
     * @param   string  $group    The field name group control value. This
↪acts as as an array
     *                            container for the field. For example if
↪the field has name="foo"
     *                            and the group value is set to "bar" then
↪the full field name
     *                            would end up being "bar[foo]".
     * @param   object  $input    An optional JRegistry object with the
↪entire data set to validate
     *                            against the entire form.
     * @param   object  $form     The form object for which the field is
↪being tested.
     *
     * @return  boolean  True if the value is valid, false otherwise.
     *
     * @since   11.1
     * @throws  JException on invalid rule.
     */
    public function test(& $element, $value, $group = null, & $input =
↪null, & $form = null)
    {
        // Check each value and return true if we get a match
        foreach ($element->option as $option) {
            if ($value == $option->getAttribute('value')) {
                return true;
            }
        }
        return false;
    }
}
```

This file is very simple. As before, this class extends the `JFormRule` class and has only one method, `test()`. The `$element` variable contains the field element and the `$value` variable contains the value entered by the user.

Inside the `test()` method, the expression `$element->option` returns an array of `JXMLElement` objects, one for each `option` element in the `field` element. We loop through each of these options and check whether `$value` (the value entered by the user) is equal to the value attribute of the option element. As soon as we find a match, we exit and return a boolean `true`. If the entered value doesn't match any of the values in the array, we return a boolean `false`.

To try this out, change the form (for example, using Firebug) to enter an invalid value for the Article Ordering (for example, "xxx" instead of "a.title"). When you try to save the form, you should get the message `Invalid Field: Article Ordering` and the form will not save. If you remove the `validate="options"` from the XML file and try this again, the form will save.

We can see that `JForm` gives us a number of options for fine-tuning the validation of our data entry fields. We can use field types to limit the possible entries, filters to fix invalid data during the save process, and validation with rules to prevent the user from saving with invalid data. We can use standard rules or create our own rules. These methods can be mixed, matched, and customized to make the form work the way you want it to.

Help File

If we are planning to distribute our module, we will want to provide an on-screen help file. One option for doing this is to include a help URL in the XML file, as follows:

```
<help url="HELP_EXTENSIONS_MODULE_JOOMPRO_ARTICLES_AUTHOR_URL"/>
```

The help element needs to be directly under the extension element. By convention, we put it after the files and languages elements. (In our example, we don't have a languages element, so it goes just after the files element.)

In the language `.ini` file, we include a line that translates the language key to the URL. For example, if we had a file called

```
mod_joompro_articles_author_help.html
```

that contained our help screen text, we would have a line like the following in our language `.ini` file:

```
HELP_EXTENSIONS_MODULE_JOOMPRO_ARTICLES_AUTHOR_URL=
↪"http://joomlaprogrammingbook.com/mod_joompro_articles_author_help.html"
```

With this setup, when the user clicks on the Help icon in the toolbar when editing the module, the designated URL will load in the help window. By putting the URL in the language file, we allow for the possibility of different help screens based on the user's language.

Packaging the Module

At this point, we have a working module. Now we want to make it available to the Joomla universe. This is easy to do and is the same procedure we followed with the plugin extension. Here are the steps:

1. Update the module XML file (`mod_joompro_articles_author.xml`) to include the `countinteger.php` file we added earlier by adding the following filename element inside the files element:

   ```
   <filename>countinteger.php</filename>
   ```

2. Copy the contents of the folder `modules/mod_joompro_articles_author` to a temporary folder on your computer.

3. Use an archive program to create a zip archive of the files in this temporary folder. The contents of the archive should be the same as the contents of the `modules/mod_joompro_articles_author` folder. By convention, the archive file would be called something like `mod_joompro_articles_author_1.0.0.zip`. The last numbers allow for version numbers, since you might be releasing updates to the module.

Test that the archive file can be installed successfully by uninstalling the existing module and then installing it from the archive file.

Review of Our Module

Let's take a moment to review what we have accomplished with our module:

- It seamlessly integrates with the rest of the Joomla site. To the user, it appears as if it is part of Joomla.
- It fully supports multiple languages. We can create the two language files for any language and the module will show in that language.
- It fully supports alternative layouts and template layout overrides. Just by using the `getLayoutPath()` method to get the name of the layout file, we provide this powerful feature for our module.
- It allows the user to enter options (parameters) that control how the module works.
- It is secure and protects against SQL injection and other possible attacks to the site. By using the field types, filtering, and validation, we control the data entered by the user and keep out malicious data.
- It provides on-screen help.
- It can be installed and uninstalled on any site running Joomla version 1.6 or later.

That is an impressive list of features! We got these features simply by taking advantage of the capabilities offered by Joomla and by designing our module to follow standard Joomla practices.

Module Best Practices

Here are some best practices for modules:

- Don't return an error if the module has a database error. The module is normally not the main content on the page, so we don't need to halt processing or scare the user. In the future, a good approach will be to log the error and continue processing. That way, the issue can be fixed without disrupting the user's experience.

- Modules generally should be small and relatively quick (or lightweight). Keep in mind that your module is one of many that might be processing for a given page.

Summary

In this chapter, we looked in detail at a core module and then created our own module. Along the way, we saw how modules can be related to components and how the different types of files in a module work together. We also demonstrated some different possible techniques for validating and filtering data entered in forms.

In creating our own module, we took advantage of many aspects of the Joomla platform. The end result is a module that integrates seamlessly with the rest of Joomla.

Components Part I: Controllers and Models

Components are typically the largest and most complex extensions and require the most knowledge and perseverance to create. If you have gotten this far in the book, you are likely ready for the challenge.

This chapter begins the in-depth look at the model-view-controller (MVC) design pattern used by all core components in Joomla!. We do this by examining the back end of the Weblinks component.

We start with an overview of the component's files and then look in detail at the different tasks that the component can do. Then we explore how these tasks are implemented in the controller and model classes. We also discuss the `JTable` class and how it is used to work with the database.

What Is a Component?

A Joomla website contains two types of building blocks. One is the content that will be entered or displayed—for example, articles, contacts, products, and so on. The other is a set of menu items. These allow you to navigate through the site and work with the content. Both of these building blocks are based on components. In the back end of Joomla, administrative components are used to manage all the content in the site. In the front end, every menu item is based on a component.

Whenever we are doing any task other than simply displaying information, we normally use a component. For example, when we enter new information into the database, such as a new article, we use a component. When we click on a menu item, we are accessing a component.

As discussed in Chapter 3, each Joomla processing cycle begins by executing a component's starting file (for example, `components/com_content/content.php`). For core components, this invokes the programs that make up the component's MVC structure.

One point of possible confusion about components in Joomla is that we use components in the back end to create and manage the site. So we use back-end components to manage both front-end and back-end components, and we use components to manage all the other extension types: modules, plugins, languages, and templates. For example, the module manager is a back-end component, but its job is to help us create and manage modules on the site.

CRUD, Get, and Post

Another way to understand components is to think in terms of what we are asking Joomla to do. If we are simply asking to display information, we can do that in a module or a plugin. However, if we want the program to take an action—for example, to save some information to the database—we normally would do this in a component. In other words, any time we press a submit or save button in Joomla, there is normally a component that will process the request.

Most HTML forms use the attribute `method="post"` to process the form's contents. This is almost always the case when you want the program to take some type of action other than simply display something. The post method places the values entered in the form into the PHP `$_REQUEST` variable. In most cases, when we process a form in Joomla with the post method, we use a component to handle the result.

CRUD is an acronym that stands for create, read, update, delete. CRUD tasks (other than read) are the parts of a component's code that add, update, or delete rows in a table. Normally in Joomla, only components handle these CRUD tasks.

Components Are Unique

To summarize, components are the primary building blocks for a Joomla site. Components are

- The main building blocks of a Joomla website
- Used to maintain both the content of a site and the menus and menu items for the site
- The normal entry point for a Joomla processing cycle
- Used in the back end to manage all the administrative setup of the site
- Used to handle all the CRUD tasks for the database
- Normally used to handle any forms that use the post method

MVC Design Pattern

Before we dive into the details of a core component, let's quickly look at the MVC design pattern that all the core components use.

As with all design patterns for object-oriented programming (OOP), the MVC design pattern attempts to maximize our ability to reuse code (classes and methods) by separating out the different types of tasks required and creating different classes to do each of these tasks. Using MVC also makes the code easier to read, understand, and maintain. People familiar with the pattern can quickly understand the organization of the code.

Let's think about a typical session in Joomla where we are entering an article. Here is a summary of the events:

User: Clicks Add button in Article Manager.

Joomla: 1. Processes the button click and submits URL for the blank form.

2. Processes URL for blank form and displays it.

User: Enters information and clicks Save & Close button.

Joomla: 1. Processes the form.

2. Saves the article and related information to the database.

3. Creates the URL for the Article Manager with success message.

4. Processes the URL to display the Article Manager with success message.

The MVC design pattern divides these programming tasks into three groups. The Controller processes the user input. The model interacts with the database and "knows" how articles work. The view displays all the content on the page. By organizing the code in this way, we can make changes in one part of the component without having to change the other parts. For example, we could add a new view without having to change the controller or the model. If we add a new user action (for example, copy), we can add these to the controller and model but don't have to modify any existing code. If we need to change how articles work (for example, it must have some minimum metadata values), we only change the model. The view and controller are unaffected.

Given this, you might expect that a Joomla component would have three files: a model, a view, and a controller. Alas, real life is more complicated than that, and a complex component has many program files, as we see in the next section. However, these files are mostly organized into these three categories, so the pattern helps us organize and understand the code.

Back-End Weblinks Component

Let's start by looking at how the core Weblinks component works in the back end. This is a typical administrative component and is similar to many of the other back-end components for managing articles, users, modules, and so on.

Table 7.1 lists the programming files for the component. All these files are in the `administator/components/com_weblinks` folder. For the rest of this chapter, all Weblinks file names are relative to this home folder unless otherwise indicated.

Most of the files are organized according to the MVC pattern. All the view files are inside the views subfolder, and the primary model and controller files are inside their respective model and controller subfolders. We also have installation, configuration, and helper files mixed in.

Table 7.1 **Back-End Weblinks Component Files (Excludes index.html Files)**

File Name	Description	MVC Group
controllers/weblink.php	Primary controller for editing a single Weblink	Controller
controllers/weblinks.php	Primary controller for the Weblinks Manager list	Controller
helpers/weblinks.php	Provides miscellaneous methods used by the controllers and views	Miscellaneous
models/fields/ordering.php	Provides a custom JFormField to show the Weblinks ordering column in the Weblinks Manager	Model
models/forms/weblink.xml	XML file used by JForm to provide the fields for the add/edit weblink screen	Model
models/weblink.php	Model for the single Weblink screen	Model
models/weblinks.php	Model for the Weblinks Manager screen	Model
sql/install.mysql.utf8.sql	SQL file for creating the Weblinks table during installation	Installation
sql/uninstall.mysql.ut8.sql	SQL file for dropping (deleting) the Weblinks table during uninstall	Installation
tables/weblink.php	Provides the WeblinksTableWeblink class	Model
views/weblink/tmpl/ edit_metadata.php	Default layout file for editing the Weblink metadata	View
views/weblink/tmpl/edit_ params.php	Default layout file for editing single Weblink options	View
views/weblink/tmpl/edit.php	Default layout file for editing a Weblink	View
views/view.html.php	Primary view class for HTML output for single Weblink	View
views/weblinks/tmpl/ default.php	Default layout file for Weblinks Manager	View
views/weblinks/view.html .php	Primary view class for HTML output for Weblinks Manager	View
access.xml	XML file to provide the list of actions for the ACL	com_config file
config.xml	XML file to provide the list of options for the component configuration	com_config file
controller.php	Primary controller class	Controller
weblinks.php	Entry point for the request	Controller
weblinks.xml	XML file to control installation process	Installation

Installation Files

Three files execute when the component is installed or uninstalled. The two SQL files are SQL database scripts that are run by the install and uninstall program. In this case, the file `sql/install.mysql.utf8.sql` creates the `#__weblinks` table and the `sql/uninstall.mysql.ut8.sql` file deletes (or drops, in database jargon) the table. For some components, we might need to run a SQL script to populate the tables with data from other tables. If so, we would include this in the install script. The weblinks.xml file performs the same function as the XML files we created to install our example plugins and modules. It has the same elements for author, creationDate, and so on, as well as a list of the files and languages.

Note that all the core components are preinstalled when you first install Joomla. The installation folder has a file called `installation/sql/mysql/joomla.sql` that is run to populate the database tables with all the core extensions. A second SQL file, `installation/sql/mysql/sample_data.sql`, is executed if you install the default sample data. However, many core extensions can be uninstalled using the Extension Manager. In this case, the installation XML file is used to control the uninstall process.

Components Menu

When we create a component, we normally require one or more menu options in the administrative back end to manage the component. Menus in the Joomla back end are created differently from menus in the front end. Front-end menu items are defined by the site administrator using the back-end com_menus component. On the back end, menu options are added to the Components menu when components are installed. These options are defined in the component's XML file.

For example, in the `weblinks.xml` file, inside the administration element, we see the following code:

```
<menu img="class:weblinks">Weblinks</menu>
 <submenu>
 <!--
  Note that all & must be escaped to &amp; for the file to be valid
  XML and be parsed by the installer
 -->
 <menu link="index.php?option=com_weblinks" view="links"
↪img="class:weblinks"
  alt="Weblinks/Links">Links</menu>
 <menu link="index.php?option=com_categories&amp;extension=com_weblinks"
  view="categories" img="class:weblinks-cat"
↪alt="Weblinks/Categories">Categories
 </menu>
</submenu>
```

These menu elements are used to add rows to the `#__menus` table when the component is installed. These rows are used to create the Components menu options in the Joomla back end, as shown in Figure 7.1.

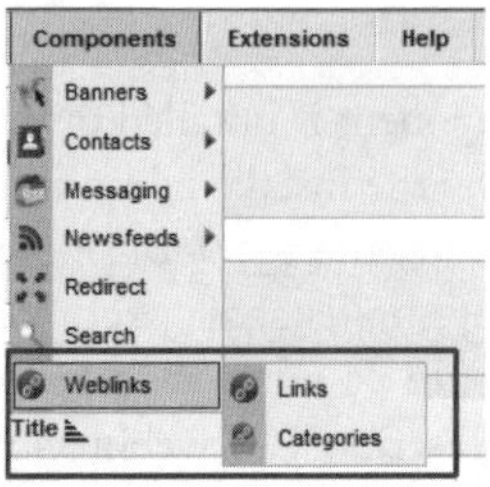

Figure 7.1   Weblinks menu options

We discuss the format of the menu element when we create our own component in Chapter 9.

Component Options (Parameters)

Component options are more complicated and more flexible than options for other extensions. For plugins, languages, modules, and templates, the `config` element from the installation XML file is read when the extension is created or edited to create the options for the extension. The set of options is defined for each instance of the extension.

For components, we can set component options at two or more levels. Global options can be set using the Options icon on the toolbar in the manager screen. Global options are used by the core components to set default options for new menu items. This process calls the back-end component com_config. It uses two XML files, `config.xml` and `access.xml`, to create a modal window with the options for the component. Each fieldset element in the `config.xml` file corresponds to a tab in the options window. By convention, the last fieldset is called permissions and has one field as follows:

```
<field name="rules" type="rules"
    component="com_weblinks"
    filter="rules"
    validate="rules"
    label="JCONFIG_PERMISSIONS_LABEL"
    section="component" />
```

We discuss this in detail when we create our front-end component in Chapter 10.

Helper Methods

Two helper methods are used in the Weblinks back end. These are provided by the file `helpers/weblinks.php.` Helper classes are used to hold small methods that might be used in several places in the component and don't fit into the model, view, or component.

The method `addSubmenu()` adds the submenu that displays on the Weblinks Manager screen, as shown in Figure 7.2.

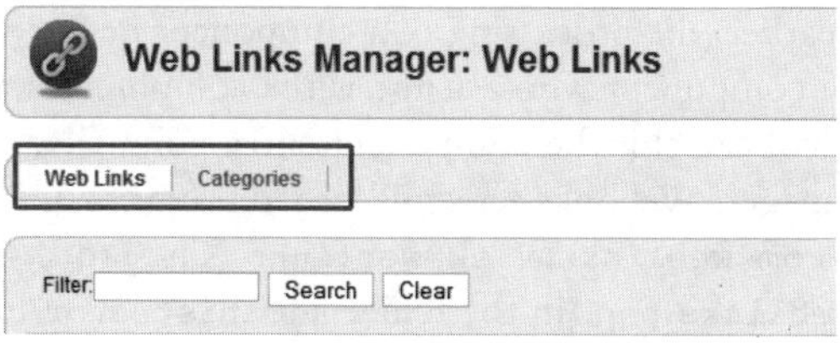

Figure 7.2   Weblinks submenu

These are not to be confused with the submenus in the Components menu, shown in Figure 7.1. Those submenus are created based on the component's XML file during the component installation. These submenus are rendered as links on the Weblinks Manager screen and provide navigation between the two manager screens: Weblinks and Categories.

The second method, `getActions()`, is used to determine what actions a user is allowed for the component. The Weblinks Manager screen has a toolbar as shown in Figure 7.3.

The Weblinks Manager: Weblink screen has the toolbar shown in Figure 7.4.

If a user doesn't have permissions for one or more of these actions, the icon is not shown in the toolbar. The `getActions()` method returns an object that lists the possible actions for the component and whether the current user has permission for the action. This is used by the views to determine which toolbars to show.

 As discussed elsewhere, it is important to remember that the feature of showing users only those toolbars that they have permissions for is a user-interface benefit but does not protect against a hacker trying an unauthorized action. These toolbar actions can still be attempted by a user who edits the PHP `$_REQUEST` variable directly in the browser, even if the button is not present. Therefore, removing the toolbar button is not a substitute for checking the user's permissions in the controller or model before performing each task.

Weblinks Component Entry Point

Now let's look more closely at the way the MVC design pattern works. We will start with the controller, because that is where the processing starts.

Figure 7.3   Weblinks Manager toolbar

Figure 7.4   Weblinks Manager: Weblink toolbar

As we have seen earlier, the processing of a component begins with the file at the root folder of the component whose name is the component name, without the "com_" letters. We will call this the component entry point file.

The Weblinks Manager: Weblinks screen is loaded using the URL administrator/ index.php?option=com_weblinks&view=weblinks. The processing of this URL starts with the file weblinks.php (in the folder administrator/com_weblinks/). This file is shown in Listing 7.1.

Listing 7.1   **administrator/com_weblinks/weblinks.php File**

```php
<?php
/**
 * @package     Joomla.Administrator
 * @subpackage com_weblinks
 * @copyright  Copyright (C) 2005 - 2012 Open Source Matters, Inc. All
➥rights reserved.
 * @license       GNU General Public License version 2 or later; see
➥LICENSE.txt
 */

// no direct access
defined('_JEXEC') or die;

// Access check.
if (!JFactory::getUser()->authorise('core.manage', 'com_weblinks')) {
        return JError::raiseWarning(404, JText::_('JERROR_ALERTNOAUTHOR'));
}

// Include dependancies
jimport('joomla.application.component.controller');

$controller = JController::getInstance('Weblinks');
$controller->execute(JRequest::getCmd('task'));
$controller->redirect();
```

This file is a PHP script and does not declare any classes. Therefore, it is executed immediately when it is loaded.

The first thing the script does, after the defined statement, is to check that the user has permission for the **core.manage** action for Weblinks. The **core.manage** action is required before a user can do any back-end management tasks for the core components. By putting this check here, we prevent an unauthorized user from accessing the screen by directly typing the URL into the browser.

The next line imports the **JController** class (libraries/joomla/application/ component/controller.php).

The last three lines of code are as follows:

```
$controller = JController::getInstance('Weblinks');
$controller->execute(JRequest::getCmd('task'));
$controller->redirect();
```

These three lines of code are very important for understanding how the Joomla MVC pattern works for components. The first line uses the `JController` class to get an instance of the controller we need for our present task. The second line uses that controller object to execute the task. The third line then executes the controller's `redirect()` method to take us to the next URL, if any.

Virtually all the core components have these same lines of code in their entry script. If we understand how this works in com_weblinks, we will have a great start in understanding MVC throughout Joomla.

Weblinks Controller in Action

Let's look as how this works when a user performs some typical actions with the Weblinks Manager in the Joomla back end.

Example 1: User Selects Components -> Weblinks Menu Option

In this example, the user selects the Weblinks option from the Components menu. The URL for this is `administrator/index.php?option=com_weblinks`. The `get-Instance()` method finds the correct controller class for the specified task. In this example, no task is specified, so we do the default task, which is "display".

For the display task, the base Weblinks controller, `WeblinksController` (`controller.php`), is used.

The second line performs the `execute()` method for the given task. Again, since the task is not specified, the default "display" task is performed. This runs the `display()` method of the `WeblinksContoller`. This method displays the Weblinks Manager screen and does not set a redirect value.

The third line executes the `WeblinksController redirect()` method. Since there is no redirect specified, this method simply returns a boolean `false` and the manager screen displays.

The key values for this example are as follows:

- URL: `administrator/index.php?option=com_weblinks`
- Task: none (defaults to display)
- Controller: WeblinksController (`controller.php`)
- Controller Method executed: `display()`
- Controller Redirect: empty

Example 2: User Clicks a Weblink Title To Edit

The information for the first part of this example is as follows:

- URL: `administrator/index.php?option=com_weblinks&task=weblink.edit&id=7`
- Task: weblink.edit
- Controller: WeblinksControllerWeblink (`controllers/weblink.php`)

- Controller Method executed: `JControllerForm->edit()`
- Controller Redirect: `index.php?option=com_weblinks&view=weblink&layout=edit&id=7`

The URL specifies the task of "weblink.edit". This tells the `getInstance()` method of `JController` to find a controller named `WebinksControllerWeblink`. This name is created as follows:

```
<component name> + Controller + <first segment of task name>.
```

The `getInstance()` method of `JController` (`libraries/joomla/application/component/controller.php`) contains the following code to process the task:

```
// Check for a controller.task command.
if (strpos($command, '.') !== false) {
 // Explode the controller.task command.
 list($type, $task) = explode('.', $command);

 // Define the controller filename and path.
 $file = self::createFileName('controller', array('name' => $type,
 ↳'format' => $format));
 $path = $basePath.'/controllers/'.$file;

 // Reset the task without the contoller context.
 JRequest::setVar('task', $task);
```

This code breaks the task name into segments using the period character. In our example, "weblink.edit" becomes an array where the type is "weblink" and the task is "edit". The type becomes the third part of the controller class name (the "Weblink" in `WeblinksCon-trollerWeblink`). Then, the request variable for task is changed to include only the second segment. In our example, `$_REQUEST['task']` is changed from `weblink.edit` to `edit`.

When we get to the `$controller->execute()` line, we are executing the edit task of the `WeblinksControllerWeblink` class. This class does not have its own `edit()` method, so it executes that method from its parent class, `JControllerForm` (`libraries/joomla/application/component/controllerform.php`). This method checks to make sure the current user can edit the given item and that the item is not checked out to another user. If everything is OK, the id of the item is saved in the user's session variable. This is used in the next step, when we process the redirect and actually load the item for editing.

The last step is to create the redirect. This gives Joomla a new URL to load. In our case, the redirect URL is

```
index.php?option=com_weblinks&view=weblink&layout=edit&id=7
```

Since we are in the back end, the word "administrator" is added to the front of the URL when it is processed by the `redirect()` method.

Processing the redirect URL starts a second request cycle. The information for this is as follows:

- URL: administrator/index.php?option=com_weblinks&view=weblink &layout=edit&id=7
- Task: none (defaults to display)
- Controller: WeblinksController (controller.php)
- Controller Method executed: WeblinksController->edit()
- Controller Redirect: none

Since the URL contains no task, we again use the base WeblinksController and we again execute the default display() method. If we look at that method, we see the following code:

```
$view = JRequest::getCmd('view', 'weblinks');
$layout = JRequest::getCmd('layout', 'default');
$id = JRequest::getInt('id');

// Check for edit form.
if ($view == 'weblink' && $layout == 'edit' &&
!$this->checkEditId('com_weblinks.edit.weblink', $id)) {
    // Somehow the person just went to the form - we don't allow that.
    $this->setError(JText::sprintf('JLIB_APPLICATION_ERROR_UNHELD_ID',
$id));
    $this->setMessage($this->getError(), 'error');
    $this->setRedirect(
JRoute::_('index.php?option=com_weblinks&view=weblinks', false));

 return false;
}
```

Recall that in the previous cycle we saved the item id in the session variable. In the checkEditId() method, we check the current item id to make sure it matches what we saved before. Why do we need to do this?

In the previous request cycle, we checked that the user was authorized to edit this item and that the item was not already checked out to another. We don't want to redo those checks, but we need to guard against a hacker who tries to edit an item by directly entering a URL like the one we used to load the edit form. By checking against the session information stored in the previous cycle, we know that this is the same user we already checked.

If everything is OK, we continue with the display() method of the WeblinksController class. This time we have a view and layout specified, so we display the edit form instead of the manager form. Since we have no redirect, the edit form displays.

To summarize, we do one request cycle to check that the user can edit this item. That process creates a redirect URL to actually display the edit form.

Example 3: User Clicks Save & Close In Edit Form

The key values for this action are as follows:

- URL: `administrator/index.php?option=com_weblinks&layout=edit&id=7`
- Task: weblink.save
- Controller: WeblinksControllerWeblink (`controllers/weblink.php`)
- Controller Method executed: `JControllerForm->save()`
- Controller Redirect: `administrator/index.php?option=com_weblinks&view=weblinks`

In this example, the URL does not contain a task segment. Instead, the task comes from the edit form. The Save & Close icon contains the following attribute:

```
onclick="javascript:Joomla.submitbutton('weblink.save')"
```

When it is clicked, it executes a JavaScript function that puts the value "weblink.save" into a form field called "task" and submits the form. This puts the task in the request array.

As before, we get the third part of the controller name from the first segment of the task, so our controller is `WeblinksControllerWeblink`. We execute the `save()` method of this controller. Because this controller doesn't have its own `save()` method, we execute the `save()` method of the parent class, `JControllerForm`.

There we get the model class for this controller. Then we again check to make sure the item id matches what we have stored in the session. As before, this ensures that a hacker hasn't tried to save an item without proper permission. Then we make sure the user has permission to save the item. Next, we validate the data using the `validate()` method of the loaded model. Next, we save the data using the model's `save()` method. If these are successful, we set the message to indicate that the save was successful.

The last thing we do is set the redirect. This depends on whether we are doing a Save, a Save & Close, or a Save & New. For the Save & Close, we remove the lock on the item and set the redirect to load the Weblinks Manager. When this redirect is executed, it will follow exactly the same cycle as in Example 1.

By separating the save into two request cycles—one for the save action and one for the redirect—we can use the same `save()` method for the different save actions. The first cycle is the same for all these actions. The difference is where the user is redirected. For the Save action, the user stays in the edit screen. For the Save & New, the user is taken to a new blank edit screen. In our example, the Save & Close, the user is taken back to the Weblinks Manager screen.

Example 4: User Trashes Some Weblinks

In this example, the user has checked the check box for one or more Weblink items in the Weblinks Manager and then presses the Trash icon in the toolbar. The key values are as follows:

- URL: `administrator/index.php?option=com_weblinks&view=weblinks`
- Task: weblinks.trash

- Controller: WeblinksControllerWeblinks (`controllers/weblinks.php`)
- Controller Method executed: `JControllerAdmin->publish()`
- Controller Redirect: `administrator/index.`
  `php?option=com_weblinks&view=weblinks`

The URL for this example simply returns us to the Weblinks Manager screen. The task "weblink.trash" comes from JavaScript, which is initiated by the onclick attribute of the toolbar icon anchor element. This attribute is as follows:

```
onclick="javascript:
if (document.adminForm.boxchecked.value==0){
  alert('Please first make a selection from the list');
} else {
  Joomla.submitbutton('weblinks.trash')
}"
```

The toolbars on the back-end manager screens are provided by the administrative module mod_toolbar. The JavaScript code for the Trash icon is created for us by the `JButtonStandard` class (`libraries/joomla/html/toolbar/button/standard.php`). It works in a manner similar to the JavaScript code in the previous example, except that this code first checks that at least one item has been selected. If so, it enters the value "weblinks. trash" in the form element whose name equals "task" and then submits the form.

Since the first segment of the task is "weblinks," we get the controller named `WeblinksControllerWeblinks`. The second segment of the task is "trash." However, the controller method we execute is `publish()`. How do we get from a task called "trash" to a method called `publish()`?

Mapping Tasks to Methods

The answer is that we use an array field called `$taskMap` in the `JController` class to map tasks to methods. This field is created in the constructor method of the controller. Then, in the `execute()` method of the `JController` class, we look up the task in the `$taskMap` array and execute the controller method for that task.

Let's look at how this works. Note: If you are unfamiliar with constructors and their role in OOP, see the sidebar called "Constructor Methods."

Constructor Methods

If you are new to OOP, it is important to understand the special role of the constructor method. A constructor is a method that executes automatically when an object is created using the new command. For example, the code

```
$registry = new JRegistry();
```

creates a new `JRegistry` object and executes the constructor method for that class before returning the object to `$registry`.

In PHP, the constructor is called "__construct." It is used to initiate values for the object. It can take arguments and doesn't return any values. A constructor can call the constructor of its parent class with the following syntax:

```
parent::__construct();
```

As with other methods, if a class contains no constructor method, the constructor of the parent class is executed, if defined. In older PHP versions, a constructor was named using the class name for the constructor method (for example, jregistry() for the JRegistry class) instead of __construct(). PHP will look for a method with the class name if no __construct() method exists. In Joomla, all constructors are named __construct().

The first line of the constructor for the JControllerAdmin class is as follows:

```
public function __construct($config = array())
{
  parent::__construct($config);
```

This calls the constructor of the parent JController class. That constructor method uses a technique known as reflection to build an array of all the class's public methods, using the following code:

```
// Determine the methods to exclude from the base class.
$xMethods = get_class_methods('JController');

// Get the public methods in this class using reflection.
$r = new ReflectionClass($this);
$rName = $r->getName();
$rMethods = $r->getMethods(ReflectionMethod::IS_PUBLIC);
$methods = array();

foreach ($rMethods as $rMethod)
{
  $mName = $rMethod->getName();

  // Add default display method if not explicitly declared.
  if (!in_array($mName, $xMethods) || $mName == 'display') {
    $this->methods[] = strtolower($mName);
    // Auto register the methods as tasks.
    $this->taskMap[strtolower($mName)] = $mName;
  }
}
```

This code populates the taskMap field with an associative array where both the key and values contain the names of all public methods in the class, excluding methods in the parent JController class. Also, a display method is always added (because it exists in the JController class). If you are new to OOP and to the idea of public, private, and protected methods and fields, see the sidebar entitled "Access Modifiers: Public, Protected, and Private."

A few lines down in the same method, we find the following code:

```
// If the default task is set, register it as such
if (array_key_exists('default_task', $config)) {
 $this->registerDefaultTask($config['default_task']);
}
else {
 $this->registerDefaultTask('display');
}
```

This code adds the default task with the key of "__default" and a value of "display". This way, if no task is specified, Joomla knows what to do with the request. For core components, this is normally the display task.

Let's look at how this works in our current example. When we run the JController::getInstance() method, we create a new WeblinksControllerWeblinks controller class. Because WeblinksControllerWeblinks has no constructor, the parent JControllerAdmin constructor is executed. The first line, as shown earlier, executes the parent constructor, which builds the taskMap array. The class Weblinks-ControllerWeblinks only defines one method, called getModel(). Because this method exists in JController, it is excluded from the taskMap array.

The parent class, JControllerAdmin, defines the following methods: checkin(), delete(), display(), publish(), reorder(), and saveorder(). Of these, only the display() method is also defined in JController, and this is explicitly added to the array. So all these methods are added to the array. Also, the JController constructor explicitly adds an element with the key of __default that defaults to display.

After the parent constructor from JController executes, taskMap has the values shown in Table 7.2.

The next section of the JControllerAdmin constructor method is as follows:

Table 7.2 **taskMap Array Values after JController Constructor**

Key (Task)	Value (Method to Execute)
delete	delete
display	display
publish	publish
reorder	reorder
saveorder	saveorder
checkin	checkin
__default	display

Table 7.3 **taskMap Array Values after registerTask Code**

Key (Task)	Value (Method to Execute)
delete	delete
display	display
publish	publish
reorder	reorder
saveorder	saveorder
checkin	checkin
__default	display
unpublish	publish
archive	publish
trash	publish
report	publish
orderup	reorder
orderdown	reorder

```
// Define standard task mappings.
$this->registerTask('unpublish',    'publish');    // value = 0
$this->registerTask('archive',      'publish');    // value = 2
$this->registerTask('trash',        'publish');    // value = -2
$this->registerTask('report',       'publish');    // value = -3
$this->registerTask('orderup',      'reorder');
$this->registerTask('orderdown',    'reorder');
```

This is where the additional tasks get mapped to the corresponding methods. For example, the highlighted line maps the "trash" task to the "publish" method by adding an element with the key "trash" and the value "publish." After this code has executed, the taskMap array has the values shown in Table 7.3.

This technique provides a combination of simplicity and flexibility. If we name our tasks to match our controller methods, we don't have to do any work to create the mapping. Joomla does it for us. If we want to modify the mapping, we can use the `registerTask()` method as shown above.

In our example, it makes sense to use the same method for the publish, unpublish, archive, trash, and report tasks. All these tasks simply change the value of the "state" column in the `#__weblinks` table.

Access Modifiers: Public, Protected, and Private

If you are new to OOP, it is important to understand the difference between public, protected, and private methods and fields.

Public methods can be called from any class or script.

Protected methods can only be called from inside an instance of the current class or a subclass of the current class.

Private methods can only be called from inside an instance of the current class.

Why do we have this distinction? The answer is that when we create a class, we typically create some methods that we expect to be used by other classes. Those will typically be the reason we created the class in the first place and those methods will normally be public.

To keep our methods small and well focused, we might also create one or more helper methods whose job is to support our main public methods. We don't want "outsiders" using these methods. For example, we might change our mind and reorganize these helper methods, and we want to be sure that we can do this without breaking some code elsewhere in the program. If we declare these helper methods private, we can be sure they won't be called from outside the current class.

Protected methods are an in-between case. They can be used by subclasses of the current class, but not by unrelated classes.

The same concept applies to fields in classes. Public fields can be accessed by any class, private fields only by instances of this class, and protected by instances of this class and its subclasses.

If a method or field is created with no access modifier, it is assumed to be public.

When we speak of the API (application programming interface) for a class, we refer to the public methods and fields. Normally, we don't want to change the API unless we need to. Protected and private methods and fields are not part of the API, so we are free to change these without affecting programs that rely on the API.

Earlier versions of PHP did not enforce this restriction. To substitute for this, a naming convention was used. If a method or field name started with an underscore "_", it was considered private and developers were not supposed to use these outside the current class. For this reason, you will see protected and private methods and fields sometimes named this way.

Using the Model

Now let's look at the `publish()` method in `JControllerAdmin`. The first part of the method is as follows:

```
function publish()
{
 // Check for request forgeries
 JRequest::checkToken() or die(JText::_('JINVALID_TOKEN'));
```

This code checks that we got to this point from within a Joomla form. This prevents a hacker from trying to access the method directly from a browser without first logging in to Joomla.

Later in the method, we have the following code:

```
// Get items to publish from the request.
$cid = JRequest::getVar('cid', array(), '', 'array');
$data = array('publish' => 1, 'unpublish' => 0, 'archive'=> 2,
➥'trash' => -2, 'report'=>-3);
$task  = $this->getTask();
```

This code gets the list of ids from the request. In our example, these are the ids that we want to change to trashed. Then we build an associative array that maps the integer values of the state column to the tasks. For example, for the "publish" task, we will change the value to 1. For the "trash" task, we will change it to −2.

Then we get the task using the getTask() method. The task value is saved when a task is executed using the following code from the JController execute() method:

```
public function execute($task)
{
 $this->task = $task;
```

Recall that the task in the request was changed in the getInstance() method so that we only have the second segment when we call the execute() method. In our example, we started with a task called "weblinks.trash" and this was changed to "trash". The line of code above saves the modified task ("trash") in the $task field of the JController class so it is available using the getTask() method when we need it.

The next line of code in the publish() method is as follows:

```
$value  = JArrayHelper::getValue($data, $task, 0, 'int');
```

This gets the value of the new state based on the associative array we created.

At this point, we know what task we are doing and we know the new value we need to set the state column equal to. The next portion of this method is as follows:

```
if (empty($cid)) {
 JError::raiseWarning(500, JText::_($this->
➥text_prefix.'_NO_ITEM_SELECTED'));
}
else {
 // Get the model.
 $model = $this->getModel();
```

This gives an error if we don't have any items to process. Otherwise, we process the task.

The next thing we do is invoke the getModel() method. This is a very important line of code. First, it is important to understand what class we are in. Even though we are executing code from the JControllerAdmin class, we are actually in the Web-linksControllerWeblinks class. We got here because the publish() method does not exist in the current class, so it is inherited from the parent class. So in the code

```
$this->getModel()
```

`$this` refers to the `WeblinksControllerWeblinks` class.

It is fundamental to the MVC design pattern that the controller "knows" how to get the right model for the task being executed. That's what `getModel()` does. In fact, if we look at the `WeblinksControllerWeblinks` class, we see that this is the *only* method in the class! The entire code for this class is as follows:

```
class WeblinksControllerWeblinks extends JControllerAdmin
{
 /**
  * Proxy for getModel.
  * @since     1.6
  */
 public function getModel($name = 'Weblink', $prefix = 'WeblinksModel',
➥$config = array('ignore_request' => true))
 {
   $model = parent::getModel($name, $prefix, $config);
   return $model;
 }
}
```

All this method—and class—does is provide the information needed to find the correct model for this controller. In this case, the model class name is `WeblinksModelWeblink` (note the second "Weblink" is singular, not plural).

Here we see a great example of how OOP and the MVC design pattern allow us to reuse code. The only thing unique about this particular controller is the name of the model it requires. So that is the only code it contains. All the other methods used by this class are inherited from its parent classes. This is true of many controllers in the back end of Joomla. For example, in Joomla version 2.5, there are 17 classes that extend the `JControllerAdmin` class. Of those, seven contain only a `getModel()` method. Most of the others also contain very little code and mostly use the code from their parent classes.

Now let's get back to the `publish()` method in the controller (`JControllerAdmin`). Once we have the model, the next block of code is as follows:

```
// Make sure the item ids are integers
JArrayHelper::toInteger($cid);

// Publish the items.
if (!$model->publish($cid, $value)) {
 JError::raiseWarning(500, $model->getError());
}
```

The first line uses a method in the `JArrayHelper` class to make sure all the array values are integers. Recall that these values came from the request, so we need to practice defensive programming to protect against hackers. Whenever we know something from the request should be an integer, it is good practice to cast it as an integer. This provides great protection, since integers cannot contain any special characters used to inject malicious code. That is also why it is a good design practice to use integers for id numbers and for columns like published state.

The next `if` block actually does the work. It calls the `publish()` method of the model, which returns a boolean `true` if the method succeeds. If the `publish()` method returns a boolean `false`, something went wrong and we show the error information from the model.

We discuss models later in this chapter and will discuss the `publish()` method there. However, it is important to note that this is the only interaction between the controller and the model for this task. First, we got the right model with the `getModel()` method. Then we called the desired method from the model. The only thing the controller "knows" about the model is its name and the name of the method to call for each task. As long as the model has the right name and the right methods, it can be modified without fear of breaking anything in the controller.

We frequently name the methods in the model to mirror the methods in the controller. Although not necessary, it makes it easier to follow the code.

The next portion of the controller's `publish()` method is as follows:

```
else {
    if ($value == 1) {
     $ntext = $this->text_prefix.'_N_ITEMS_PUBLISHED';
    }
    else if ($value == 0) {
     $ntext = $this->text_prefix.'_N_ITEMS_UNPUBLISHED';
    }
    else if ($value == 2) {
     $ntext = $this->text_prefix.'_N_ITEMS_ARCHIVED';
    }
    else {
     $ntext = $this->text_prefix.'_N_ITEMS_TRASHED';
    }
    $this->setMessage(JText::plural($ntext, count($cid)));
 }
}
```

This is the code block that is processed if the model's `publish()` method succeeds. It creates the correct message to show for each task. Note that the last line uses the `JText::plural()` method that was added in Joomla version 1.6. This method makes it easier to show messages that list counts of items with the correct plural forms for each language.

The last part of the `publish()` method is as follows:

```
$extension = JRequest::getCmd('extension');
$extensionURL = ($extension) ? '&extension=' .
```

```
↪JRequest::getCmd('extension') : '';
 $this->setRedirect(JRoute::_('index.php?option='.
↪$this->option.'&view='.$this->view_list.$extensionURL, false));
}
```

This code sets the redirect. In our example, we don't have an extension in the request, so the redirect comes from the option ("com_weblinks") and the view_list ("weblinks"). This takes us back to the Weblinks Manager screen. Because we set the message showing the success message, that message will show on that screen.

Weblinks Controller Tasks, Classes, and Methods

With this in mind, let's look at the methods in the three Weblinks controllers and how they map to the component's tasks.

As we saw earlier, the `WeblinksController` class (`controller.php`) contains the `display()` method that handles the default display task. Display is the only task this controller executes, and it is the only controller that displays anything.

The class `WeblinksControllerWeblinks` controls the Weblinks Manager screen. It extends the `JControllerAdmin` class, which in turn extends `JController`. As we discussed earlier, `WeblinksControllerWeblinks` itself contains only one method, `getModel()`. This method, although public, is not included in the taskMap array because it is also found in the `JController` class and `JController`'s methods are excluded from taskMap. Because `JControllerAdmin` extends `JController`, the methods added to taskMap are the public methods contained in `JControllerAdmin` that are not found in `JController`.

Figure 7.5 is a screenshot from the Eclipse Type Hierarchy view showing the inheritance for `WeblinksControllerWeblinks` and the methods for `JControllerAdmin`.

Here we see that the public methods (with the circle) are the ones used to perform the tasks. As discussed earlier, in the constructor method, we map some additional tasks to the `publish()` and `saveorder()` methods. The small triangle to the left of the `display()` method indicates that this is overriding a display method from a parent

Figure 7.5   JControllerAdmin methods

class. The `display()` method is explicitly added to the taskMap array even though it exists in `JController`. However, the `display()` method in `JControllerAdmin` simply returns a false value and is never executed.

The third controller class is `WeblinksControllerWeblink` (`controllers/weblink .php`). The name is the same as the previous except that the third segment is singular ("Weblink") instead of plural ("Weblinks"). This class controls the add/edit screen, where we are working with a single Weblink item. This naming convention—plural for the manager screen and singular for the edit screen—is used throughout the core Joomla components (although it is not required, as we see when we build our own component in Chapter 9).

The `WeblinksControllerWeblink` class itself only contains two private methods. The methods mapped in the taskMap array come from its parent class, `JControllerForm`. Its methods and the type hierarchy are shown in the Eclipse screenshot in Figure 7.6.

The public methods added to the taskMap are `add()`, `cancel()`, `edit()`, and `save()`. If we look at the constructor method for `JControllerForm`, we see the following code:

```
$this->registerTask('apply', 'save');
$this->registerTask('save2new', 'save');
$this->registerTask('save2copy', 'save');
```

This maps the tasks apply, save2new, and save2copy to the `save()` method.

We can now summarize all the tasks that a user may perform in the back end with the Weblinks component. Table 7.4 shows the mapping of each toolbar icon in the Weblinks Manager: Weblinks screen (the list of Weblinks).

Table 7.5 shows the mapping for the Weblinks Manager: Weblink screen (adding or editing a single Weblink).

Figure 7.6   JControllerForm methods and type hierarchy

Table 7.4 **Weblinks Manager: Weblinks Screen Tasks**

Toolbar Icon	Task	Controller	Method
New	weblink.add	WeblinksControllerWeblink	add()
Edit	weblink.edit	WeblinksControllerWeblink	edit()
Publish	weblinks.publish	WeblinksControllerWeblinks	publish()
Unpublish	weblinks.unpublish	WeblinksControllerWeblinks	publish()
Archive	weblinks.archive	WeblinksControllerWeblinks	publish()
Check In	weblinks.checkin	WeblinksControllerWeblinks	checkin()
Trash	weblinks.trash	WeblinksControllerWeblinks	publish()
Empty Trash	weblinks.delete	WeblinksControllerWeblinks	delete()
Order Up Arrow	weblinks.orderup	WeblinksControllerWeblinks	reorder()
Order Down Arrow	weblinks.orderdown	WeblinksControllerWeblinks	reorder()
Save Order	weblinks.saveorder	WeblinksControllerWeblinks	saveorder()

Table 7.5 **Weblinks Manager: Weblink Screen Tasks**

Toolbar Icon	Task	Controller	Method
Save	weblink.apply	WeblinksControllerWeblink	save()
Save & Close	weblink.save	WeblinksControllerWeblink	save()
Save & New	weblink.save2new	WeblinksControllerWeblink	save()
Save as Copy	weblink.save2copy	WeblinksControllerWeblink	save()
Close	weblink.cancel	WeblinksControllerWeblink	cancel()

With this information, we know exactly where each task is executed. If we want to add a new task, we can either map it to an existing controller method in the class constructor and add logic to the mapped method or add a new method to the controller class whose name matches the name of the new task. If we want to add a new management screen, we can add a new controller for this screen with its own tasks and methods.

Review of Controllers in Components

Let's review what we've learned about the role of controllers. The entry point of an MVC component contains three commands:

- Get the controller for this task.
- Execute the task using the controller.
- Execute the redirect, if any.

The controller class name follows rules based on the component name and the task name. If the task is something other than display, the task is executed and a redirect is set to display the desired page. If the task is not given, it defaults to display, which displays the page and doesn't have a redirect.

Tasks are mapped to methods in the controller. Executing a task runs the controller method mapped to that task. The method name can be the same as the task name or can be mapped using the `registerTask()` method.

Weblinks Models

Now that we understand how the controllers work, let's look at the Weblinks models. There are two primary model classes for Weblinks, `WeblinksModelWeblink` (models/weblink.php) and `WeblinksModelWeblinks` (models/weblinks.php). These follow the same naming convention as the controllers. `WeblinksModelWeblink` provides the methods to support the controller tasks that apply to individual Weblink items. `WeblinksModelWeblinks` provides the methods to display the list of Weblinks on the Weblinks Manager: Weblinks form.

Let's start by looking at how the controller tasks are supported by the `Weblinks ModelWeblink` class. First, we need to know which model class to use. How do we link the controllers to the models? Recall that in the `WeblinksControllerWeblinks` (plural) class, we override the `getModel()` method to explicitly load the `Weblinks ModelWeblink` model. This links this controller to this model. In the case of `Web linksControllerWeblink` (singular), we don't have a `getModel()` method. When we execute `getModel()` inside this class, we use the method from the parent class `JControllerForm`. That method is as follows:

```
public function getModel($name = '', $prefix = '',
➥$config = array('ignore_request' => true))
{
 if (empty($name)) {
    $name = $this->context;
 }

 return parent::getModel($name, $prefix, $config);
}
```

This method sets the `$name` variable from the context field of the class. The context field is set in the constructor to the word that follows the word "Controller" in the class name. In this case, since the class name is `WeblinksControllerWeblink`, the context field is set to "weblink." Then we execute the parent's (`JController`) `get Model()` method with the name equal to this value. This does a similar process to get the first part of the model name. If the `$prefix` variable is empty (which it is in our case), we use the field called `model_prefix`. This is set one of two ways: (1) from an array element in the `$config` argument for the constructor, or (2) from the first part of the class name.

In our case, we haven't specified a `model_prefix` in the `$config`, so we use the normal naming convention. The end result of all this is that the default model name is the same as the controller name with the word "Controller" replaced by the word "Model." However, you can easily override this convention. Simply specify a value for `model_prefix` in the `$config` array when the model is instantiated (created).

Next, let's look at how the model supports the tasks initiated in the controllers. Tables 7.3 and 7.4 show the controller methods that are called for each task a user can do in Weblinks. The `add()`, `edit()`, and `cancel()` methods in the `WeblinksControllerWeblink` class are called when we load or close the edit screen. There are no corresponding methods in the model.

The `add()` method just checks to see if the user is authorized to add a Weblink item. If so, it sets the redirect to open the edit screen for a new Weblink item. It does not access any of the model's methods.

The `edit()` method also checks for the user's permissions. In addition, it uses the model's `getTable()` , `checkout()`, and `getError()` methods to make sure the item is not checked out and to flag it as checked out before starting the edit session. Then the redirect is set to open the selected item for editing.

The `cancel()` method uses the model's `checkin()` method to check in the item and then it redirects back to the Weblinks Manager: Weblinks screen.

The other methods are `publish()`, `checkin()`, `delete()`, `reorder()`, `save()`, and `saveorder()`. These call corresponding methods in the model. Figure 7.7 shows the methods available in `WeblinksModelWeblink`, inherited from `JModelAdmin`.

As expected, we see these same six public methods available in the model (with the circles to indicate they are public).

Model publish() Method

Earlier, we looked at the `publish()` method in the `WeblinksControllerWeblinks` class (inherited from `JControllerAdmin`) and saw the following block of code:

Figure 7.7   JModelAdmin methods

```
// Publish the items.
if (!$model->publish($cid, $value)) {
        JError::raiseWarning(500, $model->getError());
}
```

This is where the model's publish() method is called. If successful, it returns a boolean true. If not, it returns a false and has error information that can be retrieved with its getError() method.

Let's look the model's publish() method (from JModelAdmin). We invoke it with two arguments. Recall from earlier that the variable $cid contains an array of Weblink ids that have been checked in the list. The variable $value contains the value that we want to put in the state column in the #__weblinks table.

The first part of the method is as follows:

```
function publish(&$pks, $value = 1)
{
 // Initialise variables.
 $dispatcher = JDispatcher::getInstance();
 $user = JFactory::getUser();
 $table = $this->getTable();
 $pks = (array) $pks;

 // Include the content plugins for the change of state event.
 JPluginHelper::importPlugin('content');
```

Note that we name the first argument with the & in front of it. This means that we are passing this argument as a reference. If we change this array variable $pks inside the method, the changed array variable will be available in the calling method (as the variable $cid—the one used when the publish() method was called). We will see why we do this a little later on.

The next two lines initialize the dispatcher object and the user object. Recall from Chapter 5 that the dispatcher is used to trigger events for plugins.

Then we create an object for our table. This calls the getTable() method. Keep in mind that we are inside the WeblinksModelWeblink class, even though we have been executing the publish() method code from the JModelAdmin class. Because we have a getTable() method in the WeblinksModelWeblink class, we use that. The code for this is very simple, as follows:

```
public function getTable($type = 'Weblink', $prefix = 'WeblinksTable',
↪$config = array())
{
 return JTable::getInstance($type, $prefix, $config);
}
```

This gets an object of type WeblinksTableWeblink from the folder tables. This class provides the methods used to read and write data to this table in the database.

The last line forces the `$pks` variable to be an array. In our case, it already was an array so there is no change. Having this line allows us to call the `publish()` method either for one item, as an integer, or for an array. If we call it with a single id, it is converted to an array.

The next line of code is as follows:

```
// Include the content plugins for the change of state event.
JPluginHelper::importPlugin('content');
```

This imports the content plugins so they will be executed when we trigger events. We fire the event called **onContentChangeState** when an item's published state is changed.

The next code block is as follows:

```
// Access checks.
foreach ($pks as $i => $pk) {
 $table->reset();

 if ($table->load($pk)) {
    if (!$this->canEditState($table)) {
       // Prune items that you can't change.
       unset($pks[$i]);
       JError::raiseWarning(403,
↪JText::_('JLIB_APPLICATION_ERROR_EDITSTATE_NOT_PERMITTED'));
       return false;
    }
 }
}
```

Here we loop through each of the ids and check that the user is authorized to change the published state of each of them. First we reset the table columns to their default values with the `reset()` method. Then we execute the `$table->load()` method for each id value. This reads the row from the database table and loads it into our `$table` object. If successful, this method returns a boolean `true`. In this case, we then invoke `$this->canEditState()`. This method will return boolean `true` if the user can edit the state for this Weblink item and `false` if the user is not authorized to do so.

If the user is authorized, we skip the statements inside the if block and continue. If the user is not authorized to edit the state of a Weblink, we do three things.

First, we use the PHP `unset` command to remove this id from the `$pks` array. Second, we display a warning message to the user indicating they don't have the correct permissions. Third, we exit from this method using `return false`. Note that when we use the `return` command anywhere in a method, we immediately exit and return to the calling method.

Recall that we put the `&` in front of this variable in the method signature (the first line that names the method's arguments). This indicates that we are including this variable by reference. So when we remove an array element from `$pks` with the `unset` command here, this change to the array will be visible back in the calling method. In other words, when we change $pks here in the model's publish() method, that will change $cid back in the controller where we called this method.

Recall in the publish() method of JControllerAdmin, we call the publish() method of the model with this code

```
if (!$model->publish($cid, $value)) {
```

and later we include the number of Weblinks published in this message with this line of code:

```
$this->setMessage(JText::plural($ntext, count($cid)));
```

If a user attempts to trash three Weblinks, but one of them is in a category for which the user does not have permission for the core.edit.state action, only two items will be trashed. Because we use unset to remove that item from the $pks array, and because we include that method argument by reference (with the &), changes we make to $pks inside the model publish() method are reflected in $cid in the controller publish() method. So, $cid in our example will only contain two elements and the message will correctly report that two items were trashed (instead of three).

Next let's look at the canEditState() method of WeblinksModelWeblink, whose code is as follows:

```
protected function canEditState($record)
  {
  $user = JFactory::getUser();

  if (!empty($record->catid)) {
     return $user->authorise('core.edit.state',
➥'com_weblinks.category.'.(int) $record->catid);
  }
  else {
     return parent::canEditState($record);
  }
}
```

Note that this method has the protected access modifier, so it can only be used within this class or any classes that extend this class. That means that this method is intended to support the publish method but not to be used directly from outside the class.

The ACL (access control list) security introduced in Joomla version 1.6 includes a special permission for changing an item's published state. For Weblinks, this can be set at the component level or at the category level. This method checks to see if the current record has a category. (Note that Weblinks always should have a category, so this check might be unneeded.) If so, we call the authorise() method (note the English spelling—United Kingdom English is the official language for Joomla) of the

JUser class to check if the current user is authorized to change the published state for Weblinks in the current category. The arguments for the authorise() method are the action and the name of the asset. For categories, the asset name is formed as

```
<component name> + .category. + <category id>
```

If there is no category for the current record, we execute the parent class's canEditState() method. That method (in JModelAdmin) has the following code:

```
return $user->authorise('core.edit.state', $this->option);
```

This checks the permission for the component level. The field $this->option contains the component name—in this case, com_weblinks.

Recall earlier in this chapter we looked at the access.xml file. That file contains the ACL actions for the component level and the category level for this component. In that file we define action elements with a name of "core.edit.state" for the component and category sections. The access.xml file allows us to edit those permissions for the component and the category. The code here checks those permissions.

The authorise() method returns a boolean true if the user is authorized to take the action and false otherwise. This value is returned by the canEditState() method as well.

The next block of code in the JModelAdmin publish() method is as follows:

```
// Attempt to change the state of the records.
if (!$table->publish($pks, $value, $user->get('id'))) {
    $this->setError($table->getError());
    return false;
}
```

This is the code that actually changes the value in the database. It calls the publish() method of the $table object, which again returns a boolean true or false to indicate success or failure. If this method fails, we get the error message from the method and return with a false result to indicate to the calling method that we had an error.

The next block of code processes the plugins for the onContentChangeState event, as follows:

```
$context = $this->option . '.' . $this->name;

// Trigger the onContentChangeState event.
$result = $dispatcher->trigger($this->event_change_state,
↪array($context, $pks, $value));

if (in_array(false, $result, true)) {
   $this->setError($table->getError());
   return false;
}
```

First we set the context so the plugins will be able to check this as needed. Then we use the $dispatcher object created earlier to trigger our event. The field $this-> event_change_state was set in the constructor method of the JModelAdmin class, with a default value of "onContentChangeState."

The trigger() method returns an array of results from each plugin. If any of the plugins fail, we again get the error message from the table and return with a false value to indicate an error. This is an important feature in this model. This allows a developer to customize the workflow for publishing items. If we write a custom content plugin that uses the onContentChangeState event, we can control whether or not the publish task succeeds. For example, we might want to require approval from a site admin before the user can publish an item. This process could be controlled by such a plugin.

The publish() method finishes with the following code:

```
// Clear the component's cache
$this->cleanCache();

$return true;
```

The cleanCache() method clears the cache files for the Weblinks component. When we have caching enabled, Joomla saves web pages in cache files for a period of time. That way, if a user requests the same exact web page that has already been displayed earlier, we can get it faster by using this saved cache file. When we change the data in a table, any cached files that contain data from that table might now be out of date. We need to clear these files so we don't risk showing out-of-date information to the user.

The last line of the method returns a boolean true to indicate success. Because we got this far, we know that none of the possible errors occurred.

Model save() Method

The save() method of JModelForm highlights some important aspects of saving data to the database. When we save a Weblink item after adding or editing, we invoke the save() method of JControllerForm (the parent of WeblinksControllerWeblink). This has the following code:

```
// Validate the posted data.
// Sometimes the form needs some posted data, such as for plugins and
⮑modules.
$form = $model->getForm($data, false);
if (!$form) {
  $app->enqueueMessage($model->getError(), 'error');
  return false;
}
// Test if the data is valid.
$validData = $model->validate($form, $data);
```

Here we get an instance of the JForm object. We discuss the `getForm()` method in more detail later in Chapter 8. The last line calls the `validate()` method of the model. This method is found in `JModelForm`. Recall that our model, `WeblinksModelWeblink`, extends `JModelAdmin`, which in turn extends `JModelForm`. Because our class and its parent do not have a `validate()` method, we use the method from the next class up the inheritance hierarchy (`JModelForm`).

The `validate()` method contains the following code:

```
$data   = $form->filter($data);
$return = $form->validate($data);
```

This is an important pattern to understand. The first line calls the `JForm filter()` method. This idea of filtering is to protect the database from getting harmful data, such as from a hacker. An example of filtering would be to require that an e-mail address only contains string characters.

The second line calls the `JForm validate()` method. Validation checks that the data in a field makes sense for that field. For example, to validate an e-mail address, we would check that it has some characters followed by an @ followed by a domain name.

Often when we validate data, we let the user know and require them to reenter the information. Filtering, on the other hand, can take place behind the scenes and simply remove harmful data before it gets saved.

Other Model Methods

Let's take a high-level look at some of the other methods in the `WeblinksModelWeblink` class (inherited from JModelAdmin) that support the tasks in our controller. The same pattern we saw with the `publish()` method applies to the `save()`, `delete()`, `reorder()`, `saveorder()`, and `checkin()` methods. In each case, the controller method

- Does some preliminary work
- Gets an instance of the model
- Calls the model method of the same name
- Saves a success or failure message
- Returns `true` for success or `false` for failure

It is beyond the scope of this book to go into detail about all the methods, even for one component such as Weblinks. However, by knowing how the methods work together, you can follow the processing in each one and see what it is doing.

Weblinks Table Class

If we dig deeper into the model methods, we see that they in turn use methods from the table class. For example, the `save()` method in `WeblinksModelWeblink` calls the `load()`, `bind()`, `check()`, and `store()` methods from the `WeblinksTableWeblink` class. These methods are where the actual interaction with the database happens. They are described in the following sections.

Table load() Method

This method, inherited from JTable, loads the data for a row from the database table and binds the database columns to the fields in the JTable instance. The row is loaded based on the primary key of the table—in our example, the id column of #__weblinks.

The great thing here is that all the work to do this is already done by Joomla (in the parent class). The WeblinksTableWeblink class inherits this and doesn't have to change a thing to use it.

Table bind() Method

This method takes as input an associative array or object and loads each element into a field of the JTable object. For example, when we read a row from the #__weblinks table, we end up with an associative array from this line of code in JTable::load():

```
$row = $this->_db->loadAssoc();
```

This array has a key for each column in the table with the value equal to the value for that row. The last line in that method is

```
return $this->bind($row);
```

The bind() method loads all the values from the array into the fields of the JTable object. The JTable class contains a field for each column in the table. These are created in the JTable constructor method. Because our WeblinksTableWeblink class extends JTable, we only have to code things that are unique to our table. Then we can just call the parent method to do the standard processing. This is what we do in the bind() method.

The special processing we have to do for WeblinksTableWeblink relates to the params and metadata columns in the #__weblinks table. If a table has a one-to-one mapping of columns to the fields in the JTable class, we can just use the parent JTable bind() method. However, the params and metadata columns are stored as JSON-formatted strings. Recall that JSON strings allow us to put multiple options (parameter) fields into one database column. This means we can add or remove options without having to alter the table structure in the database. This comes with a small cost, however. Before we can use these values in code, we need to unpack them into a more useful format.

The unpacking happens in the getItem() method of WeblinksModelWeblink. This method first calls the parent getItem() method (in JModelAdmin). This converts the params column from a JSON string to an array using the toArray() method of the JRegistry class. Then, back in the WeblinksModelWeblink getItem() method, we do the same thing for the metadata column. This way, we can work with the individual fields of the JSON strings as array elements inside the WeblinksTableWeblink class.

When it is time to write a row back to the #__weblinks table, we need to do the reverse operation and convert the arrays back to JSON strings. This is done in the bind() method of WeblinksTableWeblink with the following code:

```
public function bind($array, $ignore = '')
{
 if (isset($array['params']) && is_array($array['params'])) {
    $registry = new JRegistry();
    $registry->loadArray($array['params']);
    $array['params'] = (string)$registry;
 }

 if (isset($array['metadata']) && is_array($array['metadata'])) {
    $registry = new JRegistry();
    $registry->loadArray($array['metadata']);
    $array['metadata'] = (string)$registry;
 }
 return parent::bind($array, $ignore);
}
```

In this method, the variable $array is an associative array of the data fields for the #__weblinks table. The array key is the column name and the value is the value to be written back to the database. This code checks to see if there is an array in the $array['parmas'] element. If so, we convert it to a JRegistry object and then use the __toString() method of JRegistry to convert it back to a JSON-formatted string. Recall that when we cast an object as a string (here using the (string) command), we invoke the __toString() method for that object. We repeat the exact same sequence to convert the metadata from an array to a JSON string.

The last line calls the bind() method of the parent class. This is very important because this is where the rest of the work is done to bind the other columns to our table object.

Table store() Method

The store() method uses this same pattern. We do some processing that is specific to this table and then we call the parent's store() method to do the standard processing.

In our store() method, we check to see if we are editing an existing row or creating a new one. Based on this, we either update the modifed date and modified_by user columns or the created date and created_by user columns. Then we do some special processing to make sure that we don't already have an item with this same alias and category id. The alias and category are used to generate the URL for Weblinks. If there are duplicates, the URL we generate will not be unique and might point to the wrong item. So we check for this when we save the item and show an error if the problem is detected.

At this point, we have done all the special processing required for the Weblinks. So we call the parent's store() method and return its result.

Table check() Method

The check() method checks for cases where the data in a row is invalid or nonsensical. It works a bit differently from the others in two ways. First, this method is empty in the parent JTable class, so we don't call the parent's check method. Second, we try to fix up the data if possible instead of just reporting the error.

For Weblinks, we check the following:

- The URL contains only valid characters.
- The title is not blank.
- The URL starts with correct characters (adding "http://" if needed).
- We don't already have a Weblink with the same name.
- The alias is set and valid (setting it if blank).
- The start publishing date is before the end publishing date (swapping dates if they are reversed).
- Keywords, if entered, are properly formatted and don't contain any illegal characters.

If we compare the `check()` methods of the different core table classes, such as `WeblinksTableWeblink`, `ContactsTableContact`, `BannersTableBanner`, and `NewsfeedsTableNewsfeed`, we see a lot of duplicate code. For example, each one contains the same code to check and fix up the publishing dates. We could improve the design by moving this duplicate code to the parent class and calling the parent's `check()` method in each subclass's `check()` method to check, just as we do in the `store()` or `publish()` methods. Note that this would not change the way these programs function. It would just reduce the size of the code base by removing duplicate code. Duplicate code makes a program harder to maintain. For example, if we have to fix a bug in code that is duplicated, we have to do the same fix in multiple places.

The process of improving code without changing functionality is called refactoring. Refactoring can be done for a variety of reasons, including to reduce duplicate code, to make code easier to read, to reduce its complexity, and to improve standardization. In a large, complex program like Joomla, refactoring is an ongoing process. It is essential when refactoring that we do not accidentally change the way the program works and break existing functionality.

Summary

This chapter explored the use of controllers and models in the MVC design pattern, using the back end of the Weblinks component as our example. We also looked at how the `JTable` class is used to help with interacting with the database.

In the next chapter, we continue with the MVC pattern by looking at the views for the back end of Weblinks. Then we look at the front end of Weblinks and how MVC works for front-end components.

Components Part II: Views, JForm, and Front End

In the previous chapter, we looked at the controllers and models for the back end of the Weblinks component. In this chapter, we continue our look at the Weblinks component.

We start by examining the views and display methods, including an in-depth look at how the Weblinks Manager layout works. Then we explore the use of the JForm class in the Weblink Edit view. Finally, we look at the front end of Weblinks and discuss what is similar and different between the back end and front end of the component.

Views and the display() Method

Let's now examine the view part of the model-view-controller (MVC) pattern, still in the back end. Recall that a view is shown when we have no task or the task is display. In this case, the WeblinksController class (the controller.php file relative to the component's home folder administrator/components/com_weblinks/) is loaded. (All file names in this chapter are relative to this folder unless otherwise specified.) Its only method is display(), and it is responsible for displaying the two component views. The Weblinks view (plural) shows a list of Weblinks and is the default view for the component. The Weblink view (singular) allows adding or editing a single Weblink item.

Weblinks View

Let's start with the Weblinks view. The code for the display() method of Weblinks-controller is as follows:

```
public function display($cachable = false, $urlparams = false)
{
 require_once JPATH_COMPONENT.'/helpers/weblinks.php';

 // Load the submenu.
```

```
WeblinksHelper::addSubmenu(JRequest::getCmd('view', 'weblinks'));

$view    = JRequest::getCmd('view', 'weblinks');
$layout   = JRequest::getCmd('layout', 'default');
$id     = JRequest::getInt('id');

// Check for edit form.
if ($view == 'weblink' && $layout == 'edit' &&
➥!$this->checkEditId('com_weblinks.edit.weblink', $id)) {
   // Somehow the person just went to the form - we don't allow that.
    $this->setError(JText::sprintf('JLIB_APPLICATION_ERROR_UNHELD_ID',
➥$id));
    $this->setMessage($this->getError(), 'error');
    $this->setRedirect(JRoute::_
➥ ('index.php?option=com_weblinks&view=weblinks', false));

    return false;
}

parent::display();

return $this;
}
```

This method gets the view, layout, and Weblinks item id from the request. In this case, the view and layout are blank, so we get the default values of "weblinks" for the view and "default" for the layout. The id is also blank.

The next code block is skipped, since we are not in the Weblink view. Then we execute the parent's `display()` method. Finally, we return the current object. Note that the return value is not used, since we called this method without assigning the result to a variable. However, by returning the object, we allow for "method chaining." This is where we can use an object created by one method to call a second method.

For example, we could replace the following three lines of code,

```
$controller = JController::getInstance('Weblinks');
$controller->execute(JRequest::getCmd('task'));
$controller->redirect();
```

with the following single line of code:

```
JController::getInstance('Weblinks')->
➥execute(JRequest::getCmd('task')->redirect();
```

This is because the `getInstance()` method returns a controller object, and that object has an `execute()` method. Because the `execute()` method again returns the controller object, we can use that object to call the `redirect()` method. The ability to do method chaining was added in version 5 of PHP.

JController display() Method

The WeblinksController class extends JController (libraries/joomla/application/component/controller.php), so parent::display() in WeblinksController executes the display() method of JController. The first part of the code is as follows:

```
public function display($cachable = false, $urlparams = false)
{
 $document = JFactory::getDocument();
 $viewType = $document->getType();
 $viewName = JRequest::getCmd('view', $this->default_view);
 $viewLayout = JRequest::getCmd('layout', 'default');

 $view = $this->getView($viewName, $viewType, '', array('base_path' =>
➥$this->basePath, 'layout' => $viewLayout));

 // Get/Create the model
 if ($model = $this->getModel($viewName)) {
    // Push the model into the view (as default)
    $view->setModel($model, true);
 }

 $view->assignRef('document', $document);

 $conf = JFactory::getConfig();
```

This gets the document, which in our case is an instance of JDocumentHTML, and the type of view—in our case, HTML. The view name is "weblinks," the layout is "default," and the view class is WeblinksViewWeblinks. Then we get the model, which is WeblinksModelWeblinks, and we make this the default model for the view.

Then we set the layout for the view and create a class field called "document" and assign the document object ($document) to that field. Finally, we get the global configuration information and save it to a variable called $conf.

The next code block in the display() method (not shown here) checks to see if we have saved this page in a cache file and, if so, loads from the cache. If not, we execute the display() method of the view, in our case WeblinksViewWeblinks (views/weblinks/view.html.php).

WeblinksViewWeblinks display() Method

The code for this display() method is as follows:

```
public function display($tpl = null)
{
  $this->state        = $this->get('State');
  $this->items        = $this->get('Items');
  $this->pagination   = $this->get('Pagination');
```

```
// Check for errors.
if (count($errors = $this->get('Errors'))) {
    JError::raiseError(500, implode("\n", $errors));
    return false;
}

$this->addToolbar();
parent::display($tpl);
}
```

Here we actually start to create our page. The first three lines execute the `getState()`, `getItems()`, and `getPagination()` methods from our model. The `get()` method in the view finds the model name and looks for a method in the model called "get" plus the string in the argument (for example, "get" + "State"). Our model, `Weblinks ModelWeblinks`, extends `JModelList`, which in turn extends `JModel`.

In this case, the `getState()` method is inherited from the `JModel` class and `getItems()` and `getPagination()` are inherited from `JModelList`. The `getState()` method returns the state object. This represents the current state of the screen, including the filters in effect, the page number, the ordering, and so on. The `getItems()` method returns the list of Weblink items for the screen. This is the information we will display in our list. The `getPagination()` returns the pagination object. This provides for the page numbers on the screen and for navigating through the items one page at a time.

Once we have what we need from the model, we check for errors. If there are none, we add the toolbar using the `addToolbar()` method. This adds the toolbar icons such as New, Edit, Publish, and so on. Recall that the toolbar comes from the administrative module `mod_toolbar`. This module works by displaying a global toolbar object. The `addToolbar()` method creates the toolbar icons in that object so they will be available to display when the `mod_toolbar` module is rendered later in the cycle.

Then we call the parent (`JView`) `display()` method (from the file `libraries/ joomla/application/component/view.php`). This method has the following code:

```
function display($tpl = null)
{
    $result = $this->loadTemplate($tpl);
    if (JError::isError($result)) {
        return $result;
    }

    echo $result;
}
```

Here we execute the `loadTemplate()` method of `JView` and save the results in a variable called `$result`. Then we use the PHP `echo` command to send that to the browser. Recall from Chapter 3 that when we execute the component, we have already turned on the output buffer with the `ob_start()` command. So when we issue the `echo` command here, it sends the output to the buffer, not to the browser.

The `loadTemplate()` method checks for template override files and loads any required language files. Then, assuming it finds the layout file correctly, it executes this code near the end of the method:

```
// start capturing output into a buffer
ob_start();
// include the requested template filename in the local scope
// (this will execute the view logic).
include $this->_template;

// done with the requested template; get the buffer and
// clear it.
$this->_output = ob_get_contents();
ob_end_clean();
return $this->_output;
```

The `ob_start()` command turns on output buffering. Then we include the template layout file. In our case, this will be the file `views/weblinks/tmpl/default.php`. Note that if we were using the Hathor administrative template instead of the default Bluestork template, we would load the Hathor override file `administrator/templates/hathor/html/com_weblinks/weblinks/default.php`.

This layout does not declare a class, so it is executed immediately and its output (the results of the `echo` commands) is saved in the buffer. The buffer is then copied into the field `$this->_output`, which is returned to the calling method (the `$result` variable in the previous code block).

Default Layout File

Now we get to the file where we are actually displaying the component output. It is helpful to see what each part of the layout is actually displaying. Figure 8.1 shows a

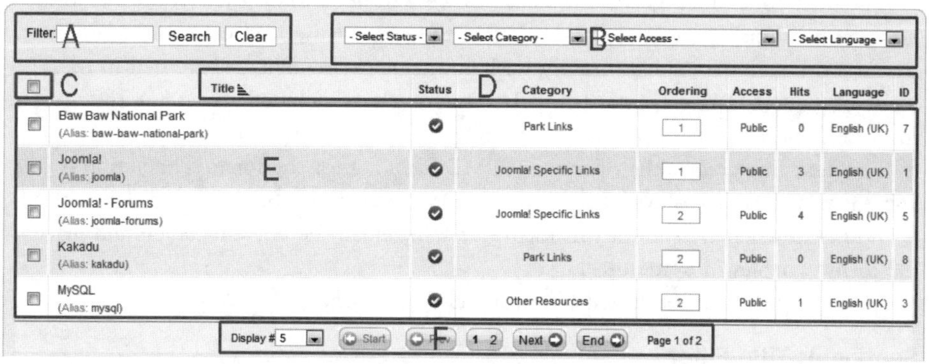

Figure 8.1   Weblinks Manager: Weblinks screenshot

screenshot of the Weblinks Manager: Weblinks screen with labels A–F on different parts of the screen. Let's look at the layout file and see how each of these parts of the screen is displayed.

Housekeeping

The first part of the file does some housekeeping tasks, as follows:

```
JHtml::addIncludePath(JPATH_COMPONENT.'/helpers/html');
JHtml::_('behavior.tooltip');
JHtml::_('script','system/multiselect.js', false, true);

$user         = JFactory::getUser();
$userId       = $user->get('id');
$listOrder    = $this->escape($this->state->get('list.ordering'));
$listDirn     = $this->escape($this->state->get('list.direction'));
$canOrder     = $user->authorise('core.edit.state',
↪'com_weblinks.category');
$saveOrder    = $listOrder == 'a.ordering';
```

The first line includes the "admnistrator/com_weblinks/helpers/html" path. This is important to understand for custom components. This allows us to include our own JHtml classes and methods that we can execute with the convenience method JHtml::_(). Recall that this method automatically loads a class for us if it hasn't been loaded yet.

To use this, we just create a class called JHtml + <component name> (for example, JHtmlWeblinks) and put the file in the helpers folder of our component. For example, if we had a method called myGrid() in a JHtmlWeblinks class, we could execute it with the command JHtml::_('weblinks.mygrid', 'argument1', 'argument2').

Back in the layout we use JHtml::_('behavior.tooltip') to add the MooTools JavaScript code needed to show tooltips and also a second JavaScript file called multiselect.js. We discuss how JavaScript works in Chapter 12.

The next code block gets some variables we will need to do the layout, including how the list should be ordered and whether the current user can change the order. Because this script is loaded directly with an include statement, we are still in the scope of the WeblinksViewWebinks class where it was included. So $this refers to an instance (object) of that class.

The next line creates the opening HTML form tag for the form. The action is our current URL (index.php?option=com_weblinks&view=weblinks) and the method is "post." So when we submit this form, we will reload the current screen and place the form variables in $_REQUEST.

Now we start to create the different parts of the form.

Section A: Title Filter

The code for section A in Figure 8.1 is as follows:

```
<div class="filter-search fltlft">
    <label class="filter-search-lbl" for="filter_search"><?php echo
↩JText::_('JSEARCH_FILTER_LABEL'); ?></label>
    <input type="text" name="filter_search" id="filter_search"
↩value="<?php echo $this->escape($this->state->get('filter.search')); ?>"
↩title="<?php echo JText::_('COM_WEBLINKS_SEARCH_IN_TITLE'); ?>" />
    <button type="submit"><?php echo JText::_('JSEARCH_FILTER_SUBMIT');
↩?></button>
    <button type="button"
↩onclick="document.id('filter_search').value='';this.form.submit();">
↩<?php echo JText::_('JSEARCH_FILTER_CLEAR'); ?></button>
</div>
```

This creates the four elements in section A: the label, the input box, and the two buttons. As with other layout files, we are mixing HTML and PHP elements on the page. The clear button just sets the input value to blank and submits the form to reload the page.

Section B: Filter Select Lists

Section B in Figure 8.1 contains four filters. These allow the user to filter the list based on published status, category, access level, and language. The code for the status filter is as follows:

```
<select name="filter_published" class="inputbox"
↩onchange="this.form.submit()">
    <option value=""><?php echo
↩JText::_('JOPTION_SELECT_PUBLISHED');?></option>
    <?php echo JHtml::_('select.options',
↩JHtml::_('jgrid.publishedOptions'), 'value', 'text',
↩$this->state->get('filter.state'), true);?>
</select>
```

This code creates an HTML select element on the form. The first option has a value of "" (empty string) and a label created by the translation of the language key "JOPTION _SELECT_PUBLISHED". Then we call the method in the highlighted line. Let's look at what this does.

In this example, `JHtml::_('select.options', . . .)` calls the method `JHtmlSelect::options()`, and `JHtml::_('jgrid.publishedOptions')` calls `JHtmlJGrid::publishedOptions()`. Recall that additional arguments after the first argument are passed as arguments to the method.

In this line of code we are calling `JHtmlSelect::options()` method. This method creates a list of option elements for an HTML select list. We pass these five arguments to the method:

- The array of values: Set as the result of `JHtmlJGrid::publishedOptions()` method, which is an array of objects for each possible published state (1 for published, 0 for unpublished, 2 for archived, −2 for trashed, and "*" for all)

- The name of the object variable: Set to "value"
- The name of the option text: Set to "text"
- The selected value: Set to `$this->state->get('filter_state')` (the current selected published state)
- Whether or not to translate the text and labels: Set to boolean `true`

The output of this code block is the following HTML code, which you can see if you look at the HTML page source for this element:

```
<select onchange="this.form.submit()" class="inputbox"
name="filter_published">
        <option value="">- Select Status -</option>
        <option value="1">Published</option>
        <option value="0">Unpublished</option>
        <option value="2">Archived</option>
        <option value="-2">Trashed</option>
        <option value="*">All</option>
</select>
```

The highlighted HTML code is produced by the `JHtmlSelect::options()` method. Because we have set the onchange attribute to `"this.form.submit()"`, the page automatically reloads any time this value is changed, using the new filter value to select the items.

Each of the filters in the form is set in the same way, using different JHtml methods to create the list of possible options for the select list:

- `JHtmlCategory::options()` builds the list of categories.
- `JHtmlAccess::assetgroups()` builds the options list of access levels.
- `JHtmlContentLanguage::existing()` builds the options list of available languages.

Section C: Check All Box

The check all box is created with the following code:

```
<input type="checkbox" name="checkall-toggle" value=""
onclick="Joomla.checkAll(this)" />
```

When clicked, this calls the JavaScript `checkAll()` method from the file **media/system/js/core.js.** This method loops through all the check box elements and sets them to the value of this check box.

Section D: Sortable Column Headings

This form has seven column headings, each of which can be clicked to sort the list by that column. If the column heading is clicked a second time, the sort order is reversed.

The following code implements the first column heading for the Weblink title:

```
<?php echo JHtml::_('grid.sort',  'JGLOBAL_TITLE', 'a.title', $listDirn,
↪$listOrder); ?>
```

This calls the method `JHtmlGrid::sort()` with the following arguments:

- title: "JGLOBAL_TITLE"
- order field: "a.title" (title column from `#__weblinks` table)
- current sort direction: `$listDirn` (set at the start of this file)
- selected ordering: `$listOrder` (set at the start of this file)

With this one line of code, we implement a great user feature. This same method is used for the other column headings.

Section E: Weblink Items

The list of Weblink items is output inside the HTML table body (tbody) element. Each Weblink is a table row (tr) and each column is a table cell (td).

As you might expect, we output the rows inside a PHP `foreach` loop as follows:

```
<?php foreach ($this->items as $i => $item) :
```

Recall that `$this->items` contains the array of items returned by the model. To start, we do some housekeeping for this item. We check the ordering, we get the category link, and then we check the user's permissions to create new items, edit existing items, check in items, and edit the state. Then we output each column for this item.

The first column uses the `JHtmlGrid::id()` method to output a check box with the value of each Weblink item's id. This method creates a check box with a name of "cid[]". The brackets after the name indicate that the results are returned as an array of ids for all boxes that are checked. Some tasks operate on an array of items, such as publish, unpublish, archive, checkin, trash, and delete. These tasks read the array from the `cid[]` element of the request.

The next cell is a bit more complicated. If the item is checked out, we output the checkout icon with this code:

```
<?php echo JHtml::_('jgrid.checkedout', $i, $item->editor,
↪$item->checked_out_time, 'weblinks.', $canCheckin); ?>
```

This calls `JHtmlJGrid::checkedout()` with the current row index, the name of the person who has checked it out, the time checked out, the task prefix (in our case, "weblinks."), and a boolean value to indicate whether this user is authorized to check in the item. Recall that `$canCheckin` was set at the start of the `foreach` loop based on whether the current user has core.manage permission for the com_checkin component or whether they are the same user who has the item checked out. If the user is authorized to check the item in, the icon is shown as a link that initiates the checkin task for this id. In this case, the method outputs the following code:

```
<a class="jgrid hasTip" href="#"
↪onclick="return listItemTask('cb0','weblinks.checkin')"
↪title="Checkin::Super User\&lt;br /&gt;Wednesday,
↪01 June 2011\&lt;br /&gt;18:15">
        <span class="state checkedout">
                <span class="text">Checked out
                </span>
        </span>
</a>
```

In this case, the image (which comes from the class "jgrid span.checkedout" CSS selector) is a link that executes the "weblinks.checkin" task and checks the item in.

If the user cannot check the item in, the output HTML code is as follows:

```
<span class="jgrid hasTip"
↪title="Checked out::Super User\&lt;br /&gt;Wednesday,
↪01 June 2011\&lt;br /&gt;18:08">
        <span class="state checkedout">
                <span class="text">Checked out
                </span>
        </span>
</span>
```

This is similar to the previous code except that there is no anchor element that links to a task.

Still in the same table cell, we show the Weblink title. If the user can edit it, we show it as a link to the item. Otherwise, we just show it as text. Finally, we show the alias for the item.

The Status column shows whether or not the item is published. We use `JHtmlJGrid::published()` to show this icon, as follows:

```
<?php echo JHtml::_('jgrid.published', $item->state, $i, 'weblinks.',
↪$canChange, 'cb', $item->publish_up, $item->publish_down); ?>
```

This outputs the class to show the correct icon based on the current published state of the item. If the current user has edit.state permission and the item is published or unpublished, the icon is a link that toggles the state between published and unpublished. All this work is done for us by the `JHtmlJGrid::published()` method.

The next table cell just shows the category title, as follows:

```
<?php echo $this->escape($item->category_title); ?>
```

 Notice that we process the title with the `$this->escape()` method. Because the title is entered in by a user, it is possible it could contain malicious code. The `escape()` method removes any characters that a hacker might enter to try to inject JavaScript or SQL code into our page. By default, subclasses of JView use the built-in

PHP function `htmlspecialchars()` as the `escape()` method. However, this can be changed to any method by setting the `$_escape` field in the class (for example, in the class constructor method).

It is good practice to escape any string data that is entered by the user. In this form, we escape the filter search value, Weblink title, Weblink alias, category title, access level, and language title. If the value contains no special characters, it will be unchanged.

The next cell is the Ordering column. This is a somewhat complicated cell because it supports a very powerful feature. If the list is ordered by the Weblinks ordering (the ordering of each Weblink item within the category), then we have the option to change the ordering of individual Weblinks. This can be done in one of two ways. We provide up and down arrows to allow a Weblink to be moved up or down one position in the list. We also provide an input box where you can enter in the desired order number for one or more items and then have the entire list reordered.

This is further complicated by the fact that the list can be sorted in ascending or descending order. If it is sorted in descending order, the up and down arrows take on the opposite meaning.

The code for this cell is as follows:

```php
<?php if ($canChange) : ?>
    <?php if ($saveOrder) :?>
        <?php if ($listDirn == 'asc') : ?>
            <span><?php echo $this->pagination->orderUpIcon($i,
➥($item->catid == @$this->items[$i-1]->catid), 'weblinks.orderup',
➥'JLIB_HTML_MOVE_UP', $ordering); ?></span>
            <span><?php echo $this->pagination->orderDownIcon($i,
➥$this->pagination->total, ($item->catid == @$this->items[$i+1]->catid),
➥'weblinks.orderdown', 'JLIB_HTML_MOVE_DOWN', $ordering); ?></span>
        <?php elseif ($listDirn == 'desc') : ?>
            <span><?php echo $this->pagination->orderUpIcon($i,
➥ ($item->catid == @$this->items[$i-1]->catid), 'weblinks.orderdown',
➥'JLIB_HTML_MOVE_UP', $ordering); ?></span>
            <span><?php echo $this->pagination->orderDownIcon($i,
➥$this->pagination->total, ($item->catid == @$this->items[$i+1]->catid),
➥'weblinks.orderup', 'JLIB_HTML_MOVE_DOWN', $ordering); ?></span>
        <?php endif; ?>
    <?php endif; ?>
    <?php $disabled = $saveOrder ?  '' : 'disabled="disabled"'; ?>
    <input type="text" name="order[]" size="5" value="<?php echo
➥$item->ordering;?>" <?php echo $disabled ?> class="text-area-order" />
<?php else : ?>
    <?php echo $item->ordering; ?>
<?php endif; ?>
```

Recall that we set the `$canChange` variable at the start of the `foreach` loop. If true, the current user can edit.state and check in the current Weblink. We need permission for the checkin action because, during the reorder, we temporarily check out the items and then check them back in after we are done.

In this case, we do the first code block inside the outer if statement. Then we check whether $saveOrder is true. Recall this was set at the start of the file and is true if we are sorting on the "a.ordering" column. If this is true, we move to the third if statement. Here we check to see if we are sorting in ascending or descending order. If ascending, we show the up arrow (from the orderUpIcon() method from our pagination object) and associate this with the weblinks.orderup task. We do the same for the order down icon, assigning it to the weblinks.orderdown task.

Things are a bit confusing if we are ordering in descending order. Because the list is reversed, the up arrow actually moves an item lower in the list. So we associate the up arrow with the weblinks.orderdown task and the down arrow with the weblinks.orderup task.

That is the end of the inner if code block. We then have two **endif** statements, so we are back in the outermost if code block. Here we set a variable called $disabled to blank if $saveOrder is true and the string "disabled='disabled'" otherwise. (Recall that we can put double quotes inside single quotes and vice versa.) This string is used to disable the order input box if we are not sorting by the ordering column. Then we show the ordering input box, which will be disabled if $saveOrder is not true.

The else code block is executed if the user doesn't have permission to edit the item. In this case, we simply show the ordering without any arrows or input box.

The last four columns are very simple. We just show the access level, the number of hits, the language title (or "All" if it is an "*"), and the id of the item.

Section F: Pagination Controls

Just before the table body element (tbody), we have the following code:

```
<tfoot>
  <tr>
    <td colspan="10">
      <?php echo $this->pagination->getListFooter(); ?>
    </td>
  </tr>
</tfoot>
```

This puts the output of the getListFooter() method of the pagination class into the table footer element. This one line of code creates all the controls shown in section F, including the Display # list, Start, Finish, page number, Next, and End buttons. That is a lot of functionality for one line of code! Recall that we got the pagination object from the getPagination() method of the model. This creates an instance of JPagination, which provides the buttons and links required to navigate through a list page by page.

Default View and Joomla! Platform

The Webinks Manager: Weblinks screen, shown in Figure 8.1, is a highly functional and easy-to-use screen that allows the site administrator to view and manage any number of Weblink items. It contains a lot of "moving parts," such as filtering, sorting, batch operations, reordering, and pagination. It is also designed to protect from malicious code, and it includes checking in and out items to control different users who try to edit the same item at the same time.

Using the built-in methods provided by the Joomla platform, we are able to create this entire screen in about 180 lines of relatively simple HTML and PHP code. From a developer's point of view, the great thing here is that we can use these exact same tools to build manager screens for our component extensions (which we do in Chapter 10).

WeblinksViewWeblink View

The last thing to understand about the back-end com_weblinks component is the display() method for WeblinksViewWeblink (views/weblink/view.html.php). Recall that this is the class used when we are adding or editing an individual Weblink item.

```php
public function display($tpl = null)
{
 $this->state   = $this->get('State');
 $this->item       = $this->get('Item');
 $this->form       = $this->get('Form');

 // Check for errors.
 if (count($errors = $this->get('Errors'))) {
    JError::raiseError(500, implode("\n", $errors));
    return false;
 }

 $this->addToolbar();
 parent::display($tpl);
}
```

This method is similar to the display() method we looked at earlier except that here we call the model's getItem() method (instead of getItems()) and getForm() (instead of getPagination()). Recall that the JView::get() method executes the method from the model with the name get + the name in the argument.

We discussed the getState() method earlier in this chapter. The getItem() method just calls the parent's (JModelAdmin) getItem() method. This method checks to see if we are editing an existing item. If so, it calls the $table->load($pk) method, where $pk is the Weblink item's id. Then it creates a JRegistry object for the item's params column.

Using JForm in Weblinks

In previous chapters, we saw examples of using the JForm class to display options—for example, when editing a template, plugin, or module. In those cases, each option was defined in an XML file and the options were rendered exactly as they were defined.

`JForm` can also be used to create complex forms with flexible layouts and dynamic properties. In Weblinks, we can see how these capabilities are used to create the form for editing an individual Weblink item.

WeblinksModel getForm() Method

The `getForm()` method gets the `JForm` object for the edit form. Figure 8.2 shows the methods called in this process.

The program flow is a bit confusing because we are executing some methods from the parent classes. Recall from Figure 7.7 that `WeblinksModelWeblink` extends `JModelAdmin`, which in turn extends `JModelForm`. `JModelForm` extends `JModel`. In this example, we find the `loadForm()` and `preprocessForm()` methods in `JModelForm` and the `bind()` method in `JForm`.

The first part of the code for `getForm()` is as follows:

```
public function getForm($data = array(), $loadData = true)
{
 // Initialise variables.
 $app   = JFactory::getApplication();

 // Get the form.
 $form = $this->loadForm('com_weblinks.weblink', 'weblink',
 array('control' => 'jform', 'load_data' => $loadData));
 if (empty($form)) {
    return false;
 }
```

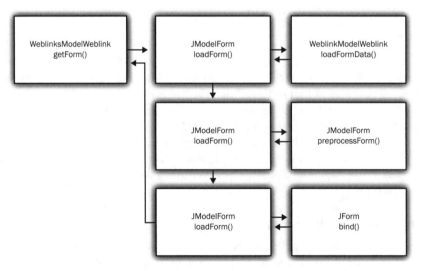

Figure 8.2   WeblinksModelWeblink getForm() methods

The highlighted line takes us to the loadForm() method of the parent class (JModelForm). The first argument, $name, is set to "com_weblinks.weblink". The second argument, $source, is "weblink", and $options is the associative array shown in the highlighted code.

In the loadForm() method, we see if we already have the form cached. If not, we execute this code using a try/catch block:

```
try {
    $form = JForm::getInstance($name, $source, $options, false, $xpath);

    if (isset($options['load_data']) && $options['load_data']) {
        // Get the data for the form.
        $data = $this->loadFormData();
    } else {
        $data = array();
    }

    // Allow for additional modification of the form, and events to be
➥triggered.
    // We pass the data because plugins may require it.
    $this->preprocessForm($form, $data);

    // Load the data into the form after the plugins have operated.
    $form->bind($data);

} catch (Exception $e) {
    $this->setError($e->getMessage());
    return false;
}
```

If you are not familiar with try/catch blocks, please see the sidebar "Exceptions and Try/Catch Blocks". We execute the getInstance() method inside the try block because this method can throw exceptions, and we have to have a catch block to process any exceptions.

Inside the getInstance() method, we check that $data is not blank. The variable $data can either be the name of an XML file or a string containing the XML for the form. In getInstance() we check the first character of $data. If it is "<," we assume it is an XML string and try to create the form using the JForm load() method. In our example, $data contains the XML file name "weblink," so we instead use the JForm loadFile() method to load the form with this file (models/forms/weblink.xml). Both of these methods create the form from the fieldset and field elements inside the XML code.

In the weblink.xml file, we define two fieldset elements that contain a number of field elements. We will see how these fields are used to render the form later in this chapter when we discuss the edit layout files.

The errors are handled cleanly in the getInstance() method. We just throw the proper type of exception for each error condition. The exceptions are handled in the catch block of the calling method, shown in the previous code block. In this case, we set the error based on the message from the exception object and return a boolean `false`.

Exceptions and Try/Catch Blocks

PHP version 5 introduced the concept of exception handling using exceptions and try/catch blocks. This is very similar to Java and other object-oriented programming (OOP) programming languages. The basic idea is this: When we are doing something in our program that is risky—in other words, that depends on things beyond our immediate control—we should check for errors. The try/catch block allows us to do that in a simple, flexible way.

Here's how it works. Risky code that can generate exceptions is put inside a try block. When you find an error condition, you execute a "throw new Exception" command. This creates an exception object and transfers program control to the catch block of code. In the catch block, you can then do what needs to be done based on the type of exception you found. This could be just to return with a false value or some processing based on the type of exception that occurred.

You can throw exceptions from inside methods without a try/catch block. In this case, you should always call that method from inside a try block. That way, if the method throws an exception, there will be a catch block to transfer control to.

Methods that throw exceptions should have this documented in the "doc block" so that programmers know to use them from inside try blocks.

This type of exception handling was not possible until Joomla version 1.6 (which requires PHP version 5.2 or higher). As new code is written for Joomla and old classes are updated, we will see this type of exception handling used more frequently in the Joomla code base.

Now, let's get back to the `loadForm()` method in the previous code block. After we have set the `$form` variable with the `JForm` object, we check to see if we are loading data to the form. In the method signature for `loadForm()`, the third argument is an associative array called `$options`. In our example, we want to preload data for the form, so we include an element called "load_data" that is set to a boolean `true`.

If so, we execute the `loadFormData()` method. This gets any previously loaded data from the session. Normally, this will be empty. If we are editing an item for the first time or creating a new item, we call `$this->getItem()`, which creates a `JObject` with the fields for the form. If we have an existing item, we get the data for that item. For a new item, we get the default values or, if no default is specified in the field, we get an empty value.

When do we use the data from the session? Suppose the user has filled out the form to add a new item but has some invalid data in the form. Maybe they have a duplicate alias field or have left out the title. In this case, the save will not be successful, so the data is not saved in the database. It would be very frustrating if the user had to reenter all the fields to fix a single error. To handle this scenario, we save the entered data in the user's session. Only after the save is successful do we clear this out of the session. That way, we either have data from the database, which we can get with **getItem()**, or we have data from the session, which we can get with **getUserState()**.

The last thing we do in the **loadFormData()** method is check if there is a category in the request or the session. If so, we set that as the default for the data. Finally, we return the **$data JObject** to the calling **loadForm()** method. If we didn't want to load data into our form, we simply set **$data** to an empty array.

The next line of code in **loadForm()** is important:

```
$this->preprocessForm($form, $data);
```

We use the method from **JModelForm** because it is not overridden in the subclasses **JModelAdmin** or **WeblinksModelWeblink**.

The code for this method is as follows:

```
protected function preprocessForm(JForm $form, $data, $group = 'content')
{
 // Import the approriate plugin group.
 JPluginHelper::importPlugin($group);

 // Get the dispatcher.
 $dispatcher    = JDispatcher::getInstance();

 // Trigger the form preparation event.
 $results = $dispatcher->trigger('onContentPrepareForm', array($form,
➥$data));

 // Check for errors encountered while preparing the form.
 if (count($results) && in_array(false, $results, true)) {
    // Get the last error.
    $error = $dispatcher->getError();

    // Convert to a JException if necessary.
    if (!JError::isError($error)) {
      throw new Exception($error);
    }
 }
}
```

This method triggers the **onContentPrepareForm** event. This event was added in Joomla version 1.6 and is used just for **JForm** objects. It allows developers to write plugins to modify **JForm** objects before they are rendered in the browser. These plugins have available to them the **JForm** object (**$form**) and the data array (**$data**). We saw an example of using this event in Chapter 5 when we created the **myregistration2.php** plugin. There we used a plugin to add some new fields to the form. We can also use plugins to remove, validate, or edit JForm objects. This means that developers can create plugin extensions to modify any core form that uses JForm.

After the plugins have been executed, we check for errors. In case a plugin has returned an error that is not an Exception object, we convert it to an Exception and use the throw exception command to report the error back to the calling method.

At this point, we are back in the loadForm() method. The next thing we do is execute the bind() method, found all the way up the class hierarchy in the JForm class (because it is not overridden by any subclasses). This method checks that our JForm object has a valid JXMLElement defined in the XML field and that our $data variable is either an object or an array. It then matches the form fields with the data elements and sets the value of each form field.

At this point, we are back again to the loadForm() method, at the end of the try block. If any of the code executed in any of the methods called threw an exception, we will have exceptions to process. In this case, we execute the catch block, as follows:

```
} catch (Exception $e) {
    $this->setError($e->getMessage());
    return false;
}
```

Here all we do is set the error message for our model and return to the loadForm() method with a value of boolean false. If we did not throw any exceptions during the execution of the try block, we skip the catch block.

Saving the JForm Object in Memory

There is one last thing to note about the loadForm() method. Before we execute the try block, we see if we already have this form saved in memory. We check this with the following code:

```
    // Create a signature hash.
    $hash = md5($source.serialize($options));

    // Check if we can use a previously loaded form.
    if (isset($this->_forms[$hash]) && !$clear) {
        return $this->_forms[$hash];
    }
```

The idea of this code is simple. We want to save this form in case we need it again in this request cycle. Retrieving the form from memory is faster than rebuilding it from the XML file. Because we could have more than one JForm object active in the same cycle, we need to create a unique identifier for this specific form.

We do this using two PHP functions: md5() and serialize(). The serialize() function converts an object to a string, keeping all the information needed to convert it back to the original object. The md5() method takes any string as input and creates a 32-character string that is unique to the input string. The md5 string is used as a key for an associative array to store the serialized object. Using this technique, we know the following:

- The same JForm instance will always produce the same hash value.
- The value will be unique to this JForm (so we can have more than one JForm in memory and keep them separate in the array).
- The hash value is suitable for using in an associative array.

In our example, $options is an associative array with two elements, control (set to "jform") and load_data (set to 1). The variable $source is "weblink". The result of serialize($options) is

```
a:2:{s:7:"control";s:5:"jform";s:9:"load_data";b:1;}
```

The result of $source.serialize($options) is

```
weblinka:2:{s:7:"control";s:5:"jform";s:9:"load_data";b:1;}
```

Finally, $hash, the result of md5($source.serialize($options)) is

```
37ceb359374f97c561de59903862618e
```

Once we have the $hash value, we can check to see if we have this specific form already saved in the $this->_forms field. If so, it means that we have already loaded this exact same form so we can get the object from memory and save having to load it from an XML file. In this case, we get the object and just return, skipping the rest of the method.

After the try/catch block, when we have a valid form, we see the following code:

```
// Store the form for later.
$this->_forms[$hash] = $form;
```

This saves the form object in the array so it will be there if we need it again.

This technique of saving objects in associative arrays using a hash as the array key is a common technique used to save processing time in various places in Joomla.

Modifying Forms Dynamically

At this point, we have loaded the JForm object inside the getForm() method of the WeblinksModelWeblink class. Now we get to see an example of how we can modify the form inside our code before the form is displayed.

If we look at the rest of the getForm() method in WeblinksModelWeblink, we see a number of $form->setFieldAttribute() methods. For example, we see the following lines:

```
// Modify the form based on access controls.
if (!$this->canEditState((object) $data)) {
  // Disable fields for display.
  $form->setFieldAttribute('ordering', 'disabled', 'true');
  $form->setFieldAttribute('state', 'disabled', 'true');
  $form->setFieldAttribute('publish_up', 'disabled', 'true');
  $form->setFieldAttribute('publish_down', 'disabled', 'true');

  // Disable fields while saving.
  // The controller has already verified this is a record you can edit.
  $form->setFieldAttribute('ordering', 'filter', 'unset');
  $form->setFieldAttribute('state', 'filter', 'unset');
  $form->setFieldAttribute('publish_up', 'filter', 'unset');
  $form->setFieldAttribute('publish_down', 'filter', 'unset');
}
```

The setFieldAttribute() is one of the powerful methods available to modify the form on the fly.

In this code block, we are checking for the case where a user can edit a Weblink item but doesn't have permission to change the state of the item. Changing the state includes changing an item's published status (state) and other information related to publishing. In this case, we want the user to still see the publishing fields on the form, but we want them to be disabled. So if the user doesn't have edit state permission, we disable the fields in the form by setting the disabled attribute for these fields to true. When the form displays, those fields will be disabled. This overrides the values set for these attributes in the form's XML file.

The second part of the code block deals with saving the form data to the database. As we have seen in previous examples, we cannot rely on HTML forms to protect our data. For example, a hacker can easily edit the form and change a disabled field to enabled. JForm contains a filter method that is triggered when you set the filter attribute. In this case, we set it to "unset," which causes any value in that field to be set to null. This has the effect of using the current value (for an existing Weblink item) or the default value (for a new item).

With this technique, we can easily fine-tune our forms dynamically before they are rendered and again during the save process. As mentioned earlier, this same technique can be used in a custom plugin extension to modify core forms (using the onContent-PrepareForm event).

Rendering the JForm

The last step in the process is rendering the form in the browser. If we look at the folder for the Weblinks layout files, views/weblink/tmpl, we see files called edit. php and edit_params.php. These files create the layout using the JForm object.

The file edit.php does the layout for most of the form. The edit_params.php file, as you might expect, displays the parameters for the Weblink item.

Edit.php File

This file shows how easy it is to display `JForm` objects. The first part of the file is as follows:

```php
defined('_JEXEC') or die;

JHtml::addIncludePath(JPATH_COMPONENT.'/helpers/html');
JHtml::_('behavior.tooltip');
JHtml::_('behavior.formvalidation');
?>
<script type="text/javascript">
   Joomla.submitbutton = function(task)
   {
     if (task == 'weblink.cancel' ||
➥document.formvalidator.isValid(document.id('weblink-form'))) {
        <?php echo $this->form->getField('description')->save(); ?>
        Joomla.submitform(task, document.getElementById('weblink-form'));
     }
     else {
       alert('<?php echo $this->escape
➥(JText::_('JGLOBAL_VALIDATION_FORM_FAILED'));?>');
     }
   }
</script>
```

As with the layout discussed earlier in this chapter, we include a helpers folder for custom JHtml methods. Then we add two behaviors: tooltip and formvalidation. Recall that the `JHtmlBehavior` class contains methods to include JavaScript functions. The `formvalidation()` method allows us to trigger JavaScript form validation from attributes set in the JForm.

The next block of code is a script element that adds the JavaScript to trigger the form validation. We discuss how this code works in Chapter 12.

The next section of code is where we start to render the form:

```php
<form action="<?php echo
➥JRoute::_('index.php?option=com_weblinks&layout=edit&id='.(int)
➥$this->item->id); ?>" method="post" name="adminForm" id="weblink-form"
➥class="form-validate">
 <div class="width-60 fltlft">
   <fieldset class="adminform">
     <legend><?php echo empty($this->item->id) ?
➥JText::_('COM_WEBLINKS_NEW_WEBLINK') : JText::sprintf(
➥'COM_WEBLINKS_EDIT_WEBLINK', $this->item->id); ?></legend>
     <ul class="adminformlist">
     <li><?php echo $this->form->getLabel('title'); ?>
     <?php echo $this->form->getInput('title'); ?></li>
```

```php
<li><?php echo $this->form->getLabel('alias'); ?>
<?php echo $this->form->getInput('alias'); ?></li>

<li><?php echo $this->form->getLabel('catid'); ?>
<?php echo $this->form->getInput('catid'); ?></li>

<li><?php echo $this->form->getLabel('state'); ?>
<?php echo $this->form->getInput('state'); ?></li>


<li><?php echo $this->form->getLabel('access'); ?>
<?php echo $this->form->getInput('access'); ?></li>

<li><?php echo $this->form->getLabel('ordering'); ?>
<?php echo $this->form->getInput('ordering'); ?></li>

<li><?php echo $this->form->getLabel('language'); ?>
<?php echo $this->form->getInput('language'); ?></li>

<li><?php echo $this->form->getLabel('id'); ?>
<?php echo $this->form->getInput('id'); ?></li>
</ul>

<?php echo $this->form->getLabel('description'); ?>
<div class="clr"></div>
<?php echo $this->form->getInput('description'); ?>
</fieldset>
</div>
```

The first line creates our HTML form element, with the action attribute pointing us back to the same URL we are on. We also define the method of post, so the form fields will go into the $_REQUEST variable. Then we create a div element and show a legend element for the div. If we have an item id, we are editing an existing Weblink. Otherwise, we are adding a new Weblink.

Then we open an unordered list (ul) element. Inside this we begin to render our form fields, each inside a list item (li) element. For each, we echo the label with the getLabel() method and the input using the getInput() method. Each form field is referenced by its name. With these two lines of code per field, we can render the entire form in any order or layout we wish.

Notice that this layout doesn't need to know what type of field is being rendered. Figure 8.3 shows the Weblinks edit screen. Title, alias, and URL are input elements. The fields category (catid), status, ordering, and language are select elements. The description form item shows the editor buttons and the area where the user can enter in a long description for the Weblink. Each of these JForm fields is rendered with the exact same two lines of code, using getLabel() and getInput().

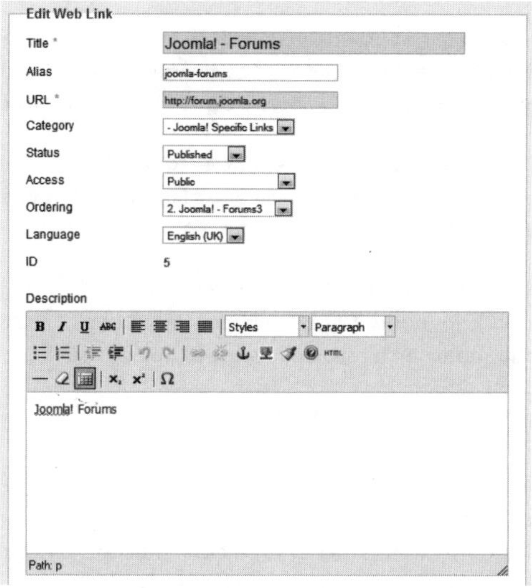

Figure 8.3   Weblinks edit screen

The next section of code displays the "sliders" on the right-hand side of the form. These are regions that can be expanded or contracted to show or hide different groups of fields. The code for the Publishing Options group is as follows:

```
<div class="width-40 fltrt">
   <?php echo JHtml::_('sliders.start','newsfeed-sliders-'.
➥$this->item->id, array('useCookie'=>1)); ?>

   <?php echo JHtml::_('sliders.panel',
➥JText::_('JGLOBAL_FIELDSET_PUBLISHING'), 'publishing-details'); ?>

   <fieldset class="panelform">
     <ul class="adminformlist">
        <li><?php echo $this->form->getLabel('created_by'); ?>
        <?php echo $this->form->getInput('created_by'); ?></li>

        <li><?php echo $this->form->getLabel('created_by_alias'); ?>
        <?php echo $this->form->getInput('created_by_alias'); ?></li>

        <li><?php echo $this->form->getLabel('created'); ?>
        <?php echo $this->form->getInput('created'); ?></li>

        <li><?php echo $this->form->getLabel('publish_up'); ?>
        <?php echo $this->form->getInput('publish_up'); ?></li>

        <li><?php echo $this->form->getLabel('publish_down'); ?>
        <?php echo $this->form->getInput('publish_down'); ?></li>
```

```php
<?php if ($this->item->modified_by) : ?>
    <li><?php echo $this->form->getLabel('modified_by'); ?>
    <?php echo $this->form->getInput('modified_by'); ?></li>

    <li><?php echo $this->form->getLabel('modified'); ?>
    <?php echo $this->form->getInput('modified'); ?></li>
<?php endif; ?>

<?php if ($this->item->hits) : ?>
    <li><?php echo $this->form->getLabel('hits'); ?>
    <?php echo $this->form->getInput('hits'); ?></li>
<?php endif; ?>

    </ul>
  </fieldset>
```

The first line uses the `JHtmlSliders::start()` method to create the slider region. The next line uses the `JHtmlSliders::panel()` method to create the slider panel. All the fields in the fieldset will show inside the panel. The slider functionality is implemented using JavaScript and the MooTools framework, both of which we discuss in Chapter 12. However, the great thing is that we can use this functionality just by calling these methods.

Then we create the fieldset element and, as before, render each field using the `getLabel()` and `getInput()` methods. Note that for the last three fields, we place the code inside an if block. In this case, we don't show these fields unless there is something in the fields to show.

The next line in `edit.php` is

```php
<?php echo $this->loadTemplate('params'); ?>
```

Recall that this looks for a layout file called `edit_params.php` and displays that layout. If we look at that file (`views/weblink/tmpl/edit_params.php`), we see the following code:

```php
$fieldSets = $this->form->getFieldsets('params');
foreach ($fieldSets as $name => $fieldSet) :
  echo JHtml::_('sliders.panel',JText::_($fieldSet->label),
➥$name.'-params');
    if (isset($fieldSet->description) && trim($fieldSet->description)) :
      echo '<p class="tip">'.
➥$this->escape(JText::_($fieldSet->description)).'</p>';
    endif;
    ?>
```

```
    <fieldset class="panelform">
      <ul class="adminformlist">
      <?php foreach ($this->form->getFieldset($name) as $field) : ?>
        <li><?php echo $field->label; ?>
        <?php echo $field->input; ?></li>
      <?php endforeach; ?>
      </ul>
    </fieldset>
<?php endforeach; ?>
```

This code demonstrates a shortcut we can use to render fields from our JForm object. Here we are rendering all the fields in order, each in an unordered list. In this case, we can loop through the fields in the JForm object instead of writing the two lines for each field.

We have two loops. The outer loop loops through each fieldset. The array of fieldsets was obtained using getFieldSets('params'). This gives us an array of all the fieldsets in the JForm in the group called "params". Recall that in the XML for the JForm, we can optionally put fieldset elements inside fields elements. In the weblink. xml file we put the parameters inside a fields element with the name of "params".

For each fieldset, we create the sliders panel using the fieldset label and show the description as a tooltip. Then we open the fieldset element and ul elements.

Then we start the inner loop, where we process each field. We use the method getFieldSet($name) to get the array of fields for that fieldset, where $name is the fieldset name attribute. Then we create the li element and again echo the field label and input. However, in this case we already have the JFormField object in the $field variable, so we use $field->label and $field->input instead of the getLabel() and getField() methods of JForm.

The advantage of using these foreach loops is that we don't have to change this code if we add or delete fieldsets or fields in the XML file. Any fieldset and field elements inside the "params" fields element will be rendered exactly as it appears in the XML file. This technique is used to render the options fields for modules, plugins, templates, and languages. Component options use a similar technique, except that each fieldset element creates a tab in the options modal screen.

JForm includes many other methods for manipulating the form. This gives the developer control over how the form works for different users or situations.

Back-End Weblinks Summary

We have now seen all the important elements of the administrator com_weblinks component, including the installation files, helper methods, and options files. We have also used it as an example to understand in detail the MVC design pattern and how the controller handles tasks and uses the models and views to make the component work.

Front-End Weblinks Component

Now let's look at the front-end side of Weblinks. Because we have examined the back-end Weblinks component in detail, here we will focus on the ways in which the front end of the component is similar to and different from the back end.

Similar Folder Structure and MVC Pattern

Table 8.1 lists the folders and top-level files for the front-end Weblinks component. These files are in the `components/com_weblinks` folder. (Note that file names for the rest of this chapter will be relative to this same folder.)

We can see that this organization is very similar to the organization of the back-end folders. As with the back end, we have folders for controllers, helpers, models, and views. Note that we don't have an installation folder here. We only need one set of installation files, and these are by convention stored in the administrative back end. Also, we don't have a tables folder. The `#__weblinks` table class only needs to be defined once. Again we have chosen to do that in the back end.

Table 8.1 **Front-End Weblinks Component Folders**

File Name	Contents	MVC Group
`controllers`	Controller for the entry screen: `weblink.php`	Controller
`helpers`	Help files: `category.php`, `icon.php`, `route.php`	Helper / Misc.
`models`	Models: `categories.php`, `category.php`, `form.php`, `weblink.php`	Model
`modesl/forms`	JForm XML file: `weblink.xml`	Model
`views/categories`	View for the Categories Menu Item: `view.html.php`	View
`views/categories/tmpl`	Layout files for the categories menu item; XML file for menu item options	View
`views/category`	Views for the single category Menu Item: `view.html.php` and `view.feed.php`	View
`views/category/tmpl`	Layout files for the single category menu item; XML file for menu item options	View
`views/form`	View for submit Weblink menu item: `view.html.php`	View
`views/form/tmpl`	Layout files for the entry form; XML file for menu item options	View
`controller.php`	Default controller for display task	Controller
`router.php`	Component router	Helper / Misc.
`weblinks.php`	Component entry point script	Controller

If we look at the top-level `weblinks.php` file, we see the following code to control the front end of the component:

```
$controller = JController::getInstance('Weblinks');
$controller->execute(JRequest::getCmd('task'));
$controller->redirect();
```

This is exactly the same three lines of code used in the back end, and the process works the same way. We get the correct controller for the task. Then we execute that task. If the task is something other than display, we set the redirect to the desired display URL and execute that URL. If the task is display, then we display the page and don't set any redirect.

As with the back end, we have a model for each view. In this case we have three views:

- Categories: Shows all the Weblinks categories in a hierarchical list
- Category: Shows the Weblinks in a single category
- Form: Displays the submit Weblink form

For each of these views, we have a model, a view class that extends `JView`, and one or more layout files that get included into the view class using the `JView loadTemplate()` method.

Two of the views, Categories and Category, only display information, so these are handled by the base controller, `WeblinksController` (`controller.php`). The Form view allows the user to enter and edit a Weblink. The controller `WeblinksControllerWeblink` handles the nondisplay tasks for this form. The tasks for this form are add, cancel, edit, and save. As with the back end, the add, cancel, and edit tasks are handled by the controller. The `save()` method calls the `save()` method of the model to actually save the data to the database.

There is one confusing thing about the file structure that is unique to this component. We have a model called `WeblinksModelWeblink` in the folder `models/weblink.php`. However, the model for the form, `WeblinksModelForm`, extends the *administrator* `WeblinksModelWeblink` class, not the front-end `WeblinksModelWeblink` class. At the start of the `WeblinksModelForm` class, we see this line of code:

```
require_once JPATH_COMPONENT_ADMINISTRATOR.'/models/weblink.php';
```

Then we see

```
class WeblinksModelForm extends WeblinksModelWeblink
```

Because we have loaded the `WeblinksModelWeblink` class from the folder `administrator/components/models/weblink.php`, when we extend the `WeblinksModelWeblink` class we are using the code from the back-end file. The `WeblinksModelForm` class inherits the `save()` method from the `JModelAdmin` class.

The front-end `WeblinksModelWeblink` is used when you click on a Weblink item. A Weblink item is different from other components. It will display an external Weblink, not a layout within this site. So we don't have a view and layout for a single Weblink item. Why even have Weblinks at all? We can display external URLs without using any component. The answer is that the component allows us to do things we couldn't do with just an external link, including the following:

- Organize our links into categories.
- Lay out the links by category.
- Restrict access levels for the links.
- Count the hits for the links.
- Allow users to submit links.
- Publish and unpublish the links.

The following is an example URL created for a Weblink item:

```
<site URL>/index.php/using-joomla/extensions/components/weblinks-
component/weblinks-single-category?task=weblink.go&id=5
```

Notice that it has the Weblinks item id and the task weblink.go. As we know from our earlier work, this executes the `go()` method in the `WeblinksControllerWeblink`. This is where we check the published status, check the access level for the user, and increment the hit counter.

To help with these tasks, we use the *front-end* `WeblinksModelWeblink` class. For example, we use the model's `getItem()` method to get the Weblink item from the database, and we use the `hit()` method to increment the item's hit counter (the number of times it has been accessed). If all this is successful, then we simply set the redirect to the external URL and it displays in the redirect cycle. Note that this is different from what we did in the back end. There, we set the redirect to link back to a screen in Weblinks (for example, the Weblinks Manager list or edit screen).

Menu Item Types

One important difference between the front and back end of Joomla is the way that menu items (the options on a menu) are created. In the back end, recall that we created three menu items in the Components menu, based on information in the menu and sub-menu elements in installation XML file (`administrator/components/com_weblinks/weblinks.xml`). We know in advance all the tasks the site administrator will need to do to use the Weblinks component, so we create the menu items to support these tasks.

In the front end, menus and menu items are completely user-defined. One site might have no menu items that use Weblinks while another site could have many menu items for different categories of Weblinks. To support this, the component provides the site administrator the tools to create and manage the menu items, but it is up to the administrator to decide which menu items to create.

Table 8.2 **Weblinks Menu Item Types**

Folder	File Name	Menu Item Type
views/categories/tmpl	default.xml	List All Weblink Categories
views/category/tmpl	default.xml	List Weblinks in a Category
views/form/tmpl	edit.xml	Submit a Weblink

The list of available menu item types is created by examining all the XML files in the layout folders of each component. In Weblinks, we have three XML files that create three menu item types, as shown in Table 8.2.

Recall in Chapter 4 that we discussed how to create alternative menu items by copying these base XML files and layout files into the template's HTML folder and modifying them as needed. The structure of the core XML files is exactly the same as for the override XML files and other extension types. The outer element is a metadata element. Here we include a layout element with language keys for the title and option. These are defined in the **administrator/language/en-GB/en-GB.com _weblinks.sys.ini** file and display when you are showing the list of menu item types. We also can define a help element, as discussed previously. The message element shows a description of the layout (which shows in the tooltip when you are viewing the list of Menu Item Types).

The layout element for the Weblinks single category menu item type is as follows:

```
<layout title="com_weblinks_category_view_default_title"
↪option="com_weblinks_category_view_default_option">
  <help
     key="JHELP_MENUS_MENU_ITEM_WEBLINK_CATEGORY"
  />
  <message>
     <![CDATA[com_weblinks_category_view_default_desc]]>
  </message>
</layout>
```

The XML file will normally include definitions for options (parameters) that can be set for this instance of the menu item type. Each option is a field inside a fieldset element, which in turn is inside a fields element. These options are organized into two possible field elements: **request** and **params**.

Request Fields Element

The first **fields** element in the single category menu item XML file is as follows:

```
<!-- Add fields to the request variables for the layout. -->
<fields name="request">
  <fieldset name="request">

    <field name="id" type="category"
```

```
        default="0"
        description="COM_WEBLINKS_FIELD_SELECT_CATEGORY_DESC"
        extension="com_weblinks"
        label="COM_WEBLINKS_FIELD_SELECT_CATEGORY_LABEL"
        required="true"
    />
  </fieldset>
</fields>
```

Option values must be stored somewhere in the database. For menu items, we use the table `#__menus` and we store the values either in the `link` column or the `params` column.

Note that name attribute of the `fields` element is "request". If we have a `fields` element with the name equal to request, we store the option in the link column, as a URL query, in the following format:

```
    <name> + = + <value>
```

In the previous example, that would be

```
    id=xx
```

where "xx" is the category id. When the URL for this menu item is loaded, this becomes part of the URL and is available in the `$_REQUEST`. The typical use for request fields is to hold the id of the main database row that is used for the menu item. For example, many menu items use category id, as above, or other item id fields, such as article or contact. In our example, the URL will point to a single category of subscriptions and we can get the category id from the request. In some cases, such as the Featured Article view, there is no single item or category id. In that case, there won't be a request fieldset element.

As with other options we have seen, these options show on the screen in the order they appear in the XML file, grouped by fieldset. Each fieldset corresponds to a "slider" that can expand and contract as needed.

Params Fields Element

The next fields element in our XML file begins with the following code:

```
<!-- Add fields to the parameters object for the layout. -->
<fields name="params">
<fieldset name="basic" label="JGLOBAL_CATEGORY_OPTIONS">
    <field name="spacer1" type="spacer" class="text"
        label="JGLOBAL_SUBSLIDER_DRILL_CATEGORIES_LABEL"
    />

    <field name="show_category_title" type="list"
        label="JGLOBAL_SHOW_CATEGORY_TITLE"
        description="JGLOBAL_SHOW_CATEGORY_TITLE_DESC"
```

```
>
    <option value="">JGLOBAL_USE_GLOBAL</option>
    <option value="0">JHIDE</option>
    <option value="1">JSHOW</option>
</field>
```

The name attribute for this fields element is `params`. This will cause all the field elements inside this fields element to be stored as a JSON-encoded string in the params column of the `#__menu` table. Recall that the `JTable` class includes code to unpack this column into a `JRegistry` object (in the `getItem()` method) and to pack the `JRegistry` object back into a JSON string (in the `bind()` method).

The `fields` element can contain any number of `fieldset` elements and `field` elements. Again, they will display in the order they appear in the XML file, grouped in sliders by `fieldset` element.

Note that menu items also have standard options that show in most cases. These are the Link Type Options, Page Display Options, and the Metadata Options. These come from the file `administrator/components/com_menus/models/forms/item _component.xml` file and are rendered on the form after the options in the layout's XML file. Some menu item types (External URL, Menu Item Alias, and Text Separator) don't show all these standard options.

Front-End Routing

Recall from Chapter 3 that a router is a class that translates between a URL and an array of commands. It has two public methods, `parse()` and `build()`. The `parse()` method returns a `JURI` object. and returns an array of commands. The `build()` method does the opposite: it takes an array of commands and returns a `JURI` object.

SEF URL Background

In the administrative back end of the site, we don't normally care about the aesthetics of the URL or whether a search engine can find the page. So a URL such as

`administrator/index.php?option=com_categories&extension=com_weblinks`

is fine as long as it gets us to where we want to go.

In the front end, things get a bit more complicated. This is because we care more about the appearance of the URL and we want search engines to be able to index the page and give it a good page ranking.

The first generation of websites were static HTML sites where each page was a separate HTML file. The URL simply contained the domain name plus the name of the HTML file—for example, `http://www.mydomain.com/homepage.html` or `http:// www.mydomain.com/cars/sportscars.html`.

When dynamic websites first appeared, they generally used the query format similar to the previous back-end URL (for example, `http://www.mydomain.com/ index.php?option=com_category&view=blog&id=23`). Initially, search engines such as Google or Yahoo were not good at indexing pages that used query strings in the URL, so dynamic pages did not achieve as high a ranking in search engines as static HTML pages. In response, Joomla and other CMS packages added the ability to use search-engine-friendly (SEF) URLs that looked more like the old static HTML URLs. In the meantime, search engines improved their ability to index URLs that contain queries. Now, search engines generally index URLs with query strings just as well as other URLs, so there is no longer a penalty for using queries in the URL.

Consequently, the term SEF URL is now somewhat of a misnomer. The main reason to use SEF URLs now is to present the website user with a more meaningful, human-friendly URL. SEF URLs have become a standard feature in most CMS software. In Joomla, the site administrator can select whether or not to use SEF URLs. In versions 1.6 and later, the default setting is to use SEF URLs. Also, a number of Joomla extensions provide alternative ways to create SEF URLs. It is believed that the great majority of Joomla sites today use SEF URLs.

A different but related subject is URL rewriting. If you have a popular website and you change the software that runs the site, you may have some pages that users have bookmarked and that have a high ranking in popular search engines. If the new software doesn't have the same exact URL structure, it might not be able to display the page with that URL. In this case, you can create a mapping from the old URL to the new URL and thereby allow users to continue to use the old URL. In Joomla, you can use the redirect component for this, or you can use the rewrite capability of the web server software (such as Apache mod_rewrite).

Best-Fit URL Method

The issue of what URL to show when we show a page seems simple at first, but it can actually be somewhat complicated. The basic problem is that, in many cases, there is more than one way to show a page with essentially the same information.

Consider this example from the Weblinks component. If we load the sample data (for example for version 2.5), we will see a category called Sample Data-Weblinks (with id of 18). It has a child category called Joomla Specific Links (with id of 32), which in turn has a child category called Other Resources (33). We have two Weblinks menu items defined, one for a categories view (which shows the subcategories of Sample Data-Weblinks) and one for a single category view. The single category menu item is defined for category 32 (Joomla Specific Links).

This setup gives us two different ways to find the Weblinks for category 32:

- Select the Weblinks Single Category menu choice from the Using Joomla menu.

- Select the Weblinks Categories menu choice and then click on the link for Joomla Specific Links.

Similarly, we can show the links for category 33 either by clicking on the Other Resources link in the Weblinks Categories page or in the Weblinks Single Category page.

In these situations, we have to decide what URL to show. We could show a different URL depending on how the user navigated to this page. In the first example, we could show the Using Joomla category as its own menu item when you get there using the menu, but show it as a subcategory of the Categories menu item when you get there via the categories menu item.

Other things equal, however, it makes more sense to have the same URL for the same page of content. It is more intuitive and it makes it easier for search engines to catalog that content.

For this reason, the standard Joomla routers use a "best-fit" strategy. This means that the system tries to find an existing menu item that shows this content. If there is one, then we always use that URL when we show the page. If not, then we try to find the menu item that most closely matches the content.

We can see how this works looking at the previous examples. When we click on the Joomla Specific Links while in the categories view, the router looks for an existing menu item for this Weblinks category. Because it finds it, we return the URL for that menu item. The result is the same page and URL as if we had selected the Single Category menu item directly from the menu.

In the second example, we don't have a menu item for category 33 (Other Resources). In this case, we have two choices. Because it is a subcategory of Joomla Specific Links, we could show it as a subcategory of the Single Category menu item. Or we could show it as a sub-subcategory of Sample Data-Weblinks from the categories menu item. In defining the router, we have decided that a single-category view is always to be preferred over the categories view. So we show the URL as a drill-down from the single category menu item. In other words, we show the URL for the single category menu item, followed by the child category id and alias.

We can see this in action with the following test. In the standard sample data, drilling down to the Other Resources category produces the following URL:

```
index.php/using-joomla/extensions/components/weblinks-component/
weblinks-single-category/33-other-resources
```

This shows the URL for the single category menu item and appends the current category's id (33) and alias (other-resources) to it. We get this same URL whether we drill down from the Weblinks Categories menu item or the Weblinks Single Category menu item.

Next, go into the back end of Joomla and unpublish the Weblinks Single Category menu item. Then click on the Other Resources category from the Weblinks Categories page. Now the URL is as follows:

```
index.php/using-joomla/extensions/components/weblinks-component/
weblinks-categories/32-joomla-specific-links/33-other-resources
```

Because we no longer have the single category available, we choose the next closest option, which is the drill-down from the categories menu item. The categories menu item is associated with category 18 (Sample Data-Weblinks). This is the grandparent category of category 33. So we show the category path from category 18 down to the current category—in this case, first category 32, then category 33.

What if we don't have any matching menu items? In the back end, unpublish both the categories and single category menu items. Now we don't have a menu item to click, but we can manually enter in a URL in query form to show the Weblinks category, as follows:

```
index.php?option=com_weblinks&view=category&id=33
```

What we get is the Other Resources page, and we get the query form of the URL, just as we typed it in. The router is able to successfully load the component and view, but it cannot find an SEF URL that matches. Note also that when we load the page, we only get modules that are assigned to all menu items. This is because we don't have an Itemid in the query. If we added one, we would get the modules, template, and language assigned to that menu item.

Building the URL

Now let's look in more detail at how this is accomplished in the code. Let's start with the layout file for the categories view. The file `views/categories/tmpl/default_items.php` is responsible for displaying the information for each individual Weblinks category. There we find the following code:

```
    <span class="item-title"><a href="<?php
➥echo JRoute::_(WeblinksHelperRoute::getCategoryRoute($item->id));?>">
        <?php echo $this->escape($item->title); ?></a>
    </span>
```

The highlighted line of code does two things. First, it executes the `getCategoryRoute()` method for the category id (`$item->id` is the category id). This creates a link in the form of a URL query. It passes the result of this link to the `JRoute::_()` method and that result is echoed as the URL inside the `href` attribute of the anchor element.

Get the Best-Fit Menu Item

In the `getCategoryRoute()` method (`helpers/route.php`), we find the menu item that is the best fit for the current category id. How do we do this?

There are two basic steps. The first step is to see if we have a single category menu item for the given category. If we find one, we return a URL that just points to that menu item and we are done.

If we don't find an exact match, we look for a Weblinks menu item that points to one of the parent categories (parent, grandparent, and so on) of the current category. To do this, we create an array of all the parent categories for our current category. Then we check each of these against the list of Weblinks menu items. We check single category views first because we consider these a better match than the categories view. If we can't find a single category for any of the parent categories, we check the categories view menu items. Finally, if we can't find any Weblinks category or categories menu items that match any of the parent categories, we just use the currently active menu item to create the link.

Now let's look at the code. The first part of **getCategoryRoute()** gets a **JCategory-Node** object for the current category. The key line of code is

```
$category = JCategories::getInstance('Weblinks')->get($id);
```

A little further on, after we have checked that we have a valid category, we see this code:

```
    $needles = array(
    'category' => array($id)
  );

  if ($item = self::_findItem($needles)) {
    $link = 'index.php?Itemid='.$item;
  }
```

This is where we try to find an exact match. We create an associative array with the view (category) and the category id. Then we see if this matches one of the existing menu items, using the **_findItem()** method.

Note that we use **self::** instead of **$this->** to call the **_findItem()** method. This is because **_findItem()** is a static method. The keyword **self** refers to "this class," whereas the variable **$this** refers to "this object." So we need to use **self** when calling static methods or referring to static fields when inside the class that defines them. The **self** keyword was introduced with PHP version 5.

If we find an exact match, we are done. If not, we execute this code block:

```
//Create the link
$link = 'index.php?option=com_weblinks&view=category&id='.$id;

if ($category) {
  $catids = array_reverse($category->getPath());
  $needles = array(
    'category' => $catids,
    'categories' => $catids
  );

  if ($item = self::_findItem($needles)) {
    $link .= '&Itemid='.$item;
  }
  else if ($item = self::_findItem()) {
    $link .= '&Itemid='.$item;
  }
}
```

Here we create the link except for the category id. Then we create the list of the parent category ids for the current id using the **getPath()** method of the **JCategoryNode** class. In our example, recall that the parent of category 33 (Other Resources) is 32

(Joomla Specific Links) and in turn its parent is 18 (Sample Data-Weblinks). The `getPath()` method returns all the parent categories in an array in the format <id> + : + <alias>. So for category 33, `getPath()` returns:

```
0 => 18:sample-data-weblinks
1 => 32:joomla-specific-links
2 => 33:other-resources
```

The `array_reverse` just reverses the order so 33 is element 0 and 18 is element 3, as shown in the following:

```
0 => 33:other-resources
1 => 32:joomla-specific-links
2 => 18:sample-data-weblinks
```

This is saved in the `$catids` variable.

Then we create an array called `$needles`, which we will use to compare to the list of Weblinks menu items. The `$needles` variable is an associative array with two elements whose keys are "category" and "categories". The value for both keys is the `$catids` array.

Then we call the method `self::_findItem($needles)` again. This time we have broadened the search to include any parent category and to include the categories menu item.

Because category is the first array key in `$needles`, we first search all the Weblinks menu items for a single category item to see if the category id matches one of the parent ids for our category. Failing that, we will repeat the process checking for Weblinks menu items with the view equal to categories.

In the `_findItem()` method, the first block of code is as follows:

```
protected static function _findItem($needles = null)
{
    $app       = JFactory::getApplication();
    $menus     = $app->getMenu('site');

    // Prepare the reverse lookup array.
    if (self::$lookup === null) {
      self::$lookup = array();

      $component = JComponentHelper::getComponent('com_weblinks');
      $items     = $menus->getItems('component_id', $component->id);
      foreach ($items as $item)
      {
        if (isset($item->query) && isset($item->query['view'])) {
          $view = $item->query['view'];

          if (!isset(self::$lookup[$view])) {
            self::$lookup[$view] = array();
          }
```

```
            if (isset($item->query['id'])) {
              self::$lookup[$view][$item->query['id']] = $item->id;
            }
          }
        }
      }
```

The variable $menus holds a JMenuSite object. The WeblinksHelperRoute class has a static field called $lookup. Because it is static, we only need to set its values once. As long as this class stays in memory, the static fields will stay defined. In the if statement we check to see whether it has already been set. If so, we don't set it again.

To set up the $lookup array, we use the getItems() method of JMenuSite to get all the menu items for the Weblinks component. This returns an array of standard class objects, each of which contains the fields for a Weblinks menu item.

Then we loop through the Weblinks menu items array and create an associative array where the key is the view from the menu item query and the value is another associative array. In this array, the key is the query id (the category id) and the value is the menu item id. In our example using the sample data, $lookup is defined as follows:

```
categories => array (0 => 438, 18 => 227)
category => array(32 => 274, 31 => 296)
```

(Note that the exact id numbers might change, based on sample data changes. However, the concept will be the same as shown here.) This shows that we have four Weblinks menu items defined: two that use the categories view and two that use the single category view. The categories menu items are 438, which points to category id 0 (the root category for the whole table), and 227, which points to category 18 (Sample Data-Weblinks). The single category menu items are 274, which points to category 32, and 296, which points to category 31.

Once we have $fields defined, we can find the best match for the current category, using the $needles array. The code for this is as follows:

```
if ($needles) {
  foreach ($needles as $view => $ids)
  {
    if (isset(self::$lookup[$view])) {
      foreach($ids as $id)
      {
        if (isset(self::$lookup[$view][(int)$id])) {
          return self::$lookup[$view][(int)$id];
        }
      }
    }
  }
}
```

We loop through the `$needles` array by view. We first look at the category view and then at the categories view.

We loop through each of the `$ids` in the category hierarchy. Recall that we reversed the array order so that the current category (33) is first, then the parent (32), then that category's parent (18), and so on. So we are looking in our exact order of preference. Therefore, as soon as we get a successful match on view and category id (in the shaded line), we simply return that menu item id, which is the value for that array element. The `return` command exits the method immediately.

Recall that the values in `$needles` include the category alias (for example, "33:other resources"). So `$id` will be in this format. For that reason, we use the (int) command to convert `$id` to just the category id (for example, 33) when we access the `$lookup` array.

The only other thing we have to do is allow for the case where there is no match. In that case, we simply return the current active menu item id. Then, back in the `getCategoryRoute()` method, we append the item id to the link (for example, "&Itemid=274") and return the link.

At this point, we have a link that points to the menu item in the site that is the best fit for the current category id. It is one of the following, in order of priority:

- A Weblinks single category menu item for this category
- A Weblinks single category menu item for one of this category's parent categories
- A Weblinks categories menu item for one of this category's parent categories
- The currently active menu item

Find the Category Path from the Menu Item

Now that we have the Itemid of the best-fit menu item, we can finish the routing process. Recall that the line of code that started this was as follows:

```
echo JRoute::_(WeblinksHelperRoute::getCategoryRoute($item->id));
```

Now we pass this link to the `JRoute::_()` method. This method first gets the router, which in the front end will be `JRouterSite` (`includes/router.php`). Then it calls the `build()` method of `JRouterSite`.

If the SEF option is set to yes, the `build()` method takes a URL with a query (for example, `index.php?option=com_weblinks&Itemid=274`) and returns an SEF URL (for example, `index.php/using-joomla/extensions/components/weblinks-component/weblinks-single-category`).

The first thing the `build()` method does is call the `build()` method of its parent, `JRouter`. When the SEF option is set to yes, we then call the protected method `_build-SefRoute()` (back in the `JRouterSite` class). This method has the following code:

```
// Use the component routing handler if it exists
$path = JPATH_SITE . '/components/' . $component . '/router.php';

// Use the custom routing handler if it exists
if (file_exists($path) && !empty($query)) {
```

```
require_once $path;
$function = substr($component, 4).'BuildRoute';
$function = str_replace(array("-", "."), "", $function);
$parts = $function($query);
```

Here we check to see if we have a router provided for the component that uses the prescribed naming convention. It needs to be a file called `router.php` in the top-level component file, and it needs to contain a function called

```
<component name (less the "com_" part)> + "BuildRoute"
```

If such a file is found, the last line in the previous code block executes the function and returns an array called `$parts`.

In Weblinks, we have this file, called `components/com_weblinks/router.php`, and it has a method called `WeblinksBuildRoute()`. Note that this file does not declare a class; it only declares the `build()` and `parse()` functions.

Recall from the previous section that when we have a single-category menu item that points to this Weblinks category, we just use the routing for that menu item. So the `WeblinksBuildRoute()` method returns an empty array when the current category matches the category used in a category menu item.

On the other hand, when we are linking to a Weblinks category that doesn't have an associated menu item, we have to find which (if any) parent category matches the best-fit menu item and then show the part of the category hierarchy that connects the menu item's category to our current category. This is done in the following code:

```
if ($category) {
   //TODO Throw error that the category either not exists or is
→unpublished
   $path = $category->getPath();
   $path = array_reverse($path);

   $array = array();
   foreach($path as $id)
   {
     if ((int) $id == (int)$menuCatid) {
       break;
     }

     if ($advanced) {
       list($tmp, $id) = explode(':', $id, 2);
     }

     $array[] = $id;
   }
   $segments = array_merge($segments, array_reverse($array));
}
```

This code is a bit tricky. At this point in the code, we know that we have a category that doesn't have its own menu item. However, one of its parent categories probably does have a menu item. We know this because this link already contains the best-matching menu item.

In the `$category` variable we have a `JCategoryNode` object for the current category. Again we use `getPath()` to return the entire hierarchy for this category. Then the `array_reverse` command reverses the order of the elements in the array, just like we saw in the previous example.

Next, we loop through the parent categories. The key to understanding this is the highlighted code. As long as we don't have a match, we add the `$id` to the `$array` variable. Then we loop again. When we finally get a match, we do the `break` command which exits the `foreach` loop.

The result is that the current category and all the parent categories up to (but not including) the matching category are added to the array. Then we reverse the order, so it is again starting at the top and working down the category hierarchy.

Finally, we use `array_merge` to add this to the `$segments` array. At the end of the method, we return this value. In our example of drilling down to the Other Resources category, `$segments` will contain one element:

```
0 => 33:other-resources
```

In the example where we unpublish the Weblinks Single Category menu item (so that the Weblinks Categories is the best fit), `$segments` will contain two elements:

```
0 => 33:other-resources, 1 => 32:joomla-specific-links
```

At this point, we return to the calling method, which is the `_buildSefRoute()` method of `JRouterSite`. There we combine these segments, putting a "/" between each, and add "component/" to the front of it. Finally, we set the path of the `JURI` object to this value.

At this point, we have created a URL that points to the closest-matching menu item. If necessary, we have also included the category path from the menu item's category down to the current category. This provides us with a URL that is consistent, logical, and user-friendly.

Parsing the URL

In the build process, we start with a Weblinks category id and build a URL to take us to the category view for that category. We also need to be able to work in the opposite direction. That is, we need to be able to take an SEF URL created by the `build()` method and get a query that will take us to the correct view.

This process is similar to the build method described previously. Here we start with the `$app->route()` command in our top-level `index.php` file. This gets our `JRouterSite` object and executes its `parse()` method. As with the previous example, we call the parent's `parse()` method, which in turn calls the `JRouterSite _parseSefRoute()` method. In this method we find the part of the SEF URL that specifies the menu item (for example, "components/weblinks-component/single-weblink-category") and set the menu item based on that. We also strip off that part of the URL (the part that points to the menu item), leaving only the category path. Then we convert the category path to an array, splitting it at the "/" character, and change each segment to the format <id> + : + <alias>.

Then we call the component's `parse()` method—in our case, `WeblinksParseRoute()`, passing the array of category path values. There we get the child categories for this menu item's category. We compare each child category's "slug" field (which is in the same format as the segments) to the passed-in array of categories. When we get a match, we create an associative array with id set to the category id and view set to "category". This is returned to the calling method and these variables are added to the query of the URL.

In our example, the SEF URL is converted to the following array:

```
Itemid => 274, option => com_weblinks, id => 33, view => category
```

This is the information Joomla needs to correctly load the component and view.

Front-End News Feed View

One other important difference between the front and back end of Weblinks is the news feed view. In the core Weblinks component, we have the option of presenting a news feed for the single category view. A news feed allows someone to subscribe to this menu item and automatically receive updates as the page changes.

Joomla has this capability built in, so we don't have to do much work to add news feeds to any component. Recall in the Edit Menu Item screen we have an option to show a feed link. If we look at the `display()` method of the `views/category/view.html.php` file, we call the method `_prepareDocument()`. At the end of that method, we see this code:

```
// Add alternative feed link
if ($this->params->get('show_feed_link', 1) == 1)
{
  $link = '&format=feed&limitstart=';
  $attribs = array('type' => 'application/rss+xml', 'title' =>
➥'RSS 2.0');
  $this->document->addHeadLink(JRoute::_($link.'&type=rss'),
➥'alternate', 'rel', $attribs);
$attribs = array('type' => 'application/atom+xml', 'title' =>
➥'Atom 1.0');
  $this->document->addHeadLink(JRoute::_($link.'&type=atom'),
➥'alternate', 'rel', $attribs);
}
```

If we have elected to show a feed link for this item, we create two links, one for the RSS 2.0 format and one for the Atom 1.0 format. We use the same `JRoute::_()`

method as before, and we use this link as the argument for the `addHeadLink()` method of the `JDocument` class. This creates the link needed for a user to subscribe to the feed. For example, in Firefox, this link shows as a feed symbol just to the right of the URL.

Notice in the link we have "format=feed". When we load that URL, that value is loaded into the request. When we create the document object for that URL, instead of our normal `JDocumentHTML` object, we create instead a `JDocumentFeed` object. In `JController`'s `display()` method, we set the `$viewType` to "feed." Then, when we execute the `getView()` method, we load the `views/category/view.feed.php` file instead of the `view.html.php` file.

The `view.feed.php` file is similar to the `view.html.php` file. The first thing to note is that it declares the same class, `WeblinksViewCategory`, as the `view.html.php` file. This is just a different format of the same information, so we give it the same class name. In any given request cycle, we will only have one of these classes loaded.

This class has one method, `display()`. Its code is very simple. We get the application and document objects and set the link field to the URL using the same method as in the previous section (`JRoute::_()` and `WeblinksHelperRoute::getCategoryRoute()`). Then we set some values for the view, including the number of items to show and the site's e-mail and editor information. This is set up in the Global Configuration screen.

Then we get our items and category from the model. We loop through the items and create a URL for each one. We also remove any HTML code from the item's title and convert the date to a string format. Then we create a new `JFeedItem` object and add the information to that object. Finally, we insert the `JFeedItem` object into our document using the `addItem()` method of `JDocumentFeed`.

That's all there is to it. All the special formatting required for news feeds is handled automatically for us by the `JDocumentFeed` and `JFeedItem` classes. This same technique allows us to add a news feed for any component.

Summary

In this chapter we completed our examination of the Weblinks core component. We started with the view classes in the administrative back end. This included looking at the layout for the manager screen and the use of `JForm` for the edit screen. Then we reviewed the front end of the component and discussed the similarities and differences of the front and back end. We looked in detail at how SEF URLs are created and decoded and looked at how news feeds are generated.

The next two chapters apply what we learned to create our own component.

Components Part III: Example Component Back End

In the previous two chapters, we looked at the Weblinks component to understand how components and the model-view-controller (MVC) design pattern work in the Joomla! core. In this chapter, we apply what we have learned and create the back-end code for our example component. We have tried to keep the example component as simple as possible while still using most of the important features we have discussed.

Note

The code for the example component may be downloaded from `http://www.joomla programmingbook.com`. You can download and install the code before reading this chapter, or you can create the component as we go along and only use the downloaded code to check your work. The second option is more work but will likely help you understand the code better.

Example Component Functional Overview

Let's first review the functional design of our component. We'll call the component JoomPro Subscriptions. Its purpose is to allow the site administrator to create subscriptions and to allow site users to subscribe to the subscriptions. Each subscription has a description, a category, and a duration (in days). Each subscription is also associated with a normal Joomla user group (as set up in Users → Groups).

When a user subscribes to the subscription, he or she is added to this group automatically. In addition, the start and end dates for this user's subscription are stored in a database table.

In this example, we are not covering what happens after a user subscribes to a subscription. Given that they are added to a group, one possibility might be that they are given access to a restricted part of the website. Also, the only thing we will require for a user to subscribe is for them to agree to the terms of service. If you understand this simple example, it should not be difficult to see how you might add features such as requiring payment.

We show almost all the code for the component in code listings in this chapter. You can download the entire component as a zip archive from the book's website, (joomlaprogrammingbook.com).

Detailed Design

To implement our design, we will need back-end manager screens to manage the subscriptions and the subscription categories. We will also need a form to add and edit subscriptions. A subscription will have the following fields: title, description, published state, category id, user group id, duration (days), and access id. We will use an integer id field for the primary key for the subscription.

We will also need a table to store the information for each user's subscription. This will need to have the user id, subscription id, and the start and end dates for the subscription.

On the front end, we will have a view of subscriptions by category. If a user is authorized to edit our subscription (using the standard access control list [ACL]), they will be able to click on the subscription and subscribe to it. If successful, a "thank-you" screen will show.

Let's summarize the design in terms of the back-end and front-end views. In the back end we will have the following:

- Subscription Manager: Subscriptions screen (called submanager)
- Subscription Manager: Categories screen (handled by the com_categories component)
- Subscription Manager: Add/Edit screen (called subscription)

In the front end, we will have the following views:

- Show subscriptions by category view (called category).
- Subscribe to a subscription (called form).

We will need to add two database tables, as follows:

- Table to hold the list of subscriptions available (called `#__joompro_subscriptions`)
- Table to hold the information for each user's subscriptions (called `#__joompro_sub_mapping`)

At this point, we have enough information about our component to start coding. Note that there is no "right" order in which to code a component. One way is to start with the database tables and then work back to the models, controllers, and views. Here we will follow the program flow. We will first look at the programs called when we use the back-end manager screen. Then we will look at the back-end add/edit programs. In the next chapter, we go to the front end and look at the category list programs and finally the subscribe programs.

Back-End Files

Table 9.1 shows the back-end files required for our component. This excludes `index.html` files, which should be present in each folder. The paths are relative to the component's base folder, `administrator/components/com_joomprosubs`.

The first thing we need to do in the back end is to create a folder called `administrator/components/com_joomprosubs`. Because all the back-end component files

Table 9.1 **Back-End Subscriptions Component Folders**

File Name	Contents
`access.xml`	Component and category level ACL actions
`config.xml`	Fields for component options
`controller.php`	JoomproSubsController class
`joomprosubs.php`	Component entry point script
`joomprosubs.xml`	Installation XML file
`controllers/subscription.php`	JoomprosubsControllerSubscription class (single item add / edit controller)
`controllers/submanager.php`	JoomprosubsControllerSubManager class (manager screen controller)
`helpers/joomprosubs.php`	JoomproSubsHelper class
`language/en-GB/en-GB.com_joomprosubs.ini`	Component language file
`language/en-GB/en-GB.com_joomprosubs.sys.ini`	System language file
`models/subscription.php`	JoomprosubsModelSubscription (single item add / edit model)
`models/submanager.php`	JoomprosubsModelSubManager class (manager screen model)
`models/forms/subscription.xml`	JForm XML file for add / edit layout
`sql/install.mysql.utf8.sql`	SQL install script
`sql/uninstall.mysql.utf8.sql`	SQL uninstall script
`tables/subscription.php`	JoomproSubsTableSubscription class (for writing rows to database)
`views/subscription/view.html.php`	JoomprosSubsViewSubscription class (single item view)
`views/subscription/tmpl/edit.php`	Layout file for single item add / edit
`views/submanager/view.html.php`	JoomprosSubsViewSubManager class (manager screen view)
`views/submanager/tmpl/default.php`	Layout file for manager screen

are in that folder, we will reference component files relative to this folder in the rest of this section.

In the component back-end folder, we will create the entry point for our component's back end, called `joomprosubs.php`. Recall that Joomla automatically loads this file when we have a back-end URL with "option=com_joomprosubs".

The code for this file is shown here:

```php
<?php
/**
 * @package     Joomla.Site
 * @subpackage com_joomprosubs
 * @copyright  Copyright (C) 2012 Mark Dexter and Louis Landry. All rights
 reserved.
 * @license     GNU General Public License version 2 or later; see
 LICENSE.txt
 */

// no direct access
defined('_JEXEC') or die;

// Access check.
if (!JFactory::getUser()->authorise('core.manage', 'com_joomprosubs')) {
        return JError::raiseWarning(404, JText::_('JERROR_ALERTNOAUTHOR'));
}

// Include dependencies
jimport('joomla.application.component.controller');

$controller = JController::getInstance('JoomproSubs');
$controller->execute(JRequest::getCmd('task'));
$controller->redirect();
```

This code should be familiar. It is identical to the `administrator/components/com_weblinks/weblinks.php` file we looked at in Chapter 7, except that we check that the user is authorized for the `com_joomprosubs` component and we get the controller for "JoomproSubs".

Subscriptions Manager: Subscriptions Screen

This screen will show the list of subscriptions that the administrator has created. A screenshot is shown in Figure 9.1. It will be similar to the Weblinks Manager and other core manager screens. Note that this screen has all the normal features of a core Joomla component manager screen. These include the following:

- A toolbar with the normal tasks (New, Edit, and so on)
- A filter box for filtering by subscription title

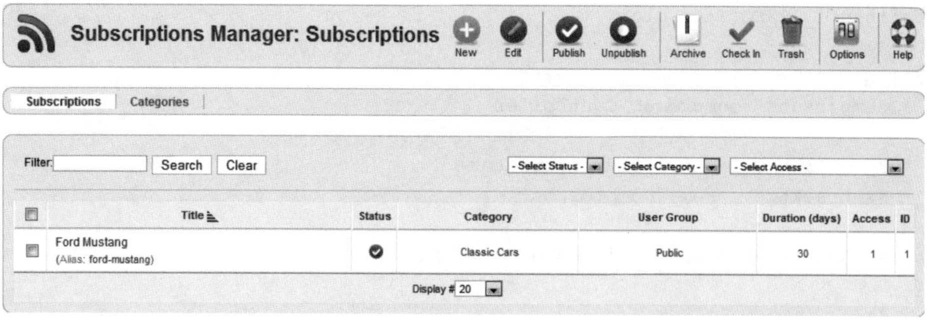

Figure 9.1   Subscriptions Manager screen

- Filter drop-downs for filtering on published status, category, and access
- Check boxes to allow the toolbars to operate on multiple items
- Column headings that allow sorting by that column
- Pagination controls

The following files are used to create this:

- controller.php (JoomproSubsController)
- views/submanager/view.html.php (JoomproSubsViewSubManager)
- helpers/joomprosubs.php (JoomproSubsHelper)
- models/submanager.php (JoomproSubsModelSubManager)
- sql/install.mysql.utf8.sql
- views/submanager/tmpl/default.php

Default Controller

When we load the manager screen, recall from Chapter 7 that the first class loaded is the default controller with the default task of display. In our case, the default controller is `JoomproSubsController`. The code for this class is shown in Listing 9.1.

Listing 9.1   **JoomproSubsController Class (controller.php)**

```php
<?php
/**
 * @package      Joomla.Administrator
 * @subpackage   com_joomprosubs
 * @copyright    Copyright (C) 2012 Mark Dexter and Louis Landry. All rights
➥reserved.
 * @license      GNU General Public License version 2 or later; see
➥LICENSE.txt
 */

// No direct access
```

```php
defined('_JEXEC') or die;

/**
 *Joomprosubs joomprosub Controller
 *
 * @package        Joomla.Administrator
 * @subpackage     com_joomprosubs
 */
class JoomproSubsController extends JController
{
    /**
     * @var     string  The default view.
     * @since   2.5
     */
    protected $default_view = 'submanager';

    /**
     * Method to display a view.
     *
     * @param    boolean     $cachable   If true, the view output will be
    cached
     * @param    array       $urlparams  An array of safe url parameters and
    their variable types, for valid values see {@link JFilterInput::clean()}.
     *
     * @return   JController This object to support chaining.
     */
    public function display($cachable = false, $urlparams = false)
    {
        JLoader::register('JoomproSubsHelper',
    JPATH_COMPONENT.'/helpers/joomprosubs.php');

        // Load the submenu.
        JoomproSubsHelper::addSubmenu(JRequest::getCmd('view', 'submanager'));

        $view = JRequest::getCmd('view', 'submanager');
        $layout = JRequest::getCmd('layout', 'default');
        $id = JRequest::getInt('id');

        // Check for edit form.
        if ($view == 'subscription' && $layout == 'edit' &&
    !$this->checkEditId('com_joomprosubs.edit.subscription', $id)) {
            // Somehow the person just went to the form - we don't allow that.
            $this->setError(JText::sprintf('JLIB_APPLICATION_ERROR_UNHELD_ID',
    $id));
            $this->setMessage($this->getError(), 'error');
            $this->setRedirect(JRoute::_(
    'index.php?option=com_joomprosubs&view=submanager', false));
```

```
        return false;
    }

    parent::display();

    return $this;
    }
}
```

This code is almost identical to the `WeblinksController` class we discussed in Chapter 7. It extends the `JController` class. Note that we include a protected field called `$default_view`, set to "submanager". This wasn't defined in the Weblinks controller. This field is where we name the default view for the back end of the component. In our example, this is "submanager". The reason we didn't need to specify this in Weblinks is that Joomla supplies a default value equal to the component name (without the "com_"). That gave us a value of "weblinks" for `com_weblinks`, which was correct. However, the default would give us a value of "joomprosubs" in this case, which is not what we want. So we define our default view using `$default_view` field.

The `JoomproSubsController` class has one method, called `display()`. This method includes our helper file. Note that we use the `JLoader::register()` method instead of `require_once`. Recall that `JLoader::register()` executes more quickly and is preferred whenever we need to load a class. We use the constant `JPATH_COMPONENT` to point to the component folder (in our case, `administrator/components/com _joomprosubs`) and then we invoke the `addSubmenu()` method of the helper class.

We then get the view, layout, and subscription id from the request. We check to make sure that the user has not tried to go directly to the edit form. Finally, we call the parent's (`JController`) `display()` method, which gets the view and executes it.

Submanager Controller and Toolbar Tasks

The default controller handles the display task, part of which is to display the toolbar (as shown in Figure 9.1). The first two toolbar icons are New and Edit. Those are handled by the subscription controller, which we discuss later in this chapter. The other tasks on the toolbar are publish, unpublish, archive, check in, trash, options, and help.

Recall from Chapter 7 that the publish, unpublish, archive, and trash tasks all map to the `publish()` method in the controller. The checkin task maps to the `checkin()` method. Also, recall that the `WeblinksControllerWeblinks` class only had one method, called `getModel()`. This is because it inherits the `publish()` and `checkin()` methods from its parent class, `JControllerAdmin`.

The same thing is true for the `JoomproSubsControllerSubManager` controller (`controllers/submanager.php`). It only needs one method—`getModel()`, as shown in Listing 9.2.

Listing 9.2   **JoomproSubsControllerSubManager Class**

```php
<?php
/**
 * @copyright   Copyright (C) 2012 Mark Dexter and Louis Landry. All rights
➥reserved.
 * @license     GNU General Public License version 2 or later; see
➥LICENSE.txt
 */

// No direct access.
defined('_JEXEC') or die;

jimport('joomla.application.component.controlleradmin');

/**
 * Joomprosubs list controller class.
 *
 * @since       2.5
 */
class JoomproSubsControllerSubManager extends JControllerAdmin
{
    /**
     * Proxy for getModel.
     */
    public function getModel($name = 'Subscription', $prefix =
➥'JoomproSubsModel', $config = array('ignore_request' => true))
    {
        $model = parent::getModel($name, $prefix, $config);
        return $model;
    }
} // end of class
```

This method allows the controller to get the correct model—in this case, `Joompro-SubsModelSubscription`. It inherits the `publish()` and `checkin()` methods from its parent class, `JControllerAdmin`. So we just use the methods for these tasks with no modification and no extra work.

The other toolbar icons are options and help. Recall that the options icon calls the com_config component using the `config.xml` file. The contents of `config.xml` are as follows:

```xml
<?xml version="1.0" encoding="utf-8"?>
<config>
    <fieldset name="permissions"
        description="JCONFIG_PERMISSIONS_DESC"
        label="JCONFIG_PERMISSIONS_LABEL"
    >
```

```
        <field name="rules" type="rules"
            component="COM_JOOMPROSUBS"
            filter="rules"
            validate="rules"
            label="JCONFIG_PERMISSIONS_LABEL"
            section="component" />
    </fieldset>
</config>
```

If we had component-level options, we would specify them here and they would show in the Options screen. In our example, we don't have any options. We only have the permissions. We specify this using a rules field.

We also need to specify the actions for our component by creating a file called `access.xml`. The contents of the file for our component are as follows:

```
<?xml version="1.0" encoding="utf-8"?>
<access component="com_joomprosubs">
    <section name="component">
      <action name="core.admin" title="JACTION_ADMIN"
→description="JACTION_ADMIN_COMPONENT_DESC" />
      <action name="core.manage" title="JACTION_MANAGE"
→description="JACTION_MANAGE_COMPONENT_DESC" />
      <action name="core.create" title="JACTION_CREATE"
→description="JACTION_CREATE_COMPONENT_DESC" />
      <action name="core.delete" title="JACTION_DELETE"
→description="JACTION_DELETE_COMPONENT_DESC" />
      <action name="core.edit" title="JACTION_EDIT"
→description="JACTION_EDIT_COMPONENT_DESC" />
      <action name="core.edit.state" title="JACTION_EDITSTATE"
→description="JACTION_EDITSTATE_COMPONENT_DESC" />
      <action name="core.edit.own" title="JACTION_EDITOWN"
→description="JACTION_EDITOWN_COMPONENT_DESC" />
    </section>
    <section name="category">
      <action name="core.create" title="JACTION_CREATE"
→description="COM_CATEGORIES_ACCESS_CREATE_DESC" />
      <action name="core.delete" title="JACTION_DELETE"
→description="COM_CATEGORIES_ACCESS_DELETE_DESC" />
      <action name="core.edit" title="JACTION_EDIT"
→description="COM_CATEGORIES_ACCESS_EDIT_DESC" />
      <action name="core.edit.state" title="JACTION_EDITSTATE"
→description="COM_CATEGORIES_ACCESS_EDITSTATE_DESC" />
      <action name="core.edit.own" title="JACTION_EDITOWN"
→description="COM_CATEGORIES_ACCESS_EDITOWN_DESC" />
    </section>
</access>
```

Because we use the same actions as Weblinks at both the component and category levels, this file is identical to the Weblinks `access.xml` file except for the component name on the second line.

Once we finish coding our component, we will be able to click the Options icon to see the permissions screen shown in Figure 9.2.

Manager View

The view for the manager screen is named `JoomproSubsViewSubManager`, which follows the naming convention discussed in Chapter 7. The third part of the name ("SubManager") is just a description of the view. We don't need to worry about another component having this name because we have already made the name unique to our component with the first segment ("JoomproSubs"). This class is in the file `views/submanager/view.html.php`, again following the same conventions as the core components.

The code for the first part of this class is as follows:

```
defined('_JEXEC') or die;

jimport('joomla.application.component.view');

/**
 * View class for a list of subscriptions.
 *
 */
class JoomproSubsViewSubmanager extends JView
{
    protected $items;
    protected $pagination;
```

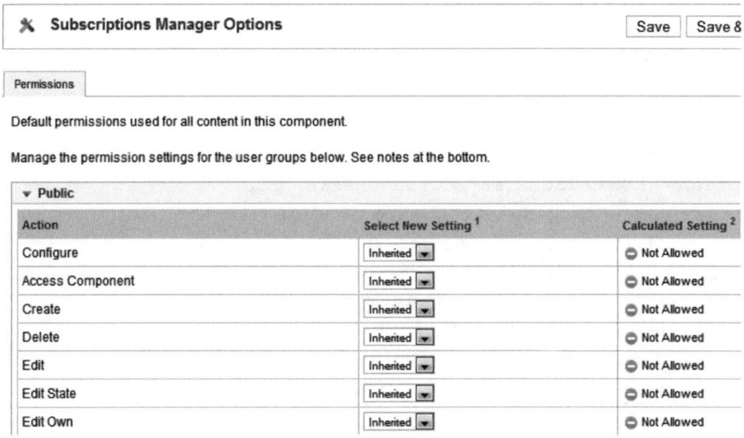

Figure 9.2   Options screen

```
   protected $state;

   /**
    * Display the view
    */
   public function display($tpl = null)
   {
      $this->state = $this->get('State');
      $this->items = $this->get('Items');
      $this->pagination = $this->get('Pagination');

      // Check for errors.
      if (count($errors = $this->get('Errors'))) {
         JError::raiseError(500, implode("\n", $errors));
         return false;
      }

      $this->addToolbar();
      parent::display($tpl);
   }
```

Again, this code is almost identical to the WeblinksViewWeblinks class, except of
course we refer to the joomprosubs component name instead of Weblinks.

The class extends JView, and we have class fields for items, pagination, and state.
The only public method for this class is display(). This method gets the state, items,
and pagination from the model, checks for errors, adds the toolbar, and then calls the
display() method of JView (its parent).

The only other method in this class is addToolbar(), shown here:

```
/**
 * Add the page title and toolbar.
 *
 * @since 2.5
 */
protected function addToolbar()
{
   JLoader::register('JoomproSubsHelper',
↪JPATH_COMPONENT.'/helpers/joomprosubs.php');

   $state  = $this->get('State');
   $canDo  = JoomprosubsHelper::getActions(
↪$state->get('filter.category_id'));
   $user   = JFactory::getUser();

   JToolBarHelper::title(JText::_(
↪'COM_JOOMPROSUBS_MANAGER_JOOMPROSUBS'), 'newsfeeds.png');
   if (count($user->getAuthorisedCategories('com_joomprosubs',
```

```
↪'core.create')) > 0) {
        JToolBarHelper::addNew('subscription.add','JTOOLBAR_NEW');
   }
   if ($canDo->get('core.edit')) {
        JToolBarHelper::editList('subscription.edit','JTOOLBAR_EDIT');
   }

   if ($canDo->get('core.edit.state')) {

        JToolBarHelper::divider();
        JToolBarHelper::publish('submanager.publish',
↪'JTOOLBAR_PUBLISH', true);
        JToolBarHelper::unpublish('submanager.unpublish',
↪'JTOOLBAR_UNPUBLISH', true);

        JToolBarHelper::divider();
        JToolBarHelper::archiveList('submanager.archive');
        JToolBarHelper::checkin('submanager.checkin');
      }

   if ($state->get('filter.state') == -2 && $canDo->get('core.delete')) {
        JToolBarHelper::deleteList('', 'submanager.delete',
↪'JTOOLBAR_EMPTY_TRASH');
        JToolBarHelper::divider();
      } else if ($canDo->get('core.edit.state')) {
        JToolBarHelper::trash('submanager.trash','JTOOLBAR_TRASH');
        JToolBarHelper::divider();
   }
   if ($canDo->get('core.admin')) {
        JToolBarHelper::preferences('com_joomprosubs');
        JToolBarHelper::divider();
   }

   JToolBarHelper::help('', '', JText::_(
↪ 'COM_JOOMPROSUBS_SUBMANAGER_HELP_LINK'));
}
```

Again, this code is almost identical to the corresponding code in Weblinks. We load the helper file and use it to create an object to hold this user's authorized actions. We then show the toolbar icons if the user's permissions authorize that action. Again, recall that checking is for the user interface but is not by itself sufficient to protect from an unauthorized user trying to perform an action. We also need to repeat these checks when we are performing each task.

If the user has permissions for the core.admin action, we add the Options toolbar button. Recall that this adds a link to the com_config component with the options specified in the config.xml file.

The last line of code creates the help icon on the toolbar. In this case, we are specifying that the help button will take the user to the URL specified in the language file for the key "COM_JOOMPROSUBS_SUBMANAGER_HELP_LINK". By making this value language dependent, we make it easy for someone to create a help screen in a different language. The `JToolBarHelper::help()` method creates the following HTML code in our page:

```
<a class="toolbar" rel="help" onclick="popupWindow(
'http://joomlaprogrammingbook.com/joompro-subscriptions-help.html', 'Help',
➥700, 500, 1)" href="#">
<span class="icon-32-help">
</span>
Help
</a>
```

The URL comes from the translation of our language key "COM_JOOMPRO-SUBS_SUBMANAGER_HELP_LINK". When clicked, this opens the link in a pop-up window, as shown in Figure 9.3.

We could also point to a local help file if we preferred. To do that, we would specify the file name in the second argument of the method. We could again use `JText::_` () to allow for different files for different languages.

Helper Class

Note in the previous file we invoked the `JoomprosubsHelper::getActions()` method from the file `helpers/joomprosubs.php`. The first part of the code for this file is as follows:

```
defined('_JEXEC') or die;

/**
 *Joomprosubs helper.
 *
 */
class JoomproSubsHelper
{
```

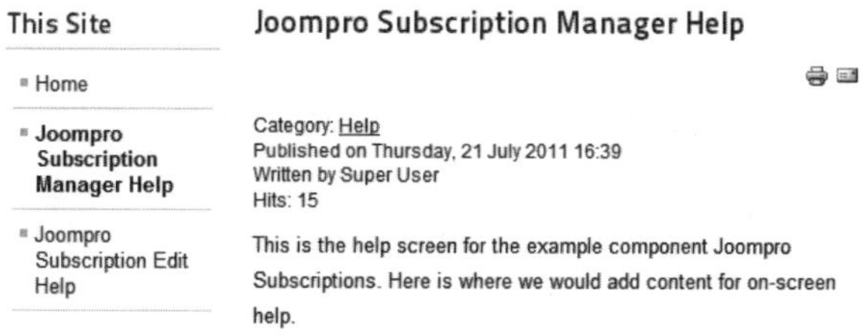

This Site	Joompro Subscription Manager Help
▪ Home	
▪ **Joompro Subscription Manager Help**	Category: Help Published on Thursday, 21 July 2011 16:39 Written by Super User Hits: 15
▪ Joompro Subscription Edit Help	This is the help screen for the example component Joompro Subscriptions. Here is where we would add content for on-screen help.

Figure 9.3   Component help screen

```
/**
 * Configure the Linkbar.
 *
 * @param string  The name of the active view.
 */
public static function addSubmenu($vName = 'submanager')
{
    JSubMenuHelper::addEntry(
        JText::_('COM_JOOMPROSUBS_SUBMENU_JOOMPROSUBS'),
        'index.php?option=com_joomprosubs&view=submanager',
        $vName == 'submanager'
    );
    JSubMenuHelper::addEntry(
        JText::_('COM_JOOMPROSUBS_SUBMENU_CATEGORIES'),
        'index.php?option=com_categories&extension=com_joomprosubs',
        $vName == 'categories'
    );
    if ($vName=='categories') {
        JToolBarHelper::title(
➥JText::sprintf('COM_CATEGORIES_CATEGORIES_TITLE',
➥JText::_('com_joomprosubs')),
            'joomprosubs-categories');
    }
}
```

This method is used to create the submenus for the manager screen. These allow the user to navigate between the Subscriptions and Categories manager screens. It is important to note that the categories screen is created by the `com_categories` component, so there is no code in our component for this screen. The previously given URL `'index.php?option=com_categories&extension=com_joomprosubs'` tells the `com_categories` component all it needs to know to create a complete management screen for our categories.

The last method in the helper class is as follows:

```
/**
 * Gets a list of the actions that can be performed.
 *
 * @param int     The category ID.
 * @return JObject
 */
public static function getActions($categoryId = 0)
{
 $user = JFactory::getUser();
 $result = new JObject;

 if (empty($categoryId)) {
    $assetName = 'com_joomprosubs';
```

```
  } else {
    $assetName = 'com_joomprosubs.category.'.(int) $categoryId;
  }

  $actions = array(
    'core.admin', 'core.manage', 'core.create', 'core.edit',
↪'core.edit.own', 'core.edit.state', 'core.delete'
  );

  foreach ($actions as $action) {
    $result->set($action,  $user->authorise($action, $assetName));
  }

  return $result;
}
```

This method creates an object that tells us which actions the current user is autho-rized to perform. The result is used to tell the view which toolbars to show on the manager screen.

Manager Model

In the `display()` method of the view, we called three methods from the model: `get-State()`, `getItems()`, and `getPagination()`. The model for this view is `JoomproSubsModelSubManager` (`models/submanager.php`). The first part of this file is as follows:

```
defined('_JEXEC') or die;

jimport('joomla.application.component.modellist');

/**
 * Methods supporting a list of joomprosub records.
 *
 */
class JoomproSubsModelSubManager extends JModelList
{

    /**
     * Constructor.
     *
     * @param    array   An optional associative array of configuration
↪settings.
     * @see      JController
     * @since    2.5
     */
    public function __construct($config = array())
    {
```

```
    if (empty($config['filter_fields'])) {
      $config['filter_fields'] = array(
         'id', 'a.id',
         'title', 'a.title',
         'alias', 'a.alias',
         'checked_out', 'a.checked_out',
         'checked_out_time', 'a.checked_out_time',
         'catid', 'a.catid', 'category_title',
         'published', 'a. published ',
         'access', 'a.access', 'access_level',
         'created', 'a.created',
         'created_by', 'a.created_by',
         'publish_up', 'a.publish_up',
         'publish_down', 'a.publish_down',
         'group_title', 'g.title',
         'duration', 'a.duration'
      );
    }

    parent::__construct($config);
  }
```

 As with Weblinks, this model extends JModelList. Also, in the constructor we build an array of valid filter fields and then call the parent's constructor. Recall that the 'filter_fields' array allows us to guard against SQL injection hacks by filtering out invalid column names in the order-by part of the request. If a hacker tries to put some SQL code into the form or URL, it will be removed because it does not match one of the valid values in this array.

The next method in our model is populateState(), as follows:

```
/**
 * Method to auto-populate the model state.
 *
 * Note. Calling getState in this method will result in recursion.
 *
 */
protected function populateState($ordering = null, $direction = null)
{
  // Initialise variables.
  $app = JFactory::getApplication('administrator');

  // Load the filter state.
  $search = $this->getUserStateFromRequest($this->context
➥.'.filter.search', 'filter_search');
  $this->setState('filter.search', $search);

  $accessId = $this->getUserStateFromRequest($this->context
➥.'.filter.access', 'filter_access', null, 'int');
```

```
        $this->setState('filter.access', $accessId);

        $published = $this->getUserStateFromRequest($this->context
    ↪.'.filter.state', 'filter_published', '', 'string');
        $this->setState('filter.state', $published);

        $categoryId = $this->getUserStateFromRequest($this->context
    ↪.'.filter.category_id', 'filter_category_id', '');
        $this->setState('filter.category_id', $categoryId);

        // Load the parameters.
        $params = JComponentHelper::getParams('com_joomprosubs');
        $this->setState('params', $params);

        // List state information.
        parent::populateState('a.title', 'asc');
    }
```

Recall that in our manager we have filters for the search field, the published state, the category, and the access level. This method reads the different state variables from the request and saves them in the state field of the model. It also saves the parameters for the component. Then it calls the parent's populateState() method. There we add the list limit and limit start values (for when we are paging through the list). We also use the 'filter_fields' array we created in the constructor to validate the ordering.

The next method in the model is getStoreId(), as follows:

```
/**
 * Method to get a store id based on model configuration state.
 *
 * This is necessary because the model is used by the component and
 * different modules that might need different sets of data or
↪different
 * ordering requirements.
 *
 * @param       string $id      A prefix for the store id.
 * @return      string          A store id.
 */
protected function getStoreId($id = '')
{
    // Compile the store id.
    $id.= ':' . $this->getState('filter.search');
    $id.= ':' . $this->getState('filter.access');
    $id.= ':' . $this->getState('filter.state');
    $id.= ':' . $this->getState('filter.category_id');

    return parent::getStoreId($id);
}
```

Recall that this method is used to create a unique key for a cached version of the list of items, the query, the total count, or the pagination object. In our case, the uniqueness of a list of items is determined by the combination of the four possible filters we use plus the start, limit, ordering, and ordering direction (which are added in the parent's `getStoreID()` method). These are converted to an `md5` hash and saved. Then, if we are showing exactly the same screen that we already have saved in memory, we can save some processing time by just using the saved copy. Note that most of the work for this is done for us by the `JModelList` class. All we have to do is add a `getStoreId()` method that includes all the possible filter values.

The last method in our model is `getListQuery()`, as follows:

```
/**
 * Build a SQL query to load the list data.
 *
 * @return     JDatabaseQuery
 */
protected function getListQuery()
{
  // Create a new query object.
  $db    = $this->getDbo();
  $query = $db->getQuery(true);

  // Select the required fields from the table.
  $query->select('a.*');
  $query->from($db->quoteName('#__joompro_subscriptions').' AS a');

  // Join over the users for the checked out user.
  $query->select('uc.name AS editor');
  $query->join('LEFT', $db->quoteName('#__users').' AS uc
➥ON uc.id=a.checked_out');

  // Join over the user groups to get the group name
  $query->select('g.title as group_title');
  $query->join('LEFT', $db->quoteName('#__usergroups').' AS g
➥ON a.group_id = g.id');
  // Join over the categories.
  $query->select('c.title AS category_title');
  $query->join('LEFT', $db->quoteName('#__categories').' AS c
➥ON c.id = a.catid');

  // Filter by access level.
  if ($access = $this->getState('filter.access')) {
     $query->where('a.access = '.(int) $access);
  }

  // Filter by published state
  $published = $this->getState('filter.state');
```

```
    if (is_numeric($published)) {
        $query->where('a.published = '.(int) $published);
    } else if ($published === '') {
        $query->where('(a.published IN (0, 1))');
    }


    // Filter by category.
    $categoryId = $this->getState('filter.category_id');
    if (is_numeric($categoryId)) {
        $query->where('a.catid = '.(int) $categoryId);
    }


    // Filter by search in title
    $search = $this->getState('filter.search');
    if (!empty($search)) {
        if (stripos($search, 'id:') === 0) {
            $query->where('a.id = '.(int) substr($search, 3));
        } else {
            $search = $db->Quote('%'.$db->getEscaped($search, true).'%');
            $query->where('(a.title LIKE '.$search.'
OR a.alias LIKE '.$search.')');
        }
    }


    // Add the list ordering clause.
    $orderCol = $this->state->get('list.ordering');
    $orderDirn = $this->state->get('list.direction');
    $query->order($db->getEscaped($orderCol.' '.$orderDirn));

    return $query;
}
```

Here we build the query to retrieve the rows from the database table. We create a new JDatabaseQuery object using $db->getQuery(true). This is important. Starting in Joomla version 1.7, which uses the Platform version 11.1, JDatabaseQuery is an abstract class. This means that you cannot instantiate a new object of this type, so you cannot use new JDatabaseQuery() to create a new query object. Using $db-> getQuery() creates a JDatabaseQuery object specific to your database type (for example, JDatabaseQueryMySQLi). This is needed to allow Joomla to work with multiple databases.

Then we select all the columns for our main table (#__joompro_subscriptions) using the SQL construct 'a.*'. We then join the #__users table so we can get the name of the user who has checked out a subscription for editing. We join the #__ usergroups and #__categories tables so we can show the titles for the user group and category for the subscriptions.

It is important that we use the prefix "#___" in our queries because we don't know what table prefix will be in use in the website. Joomla substitutes the correct table prefix before the query is passed to the database.

Also, notice that we put the table names inside the $db->quoteName() method. This allows for the possibility that different databases use different quote characters to escape table and column names. For example, MySQL uses the back-quote "`" for this. We discuss this more in Chapter 11.

All the joins are LEFT joins, which means that the row from the primary table, #__joompro_subscriptions, will show even if there is no matching row in one of these tables. Note that this should never happen in our case, because we should always have a valid category, user, and user group.

Then we check our access, published state, category, and search filters. If any of these are set, we add the appropriate WHERE clause to the database query to limit the query results. Note that we have special code to allow a search by id number. We check to see if the first three characters in the search field match "id:". If so, we look for an integer and try to find an id that matches. If not, we assume it is a partial text match on the title. Finally, we add the query ordering according to the state variables for ordering and direction.

Database Tables

In the previous section, we did a query on one of our new database tables. Let's see where these are created. To create the tables automatically when our component is installed, we create a file called sql/install.mysql.utf8.sql. The file is as follows:

```
CREATE TABLE IF NOT EXISTS `#__joompro_subscriptions` (
  `id` int(10) unsigned NOT NULL AUTO_INCREMENT COMMENT 'Automatic
↪incrementing key field',
  `catid` int(11) NOT NULL DEFAULT '0' COMMENT 'Foreign key to
↪#__categories=table',
  `title` varchar(250) NOT NULL DEFAULT '' COMMENT 'Title of Subscription',
  `alias` varchar(255) NOT NULL DEFAULT '' COMMENT 'Alias value, used for
↪SEF URLs',
  `description` text NOT NULL COMMENT 'Description (will be edited using
↪editor)',
  `group_id` int(11) NOT NULL DEFAULT '0' COMMENT 'Foreign key to
↪#__usergroups  table',
  `duration` int(11) NOT NULL DEFAULT '0' COMMENT 'Number for days that
↪subscription lasts',
  `published` tinyint(1) NOT NULL DEFAULT '0' COMMENT 'Published state
↪(1=published, 0=unpublished, -2=trashed)',
  `checked_out` int(11) NOT NULL DEFAULT '0',
  `checked_out_time` datetime NOT NULL DEFAULT '0000-00-00 00:00:00',
  `access` int(11) NOT NULL DEFAULT '1' COMMENT 'Used to control access to
↪subscriptions',
  `params` text NOT NULL COMMENT 'For possible future use to add item-level
↪parameters (JSON string format)',
```

```
`language` char(7) NOT NULL DEFAULT '' COMMENT 'For possible future use to
↪add language switching',
`created` datetime NOT NULL DEFAULT '0000-00-00 00:00:00',
`created_by` int(10) unsigned NOT NULL DEFAULT '0' COMMENT 'Foreign key to
↪#__users table for user who created this item',
`created_by_alias` varchar(255) NOT NULL DEFAULT '',
`modified` datetime NOT NULL DEFAULT '0000-00-00 00:00:00',
`modified_by` int(10) unsigned NOT NULL DEFAULT '0' COMMENT 'Foreign key
↪to #__users table for user who modified this item',
`publish_up` datetime NOT NULL DEFAULT '0000-00-00 00:00:00' COMMENT 'Date
↪to start publishing this item',
`publish_down` datetime NOT NULL DEFAULT '0000-00-00 00:00:00' COMMENT
↪'Date to stop publishing this item',
PRIMARY KEY (`id`),
KEY `idx_access` (`access`),
KEY `idx_checkout` (`checked_out`),
KEY `idx_published` (`published`),
KEY `idx_catid` (`catid`),
KEY `idx_createdby` (`created_by`),
KEY `idx_language` (`language`)
) ENGINE=MyISAM DEFAULT CHARSET=utf8 AUTO_INCREMENT=1 ;

CREATE TABLE IF NOT EXISTS `#__joompro_sub_mapping` (
`subscription_id` int(11) NOT NULL DEFAULT '0' COMMENT 'Foreign Key to
↪#__joompro_subscriptions.id',
`user_id` int(11) NOT NULL DEFAULT '0' COMMENT 'Foreign Key to
↪#__users.id',
`start_date` datetime NOT NULL DEFAULT '0000-00-00 00:00:00',
`end_date` datetime NOT NULL DEFAULT '0000-00-00 00:00:00',
PRIMARY KEY (`subscription_id`, `user_id`)
) ENGINE=MyISAM DEFAULT CHARSET=utf8;
```

This file creates our two new database tables. We will reference this file in our component's XML file as an installation file to be run automatically when we install our component. There are several things to note about this file:

- It is not a PHP file. It is a SQL script, meaning that it contains SQL commands in plain text.

- It is specific to one database—MySQL. To support installation for a different database, we would supply a separate file for each one.

- It references the tables with the prefix #__. Therefore, it is designed to be run from within Joomla, where the JDatabase object will convert the prefix to the correct one for each Joomla site. (For testing purposes, you can easily run this script against your test database using a database management program such as phpMyAdmin. Just load the file into a text editor and do a search/replace replacing "#__" with the table prefix for your Joomla site.)

We will discuss creating tables in detail in Chapter 11. For now, you can create the table by installing the component from the archive file or by running this script from phpMyAdmin (after changing the table prefix).

If a user uninstalls our component, we don't want to keep the database tables in the database. So we provide an uninstall file called `sql/uninstall.mysql.utf8.sql` with the following code:

```
DROP TABLE IF EXISTS `#__joompro_subscriptions`;
DROP TABLE IF EXISTS `#__joompro_sub_mapping`;
```

This deletes our two tables from the database. We discuss this code in Chapter 11.

Manager Screen Layout

The last program for displaying the manager screen is the layout, `views/submanager/tmpl/default.php`. This file, like the others, is closely modeled on the corresponding file for Weblinks (`administrator/components/com_weblinks/views/weblinks/tmpl/default.php`). The first part of the layout file is as follows:

```php
defined('_JEXEC') or die;

JHtml::addIncludePath(JPATH_COMPONENT.'/helpers/html');
JHtml::_('behavior.tooltip');
JHtml::_('script','system/multiselect.js', false, true);

$user = JFactory::getUser();
$userId = $user->get('id');
$listOrder = $this->escape($this->state->get('list.ordering'));
$listDirn = $this->escape($this->state->get('list.direction'));
?>
```

This just does some housekeeping and gets the current ordering for the list. The next part of the file is as follows:

```php
<div class="joomprosubs-manager">
<form action="<?php echo
➥JRoute::_('index.php?option=com_joomprosubs&view=submanager'); ?>"
  method="post" name="adminForm" id="adminForm">
  <fieldset id="filter-bar">
     <div class="filter-search fltlft">
        <label class="filter-search-lbl" for="filter_search"><?php echo
➥JText::_('JSEARCH_FILTER_LABEL'); ?></label>
        <input type="text" name="filter_search" id="filter_search"
➥value="<?php echo $this->escape($this->state->get('filter.search')); ?>"
➥title="<?php echo JText::_('COM_JOOMPROSUBS_SEARCH_IN_TITLE'); ?>" />
        <button type="submit"><?php echo
➥JText::_('JSEARCH_FILTER_SUBMIT');
```

```
↪?></button>
        <button type="button" onclick=
↪"document.id('filter_search').value='';this.form.submit();">
↪<?php echo JText::_('JSEARCH_FILTER_CLEAR'); ?></button>
    </div>
    <div class="filter-select fltrt">

        <select name="filter_published" class="inputbox"
↪onchange="this.form.submit()">
            <option value=""><?php echo
↪JText::_('JOPTION_SELECT_PUBLISHED');?></option>
            <?php echo JHtml::_('select.options',
↪JHtml::_('jgrid.publishedOptions'), 'value', 'text',
↪$this->state->get('filter.state'), true);?>
        </select>

        <select name="filter_category_id" class="inputbox"
↪onchange="this.form.submit()">
            <option value=""><?php echo
↪JText::_('JOPTION_SELECT_CATEGORY');?></option>
            <?php echo JHtml::_('select.options',
↪JHtml::_('category.options', 'com_joomprosubs'), 'value', 'text',
↪$this->state->get('filter.category_id'));?>
        </select>

         <select name="filter_access" class="inputbox"
↪onchange="this.form.submit()">
            <option value=""><?php echo
↪JText::_('JOPTION_SELECT_ACCESS');?></option>
            <?php echo JHtml::_('select.options',
↪JHtml::_('access.assetgroups'), 'value', 'text',
↪$this->state->get('filter.access'));?>
        </select>


    </div>
  </fieldset>
  <div class="clr"> </div>
```

This code creates the search and other filters. It is modeled after the same code in Weblinks. Note that we put a div element with a class of "joomprosubs-manager" around the entire layout. This allows a designer to create CSS styling specific to this screen.

The next part of the file is as follows:

```
<table class="adminlist">
  <thead>
    <tr>
```

```
        <th style="width: 1%;">
         <input type="checkbox" name="checkall-toggle" value=""
↪onclick="checkAll(this)" />
        </th>
        <th class="title">
         <?php echo JHtml::_('grid.sort',  'JGLOBAL_TITLE', 'a.title',
↪$listDirn, $listOrder); ?>
        </th>
        <th style="width: 5%;">
          <?php echo JHtml::_('grid.sort',  'JSTATUS', 'a.published',
↪$listDirn, $listOrder); ?>
        </th>

        <th style="width: 20%;">
          <?php echo JHtml::_('grid.sort',  'JCATEGORY',
↪'category_title', $listDirn, $listOrder); ?>
        </th>

        <th style="width: 20%;">
                          <?php echo JHtml::_('grid.sort',
↪'COM_JOOMPROSUBS_FIELD_USERGROUP_LABEL', 'g.title', $listDirn,
↪$listOrder); ?>
        </th>

        <th style="width: 10%;">
          <?php echo JHtml::_('grid.sort',
↪'COM_JOOMPROSUBS_FIELD_DURATION_LABEL', 'a.duration', $listDirn,
↪$listOrder); ?>
        </th>

        <th style="width: 5%;">
          <?php echo JHtml::_('grid.sort',  'JGRID_HEADING_ACCESS',
↪'a.access', $listDirn, $listOrder); ?>
        </th>

        <th style="width: 5%;" class="nowrap">
          <?php echo JHtml::_('grid.sort',  'JGRID_HEADING_ID', 'a.id',
↪$listDirn, $listOrder); ?>
        </th>
   </tr>
   </thead>
```

This creates the sortable column headings, just like in the Weblinks Manager screen. The only difference is that we have used the preferred syntax for the in-line styling of the width.

The next part creates the pagination at the bottom of the screen, as follows:

```
<tfoot>
  <tr>
    <td colspan="10">
      <?php echo $this->pagination->getListFooter(); ?>
    </td>
  </tr>
</tfoot>
```

The next section starts a **foreach** loop to process each subscription in the list, as follows:

```
<tbody>
<?php foreach ($this->items as $i => $item) :
   $ordering = ($listOrder == 'a.ordering');
   $item->cat_link =
↪JRoute::_('index.php?option=com_categories&extension=com_joomprosubs
↪&task=edit&type=other&cid[]='. $item->catid);
   $canCreate = $user->authorise('core.create',
↪'com_joomprosubs.category.'.$item->catid);
   $canEdit = $user->authorise('core.edit',
↪'com_joomprosubs.category.'.$item->catid);
   $canCheckin = $user->authorise('core.manage', 'com_checkin') ||
↪$item->checked_out==$user->get('id') || $item->checked_out==0;
   $canChange = $user->authorise('core.edit.state',
↪'com_joomprosubs.category.'.$item->catid) && $canCheckin;
   ?>
```

This checks whether the current user has permission to create, edit, check in, and publish each item.

The next section of code displays the information for each subscription in the list, as follows:

```
<tr class="row<?php echo $i % 2; ?>">
  <td class="center">
    <?php echo JHtml::_('grid.id', $i, $item->id); ?>
  </td>
  <td>
    <?php if ($item->checked_out) : ?>
    <?php echo JHtml::_('jgrid.checkedout', $i,
↪$item->editor, $item->checked_out_time, 'submanager.', $canCheckin); ?>
    <?php endif; ?>
    <?php if ($canEdit) : ?>
      <a href="<?php echo
↪JRoute::_('index.php?option=com_joomprosubs&task=subscription.edit&id='.
↪(int) $item->id); ?>">
        <?php echo $this->escape($item->title); ?></a>
      <?php else : ?>
```

```
        <?php echo $this->escape($item->title); ?>
      <?php endif; ?>
      <p class="smallsub">
      <?php echo JText::sprintf('JGLOBAL_LIST_ALIAS',
➥$this->escape($item->alias));?></p>
    </td>
    <td class="center">
      <?php echo JHtml::_('jgrid.published', $item->published,
➥$i, 'submanager.', $canChange, 'cb', $item->publish_up,
➥$item->publish_down); ?>
    </td>
    <td class="center">
      <?php echo $this->escape($item->category_title); ?>
    </td>

    <td class="center">
      <?php echo $this->escape($item->group_title); ?>
    </td>

    <td class="center">
      <?php echo $this->escape($item->duration); ?>
    </td>

    <td class="center">
      <?php echo $this->escape($item->access); ?>
    </td>
    <td class="center">
      <?php echo (int) $item->id; ?>
    </td>
    </tr>
    <?php endforeach; ?>
  </tbody>
</table>
```

This code reads each row from the `$item` object and displays it inside a table cell (td) HTML element.

The last section of code outputs hidden fields for `task`, `boxchecked`, `filter_order`, and `filter_order_dir`, as follows:

```
  <div>
    <input type="hidden" name="task" value="" />
    <input type="hidden" name="boxchecked" value="0" />
    <input type="hidden" name="filter_order" value="<?php echo
➥$listOrder; ?>" />
    <input type="hidden" name="filter_order_Dir" value="<?php echo
➥$listDirn; ?>" />
    <?php echo JHtml::_('form.token'); ?>
```

```
        </div>
    </form>
</div>
```

It also closes the initial div element we used for possible styling.

This is a lot of code, but it is closely based on similar files for Weblinks and other core components.

At this point, we have all the files we need to do the default task: display the manager screen.

Subscriptions Manager: Add and Edit

Next let's look at the code for adding and editing a subscription. This uses the following files, which are discussed in this section:

- `controllers/subscription.php` (JoomprosubsControllerSubscription)
- `views/subscription/view.html.php` (JoomprosubsViewSubscription)
- `models/subscription.php` (JoomproSubsModelSubscription)
- `views/subscription/tmpl/edit.php`
- `models/forms/subscription.xml`
- `tables/subscription.php` (JoomprosubsTableSubscription)

Controller Tasks

In the manager screen, the toolbar task for add and edit are subscription.add and subscription.edit. Recall from Chapter 7 that this means we invoke the `add()` and `edit()` methods of the controller class `JoomprosubsControllerSubscription` (`controllers/subscription.php`). This class extends JControllerForm and only overrides two methods: `allowAdd()` and `allowEdit()`. These are called from the `add()` and `edit()` methods of `JControllerForm` to check whether the user is authorized to perform these actions.

The first part of `JoomprosubsControllerSubscription` defines the `allowAdd()` method, as follows:

```
defined('_JEXEC') or die;

jimport('joomla.application.component.controllerform');

/**
 * Joomprosubs controller class.
 *
 */
class JoomproSubsControllerSubscription extends JControllerForm
{
  /**
```

```
 * The URL view list variable.
 *
 * @var     string
 */
protected $view_list = 'submanager';

/**
 * Method override to check if you can add a new record.
 *
 * @param     array       $data    An array of input data.
 * @return boolean
 */
protected function allowAdd($data = array())
{
    // Initialise variables.
    $user = JFactory::getUser();
    $categoryId = JArrayHelper::getValue($data, 'catid',
↪JRequest::getInt('filter_category_id'), 'int');
    $allow = null;

    if ($categoryId) {
        // If the category has been passed in the URL check it.
        $allow  = $user->authorise('core.create',
↪$this->option.'.category.'.$categoryId);
    }

    if ($allow === null) {
        // In the absense of better information, revert to the component
↪permissions.
        return parent::allowAdd($data);
    } else {
        return $allow;
    }
}
```

Here we define the class and the first method. Note that we define a field called $view_list, set to "submanager". We didn't need this field in the WeblinksCon-trollerWeblink class because it defaulted to the component name without the plural ("weblink"). In our case, that rule doesn't work. If we called the default view "joom-prosubs", we wouldn't need this field or the $default_view field we defined in the JoomproSubsController class. However, two lines of code is a small price to pay for having meaningful class and file names, and "submanager" is more meaningful than "joomprosubs".

The allowAdd() method is very similar to the same method in WeblinksCon-trollerWeblink class. We try to read a category id from the request. If we are filtering on a category, there will be one. If we find a category id, we check to see if the current user is authorized to add an item in this category. If not, we just check the permissions at the component level, which we do by calling the parent's `allowAdd()` method.

The rest of the code for this class defines the `allowEdit()` method, as follows:

```
/**
 * Method to check if you can add a new record.
 *
 * @param   array   $data  An array of input data.
 * @param   string  $key   The name of the key for the primary key.
 *
 * @return  boolean
 */
protected function allowEdit($data = array(), $key = 'id')
{
    // Initialise variables.
    $recordId = (int) isset($data[$key]) ? $data[$key] : 0;
    $categoryId = 0;

    if ($recordId) {
        $categoryId = (int) $this->getModel()->getItem($recordId)->catid;
    }

    if ($categoryId) {
        // The category has been set. Check the category permissions.
        return JFactory::getUser()->authorise('core.edit',
$this->option.'.category.'.$categoryId);
    } else {
        // Since there is no asset tracking, revert to the component
permissions.
        return parent::allowEdit($data, $key);
    }
}
}
```

Normally, when we are in this method, we should have a valid subscription id. In this case, we read the category id from the subscription and check that the user is authorized to edit subscriptions in this category. If for some reason we don't have a valid subscription id, we check that the user has edit permission at the component level.

Add and Edit View

Assuming the user is authorized to add or edit, the parent controller sets the redirect to

```
administrator/index.php?option=com_joomprosubs&view=subscription
&layout=edit.
```

This will execute the display task using the `JoomproSubsViewSubscription` class (views/subscription/view.html.php).

The first part of this file is as follows:

```php
defined('_JEXEC') or die;
jimport('joomla.application.component.view');

/**
 * View to edit a contact.
 *
 * @package        Joomla.Administrator
 * @subpackage     com_joomprosubs
 */
class JoomprosubsViewSubscription extends JView
{
 protected $form;
 protected $item;
 protected $state;

 /**
  * Display the view
  */
 public function display($tpl = null)
 {
     // Initialiase variables.
     $this->form     = $this->get('Form');
     $this->item     = $this->get('Item');
     $this->state    = $this->get('State');

     // Check for errors.
     if (count($errors = $this->get('Errors'))) {
        JError::raiseError(500, implode("\n", $errors));
        return false;
     }

     $this->addToolbar();
     parent::display($tpl);
 }
```

This is similar to the corresponding file for Weblinks. Here, we extend `JView` and then define our `display()` method. This method gets the form object, the item, and the state from the model. It then checks for errors. If none are found, it adds the toolbar and then calls the parent's display method.

The last part of the file is as follows:

```php
 protected function addToolbar()
 {
```

```
    JRequest::setVar('hidemainmenu', true);

    $user = JFactory::getUser();
    $isNew = ($this->item->id == 0);
    $checkedOut = !($this->item->checked_out == 0 ||
⮑$this->item->checked_out == $user->get('id'));
    $canDo = JoomprosubsHelper::getActions(
⮑$this->state->get('filter.category_id'), $this->item->id);

    JToolBarHelper::title(JText::_('COM_JOOMPROSUBS_MANAGER_JOOMPROSUB'),
⮑'newfeeds.png');

    // If not checked out, can save the item.
    if (!$checkedOut && ($canDo->get('core.edit')||
⮑ (count($user->getAuthorisedCategories('com_joomprosubs',
⮑'core.create')))))
    {
        JToolBarHelper::apply('subscription.apply', 'JTOOLBAR_APPLY');
        JToolBarHelper::save('subscription.save', 'JTOOLBAR_SAVE');
    }
    if (!$checkedOut && (count($user->getAuthorisedCategories(
⮑'com_joomprosubs', 'core.create')))){
        JToolBarHelper::custom('subscription.save2new', 'save-new.png',
⮑'save-new_f2.png', 'JTOOLBAR_SAVE_AND_NEW', false);
    }
    // If an existing item, can save to a copy.
    if (!$isNew && (count($user->getAuthorisedCategories(
⮑'com_joomprosubs', 'core.create')) > 0)) {
        JToolBarHelper::custom('subscription.save2copy', 'save-copy.png',
⮑'save-copy_f2.png', 'JTOOLBAR_SAVE_AS_COPY', false);
    }
    if (empty($this->item->id)) {
        JToolBarHelper::cancel('subscription.cancel', 'JTOOLBAR_CANCEL');
    }
    else {
        JToolBarHelper::cancel('subscription.cancel', 'JTOOLBAR_CLOSE');
    }

    JToolBarHelper::divider();
    JToolBarHelper::help('', '',
⮑JText::_('COM_JOOMPROSUBS_SUBSCRIPTION_HELP_LINK'));
  }
}
```

As with the corresponding method for Weblinks, here we check the user's permissions before showing the Save, Save & Close, Save & New, and Save as Copy icons. We also show the Cancel/Close and Help icons. Remember that this is to improve the user interface and is not a substitute for rechecking the user's permissions for these actions after they have been initiated.

Add and Edit Model

In the view, we called the model's `getForm()`, `getItem()`, and `getState()` methods. Let's look at the model class next. This is the `JoomproSubsModelSubscription` class in the file `models/subscription.php`. Note that the `getItem()` and `getState()` methods for this class are inherited from `JModelAdmin` and `JModel`, respectively. In addition, this model defines six methods.

The first part of the file defines the class and the `canDelete()` method, as follows:

```php
defined('_JEXEC') or die;

jimport('joomla.application.component.modeladmin');

/**
 *Joomprosubs model.
 *
 * @package    Joomla.Administrator
 * @subpackage com_joomprosubs
 * @since      2.5
 */
class JoomproSubsModelSubscription extends JModelAdmin
{
  /**
   * @var  string  The prefix to use with controller messages.
   */
  protected $text_prefix = 'COM_JOOMPROSUBS';

  /**
   * Method to test whether a record can be deleted.
   *
   * @param    object A record object.
   * @retur    Boolean True if allowed to delete the record. Defaults to
→the permission set in the component.
   */
  protected function canDelete($record)
  {
    if (!empty($record->id)) {
      if ($record->published != -2) {
        return ;
      }
      $user = JFactory::getUser();

      if ($record->catid) {
        return $user->authorise('core.delete',
```

```
➥'com_joomprosubs.category.'.(int) $record->catid);
        }
        else {
            return parent::canDelete($record);
        }
    }
}
```

This method is called during the delete task. It simply checks whether a user has delete permission for the item. Note that we only check the permission for the category. Because the Joomla ACL is hierarchical, we only need to check the category permission. If there is no permission for this action set at the category level, it will automatically inherit the component level permission. So we don't need to check both levels.

The next method in this class is **canEditState()**, as follows:

```
/**
 * Method to test whether a record can have its state changed.
 *
 * @param      object A record object.
 * @return     Boolean True if allowed to change the state of the record.
➥Defaults to the permission set in the component.
 */
protected function canEditState($record)
{
    $user = JFactory::getUser();

    if (!empty($record->catid)) {
        return $user->authorise('core.edit.state',
➥'com_joomprosubs.category.'.(int) $record->catid);
    }
    else {
        return parent::canEditState($record);
    }
}
```

This method is called whenever the published state is changed. Again, this method just checks the user for this permission for the item's category.

The next method is **getTable()**, as follows:

```
/**
 * Returns a reference to the a Table object, always creating it.
 *
 * @param  type      The table type to instantiate
 * @param  string    A prefix for the table class name. Optional.
 * @param  array     Configuration array for model. Optional.
 * @return JTable     A database object
 */
```

```
public function getTable($type = 'subscription',
↪$prefix = 'JoomproSubsTable', $config = array())
{
    return JTable::getInstance($type, $prefix, $config);
}
```

This method is called whenever we are going to write to the table. It simply provides the correct table name for the table and then gets an instance of the table using the JTable class.

The next method is getForm(), as follows:

```
/**
 * Method to get the record form.
 *
 * @param  array    $data An optional array of data for the form to
↪interogate.
 * @param  boolean  $loadData  True if the form is to load its own
↪data (default case), false if not.
 * @return  JForm   A JForm object on success, false on failure
 */
public function getForm($data = array(), $loadData = true)
{
// Initialise variables.
$app   = JFactory::getApplication();

// Get the form.
$form = $this->loadForm('com_joomprosubs.subscription',
↪'subscription', array('control' => 'jform', 'load_data' => $loadData));
if (empty($form)) {
    return false;
}

// Determine correct permissions to check.
if ($this->getState('subscription.id')) {
    // Existing record. Can only edit in selected categories.
    $form->setFieldAttribute('catid', 'action', 'core.edit');
} else {
    // New record. Can only create in selected categories.
    $form->setFieldAttribute('catid', 'action', 'core.create');
}

// Modify the form based on access controls.
if (!$this->canEditState((object) $data)) {
    // Disable fields for display.
    $form->setFieldAttribute('published', 'disabled', 'true');
    $form->setFieldAttribute('publish_up', 'disabled', 'true');
    $form->setFieldAttribute('publish_down', 'disabled', 'true');
```

```
    // Disable fields while saving.
    // The controller has already verified this is a record you can
↪edit.
    $form->setFieldAttribute('published', 'filter', 'unset');
    $form->setFieldAttribute('publish_up', 'filter', 'unset');
    $form->setFieldAttribute('publish_down', 'filter', 'unset');
 }

 return $form;
}
```

This method is called at two points in the cycle:

- When we open a form for editing
- When we are saving form data

Here we get the data for the form and check that the user has permission to either edit or create an item. Then, we check if the user has edit state permission. If not, we do two things:

- We disable the fields so they don't show on the form, by setting the disabled attribute in the form to true.
- We filter out any changes that might have been entered in these fields, by setting the filter attribute to unset.

We previously discussed the fact that we need to check input coming from users before processing the information. Even if a form does not allow a user to enter something, a hacker can easily modify the HTML of the page to change the form and bypass this control. That is why we need to also check form values after the form has been submitted.

JForm makes this very easy to do. When we set the filter attribute to unset, we are telling JForm to remove any data that might have been entered by a user. In this case, because we already disabled those form fields to prevent normal entry, we know this information must have been entered by someone who modified the form in their browser. This code protects us from this type of hacking attempt. No further checking of input is required. This is a great example of using JForm to change things on the fly and to protect against hacking.

The next method is getFormData(), as follows:

```
/**
 * Method to get the data that should be injected in the form.
 *
 * @return mixed   The data for the form.
 */
protected function loadFormData()
{
```

```
   // Check the session for previously entered form data.
   $data = JFactory::getApplication()->getUserState
→('com_joomprosubs.edit.subscription.data', array());

   if (empty($data)) {
      $data = $this->getItem();

      // Prime some default values.
      if ($this->getState('subscription.id') == 0) {
          $app = JFactory::getApplication();
          $data->set('catid', JRequest::getInt('catid',
→$app->getUserState('com_joomprosubs.submanager.filter.category_id')));
      }
   }

   return $data;
}
```

First, we get any data that may have been saved in the session. Recall that we do this so the user doesn't have to reenter all the form's data if one field is invalid. If there isn't data already in the session, we get the data using the `getItem()` method. If we are entering a new item, we check whether we are filtering on a category. If so, we use that category id as the default for the form.

The last part of the class has the `prepareTable()` method, as follows:

```
   /**
    * Prepare and sanitise the table prior to saving.
    *
    */
   protected function prepareTable(&$table)
   {
      $table->alias = JApplication::stringURLSafe($table->alias);
      if (empty($table->alias)) {
          $table->alias = JApplication::stringURLSafe($table->title);
      }
   }
} // end of class
```

Here, we are making sure the alias column is safe to be in a URL. This is because we use the alias in the URL when we have the SEF URL option set to yes. We also set the URL automatically, based on the title, if it is not already set. This way the user can skip this field if they just want to use the title as the alias.

Add and Edit Form

When we render the form on the screen, the layout for the form is `views/subscription/tmpl/edit.php`. This is a script, not a class. The first part of the code for this file is as follows:

```php
<?php
/**
 * @copyright  Copyright (C) 2011 Mark Dexter and Louis Landry. All rights
reserved.
 * @license    GNU General Public License version 2 or later; see
LICENSE.txt
 */

// no direct access
defined('_JEXEC') or die;

JHtml::addIncludePath(JPATH_COMPONENT.'/helpers/html');
JHtml::_('behavior.tooltip');
JHtml::_('behavior.formvalidation');
?>
<script type="text/javascript">
  Joomla.submitbutton = function(task)
  {
     if (task == 'subscription.cancel' ||
document.formvalidator.isValid(document.id('subscription-form'))) {
        <?php echo $this->form->getField('description')->save(); ?>
        Joomla.submitform(task, document.getElementById(
'subscription-form'));
     }
     else {
        alert('<?php echo $this->escape(
JText::_('JGLOBAL_VALIDATION_FORM_FAILED'));?>');
     }
  }
</script>
```

As with earlier examples of using `JForm`, we include two JavaScript behaviors, one for tooltips and one for validating our form. Then we define a script that will run the form validation when we submit the form. We discuss how this works in Chapter 12.

The next part of the file is as follows:

```php
<form action="<?php echo
JRoute::_('index.php?option=com_joomprosubs&layout=edit&id='.(int)
$this->item->id); ?>" method="post" name="adminForm"
id="subscription-form" class="form-validate">
```

```
<div class="width-60 fltlft">
  <fieldset class="adminform">
    <legend><?php echo empty($this->item->id) ?
JText::_('COM_JOOMPROSUBS_NEW_JOOMPROSUB') :
JText::sprintf('COM_JOOMPROSUBS_EDIT_JOOMPROSUB', $this->item->id); ?>
</legend>
    <ul class="adminformlist">
    <li><?php echo $this->form->getLabel('title'); ?>
    <?php echo $this->form->getInput('title'); ?></li>

    <li><?php echo $this->form->getLabel('alias'); ?>
    <?php echo $this->form->getInput('alias'); ?></li>

    <li><?php echo $this->form->getLabel('catid'); ?>
    <?php echo $this->form->getInput('catid'); ?></li>

    <li><?php echo $this->form->getLabel('group_id'); ?>
    <?php echo $this->form->getInput('group_id'); ?></li>

    <li><?php echo $this->form->getLabel('duration'); ?>
    <?php echo $this->form->getInput('duration'); ?></li>

    <li><?php echo $this->form->getLabel('published'); ?>
    <?php echo $this->form->getInput('published'); ?></li>

    <li><?php echo $this->form->getLabel('access'); ?>
    <?php echo $this->form->getInput('access'); ?></li>

    <li><?php echo $this->form->getLabel('id'); ?>
    <?php echo $this->form->getInput('id'); ?></li>
    </ul>

    <?php echo $this->form->getLabel('description'); ?>
    <div class="clr"></div>
    <?php echo $this->form->getInput('description'); ?>

  </fieldset>
</div>
```

Here we define the form action to load the same URL we are already on, with our current item id. Then we define the post method for the form and define the name, id, and class attributes for the form element. Then we output the first seven form elements as an unordered HTML list. In each case, we just get the form label and input from the form's XML file. These are the elements that show on the left side of the form.

The last part of this file is as follows:

```
    <div class="width-40 fltrt">
        <?php echo JHtml::_('sliders.start','joomprosubs-sliders-'.
↪$this->item->id, array('useCookie'=>1)); ?>

        <?php echo JHtml::_('sliders.panel',JText::_(
↪'JGLOBAL_FIELDSET_PUBLISHING'), 'publishing-details'); ?>

        <fieldset class="panelform">
            <ul class="adminformlist">
                <li><?php echo $this->form->getLabel('created_by'); ?>
                <?php echo $this->form->getInput('created_by'); ?></li>

                <li><?php echo $this->form->getLabel('created_by_alias'); ?>
                <?php echo $this->form->getInput('created_by_alias'); ?></li>

                <li><?php echo $this->form->getLabel('created'); ?>
                <?php echo $this->form->getInput('created'); ?></li>

                <li><?php echo $this->form->getLabel('publish_up'); ?>
                <?php echo $this->form->getInput('publish_up'); ?></li>

                <li><?php echo $this->form->getLabel('publish_down'); ?>
                <?php echo $this->form->getInput('publish_down'); ?></li>

                <?php if ($this->item->modified_by) : ?>
                    <li><?php echo $this->form->getLabel('modified_by'); ?>
                    <?php echo $this->form->getInput('modified_by'); ?></li>

                    <li><?php echo $this->form->getLabel('modified'); ?>
                    <?php echo $this->form->getInput('modified'); ?></li>
                <?php endif; ?>

            </ul>
        </fieldset>

        <?php echo JHtml::_('sliders.end'); ?>

        <input type="hidden" name="task" value="" />
        <?php echo JHtml::_('form.token'); ?>
    </div>
    <div class="clr"></div>
</form>
```

Here we define a slider for the publishing information. We use the
JHtmlSliders::start() and JHtmlSliders::panel() methods to create the slider.
Then we use getLabel() and getInput() again to output the seven form fields for
publishing information. Then we close the slider and add a hidden field for the form

token. Recall that this field is used to check against the token saved in the session to make sure we are saving the correct information.

Next, let's look at the XML file (models/forms/subscription.xml) that we read the fields from. The first part is as follows:

```xml
<?xml version="1.0" encoding="utf-8"?>
<form>
   <fieldset>
      <field name="id" type="text" default="0"
➥label="JGLOBAL_FIELD_ID_LABEL"
         readonly="true" class="readonly"
         description="JGLOBAL_FIELD_ID_DESC"/>

      <field name="title" type="text" class="inputbox"
         size="40" label="JGLOBAL_TITLE"
         description="COM_JOOMPROSUBS_FIELD_TITLE_DESC" required="true" />

      <field name="alias" type="text" class="inputbox"
         size="40" label="JFIELD_ALIAS_LABEL"
         description="COM_JOOMPROSUBS_FIELD_ALIAS_DESC" />

      <field name="catid" type="category" extension="com_joomprosubs"
         label="JCATEGORY"
         description="COM_JOOMPROSUBS_FIELD_CATEGORY_DESC"
         class="inputbox" >
      </field>

      <field name="group_id" type="usergroup"
         label="COM_JOOMPROSUBS_FIELD_USERGROUP_LABEL"
         description="COM_JOOMPROSUBS_FIELD_USERGROUP_DESC"
         default="0" size="1" >
      </field>

      <field name="duration" type="integer" filter="integer"
         first="15" last="90" step="15" default="30"
         label="COM_JOOMPROSUBS_FIELD_DURATION_LABEL"
         description="COM_JOOMPROSUBS_FIELD_DURATION_DESC" />

      <field name="description" type="editor" buttons="true"
         hide="pagebreak,readmore"
         class="inputbox"
         filter="safehtml"
          label="JGLOBAL_DESCRIPTION"
          description="COM_JOOMPROSUBS_FIELD_DESCRIPTION_DESC" />
```

Here we define the first seven fields for our form. For the catid field, we set the type to category and the extension to our extension name. That provides us with the list of subscription categories in a drop-down list box. Similarly, we specify a type of user group for the user group field.

The duration field uses the "integer" type and also the "integer" filter. This type allows us to specify a lower and upper bound and a step. In this case, we start with 15 days and go by increments of 15 up to 90 days. Note that we set the filter to integer. This means that even if a hacker bypasses our list box and enters in something else in the form, it will be converted to an integer when the data is saved to the table.

Finally, the description has a type of "editor". This means that the user's default editor will be used to edit this field. We specify a filter of "safehtml" to filter the user's input to be safe to render on an HTML page.

The last part of this XML file is as follows:

```
<field
  name="published"
  type="list"
  label="JSTATUS"
  description="COM_JOOMPROSUBS_FIELD_STATE_DESC"
  class="inputbox"
  size="1"
  default="1">
  <option
    value="1">JPUBLISHED</option>
  <option
    value="0">JUNPUBLISHED</option>
  <option
    value="-2">JTRASHED</option>
</field>

<field name="access" type="accesslevel" label="JFIELD_ACCESS_LABEL"
  description="JFIELD_ACCESS_DESC" class="inputbox" size="1" />

<field name="created" type="calendar"
  label="JGLOBAL_FIELD_CREATED_LABEL"
  description="JGLOBAL_FIELD_CREATED_DESC"
  class="inputbox" size="22" format="%Y-%m-%d %H:%M:%S"
  filter="user_utc" />

<field name="created_by" type="user"
  label="JGLOBAL_FIELD_CREATED_BY_LABEL"
  description="JGLOBAL_FIELD_CREATED_BY_Desc" />

<field name="created_by_alias" type="text"
  label="JGLOBAL_FIELD_CREATED_BY_ALIAS_LABEL"
  description="JGLOBAL_FIELD_CREATED_BY_ALIAS_DESC"
  class="inputbox" size="20" />

<field name="modified" type="calendar" class="readonly"
  label="JGLOBAL_FIELD_MODIFIED_LABEL"
```

```
          description="COM_JOOMPROSUBS_FIELD_MODIFIED_DESC"
          size="22" readonly="true" format="%Y-%m-%d %H:%M:%S"
          filter="user_utc" />

      <field name="modified_by" type="user"
        label="JGLOBAL_FIELD_MODIFIED_BY_LABEL"
        class="readonly" readonly="true" filter="unset"  />


      <field name="checked_out" type="hidden" filter="unset" />


      <field name="checked_out_time" type="hidden" filter="unset" />


      <field name="publish_up" type="calendar"
        label="JGLOBAL_FIELD_PUBLISH_UP_LABEL"
        description="JGLOBAL_FIELD_PUBLISH_UP_DESC"
        class="inputbox" format="%Y-%m-%d %H:%M:%S" size="22"
        filter="user_utc" />

      <field name="publish_down" type="calendar"
        label="JGLOBAL_FIELD_PUBLISH_DOWN_LABEL"
        description="JGLOBAL_FIELD_PUBLISH_DOWN_DESC"
        class="inputbox" format="%Y-%m-%d %H:%M:%S" size="22"
        filter="user_utc" />

  </fieldset>

</form>
```

This defines the last seven fields in our form. Note that we use the type of "calendar" for our dates. This provides a pop-up calendar widget. We also include two hidden fields for checked_out and checked_out_time. These cannot be entered from the form because we set the filter attribute to unset. These are included specifically to prevent them from being entered by a hacker.

Table Class

The last file to review for the add/edit process is **JoomprosubsTableSubscription** (**tables/subscription.php**). This file defines any special processing we need to do when we save a row in our table. The first part of the file is as follows:

```
defined('_JEXEC') or die;

class JoomprosubsTableSubscription extends JTable
{
  /**
   * Constructor
   *
   * @param JDatabase A database connector object
```

```
 */
public function __construct(&$db)
{
  parent::__construct('#__joompro_subscriptions', 'id', $db);
}
```

This defines the class and gives the database table name as the first argument in the constructor. Note that we use an ampersand (&) in front of the $db in the argument list. Recall that this means that if we change the $db object during this method, the changed object will be passed back to the calling method.

The next part of the class defines the store() method, as follows:

```
/**
 * Overload the store method for the Subscriptions table.
 *
 * @param  boolean    Toggle whether null values should be updated.
 * @return boolean    True on success, false on failure.
 */
public function store($updateNulls = false)
{
  $date = JFactory::getDate();
  $user = JFactory::getUser();
  if ($this->id) {
     // Existing item
     $this->modified     = $date->toSQL();
     $this->modified_by  = $user->get('id');
  } else {
     // New subscription. Created and created_by field can be set by
  the user,
     // so we don't touch either of these if they are set.
     if (!intval($this->created)) {
        $this->created = $date->toSQL();
     }
     if (empty($this->created_by)) {
        $this->created_by = $user->get('id');
     }
  }

  // Verify that the alias is unique
  $table = JTable::getInstance('subscription', 'JoomprosubsTable');
  if ($table->load(array('alias'=>$this->alias,'catid'=>$this->catid))
  && ($table->id != $this->id || $this->id==0)) {
     $this->setError(JText::_('COM_JOOMPROSUBS_ERROR_UNIQUE_ALIAS'));
     return false;
  }
  // Attempt to store the user data.
  return parent::store($updateNulls);
}
```

This method is used when we save a row in the table. If we are editing an existing row, we set the modified date to the current time and the modified-by user to the current user. If we are adding a new row, we set the created-by user and time. Then we check that the alias is unique for this category. This is to prevent problems when a user inadvertently creates two items in the same category with the same alias. If that happens, only one of them can be displayed on the front end, because they both have the same URL. This check prevents that from happening by giving the user an error message.

Finally, we call the `store()` method of the parent class to do the standard table processing. This includes setting the key field and updating the assets table if needed.

The last part of this class defines the `check()` method, as follows:

```
/**
 * Overloaded check method to ensure data integrity.
 *
 * @return    boolean True on success.
 */
public function check()
{
    // check for existing name
    $db = $this->_db;
    $query = $db->getQuery(true);
    $query->select('id');
    $query->from($db->quoteName('#__joompro_subscriptions'));
    $query->where('title = ' . $db->quote($this->title) .
       ' AND catid = ' . (int) $this->catid);
    $db->setQuery($query);

    $xid = intval($db->loadResult());
    if ($xid && $xid != intval($this->id)) {
        $this->setError(JText::_('COM_JOOMPROSUBS_ERR_TABLES_NAME'));
        return false;
    }

    if (empty($this->alias)) {
        $this->alias = $this->title;
    }
    $this->alias = JApplication::stringURLSafe($this->alias);
    if (trim(str_replace('-','',$this->alias)) == '') {
        $this->alias = JFactory::getDate()->format("Y-m-d-H-i-s");
    }

    // Check the publish down date is not earlier than publish up.
    if (intval($this->publish_down) > 0 && $this->publish_down <
↪$this->publish_up) {
        // Swap the dates.
```

```
        $temp = $this->publish_up;
        $this->publish_up = $this->publish_down;
        $this->publish_down = $temp;
    }

    return true;
    }
}
```

Here we check that the name of the subscription is unique, again for this category. This helps prevent duplicate alias values. We also check that the publish start date is before the stop date.

At this point, we have defined all the files required to add or edit a subscription item in the back end of our component.

Language Files

We need two language files for the back end. We have chosen to keep these files in the component's language folder (administrator/components/com_joomprosubs/ language/en-GB/) instead of in the common administrator/language folder. The first file is language/en-GB/en-GB.com_joomprosubs.ini. This contains all the translations for the language keys used for the component. Its contents are as follows:

```
COM_JOOMPROSUBS_CATEGORY_LIST_HELP_LINK="http://joomlaprogrammingbook.com/
➥joompro-category-list-help.html"
COM_JOOMPROSUBS_CATEGORY_VIEW_DEFAULT_TITLE="Category List"
COM_JOOMPROSUBS_CONFIGURATION="Subscriptions Manager Options"
COM_JOOMPROSUBS_EDIT_JOOMPROSUB="Subscription Edit"
COM_JOOMPROSUBS_FIELD_ALIAS_DESC="Alias for the item. You can leave this
➥blank and the system will create an alias for you."
COM_JOOMPROSUBS_FIELD_CATEGORY_DESC="Select the category from the list."
COM_JOOMPROSUBS_FIELD_DESCRIPTION_DESC="Enter an optional description for
➥the subscription."
COM_JOOMPROSUBS_FIELD_DURATION_DESC="Select the number of days that this
➥subscription will be active."
COM_JOOMPROSUBS_FIELD_DURATION_LABEL="Duration (days)"
COM_JOOMPROSUBS_FIELD_MODIFIED_DESC="Date this subscription was last
➥modified."
COM_JOOMPROSUBS_FIELD_SELECT_CATEGORY_DESC="Select the category from the
➥list."
COM_JOOMPROSUBS_FIELD_SELECT_CATEGORY_LABEL="Category"
COM_JOOMPROSUBS_FIELD_STATE_DESC="Published state for this subscription."
COM_JOOMPROSUBS_FIELD_TITLE_DESC="Title of the subscription."
COM_JOOMPROSUBS_FIELD_USERGROUP_DESC="Select the User Group that is
➥associated with this subscription."
COM_JOOMPROSUBS_FIELD_USERGROUP_LABEL="User Group"
```

```
COM_JOOMPROSUBS_MANAGER_JOOMPROSUB="Subscription Manager: Subscription
↪Entry"
COM_JOOMPROSUBS_MANAGER_JOOMPROSUBS="Subscriptions Manager: Subscriptions"
COM_JOOMPROSUBS_N_ITEMS_ARCHIVED_1="%d subscription successfully archived"
COM_JOOMPROSUBS_N_ITEMS_ARCHIVED="%d subscriptions successfully archived"
COM_JOOMPROSUBS_N_ITEMS_CHECKED_IN_0="No subscription successfully checked
↪in"
COM_JOOMPROSUBS_N_ITEMS_CHECKED_IN_1="%d subscription successfully checked
↪in"
COM_JOOMPROSUBS_N_ITEMS_CHECKED_IN_MORE="%d subscriptions successfully
↪checked in"
COM_JOOMPROSUBS_N_ITEMS_DELETED_1="%d subscription successfully deleted"
COM_JOOMPROSUBS_N_ITEMS_DELETED="%d subscriptions successfully deleted"
COM_JOOMPROSUBS_N_ITEMS_PUBLISHED_1="%d subscription successfully
↪published"
COM_JOOMPROSUBS_N_ITEMS_PUBLISHED="%d subscriptions successfully
↪published"
COM_JOOMPROSUBS_N_ITEMS_TRASHED_1="%d subscription successfully trashed"
COM_JOOMPROSUBS_N_ITEMS_TRASHED="%d subscriptions successfully trashed"
COM_JOOMPROSUBS_N_ITEMS_UNPUBLISHED_1="%d subscription successfully
↪unpublished"
COM_JOOMPROSUBS_N_ITEMS_UNPUBLISHED="%d subscriptions successfully
↪unpublished"
COM_JOOMPROSUBS_NEW_JOOMPROSUB="Subscription Add"
COM_JOOMPROSUBS_SEARCH_IN_TITLE="Searh in title."
COM_JOOMPROSUBS_SUBMANAGER_HELP_LINK="http://joomlaprogrammingbook.com/
↪joompro-subscription-manager-help.html"
COM_JOOMPROSUBS_SUBMENU_CATEGORIES="Categories"
COM_JOOMPROSUBS_SUBMENU_JOOMPROSUBS="Subscriptions"
COM_JOOMPROSUBS_SUBSCRIPTION_HELP_LINK="http://joomlaprogrammingbook.com/
↪joompro-subscription-edit-help.html"
COM_JOOMPROSUBS_TOOLBAR_CSVREPORT="Report"
COM_JOOMPROSUBS="Subscriptions"
```

The second file, `language/en-GB/en-GB.com_joomprosubs.sys.ini`, contains the language strings needed when we are not in the component. It is as follows:

```
CATEGORIES="Categories"
COM_JOOMPROSUBS="JoomPro Subscriptions"
COM_JOOMPROSUBS_XML_DESCRIPTION="This is an example component for the
↪Joomla! Programming book."
COM_JOOMPROSUBS_CATEGORY_VIEW_DEFAULT_DESC="Lists all subscriptions in a
↪category."
COM_JOOMPROSUBS_CATEGORY_VIEW_DEFAULT_OPTION="Default Layout"
COM_JOOMPROSUBS_CATEGORY_VIEW_DEFAULT_TITLE="Category List"
```

Installation and Configuration

The last file in the back end is the `joomprosubs.xml` file in the `administrator/components/com_joomprosubs` folder. We are going to build this file in two stages. For now, we will include only the back-end files. This will allow us to install and test the back end of the component before moving on to the front end. We will add the front-end files to the installation file in the next chapter.

The first part of this file is as follows:

```xml
<?xml version="1.0" encoding="utf-8"?>
<extension type="component" version="2.5.0" method="upgrade">
   <name>com_joomprosubs</name>
   <author>Mark Dexter and Louis Landry</author>
   <creationDate>January 2012</creationDate>
   <copyright>(C) 2012 Mark Dexter and Louis Landry. All rights reserved.
   </copyright>
   <license>GNU General Public License version 2 or later; see
      LICENSE.txt</license>
   <authorEmail>admin@joomla.org</authorEmail>
   <authorUrl>www.joomla.org</authorUrl>
   <version>2.5.0</version>
   <description>COM_JOOMPROSUBS_XML_DESCRIPTION</description>

   <install> <!-- Runs on install -->
      <sql>
         <file driver="mysql"
charset="utf8">sql/install.mysql.utf8.sql</file>
      </sql>
   </install>
   <uninstall> <!-- Runs on uninstall -->
      <sql>
         <file driver="mysql"
charset="utf8">sql/uninstall.mysql.utf8.sql</file>
      </sql>
   </uninstall>
```

First, we define various descriptive elements, including name, author, and so on, down to description. Then we define the install and uninstall elements. These name the database scripts to run when the component is installed or uninstalled. In our example, recall that these scripts create and drop the two tables for our component.

The next section is as follows:

```xml
<administration>
   <menu img="class:newsfeeds">COM_JOOMPROSUBS</menu>
   <submenu>
      <!--
         Note that all & must be escaped to &amp; for the file to be valid
```

```
    XML and be parsed by the installer
    -->
    <menu link="option=com_joomprosubs" view="submanager"
⇥img="class:newsfeeds"
        alt="Subscriptions/Subscriptions">COM_JOOMPROSUBS</menu>
    <menu link="option=com_categories&amp;extension=com_joomprosubs"
        view="categories" img="class:newsfeeds-cat"
        alt="Subscriptions/Categories">Categories</menu>
  </submenu>
```

This starts the administrator element, which defines the back-end menus and files.
The first part defines the menu and submenu elements. These are exactly the same as
discussed in Chapter 7 for Weblinks except that we use our component name. Here
we add one top-level option and two submenu options for our component, which will
display as shown in Figure 9.4.

The last section of the installation XML file is as follows:

```
    <files folder="admin">
        <folder>controllers</folder>
        <folder>helpers</folder>
        <folder>language</folder>
        <folder>models</folder>
        <folder>sql</folder>
        <folder>tables</folder>
        <folder>views</folder>
        <filename>access.xml</filename>
        <filename>config.xml</filename>
        <filename>controller.php</filename>
        <filename>index.html</filename>
        <filename>joomprosubs.php</filename>
    </files>
  </administration>
</extension>
```

This defines the files for the back end of our component. Again, we only have to define
the top-level folders and files. Then we close the administrator and extension elements.

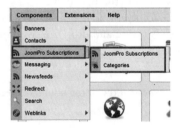

Figure 9.4   Subscriptions menu options

At this point, we can use the Discover and Install options from the Extension Manager → Discover screen to install and test the back-end part of our component.

Summary

In this chapter, we created the entire back end of our example component. This included the manager screen, the add/edit screen, installation files, and the miscellaneous files we need. If you understand how this works, you will be able to create your own components using the same techniques covered here.

10

Components Part IV: Example Component Front End

In the previous chapter, we created the back end of our example component. In this chapter, we create the front end of the component and create an installable zip archive file. Then we will add a new report to the component to demonstrate how the model-view-controller (MVC) design pattern makes it easy to add to the component's functionality.

Files Overview

Table 10.1 shows the front-end files for our component, excluding index.html files. The file names are relative to the `components/com_joomprosubs` folder.

Installation XML File

In the previous chapter, we created the file `administrator/components/com_joomprosubs/joomprosubs.xml` with the information needed for the back-end files. We left out the front-end files so we could install and test just the administrative back end of the component.

In this chapter, we complete the front end of the component. So let's begin by adding the front-end (or site) files to the XML file, as follows:

```
   . . .
   </uninstall>
   <files folder="site">
     <folder>controllers</folder>
     <folder>helpers</folder>
     <folder>language</folder>
     <folder>models</folder>
     <folder>views</folder>
     <filename>controller.php</filename>
     <filename>index.html</filename>
```

```
<filename>joomprosubs.php</filename>
</files>
<administration>
  . . .
```

The highlighted lines are the new lines in the file. This adds a files element between the uninstall and administration elements. As before, this lists top-level files and folders only. The folder attribute of "site" tells the installer to copy these folders in the front-end components folder.

Component Entry Point

The first thing we need to do is create our front-end component folder, `components/ com_joomprosubs`. Because all the front-end files are in this folder, we will refer to the front-end files relative to this location.

Table 10.1 **Front-End Subscriptions Component Folders**

File Name	Contents
`controller.php`	`JoomproSubsController` class
`joomprosubs.php`	Component entry script
`controllers/subscription.php`	`JoomproSubsControllerSubscription` class
`helpers/category.php`	`JoomproSubsCategories` class
`language/en-GB/en-GB.com _joomprosubs.ini`	Language file
`models/category.php`	`JoomprosubsModelCategory` class (for single-category menu item)
`models/form.php`	`JoomprosubsModelForm` class (for subscription sign-up form)
`models/forms/subscription.xml`	XML file for form
`views/category/view.html.php`	`JoomprosubsViewCategory` class (for single-category menu item)
`views/category/tmpl/default.php`	Layout for single-category menu item
`views/category/tmpl/default.xml`	XML options file for single-category menu item
`views/category/tmpl/default _items.php`	Sublayout file for single-category menu item
`views/form/view.html.php`	`JoomprosubsViewForm` class (for subscription submit form)
`views/form/tmpl/edit.php`	Layout file for subscription submit form
`views/form/tmpl/thankyou.php`	Layout file for thank-you message

The entry point for the front end of our component is the file `joomprosubs.php`. This has the expected code as follows:

```
defined('_JEXEC') or die;

jimport('joomla.application.component.controller');

$controller = JController::getInstance('Joomprosubs');
$controller->execute(JRequest::getCmd('task'));
$controller->redirect();
```

Default Controller

Our default controller, which handles the display task, is a class called JoomproSubsController (`controller.php`). The code for this class is as follows:

```
defined('_JEXEC') or die;

jimport('joomla.application.component.controller');

/**
 * Joomprosubs Component Controller
 *
 */
class JoomproSubsController extends JController
{
    /**
     * Method to display a view.
     *
     * @param   boolean    If true, the view output will be cached
     * @param   array      An array of safe url parameters and their
    variable types, for valid values see {@link JFilterInput::clean()}.
     *
     * @return  JController   This object to support chaining.
     */
    public function display($cachable = false, $urlparams = false)
    {
        // Initialise variables.
        $cachable = true;
        $user = JFactory::getUser();

        // Set the default view name and format from the Request.
        // Note we are using sub_id to avoid collisions with the router and
    the return page.
        $id = JRequest::getInt('sub_id');
        $vName = JRequest::getCmd('view', 'category');
        JRequest::setVar('view', $vName);
```

```
        if ($user->get('id')) {
            $cachable = false;
        }

        $safeurlparams = array(
            'id'                => 'INT',
            'limit'             => 'INT',
            'limitstart'        => 'INT',
            'filter_order'      => 'CMD',
            'filter_order_Dir'  => 'CMD',
            'lang'              => 'CMD'
        );

        // Check for edit form.
        if ($vName == 'form' && !$this->checkEditId(
    'com_joomprosubs.edit.subscription', $id)) {
            // Somehow the person just went to the form - we don't allow
    that.
            return JError::raiseError(403,
    JText::sprintf('JLIB_APPLICATION_ERROR_UNHELD_ID', $id));
        }

        return parent::display($cachable,$safeurlparams);
    }
}
```

This class is almost the same as the Weblinks front-end default controller. We need to determine whether or not the view will be cacheable—whether we can save a previous copy of the view in a quick-loading cache file. If the user is logged in, we won't try to use a cache file. In that case, we need to check the database each time to see what permissions the user might have for subscribing to an item, so caching won't work.

The other thing we do here is get the subscription id and the view name. We set the default view to category in case we don't have one in the request. In our example, we only have one view, called category.

We also create an array called $safeurlparams. This contains all the valid parameters for the URL. Any other parameters in the URL are invalid, so this allows us to remove any invalid code from the URL.

Finally, as we have seen elsewhere, we return the result of the parent's (JController) display() method. That method returns the variable $this. As discussed previously, returning $this allows us to do method chaining.

Subscription-Category View

Our component only has one front-end view, called category. This is similar to core category list views. It shows all the subscriptions in a single category. Let's first look at how we create a menu item for this view.

Menu Item XML File

Each menu item provides a set of options (also called parameters) that control the display of the menu item. As with other options, these are specified in an XML file. The XML file is located in the `tmpl` subfolder of the view and is named the same as the layout file for that menu item.

In our example, this file is called `views/category/tmpl/default.xml`. Its contents are as follows:

```xml
<?xml version="1.0" encoding="utf-8"?>
<metadata>
  <layout title="COM_JOOMPROSUBS_CATEGORY_VIEW_DEFAULT_TITLE"
    option="COM_JOOMPROSUBS_CATEGORY_VIEW_DEFAULT_OPTION">
    <help url="COM_JOOMPROSUBS_CATEGORY_LIST_HELP_LINK"
    />
    <message>
      <![CDATA[COM_JOOMPROSUBS_CATEGORY_VIEW_DEFAULT_DESC]]>
    </message>
  </layout>

  <!-- Add fields to the request variables for the layout. -->
  <fields name="request">
    <fieldset name="request">
      <field name="id" type="category"
        default="0"
        description="COM_JOOMPROSUBS_FIELD_SELECT_CATEGORY_DESC"
        extension="com_joomprosubs"
        label="COM_JOOMPROSUBS_FIELD_SELECT_CATEGORY_LABEL"
        required="true"
      />
    </fieldset>
  </fields>

  <!-- Add fields to the parameters object for the layout. -->
  <fields name="params">
    <fieldset name="basic" label="JGLOBAL_CATEGORY_OPTIONS">
      <field name="show_description" type="list"
        description="JGLOBAL_SHOW_CATEGORY_DESCRIPTION_DESC"
        label="JGLOBAL_SHOW_CATEGORY_DESCRIPTION_LABEL"
      >
        <option value="0">JHIDE</option>
```

```
            <option value="1">JSHOW</option>
          </field>
        </fieldset>
      </fields>
</metadata>
```

The layout element specifies the title and description that will show when the list of available menu items is displayed. Here we are again using a URL for the help file. When we are adding or editing a subscription-category list menu item and click the Help icon in the toolbar, the URL specified in our language file will be loaded in a new browser window. This allows us to have language-specific help sites.

We then have two `fields` elements. The first one is called request and has a field-set element called request. This element will be added to the request variable when this menu item is loaded. Typically, we have one request field in a menu item, such as category id or article id. In this case, we specify the type as category and the extension as com_joomprosubs. This uses the core `JFormFieldCategory` class (in the core file `libraries/joomla/form/fields/category.php`) to present the user with a list box of all categories for this component.

The folder `libraries/joomla/form/fields` contains class files that support the predefined types for `JForm` fields. In Chapter 6 we created a custom `JFormRule` class that worked when we set the validate attribute in a `JForm` field element. In a similar fashion we can, if needed, create custom `JFormField` classes. To do this, we include an attribute called "addfieldpath" in the `JForm` fieldset element that points to the folder of the custom class. The type attribute of a field matches the file name of the custom field class. This technique is used in a few places in Joomla!—for example, in `administrator/components/com_content/config.xml`.

Back in our menu item's XML file, we have a second `fields` element called params. We have one fieldset, called basic, and one field, called show_description. This is exactly the same as other parameter fields we have seen previously. Here we give the user the option to display the category description.

Figure 10.1 shows screenshots of these two options when you create a new subscription-category list menu item.

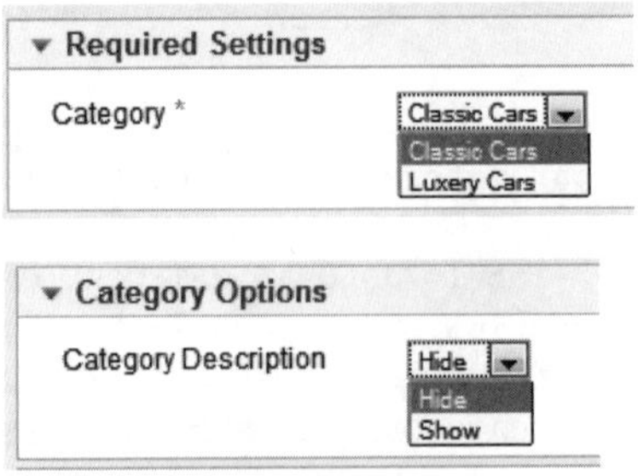

Figure 10.1   Menu item options (both shown expanded)

Category View

Next let's look at the view class, `JoomproSubsViewCategory`. This is the file `views/category/view.html.php`. The first part of the code in this file is as follows:

```php
defined('_JEXEC') or die;

jimport('joomla.application.component.view');

/**
 * HTML View class for the JoomproSubs component
 *
 */
class JoomprosubsViewCategory extends JView
{
    protected $state;
    protected $items;
    protected $category;
    protected $children;
    protected $pagination;

    function display($tpl = null)
    {
      $app = JFactory::getApplication();
      $params = $app->getParams();

      // Get some data from the models
      $state = $this->get('State');
      $items = $this->get('Items');
      $category = $this->get('Category');
      $pagination = $this->get('Pagination');

      // Check for errors.
      if (count($errors = $this->get('Errors'))) {
        JError::raiseError(500, implode("\n", $errors));
        return false;
      }

      if ($category == false) {
        return JError::raiseWarning(404,
➥JText::_('JGLOBAL_CATEGORY_NOT_FOUND'));
      }
```

This code is similar to the category view for Weblinks. We have some fields for the class and a method called `display()`. Recall that this method is called from the `display()` method of the controller. We get the state, list of items, category, and pagination from the model. Then we check for errors.

The next section of the `display()` method is as follows:

```
// Check whether category access level allows access.
$user = JFactory::getUser();
$groups = $user->getAuthorisedViewLevels();
if (!in_array($category->access, $groups)) {
   return JError::raiseError(403, JText::_('JERROR_ALERTNOAUTHOR'));
}

// Prepare the data.
// Compute the joomprosub slug & link url.
for ($i = 0, $n = count($items); $i < $n; $i++)
{
   $item = &$items[$i];
   $item->slug  = $item->alias ? ($item->id.':'.$item->alias) :
$item->id;
}

// Setup the category parameters.
$cparams = $category->getParams();
$category->params = clone($params);
$category->params->merge($cparams);

$this->state = $state;
$this->items = $items;
$this->category = $category;
$this->params = $params;
$this->pagination = $pagination;

//Escape strings for HTML output
$this->pageclass_sfx = htmlspecialchars(
$params->get('pageclass_sfx'));
```

First, we check that the user is authorized to view this category. We use the `get-AuthorisedViewLevels()` method of the `JUser` class to get an array of the view levels and then check that the view level for this category is in that array. Otherwise, we show a 403 error.

Next we loop through each item and calculate its "slug" value. This is item id followed by a colon and the alias. Then we merge the category parameters with the menu item parameters. In our example, we don't have any special category parameters. However, we might want to allow the site administrator to specify parameters at the category and component levels and then merge these with the parameters for this menu item.

It is important to understand how the `JRegistry merge()` method works. This method is the key to understanding how hierarchical parameters are implemented in Joomla. In this example, we have this code:

```
$cparams = $category->getParams();
$category->params = clone($params);
$category->params->merge($cparams);
```

The first line puts the category-level parameters in `$cparams`. The second line uses the PHP `clone()` function to make a new copy of the current component-level parameters and stores this in the params field of the `JCategory` object. We use the `clone()` function so that we don't change the original `$params` object. The last line does the merge.

When we call the merge method for a `JRegistry` object, we have the calling object (in this case `$category->params`) and the object being merged (in this case `$cparams`). The logic for merging the two objects is as follows:

- If a value is set in one object and not set (or undefined) in the other, the set value is used.

- If a value is set in both objects, the calling object's value takes priority over the argument object's value.

In core components, we use this to inherit global settings at lower levels in the hierarchy. The value "Use Global" equates to a blank or unset value. For example, if we had menu item parameters, they would take priority over component-level parameters. When the `JRegistry` objects are merged, the `JRegistry` object for menu item parameters is the calling object and the component level is the merged object. If the menu item has a blank value (equating to Use Global), the component-level value will be applied to the merged object. If both objects have a value set, the menu item value is used (because it is the calling object).

The next block sets the class fields for state, items, category, params, and pagination. This allows them to be available when we are inside the layout scripts. Then we add the page class suffix, using the `htmlspecialchars()` function to escape it to protect against any embedded code.

The last part of the `display()` method is as follows:

```
    // Check for layout override only if this is not the active menu item
    // If it is the active menu item, then the view and category id will
➥match
    $active = $app->getMenu()->getActive();
    if ((!$active) || (strpos($active->link, 'view=category') === false))
➥{
        if ($layout = $category->params->get('category_layout')) {
        $this->setLayout($layout);
        }
    }
    elseif (isset($active->query['layout'])) {
        // We need to set the layout in case this is an alternative menu
➥item (with an alternative layout)
        $this->setLayout($active->query['layout']);
```

```
    }

    $this->_prepareDocument();

    parent::display($tpl);
}
```

This checks for alternative layout files. In our example, this logic is not strictly needed. However, it is important to understand. It comes into play when (a) there is more than one type of layout possible for a category and (b) you link to a category layout that doesn't have an associated menu item.

In this case, we need to know which layout to use for the category. This can be set at the component or the category level. For example, if you look at the Article Manager → Options → Category, there is an option called Choose Layout that lets you choose whether to use a Blog or List layout as the default.

The logic in the code is as follows. If we are in the active menu item, we know we have a menu item. If we are not processing a category view, we don't have to worry about it. If we (a) are not in the active menu item and (b) are processing a category view, then we get the alternative layout for the category and use that. Otherwise, we check if there is a layout specified in the URL query and use that.

After we have processed the alternative layout logic, we call the _prepareDocument() method and then the parent's display() method. The _prepareDocument() method is similar to the corresponding method in the Weblinks component. The first part of this method is as follows:

```
protected function _prepareDocument()
{
  $app = JFactory::getApplication();
  $menu = $app->getMenu()->getActive();
  $pathway = $app->getPathway();
  $title = null;

  if ($menu) {
     $this->params->def('page_heading', $this->params->get
↪('page_title', $menu->title));
  }
  else {
     $this->params->def('page_heading',
↪JText::_('COM_JOOMPROSUBS_DEFAULT_PAGE_TITLE'));
  }

  $title = $this->params->get('page_title', '');

  if (empty($title)) {
     $title = $app->getCfg('sitename');
  }
```

```
  elseif ($app->getCfg('sitename_pagetitles', 0)) {
      $title = JText::sprintf('JPAGETITLE', $app->getCfg('sitename'),
➥$title);
  }
  elseif ($app->getCfg('sitename_pagetitles', 0) == 2) {
      $title = JText::sprintf('JPAGETITLE', $title,
➥$app->getCfg('sitename'));
  }


  $this->document->setTitle($title);
```

This sets the page title based on a hierarchy, starting with the menu title, then the component default, then the site name, and then some global configuration. The idea here is to have the most specific page title that is defined, but also to make sure you have something in the page title.

The remainder of this method and this class is as follows:

```
    if ($this->category->metadesc) {
        $this->document->setDescription($this->category->metadesc);
    }
    elseif (!$this->category->metadesc && $this->params->get(
➥'menu-meta_description')) {
        $this->document->setDescription($this->params->get(
➥'menu-meta_description'));
    }

    if ($this->category->metakey) {
        $this->document->setMetadata('keywords',
➥$this->category->metakey);
    }
    elseif (!$this->category->metakey && $this->params->get(
➥'menu-meta_keywords')) {
        $this->document->setMetadata('keywords',
➥$this->params->get('menu-meta_keywords'));
    }

    if ($this->params->get('robots')) {
        $this->document->setMetadata('robots',
➥$this->params->get('robots'));
    }

    if ($app->getCfg('MetaTitle') == '1') {
        $this->document->setMetaData('title',
➥$this->category->getMetadata()->get('page_title'));
    }

    if ($app->getCfg('MetaAuthor') == '1') {
```

```
            $this->document->setMetaData('author',
➥$this->category->getMetadata()->get('author'));
    }

    $mdata = $this->category->getMetadata()->toArray();

    foreach ($mdata as $k => $v)
    {
        if ($v) {
            $this->document->setMetadata($k, $v);
        }
    }
  }
} // end of class
```

This adds the metadata to the document from the category or the menu item.
Again, the idea is to use the most specific metadata that is available.

Model

In the previous section, we called the methods getState(), getItems(), getCate-
gory(), and getPagination() from the model. Our model is JoomproSubsModelCat-
egory (models/category.php). Let's review its code.

The first section is as follows:

```
defined('_JEXEC') or die;

jimport('joomla.application.component.modellist');
jimport('joomla.application.categories');

/**
 * Joomprosubs Component Joomprosub Model
 *
 * @package        Joomla.Site
 * @subpackage com_joomprosubs
 */
class JoomprosubsModelCategory extends JModelList
{
    /**
     * Category items data
     *
     * @var array
     */
    protected $_item = null;

    /**
     * Constructor.
```

```
     *
     * @param    array    An optional associative array of configuration
→settings.
     * @see      JController
     */
    public function __construct($config = array())
    {
        if (empty($config['filter_fields'])) {
            $config['filter_fields'] = array(
                'id', 'a.id',
                'title', 'a.title',
                'g.title', 'group_title',
                'duration', 'a.duration'
            );
        }


        parent::__construct($config);
    }
```

Our model extends `JModelList`, which in turn extends `JModel`. Note that we inherit the `getState()` method from `JModel` and the `getPagination()` method from `JModelList`. Note also that we import the `JCategories` class, which we will use in the `getCategory()` method. We have one field called `$_item`. We will use this to save the category object.

The constructor creates an array of filter fields that we use to check that the ordering column is valid. Then we call the parent's constructor.

The next method in the class is `getListQuery()`. The first part of this method is as follows:

```
    protected function getListQuery()
    {
        $user = JFactory::getUser();
        $groups = implode(',', $user->getAuthorisedViewLevels());

        // Create a new query object.
        $db       = $this->getDbo();
        $query    = $db->getQuery(true);

        // Select required fields from the categories.
        $query->select($this->getState('list.select', 'a.*'));
        $query->select('g.title as group_title');
        $query->from($db->quoteName('#__joompro_subscriptions').' AS a');

        // Join on groups to get title of group
        $query->join('LEFT', $db->quoteName('#__usergroups').' AS g ON
a.group_id = g.id');
        $query->where('a.access IN ('.$groups.')');
```

```
      // Filter by category.
      if ($categoryId = $this->getState('category.id')) {
          $query->where('a.catid = '.(int) $categoryId);
          $query->join('LEFT', $db->quoteName('#__categories').' AS c ON
c.id = a.catid');
          $query->where('c.access IN ('.$groups.')');

          //Filter by published category
          $cpublished = $this->getState('filter.c.published');
          if (is_numeric($cpublished)) {
              $query->where('c.published = '.(int) $cpublished);
          }
      }
```

In this method, we build the query for the list layout. We include all columns from the #__joompro_subscriptions table and the title from the user groups table. We only include subscriptions in an access level group to which the current user is allowed access. Then we filter on category id and the category published state.

The last part of the method is as follows:

```
   // Filter by state
   $state = $this->getState('filter.state');
   if (is_numeric($state)) {
      $query->where('a.published = '.(int) $state);
   }

   // Filter by search
   if ($this->getState('list.filter') != '') {
       $filter = JString::strtolower($this->getState('list.filter'));
       $filter = $db->quote('%'.$filter.'%', true);
       $query->where('a.title LIKE ' . $filter);
   }

   // Filter by start and end dates.
   $nullDate = $db->quote($db->getNullDate());
   $nowDate = $db->quote(JFactory::getDate()->toSQL());

   if ($this->getState('filter.publish_date')){
       $query->where('(a.publish_up = ' . $nullDate . '
⮡OR a.publish_up <= ' . $nowDate . ')');
       $query->where('(a.publish_down = ' . $nullDate . '
⮡OR a.publish_down >= ' . $nowDate . ')');
   }

   // Add the list ordering clause.
```

```
    $query->order($db->getEscaped($this->getState('list.ordering',
'a.title')).
        ' '.$db->getEscaped($this->getState('list.direction', 'ASC')));
    return $query;
}
```

Here we add WHERE clauses to our query to filter on the published state of the category, any filtering text the user typed in, and the start and stop publishing dates for the subscription. Finally, we order the list based on the column clicked by the user and return the query object.

 The list filter is text the user types in to filter the list. For example, they might type in "Chevy" to only show subscriptions with "Chevy" in the title. This text gets incorporated into our SQL query, so we have to be careful to filter out malicious SQL code. We do this using the quote() method of the database object. By setting the second argument to true, we tell the method to run its escape() method on the first argument. This escapes any special characters that could be used to inject malicious SQL code into our query.

Next is the populateState() method, which is as follows:

```
    protected function populateState($ordering = null, $direction = null)
    {
        // Initialise variables.
        $app    = JFactory::getApplication();
        $params         = JComponentHelper::getParams('com_joomprosubs');

        // List state information
        $limit = $app->getUserStateFromRequest('global.list.limit',
'limit', $app->getCfg('list_limit'));
        $this->setState('list.limit', $limit);

        $limitstart = JRequest::getVar('limitstart', 0, '', 'int');
        $this->setState('list.start', $limitstart);

        $orderCol = JRequest::getCmd('filter_order', 'title');
        if (!in_array($orderCol, $this->filter_fields)) {
            $orderCol = 'ordering';
        }
        $this->setState('list.ordering', $orderCol);

        $listOrder = Request::getCmd('filter_order_Dir', 'ASC');
        if (!in_array(strtoupper($listOrder), array('ASC', 'DESC', ''))) {
            $listOrder = 'ASC';
        }
        $this->setState('list.direction', $listOrder);

        $this->setState('list.filter', JRequest::getString(
'filter-search'));
```

```
        $$id = JRequest::getInt('id', 0);
        $this->setState('category.id', $id);


        $user = JFactory::getUser();
        if ((!$user->authorise('core.edit.state', 'com_joomprosubs')) &&
    (!$user->authorise('core.edit', 'com_joomprosubs'))){
            // limit to published for people who can't edit or edit.state.
            $this->setState('filter.state',   1);


            // Filter by start and end dates.
            $this->setState('filter.publish_date', true);
        }
    }
```

Here, we set the state object's fields based on the request variable. We use the
`getUserStateFromRequest()` method to get the setting for the list limit (the number
of items to display on the page). This reads this value from the session object. Using
this method allows us to save the value in the session and "remember" what the user
has specified for this screen.

Next we get the limit start. This tells the database where to start when we are paging through a long list. Note that we use the `getInt()` method of `JRequest` to guar-
antee that we have an integer for this.

Then we get the ordering column and direction. Note that we use the field called
filter_fields, which we created in the constructor to validate the ordering column. We
also validate the direction to be either ASC or DESC.

Then we set the list.filter field of the state based on input the user typed in to filter
the list. This is a point of potential vulnerability in our application. The user can type
any string in this field, and the `getString()` method only checks that we have a valid
string and does not do any filtering of malicious content. That is why we used the
`$db->quote()` method when we built the query.

Next we get the category id from the request and set it in the state. Finally, if the
user does not have permission to edit state, we only allow them to see published items.

The last method in the file is `getCategory()`, as follows:

```
    public function getCategory()
    {
        if(!is_object($this->_item))
        {
            $categories = JCategories::getInstance('Joomprosubs');
            $this->_item = $categories->get($this->getState('category.id',
    'root'));
        }

        return $this->_item;
    }
} // end of class
```

Here we simply get the category object based on the category id. Note that we only do this once and save it in the field $_item. If we need it again, we just get it from the field.

Category Helper File

Note that when we call the `getInstance()` method of `JCategories`, we in turn call the `__construct()` method of the `JoomproSubsCategories` class (`helpers/category.php`). This class has the following code:

```php
defined('_JEXEC') or die;

// Component Helper
jimport('joomla.application.component.helper');
jimport('joomla.application.categories');

/**
 * Joomprosubs Component Category Tree
 *
 * @static
 * @package     Joomla.Site
 * @subpackage com_joomprosubs
 */
class JoomproSubsCategories extends JCategories
{
    public function __construct($options = array())
    {
        $options['table'] = '#__joompro_subscriptions';
        $options['extension'] = 'com_joomprosubs';
        $options['statefield'] = 'published';
        parent::__construct($options);
    }
} // end of class
```

This file provides the specific information needed for categories for this extension, including the table name, the extension name, and the fact that we have a column called published where we store our state information.

Category Layout Files

Two layout files are used to render the category list. The entry point is the file `views/category/tmpl/default.php`, whose code is as follows:

```php
<?php
/**
 * @package     Joomla.Site
 * @subpackage com_joomprosubs
```

```
 * @copyright  Copyright (C) 2012 Mark Dexter and Louis Landry. All rights
⇥reserved.
 * @license    GNU General Public License version 2 or later; see
⇥LICENSE.txt
 */
// no direct access
defined('_JEXEC') or die;
JHtml::addIncludePath(JPATH_COMPONENT.'/helpers'); ?>
<div class="joomprosub-category<?php echo $this->pageclass_sfx;?>">
<?php if ($this->params->def('show_page_heading', 1)) : ?>
<h1>
    <?php echo $this->escape($this->params->get('page_heading')); ?>
</h1>
<?php endif; ?>
<?php if($this->params->get('show_category_title', 1)) : ?>
<h2>
    <?php echo JHtml::_('content.prepare', $this->category->title); ?>
</h2>
<?php endif; ?>
<?php if ($this->params->get('show_description', 1) ||
⇥$this->params->def('show_description_image', 1)) : ?>
    <div class="category-desc">
    <?php if ($this->params->get('show_description_image') &&
⇥$this->category->getParams()->get('image')) : ?>
        <img src="<?php echo $this->category->getParams()->get('image');
⇥?>"/>
    <?php endif; ?>
    <?php if ($this->params->get('show_description') &&
⇥$this->category->description) : ?>
        <?php echo JHtml::_('content.prepare',
⇥$this->category->description); ?>
    <?php endif; ?>
    <div class="clr"></div>
    </div>
<?php endif; ?>
<?php echo $this->loadTemplate('items'); ?>
</div>
```

Again, this is similar to the corresponding file for Weblinks or the other category list layouts. We display the category description and image. Then we use the `load-Template()` method to load the `default_items.php` layout file.

The first part of the `default_items.php` file is as follows:

```
<?php
/**
 * @subpackage  com_joomprosubs
 * @copyright   Copyright (C) 2012 Mark Dexter and Louis Landry. All
```

```
➥rights reserved.
 * @license      GNU General Public License version 2 or later; see
➥LICENSE.txt
 */

// no direct access
defined('_JEXEC') or die;
// Code to support edit links for joomaprosubs
// Create a shortcut for params.

JHtml::addIncludePath(JPATH_COMPONENT.'/helpers/html');
JHtml::_('behavior.tooltip');
JHtml::core();

// Get the user object.
$user = JFactory::getUser();
// Check if user is allowed to add/edit based on joomprosubs permissions.
$canEdit = $user->authorise('core.edit', 'com_joomprosubs.category.' .
➥$this->category->id);

$listOrder = $this->escape($this->state->get('list.ordering'));
$listDirn = $this->escape($this->state->get('list.direction'));
$listFilter = $this->state->get('list.filter');
?>

<?php if (empty($this->items)) : ?>
  <p> <?php echo JText::_('COM_JOOMPROSUBS_NO_JOOMPROSUBS'); ?></p>
<?php else : ?>

<form action="<?php echo htmlspecialchars(JFactory::getURI()->
➥toString()); ?>"
  method="post" name="adminForm" id="adminForm">
  <fieldset class="filters">
  <legend class="hidelabeltxt"><?php echo
➥JText::_('JGLOBAL_FILTER_LABEL'); ?></legend>
  <div class="filter-search">
     <label class="filter-search-lbl" for="filter-search">
     <?php echo JText::_('COM_JOOMPROSUBS_FILTER_LABEL').' ';
➥?></label>
     <input type="text" name="filter-search" id="filter-search"
        value="<?php echo $this->escape($this->state->get('list.filter'));
➥?>"
        class="inputbox" onchange="document.adminForm.submit();"
        title="<?php echo JText::_('COM_CONTENT_FILTER_SEARCH_DESC'); ?>"
➥/>
  </div>
<div class="display-limit">
```

```
    <?php echo JText::_('JGLOBAL_DISPLAY_NUM'); ?>
    <?php echo $this->pagination->getLimitBox(); ?>
</div>
</fieldset>
```

We start with some housekeeping to load the helper files, the JavaScript tooltip behavior, and the core JavaScript behavior. Then we check if the user can edit this category. If so, we will show the category as a link to subscribe. Otherwise, we will just show the category as text.

Next we get the sort ordering field and direction and then the filter text, if any. Recall that the user can sort the list by clicking on the column headings.

Next we check to see if we have any items to process. If not, we output a message saying there are no subscriptions in this category. Otherwise, we proceed with the layout for the items.

Next we create the form element. The action is the URL back to this same page. We need a form to process the sorting by column and filtering based on user input. Then we render the filter text box and the display limit list box.

The next code block is as follows:

```
<table class="category">
  <thead><tr>
    <th class="title">
        <?php echo JHtml::_('grid.sort', 'COM_JOOMPROSUBS_GRID_TITLE',
        'a.title', $listDirn, $listOrder); ?>
    </th>
    <th class="group">
      <?php echo JHtml::_('grid.sort', 'COM_JOOMPROSUBS_GRID_GROUP',
        'g.title', $listDirn, $listOrder); ?>
    </th>
    <th class="duration">
      <?php echo JHtml::_('grid.sort', 'COM_JOOMPROSUBS_GRID_DURATION',
        'a.duration', $listDirn, $listOrder); ?>
    </th>
</tr></thead>
```

This renders the sortable column headings.

The next block is as follows:

```
  <tbody>
  <?php foreach ($this->items as $i => $item) : ?>
    <tr class="cat-list-row<?php echo $i % 2; ?>" >
    <td class="title">
      <?php if ($canEdit) : ?>
        <a href="<?php echo JRoute::_(
↪'index.php?option=com_joomprosubs&task=subscription.edit
↪&sub_id='. $item->id.'&catid='.$item->catid); ?>">
```

```
      <?php echo $item->title; ?></a>
    <?php else: ?>
      <?php echo $item->title;?>
    <?php endif; ?>
    <?php if ($this->params->get('show_description')) : ?>
      <?php echo nl2br($item->description); ?>
    <?php endif; ?>
  </td>
  <td class="item-group">
    <?php echo $item->group_title; ?>
  </td>
  <td class="item-duration">
    <?php echo $item->duration; ?>
  </td>
  </tr>
  <?php endforeach; ?>
</tbody>
</table>
```

This loops through the array of items and renders each of the rows of the table. This includes the title, the description (if the parameter is set to show description), the subscription title, and the duration.

The last section of the file is as follows:

```
<div class="pagination">
  <p class="counter">
  <?php echo $this->pagination->getPagesCounter(); ?>
  </p>
  <?php echo $this->pagination->getPagesLinks(); ?>
</div>
<div>
  <input type="hidden" name="filter_order"
→value="<?php echo $listOrder; ?>" />
  <input type="hidden" name="filter_order_Dir"
→value="<?php echo $listDirn; ?>" />
</div>
</form>
<?php endif; ?>
```

This renders the pagination controls, closes the form, and ends the if-else block. An example of this layout is shown in Figure 10.2.

Subscription View

Next let's look at the subscription view. This is where a user can subscribe to one of our subscriptions. If a user who has permission to edit this subscription category is

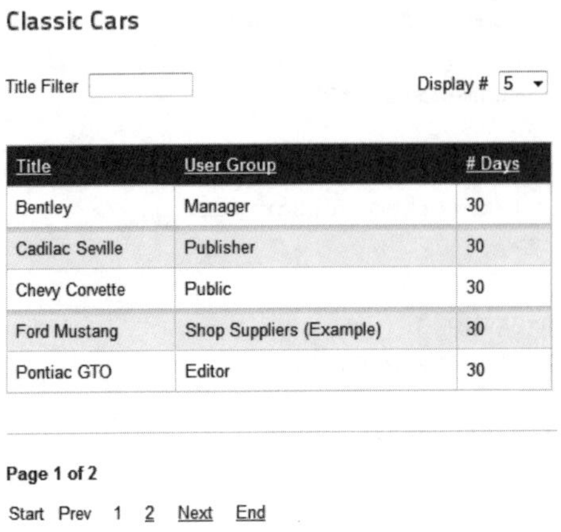

Classic Cars

Title Filter		Display # 5 ▾

Title	User Group	# Days
Bentley	Manager	30
Cadilac Seville	Publisher	30
Chevy Corvette	Public	30
Ford Mustang	Shop Suppliers (Example)	30
Pontiac GTO	Editor	30

Page 1 of 2

Start Prev 1 2 Next End

Figure 10.2   Example of subscription layout

logged in to the site, the subscription titles display as links to the subscribe form. For example, a subscription with an id of 3 shows the following link:

```
index.php/subscriptions?task=subscription.edit&sub_id=3
```

Clicking this link causes the screen in Figure 10.3 to appear.

Subscription Edit Controller Methods

We know from earlier work that the task "susbscription.edit" will cause the `edit()` method of the `JoomproSubsControllerSubscription` (controllers/subscription. php) class to be run. So clicking on this link will initiate this method. Let's follow the logic for this view, starting with the controller.

The first part of the code is as follows:

```
<?php
/**
 * @copyright   Copyright (C) 2012 Mark Dexter and Louis Landry. All
→rights reserved.
 * @license     GNU General Public License version 2 or later; see
```

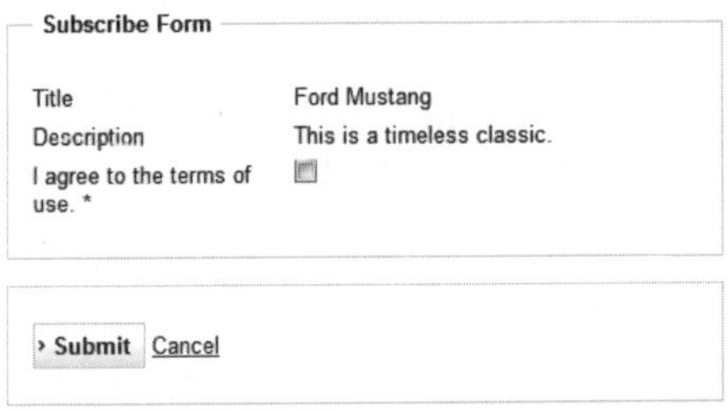

Subscribe Form

Title	Ford Mustang
Description	This is a timeless classic.
I agree to the terms of use. *	▣

› **Submit** Cancel

Figure 10.3   Subscribe form

```
↪LICENSE.txt
 */

// no direct access
defined('_JEXEC') or die;

jimport('joomla.application.component.controllerform');
jimport('joomla.user.helper');

class JoomproSubsControllerSubscription extends JControllerForm
{

    protected $view_item = 'form';
```

This imports the classes we will need and creates a field, $view_item, that we will use later in the class.

The next block of code defines the edit() method that is called when the subscription link is clicked. Here is the code:

```
public function edit($key = null, $urlVar = 'sub_id')
{
    $result = false;
    $itemid = JRequest::getInt('Itemid');
    $catid = JRequest::getInt('catid');
    if (($catid) && ($this->allowEdit($catid))) {
        $result = parent::edit($key, $urlVar);

        // Check in the subscription, since it was checked out in the
↪edit method
        $this->getModel()->checkIn(JRequest::getInt($urlVar));
    }
    return $result;
}
```

This method gets the current menu item id and category id from the request. Then, if we have a category id and if the allowEdit() method for this category id returns a boolean true, we call the edit() method of the parent class. Because this method checks out the item, we immediately check it back in using our model. (Notice that we use method chaining to call the checkIn() method of the model.) We don't need to hold the row for editing because we do not change the row for this subscription. As we will see, instead we add a row to the mapping table.Finally, we return the result, which will be true if the method was successful and otherwise false.

The next method in the controller that we use at this point in the process is getRedirectToItemAppend(). This method is called from the parent's (JControllerForm) edit() method and is used to append the current Itemid to the redirect URL. Because we override this method in our class (`JoomproSubsControllerSubscription`), the override code in our class gets executed. The code is as follows:

```php
protected function getRedirectToItemAppend($recordId = null,
$urlVar = null)
{
    $append = parent::getRedirectToItemAppend($recordId, $urlVar);
    $itemId = JRequest::getInt('Itemid');
    if ($itemId) {
        $append .= '&Itemid='.$itemId;
    }
    return $append;
}
```

This calls the parent's method first. Then it appends the current Itemid and returns the result. This means that we keep the same Itemid value in our redirect so the modules and template that are assigned to this menu item will still show when we are redirected to the form.

The `allowEdit()` method of the controller is as follows:

```php
protected function allowEdit($catid)
{
    return JFactory::getUser()->authorise('core.edit',
$this->option.'.category.'.$catid);
}
```

This just checks that the current user has permissions in the access control list (ACL) to edit this category of subscriptions.

The `getModel()` method of the controller is as follows:

```php
public function getModel($name = 'form', $prefix = '',
$config = array('ignore_request' => true))
{
    $model = parent::getModel($name, $prefix, $config);
    return $model;
}
```

This just specifies that our model's name is "form", meaning that the full model name will be `JoomproSubsModelForm`.

Edit View and Form

The next step in the process is to execute the `display()` method of the view `JoomproSubsViewForm` (`views/form/view.html.php`). The first part of this class is as follows:

```php
<?php
/**
```

```
 * @package    Joomla.Site
 * @subpackage com_joomprosubs
 * @copyright  Copyright (C) 2012 Mark Dexter and Louis Landry. All rights
⮞reserved.
 * @license    GNU General Public License version 2 or later; see
⮞LICENSE.txt
 */

// no direct accessdefined('_JEXEC') or die;
jimport('joomla.application.component.view');

/**
 * HTML View class for the JoomproSubs component
 *
 */
class JoomprosubsViewForm extends JView{
    protected $state;
    protected $item;
    protected $category;

    function display($tpl = null)
    {
        $app = JFactory::getApplication();
        $params = $app->getParams();
        $user = JFactory::getUser();


        // Get some data from the model
        $item = $this->get('Item');
        $this->form = $this->get('Form');
```

Here we declare the class fields and start the **display()** method. We do some standard housekeeping and then get the item and form from the model.

Our model, **JoomproSubsModelForm**, extends the back-end model **JoomproSubs ModelSubscription**. The back-end model has a **getForm()** method and inherits **get-State()** and **getItem()**. When called from our front-end class, the **getForm()** method loads the **subscription.xml** file from the folder **components/com_joomprosubs/ models/forms** (not from the **administrator/components folder**). This is because we use the constant JPATH_COMPONENT, which has a different value when we are in the front or back end of the site.

The form's XML file, **models/forms/subscription.xml**, is as follows:

```
<?xml version="1.0" encoding="UTF-8"?>
<form>
    <fields>
    <fieldset>
        <field name="subscription_terms" type="checkbox"
```

```
          default="0" filter="bool"
          label="COM_JOOMPROSUBS_FORM_TERMS_LABEL"
          desc="COM_JOOMPROSUBS_FORM_TERMS_DESC"
          required="true"
          value="1"
      />
    </fieldset>
    </fields>
</form>
```

This file defines one form field, which is a check box called `subscription_terms`.

Back in the view `JoomproSubsViewForm` (`views/form/view.html.php`), the rest of the `display()` method is as follows:

```
$authorised = $user->authorise('core.edit', 'com_joomprosubs.category.'
↪. $item->catid);

if ($authorised !== true) {
    JError::raiseError(403, JText::_('JERROR_ALERTNOAUTHOR'));
    return false;
}

$this->form->bind($item);

// Check for errors.
if (count($errors = $this->get('Errors'))) {
    JError::raiseWarning(500, implode("\n", $errors));
    return false;
}

//Escape strings for HTML output
$this->pageclass_sfx = htmlspecialchars(
↪$params->get('pageclass_sfx'));

$this->params = $params;
$this->user = $user;
$this->item = $item;

$this->_prepareDocument();
parent::display($tpl);
}
```

Here we make sure the user has edit permissions for this category. Note that this is not strictly needed in this case. We have already checked this permission in the controller's `edit()` method. However, it is good practice to put this check in the view as well. That way, if we use this method in a different context, it will ensure that the user has the correct permissions.

Then we call the **bind()** method and check for errors. Then we escape the page class suffix to eliminate any malicious code. Next we save the params, user, and item as fields so we can use them in the layout files. Finally, we call the **_prepareDocument()** method and the parent's display method to invoke the layout files.

The **_prepareDocument()** method is also in this class. It has the following code:

```
protected function _prepareDocument()
{
    $app = JFactory::getApplication();
    $menus = $app->getMenu();
    $pathway = $app->getPathway();
    $title = null;

    // Because the application sets a default page title,
    // we need to get it from the menu item itself
    $menu = $menus->getActive();

    $head = JText::_('COM_JOOMPROSUBS_FORM_SUBMIT_SUB');

    if ($menu) {
        $this->params->def('page_heading',
➥$this->params->get('page_title', $menu->title));
    } else {
        $this->params->def('page_heading', $head);
    }

    $title = $this->params->def('page_title', $head);
    if ($app->getCfg('sitename_pagetitles', 0)) {
        $title = JText::sprintf('JPAGETITLE', $app->getCfg('sitename'),
➥$title);
    }
    $this->document->setTitle($title);

    if ($this->params->get('menu-meta_description'))
    {
        $this->document->setDescription($this->params->get(
➥'menu-meta_description'));
    }

    if ($this->params->get('menu-meta_keywords'))
    {
        $this->document->setMetadata('keywords',
➥$this->params->get('menu-meta_keywords'));
    }

    if ($this->params->get('robots'))
    {
```

```
          $this->document->setMetadata('robots',
↪$this->params->get('robots'));
      }
   }
} // end of class
```

This method sets the document page heading, page title, description, keywords, and robots. It is almost exactly the same as the method in the other views. Note that this is a strong indication that we could eliminate some duplicate code if we created a method in the parent class and called that method.

Edit Layout

The subscribe layout is the file **edit.php** in the folder **views/tmpl**. Its code is as follows:

```php
<?php

/**
 * @copyright  Copyright (C) 2012 Mark Dexter and Louis Landry. All rights
↪reserved.
 * @license    GNU General Public License version 2 or later; see
↪LICENSE.txt
 */
defined('_JEXEC') or die;
JHtml::_('behavior.keepalive');
JHtml::_('behavior.formvalidation');
JHtml::_('behavior.tooltip');
$itemid = JRequest::getInt('Itemid');
?>

<div class="edit joomprosubs-edit<?php echo $this->pageclass_sfx; ?>">
  <form action="<?php echo JRoute::_('index.php'); ?>"
     id="adminForm" name="adminForm" method="post" class="form-validate">
    <fieldset>
    <legend><?php echo JText::_('COM_JOOMPROSUBS_FORM_LABEL'); ?></legend>
      <dl>
        <dt><?php echo JText::_('COM_JOOMPROSUBS_GRID_TITLE'); ?></dt>
        <dd><?php echo $this->escape($this->item->get('title')); ?></dd>
        <dt><?php echo JText::_('COM_JOOMPROSUBS_GRID_DESC'); ?></dt>
        <dd><?php echo $this->escape(strip_tags($this->
↪item->get('description'))); ?></dd>
        <dt><?php echo $this->form->getLabel('subscription_terms');
↪?></dt>
        <dd><?php echo $this->form->getInput('subscription_terms');
↪?></dd>
      </dl>
    </fieldset>
```

```
      <fieldset>
        <button class="button validate" type="submit"><?php echo
➥JText::_('COM_JOOMPRPOSUBS_FORM_SUBMIT'); ?></button>
        <a href="<?php echo
➥JRoute::_('index.php?option=com_joomprosubs&Itemid='. $itemid); ?>">
          <?php echo JText::_('COM_JOOMPRPOSUBS_FORM_CANCEL'); ?></a>
        <input type="hidden" name="option" value="com_joomprosubs" />
        <input type="hidden" name="task" value="subscription.subscribe" />
        <input type="hidden" name="sub_id" value="<?php echo
➥$this->item->id; ?>" />
        <?php echo JHtml::_( 'form.token'); ?>
      </fieldset>
    </form>
</div>
```

This creates a form and then renders the one form field using the `getLabel()` and `get-Input()` methods. It then creates a submit button that sets the task equal to "subscription.subscribe". Recall in our `subscription.xml` file we set the required attribute for the check box to `true`. If the user clicks the submit button without checking this box, this will give an error message "Field required: I agree to the terms of use." Also, note that we have provided a cancel link that takes us back to the original menu item.

Subscribe Task

If a user clicks the submit button in the edit form, we execute the `subscribe()` method in the controller. The code for this is in the `JoomproSubsControllerSubscription` class (`controllers/subscription.php`) . The first part of this method is as follows:

```
    /**
     * Subscribe to a subscription.
     *
     * @param  string   $key     The name of the primary key of the URL
➥variable.
     * @param  string   $urlVar  The name of the URL variable if different
➥from the primary key
     *
     * @return   string   The return URL.
     */
public function subscribe ($key = null, $urlVar = 'sub_id')
{
    // Check that user is authorized
    $user = JFactory::getUser();
    if (!$user->authorise('core.edit', 'com_joomprosubs.category.' .
➥$this->category->id)) {
        JError::raiseError(403, JText::_('JERROR_ALERTNOAUTHOR'));
        return false;
    }
```

```
// Check that form data is valid
if(!$this->validate()) {
    return false;
}

// Add user to group if not already a member
$model = $this->getModel();
$id = JRequest::getInt('sub_id');
$subscription = $model->getItem($id);

// Set redirect without id in case of an error
$this->setRedirect(JRoute::_(
↪'index.php?option=com_joomprosubs&view=form&layout=thankyou', false));
```

Once again, we check that the user has permissions. Recall that a hacker could simply alter the form to enter in the task and id, so we need to check that this is a legitimate user. Then we execute the **validate()** method to make sure the data is valid. We discuss this method a bit later. Then we use the model to get the subscription item.

Finally, we set the redirect link omitting the id number. As we will see a bit later, this indicates to the thank-you layout that we were not successful, so we can show the user a message to that effect.

Note that we call **JRoute::_()** with a second argument of boolean **false**. This argument defaults to **true**, in which case the **htmlspecialchars** command is run on the URL to escape special characters. Recall that this changes "&" to "&". Normally, when we use **JRoute::_()** to build a URL, we omit the second argument and take the default value. However, when we are using **JRoute::_()** to build a URL for a redirect, we need to specify a **false** value so that the URL does not get escaped. Otherwise, when the redirect is processed, the URL query variables will be wrong (for example, in the **$_REQUEST** array, instead of a key equal to "Itemid" you will have "&Itemid").

The rest of the **subscribe()** method is as follows:

```
if (!in_array($subscription->group_id, $user->groups)) {
    if (!JUserHelper::addUserToGroup($user->id,
↪$subscription->group_id)) {
        $this->setMessage($model->getError(), 'error');
        return false;
    }
}

// Add or update row to mapping table
if (!$result = $model->updateSubscriptionMapping($subscription,
↪$user)) {
    $this->setMessage($model->getError(), 'error');
    return false;
}
```

```
    // At this point, we have succeeded
    // Trigger the onAfterSubscribe event
    JDispatcher::getInstance()->trigger('onAfterSubscribe',
↪array(&$subscription));

    // Include id in redirect for success message
    $this->setRedirect(JRoute::_(
↪'index.php?option=com_joomprosubs&view=form&layout=thankyou
↪&sub_id='.$id, false));
    return true;
}
```

Now we actually change the database to reflect that the user has subscribed. Recall that there are two actions we need to take to create the subscription. First, we add the user to the ACL group for this subscription. Second, we add a row to the mapping table to record the subscription details.

We start by checking whether the user is already in this group. If not, we use the `JUserHelper::addUserToGroup()` method to add the user to the group. If that is not successful, we set the error message and return false.

The next line calls the `updateSubscriptionMapping()` method of our model and sets the error if it returns false. We discuss this a bit later.

Next we trigger an event for our component, called `onAfterSubscribe`. This will look for any plugins with a method of this name and invoke them. This event is not essential for the component to work. It just creates an event that we can use if we like.

Finally, we set the redirect route to the full value, including the id. The layout will use this value to check that our task was successful. Note that again we set the second argument of `JRoute::_()` to `false`.

Controller Validate Method

In the `subscribe()` method we called the controller's `validate()` method to check that the data was valid. The code for this method is as follows:

```
/**
 * Validate the data
 *
 * @return   boolean   true if data is valid, false otherwise
 */
protected function validate()
{
    $app = JFactory::getApplication();
    $model = $this->getModel();
    $data = JRequest::getVar('jform', array(), 'post', 'array');
    $form = $model->getForm($data, false);
    $validData = $model->validate($form, $data);
```

```
        $recordId = JRequest::getInt('sub_id');

        // Check for validation errors.
        if ($validData === false) {
            // Get the validation messages.
            $errors    = $model->getErrors();

            // Push up to three validation messages out to the user.
            for ($i = 0, $n = count($errors); $i < $n && $i < 3; $i++)
            {
                if (JError::isError($errors[$i])) {
                    $app->enqueueMessage($errors[$i]->getMessage(), 'warning');
                }
                else {
                    $app->enqueueMessage($errors[$i], 'warning');
                }
            }

            // Save the data in the session.
            if (isset($data[0])) {
                $app->setUserState($context.'.data', $data);
            }

            // Redirect back to the edit screen.
            $this->setRedirect(JRoute::_('index.php?option='.
➥$this->option.'&view='.$this->view_item.
➥$this->getRedirectToItemAppend($recordId, 'sub_id'), false));
            return false;
        }
        return true;
    }

} // end of class
```

Here we get the form data from the request and then call the model's **validate()** method. Recall from earlier that this executes the **filter()** and **validate()** methods of the form object. If either of these methods finds an error, the model's **validate()** method will return false. In that case, the controller **validate()** method displays up to three different error messages and then sets the redirect back to the form.

If everything is OK, we return **true**.

Form Model

Recall from our basic discussion of the MVC design pattern that the model is typically where we interact with the database. In this case, we call the **updateSubscriptionMapping()** method of the model to handle the database changes to the mapping table.

The model class is `JoomproSubsModelForm` in the file `models/form.php`. The first part of this model class is as follows:

```
<?php
/**
 * @copyright Copyright (C) 2012 Mark Dexter and Louis Landry. All rights
➥reserved.
 * @license   GNU General Public License version 2 or later; see
➥LICENSE.txt
 */

// No direct access.
defined('_JEXEC') or die;
JLoader::register('JoomproSubsModelSubscription',
   JPATH_COMPONENT_ADMINISTRATOR.'/models/subscription.php');

/**
 * Joomprosubs model.
 *
 * @package     Joomla.Site
 * @subpackage  com_joomprosubs
 */
class JoomproSubsModelForm extends JoomproSubsModelSubscription
{
```

Note that we extend the back-end model class. This gives us the methods we need for getting subscription items. Note also that we use the preferred `JLoader::register()` method instead of `require_once`.

The only public method in the model is `updateSubscriptionMapping()`. Its code is as follows:

```
   /**
    *
    * Method to add or update the subscription mapping table
    * If the row already exists, update the start and end date.
    * If the row doesn't exist, add a new row.
    *
    * @param JObject  $subscription   Subscription object
    * @param JUser    $user User object
    * @return  Boolean  true on success, false on failure
    */
   public function updateSubscriptionMapping($subscription, $user)
   {
      // Check that we have valid inputs
      if (((int) $subscription->id) && ((int) $subscription->duration)
            && ((int) $user->id)) {
```

```
        $today = JFactory::getDate()->toSQL();
        $endDate = JFactory::getDate('+ ' . (int)
➥$subscription->duration . ' days')->toSQL();

        // Check whether the row exists
        $mapRow = $this->getMapRow($subscription->id, $user->id);
        if ($mapRow === false) {
            // We have a database error
            return false;
        } else if ($mapRow) {
            // The row already exists, so update it
            if (!$this->updateMapRow($subscription->id, $user->id, $today,
➥$endDate)) {
                return false;
            }
        } else {
            // The row doesn't exist, so add a new map row
            if (!$this->addMapRow($subscription->id, $user->id, $today,
➥$endDate)) {
                return false;
            }
        }

        // At this point, we have successfully updated the database
        return true;
    }
}
```

First, we check that we have valid nonzero integers for the subscription and user ids and the duration. Then we calculate the subscription ending date using the **JFactory** **getDate()** method. This method accepts a time interval relative to the current time, such as "+ 10 minutes" or "+ 30 days." In this case, we are passing "+ xx days" where xx is the duration of our subscription.

Next we call **getMapRow()** to see if this user already has a row in the table. If so, we call **updateMapRow()** to update the fields. Otherwise, we call **addMapRow()** to add a new row.

The **getMapRow()** method is as follows:

```
protected function getMapRow($subID, $userID)
{
    $db = $this->getDbo();
    $query = $db->getQuery(true);
    $query->select('subscription_id, user_id, start_date, end_date');
    $query->from($db->nameQuote('#__joompro_sub_mapping'));
    $query->where('subscription_id = ' . (int) $subID);
    $query->where('user_id = ' . (int) $userID);
    $db->setQuery($query);
```

```
    $data = $db->loadObject();
    if ($db->getErrorNum()) {
        $this->setError(JText::_('COM_JOOMPROSUBS_GET_MAP_ROW_FAIL'));
        return false;
    } else {
        return $data;
    }
}
```

Here we do a select query to get the row using the subscription and user ids and return it as a standard object. Recall that this table has these values as the primary key. That means that there can only be one row for each combination of subscription id and user id.

The updateMapRow() method is as follows:

```
protected function updateMapRow($subID, $userID, $startDate, $endDate)
{
    $db = $this->getDbo();
    $query = $db->getQuery(true);
    $query->update($db->nameQuote('#__joompro_sub_mapping'));
    $query->set('start_date = ' . $db->quote($startDate));
    $query->set('end_date = ' . $db->quote($endDate));
    $query->where('subscription_id = ' . (int) $subID);
    $query->where('user_id = ' . (int) $userID);
    $db->setQuery($query);
    if ($db->query()) {
        return true;
    } else {
        $this->setError(
 ➥JText::_('COM_JOOMPROSUBS_UPDATE_MAP_ROW_FAIL'));
        return false;
    }
}
```

Here we create an update query to update the start and end dates for the row. Again, by specifying the subscription id and user id columns, we know we have the correct database row.

The addMapRow() method is as follows:

```
protected function addMapRow ($subID, $userID, $startDate, $endDate)
{
    $db = $this->getDbo();
    $query = $db->getQuery(true);
    $query->insert($db->nameQuote('#__joompro_sub_mapping'));
    $query->set('subscription_id = ' . (int) $subID);
    $query->set('user_id = ' . (int) $userID);
    $query->set('start_date = ' . $db->quote($startDate));
```

```
    $query->set('end_date = ' . $db->quote($endDate));
    $db->setQuery($query);
    if ($db->query()) {
        return true;
    } else {
        $this->setError(JText::_('COM_JOOMPROSUBS_ADD_MAP_ROW_FAIL'));
        return false;
    }
}
```

Here we create an insert query and set the columns for the subscription and user ids as well as the start and end dates. Then we set the error message if the query fails. Note that we use the JDatabase **quote()** method for the dates. In our case, the dates are in the format "yyyy-mm-dd<space>hh:mm:ss" (for example, "2012-08-10 22:40:45"). We need to put this in quotes because it contains a space character.

The last method in the model is the **populateState()** method. This is called when we call the **get('Item')** method in the view. The **populateState()** method is as follows:

```
protected function populateState()
{
    $app = JFactory::getApplication();

    // Load state from the request.
    $pk = JRequest::getInt('sub_id');
    $this->setState('joomprosub.sub_id', $pk);
    // Add compatibility variable for default naming conventions.
    $this->setState('form.id', $pk);

    $return = JRequest::getVar('return', null, 'default', 'base64');

    if (!JUri::isInternal(base64_decode($return))) {
        $return = null;
    }

    $this->setState('return_page', base64_decode($return));

    // Load the parameters.
    $params = $app->getParams();
    $this->setState('params', $params);
    $this->setState('layout', JRequest::getCmd('layout'));
}
```

Here we set state variables for the sub_id, the form id, return page, params, and layout. Note that we don't currently use the params object. This is included in case we wish to add parameters at a later time.

Thank-You Layout

The last step in the subscribe task is to communicate to the user that the task has been successful. This is done by displaying the thank-you layout. In the controller's **subscribe()** method, recall that we set the redirect to the URL to

```
$this->setRedirect(JRoute::_('index.php?option=com_joomprosubs
&view=form&layout=thankyou&sub_id='.$id, false));
```

If the subscribe task was not successful, we omitted the **sub_id** number.

When this redirect is loaded, it starts a new execution cycle to load the view with the layout file **views/form/tmpl/thankyou.php**. The listing of this file is as follows:

```php
<?php
/**
 * @package       Joomla.Site
 * @subpackage    com_joomprosubs
 * @copyright     Copyright (C) 2012 Mark Dexter and Louis Landry. All
➥rights reserved.
 * @license       GNU General Public License version 2 or later; see
➥LICENSE.txt
 */

// no direct access
defined('_JEXEC') or die;
$id = (int) $this->item->id;
$name = $this->escape(JFactory::getUser()->get('name'));
$title = $this->escape($this->item->title);
$duration = (int) $this->item->duration;
$itemid = JRequest::getInt('Itemid');
?>
<?php if ($id) :?>
    <h1><?php echo JText::sprintf('COM_JOOMPROSUBS_THANK_YOU_NAME',
➥$name)?></h1>
    <p><?php echo JText::sprintf('COM_JOOMPROSUBS_THANK_YOU_TITLE',
➥$title)?></p>
    <p><?php echo JText::sprintf('COM_JOOMPROSUBS_THANK_YOU_DURATION',
➥$duration)?></p>
<?php else : ?>
    <p><?php echo JText::sprintf('COM_JOOMPROSUBS_THANK_YOU_ERROR')?></p>
<?php endif; ?>
<br/>
<a href="<?php echo JRoute::_('index.php?option=com_joomprosubs&Itemid=' .
➥$itemid); ?>" >
<?php echo JText::_('COM_JOOMPROSUBS_RETURN_TO_LIST')?></a>
```

Here we echo the user's name and see a message indicating the success or failure of the subscribe task. Figure 10.4 shows the screen after a successful subscribe task.

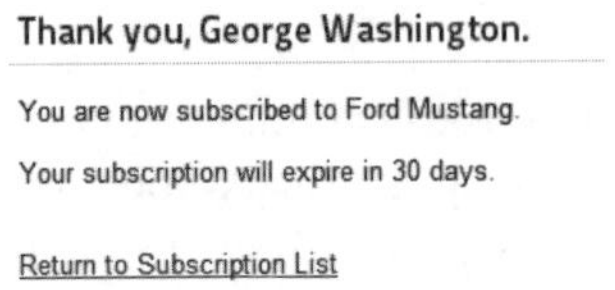

Thank you, George Washington.

You are now subscribed to Ford Mustang.

Your subscription will expire in 30 days.

Return to Subscription List

Figure 10.4   Successful subscribe thank-you screen

Figure 10.5 shows the screen if the subscribe task is not successful. Note that you won't be able to see these screens fully translated until you have finished coding the component, including the language file.

Normally, the task should always be successful. So how do we test the unsuccessful condition? There are several ways we can do this. One simple way is to temporarily change the code so we know the method will fail. For example, in the `subscribe()` method of the controller we have this block of code:

```
// Set redirect without id in case of an error
   $this->setRedirect(JRoute::_(
➥'index.php?option=com_joomprosubs&view=form&layout=thankyou', false));
   if (!in_array($subscription->group_id, $user->groups)) {
       if (!JUserHelper::addUserToGroup($user->id,
➥$subscription->group_id)) {
          $this->setMessage($model->getError(), 'error');
          return false;
       }
   }
```

If we insert the line

```
return false;
```

after the `setRedirect()`, the method will always return false and we should always go to the thank-you layout with no id. (Remember to remove the line when you are done testing!)

Language File

In the front end, we have only one language file per language. The default English language file is called `language/en-GB/en-GB.com_joomprosubs.ini`. We have again chosen to keep the language file in the component folder instead of the common languages folder.

The language file listing is as follows:

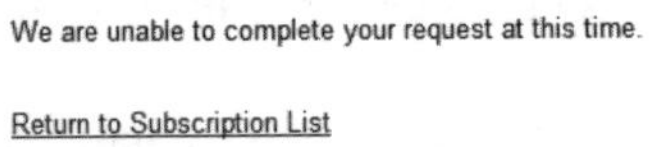

We are unable to complete your request at this time.

Return to Subscription List

Figure 10.5   Unsuccessful subscribe thank-you screen

```
COM_JOOMPROSUBS_ADD_MAP_ROW_FAIL="Error trying to add row to
↪mapping table."
COM_JOOMPROSUBS_DEFAULT_PAGE_TITLE="Subscriptions"
COM_JOOMPROSUBS_EDIT="Edit Subscription"
COM_JOOMPROSUBS_ERR_TABLES_NAME="There is already a Subscription with that
↪name in this category. Please try again."
COM_JOOMPROSUBS_ERR_TABLES_PROVIDE_URL="Please provide a valid URL"
COM_JOOMPROSUBS_ERR_TABLES_TITLE="Your Joomprosub must contain a title."
COM_JOOMPROSUBS_ERROR_CATEGORY_NOT_FOUND="Subscription category not found"
COM_JOOMPROSUBS_ERROR_JOOMPROSUB_NOT_FOUND="Subscription not found"
COM_JOOMPROSUBS_ERROR_JOOMPROSUB_URL_INVALID="Invalid Subscription URL"
COM_JOOMPROSUBS_ERROR_UNIQUE_ALIAS="Another Joomprosub from this category
↪has the same alias"
COM_JOOMPROSUBS_FIELD_ALIAS_DESC="The alias is for internal use only.
↪Leave this blank and Joomla! will fill in a default value from the
↪title. It has to be unique for each subscription in the same category."
COM_JOOMPROSUBS_FIELD_CATEGORY_DESC="You must select a Category."
COM_JOOMPROSUBS_FIELD_DESCRIPTION_DESC="You may enter here a description
↪for your Subscription"
COM_JOOMPROSUBS_FIELD_TITLE_DESC="Your Subscription must have a Title."
COM_JOOMPROSUBS_FILTER_LABEL="Title Filter"
COM_JOOMPROSUBS_FORM_DURATION_DESC="Number of days the subscription will
↪be active."
COM_JOOMPROSUBS_FORM_DURATION_LABEL="Duration (Days)"
COM_JOOMPROSUBS_FORM_LABEL="Subscribe Form"
COM_JOOMPROSUBS_FORM_SUBMIT_SUB="Subscribe Form"
COM_JOOMPROSUBS_FORM_TERMS_DESC="Terms for the subscription."
COM_JOOMPROSUBS_FORM_TERMS_LABEL="I agree to the terms of use."
COM_JOOMPROSUBS_FORM_TITLE_DESC="Form to subscribe to a group."
COM_JOOMPROSUBS_FORM_TITLE_LABEL="Subscribe To The Group"
COM_JOOMPROSUBS_GET_MAP_ROW_FAIL="Error trying to retrieve a row from
↪mapping table."
COM_JOOMPROSUBS_GRID_DESC="Description"
COM_JOOMPROSUBS_GRID_DURATION="# Days"
COM_JOOMPROSUBS_GRID_GROUP="User Group"
COM_JOOMPROSUBS_GRID_TITLE="Title"
COM_JOOMPROSUBS_LINK="Subscription"
COM_JOOMPROSUBS_NAME="Name"
COM_JOOMPROSUBS_NO_JOOMPROSUBS="There are no Subscriptions in this
↪category"
COM_JOOMPROSUBS_NUM="# of subscriptions:"
COM_JOOMPROSUBS_RETURN_TO_LIST="Return to Subscription List"
COM_JOOMPROSUBS_THANK_YOU_DURATION="Your subscription will expire in %s
↪days."
COM_JOOMPROSUBS_THANK_YOU_ERROR="We are unable to complete your request at
↪this time."
COM_JOOMPROSUBS_THANK_YOU_NAME="Thank you, %s."
```

```
COM_JOOMPROSUBS_THANK_YOU_TITLE="You are now subscribed to %s."
COM_JOOMPROSUBS_UPDATE_MAP_ROW_FAIL="Error trying to update a row in the
➥mapping table."
COM_JOOMPRPOSUBS_FORM_CANCEL="Cancel"
COM_JOOMPRPOSUBS_FORM_SUBMIT="Submit"
```

Note that a few of the tags, such as COM_JOOMPROSUBS_THANK_YOU_NAME, have the characters %s in them. This means that a variable will be added to the tag when it is translated. In the thank-you layout, we saw this code:

```
<h1><?php echo JText::sprintf('COM_JOOMPROSUBS_THANK_YOU_NAME', $name)?></h1>
```

Here we use the sprintf() method of JText (instead of the _() method). The second argument of the method is the variable to add to the text—in this case, the user's name.

This type of construct is more flexible than hard-coding the word order in the layout. For example, we could have used something like this:

```
<h1><?php echo JText::_('COM_JOOMPROSUBS_THANK_YOU_NAME') . ' ' . $name)?></h1>
```

However, that would assume that the name would always come after the thank-you message. In some languages, it might be better to have the name before the text or in the middle of the text. Using the sprintf() method allows the translator greater flexibility when translating phrases with embedded data.

Packaging the Component

At this point, our component is complete. A next logical step is to package the component so that it can easily be installed in any Joomla site running a compatible version (for example, versions 2.5.0 or higher). To do this, we need to make an archive file like we did for the example module and plugin extensions. Here are the steps:

- Create a working folder for your archive file (for example, temp) and then create two subfolders, called admin and site.
- From the Joomla site where the component is installed, copy the files and folders from administrator/components/com_joomprosubs to temp/admin.
- Copy the files and folders from components/com_joomprosubs to temp/site.
- Move the file temp/admin/joomprosubs.xml to temp/joomprosubs.xml. At this point, the temp folder should have the two subfolders plus the XML file.
- Create a zip archive of the entire temp folder (for example, called com_joomprosubs_1.0.0.zip).

The zip file should be now installable from the Extension Manager.

New Functionality: Back-End Subscriber Report

At this point, our basic component is complete. In the real world, however, most software is never actually complete. The most common tasks in software development are fixing bugs and adding or changing functionality. One of the primary goals of design patterns such as MVC is to make it easy to expand functionality while minimizing the risk of unintended side effects.

Let's look at a real example of adding some new functionality to our component. In this case, we will add a new report showing all the subscribers for each subscription. The report will be in a comma-separated values (CSV) formatted file that is downloaded to the browser. It will show a list of our subscriptions and the subscribers for each one. It will be an option from the Subscription Manager screen in the back end.

To make the report more useful, we will use the Subscription Manager filters to prepare the report. In other words, if we have filters set in the manager, the report will use them to filter the report results.

Here are the changes we need to make to implement this new functionality. The file paths are relative to **administrator/components/com_joomprosubs** (because we are in the back end):

- In `JoomproSubsViewSubmanager` (`views/submanager/view.html.php`), add a new toolbar button in the toolbar to download the report file.

- In `JoomproSubsControllerSubManager` (`controllers/submanager.php`), add a new method to the controller for the new task.

- Add a new model, `JoomproSubsModelCSVReport` (`models/csvreport.php`), to prepare the data for the report.

- Add a new method to the `JoomproSubsControllerSubManager`, called `export-Report()`, to render the report (used instead of a layout).

Note that we don't need a new layout. Instead, the `exportReport()` method in the controller will create the CSV file and send it to the browser.

New Toolbar Button

Recall that the toolbar for the Subscription Manager screen is created in the `addTool-Bar()` method of the view `JoomproSubsViewSubmanager` (`views/submanager/view.html.php`). To add the new toolbar, use the following code:

```
// Add export toolbar
$bar = JToolBar::getInstance('toolbar');
$bar->appendButton('Link', 'export', 'COM_JOOMPROSUBS_TOOLBAR_CSVREPORT',
    'index.php?option=com_joomprosubs&task=submanager.csvreport');
```

We can add this anywhere in the toolbar—for example, between the Edit and Publish icons.

Note that we use different commands to add this button. For the standard buttons, we have helper methods in `JToolBarHelper`, such as `editList()` and `custom()`. These let us add a toolbar with a single line of code.

In this case, we have decided to add the button as a link. This will create a new request cycle to run the report. That way, the state of our manager screen is not changed by running the CSV report. To do this, we specify the arguments for the `appendButton()` method as follows:

- button type = `'Link'`—creates a JButtonLink button
- task = `'export'`—sets the button to toolbar-export (used to get the button image)
- text = `'COM_JOOMPROSUBS_TOOLBAR_CSVREPORT'`—used for the button text
- URL = `'index.php?option=com_joomprosubs&task=submanager.csvreport'`—the URL to link to (which initiates the csvreport task)

You can see an example of how `JButtonLink` works by reviewing the `back()` method of `JToolBarHelper` class.

Controller Method for New Task

When our new button is pressed, it starts a new request cycle with the URL shown earlier. The task in the URL tells Joomla to execute a method called `csvReport()` in the controller class `JoomproSubsControllerSubManager` (`controllers/submanager.php`). The code for this new method is as follows:

```
public function csvReport()
{
    $model = $this->getModel('CSVReport', 'JoomproSubsModel',
        array('ignore_request' => true));
    $model->setModelState();
    $data = $model->getItems();
    $this->exportReport($data);
}
```

This code is short and simple. We get our new model class. Then we call the `setModelState()` method. This method sets the model's state field based on the current state of the manager screen. We use the state values when creating the query. Next we get the data from the model. Finally, we pass that data to our new `exportReport()` method.

New Model Class

We need to create a new class called `JoomproSubsModelCSVReport` (`models/csvreport.php`). The first part of the code for this class is as follows:

```
<?php
/**
```

```
 * @copyright    Copyright (C) 2012 Mark Dexter and Louis Landry. All
↪rights reserved.
 * @license      GNU General Public License version 2 or later; see
↪LICENSE.txt
 */

defined('_JEXEC') or die;

jimport('joomla.application.component.modellist');
JLoader::register('JoomproSubsModelSubManager',
   JPATH_COMPONENT.'/models/submanager.php');

/**
 * Methods supporting a list of joomprosub records.
 *
 */
class JoomproSubsModelCSVReport extends JoomproSubsModelSubManager
{
   /**
    * Method to set the state using the values from the submanager view
    */
   public function setModelState()
   {
      $this->context = 'com_joomprosubs.submanager';
      parent::populateState();
   }
}
```

Note that we extend `JoomproSubsModelSubManager`, the model for the manager screen. That way, we can use the constructor and the `populateState()` methods we already wrote for that class. Recall that the constructor includes a list of valid columns for sorting the data. This was done to protect against hacking.

The first method is `setModelState()`. Recall that we want to filter and order our CSV report using the values that have been set in the manager screen. To do this, we need to call `populateState()` with the manager screen's context value. However, we have a slight problem. Recall that `populateState()` is a protected method, so we can't call it directly from the controller class. Also, we can't override this method (create a method with the same name) and change its access modifier to public. When you override a parent class's method in a subclass, it has to have the same access modifier as the method in the parent class.

However, we *can* call `populateState()` from our current model, because our model is a subclass of `JoomproSubsModelSubManager`. So, the solution to our problem is to make a *new public* method (not an override) in our class that in turn calls the *protected* method of the parent class. We create a public method called `setModelState()` in `JoomproSubsModelCSVReport` and use that to call the protected `populateState()` method of the parent class. Then we will be able to call the public method `setModelState()` from the controller.

The other method in our model is **getListQuery()**. This method overrides the same method in the parent class. For this reason, it must have the same access modifier as the method in the parent class—in this case, protected. The first part of this method is as follows:

```
/**
 * Build a SQL query to load the list data.
 *
 * @return   JDatabaseQuery
 */
protected function getListQuery()
{
    // Create a new query object.
    $db = $this->getDbo();
    $query = $db->getQuery(true);

    // Select the required fields from the table.
    $query->select('a.id AS subsciption_id,
        a.title AS subscription_title,
        g.title AS group_title, c.title AS category_title,
        a.alias AS subscription_alias,
        a.description AS subscription_description, a.duration,
        a.published AS subscription_published,
        a.access AS subscription_access,
        uc.name AS subscriber_name');
    $query->from($db->quoteName('#__joompro_subscriptions').' AS a');
```

Here we create a new **JDatabaseQuery** object and add our selected columns to the select field of the query. We list all the columns we want in our report, in the order that we want them. Then we add the primary table into the from field of the query.

The next part of the code is as follows:

```
    // Join over the mapping table to get subscribers
    $query->select('m.user_id as subscriber_id, m.start_date, m.end_date');
    $query->join('LEFT', $db->quoteName('#__joompro_sub_mapping').' AS m
 ON m.subscription_id = a.id');

    // Join over the users for the subscribed user.
    $query->join('LEFT', $db->quoteName('#__users').' AS uc
 ON uc.id = m.user_id');

    // Join over the user groups to get the group name
    $query->join('LEFT', $db->quoteName('#__usergroups').' AS g
 ON a.group_id = g.id');

    // Join over the categories.
    $query->join('LEFT', $db->quoteName('#__categories').' AS c ON c.id =
 a.catid');
```

Here we add the user id, start date, and end date columns from the mapping table. Then we add left joins for the mapping user, user group, and categories tables.

The next part of the code is as follows:

```
// Filter by access level.
if ($access = $this->getState('filter.access')) {
    $query->where('a.access = '.(int) $access);
}

// Filter by published state
$published = $this->getState('filter.state');
if (is_numeric($published)) {
    $query->where('a.published = '.(int) $published);
} else if ($published === '') {
    $query->where('(a.published IN (0, 1))');
}

// Filter by category.
$categoryId = $this->getState('filter.category_id');
if (is_numeric($categoryId)) {
    $query->where('a.catid = '.(int) $categoryId);
}

// Filter by search in title
$search = $this->getState('filter.search');
if (!empty($search)) {
    if (stripos($search, 'id:') === 0) {
        $query->where('a.id = '.(int) substr($search, 3));
    } else {
        $search = $db->Quote('%'.
➥$db->getEscaped($search, true).'%');
        $query->where('(a.title LIKE '.$search.'
➥OR a.alias LIKE '.$search.')');
    }
}
```

Here we use the filter fields from the manager screen's state field to filter the report results. We add WHERE clauses to filter by access, published state, category id, and search text. Note that there is some tricky processing in the search text filter. If the first three characters of the text are "id:", then we search for an integer id. For example, if you put "id:6" in the search text, it will only find rows where the subscription id is equal to "6". Otherwise, we use a SQL wild-card search to match characters in the title column.

The last part of the method is as follows:

```
$orderCol = $this->state->get('list.ordering', 'a.title');
$orderDirn = $this->state->get('list.direction', 'ASC');
```

```
    $query->order($db->getEscaped($orderCol.' '.$orderDirn));

    return $query;
  }
} // end of class
```

Here we set the order field for the query, defaulting to ordering by subscription title.

Controller Method to Export File

At this point, we have the data for our export file. The last step is to create the file and send it to the browser. We do this in the `exportReport()` method in the controller class `JoomproSubsControllerSubManager` (`controllers/submanager.php`). The code for this method is as follows:

```
    protected function exportReport($data)
  {
      // Set headers
      header('Content-Type: text/csv');
      header(
➥'Content-Disposition: attachment;filename='.'subscriptions.csv');

      if ($fp = fopen('php://output', 'w')) {

          // Output the first row with column headings
          if ($data[0]) {
              fputcsv($fp,
➥array_keys(JArrayHelper::fromObject($data[0])));
          }

          // Output the rows
          foreach ($data as $row) {
              fputcsv($fp, JArrayHelper::fromObject($row));
          }

          // Close the file
          fclose($fp);
      }
      JFactory::getApplication()->close();
    }
} // end of class
```

The first two lines use the PHP `header()` function to send a raw HTTP header to the browser. The format for these lines must be exactly as shown. The first line tells the browser that we are sending a CSV text file. The second line tells the browser that we will be sending a file named "subscriptions.csv" as an attachment. Depending on your browser settings, this will give you the option to open or save the CSV file.

Then we use the PHP command `fopen()` to create a file object you can write to. We have two arguments. The first is the file name. Here we use a special name called `php://output`. This allows us to write to the output buffer. We use this because we already created the file name in the http header. The second argument is the mode. Here we use "w" to indicate that this is a write–only stream.

We put this inside an `if` statement because we don't want to do any file operations if for some reason the `fopen()` is not successful. Inside the `if` block, we check the first array element to see whether or not we have any data. If so, we use the PHP command `fputcsv()` to write out the array keys as column headers for our CSV file. The `fputcsv()` command does the work of creating the CSV-formatted text, and it uses the `$fp` object we created with the `fopen()` command.

Notice that we use the `JArrayHelper fromObject()` method to convert the object to an array. Then we use the PHP function `array_keys()` to get the keys of the array. This way, we get a list of all the column names to put in the first row of our file.

Once we have the first row, we do a `foreach` loop through all the array elements and write a row to our file for each element. Again we use the `fromObject()` method to convert the object to an array before passing it to the `fputcsv()` function. And again we use the `$fp` object as the first argument.

Finally, we use the `fclose()` method to close the file buffer. Then we call the `close()` method for the Joomla application object. This closes this request cycle and sends the file to the browser.

Report in Action

When you click the Report button, you see something similar to what's shown in Figure 10.6. If you save the file and then open it (for example, as a spreadsheet), you should see your subscriptions listed in a format similar to that shown in Figure 10.7 and Figure 10.8.

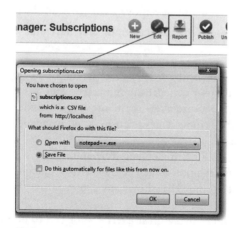

Figure 10.6 New report button and file download dialog

A	B	C	D	
subsciption_id	subscription_title	group_title	category_title	su
3	Bentley	Manager	Classic Cars	be
4	Cadilac Seville	Publisher	Classic Cars	ca
5	Chevy Corvette	Public	Classic Cars	ch
2	Ford Mustang	Shop Suppliers (Example)	Classic Cars	for
2	Ford Mustang	Shop Suppliers (Example)	Classic Cars	for
1	Pontiac GTO	Editor	Classic Cars	po

Figure 10.7   Example CSV file part I

J	K	L	M
subscriber_name	subscriber_id	start_date	end_date
George Washington	43	2011-08-11 17:12:48	2011-09-10 17:
Super User	42	2011-08-11 17:13:46	2011-09-10 17:
George Washington	43	2011-08-11 17:12:41	2011-09-10 17:

Figure 10.8   Example CSV file part II

This exercise illustrates part of the value of the MVC design pattern. It was relatively easy to add this new functionality to the existing component. Moreover, we didn't have to change any existing code to do this. That minimizes the chance that something we added might break some existing functionality.

Real-World Considerations

This realistic example illustrates most of the aspects of building a real-life component. However, to reduce the amount of code, some functions that you would want to have in a real component have been left out, such as the following:

- A way for users to unsubscribe from a subscription in the front end
- A way for managers to add or remove users from a subscription in the back end
- A way for users to see what subscriptions they have and when they are due to expire

A simple way to implement the first of these would be to alter the category list layout to indicate whether a user was already subscribed and, if so, when their subscription expired. This would require altering the model to include the mapping table and adding some fields to the layout. A new button could be added to unsubscribe, which would require a new task.

The second feature could be implemented by adding a new mapping table manager screen, similar to the subscription screen. One way to implement the third feature would be with a simple module that shows any subscriptions the user has, along with their expiration dates.

Any or all of these would make great exercises for you to do on your own, applying the knowledge you have gained from the past four chapters.

Summary

In this chapter, we finished the example component by building the front end. We followed the MVC pattern we learned from examining the Weblinks component. Finally, we modified our component to add a new report. This demonstrated how the MVC pattern makes it relatively easy to add and modify existing components.

11

Working with Your Database

In this chapter, we discuss the basics of SQL databases and how to work with them in Joomla!. We start with a "crash course" on SQL databases and how to work with a database outside of Joomla using phpMyAdmin. We discuss creating tables and then move on to an overview of SQL queries. Once we understand how SQL queries work outside of Joomla, we look at how queries are built and used inside Joomla. We cover how to use the `JDatabaseQuery` class to build queries that will work with any supported database. Then we look at how to execute a query and work with the query results inside Joomla.

We will use the MySQL database for our example, but the concepts apply to any SQL database. There are many aspects and subtleties of working with SQL databases that are beyond the scope of this book. There are a number of online and print resources for learning more about MySQL and SQL databases in general. Here we focus on the practical basics, especially as it relates to Joomla development.

In this chapter, we refer to tables with the old default prefix `jos` (for example, `jos_categories`) when working with tables outside Joomla. We use the standard `#__` prefix when working with tables in Joomla code. Remember to always use the `#__` prefix when referencing database tables inside a Joomla application.

If you are already familiar with SQL databases and MySQL, you might want to skip or just skim the first part of this chapter and focus on the section, "Working with the Database Inside Joomla."

Database Overview

SQL databases (also known as relational databases) are the primary way to store data in Joomla and other content management system (CMS) packages. SQL is the language used to interact with SQL databases.

The basic idea of a SQL database is to allow a program or user to interact with the data purely from a logical point of view, without any regard for how the data is physically stored on the computer. The logical units of data storage are as follows:

- **Database**: A collection of tables. A Joomla site normally uses one database whose name is given when we first install Joomla. We don't have to specify the database name once Joomla is running. Joomla automatically connects us to the correct database using the database name and login information from the `configuration.php` file.

- **Table**: A collection of rows. A table can be thought of as a spreadsheet, with rows and columns. Each row stores a set of data with one value for each column.

- **Row**: A set of data with one value for each column. A row has one or more columns of actual data. Each row has exactly the same column structure, just like a spreadsheet. Normally a row will have all the different pieces of data (also called attributes) for one thing. For example, a row might have the data for one article, one user, or one log entry.

- **Column**: A set of data with one value for each row. A column is a specific type of data (such as date, text, or integer). For example, one column might store the hit count of each article, the name of each user, or the timestamp (date and time) of each log entry.

Just as with a spreadsheet, we can think of tables either horizontally, by row, or vertically, by column. When we look at data by row, we generally see different types of information (for example, title, description, date created) about one thing. When we look at data by column, we see the same piece of information (for example, a title) for multiple items (for example, multiple articles).

The structure of a database table is rigid. Every row has exactly the same columns available. A column is always defined as one type of data—for example, a date, text, or integer. All the data in the column must be of this same type.

All the interaction with the database is done using SQL commands. These commands tell the database *what* to do, but leave it up to the database *how* to do it. For example, we don't have to tell the database where on the file system the data is stored. The database finds the table for us. In fact, most programmers who write code for SQL databases have no idea what the physical file structure is for the database (for example, one file per table, one file for the database, or multiple files for a table) or where the files are stored on the server's file system. The commands for working with SQL databases don't change when we change operating systems or programming languages or if the database is moved to a different folder or server.

SQL commands fall into two general types. Data definition language (DDL) commands are used to create or modify the structure of tables. Data manipulation language (DML) commands are used to query, add, update, or delete the data inside tables. We use DDL commands to initially create the database structure and DML commands to work with the actual data.

Creating and Modifying Tables with DDL Commands

DDL commands are used to create or modify the structure of tables. In Joomla applications, we normally only use DDL commands when we install, uninstall, or update an extension. So DDL commands will normally only be in the install and uninstall scripts, not in the actual extension's PHP code.

Although it is possible to use DDL commands dynamically during an execution cycle, it is normally not recommended. For most applications, the database tables should be created once, when an extension is installed or updated. For this reason, we don't normally see DDL commands used during normal processing.

In Chapter 9, we created two scripts called `sql/install.mysql.utf8.sql` and `sql/uninstall.mysql.utf8.sql`. Note that these scripts are specific to the MySQL database. An install script for Microsoft SQL Server would be called `sql/install.sqlserver.utf8.sql`. Why do we need different scripts for different SQL databases?

The answer is that the DDL SQL command syntax, although similar, is slightly different across SQL databases, such as MySQL, Microsoft SQL Server, Oracle, and PostgreSQL. A script that works in one database may not work in another. The safest approach in this case is to use different scripts for different databases.

Our example extension install script uses the `CREATE TABLE` command to create the two tables for our example extension. The uninstall script uses the `DROP TABLE` command to drop or delete the table from the database. Note that it is normal convention to show SQL commands in uppercase. The commands can be entered in uppercase or lowercase.

In the Joomla core distribution, the file `installation/sql/mysql/joomla.sql` contains all the DDL commands used to create the entire Joomla database, including the core extensions. Note that this is again specific to the MySQL database. A different folder name would be used for a different database. Note also that this script also uses the `DML INSERT` command to load some data into the core tables. We discuss the `INSERT` command later in this chapter.

The most common `DDL` commands used for Joomla applications are `CREATE TABLE`, `ALTER TABLE`, and `DROP TABLE`.

CREATE TABLE Command

The `CREATE TABLE` command is the main command to understand for building a database. The syntax for this command in MySQL is as follows:

```
CREATE TABLE <table name> (<list of columns> , <list of indexes>)
<character set>
```

Let's look at the command for creating the core table `#__banner_clients`, in the file `installation/sql/mysql/joomla.sql`. The code is as follows:

```
CREATE TABLE `#__banner_clients` (
```

```
`id` INTEGER NOT NULL auto_increment,
`name` VARCHAR(255) NOT NULL DEFAULT '',
`contact` VARCHAR(255) NOT NULL DEFAULT '',
`email` VARCHAR(255) NOT NULL DEFAULT '',
`extrainfo` TEXT NOT NULL,
`state` TINYINT(3) NOT NULL DEFAULT '0',
`checked_out` INTEGER UNSIGNED NOT NULL DEFAULT '0',
`checked_out_time` DATETIME NOT NULL default '0000-00-00 00:00:00',
`metakey` TEXT NOT NULL,
`own_prefix` TINYINT NOT NULL DEFAULT '0',
`metakey_prefix` VARCHAR(255) NOT NULL default '',
`purchase_type` TINYINT NOT NULL DEFAULT '-1',
`track_clicks` TINYINT NOT NULL DEFAULT '-1',
`track_impressions` TINYINT NOT NULL DEFAULT '-1',
PRIMARY KEY (`id`),
INDEX `idx_own_prefix` (`own_prefix`),
INDEX `idx_metakey_prefix` (`metakey_prefix`)
) DEFAULT CHARSET=utf8;
```

The first thing to note is that the table name uses the prefix "#__". Recall that this is a placeholder prefix. Joomla will convert it to the actual database prefix for the specific Joomla site before the command is passed to the database.

Next, note that table name and the column names are enclosed in back quotes (`). This is not strictly necessary in many cases, but it is good practice. For example, reserved words can be used for table or column names, as long as you enclose the names in back quotes. If you use a reserved word without back quotes, you may get errors. MySQL has over 200 reserved words, such as BOTH, CHECK, CASCADE, and SENSITIVE, so it is easy to use one of them without realizing it. Also, new reserved words are sometimes added with new MySQL versions, so a word that was not reserved can suddenly become a reserved word. Later in this chapter, we will show you how to use phpMyAdmin to create DDL scripts that automatically include back quotes. The use of back quotes is specific to MySQL. Other databases may use different quote characters.

Primary Keys, Auto_Increment, and Foreign Keys

The first column in our table is defined as follows:

```
`id` INTEGER NOT NULL auto_increment
```

Typically, the first column in a table is an id just like this and plays a special role in the table. The data type is INTEGER and it has two attributes, NOT NULL and AUTO_INCREMENT. The NOT NULL attribute indicates that this column must have a value. The AUTO_INCREMENT attribute is special and is linked to the PRIMARY KEY definition, which we see defined further down in the script, after the last column definition.

A primary key is a unique value for each row in the table. If you try to insert a new row that duplicates an existing primary key value (in this example, an id that is the same as an existing id value), you will get an error message and the insert will fail.

Primary keys are very useful. When we select a row based on the primary key, we know we will get at most one row that matches. Normally, the primary key column will not change. It is the identifier for that row as long as that row exists in the table.

Primary keys are often used as foreign keys. A foreign key is a column in table A that is the same value as the primary key in table B. For example, in the Joomla database, the #__weblinks table has a column called catid. This is a foreign key to the #__categories table. In the #__categories file, we use the id column as the primary key. In the sample data we have a category called Joomla Specific Links that has an id of 32. In the #__weblinks table, the foreign key column called catid matches the value of the id in the #__categories table. So when a Weblink is assigned to the Joomla Specific Links category, its catid column is set to 32 to match the id in the #__categories table. As we see later in this chapter, we use foreign keys to join multiple tables in a single query.

If every primary key value must be unique across the entire table, how do we make sure we use an id that is not already used for another row? That's where the AUTO_INCREMENT attribute comes in. It tells the database to automatically create a unique value for this column (normally the next unused integer). When we insert a new row, we don't have to worry about what the value of the id is. We can just leave it unset or set it to NULL. MySQL will get the next unused value for us and make sure we have a unique id column.

Note that we don't do this in the joomla.sql and sample_data.sql scripts. In these scripts, we *do* supply specific values for primary key columns. This is a special case where we know we are starting with an empty table, so we can supply values for the primary key columns and know they will be unique. Once a database has been in use, we don't know what id values may already be used, so we need to let the database provide the values for us.

It is good practice to define every table with a primary key. In most cases, it works well to use the scheme indicated here, using an INTEGER data type with NOT NULL, AUTO_INCREMENT, and defined as the primary key. We will discuss this more later in the chapter.

If we look at the rest of the column definitions, we see the data types VARCHAR, TEXT, TINYINT, and DATETIME. The different data types are discussed later in this chapter.

Indexes

The next part of the CREATE TABLE command defines the indexes. The first one is the PRIMARY KEY, which is specified as the `id` column. You can think of the primary key as the preferred way to find one row in the table. Often this uses an INTEGER column with the AUTO_INCREMENT attribute, as discussed earlier.

In this example we create two additional indexes, `idx_own_prefix` and `idx_metakey_prefix`. By convention, index names start with `idx_` to keep them different from column names or other names used in the database. Each index is defined as a list of one or more columns.

Indexes help speed up database queries. On the other hand, indexes make updates to the table slightly slower. So we only want to use indexes where it will help our queries. The subject of using indexes in database tables can get complicated, but there are some good general guidelines:

- The more rows a table will have, the more important indexes are. A table with only 10 or 20 rows doesn't need any indexes (other than the primary key, which technically is an index).
- Index on columns that are used for selecting, ordering, or grouping. For example, in the `#__content` table, we have indexes on access, checked_out, state, catid, created_by, and language for this reason.
- Don't index on columns that we normally just display and don't use for selecting, ordering, or grouping. Also, don't index on very long columns, such as columns of type `TEXT` or `MEDIUMTEXT`.
- As discussed earlier, using a `UNIQUE` index allows the database to require that a column or group of columns is unique in a table. This is a good technique for preventing duplicate data. For example, in the table `#__menu` we use a unique index to ensure that we can't have two menu options (rows) at the same menu level with the same alias and language.
- If a column is a foreign key that will be used to join other tables, an index on this column can be helpful. This is another reason to have an index on catid, for example.

There are some potentially confusing things about the index syntax. The words `INDEX` and `KEY` are interchangeable. So, for example, we could use

```
KEY `idx_own_prefix` (`own_prefix`),
```

instead of

```
INDEX `idx_own_prefix` (`own_prefix`),
```

Also, if you substitute the word `UNIQUE` for `INDEX`, it tells MySQL to make sure that the value of this combination of columns is unique in the table. For example, in the definition of the `#__menu_types` table, we see this code:

```
UNIQUE `idx_menutype` (`menutype`)
```

If we try to add a row that duplicates the value of an existing `menutype` column, we will get a database error.

The last thing in the `CREATE TABLE` script is the character set—in this case, `DEFAULT CHARSET=utf8`. We always use the UTF-8 character set for Joomla tables, because this allows the database to store data in languages that use non–Latin characters.

Data Types

Deciding which data type to use for a column is normally straightforward. The following is a short discussion about the most commonly used types for Joomla applications.

INT/INTEGER

INT and INTEGER are exact synonyms and refer to the same data type. As discussed earlier, this is the type normally used for primary keys where you just need a unique id for a row. You should also use this data type when referring to a key column in another table. For example, we use the column catid to refer to the category id in several tables (for example, #__content and #__contacts). We define catid as INT to match the data type for id in the #__categories table.

INT can either be signed (positive and negative values) or unsigned (positive values only). When used with AUTO_INCREMENT, it is always unsigned.

Sometimes you will see INT or INTEGER as INT(10). In this case, the number 10 is used to indicate how big to display the column in a query. It does not affect the maximum value that can be stored in the column.

TINYINT

TINYINT is similar to INT except that it only allows for the numbers −127 to +127 (or 0 to 255 if unsigned). TINYINT is used for columns where there are a small number of valid values, such as published state or yes/no conditions.

Using integers for these types of values offers two important advantages over using text strings, like VARCHAR. First, when we retrieve integers from an untrusted source (such as a form or the URL), they are very easy to sanitize in PHP. We just use (int) to cast them as integers. Second, in Joomla, we normally want to translate any words used in the application. We can easily associate integers with language keys and make the meaning of each value language neutral and translatable.

VARCHAR

VARCHAR is used to store text fields up to a given length, to a maximum of 21,844 characters. The maximum number of characters allowed is specified by the number in parentheses. For example, VARCHAR(20) would allow up to 20 characters. VARCHAR columns are variable length and only use the amount of space required to store the entered data. If a column is VARCHAR(100) but only seven characters are entered, it only uses seven characters of storage on the disk.

As discussed earlier, we use the CHARSET=utf8 for all Joomla tables. Because UTF-8 characters can take up to three bytes to store one character, the maximum size for VARCHAR columns is 21,844 (instead of 65,535 for Latin characters).

CHAR

CHAR columns also store text fields but are fixed length. So a CHAR(100) column always uses 100 characters of storage. The maximum size of a CHAR field is 255 characters. In Joomla, the CHAR data type is rarely used and VARCHAR is normally preferred.

DATETIME

DATETIME does just what it says. It stores a date and time in the format 'YYYY-MM-DD HH:MM:SS'. There is also a data type called DATE if you just want to store the date and don't need the time. Note that you can easily extract just the date portion of a DATE-TIME column using the date() function.

TEXT

The TEXT data type is similar to VARCHAR except that it always stores up to 65,000 characters. In Joomla, the TEXT data type is used for columns where the length could be more than, say, 2,000 characters but not more than about 10,000 characters. This includes columns such as parameters (JSON-formatted strings) and keywords. If a column will be used in an index, it should normally be VARCHAR and not text.

MEDIUMTEXT

MEDIUMTEXT is exactly like TEXT except that the maximum length is about 16 megabytes. MEDIUMTEXT is used only when the length of a text column can be very large. In Joomla, it is used for the text for articles and the category description, for example.

DECIMAL

If you are tracking exact decimal numbers, such as monetary amounts, use the DECIMAL data type. For example, to store dollar amounts to the nearest penny up to a maximum of 9,999,999,999.99, use DECIMAL(10,2).

FLOAT and DOUBLE

FLOAT is used for scientific calculations where you need a high level of precision. FLOAT provides 23 significant digits and DOUBLE provides up to 53 significant digits. You should *not* use FLOAT or DOUBLE when you need exact amounts, based on a fixed number of decimal places. Use DECIMAL instead. If you use FLOAT for dollar amounts, you can get small rounding errors that are difficult to debug.

Column Attributes

When you define a column, you can specify attributes as well as the data type. Common attributes include NOT NULL, AUTO_INCREMENT, DEFAULT, and unsigned.

NOT NULL

When you create a column, by default a null value is allowed in that column. Note that in SQL databases, a null value is different from a blank or zero value and may give results you don't expect or want. For example, if you calculate a total on a numeric column and *any* of the values is null, the total will also be null.

In many cases, it is preferred to not allow a column to be null. To do this, include the attribute NOT NULL after the data type. Often, when you specify NOT NULL, you will also specify AUTO_INCREMENT or a DEFAULT value.

AUTO_INCREMENT

As discussed earlier, this attribute creates an automatic primary key number (normally 1, 2, 3, and so on). It is used in conjunction with an INTEGER data type and the NOT NULL attribute.

DEFAULT

This attribute specifies a default value for the column. This value is used if a new row is inserted without specifying a value for this column. For example, if we are tracking article hits or banner clicks, we want to start with zero, not null. So we specify that as follows:

```
`clicks` INTEGER NOT NULL DEFAULT '0'
```

That way, if we include this value in a calculation, it will be treated as zero and give us the desired result.

A similar technique is used with publish start and stop dates, where a "zero" value is treated like the beginning or end of time. In these cases, we see the following code to create the columns:

```
`publish_up` DATETIME NOT NULL DEFAULT '0000-00-00 00:00:00',
`publish_down` DATETIME NOT NULL DEFAULT '0000-00-00 00:00:00',
```

Note that we do not use a DEFAULT value when we have an AUTO_INCREMENT attribute set.

UNSIGNED

This attribute is used with INTEGER or TINYINT to tell the database to store the value as a positive integer. Setting an integer as unsigned allows it to store a higher maximum value. This is used, for example, when we have a foreign key.

ALTER TABLE Command

The ALTER TABLE command is similar to the CREATE TABLE command except that it is used to change the structure of a table. The most common examples in Joomla are either adding new columns to a table or changing the data type of an existing table. For example, in the file installation/sql/mysql/joomla_update_16beta13.sql, we see the following code:

```
ALTER TABLE `#__template_styles`
 CHANGE `params` `params` varchar(10240) NOT NULL DEFAULT '';

ALTER TABLE `#__menu`
 ADD COLUMN `client_id` TINYINT(4) NOT NULL DEFAULT 0 AFTER `language`;

ALTER TABLE `#__menu`
 ADD UNIQUE `idx_alias_parent_id` (`client_id`,`parent_id`,`alias`);
```

The first command changes the data type for params to VARCHAR(10240). Running this command will not alter or remove data as long as the data in the table fits into the new data type. Normally, we are increasing the size of columns, not decreasing them. In this case, our existing data will be preserved.

The second command adds a new column to the #__menu table. Note that we have set it to NOT NULL DEFAULT 0. After this command is run, the client_id column will be zero for every row in the table (instead of NULL). Notice here we specify the default value as a zero without the single quotes whereas in a previous example we used zero inside single quotes. MySQL supports either usage, although the usage with single quotes is preferred.

The third command adds a unique index to the #__menu table. Note that this command will not succeed if there is existing data that is not unique. In this case, if there are two or more rows with the same client_id, parent_id, and alias, this command will fail with an error message.

DROP TABLE Command

The DROP TABLE command is simple and should be used with care. It deletes the table from the database and any data in the table is permanently deleted. The syntax for DROP TABLE is

```
DROP TABLE <table name>;
```

Using phpMyAdmin

You can use MySQL from the command line, but it is easier for most people to work with a program such as phpMyAdmin. phpMyAdmin is distributed as part of popular LAMP packages, such as XAMPP, and is available on most web hosts. You can also download it as a separate package from http://www.phpmyadmin.net. Complete documentation on how to use phpMyAdmin is available on their website. Here we will do a brief introduction to show you how you can use it to help you test and debug SQL queries, create DDL scripts, and back up or move your database to a different server.

Test and Debug SQL Queries

You normally start phpMyAdmin by clicking on a link from your host or from the local host page. Depending on your setup, you may need to log in with your MySQL user name and password. Figure 11.1 shows an example of the phpMyAdmin start screen.

Figure 11.1   phpMyAdmin start screen

The left side of the screen shows the available databases that you have access to on this server. Normally, you will work in one database at a time. When you click on a database in the left, the screen will show something similar to Figure 11.2.

Now that we have a database selected, we see the tables in the left column. Also, we can now do SQL queries without needing to specify which database to use.

If we click on the SQL tab at the top, we get an entry text box where we can enter and execute SQL commands. For example, if we enter the command

```
SELECT * FROM jos_content
```

and press the Go button in the lower right corner, we see a screen similar to Figure 11.3.

If the query is successful, we see a message "Showing rows . . ." that gives you the total number of rows returned by the query. We also see the first group of rows in a table. If there is an error in the query syntax, we would see the error message.

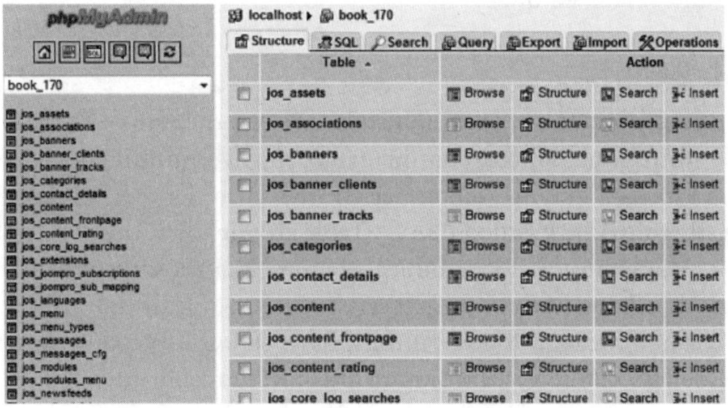

Figure 11.2   Screen with a database selected

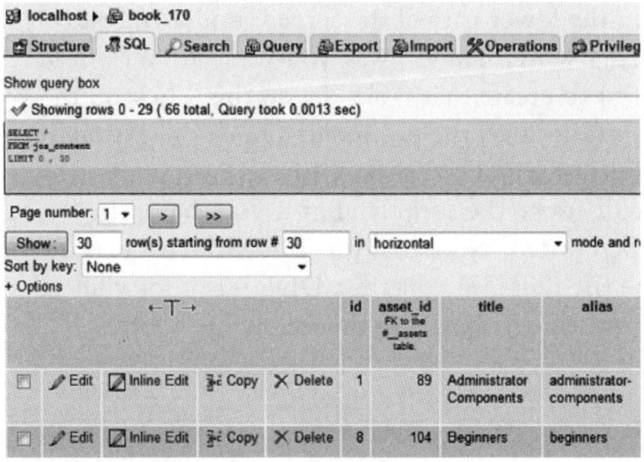

Figure 11.3   Results of SQL query

When we are working on the SQL queries we need for a Joomla programming project, it is often helpful to write the queries first in SQL and test them in this manner. That way, we know that the query works as expected.

You can also use phpMyAdmin to debug a Joomla query. You can do this with the following steps:

- Navigate to the System tab of the Global Configuration screen in the administrative back end of your Joomla site and set Debug System to "Yes".

- Navigate to the screen where the desired query is executed. The SQL queries for the screen will display below the normal page display.

- Select and copy the desired query from the debug display and paste it into the SQL field in phpMyAdmin.

- Press the Go button to execute the query directly in phpMyadmin.

At this point, you can easily work with the query and test different options until you find the problem. Then you can go back to the Joomla PHP code and change the code to create the corrected query.

Create DDL Scripts

You can also use phpMyAdmin to simplify the process of writing the DDL scripts for creating or editing the structure of our tables. phpMyAdmin allows you to create or modify tables using a graphical interface. In the lower left corner, under the last database table, there is a link called Create Table. If you click this, you get a form that allows you to create a table and its columns. Figure 11.4 shows a screenshot where we are about to create a table with two columns.

In the lower right corner are two buttons, Save and Go. Pressing the Save button saves the table. To add more columns, press the Go button.

You can also add, edit, or drop (delete) columns of an existing table. To do this, select a table and then click on the structure tab. Figure 11.5 shows the links for changing, deleting, or adding columns.Note that you can also add or edit indexes using the buttons in the lower part of the screen, under Indexes.

Once you have a table defined the way you want it, you can have phpMyAdmin create the DDL script to create that table. To do this, click on the Export button. At this point, you get a form with the option for Quick or Custom. Select Quick and select SQL in the Format list. Then press Go.

phpMyAdmin will create the script and give you the option to open the file or save it. A text file will be created. Note that this file will have extra information you don't need. However, the file will also contain a DDL script for your table. For example, the listing for the jos_test table is shown in the following:

```
--
-- Table structure for table `jos_test`
--
```

```
CREATE TABLE IF NOT EXISTS `jos_test` (
  `test_id` int(10) unsigned NOT NULL AUTO_INCREMENT COMMENT 'Primary
➥Key',
  `test_title` varchar(100) DEFAULT NULL COMMENT 'Title',
  PRIMARY KEY (`test_id`)
) ENGINE=MyISAM DEFAULT CHARSET=utf8 AUTO_INCREMENT=1 ;
```

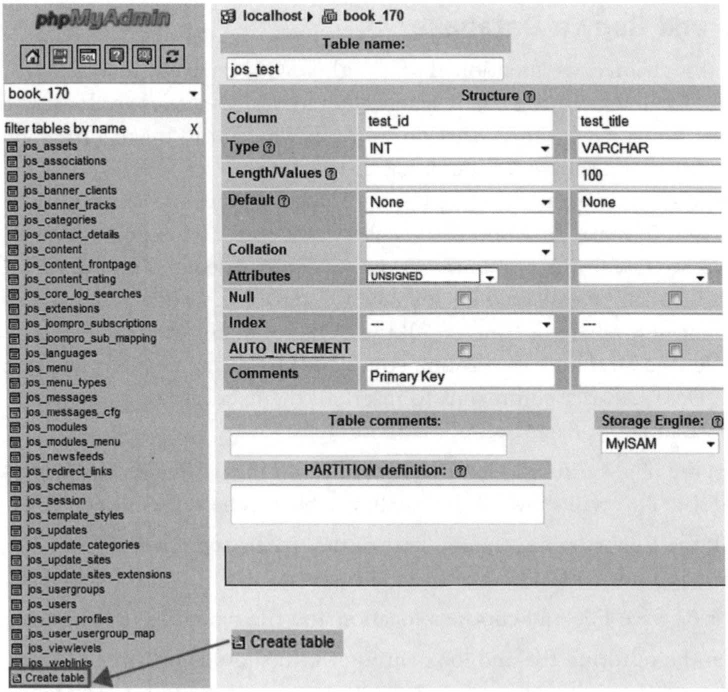

Figure 11.4   Creating a table with phpMyAdmin

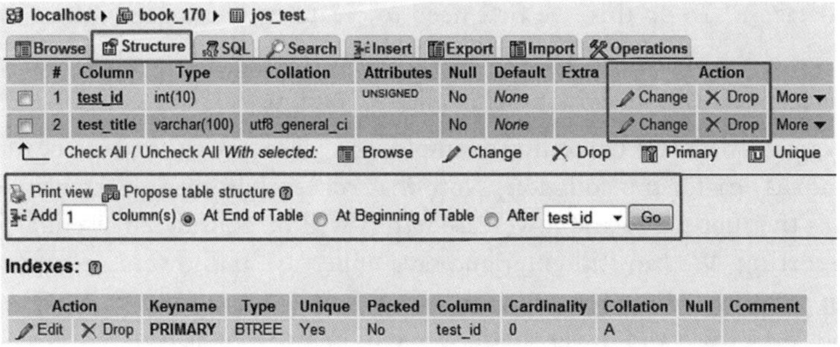

Figure 11.5   Add, change, or delete columns with phpMyadmin

Important Note

When working with tables in phpMyAdmin, you need to use the actual table prefix for your current Joomla database (in this example, "jos_"). When you use the same script inside your Joomla application, remember to change the prefix to "#__" so that Joomla will automatically substitute the correct prefix for each site.

Backup and Copy a Database

Earlier in this chapter, we mentioned that with a SQL database, such as MySQL, we don't need to know anything about where the physical data files are located or how they are organized. Given this, what do we do if we want to make a backup copy of a database or move a database from one server to another?

The answer is that we use the export and import feature of the database to accomplish this task. To make a backup of a database, we create an export file of the entire database. As we saw in the previous section, an export file contains a series of SQL commands that can be executed by any MySQL database. When we create an export file for an entire database, it contains all the SQL commands to re-create the database. This includes the DDL `CREATE TABLE` commands to create all the tables' structure as well as the DML `INSERT` commands to insert all the data into these tables.

To export an entire database, follow these steps:

- From the phpMyAdmin Home screen, click on the desired database in the left-hand list. This will show all the database tables in the list, as shown in Figure 11.2.
- Click the Export tab in the top part of the screen and select Export Method: Quick and Format: SQL. Press the Go button.
- Click on Save File and choose a location and file name for the export file.
- Open the resulting file and look through it. It should contain a `CREATE TABLE` command for each table and an `INSERT INTO` command for each table that contains data.

Next, let's use this export file to create a new database that is an exact copy of the exported database. To do this, we first need to create our new database, as follows:

- From the phpMyAdmin Home screen, select the Databases tab in the top part of the screen. This will show a field called Create new database.
- Select your database name (for example, `jos_test_copy`) and select `utf8 _general_ci` for the collation. Note that "ci" stands for case insensitive. This means that uppercase and lowercase letters will be considered as equal for database sorting. We can still enter and save uppercase and lowercase letters and see them correctly. However, when we use the `ORDER BY` clause in a SQL command, uppercase and lowercase letters will be ordered as if they were all the same case. This is the default and preferred behavior for most SQL databases.

- Press the Create button. You should get a message saying that the database was created successfully.

- Select the new database and press the Import button in the top row of the screen.

- Browse to the export file created when we exported the entire database previously.

- Press the Go button. The system will work for a minute and then will give you a success message.

- Check that the new database now has all the tables and data that the original database had.

Using SQL Data with DML Commands

We work with the data in tables by writing queries. The main query commands are SELECT, UPDATE, INSERT, UNION, and DELETE. The subject of writing SQL queries is a large and complex one. Here we will cover the basics that will help you write most of the queries you will need for Joomla applications.

SELECT Queries

SELECT queries are the most frequently used in Joomla applications. They are used to retrieve data from the tables in the database. The data retrieved from a SELECT query is called a data set. The basic structure of a SELECT query is as follows:

> SELECT <list of columns and expressions>
>
> FROM <primary table>
>
> JOIN <list of join clauses>
>
> WHERE <where conditions>
>
> ORDER BY <order by columns>
>
> LIMIT <offset, row count>

A SELECT query doesn't have to have all these clauses. However, if present, they must be in the order listed.

As we see later in this chapter, one of the benefits of using the Joomla JDatabase-Query class for building queries inside our code is that we can build the query's clauses in any order we like. However, when we run queries directly in the database (for example, with phpMyAdmin), we need to follow the required order of the different SQL clauses.

List of Columns

The first part of a SELECT query includes a list of columns and expressions that will display in the query. These will be the column headings for the rows that are returned.

We normally use an alias to identify which table a column comes from. For example, in the query

```
SELECT a.id, a.name FROM jos_content AS a
```

we have identified **a** as the alias for **jos_content**. Note that, by convention, we type SQL key words in all uppercase. SQL queries are case insensitive, so this convention is just to make it easier to read the query.

We can also create aliases for column names. By default, the query column name is the same as the table column name. In many cases, this is fine. However, in some cases, we want the query column name to be different (for example, if two tables have the same column names or if we are using an expression for a column). We create an alias for the column name using the **AS** keyword, as follows:

```
SELECT a.id AS article_id, a.name FROM jos_content AS a
```

In this example, the id column will show as **article_id**. Note that because we use a period between the table alias and the column name, we can't use periods in the column or alias names unless we enclose the alias in quotes.

If you like, you can omit the **AS** keyword and it will be assumed. For example, the following query is equivalent to the previous example:

```
SELECT a.id article_id, a.name FROM jos_content a
```

Explicitly including the **AS** command is generally preferred because it makes the query easier to read.

We can also use an asterisk (*) to indicate all the columns from a table. For example,

```
SELECT a.* FROM jos_content AS a
```

will return all the rows from a table. In this case, you cannot create column aliases.

Finally, we can include expressions as query columns. This is frequently done when we use the **GROUP BY** clause, discussed later in this section.

FROM Clause

In the **FROM** clause, we list one or more tables from which we will pull our data. One confusing thing about SQL syntax is that there are two equivalent ways to create joins between tables. One way is to list all the tables in the **FROM** clause and include the join conditions in the **WHERE** clause. The preferred method, at least for Joomla, is to use the **JOIN** command. It is preferred because it is clearer to the reader what the query is doing. So that is the syntax we will use here.

When we are using the **JOIN** statement for our secondary tables, the **FROM** clause will only include the primary table for the query. Which table is the primary table? In most cases, it is reasonably intuitive. Typically, we are trying to get information mainly for one thing, like articles or users. So we start with the main table for that item and then add related tables as needed to pull in related information. So that main table is the primary table for our query.

As mentioned earlier, we normally create a short alias using the AS command—for example, FROM jos_content AS a.

JOIN Clause

JOIN statements are used to combine columns from two or more different tables. This is something we do in most queries. When designing SQL databases, it is good practice to put only one type of data in one table. This means that we often need information from more than one table in a single query.

For example, in Joomla, we keep category data in a separate category table (jos_categories). In related tables, such as jos_content, we only store the category id (as a foreign key). When we write a query to see articles from jos_content, we will often want to display the category name or other category information, not just the category id. We do this by joining the category table to the query. Doing so gives us the ability to show the category name or any other category column.

JOIN statements can be confusing when you are learning about SQL queries. The two join types that are most frequently used are INNER joins and LEFT joins (sometimes referred to as LEFT OUTER joins). By default, if no join type is specified, an INNER join is assumed.

Let's look at a simple query where we show articles and their categories, as follows:

```
SELECT a.title, c.title AS category_title
FROM jos_content AS a
INNER JOIN jos_categories AS c
ON a.catid = c.id
```

Here we are showing the article title and category title for each article. Note that we use the AS command to create an alias for each table and to create an alias for the category title. Otherwise, we would have two columns in the query called title.

Note that we use an INNER JOIN. We could simply use JOIN and get the same result, because INNER is assumed by default. However, it is preferred to explicitly state the type of join.

The last line, with the ON statement, is very important. Here we specify how the two tables are related for this query. *We always have an ON statement with a JOIN clause.* Otherwise, we don't get the result we expect. In this example, if we omit the ON statement, we would get a row in our query for each combination of rows in the two tables. For example, in the version 2.5 sample data, we have 66 rows in the jos_content table and 69 rows in the jos_categories table, so if we omit the ON statement we get 4,554 rows in our query!

The ON statement often uses a foreign key column to relate the two tables. In this example, a.catid is a foreign key to the jos_categories table. There are many other examples of foreign key relationships in the Joomla database, including `jos_banners` to `jos_categories`, `jos_banners` to `jos_banner_clients`, `jos_contact_details` to `jos_users`, and so on.

Next, let's explore the difference between an INNER join and a LEFT join. With an INNER join, we require that rows exist in both tables. In the previous, every article listed in the query will have a corresponding category. In a normal Joomla database, this will always be true. Every article has exactly one category. In this case, an INNER and LEFT join will give exactly the same results.

Let's look at a different example. Say we wanted a list of articles including whether or not they are flagged for the front page featured blog. The table `jos_content_frontpage` contains a row for every featured article, including its id and an ordering number. Here is the first version of the query:

```
SELECT a.title, f.ordering
FROM jos_content AS a
INNER JOIN jos_content_frontpage AS f
ON a.id = f.content_id
```

Here we show the article's title and its front-page ordering. By specifying an inner join, we only include articles with a row in the `jos_content_frontpage` table. With the version 2.5 sample data, we will get four rows as follows:

```
title           ordering
Beginners          2
Professionals      4
Joomla!            1
Upgraders          3
```

Now let's see what happens when we use A LEFT join, as follows:

```
SELECT a.title, f.ordering
FROM jos_content AS a
LEFT JOIN jos_content_frontpage AS f
ON a.id = f.content_id
```

Now we get all the articles from `jos_content`, even if they don't have a corresponding row in `jos_content_frontpage`. In that case, the value for `f.ordering` is NULL (meaning it doesn't exist).

We could change this query to indicate whether or not an article was flagged for the front page using an expression with the SQL CASE function, as follows:

```
SELECT a.title,
CASE WHEN (f.content_id IS NULL) THEN 'No' ELSE 'Yes' END AS front_page
FROM jos_content AS a
LEFT JOIN jos_content_frontpage AS f
ON a.id = f.content_id
```

The second line shows the use of an expression in the SELECT list. The CASE function allows us to display different values based on different boolean tests. Here we test whether the f.content_id is null. If so, we know that the article is not in the jos_content_frontpage table and we show a value of 'No'. Otherwise, we know it is in the table and show the value of 'Yes'. The first five rows returned by this query are as follows:

```
title                              front_page
Administrator Components               No
Beginners                              Yes
Archive Module                         No
Banner Module                          No
Article Categories Module              No
```

We can have as many JOIN clauses as we need to bring in the data from each of the desired tables. Each table alias must be unique in the query.

WHERE Clause

This is where we can filter the rows of the query to include only those rows that match specific conditions. WHERE clauses can be simple or complex. In the following example, we have added a WHERE clause to include only published articles:

```
SELECT a.title, c.title AS category_title
FROM jos_content AS a
INNER JOIN jos_categories AS c
ON a.catid = c.id
WHERE a.state = 1
```

We can connect multiple statements in the WHERE clause with AND or OR. For example, the following query will show articles that are published *and* have a nonzero publish_down date:

```
SELECT a.title, c.title AS category_title
FROM jos_content AS a
INNER JOIN jos_categories AS c
ON a.catid = c.id
WHERE a.state = 1
AND a.publish_up != '0000-00-00 00:00:00'
```

Recall that the publish_down column has a default value of '0000-00-00 00:00:00', which means never unpublish the article. In the sample data, no articles will fit these conditions. To test the query, go into the Article Manager and add a stop-publishing date to an article. When you rerun the query, it should show this article.

We can use OR to connect statements in a WHERE clause. In this case, it gives us rows that match *any* of the conditions. For example, the following query gives us rows where either the created-by alias is "Parks Webmaster" *or* the category title is "Plugins":

```
SELECT a.title, c.title AS category_title, a.created_by_alias
FROM jos_content AS a
INNER JOIN jos_categories AS c
ON a.catid = c.id
WHERE a.created_by_alias = 'Parks Webmaster'
OR c.title = 'Plugins'
```

Note that we can use columns from any table in the WHERE clause.

If we need to use both AND and OR connectors in our WHERE clause, we group them using parentheses. For example, the following query includes rows from the previous example but adds the conditions that the article's title must begin with the letters "Ed" *or* "Au".

```
SELECT a.title, c.title AS category_title, a.created_by_alias
FROM jos_content AS a
INNER JOIN jos_categories AS c
ON a.catid = c.id
WHERE
    (a.created_by_alias = 'Parks webmaster'
    OR c.title = 'Plugins')
AND
    (a.title LIKE 'Ed%'
    OR
    a.title LIKE 'Au%')
```

Note that LIKE allows us to use a wild-card match, where the percent sign means match any character. If we used a.title LIKE '%abc%' we would match any column that contained "abc" anywhere in the text, while a.title LIKE '%abc' would match any text ending with "abc".

ORDER BY Clause

The ORDER BY clause is used to sort the query rows in the desired order. You can specify the direction of ordering, using ASC for normal ascending (A to Z) order or DESC for reverse or descending (Z to A) order. You can list more than one column, separated by commas. For example, the ORDER BY clause

```
ORDER BY a.created_by_alias ASC, d.created DESC
```

would cause the query rows to be ordered alphabetically by created_by_alias. If two or more articles had the same created_by_alias value, they would then be ordered by the date and time created, with the most recently created articles first.

LIMIT Clause

MySQL includes the option to limit the rows returned by a query with the LIMIT clause. This goes after the ORDER BY clause. The syntax is LIMIT xx, yy, which limits the query to the first yy rows, starting with row xx + 1.

For example, to limit our query to return the rows 6–15, we would add `LIMIT 5, 10` to the query. We prepare the query, we skip the first five rows, and then we return the next ten rows. Similarly, `LIMIT 0,10` would return the first ten rows. If you don't want to skip any rows, you can omit the first argument and write `LIMIT 10`.

Aggregate Queries with GROUP BY

In normal `SELECT` queries, our rows are returned at the same level of detail as the tables being queried. If we want summarized data, we use the `GROUP BY` clause. A query that includes a `GROUP BY` clause is called an aggregate query. If present, the `GROUP BY` clause goes after the `WHERE` clause and before the `ORDER BY`.

Using a `GROUP BY` clause affects the columns you can list in the column list. You can only list (a) columns that are used for the grouping or (b) columns that are aggregate expressions. If we think about it, this makes sense. Because the query is summarizing multiple rows into one row, the database has to know how to summarize the values. Aggregate expressions tell the database how we want to do that.

Let's look at an example. Let's say we wanted to get a count of the articles for each `created_by_alias` value. The query is as follows:

```
SELECT a.created_by_alias, COUNT(*) AS article_count
FROM jos_content AS a
GROUP BY a.created_by_alias
```

This query returns the following result:

created_by_alias	article_count
	12
Fruit Shop Webmaster	4
Joomla!	40
Joomla! 1.5	1
Parks webmaster	9

This query has two columns, the `created_by_alias` and an aggregate function called `COUNT`. The argument for this function is "`*`". This function counts the number of rows in the table for each different value of `created_by_alias`. Note that 12 of the articles don't have a `created_by_alias` so they show as blank.

MySQL and other SQL databases provide a number of useful aggregate functions, including `MIN()`, `MAX()`, `AVG()`, `SUM()`, `COUNT()`, and `COUNT(DISTINCT)`.

Let's say we wanted to modify our query to show the most recent date for each author's articles. We could just add the column

```
MAX(created) as last_create_date
```

to our query columns.

Say we wanted to exclude articles with no `created_by_alias`. We can do this by including a `WHERE` clause to check that we have something in this column. Here we get into a subtle point about SQL data columns. If we look at the definition for this column in the database, we see that NULL values are not allowed and that the default value is an empty string '' (two single quotes with no space in between). Because of this, we cannot test for NULL values—there won't be any. Instead, we can test for the value being greater than an empty string.

Our query is as follows:

```
SELECT a.created_by_alias, COUNT(*) as article_count,
MAX(a.created) as last_create_date
FROM jos_content AS a
JOIN jos_categories AS c
ON a.catid = c.id
WHERE a.created_by_alias > ''
GROUP BY a.created_by_alias
```

This query omits the row showing the 12 articles with no created_by_alias.

What if we wanted to only show rows where we have at least two articles? We can't do this in a WHERE clause, because that examines each row one at a time. At that point in the query, we don't know how many articles we might end up with for each created_by_alias.

To solve this, SQL provides a HAVING clause that can come right after the GROUP BY and before the ORDER BY. The HAVING clause is like a WHERE clause except that it tests for the values of aggregate functions. To limit our query to only those rows having two or more articles, we modify the query as follows:

```
SELECT a.created_by_alias, COUNT(*) as article_count,
MAX(a.created) as last_create_date
FROM jos_content AS a
JOIN jos_categories AS c
ON a.catid = c.id
WHERE a.created_by_alias > ''
GROUP BY a.created_by_alias
HAVING COUNT(*) >= 2
```

Now the query will only show rows where the count is two or more.

We can also use aggregate functions in our ORDER BY. Say we want to order the list showing the rows with the most articles first. To do this, we add

```
ORDER BY COUNT(*) DESC
```

to the end of the query. Now we get the rows ordered from the highest article count to the lowest count.

UPDATE Queries

UPDATE queries allow you to modify the contents of columns in a table. The general form of an UPDATE query is as follows:

UPDATE <table>

SET <list of column names and values>

WHERE <where conditions>

For example, to do a search-and-replace for the **created_by_alias** column, you would do the following query:

```
UPDATE jos_content
SET created_by_alias = 'Site Administrator'
WHERE created_by_alias = 'Joomla!'
```

To update more than one column, you separate the column-value pairs with a comma. For example, the following query would also update the **date_created** to January 1, 2014:

```
UPDATE jos_content
SET created_by_alias = 'Site Administrator',
        created = '2014-01-01 12:00:00'
WHERE created_by_alias = 'Joomla!'
```

The WHERE clause syntax for UPDATE queries is exactly the same as for SELECT queries.

INSERT Queries

INSERT queries are used to add new rows into a database table. The general form of an INSERT query is as follows:

```
INSERT INTO <table>
(<column1, column2, . . . >)
VALUES (<value list for row 1>), (<value list for row 2>)
```

If you omit the column list, it is assumed that the values list includes all the columns in the order defined for the table.

We can see many examples of INSERT queries in the file **joomla.sql** and **sample _data.sql** files in the folder **installation/sql/mysql** and in the export file we created earlier in this chapter. For example, the export file includes this INSERT query for the **jos_content_frontpage** table:

```
INSERT INTO `jos_content_frontpage` (`content_id`, `ordering`) VALUES
(8, 2),
(35, 4),
(24, 1),
(50, 3);
```

Note that table name and column names are enclosed in back quotes. As discussed previously, this is good practice although it is not necessary unless you use a key word or special character in the name (like a period or a space).

One important thing to be aware of when inserting rows is the possibility of duplicate keys or duplicate indexes. If you have a primary key defined and you try to insert a row with a primary key that is a duplicate of an existing row, you will get an error.

Also, if you have a primary key defined as `AUTO_INCREMENT`, you can specify a value of `NULL` for that key and the database will automatically put the next available value into the column. This is what you normally need to do when you are inserting a row into a table of an existing database, where you don't know what primary keys are already in the table. As discussed earlier, when we are creating a new table and we know it is empty, we can specify the id column. This is the case in the `joomla.sql` and `sample_data.sql` scripts and also in our backup script.

DELETE Queries

`DELETE` queries are used to permanently delete rows from the database. The general form of a `DELETE` query is as follows:

```
DELETE FROM <table name>
WHERE <where conditions>
```

For example, the syntax to delete one row from the `jos_content_frontpage` table would be as follows:

```
DELETE FROM jos_content_frontpage
WHERE content_id = 35
```

The syntax of the `WHERE` clause is the same as for `SELECT` queries. Warning: if you omit the `WHERE` clause, *all* rows in the table will be deleted.

UNION Queries

`UNION` queries allow you to combine like columns in two or more tables into one query. They are rarely used in Joomla applications. The general form of a `UNION` query is as follows:

```
<SELECT query 1>
UNION
<SELECT query 2> . . .
```

For example, to see a list of all Weblink and news feed items in one query, you could do a `UNION` query as follows:

```
SELECT 'Weblink' as type, w.title AS title
FROM jos_weblinks w
UNION
SELECT 'Newsfeed' as type, n.name as title
FROM jos_newsfeeds n
```

In a UNION query, the column names for each SELECT query must be the same and in the same order.

Expressions in Queries

Expressions can be used instead of column names in most places. Exceptions are where you are using a column name to designate where a value is to be written, such as the SET clause of an UPDATE or INSERT query.

MySQL and other SQL databases provide a number of useful functions. These include string functions like UPPER(), LOWER(), LENGTH(); date and time functions like DATE_ADD(), DATE(), and DATEDIFF(); and the CASE() function, as seen earlier, for conditional logic. For a complete list of expressions available in MySQL, check the MySQL documentation at http://dev.mysql.com/doc/refman/5.1/en/functions.html.

Designing the Table Structure

Designing the table structure is an important part of designing a Joomla extension. The general idea of database design is to have a table for every type of entity in the database, and to only have one type of entity in a given table.

Let's consider the example of a database for a school. The purpose of the database will be to track students, teachers, and their classes. We can divide the types of tables into groups based on the type of information they will hold. Three typical table types are as follows:

- **Reference table**: Typically holds static information about an entity. Examples include customers, contacts, and articles. Reference tables will typically be maintained by users entering and editing rows—for example, with a form.

- **Mapping table**: Used to map from one table to another. Examples include mapping users to groups or mapping students to classes. Mapping tables will typically be maintained by the system, based on user actions.

- **History table**: Used to record detailed information. Examples include event logs, purchase history, or class history. History tables will typically be written to automatically by the system.

We will show examples of these different table types.

Reference Tables

In our example, we will start with four reference tables, as follows:

- **Students**: All static information for each student, such as name, address, age, and grade level would go into the students table. We will not include dynamic information, such as classes taken or past grades.

- **Teachers**: All static information for each teacher, such as name, address, department, and pay rate. Again, we will not include dynamic or historical information here.

- **Classes**: All static information for each class, such as class title, description, department, meeting time, room number, dates held, and maximum students allowed.

- **Department**: All static information for each department. This might include the department name and description.

Each of these tables has a simple structure. One row in the table will represent one student, teacher, class, or department. The system users will typically add and edit these tables directly using forms.

Key Fields and Foreign Keys

In the tables just listed, it makes sense to identify each entity using an id column. The standard way this is done in Joomla is using an auto-incrementing integer as the primary key, as discussed earlier in this chapter.

In our example, each teacher is a member of exactly one department. In this case, we can include the key field for the department table (for example, department id) as a column in the teacher department. If we need to get other information from the department table, we can add a `JOIN` on this column in our query.

If the tables are expected to contain a large number of rows (for example, more than 1,000), we would probably want to create indexes on the foreign key columns. This will speed up queries where we join tables based on these columns.

Mapping Tables

Foreign keys work well to relate one row in one table to one row in another table. In some cases, however, we need to map multiple rows in one table to multiple rows in a second table.

In our example, consider the relationship of the students and classes tables. Each student will take multiple classes and each class will have multiple students assigned to it. This is known as a many-to-many relationship. The normal way to handle this is with a mapping table. In this case, we could create a table called `student_class_map` with two columns, `student_id` and `class_id`. We would create a primary key that combines the two columns. In other words, a given student could be assigned to a given class only once.

Each time a student is added to a class, a new row with the student and class id columns is added to the table automatically by the system. If a student drops the class, the row could be deleted automatically.

With the mapping table, we can easily do two types of queries. We can get a list of students in a single class (`class id = 123`) with the following query:

```
SELECT c.class_name, s.student_name
FROM student_class_map AS m
INNER JOIN classes AS c ON m.class_id = c.id
INNER JOIN students AS s ON m.student_id = s.id
```

```
WHERE m.class_id = 123
ORDER BY s.student_name;
```

Similarly, we can get a list of all classes that a student (`id` = 234) is enrolled in with the following query:

```
SELECT s.student_name, c.class_name
FROM student_class_map AS m
INNER JOIN classes AS c ON m.class_id = c.id
INNER JOIN students AS s ON m.student_id = s.id
WHERE m.student_id = 234
ORDER BY c.class_name;
```

Note that we use the `student_class_map` table as the primary table in both of these queries, even though the displayed columns come from the other tables. This is because we want one row in our query for each row in the `student_class_map` table.

We could have a similar mapping table mapping teachers to classes. This is also a many-to-many relationship. As with the reference tables, we might want to create indexes on the `class_id` and `student_id` columns to speed up queries where we use these columns as foreign keys.

History Tables

A third type of table is a history or transaction table. In our example, one such table would be a history of the classes completed by students. In most cases, an `AUTO_INCREMENT` primary key column works well for this type of table. A partial structure for the student class history table might be as follows:

- `history_id`: INT, AUTO_INCREMENT, PRIMARY KEY
- `student_id`: foreign key to students table
- `class_id`: foreign key to classes table
- `semester`: varchar(6) (format: yyyyxx, where yyyy is the year and xx is 01, 02, 03)
- `date_completed`: date
- `class_grade`: varchar(2)
- `comments`: varchar(1024)

At the completion of each class, when the final grade is posted, a row would be added for each student and class combination. We could get a student transcript (list of completed classes) with the following query:

```
SELECT c.name, h.semester, h.class_grade
FROM student_class_history AS h
INNER JOIN students AS s ON s.id = h.student_id
INNER JOIN classes AS c ON c.id = h.class_id
```

```
WHERE h.student_id = 234
ORDER BY h.semester ASC, c.name ASC
```

A similar history table could be added to record the classes taught by each teacher.

For the history table, we might want to include indexes on `student_id` and `class_id`. Because we might build queries to filter the rows by `semester_id`, this could also be a candidate for an index. Similarly, if we expected to query based on date_completed, we could do an index on this column as well.

Working with the Database Inside Joomla

Now that we have a good understanding of how SQL queries work, we can look at how we create and work with queries inside Joomla.

In Joomla applications, we work mostly with `SELECT` queries. The SQL queries for `INSERT`, `UPDATE`, and `DELETE` tasks are often done for us by the `JTable` class. In our example component, this was the case for our `#__joompro_subscriptions` table. However, in the case of our `#__joompro_sub_mapping` table, we had to create our own `INSERT`, `UPDATE`, and `DELETE` queries.

In Joomla, the `JDatabaseQuery` class is used to create the SQL queries, and the `JDatabase` class is used to execute the query and return the query results.

Using JDatabaseQuery

The `JDatabaseQuery` class was introduced in Joomla version 1.6 to make it easier to create SQL queries in Joomla version 2.5 introduced the classes needed to support multiple databases. This includes subclasses for each supported database (for example, `JDatabaseQueryElementMySQLi` for the MySQLi driver, `JDatabaseQuerySQLSrv` for Microsoft SQL Server). These subclasses deal with the subtle SQL syntax differences among different supported databases. The great news for developers is this: as long as we use the `JDatabaseQuery` class to build our query and follow a few simple rules, our query will *automatically* work across all supported databases! We can still build our queries manually if we prefer, but if we do they will not support multiple databases.

Creating the JDatabaseQuery Object

We create our query object using the `getQuery()` method of the `JDatabase` object. For example, this code will create an empty query object:

```
$query = JFactory::getDbo()->getQuery(true);
```

Including the boolean `true` as an argument erases any prior query and gives you a blank query to start with, which is what you normally want.

Recall that we create our `JDatabase` object using the code `JFactory::getDbo()`. This gives us the type of database object for our configured database driver. In turn, the database object knows how to create the correct `JDatabaseQuery` object for our configured database.

Note that we do *not* want to use the following code to create an empty query:

```
$query =  new JDatabaseQuery(); // Do NOT use this code!
```

This will not create the correct type of object for different database drivers and therefore will not work correctly with different databases.

SELECT Queries with JDatabaseQuery

If we understand how to create SELECT queries in SQL, creating them with JDatabaseQuery is very easy. Table 11.1 shows the JDatabaseQuery method for each clause in a SELECT query.

As discussed earlier, the ordering of the various query clauses in SQL is rigid. With JDatabaseQuery, we can build our query object in any order we prefer. When the query is passed to the database, the __toString() method of JDatabaseQuery puts the clauses in the correct order for us.

Similarly, we can easily add more columns to our query. For example, we could start with the following list of columns:

```
$query->select('a.id, a.title');
```

Later on, perhaps when we have added the category table to the query, we could add more columns as follows:

```
$query->select('c.id AS catid, c.title AS cat_title');
```

Table 11.1 **JDatabaseQuery Methods for Select Queries**

SELECT Query Clause	JDatabaseQuery Method	Example Argument
list of columns	select()	'a.title, c.title AS category_title'
FROM	from()	'#__content AS a'
INNER JOIN	innerJoin()	'#__categories AS c ON a.catid = c.id'
LEFT JOIN	leftJoin()	'#__categories AS c ON a.catid = c.id'
WHERE	where()	'a.published = ' . (int) $published
ORDER BY	order()	$db->getEscaped($orderCol.' '.$orderDirn)
GROUP BY	group()	'c.id'
LIMIT	Implemented in JDatabase object	$dbo->setQuery($query, $limitstart, $limit);

This allows us to create the query in a way that is easy to understand and that follows the flow of the program code.

This is also true of the join methods. Note that we have separate methods for INNER and LEFT joins and then we pass the ON conditions in the argument. We can do the joins one at a time and, if we prefer, add the columns from the joined table at that point in the code.

In the where() method, we can specify a connector (AND or OR) in the second argument. The default is AND. If we need to create complex WHERE clauses—for example, with an OR condition nested inside an AND condition—we do this with parentheses just like we would in a SQL WHERE clause. For example, to reproduce the following SQL WHERE clause

```
WHERE
    (a.created_by_alias = 'Parks Webmaster'
    OR c.title = 'Plugins')
AND
    (a.title LIKE 'Ed%'
    OR
    a.title LIKE 'Au%')
```

we would use the following code:

```
$query->where('(a.created_by_alias = 'Parks Webmaster'
    OR c.title = 'Plugins')');
$query->where('(a.title LIKE 'Ed%' OR a.title LIKE 'Au%')');
```

Here we pass the nested OR conditions as arguments with the default AND connector. Note that we use parentheses to make sure the expressions are evaluated the way we want. In the select() and order() methods, each column name or expression is separated by a comma. In the order() method, you specify the sort order using ASC or DESC, just as in the SQL code.

Protecting against Hackers

When we use JDatabaseQuery to build queries, we still need to protect ourselves from hackers entering malicious code. For example, if a value used in a WHERE or ORDER BY clause comes from an untrusted source, such as an HTML form or the URL (both of which can be used by hackers to enter malicious code), we need to sanitize the value before we use it in a query. If a value in a WHERE clause should be an integer, we should cast it as an integer using (int). In the following example, we know that $catid should be an integer, so we make sure it is, as follows:

```
$query->where('a.catid = ' . (int) $catid);
```

If the value is text, we should use the quote() method of JDatabase to put quotes around it and to "escape" any special characters. Escaping text means to check for characters that have special meaning for a particular language—in this case, SQL. When we escape a value, we display any special characters in a way so that they lose their special meaning for the language. In SQL, for example, this is done by putting a back slash ("\") in front of quote characters (single and double quotes). This allows the quote to be displayed, but it tells the database not to interpret it as a special character. Escaping text values prevents a hacker from using quotes or other special characters to change the meaning of our query and inject their own SQL into our code. As we have seen in other chapters, we can also escape text with respect to HTML or JavaScript.

Let's say we use a variable called `$created_by` in our `WHERE` clause, and say this variable comes from an untrusted source. In this case, we would do something like the following:

```
$query->where('a.created_by_alias = ' . $db->quote($created_by));
```

If a hacker puts malicious code into `$created_by`, it will be rendered harmless by the `quote()` method and our query will be safe.

If we are using a variable as part of a `WHERE` clause with a wild card, we need to take care about where we put the quotes. For example, say we want to do a `WHERE` clause as follows:

```
WHERE a.title LIKE '%abc%'
```

where `'abc'` is from a user-entered variable called `$search`. In this case, we need to make sure to put the percent signs inside the argument passed to the `quote()` method, as follows:

```
$query->where('a.title LIKE ' . $db->quote('%' . $search . '%'));
```

That way, the quotes end up outside the percent signs, but the `$search` value is still escaped.

Where passing untrusted data to an `ORDER BY` clause, we have to make sure that the values are valid column names. Otherwise, we get a SQL error that can disclose information about our site to potential hackers. We discussed one way to do this in Chapter 10, using the model's constructor to create an array of valid column names and then checking the input against this list.

Method Chaining

The `JDatabaseQuery` methods return a value of `$this`, which means that they support method chaining. So, for example, the following code snippet

```
$query = JFactory::getDbo()->getQuery(true);
$query->select('a.id, a.title');
$query->from('#__content AS a');
$query->where('a.catid = ' . (int) $catid);
```

does the same thing as this snippet:

```
$query = JFactory::getDbo()->getQuery(true);
$query->select('a.id, a.title')->from('#__content AS a')
    ->where('a.catid = ' . (int) $catid);
```

In the second example, the `select()` method returns a `JDatabaseQueryElement` object, so it can be used to call the `from()` method. Again, the `from()` method returns an object that can call the `where()` method. In the Joomla core, the first approach is used in most places, but you will see examples of the second approach as well.

The `LIMIT` clause of the query is not created in the `JDatabaseQuery` class. Instead it is done when the query is passed to the `JDatabase` object for processing. That is covered later in this chapter.

Group by Queries with JDatabaseQuery

Aggregate queries (queries with the `GROUP BY` clause) are created using the `group()` method. This works just like the `GROUP BY` clause. When you create an aggregate query, you need to make sure that only columns that are used for grouping, as well as expressions using aggregate functions, are present in the column list (created by the `select()` method).

For example, the following SQL query

```
SELECT a.created_by_alias, COUNT(*) AS article_count
FROM jos_content AS a
GROUP BY a.created_by_alias
```

could be written using `JDatabaseQuery` as follows:

```
$query = JFactory::getDbo()->getQuery(true);
$query->group('a.created_by_alias');
$query->from('#__content AS a');
$query->select('a.created_by_alias, COUNT(*) AS article_count');
```

Insert Queries with JDatabaseQuery

`JDatabaseQuery` provides two alternatives for creating `INSERT` queries. One uses the `set()` method to set each column individually. The second method uses the `columns()` and `values()` methods to set the columns as a group.

The following is a SQL `INSERT` query for adding a row to the `jos_joompro_sub_mapping` table:

```
INSERT INTO jos_joompro_sub_mapping
(subscription_id, user_id, start_date, end_date)
VALUES (123, 234, '2014-01-01 12:00:00', '2014-12-31 12:00:00');
```

Here is the code for building the same query using the `set()` method of `JDatabaseQuery`:

```
$query = $db->getQuery(true);
$query->insert('#__joompro_sub_mapping');
$query->set('subscription_id = ' . (int) $subID);
$query->set('user_id = ' . (int) $userID);
$query->set('start_date = ' . $db->quote($startDate));
$query->set('end_date = ' . $db->quote($endDate));
```

The argument for the `set()` method is a string containing the column name, an equals sign, and the literal value to use for the column. In this example, each column is set with a separate `set()` method. We can also set multiple columns in one line by putting the strings together in a comma-delimited list.

Alternatively, we can use the `columns()` and `values()` methods to accomplish the same thing. Here is the code for doing this:

```
$query = $db->getQuery(true);
$query->insert('#__joompro_sub_mapping');
$query->columns('subscription_id, user_id, start_date, end_date');
$query->values((int) $subID . ',' . (int) $userID . ','
    . $db->quote($startDate) . ',' . $db->quote($endDate));
```

Here we use the `columns()` methods to name the columns that will be set. If we omit this, the entire column list for the table is assumed. Then we use the `values()` method to create a comma-delimited list of values for each column.

Update Queries with JDatabaseQuery

`UPDATE` queries with `JDatabaseQuery` use the `update()`, `set()`, and `where()` methods to create a query. Here is an example `UPDATE` query using SQL:

```
UPDATE jos_joompro_sub_mapping
SET start_date = '2015-01-01 12:00:00', end_date = '2015-12-31 12:00:00'
WHERE subscription_id = 123 AND user_id = 234;
```

Here is the same query using `JDatabaseQuery`:

```
$query = $db->getQuery(true);
$query->update('#__joompro_sub_mapping');
$query->set('start_date = ' . $db->quote($startDate));
$query->set('end_date = ' . $db->quote($endDate));
$query->where('subscription_id = ' . (int) $subID);
$query->where('user_id = ' . (int) $userID);
```

We use the `set()` method to set the value of each column to be updated. We use the `where()` method to indicate which rows to update. As with `INSERT` queries, the `set()` method can either set one column or multiple columns. To set multiple columns, we separate each column-value pair with a comma.

Delete Queries with JDatabaseQuery

Creating DELETE queries uses three methods: delete(), from(), and where(). The delete() method has no arguments. It just tells the class that we are creating a DELETE query.

The from() method names the table from which to delete the rows. The where() method has the usual syntax for creating the WHERE clause, so select the rows to be deleted.

Here is an example SQL DELETE query to remove one row from the jos_joompro _sub_mapping table:

```
DELETE FROM jos_joompro_sub_mapping
WHERE subscription_id = 98 AND user_id = 76;
```

The same query would be created in JDatabaseQuery with the following code:

```
$query = $db->getQuery(true);
$query->delete();
$query->from('#__joompro_sub_mapping');
$query->where('subscription_id = ' . (int) $subid);
$query->where('user_id = ' . (int) $userid);
```

Union Queries with JDatabaseQuery

At this time, JDatabaseQuery does not support UNION queries. As discussed earlier, these queries are rarely used in Joomla applications.

Working with Query Data

Once we have built our query, we need to pass it to the database, execute it, check for errors, and return the query results, if any.

The query is passed to the database using the setQuery() method. For INSERT, UPDATE, or DELETE queries, we need to execute the query and check for errors. For SELECT queries, we also need to return the query results to the program.

INSERT, UPDATE, and DELETE Queries

These queries modify the database but do not return any data to the calling program. The steps for executing a query of this type are as follows:

- Use the setQuery() method to pass the query to the database object.
- Use the query() method to execute the query.
- Check for any database errors and process them if needed.

The following is a typical example of code used to accomplish this. In this example, an UPDATE query has been created and loaded into the variable $query.

```
$db->setQuery($query);
if ($db->query()) {
```

```
    return true;
} else {
    $this->setError(JText::_('COM_JOOMPROSUBS_ADD_MAP_ROW_FAIL'));
    return false;
}
```

The first line passes our query to the database object. If $query is a JDatabaseQuery object, its __toString() method is executed automatically. This method creates the query with the required syntax for the specific database in use.

The query() method executes the query and returns a boolean true if the query is executed successfully. So we can use the return value to check for database execution errors. If found, we handle the error condition. Note that we can use the methods $db>getErrorNum() and $db->getErrorMsg() to get more information about the database error.

SELECT Queries

The steps needed to process a SELECT query are as follows:

- Use the setQuery() method to pass the query to the database object. We also use this method to optionally limit the number of rows returned by the query.

- Use one of the load methods to process the query and return the results to a PHP variable.

- Check for any database errors and process them if needed.

The following is a typical example of code to accomplish this:

```
$db->setQuery($query, $limitstart, $limit);
$data = $db->loadObjectList();
if ($db->getErrorNum()) {
    $this->setError(JText::_('COM_MYCOMPONENT_ERROR_MSG'));
    return false;
} else {
    return $data;
}
```

As before, the first line passes the query to the database object. Here we have also included the optional arguments ($limitstart and $limit). These values are designed to support pagination and to otherwise limit the query's data set to a fixed number of rows.

In this example, $limitstart tells the database how many rows in the query's data set to skip. The value of $limit tells the database the maximum number of rows to return. For example, if $limitstart is 0 and $limit is 15, we would return *up to* the first 15 rows of the data set. If $limitstart is 15 and $limit is 5, we would skip the first 15 rows and return *up to* the next 5 rows (16–20), assuming the query's data set had that many rows. If $limitstart is greater than the number of rows in the data set, no rows will be returned by the query.

The second line uses the loadObjectList() method to return the rows of the query results as an array of objects. We discuss the different options for returning SELECT query results in the next section.

In the third line, we use the the the getErrorNum() method to check for a database error. If we find an error, we set the error message and return a false. Otherwise, we return the results of the query in the variable called $data. Whether we check for database errors and how we respond to them depends on the situation. In some cases, we continue with normal processing. In others, we report an error to the user. Going forward with the new logging functionality in the platform, we will implement logging of noncritical database errors so the site administrator can correct these without adversely affecting the user's experience.

Returning Query Results

SELECT queries return rows and columns of data. Depending on the query, a single value, a single row, or multiple rows may be returned. The JDatabase class provides a number of methods we can use to retrieve the data from a SELECT query. Table 11.2 lists the most commonly used methods for returning the results of SELECT queries.

The most frequently used load methods in Joomla are loadObjectList() and loadResult(). The loadObjectList() is used when the query can return multiple rows and columns. The return type is an indexed array (0-n) of standard objects. The fields in the standard objects are the column names and the values are the column values.

To use the return value in PHP, we could use a foreach loop as illustrated in the following code:

```
$data = $dbo->loadObjectList();
foreach ($data as $row) {
```

Table 11.2 **JDatabase Methods for Returning Query Data**

JDatabase Method	Return Type	Description
loadObject()	Standard object	Returns first row of query
loadObjectList()	Indexed array of standard objects	Returns all rows of query
loadResult()	Mixed	Returns first column of first row
loadColumn()	Array	Returns array of one column of the query
loadAssoc()	Associative array	Returns first row of query
loadAssocList()	Indexed array of associative arrays	Returns all rows of query
loadRow()	Indexed array	Returns first row of query as indexed array
loadRowList()	Indexed array of indexed arrays	Returns all rows of query

```
$title = $row->get('title');
$id = $row->get('id');
. . .
```

Here $row is the standard object for one row of the query's data set. We can use the get() method of the standard object to get the different columns of data for the row, based on the column name from the query.

The loadResult() method is normally used when we expect the query to return only one value (one row with one column). An example might be getting the title for a single category. In this case, we just assign it to a single variable.

The loadObject() method is similar to the loadObjectList() method except that only the first row from the query is returned. We would use this when we only expect one row from the query (or we only care about the first row). The results are returned as a standard object, again with the object field names set to the query's column names.

The loadAssocList() method is very similar to the loadObjectList() method. The loadAssocList() method returns an array where each array element is an associative array containing the data for one row. The following code illustrates how to use this type of result:

```
$data = $dbo->loadAssocList();
foreach ($data as $row) {
    $title = $row['title'];
    $id = $row['id'];
    . . .
```

This code is the same as that for the loadObjectList() method except that each row's data is accessed as an associative array instead of a standard object.

The loadAssoc() method is like the loadObject() method. Both methods return only the first row of the query. The loadAssoc() returns the row as an associative array.

The loadRowList() is like the loadAssocList() method except that it returns an indexed array instead of an associative array. The following code illustrates how to use this type of result:

```
$data = $dbo->loadRowList();
foreach ($data as $row) {
    $first_column = $row[0];
    $second_column = $row[1];
    . . .
```

The loadColumn() method allows you to work with one column of the data set as an indexed array. This would normally be used when the query contains multiple rows with one column each. This method returns an indexed array where each element is this column's data for the row for that index value. For example, if the query returned three rows, $data[0] would be the value for the first row, $data[1] for the second row, and $data[2] for the third row.

Summary

In this chapter, we covered basic information about SQL databases in general, including how to create and design database tables and how to write SQL queries to update and access database data. We also covered the specifics of how to write queries inside a Joomla application and how to retrieve and use the data from these queries.

JavaScript and MooTools in Joomla!

JavaScript enables improved user interaction with web applications and is becoming an increasingly important part of Joomla!. JavaScript is also a key component of AJAX (asynchronous JavaScript and XML). MooTools is a JavaScript framework that is included with Joomla. Using MooTools simplifies the process of creating and maintaining JavaScript functionality that works reliably across different browsers.

In this chapter, we discuss some basic concepts related to JavaScript and MooTools and how they are integrated into Joomla. Then we discuss the specific JavaScript features that are built into Joomla and how you can use these features in your programs. Finally, we show an example of using JavaScript to create an AJAX update of a Joomla page.

JavaScript is a full-featured programming language with its own subtleties and complexity. MooTools is a powerful framework with many core features and many more extensions. Trying to teach JavaScript and MooTools is beyond the scope of this book. Fortunately, Joomla is designed so that we can take advantage of many JavaScript and MooTools features without in-depth knowledge of JavaScript.

What Is JavaScript?

JavaScript is an event-driven programming language that runs inside the web browser. Like PHP, JavaScript is an interpreted language, meaning that the script files are executed directly, without being compiled. Unlike PHP, which runs on the web server, JavaScript runs on the client machine—for example, the user's PC. Every modern browser includes a built-in JavaScript interpreter that can execute any JavaScript code that is included in a web page. Because it runs locally on the client machine, JavaScript can respond to events instantly, without requiring any communication with the server. For this reason, programs written in JavaScript work and feel more like desktop programs written in C, Java, or Basic than like typical web-based applications.

How Does JavaScript Work?

In Joomla, JavaScript code works along with PHP code. It does not replace PHP code or functionality. Instead, it enhances the functionality. JavaScript allows web-based Joomla applications to be more interactive than they would be with only PHP and HTML.

JavaScript works on the client side by modifying the HTML document on the fly. This can include adding, altering, or deleting HTML elements and attributes. JavaScript responds to events—things the user does or things the web browser does. Events include the following:

- Moving the mouse to or away from a specific HTML element
- Clicking on something
- Changing the value of a form
- Submitting a form
- Completing the process of loading a new HTML document

For example, when the mouse is moved over an element on the page, a JavaScript function can modify the HTML document in the browser's memory to display a tooltip. The JavaScript function adds the tooltip HTML elements to the document and the tooltip shows on the page. When the mouse moves away from the element, the HTML is modified to remove the elements for the tooltip, and the tooltip disappears. This happens instantly, inside the browser's working memory, without requiring any communication with the server.

JavaScript can also be used for AJAX requests. These are requests to the web server, similar to normal page load requests. The difference is that AJAX requests are done in the background, without interrupting the program flow. The user can continue using the application while the request is sent to the server and while the response comes back from the server.

These two capabilities of JavaScript—instant interaction with the user and background communication with the web server—allow developers to create a richer user experience in their web applications than would otherwise be possible.

JavaScript programs are included in an HTML page using the script element. The preferred method for adding JavaScript code to an HTML web page is to add one or more script elements to the head element of the page. In Joomla, this is often done using the JHTML behavior methods. For example, the code

```
JHtml::_('behavior.tooltip');
```

adds the required JavaScript code for displaying tooltips to the HTML page.

What Is MooTools?

MooTools is a JavaScript framework. There are two important benefits of using a framework like MooTools. First, the framework provides a lot of built-in functionality.

It includes built-in functions for things like sliders, tooltips, expandable trees, and other commonly used user-interface features. We can use these features in Joomla with simple application programming interface (API) calls, without having to write all the underlying JavaScript code.

The second benefit is browser compatibility. Although all modern browsers can run JavaScript, there are enough small differences in how JavaScript works in different browsers to make it difficult (and tedious) to write JavaScript code that works reliably in all environments. With a framework such as MooTools, the framework developers make sure that all its features work consistently in all supported browsers. Where there are compatibility problems in specific browsers, the code to work around those problems is built into the framework. The MooTools developers are experts in the nuances of different browsers' JavaScript interpreters. That means users of MooTools (like us) don't have to be. The code we write using the MooTools API will work correctly in all supported browsers.

In short, using a framework like MooTools saves us time when we are developing the application because we can take advantage of its built-in functionality. It also saves us time and problems maintaining the application because we don't have to worry about testing and debugging problems arising from JavaScript differences in different browsers.

There are a number of other popular JavaScript frameworks available, including jQuery, Dojo, and Prototype. Each has its strengths and weaknesses and each has its supporters. Starting with version 1.5, the Joomla project decided to use MooTools. The main benefits of MooTools are as follows:

- It is lightweight and modular. We can use just the pieces we need and page loads are not slowed down noticeably.

- Like Joomla, MooTools uses object-oriented programming (OOP), so it is a good fit from a software engineering perspective.

- MooTools is closely aligned with how JavaScript works natively. It extends JavaScript but does not change the way you write JavaScript. Learning MooTools is a natural extension of learning JavaScript.

These benefits were important considerations in 2007, when the Joomla project leadership decided to use MooTools. It is the judgment of the Joomla Production Leadership Team that these advantages still pertain in 2012 and beyond. At this time, MooTools is a healthy open-source project that continues to be developed and improved, and there are no plans for Joomla to change to a different JavaScript framework in the foreseeable future.

As we discuss later in this chapter, it is possible for designers or extension developers to include other JavaScript frameworks in Joomla templates and extensions. Changes made to MooTools and to Joomla since version 1.6 make this process relatively easy. However, because MooTools is already included in every Joomla installation, and because it is integrated into the Joomla platform and content management system (CMS), Joomla developers are encouraged to use MooTools.

How JavaScript and MooTools Are Used in Joomla

Joomla is designed to follow the standards for unobtrusive JavaScript. This means the following

- The JavaScript code is separate from the HTML markup and selects the HTML elements to alter, based on element attributes, such as id or class.
- Most pages in Joomla are designed to "degrade gracefully." If the browser's JavaScript is disabled, the user should still be able to have access to all the site's functionality, although perhaps with a less elegant user interface.
- The pages and functionality in Joomla should be accessible to people with visual or other disabilities. Enhancing the user experience with JavaScript should not, for example, interfere with screen readers for the visually impaired or prevent someone from using the application entirely with the keyboard (without a mouse).

Implementing JavaScript in Joomla normally involves invoking one of the JHTML-Behavior methods—for example, JHtml::_('behavior.tooltip'). The JHTMLBehaviour methods load the required JavaScript code into the HTML document header so it is available to be executed if called.

For some features, such as keep alive, that's all we need to do. For others, such as tooltip, we need to make sure we have the right HTML markup to invoke the JavaScript behavior.

Built-In JavaScript Features

Table 12.1 shows the standard JavaScript behaviors available in Joomla version 2.5.

The JavaScript files are found in the folder media/system/js. Note that two copies of each JavaScript file are included in the Joomla package. The files listed in Table 12.1 are the files actually used in Joomla. They are compressed to minimize the file load times. For example, all spaces and comments are removed. A second copy of each file, with the text "-uncompressed" added to the file name, is included as well. The uncompressed copy has comments and normal formatting and is used for debugging, reading, and working on the code.

Each of these behaviors is discussed in the following sections.

Calendar

The calendar behavior creates the pop-up calendar, which allows the user to enter a date using a visual calendar widget. Figure 12.1 shows an example of the calendar widget from the article edit screen.

This widget can be added to a page in one of two ways. The easiest way is to use a JForm field whose type attribute is set to calendar. For example, the following code is from the file administrator/components/com_content/models/forms/article.xml:

```
<field name="created" type="calendar"
label="COM_CONTENT_FIELD_CREATED_LABEL"
 description="COM_CONTENT_FIELD_CREATED_DESC" class="inputbox" size="22"
 format="%Y-%m-%d %H:%M:%S" filter="user_utc" />
```

Table 12.1 **Built-In JavaScript Behaviors**

Behavior Name	Description	JavaScript File
calendar	Provides a pop-up calendar to enter dates with a mouse click	`calendar.js`
caption	Creates image captions when page is loaded	`caption.js`
colorpicker	Provides a pop-up color selector.	`mooRainbow.js`
formvalidation	Provides validation for JForm forms	`validate.js`
framework	Loads the MooTools core framework Needed when custom JavaScript scripts use MooTools core; one example being the check-all control	`mootools.js`
highlighter	Highlights words using a background color	`highlighter.js`
keepalive	Keeps a session alive, for example, when performing a long editing task	`none (uses mootools.js)`
modal	Provides a pop-up modal window without requiring a page refresh	`modal.js`
multiselect	Lets you select a range of checkboxes on the screen using Shift+Left Click	`multiselect.js`
noframes	Prevents a page from being loaded inside an iframe (for example, to prevent site hijacking)	`none (uses mootools.js)`
switcher	Provides tab-like panes in screens (for example, in Global Configuration)	`switcher.js`
tooltip	Provides pop-up tooltips based on mouse hovering	`none (uses mootools.js)`
tree	Provides an expandable tree control	`mootree.js`
uploader	Provides a multiple file uploader (for example, in Media Manager)	`uploader.js`

Figure 12.1   Calendar pop-up

The highlighted code tells JForm to render this field with a pop-up calendar. Recall that the type attribute determines which JFormField class is used for the field. Here we call the getInput() method of the JFormFieldCalendar class. Note that the last line of its getInput() method is as follows:

```
return JHtml::_('calendar', $this->value, $this->name, $this->id, $format,
➥$attributes);
```

This calls the JHtml::calendar() method to render the calendar field.

If we need to use a calendar outside a JForm form, we can call the JHtml::calendar() method directly. In this case, we pass it arguments for the date value, the field name, the field id, the date format, and an array of any additional HTML attributes we want for the field. For example, the following code from the file administrator/components/com_banners/views/tracks/tmpl/default.php creates the begin date for the date filter in the Banner Manager: Tracks screen:

```
<?php echo JHtml::_('calendar',$this->state->get('filter.begin'),
➥'filter_begin','filter_begin','%Y-%m-%d' ,
➥array('size'=>10,'onchange'=>"this.form.fireEvent(
➥'submit');this.form.submit()"));?>
```

In the HTML attributes array argument for this example, we are specifying a size of 10 and the onchange attribute. Here we cause the form to be submitted whenever this field is changed. That way, we reload the page with the correct items when we change the filter_begin field.

Either way that we use to create a calendar, it is not necessary to insert the JHtml::_('behavior.calendar') command. This is done for us in the JHtml::calendar() method.

Caption

The caption behavior automatically adds caption text below an image. To use this, we add two attributes to an img element:

- class="caption": Used as the selector for the JavaScript function
- title="<desired caption title>": The text to display in the caption

If the caption behavior is enabled, the following script element is added to the page:

```
<script type="text/javascript"
src="/joomla_development/j16_trunk/media/system/js/caption.js">
```

This JavaScript automatically selects any img elements with a class of "caption" and creates a centered caption under the image using the value of the title attribute for the caption text.

The caption behavior is a good example of unobtrusive JavaScript. Nothing is required to invoke the behavior other than the presence of these attributes. If the JavaScript is disabled, the behavior fails gracefully. The only impact is that the caption doesn't display.

Colorpicker

This behavior, new in version 2.5, creates a pop-up control that allows a user to select a color value. Figure 12.2 shows an example of a colorpicker pop-up. The color is selected visually, by sliding the control across the color palette. The result is a standard six-digit hex color code.

We can easily create a colorpicker control using `JForm` simply by specifying the type attribute as "color". To create a colorpicker control without `JForm`, simply follow these two steps:

1. Add the code `JHtml::_('behavior.colorpicker');` to load the required Java-Script file.

2. Create an input element with a type of "text" and a CSS class of "input-colorpicker".

Form Validation

This behavior allows us to validate fields in forms using JavaScript. The advantage of validating with JavaScript is that we can immediately notify the user when a field is invalid, without waiting for the user to submit the form.

Figure 12.3 shows an example of the form validation behavior in the front-end Edit Your Profile screen.

Here we entered an invalid password and e-mail address. In both cases, the fields are highlighted as soon as they are changed. We don't have to click on the Submit button to see the errors.

Let's look at how this works. In the XML file for this JForm (`components/com_users/models/forms/profile.xml`), we see the following code for the Password field:

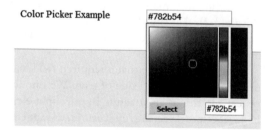

Figure 12.2   Colorpicker pop-up control example

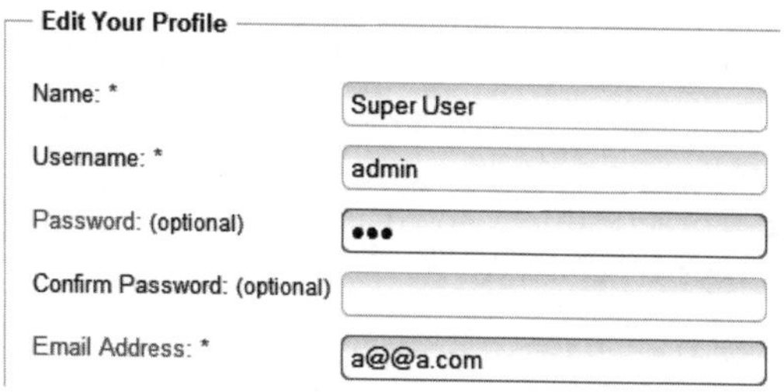

Figure 12.3   Form validation example

```
<field name="password1" type="password"
    autocomplete="off"
    class="validate-password"
    description="COM_USERS_DESIRED_PASSWORD"
            field="password2"
    filter="raw"
    label="COM_USERS_PROFILE_PASSWORD1_LABEL"
    message="COM_USERS_PROFILE_PASSWORD1_MESSAGE"
    size="30"
    validate="equals"
/>
```

By setting the class attribute to **validate-password**, we invoke the JavaScript password validation.

The XML code for the E-mail field is as follows:

```
<field name="email1" type="email"
    description="COM_USERS_PROFILE_EMAIL1_DESC"
    filter="string"
    label="COM_USERS_PROFILE_EMAIL1_LABEL"
    message="COM_USERS_PROFILE_EMAIL1_MESSAGE"
    required="true"
    size="30"
    unique="true"
    validate="email"
/>
```

Here we set the type attribute to e-mail. This tells **JForm** to use the **JFormFieldE-Mail** class to render this field. In that file (**libraries/joomla/form/fields/email.php**), we set the class attribute of this field to "validate-email." This triggers the JavaScript e-mail validation.

We can also use this behavior to validate that a required field has been entered. To do that, we add a required attribute with a value of true. We can do this in the XML file for a **JForm** field or just add this as an attribute in our input element. All these validations are done in the JavaScript file **media/system/js/validate.js**. For the form validation behavior to work, we do the following:

- Call the **JHtml::_('behavior.formvalidation')** method to load the JavaScript into the page header.
- Make sure the form element includes a class attribute of "form-validate."
- Make sure the field includes either a required attribute equal to true or a class attribute equal to one of the values listed in Table 12.2. This is done in the XML file for a **JForm** field. (As noted above, the class attribute is added for us if the **JForm** field type is "email.")

Note that this JavaScript validation is separate from the validation done by the **JFormRule** class, which is triggered by the validate attribute of **JForm** fields. As

Table 12.2 **Built-In Field Validation Types**

Class Attribute	Description
validate-username	Does not allow the following characters in the field: less than or greater than (< or >), single or double quotes (" or '), percent sign (%), semicolon (;), parentheses ("(" or ")"), or ampersand (&)
validate-password	Must be at least four characters (and not more than 196 characters) starting with a nonwhitespace character
validate-numeric	Must contain only digits (0–9), minus sign (–), comma (,), or period (.)
validate-email	Must be a string in the format xxx@yyy.zzz where xxx, yyy, and zzz contain only letters, numbers, periods, and dashes. xxx and yyy must be at least one character long. zzz must be between two and four characters long.

discussed in Chapter 6, when we add a validate attribute in a `JForm` field, it invokes the `test()` method of the corresponding `JFormRule` class. In our e-mail example, we set the validate attribute to "email," so we invoke the `test()` method of the `JFormRuleEMail` class. This method is run after we press the Submit button. Also note that this is different from filtering. Filtering actually changes values during the save process to remove potentially harmful characters.

 Recall from other discussions in this book that we cannot rely on any type of form validation to protect us from hackers. This type of validation is important to provide a good user interface, but we still need to validate and filter data after the form is submitted to protect against malicious code.

Disabling the Submit or Save Action

As we have discussed, the JavaScript validation works locally in the browser. It doesn't require us to press the Submit or Save button in order to validate the fields in the form. If we know from the JavaScript validation that some of the data on our form is invalid, we may want to disable the submit action until the form contains all valid data.

If we submit a form with invalid data, we should get validation errors back from the server and the form will not be accepted. So there is no point in submitting a form with invalid data, and it is less confusing to the user only to show one set of validation errors (rather than getting one set of error messages before the form is submitted and then a different set of messages after the form is submitted).

In the Joomla core programs, we normally disable the submit function when form validation has found errors. This is accomplished in two different ways, as follows:

- If the form has a button element with a type attribute of "submit" and class attribute of "validate," the form validation will automatically validate the entire form and disable the submit action of this button if the form contains any invalid data.

- If the form doesn't have a submit button, we can create a JavaScript function to intercept the submit action and only submit the form if the form is valid. This is the case for the back-end manager screens that have toolbars with multiple buttons for different tasks.

An example of the second method can be found in the back-end User Manager: Edit screen (administrator/components/com_users/views/user/tmpl/edit.php). There we see the following code:

```
<script type="text/javascript">
   Joomla.submitbutton = function(task)
   {
       if (task == 'user.cancel' ||
➥document.formvalidator.isValid(document.id('user-form'))) {
           Joomla.submitform(task, document.getElementById('user-form'));
       }
   }
</script>
```

This code creates a JavaScript function called `Joomla.submitbutton`. When the user clicks on any of the toolbar icons that submit the form, such as Save, Cancel, or Save & Close, this function is called. If the task is equal to "user.cancel", or if the form is valid, the form is submitted by calling the `Joomla.submitform` function (which is defined in the `media/system/js/core.js` file). Otherwise, nothing happens, so the form is not submitted. This way the user is required to fix any invalid data before the form can be submitted.

Note that this is another example of unobtrusive JavaScript. The application is not relying on the JavaScript validation to ensure that the fields are valid. There are other methods that check for valid data—for example, `JFormRule` classes and the `JTable` validation methods. The JavaScript methods just improve the user interface by giving the user immediate feedback when invalid data is entered. If JavaScript is disabled, the form will still work, but with a less elegant user interface.

Framework

This behavior simply loads the MooTools framework as a script tag in the page header. You would use this when adding custom JavaScript code that relies on MooTools. It is not associated with any specific JavaScript functions. The code is as follows:

```
JHtml::_('behavior.framework');
```

Highlighter

The highlighter behavior allows you to easily highlight selected words on the page. This is used in the Smart Seach component to highlight the search terms in an article, as shown in Figure 12.4.

To use the highlighter behavior, follow these steps:

1. Add the command JHtml::_('behavior.highlighter', $wordArray), where $wordArray is an array of the words you want to highlight.

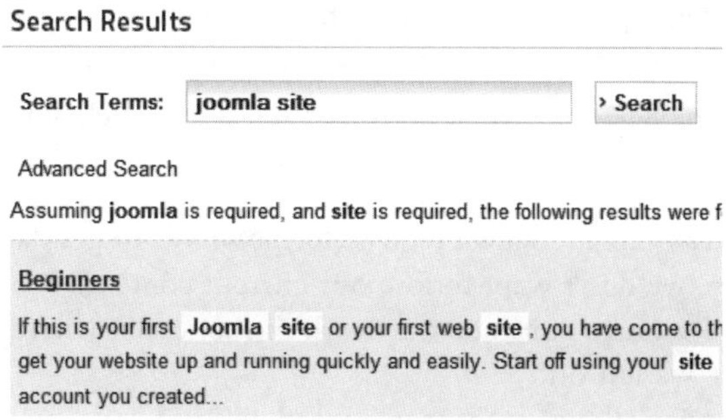

Figure 12.4   Highlighter example

2. Add the HTML code `<br id="highlighter-start" />` just before the section of the document to be highlighted.

3. Add the HTML code `<br id="highlighter-end" />` just after the section of the document to be highlighted.

Keepalive

This behavior allows Joomla to keep a session active for an indefinite period of time. Normally, when a user is using Joomla, we want the session to expire after a given amount of time. The default setting is 15 minutes. This is a security feature. For example, if a user is logged in to a sensitive area and leaves the computer without logging out, we would want the session to time out to lessen the chance of an unauthorized person gaining access to the site.

In some cases, however, the session timeout can cause problems. For example, a user might be editing a long article. It is easy to imagine a case where someone goes 15 minutes or longer without saving. If the session were to expire during this time, the user could lose all their work. What's worse, the user would only find out about the problem after hitting the Save button (when it would be too late!).

To prevent this, we can invoke the keepalive behavior. All we need is the single line of code as follows:

```
JHtml::_('behavior.keepalive');
```

This uses a built-in MooTools method to automatically make an AJAX request to the server one minute before the session would otherwise expire. The request is done in the background and causes the server to reset the session timeout. This has the effect of keeping the session alive indefinitely. Many of the component edit screens in Joomla use this behavior.

Modal

The modal behavior is used when we need to show a self-contained pop-up window inside a containing screen. Two examples in the Joomla core are as follows:

- Clicking on the Options toolbar icon in User Manager and other manager screens to edit the component-level configuration options

- Clicking on the Select/Change button to select an article for a Single Article menu item

In these cases, we need to make a request to the server to get data and then show that data. However, we don't want to lose our current context. When we close the modal window, we want to continue our work in the screen where we opened the modal, right where we left off.

The modal behavior allows us to open a window inside our current document, work in that window, and close it when we are ready. When we close the modal window, we are returned to the parent window. As long as the modal window is open, we cannot work in the parent window.

In many cases, we display the modal window inside an iframe element. This allows us to have a second document inside the parent document.

To create a modal in Joomla, we need to do the following:

- Add the command `JHtml::_('behavior.modal')` to insert the JavaScript into the page header. We can pass a CSS class selector as an optional second argument. It defaults to "a.modal," which will select an anchor element with a class attribute of "modal."

- Create an anchor element with a class attribute of "modal" (or that matches the second argument of the behavior.modal command) and an href attribute that points to the URL to load in the modal window. If the modal will be rendered in an iframe element, include a rel attribute with the handler and size information.

- Create the view and layout for the contents of the modal. These are just like normal view and layout programs.

Let's look at our two examples to see how this works.

User Configuration Modal

This screen is opened by clicking on the Options icon in the User Manager toolbar. Figure 12.5 shows an example of this screen.

Recall that the code for this button comes from the **addToolbar()** method of the **UsersViewUsers** class (**administrator/components/com_users/views/users/view .html.php**). There, we see this code:

```
JToolBarHelper::preferences('com_users');
```

In that method, we see the following line of code:

```
$bar->appendButton('Popup', 'options', $alt,
⮱'index.php?option=com_config&amp;view=component&amp;component='.
⮱$component.'&amp;path='.$path.'&amp;tmpl=component', $width, $height,
⮱$top, $left, $onClose);
```

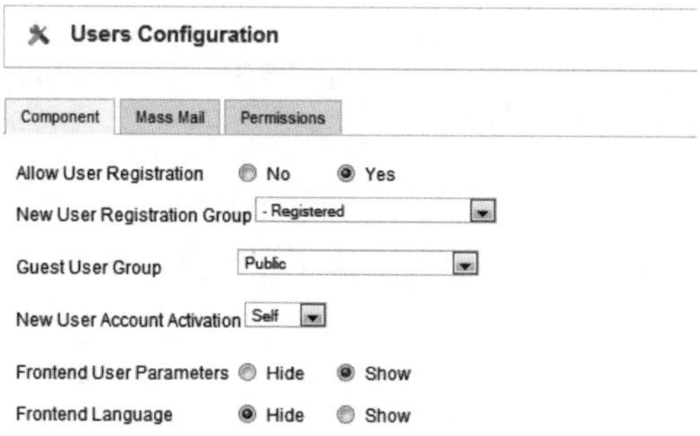

Figure 12.5   Users configuration modal example

This calls the `fetchButton()` method of the `JButtonPopup` class (`libraries/joomla/html/toolbar/button/popup.php`), passing the URL as the fourth argument. The URL points to the default layout of the component view in the `com_config` component.

In the `fetchButton()` method we find the following code to add the modal behavior:

```
JHtml::_('behavior.modal');
```

Because the second argument is omitted, the default select of "a.modal" is used. Further on in the method we find the following code:

```
$html = "<a class=\"modal\" href=\"$doTask\"
➥rel=\"{handler: 'iframe', size: {x: $width, y: $height},
➥onClose: function() {".$onClose."}}\">\n";
    $html .= "<span class=\"$class\">\n";
```

Here we create the anchor with the class attribute of modal and with the URL in the href attribute. We also create an optional `onClose` function. This gives us the opportunity to call a JavaScript function when the modal window is closed. In this case, the function is empty, so no special processing occurs when the modal window is closed.

The end result is that we render the layout file `administrator/components/com_config/views/component/tmpl/default.php` inside the modal window in an iframe element. The great thing about this approach is that the code for this layout is just like a normal layout and is not affected by the fact that it is running in the modal window. The layout is opened inside the modal window when the Options button is clicked, and returns control to the parent window when it is closed.

Article Selector Modal

This screen is similar to the Article Manager except that it runs inside a modal window. It allows the user to search for and select one article. One place this is used is when you create a Single Article menu item, as shown in Figure 12.6.

A site might contain thousands of articles, far more than we would want to show in a list box. This modal window allows the user to select an article in a pop-up window that has the same pagination, search, and filtering options used in the Article Manager screen. This allows the user to find the desired article even when there are many to

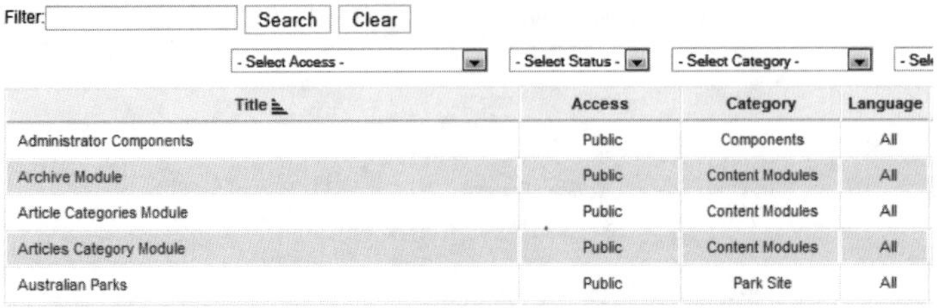

Figure 12.6   Article select modal example

choose from. Note that this example is a bit different from the previous one because here we need to pass information about the selected article back to the parent window. Let's look at how this works.

The Single Item Menu Item screen is a `JForm` that uses the XML file `components/com_content/views/article/tmpl/default.xml`. The element that renders the Select/Change Article modal is as follows:

```
<fields name="request">
 <fieldset name="request"
   addfieldpath="/administrator/components/com_content/models/fields">
    <field name="id" type="modal_article"
       label="COM_CONTENT_FIELD_SELECT_ARTICLE_LABEL"
       required="true"
       description="COM_CONTENT_FIELD_SELECT_ARTICLE_DESC"
   />
 </fieldset>
</fields>
```

The type attribute loads the field from the `getInput()` method of `JFormFieldModal_Article` (`administrator/components/com_content/models/fields/modal/article.php`).

In that method, we first see code that is used to create a JavaScript function in the parent window called `jSelectArticle_` plus the form's id attribute. In this example, the function name will be `jSelectArticle_jform_request_id`. This code is as follows:

```
// Build the script.
$script = array();
$script[] = '    function jSelectArticle_'.$this->id.'(id, title, catid,
↪object) {';
$script[] = '        document.id("'.$this->id.'_id").value = id;';
$script[] = '        document.id("'.$this->id.'_name").value = title;';
$script[] = '        SqueezeBox.close();';
$script[] = '    }';

// Add the script to the document head.
JFactory::getDocument()->addScriptDeclaration(implode("\n", $script));
```

This creates the text of the JavaScript function and adds it to the document's script element. The JavaScript function adds the article's id and title to the document's id and name form fields. This JavaScript function is added to the parent window's document. We will see later that this function is called when the user clicks the article's title in the modal window.

Later in the `getInput()` method we see this line of code creating the href URL:

```
$link = 'index.php?option=com_content&amp;view=articles&amp;
↪layout=modal&amp;tmpl=component&amp;function=jSelectArticle_'.$this->id;
```

This points to the modal layout in the articles view of the com_content component.

Then we see this code creating the anchor element:

```
$html[] = ' <a class="modal" title="'.
↪JText::_('COM_CONTENT_CHANGE_ARTICLE').'"  href="'.$link.
↪'&amp;'.JSession::getFormToken().'=1"
↪'" rel="{handler: \'iframe\', size: {x: 800, y: 450}}">'.
↪JText::_('COM_CONTENT_CHANGE_ARTICLE_BUTTON').'</a>';
```

As we expect, we have an anchor element with a class attribute set to "modal" and a rel attribute setting up the iframe information.

Notice that we add a function variable to the URL that loads the modal. This variable has the name of the parent's JavaScript function (jSelectArticle_jform_ request_id). The modal's document does not include this JavaScript function. So what is this variable used for? The answer is that we need to know this function name when we create the anchor element for each listed article inside the modal window. Notice that we also add a form token to the URL. This allows us to ensure that this form is called from within a Joomla session.

At this point, we have the code in the parent window that creates the modal window and processes the return values from that window. The last step is the layout code for the modal window itself.

The modal window layout file in this case is **administrator/components/com_ content/views/articles/tmpl/modal.php**. This code is very similar to the Article Manager layout (**administrator/components/com_content/views/articles/tmpl/ default.php**) and also similar to the Weblinks Manager we discussed in Chapter 7. The main difference is what happens when the link for an article is clicked. In the Article Manager, when the user clicks the link for the article's title, the article is opened for editing. In the modal window, clicking the link invokes the **jSelectArticle_jform _request_id** JavaScript function in the parent window. This passes the article's id and title to the parent window, closes the modal window, and returns control to the parent window. Let's see how that works.

The first thing we need to do is get the name of the JavaScript function we need to call when the link is clicked. Recall that this is included in the URL in a variable called function. The code that reads the function name is as follows:

```
$function = JRequest::getCmd('function', 'jSelectArticle');
```

Recall from the discussion in Chapter 7 about the Weblinks Manager that the manager screen is a form that, when submitted, calls its own URL. This allows us to use the search and filtering features of the screen. We do the same technique in the modal screen as shown in the following code:

```
<form action="<?php echo
➥JRoute::_('index.php?option=com_content&view=articles&layout=modal
➥&tmpl=component&function='.$function.'&'.JSession::getFormToken().'=1');
➥?>" method="post" name="adminForm" id="adminForm">
```

Note that we again include the function name in the URL. Also note that we again include the form token.

The key part of this layout that makes it different from the Article Manager is the link for each article. The code for this is as follows (inside the `foreach` loop):

```
<a class="pointer" onclick="if (window.parent)
➥window.parent.<?php echo $this->escape($function);?>
➥ ('<?php echo $item->id; ?>',
➥'<?php echo $this->escape(addslashes($item->title)); ?>',
➥'<?php echo $this->escape($item->catid); ?>');">
        <?php echo $this->escape($item->title); ?></a>
```

Here we add a JavaScript function linked to the onclick event for the anchor element. In that function, we check that the parent window exists (meaning that we are indeed inside a modal window). If so, we execute a function called `window.parent._jSelectArticle_jform_request_id` function. This calls the `jSelectArticle_jform_request_id` function of the parent window. We pass the current article's id, title, and category id to this function. (Note that we only use the first two arguments in this function. The category id argument is not used.)

Keep in mind that the parent window is loaded into memory the entire time we are working inside the modal window. So after the user selects the desired article (or closes the modal), the parent window continues to process at the point where the modal was opened.

The end result is that we get a pop-up modal window inside an iframe that allows the user to select an article. The modal window includes filters and pagination controls that allow the user to find and select the desired article, even if there are a large number of articles in the site. The modal screen is coded almost identically to the corresponding manager screen, making it easy to understand and maintain. Similar modal screens are used for selecting modules, contacts, and users.

Check All and Multiselect

These behaviors allow users to toggle on or off multiple check boxes on a form. The Check All allows you to add a "check all" check box to a form. This acts as a toggle to check or uncheck all the checkboxes on the form. The multiselect behavior allows the user to toggle a range of consecutive checkboxes.

Check All

Figure 12.7 shows an example from the Weblinks Manager screen with the arrow pointing to the check-all toggle.

To implement this behavior, follow these steps:

1. Make sure the core.js file is loaded—for example, with JHtml::_('behavior.framework') or one of the behaviors that includes loading the framework.

2. Add an input control of type check box with the onclick attribute equal to "Joomla.checkAll(this)."

3. Make sure the check boxes to be toggled on and off include the letters "cb" in the id attribute. For example, the standard for core manager screens is to label the checkboxes for each row "cbx," where x is the row number 0-n.

Multiselect

Multiselect allows the user to toggle on or off a range of check boxes using Shift+Left Click. For example, if all the checkboxes are unchecked and you want to click boxes 2–8, you can click on box 2 and Shift+Left Click on box 8. This will check boxes 2–8. You can use the same technique to uncheck a consecutive group of boxes.

To enable this behavior, just add the code JHtml::_('behavior.multiselect') to the script.

Noframes

This behavior prevents a page from being loaded inside an iframe. This is a security feature to help prevent phishing attacks. For example, a link might direct a user to a site where the login screen is being run inside an iframe. To the user, the login could look exactly like the real site, and the hackers could collect sensitive login credentials. The noframes behavior prevents this type of forgery. In core it is used in the back-end login screens.

To implement this behavior, simply add the code JHtml::_('behavior.noframes') to the program file.

Switcher

This behavior allows the developer to create a tab-like interface in an HTML page. This is convenient when we want to show more information on a screen than will

Figure 12.7   Multiselect example

fit on one page. Figure 12.8 shows the Global Configuration screen, which uses the switcher behavior.

This is similar in function to submenus. When you click on each link, the information related to that "panel" (a div element in the document) of the form is displayed. The difference is, with the switcher, all the information for the entire screen is loaded in one request cycle. Only one panel of output is shown at a time, but they are all there in the document. So switching between panels is very fast and doesn't require a new page load from the server. It is accomplished by unobtrusive JavaScript that changes the style attribute to hide all the panels except the one in view.

Let's look at how this works in Global Configuration. If we look at the folder `administrator/components/com_config/views/application/tmpl`, we see 17 different layout files. The `default.php` is the first file loaded. The first part of that file is as follows:

```
defined('_JEXEC') or die;

// Load tooltips behavior
JHtml::_('behavior.formvalidation');
JHtml::_('behavior.switcher');
JHtml::_('behavior.tooltip');

// Load submenu template, using element id 'submenu' as needed by
➥behavior.switcher
$this->document->setBuffer($this->loadTemplate('navigation'), 'modules',
➥'submenu');
```

Here we include the `behavior.switcher` to load the required JavaScript. Then we create the submenu links with the highlighted line of code. That code executes the `default-navigation.php` file and puts the output from that into the module position called submenu.

The `default-navigation.php` file has the following code:

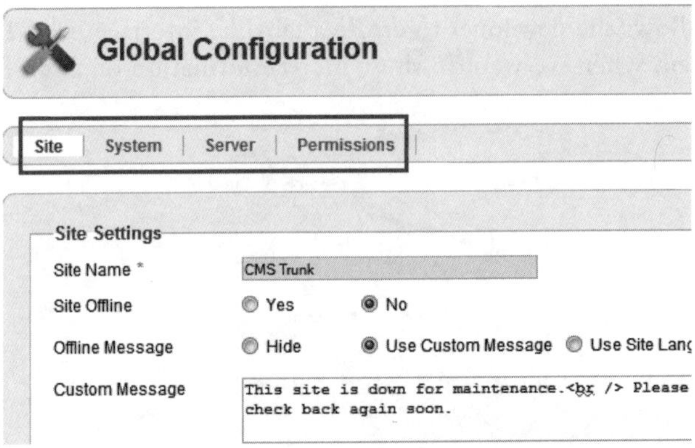

Figure 12.8   Switcher example screen

```
<ul id="submenu" class="configuration">
    <li><a href="#" onclick="return false;" id="site" class="active">
↪<?php echo JText::_('JSITE'); ?></a></li>
    <li><a href="#" onclick="return false;" id="system">
↪<?php echo JText::_('COM_CONFIG_SYSTEM'); ?></a></li>
    <li><a href="#" onclick="return false;" id="server">
↪<?php echo JText::_('COM_CONFIG_SERVER'); ?></a></li>
    <li><a href="#" onclick="return false;" id="permissions">
↪<?php echo JText::_('COM_CONFIG_PERMISSIONS'); ?></a></li>
</ul>
```

This creates a ul element with an id of submenu. This is important. That is used by the JavaScript selector to indicate that this list of links will be used to switch between the different panels.

Each of the li elements has a link to one of the panels in the switcher screen. The id attribute corresponds to the name of each panel. Notice that the first link has a class attribute set to active. This indicates to the user that this is the active panel.

Now let's go back to the default.php file. The next section of code there adds the JavaScript that enables the form validation behavior discussed earlier in this chapter. Then we see the following code:

```
<form action="<?php echo JRoute::_('index.php?option=com_config');?>"
↪id="application-form" method="post" name="adminForm"
↪class="form-validate">
    <?php if ($this->ftp) : ?>
        <?php echo $this->loadTemplate('ftplogin'); ?>
    <?php endif; ?>
    <div id="config-document">
        <div id="page-site" class="tab">
            <div class="noshow">
                <div class="width-60 fltlft">
                    <?php echo $this->loadTemplate('site'); ?>
                    <?php echo $this->loadTemplate('metadata'); ?>
                </div>
                <div class="width-40 fltrt">
                    <?php echo $this->loadTemplate('seo'); ?>
                    <?php echo $this->loadTemplate('cookie'); ?>
                </div>
            </div>
        </div>
    </div>
```

The first line creates a normal form. Then we load the ftp login page if the ftp option is enabled.

The next two lines of code are important for the switcher. The first highlighted line creates a div element with an id of "config-document." This is the container element for all the panels that will be controlled by the switcher.

The second highlighted line creates the first panel. This is a div element with the id of **page-xxx**, where **xxx** matches the id of the anchor element in the submenu. It also needs to have a class of tab. Further down, we see the four highlighted lines of code. Each of these loads a layout into the desired place on the page. For example, the first one loads the **default-site.php** layout, and the second one loads the layout file called **default-metadata.php**.

The next line of code is as follows:

```
<div id="page-system" class="tab">
```

This creates the second panel that corresponds to the system link in the submenu. Further down we create the panel called page-server and then page-permissions. Each of these loads one or more layout scripts.

When the page is first loaded, the JavaScript function checks to see which panel should be visible. A cookie is used to remember which one the user was working in last. If there is no cookie, the first panel is visible by default.

The JavaScript function works as follows. It builds an array of the div elements with a class attribute of tab. These are the container elements for each tab panel. For the one visible panel, it dynamically creates a style attribute equal to **"display: block;"**. For all the others, it creates one equal to **"display: none;"**.

When the user clicks on a submenu link, this process is repeated. The div element corresponding to the clicked link is made visible (**style = "display: block;"**) and the others are all made invisible (**style = "display: none;"**). This is done almost instantly in the working memory of the browser.

This approach is relatively simple and very flexible. Each individual layout file is very simple. If we need to move things around on the page or create new tabs, it is very easy to do. This technique is also used in core in the Site → System Information screen.

The following summarizes the requirements to use the switcher behavior:

- Add the switcher behavior to the layout.
- Create a layout similar to the **default-navigation.php** file discussed earlier. This should have a ul element with an id of "submenu" and class of "configuration." In that, add li elements with anchor elements where each anchor element's id is the name of the panel (for example, "site," "system," and so on).
- In the default layout, load this navigation layout (for example, in the submenu module position).
- Create one or more layouts for each of the panels.
- In the default layout, create a div element with an id of "config-document."
- Inside that, create one div element for each of the panels. Each of these should have an id of "page-xxx" and a class of "tab."
- Inside each of these div elements, use the **loadTemplate()** method to load the layout files for each part of the page.

Tooltip

The tooltip behavior allows you to create tooltip pop-up displays that show when the user hovers the mouse on a form element. This is normally used in Joomla to provide help text, as shown in Figure 12.9.

All that is required to create a tooltip is to invoke the tooltip behavior and then create an element with a class attribute of "hasTip." The text in the element's title attribute will show in the tooltip. As an option, you can create a title and body text in the tooltip by creating a title attribute in the following format:

```
<title>::<body>
```

For example, in Figure 12.9 the title attribute is set as follows:

```
title="Meta Description::An optional paragraph to be used as the
▸description of the page in the HTML output. This will generally display
▸in the results of search engines."
```

Tooltips are created automatically by `JForm`. In this case, the label attribute is used as the tooltip title and the description attribute is used for the tooltip text. Recall that if these values are keys in the language file, they will be translated in the tooltip.

Yet another way to create a tooltip is by using the `JHtml::tooltip()` method. For example, the following line of code

```
echo JHtml::_('tooltip', 'My tooltip text.', 'My Tooltip Title', '',
▸'Hover on this text to see the tooltip.');
```

produces the following HTML out produces the following HT put:

```
<span class="hasTip" title="My Tooltip Title::My tooltip text.">Hover on
▸this text to see the tooltip.</span>
```

Tree

This behavior is used in the Media Manager to show the folders containing media files in a tree control. The user can click on the plus or minus icon to expand or collapse the tree. Figure 12.10 shows an example of this screen, with the tree fully expanded.

The tree behavior works like this. In our layout, we create an unordered list (`ul`) element with an anchor (`a`) element inside each list (`li`) element. These can be nested, so that inside an li element we could have another ul element and so on. An example of this structure is as follows:

Figure 12.9   Tooltip example

Figure 12.10   Tree behavior example

```
<ul id="testtree">
   <li><a href="test.html">Item One</a></li>
   <li><a href="test.html">Item Two</a>
      <ul>
         <li><a href="test.html">Item Two Point One</a></li>
         <li><a href="test.html">Item Two Point Two</a></li>
      </ul>
   </li>
   <li><a href="test.html">Item Three</a>
   </li>
</ul>
```

The JavaScript function reads the outer ul element based on its id attribute, creates a corresponding tree object, and hides the entire ul element. So we see the tree and not the list. The anchor values become the link URLs to use when the tree item is clicked. If the li element has a nested ul element, clicking on the +/– toggle expands or hides the nested list.

Trees can be useful when we are dealing with items in nested hierarchies, such as files or categories. Let's look at how we could use the tree behavior to view article categories as a tree. To illustrate this, we will create a template override for the Articles → List all Categories menu item and change the layout to show a simple tree.

First, we need to create the override folder called `templates/beez_20/html/com_content/categories`. Then we create a file in this folder called `default.php` with the following code:

```
<?php
// no direct access
defined('_JEXEC') or die;
JHtml::addIncludePath(JPATH_COMPONENT.'/helpers');

// testtree is the name of the div with the ul element to
```

```
↪be converted to the tree
// Article Categories is the title for the root node of the tree
JHtml::_('behavior.tree', 'testtree', array(),
↪array('text' => 'Article Categories'));
?>


<h1>MooTree Example Template Override</h1>
<div id="testtree_tree"></div>


<?php echo $this->loadTemplate('items'); ?>
```

This file calls the `behavior.tree` function with three arguments. The first argument, "testtree", is the id of the `ul` element to convert to the tree. The second (`array()`) is some optional parameters that we don't use. The third argument allows us to specify the wording for the top-level node in the tree (in an associative array with a key of text). This defaults to "Root," but in our example, we set it to `Article Categories`.

Then we create a heading element and an empty div element with the id attribute of `"testtree_tree"`. This is required and will be the div element where the tree is created. The id of this div is the ul id plus `_tree` (in our example, `testtree_tree`).

The last line calls the layout file `default_items.php`, which we create in the same directory. The listing for that file is as follows:

```
<?php
// no direct access
defined('_JEXEC') or die;
?>
<ul id="testtree">
<?php foreach($this->items[$this->parent->id] as $id => $item) : ?>
   <li><a href="<?php echo
↪JRoute::_(ContentHelperRoute::getCategoryRoute($item->id));?>">
       <?php echo $this->escape($item->title); ?> </a>
    <?php if ($children = $item->getChildren(false)) : ?>
       <ul>
        <?php foreach ($children as $child) : ?>
           <li><a href="<?php echo
↪JRoute::_(ContentHelperRoute::getCategoryRoute($child->id));?>">
               <?php echo $this->escape($child->title); ?> </a>
           </li>
        <?php endforeach; ?>
       </ul>
    <?php endif; ?>
   </li>
<?php endforeach; ?>
</ul>
```

Here we are creating a ul element with an id of "testtree" that will be used to create the tree. We have two foreach loops. The outer loop creates an li element for each category in the list, using the category route for the anchor URL.

Then we check to see if there are child categories for each category. If so, we create an inner ul element for the child categories. Note that we only go one level down in this example, but we could continue down the tree in this same manner to any number of levels.

We can see this layout in action by navigating in the sample data to Home → Using Joomla! → Using Extensions (book_170/index.php/using-joomla/extensions). Figure 12.11 shows the override layout with the tree.

Uploader

This behavior is used in Media Manager when the Enable flash uploader option is set to yes. The uploader behavior displays the information about the files being uploaded and the progress of the operation. An example screen is shown in Figure 12.12.

This behavior is closely linked to the media manager component and is not designed for general use. The MooTools library does include a number of status bars and related widgets to let the user know the status of a background process.

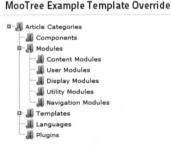

Figure 12.11   MooTree example

Figure 12.12   Media Manager upload status example

Using MooTools Extensions

In addition to the core MooTools functionality, MooTools maintains a website, http://mootools.net/forge, that lists many extensions to the basic framework. These extensions can be downloaded and used in your Joomla website.

Let's demonstrate this with an easy-to-use extension written by Rouven Wessling called Grayscale Image Hover. This function changes an image from grayscale to color when you hover the mouse over it. Here are the steps to see this function work:

1. Download the archive file from http://mootools.net/forge/p/ grayscale_image_hover.

2. Extract the files from this archive and copy the source code file grayscale-hover.js to the folder templates/beez_20/javascript.

3. Add the following code to the template's index.php file (templates/beez_20/ index.php) after the last addScript() call:

```
$doc->addScript($this->baseurl.
➦'/templates/beez_20/javascript/grayscalehover.js', 'text/javascript',
➦true);
$grayscaleHover = "
        window.addEvent('domready', function() {
                new GrayscaleImages('img');
        });
";
$doc->addScriptDeclaration($grayscaleHover);
```

Here we add the new JavaScript source file so that we can use its functions. Then we add the JavaScript code to attach the new function to the domready event. In this example, we will change every img element to use the new function when the page is loaded.

To see this in action, navigate to the Australian Parks page in the sample data. The image initially shows in grayscale. If you hover the mouse over the image, the image gradually changes to color.

Other MooTools extensions can be added to your Joomla site following the same steps.

Using AJAX in Joomla

As previously mentioned, JavaScript is also used to handle asynchronous requests to the server. The advantage of this type of request is that it can be done in the background and doesn't require a full page refresh. The JavaScript program runs continuously in the browser and can control the entire process.

One place where AJAX is used in Joomla is in the installation. It is beyond the scope of this chapter to present detailed instructions for creating AJAX-based extensions, and we won't go into the details of how the JavaScript code works. Instead, we will look at the outlines of how this works, especially how the PHP and JavaScript work together.

The Joomla installation is a separate application with its own folder. These programs are normally executed once to install an instance of Joomla, and then the entire installation folder is deleted (for security purposes).

The entry point for a new Joomla installation is the file `installation/index.php`. That in turn runs the file `installation/controller.php`. There we load the required platform classes and path variables and then set the default view to "language" (the first screen in the Joomla installation). This executes the view `JInstallationViewLanguage` (`installation/views/language/view.html.php`) and the layout `installation/views/language/tmp/default.php`. The template for the installation is `installation/template/index.php`.

In the template `index.php` file, we see the following code to load the required JavaScript files:

```
// Load the JavaScript behaviors
JHtml::_('behavior.framework', true);
JHtml::_('behavior.keepalive');
JHtml::_('behavior.tooltip');
JHtml::_('behavior.formvalidation');
JHtml::_('script', 'installation/template/js/installation.js', true,
↪false, false, false);
?>
```

The last line loads the `installation.js` file, which is used to control the entire installation process.

Later in the `index.php` file we see the following JavaScript code in a script element:

```
<script type="text/javascript">
 window.addEvent('domready', function() {
  window.Install = new Installation('rightpad',
↪'<?php echo JURI::current(); ?>');

  Locale.define('<?php echo JFactory::getLanguage()->getTag(); ?>',
↪'installation', {
     sampleDataLoaded: '<?php echo JText::_('INSTL_SITE_SAMPLE_LOADED',
↪true); ?>'
  });
  Locale.use('<?php echo JFactory::getLanguage()->getTag(); ?>');
 });
</script>
```

This code adds a JavaScript command to the "domready" event. This event fires when the HTML document is completely loaded. The code here creates a new `Installation` object, called `Install`, using the JavaScript file `installation/template/js/installation.js`. This file will take over control of the entire installation process from this point on. The language view, shown in Figure 12.13, has a Next button in the upper right corner.

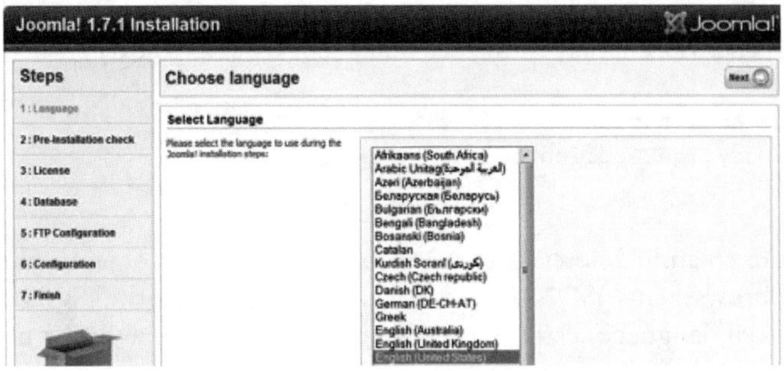

Figure 12.13   Installation screen

The onclick attribute for the Next button is `Install.submitform()`. This executes the `submitform()` function for the JavaScript `Install` object (created from the dom-ready event when this page was loaded).

At this point, the JavaScript `Install` object is running the process. Instead of the pages being loaded by separate requests from the browser to the server, the `Install` object will send asynchronous requests to the server to update the existing data on the page.

The `submitform()` method of the `Install` object reads the task from the form (the element whose name attribute equals "task") and uses that for the task in the request. The first request sent by `Install` includes `task=setup.setlanguage&format=json`. This is sent after the user clicks on the Next button in the Choose Language screen shown in Figure 12.13. This request is then sent asynchronously to the server. This means that the JavaScript program continues to run while the task is executed by the server.

This request is processed by the server just like a normal browser request, and we are back to running the normal Joomla PHP programs. In this case, we run the `setlanguage()` method of the `JInstallationControllerSetup` class (`installation/controllers/setup.json.php`). Note that the `format=json` in the URL causes the `setup.json.php` file to be loaded.

The `setlanguage()` method gets some data from the model, checks for errors, and then ends with the following code:

```
// Redirect to the next page.
$r->view = 'preinstall';
$this->sendResponse($r);
```

Here the variable `$r` is a `JObject` with the view field set to "preinstall," the name of the next view in the installation process. We then call the `sendResponse()` method. This is where things get interesting.

The `sendResponse()` method checks for errors and then ends with the following code:

```
// Send the JSON response.
echo json_encode(new JInstallationJsonResponse($response));

// Close the application.
$app = JFactory::getApplication();
$app->close();
```

Here we are creating a new `JInstallationJsonResponse` object and echoing this object to the browser in a JSON-encoded format. In this case, the JSON text contains the session token, language, error status, and data with the name of the next view to display, similar to the following:

```
{"token":"c8de8295d8be5a299c66045157ba29df","lang":
↪"en-US","error":false,"data":{"view":"preinstall"}}
```

After we echo this text to the browser, we *close the application!* In a normal request cycle, we might expect at this point to see some JSON-encoded text displayed in the browser. Instead, we are taken to the preinstall screen in the installation process. How does this work?

The key to understanding this is that this PHP code is running under the control of the JavaScript `Installation` class (the `Install` object). The AJAX request is sent using the `post()` method of the MooTools class `Request.JSON`. That class includes an event called `onSuccess` that is triggered when the request completes. At that time, the JavaScript program continues with the code for the `onSuccess` event for this request.

When we close the Joomla PHP application with the `$app->close()` method, control passes back to the JavaScript `Install` object, specifically to the code for the `onSuccess` event for this request. That code reads the JSON string echoed to the browser by the `sendResponse()` method. The code then gets the view from the data element of the JSON string—in this case, "preinstall"—and calls the `goToPage()` method, passing the view name as an argument. The `goToPage()` method then issues a new AJAX request to load the preinstall view, the next view in the installation process.

In the preinstall view, the Next button is defined to call the JavaScript function `goToPage('license')`. That directly loads the next view, called "license."

As we go through the different installation screens, the pattern is as follows. If the screen needs to do a task other than display,

- The Next button invokes the `submitform()` method of the JavaScript Install object. That method reads the task from the task element of the form (normally a hidden element).

- The `submitform()` method sends a new AJAX request to process that task. After the task has completed, the PHP program for the task echoes a JSON-formatted string to the browser and closes the PHP application.

- The `onSuccess` event is fired and the Install object continues processing with the code for this event. In this case, the name of the next view to load is read from the JSON string and the view is loaded with another AJAX request.

If the screen just needs to load the next view, without any processing,

- The Next button invokes the `goToPage()` method of the JavaScript `Install` object for the next view.

- The `goToPage()` method creates an AJAX request to load the next view.

The process continues in this fashion until the installation is completed or the user terminates the process. The entire process is done with only two full page loads. The first one loads the initial language view. The second page load is done after the user deletes the installation folder and navigates to either the back or front end of the newly installed site.

We can see that this process is similar to the normal model-view-controller (MVC) pattern in Joomla, where one request cycle might be to run a task and the following cycle causes a layout to be displayed. The difference here is that the requests are asynchronous and the same JavaScript program is in memory the entire time and controls the entire process.

Using Other JavaScript Frameworks

It is relatively easy to use other JavaScript frameworks with Joomla. Here we will show an example of using the popular jQuery framework and MooTools on the same page. Here are the steps for the example:

1. In a test Joomla website, create a folder called **components/com_test**. This will hold our example files.

2. Download the jQuery framework from the jQuery website (**http://docs .jquery.com/Downloading_jQuery#Download_jQuery**). Here we use the file called **jquery-1.6.4.js**. Copy this file into the **com_test** folder.

3. In the **com_test** folder, create a file called **noconflict.js** with the following code:

```
/**
 * noconflict.js file to demonstrate loading jQuery with MooTools
 */
jQuery.noConflict();
```

4. Also in the **com_test** folder, create a file called **test.php** with the following code:

```
<?php
// Test file to demonstrate loading MooTools and jQuery libraries

JHtml::_('behavior.framework');
$document = JFactory::getDocument();
$document->addScript(JURI::root(true).
↪'/components/com_test/jquery-1.6.4.js');
```

```
$document->addScript(JURI::root(true).
→'/components/com_test/noconflict.js');

$mootoolsStyle = "
// MooTools change font style on domready event
    window.addEvent('domready',function() {
        $$('p.test').setStyle('font-style','italic');
    }); ";
$document->addScriptDeclaration($mootoolsStyle);

$jqueryStyle = "
// jQuery change background color on document ready event
        jQuery(document).ready(function($){
                jQuery('p.test').css('background-color','#fafa99');
        }); ";
$document->addScriptDeclaration($jqueryStyle);
?>


<p class="test">MooTools sets this paragraph's text to italic,
and jQuery sets the background to yellow.</p>
```

In our `test.php` file, we use the `behavior.framework` to load MooTools. Then we use the `addScript()` method of `JDocument` to load the jQuery framework file (`jquery-1.6.4.js`) and the `noconflict.js` file. This second file causes jQuery to run in "no conflict" mode. By default, both jQuery and MooTools use "$" as a shortcut in the framework. When you use jQuery in no conflict mode, the "$" can still be used in MooTools. In this case, you can use jQuery (or some other assigned variable) to reference jQuery functions. It is important that the `addScript()` method for the `noconflict.js` file execute immediately after the `addScript()` for the jQuery framework file.

After we load the two frameworks and the no-conflict file, we demonstrate using both frameworks on the same page. Here we have created two functions. The first one uses MooTools to change our paragraph's font style to italic. The second function uses jQuery to change the background color to yellow. Both functions are attached to the document ready event, so they are both called as soon as the document is loaded.

Finally, we include a paragraph element with a class called test. This is the element that both JavaScript functions will modify.

To see the results, load your test website with the URL `<your URL>/index.php?option=com_test`. Recall that this executes the file `components/com_test/test.php`. You should see a screen similar to Figure 12.14.

(Note that we have error notices because our `com_test` component doesn't have a row in the `#__extensions` table.)

As discussed earlier, it is recommended to use MooTools if possible for Joomla work because it is already included and saves having to load and maintain code for another framework. However, if needed, another framework can be used alongside MooTools, as demonstrated in this example.

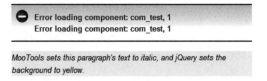

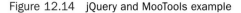

Figure 12.14   jQuery and MooTools example

Summary

In this chapter, we discussed what JavaScript and MooTools are and how they are used in Joomla websites. We looked at specific user-interface features that can be implemented with existing JavaScript methods. Finally, we outlined how AJAX can be used in Joomla, using the installation program as an example.

JavaScript offers the potential for building more user interaction into Joomla and for taking advantage of the benefits of AJAX. JavaScript is also a key component of building web services that can allow Joomla websites to serve information to other programs, such as mobile apps or other web servers. For these reasons, it is expected to grow in importance in Joomla applications in the future.

Using the Joomla! Platform as an Application Framework

With the release of Joomla! 1.7.0 in July 2011, the Joomla platform officially became its own project, separate from the Joomla content management system (CMS). This allows the platform to be developed independently of the Joomla CMS and makes it easier for the platform to be deployed on its own to develop and power a wide variety of web applications.

The Joomla platform is a large topic and deserves its own book. This chapter is intended to give an overview of the platform and some simple examples of its use.

What Is the Joomla Platform?

Joomla version 1.5 was designed so that classes that performed fundamental functions were placed in a folder called `libraries/joomla`. Although used in various places in the CMS, these classes perform functions that are common to most web applications and not specific to a CMS application. Examples include authenticating users, translating text into other languages, filtering input and output, and working with the server's file system.

This initial separation of these programs went a long way toward allowing the Joomla platform to be used separately from the CMS. However, there were still a number of places where programs in the platform folder depended on programs in other places in the CMS to function correctly.

With the release of the platform as a separate project, these dependencies have been eliminated and now it is easy to install and use the platform without installing the Joomla CMS. The platform has its own code repository at the website `https://github.com/joomla/joomla-platform`. It can be downloaded and used on its own.

Why Have a Separate Project?

There are two overriding reasons for officially separating out the platform project from the CMS project.

The first reason is to make the project more attractive to developers. The Joomla CMS is a mature product with millions of users. Although there is exciting work yet to do to improve the CMS, it has been around since 2005 and it was created as a fork of the Mambo project, which was started in 2000. So the Joomla CMS is at a stage where most changes are incremental. Moreover, the entire CMS industry is at a relatively mature stage at this time, at least compared to many other types of web applications.

By contrast, the Joomla platform presents a unique opportunity for developers. It is a new project where developers can participate in working on exciting new functionality without the constraints of existing code. There are many opportunities to create new code and functionality from scratch.

On the other hand, because the platform is already used in millions of Joomla websites, it is well tested and has a lot of credibility. New functionality in the platform will, in many cases, be made available to the entire Joomla CMS user base over time, as the CMS takes advantage of new platform features. This means that developers who add important features to the platform will potentially see those features get used by millions of people.

The second important reason for creating the platform project is to make it very easy for developers to use the platform for non-CMS applications. Content management is an important type of web application, but it is only one of many possible application types. Today, the web is used for many things beyond creating websites for sharing information, and these include many of the most innovative web applications.

Most web applications need basic functionality, such as user authentication, file system interaction, filtering, and others. When a team is developing a new web application, instead of creating this functionality for themselves, they can use the Joomla platform to get a head start on the project. By deploying a set of programs that already includes methods for many common requirements, they can focus on the parts of the project that are unique and not spend time "reinventing the wheel."

What Can the Platform Be Used For?

Today, many types of applications are being performed on the web. Just some of the examples are as follows:

- E-commerce programs designed to act as the "back-room" processing for any website that includes a shopping feature
- Web-based enterprise resource planning (ERP) systems, designed to provide financial accounting and related functions to various types of businesses and organizations
- Applications that allow websites to be modified by running a program at a server's command-line console.
- User forums and bulletin-board systems.

The Joomla platform can be used as the foundation for developing almost any type of web application. One way to think about it is this: if your application will need to do any of the functionality built into the platform, then the platform can be a great starting point for your application.

Platform Example Programs

The best way to understand the platform is to see some examples. Note that there are a number of example applications available from the Joomla platform code repository here: `https://github.com/joomla/joomla-platform-examples`. We will start with two very simple examples, one that uses the browser and one that uses the system command-line interface (CLI). CLI programs are run from the command console, not from the browser.

Set Up Platform Project

The first thing we need to do is download the platform files and set up our folder structure. One simple way to do this is as follows:

1. Create a folder to hold the project files. We'll call our folder `platform-test`. If you want to test the platform with browser applications as well as CLI applications, put this folder under your web server's DocumentRoot folder (for example, under the `htdocs` folder).

2. Download the platform. One easy way to do this is to navigate to `https://github.com/joomla/joomla-platform` and press the Tags button. This will give you a list of the official release versions (for example, 11.4.zip). Alternatively, you can download the latest repository version by pressing Downloads → Download as zip.

3. Unpack the archive in the `platform-test` folder. The top-level folder in the archive is the same as the archive name, in the format joomla-joomla-platform-<version>-<changeset number> (for example, `joomla-joomla-platform-11.4-0-g4329ba0.zip`). After unpacking, rename this folder to `joomla-platform`. At this point, `platform-test` should have a subfolder called `joomla-platform`, which should have subfolders called `build`, `docs`, `libraries`, `media`, and `tests`. Note that you only need the `libraries` and `media` folders to run the platform. The other folders are for development.

4. Download the examples. To do this, navigate to `https://github.com/joomla/joomla-platform-examples`, press Download → Download as zip. This will download a file called something like `joomla-joomla-platform-examples-544306f.zip`.

5. Unpack this archive in a temporary folder and copy the `cli` and `web` folders to the `platform-test` folder. Also copy the `bootstrap.dist.php` file to the `platform-test` folder.

6. At this point, `platform-test` should have three subfolders: `cli`, `joomla-platform`, and `web`. You should also have a file called `bootstrap.dist.php`.

7. Copy the `bootstrap.dist.php` file to `bootstrap.php`. Edit this file to contain the following line of code:

```
require dirname(__FILE__).'/joomla-platform/libraries/import.php';
```

> This code tells the platform where to find the import script. It uses the PHP `dirname()` command to get the directory name of the current file (`bootstrap.php`) and then uses that to create the full path name of the import script. In our setup, the `bootstrap.php` file is in the same folder as the `joomla-platform` folder.

At this point, you should be able to run all the example programs. To test this, try out the Hello World example, as follows:

- Open a command-line session in your computer and change to the directory `platform-test/cli/101-hello-world`.
- Make sure your PHP program is executable from the command line. If needed, add it to the execution path.
- At the command prompt enter the command `php run.php`
- You should see "Hello World!" output to the console.

If this doesn't work, check the `bootstrap.php` file and the require statement that loads the bootstrap file.

If the `platform-test` folder is under your web server's DocumentRoot folder, you should also be able to run the web applications. For example, to run the detect-client example web application, enter the following URL in your browser:

```
<path to the platform-test folder>/web/detect-client/index.php
```

For example, if your `platform-test` is a subfolder of `htdocs` on your local machine, the URL would be

```
http://localhost/platform-test/web/detect-client/index.php
```

You should see something like the following output in your browser:

```
Welcome to the Joomla! Platform's JWeb class.

    * User-agent: Mozilla/5.0 (Windows; U; Windows NT 6.0; en-US;
↪rv:1.9.2.23) Gecko/20110920 Firefox/3.6.23 ( .NET CLR 3.5.30729;
↪ .NET4.0C)
    * Is a mobile device? No
    * Platform: 1
    * Engine: 13
    * Browser: 18 (3.6.23)
```

Again, if you get an error, check that the `bootstrap.php` file is correct.

Hello World CLI Application

Next, let's look at the code for the hello world application (in the file `platform-test/joomla-platform/cli/101-hello-world/run.php`). The first part of the code is as follows:

```
// We are a valid Joomla! entry point.
// This is required to load the Joomla! Platform import.php file.
define('_JEXEC', 1);

// Setup the base path related constant.
// This is one of the few, mandatory constants needed for the Joomla!
➥Platform.
define('JPATH_BASE', dirname(__FILE__));

// Bootstrap the application.
require dirname(dirname(dirname(__FILE__))).'/bootstrap.php';

// Import the JCli class from the platform.
jimport('joomla.application.cli');
```

Here we define the _JEXEC constant. This tells subsequent program files that we are inside a Joomla application. This constant is required for the platform files to execute.

The next thing we do is define the JPATH_BASE constant. This constant needs to be defined, although its use is up to the application. It will normally point to the root folder of the application. In this case, we aren't using it, so we define it to just point to the current folder.

The next command includes the bootstrap.php file we edited earlier. In this case, we have that file in the root folder of our structure (platform_test), which is three folders up from the current path (platform_test/cli/101-hello-world). So we use three dirname() commands to get to this folder. Note that we can put the bootstrap.php file anywhere we like. This is just the structure that the example programs use.

The bootstrap.php file loads the libraries/import.php file, which in turn creates a number of platform constants and loads some basic platform classes.

The last command imports the cli.php file from the libraries/joomla/application folder. This is the class that all platform CLI applications will normally extend.

The rest of the code for our Hello World example is as follows:

```
class HelloWorld extends JCli
{
    /**
     * Execute the application.
     *
     * The 'execute' method is the entry point for a command line
➥application.
```

```
    *
    * @return   void
    *
    * @since    11.3
    */
   public function execute()
   {
      // Send a string to standard output.
      $this->out('Hello world!');
   }
}
// Instantiate the application object, passing the class name to
↪JCli::getInstance
// and use chaining to execute the application.
JCli::getInstance('HelloWorld')->execute();
```

Here we create our class, which extends the `JCli` class. We have one method called `execute()`. In this case, it uses the `out()` method of the `JCli` class to output the message to the console. Then we close the method declaration and the class declaration.

The last line of the file uses method chaining to do two things. First, it gets a new `JCli` object using the `getInstance()` method. Then it calls the `execute()` method of that object. The end result is that "Hello world!" is shown on the console. Note that this last line is outside the class declaration and is executed immediately.

Web Hello WWW Application

This application, `web/101-hello-www/index.php`, outputs a simple text message in the browser. The first part of the code is as follows:

```
// We are a valid Joomla! entry point.
define('_JEXEC', 1);

// Setup the base path related constant.
define('JPATH_BASE', dirname(__FILE__));

// Increase error reporting to that any errors are displayed.
// Note, you would not use these settings in production.
error_reporting(E_ALL);
ini_set('display_errors', true);

// Bootstrap the application.
require dirname(dirname(dirname(__FILE__))).'/bootstrap.php';

// Import the JWeb class from the platform.
jimport('joomla.application.web');
```

As before, we define our constants. The next two lines set up maximum error reporting. This is helpful during development to allow you to see any code that violates PHP strict standards. Also, note that the platform is designed to run for PHP versions 5.3 and higher.

The next two lines require the **bootstrap.php** file from our project root folder and then import the file **libraries/application/web.php** file. This defines the JWeb class.

The rest of the **index.php** file is as follows:

```
class HelloWww extends JWeb
{
    /**
     * Overrides the parent doExecute method to run the web application.
     *
     * This method should include your custom code that runs the
 →application.
     *
     * @return   void
     *
     * @since    11.3
     */
      protected function doExecute()
    {
        // This application will just output a simple HTML document.
        // Use the setBody method to set the output.
        // JWeb will take care of all the headers and such for you.

        $this->setBody('<html>
           <head>
              <title>Hello WWW</title>
           </head>
           <body style="font-family:verdana;">
              <p>Hello WWW!</p>
           </body>
           </html>'
        );
    }
}
// Instantiate the application object, passing the class name to
 →JWeb::getInstance
// and use chaining to execute the application.
JWeb::getInstance('Hellowww')->execute();
```

This creates the **HelloWww** class, extending the **JWeb** class. Most web applications using the platform will extend the **JWeb** class.

Then we create a protected method called **doExecute()**. This overrides the **doExecute()** method of the **JWeb** class. Recall in the CLI Hello World example we created an **execute()** method. We can use either method to execute code inside the class. However, there is an important difference. If you look at the code for the execute() method of the JWeb class, you will see that it triggers events before and after the doExecute() method is called. Then it renders the document and triggers some more events. Finally, it sends the response to the client, again with before and after events triggered. Because these are steps we normally want done when we are working with HTML documents, the preferred approach is to override the doExecute() method and let the JWeb execute() method do the rest of this work.

The code in the doExecute() method uses the setBody() method of JWeb to add our HTML to show the hello message. JWeb includes various methods for working with the document header and body.

The last line of our file is similar to the prior example. We get an instance of the object and then run its execute() method. The result is that the message displays in an HTML document in our browser.

Subscription Monitoring Example

Now that we understand the basics of using the platform CLI, let's look at a realistic example using the Joompro Subscriptions component we created earlier in the book. Recall that this component creates subscriptions that expire after a certain number of days. In a real-life situation, we would want to have a way to monitor and manage these subscriptions.

In this example, we will create a CLI application that does two things. First, it checks the database for subscriptions that will expire in the next five days and sends the subscriber a reminder e-mail. Second, if a subscription has expired, it deletes the subscription row from the mapping table and removes the user from the subscription's group.

We will assume that the application will be run unattended on a schedule (for example, using the Linux cron command). For this reason, we will record the results of the program in a log file for the system administrator to review (instead of printing information out in the console).

Project Structure

For this example, we will use a somewhat different project structure from those the earlier examples used. We will put our program files in a folder called src under the joomla-platform folder. The src folder will hold our program files and log files.

To set this up, create a new folder called platform-test/joomla-platform/src. Then under the src folder create a folder called logs to hold the log files.

In the src folder, we will have three files and one folder, as follows:

- monitor.php: The program to run from the command line
- subscriptionmonitor.php: The program that does the subscription checking
- configuration.php: The file that holds the site-specific configuration data
- logs: The folder where our log files will be created

Configuration File

The first file we need to create is our configuration file. This has the exact same structure as the Joomla CMS configuration file (and in fact you can copy the configuration.php file from the root folder of a Joomla installation). In this example, we only require the fields needed to connect to the CMS database and send an e-mail, but we have included the other fields as well.

The code for configuration.php is as follows:

```php
<?php

// Prevent direct access to this file outside of a calling application.
defined('_JEXEC') or die;
class JConfig
{
    public $dbtype      = 'mysqli';
    public $host        = '127.0.0.1';
    public $user        = 'test';
    public $password    = 'password';
    public $db          = 'book_170';
    public $dbprefix    = 'jos_';
    public $ftp_host    = '127.0.0.1';
    public $ftp_port    = '21';
    public $ftp_user    = '';
    public $ftp_pass    = '';
    public $ftp_root    = '';
    public $ftp_enable = 0;
    public $tmp_path    = '/tmp';
    public $log_path    = '/var/logs';
    public $mailer      = 'smtp';
    public $mailfrom    = 'admin@yoursite.com';
    public $fromname    = 'Joomla! Programming';
    public $sendmail    = '/usr/sbin/sendmail';
    public $smtpauth    = '1';
    public $smtpuser    = '<gmail user name>';
    public $smtppass    = '<gmail password>';
    public $smtphost    = 'smtp.gmail.com';
    public $smtpsecure = 'ssl';
    public $smtpport    = '465';
    public $debug       = 0;
    public $caching     = '0';
    public $cachetime   = '900';
    public $language    = 'en-GB';
    public $secret      = null;
    public $editor      = 'none';
    public $offset      = 0;
    public $lifetime    = 15;
}
```

You will need to change the settings to match your environment. These will include $user (database user name), $password (database password), $db (database name), and $dbprefix (database table prefix) and possibly the e-mail settings (depending on your system). You can run the example code here without e-mail if needed. The e-mail settings shown here are for a Google Gmail account.

Monitor File

This file is the entry point for our application. It is the command that will be run from the command line. The first part of the code is as follows:

```php
<?php
// Declare that we are a valid Joomla! entry point if not declared.
if (!defined('_JEXEC'))
{
        define('_JEXEC', 1);
}
// Setup the application base path constant if not already set.
if (!defined('JPATH_BASE'))
{
        define('JPATH_BASE', dirname(__FILE__));
}
// Import the Joomla! Platform.
require dirname(dirname(__FILE__)) . '/libraries/import.php';
// Import library dependencies.
jimport('joomla.log.log');
require JPATH_BASE . '/subscriptionmonitor.php';
```

Here we make sure that the _JEXEC and JPATH_BASE constants are defined. Then we require the libraries/import.php file. Note that we don't use a bootstrap.php file in this example. Instead, we just require the import file. Note also that we adjust the command to find the import.php file relative to the location of the current file (monitor.php).

Once we have the import.php file loaded, we can import the library classes we need for this program. In this case, it's just the JLog class. Then we require the subscriptionmonitor.php program.

The next part of the file is as follows:

```php
// Load the configuration.php file
$config = JFactory::getConfig(JPATH_BASE.'/configuration.php');

// Create the log file
// Get the date so that we can roll the logs over a time interval.
$date = JFactory::getDate()->format('Y-m-d');

// Add the logger.
JLog::addLogger(
```

```
    // Pass an array of configuration options.
    // Note that the default logger is 'formatted_text' - logging to a
↪file.
    array(
    // Set the name of the log file.
        'text_file' => 'monitor-.'.$date.'.php',
        // Set the path for log files.
        'text_file_path' => __DIR__.'/logs/'
        )
    );
```

Here we set the configuration using the configuration.php file we created. Note that we don't use the $config object. However, executing this method creates the JConfig object (JFactory::$config), which is used in the JFactory::getDate() and JFactory::getMailer() methods we use later on. By setting this at the start of our program, we know it will be set with the desired configuration.php file. If, for example, we call JFactory::getDate() before creating JConfig, it will load configuration.php from the default location (JPATH_PLATFORM), which is not what we want.

Next we create the log file using the JLog class. We make the current date part of the file name. That way, we get a new file every day. We place this file in the logs folder we created earlier.

The next part of the file is as follows:

```
// Wrap the execution in a try statement to catch any exceptions thrown
↪anywhere in the script.
try
{
        // Instantiate and execute the application.
        JCli::getInstance('SubscriptionMonitor')->execute();
}
catch (Exception $e)
{
        // An exception has been caught, add the message to the log.
        JLog::add($e->getMessage(), JLog::ERROR);
        exit($e->getCode());
}
```

Here we create a try/catch block and call the execute() method of the SubscriptionMonitor class inside the try block. As we will see, several methods in the SubscriptionMonitor class throw exceptions. By calling the execute() method inside the try block, we ensure that any exceptions thrown anywhere in the method are caught and handled.

In the catch block, we add the exception message to the log. Keep in mind that this program will normally be run automatically by the server, so logging errors in a log file is preferable to showing them in the console.

We could have put all the code for checking the subscriptions in this one file instead of creating a second file. The approach used here has an important advantage: It makes it very easy to add more monitoring functions. Say, for example, we also wanted to monitor the stop publishing date for articles. All we would do is create the new article monitoring class and add the line to execute it in the try block of monitor.php. This one monitor.php file could run all our monitoring functions for the entire site and could be run by the server as one simple cron job.

Subscription Monitoring File

This file, subscriptionmonitor.php, actually does the work of checking and updating the database and sending the e-mails. The first part of this file is as follows:

```php
jimport('joomla.application.cli');
jimport('joomla.database.database');


/**
 * A Joomla! Platform application to monitor subscription status and take
 ↪action when necessary.
 *
 * @package  Subscriptions
 * @since    1.0
 */
class SubscriptionMonitor extends JCli
{
        /**
         * @var    JDatabase  The application database connection object.
         * @since  1.0
         */
        protected $db;
```

This imports the JCli and JDatabase classes and then declares the Subscription-Monitor class as a subclass of JCli. Finally, we add a protected member to hold the JDatabase object for the class.

The next part of the code is the class constructor, as follows:

```php
public function __construct(JInputCli $input = null, JRegistry $config =
↪null, JDispatcher $dispatcher = null, JDatabase $db = null)
{
    // Call the parent constructor for basic setup of the object.
    parent::__construct($input, $config, $dispatcher);

    // If a database connection object is given use it.
    if ($db instanceof JDatabase)
    {
        $this->db = $db;
    }
```

```
    // Create the database connection based on the application logic.
    else
    {
        $this->loadDatabase();
    }

}
```

The constructor has four arguments in its method signature: $input, $config, $dispatcher, and $db. We don't use these arguments in this example, but they are there in case we later want to reuse this class in a different context. For example, the first argument allows you to pass a JInputCli object to the constructor. This object simulates command-line arguments. The other arguments allow you to call the constructor with your own configuration file, dispatcher class, and database class.

Note that there is something different about the method signature from what we have seen before. Here we indicate the class name before each variable (for example, JInputCli $input). This is known in PHP as type hinting. It tells the PHP interpreter (and someone reading the code) that this argument must be an object of that type. Otherwise, you will get a fatal error when executing the method. Note that type hinting is only available in PHP 5.3 and later.

The constructor code calls the parent constructor and then checks whether the $db field has been set. If not, it calls the loadDatabase() method to set this field.

The next method in this class is doExecute(). Recall that this method is run by the execute() method of the JCli class. The code for this is as follows:

```
protected function doExecute()
{
    // Log start of program
    JLog::add('Subscription monitoring started');

    // Get a list of the ended subscriptions and remove them.
    $ended = $this->getEndedSubscriptions();
    foreach ($ended as $sub)
    {
        $this->doEndSubscription($sub);
    }

    // Get a list of the ending subscriptions and send a notification.
    $ending = $this->getEndingSubscriptions();
    foreach ($ending as $sub)
    {
        $this->doSendSubscriptionEndingNotification($sub);
    }

    // Log end of program
```

```
     JLog::add('Subscription monitoring ended');
}
```

This is the method that actually controls the program flow and does the work. We start by adding a log entry indicating the program has started. Then we call the **getEndedSubscriptions()** method to get a list of subscriptions that have expired. Then we loop through each of these and call the **doEndSubscription()** to actually process each expired subscription.

There is an interesting point about using **foreach** loops in this context. It is quite possible in normal use that there could be no expiring subscriptions. In this case, **$ended** will be an empty array. In that case, the **foreach** loop is simply skipped, and there are no errors or notices.

After we process the expired subscriptions, we call the **getEndingSubscriptions()** to get a list of subscriptions that are close to expiration. Again, we process the list in a **foreach** loop, calling the **doSendSubscriptionEndingNotification()** method for each one in the list. The last thing we do is add a log entry indicating that we have finished.

The next method in the class is **getEndedSubscriptions()**. This method queries the database to get a list of expired subscriptions. The code is as follows:

```
protected function getEndedSubscriptions()
{
    // Get a date object for now.
    $now = JFactory::getDate($this->get('execution.datetime'));

    // Get the query builder class from the database.
    $query = $this->db->getQuery(true);

    // Set up a query to select subscriptions that have end dates
➥before now.
    $query->select('*')
        ->from($this->db->qn('#__joompro_sub_mapping'))
        ->where($this->db->qn('end_date') . ' < ' .
➥$this->db->q($now->toSQL()))
        ->where($this->db->qn('end_date') . ' > ' .
➥$this->db->q('0000-00-00 00:00:00'));

    // Set the database query object to the database connection
➥object.
    $this->db->setQuery($query);

    // Get all the returned rows from the query as an array of
➥objects.
    $rows = $this->db->loadObjectList();

    return $rows;
}
```

Here we get the current date and time and then build a query that selects all rows in the mapping table that have an **end_date** column that is less than the current date and time. Notice that we use the code

```
($this->get('execution.datetime')
```

to get the current time. This calls the **get()** method of the **JCli** class. That method has the following code:

```
public function get($key, $default = null)
{
    return $this->config->get($key, $default);
}
```

Here we are calling the **get()** method of the config field of the class. Where is the execution.datetime being set? The answer is in the contructor of the **JCli** class. There we see the following line of code:

```
$this->set('execution.datetime', gmdate('Y-m-d H:i:s'));
```

The **set()** method adds the results of the **gmdate()** method to the config field of the class. The **gmdate()** method returns the current time for the Greenwich Mean Time (GMT) time zone. Why do we save this value in the config field instead of just calling **gmdate()** each time we need the current time? The answer is that the **gmdate()** method will return a different value each time it is called. By calling it once in the constructor, we have one time value to use in both of our queries, so they will always give a consistent result.

Note that we also check that the end date is greater than a zero date. Recall that in the Joomla CMS we use the convention of a zero date indicating an indefinite expiration date. Adding this would allow us to use the same convention for subscriptions.

Here we use method chaining to build the query. The entire query is built with one command, using the results of one query method as the object to call the next method. Alternatively, we could have used separate lines of code to call the **select()**, **from()**, and the two **where()** methods.

After we build the query, we pass it to the database object and return the results using **loadObjectList()**. Recall that this method returns an array of objects.

There is one last interesting thing to notice about this code. In several places, we use the **JDatabase qn()** method. However, if we look at the **JDatabase** class (**libraries/joomla/database/database.php**), we don't see any method called **qn()**. The **JDatabase** class doesn't extend another class, so it isn't coming from a parent class. Where is **qn()** defined?

The answer is in the **__call()** method of **JDatabase**. This method is one of several "magic" methods in PHP. It is called any time we call a method that doesn't exist in the current class. One common use for the **__call()** method is to create aliases for commonly used methods. If we look at this method, we see the following code:

```
switch ($method)
{
    case 'q':
        return $this->quote ($args[0], isset($args[1]) ? $args[1] :
true);
        break;
    case 'nq':
    case 'qn':
            return $this->quoteName ($args[0]);
        break;
}
```

Here we test for methods called q, nq, and qn and in turn calling either the
quote() method or the quoteName() method. So the qn() method is just an alias for
the quoteName() method. Note that we have to be careful to pass the arguments (an
array called $args) through to the quote() and quoteName() methods.

The next method in the SubscriptionMonitor class is getEndingSubscrip-
tions(). This is similar to the previous method, except that it selects subscriptions that
will expire within the next five days. Here is the code:

```
protected function getEndingSubscriptions()
{
    // Get a date object for now and five days into the future.
    $now    = JFactory::getDate($this->get('execution.datetime'));
    $future = JFactory::getDate($this->get('execution.datetime'));
    $future->add(new DateInterval('P5D'));

    // Get the query builder class from the database.
    $query = $this->db->getQuery(true);

    // Set up a query to select subscriptions that have end dates
between now and 5 days from now.
    $query->select('*')
        ->from($this->db->qn('#__joompro_sub_mapping'))
        ->where($this->db->qn('end_date') . ' < ' .
$this->db->q($future->toSQL()))
        ->where($this->db->qn('end_date') . ' > ' .
$this->db->q($now->toMySQL()));

    // Set the database query object to the database connection
object.
    $this->db->setQuery($query);

    // Get all the returned rows from the query as an array of
objects.
    $rows = $this->db->loadObjectList();
```

```
    return $rows;
}
```

The first thing we do is calculate a date and time that is five days in the future. We create a date called $future equal to the current date and then we add five days to it using its add() method. To get the five-day interval, we use the PHP DateInterval class. This takes an argument in the form

```
P + <number> + <time interval>
```

In our example, we use P5D to indicate five days. The result is that $future now holds a date-time object five days later than $now.

Now we use these date-time values to build a query that selects any subscriptions with ending dates later than now but before five days from now. As before, we return these as an array of objects.

Notice that there is a potential design problem with this query. If we run our monitor program on a daily basis, a subscriber would get an e-mail every day for up to five days, which could be annoying. If we didn't want that result, we could run the monitor program less often (say every five days) or we could change the query to select subscriptions in a narrower time window (for example, subscriptions that will expire in between four and five days). Alternatively, we could record in the database that a reminder e-mail has been sent and use that to filter the query results.

The next method is doEndSubscriptions(). This method does several things:

- Gets the subscription title and user name for the e-mail
- Deletes the row for the user-to-usergroup mapping table (thereby removing the user from the group)
- Deletes the row from the mapping table (thereby removing the subscription)
- Sends an e-mail to the user to notify them the subscription has been removed

The first part of the method is as follows:

```
  protected function doEndSubscription($subscriptionMapping)
  {
      $subscription = $this->getSubscription(
➥$subscriptionMapping->subscription_id);
        $user = $this->getUser($subscriptionMapping->user_id);
```

Here we call the getSubscription() and getUser() methods. These check that the subscription and user ids are valid and also give us the subscription title and user name for the e-mail.

The next section of code is as follows:

```
// Set up a query to remove the user group mapping.
$query = $this->db->getQuery(true);
```

```
$query->delete()
    ->from($this->db->qn('#__user_usergroup_map'))
    ->where($this->db->qn('group_id') . ' = ' . (int)
➡$subscription->group_id)
    ->where($this->db->qn('user_id') . ' = ' .
➡ (int) $subscriptionMapping->user_id);

// Set the database query object to the database connection object.
$this->db->setQuery($query);

// Execute the query.
$this->db->query();
```

At this point, we know that the subscription and user from the mapping table are valid. Now we begin updating the database. We build a new delete query to delete the row for the user in the user-to-user group mapping table. Then we execute the query. By deleting this row, we remove the user from the group. Recall that the user was added to the group when the user subscribed to the subscription.

The next code block is as follows:

```
// Get the query builder class from the database.
$query = $this->db->getQuery(true);

// Set up a query to remove the subscription mapping.
$query->delete()
    ->from($this->db->qn('#__joompro_sub_mapping'))
    ->where($this->db->qn('subscription_id') . ' = ' .
➡(int) $subscriptionMapping->subscription_id)
    ->where($this->db->qn('user_id') . ' = ' .
➡(int) $subscriptionMapping->user_id);

// Set the database query object to the database connection
➡object.
$this->db->setQuery($query);

// Execute the query.
$this->db->query();
```

Here we create a new delete query—this time, to remove the row from the subscription mapping table. This unsubscribes the user from this subscription.

The last portion of the method is as follows:

```
    // Build expiration email.
    $subject = 'Your subscription has expired.';
    $body[] = 'Hi, '.$user->name.',';
    $body[] = '';
    $body[] = 'Your subscription to '.$subscription->title.' has
```

```
➥expired.';
     $body[] = '';
     $body[] = 'Regards,';
     $body[] = $this->get('fromname');

     // Send the notification email.
     $this->sendNotificationEmail($user->email, $subject,
➥implode("\n", $body));
     JLog::add('Subscription removed for user='.$user->name.',
➥title='.$subscription->title);
}
```

Here we build the contents of the notification e-mail to the user. Then we call the sendNotificationEmail() method to send the e-mail. Finally, we add a log entry to indicate that this user's subscription was removed.

Next comes the doSendSubscriptionEndingNotification() method. Its code is as follows:

```
protected function doSendSubscriptionEndingNotification($subscriptionMapping)
     {
         $subscription = $this->getSubscription(
➥$subscriptionMapping->subscription_id);
         $user = $this->getUser($subscriptionMapping->user_id);

         $subject = 'Your Subscription is ending soon.';
         $body[] = 'Hi, '.$user->name.',';
         $body[] = '';
         $body[] = 'Your subscription to '.$subscription->title.
➥' will end on '.$subscriptionMapping->end_date.'.';
         $body[] = '';
         $body[] = 'Regards,';
         $body[] = $this->get('fromname');

         // Send the notification email.
         $this->sendNotificationEmail($user->email, $subject, implode("\n",
➥$body));

         // Log the notification
         JLog::add('Subscription ending notification sent for user='.
➥$user->name.', title='.$subscription->title);
     }
```

Again, we start by getting the user and subscription objects. Then we build the e-mail to send and send it using the sendNotificationEmail() method. Finally, we log that this has been done. Note that in this case we aren't changing the database. We are just sending the user a reminder.

The next method is getSubscription(), as follows:

```
protected function getSubscription($subID)
{
    // Set up a query to get the group_id from the subscription
➥record.
    $query = $this->db->getQuery(true);
    $query->select('*')
        ->from($this->db->qn('#__joompro_subscriptions'))
        ->where($this->db->qn('id') . ' = ' . (int) $subID);

    // Set the database query object to the database connection
➥object.
    $this->db->setQuery($query);

    // Validate that the subscription exists.
    $subscription = $this->db->loadObject();
    if (empty($subscription))
    {
        throw new Exception('Invalid Subscription.');
    }
    return $subscription;
}
```

Here we build a query to read the row from the subscriptions table using the subscription id. Recall that the id must be unique, so this query will return at most one row. If the subscription doesn't exist for this item, we throw an exception to log this event. At the end, we return the $subscription object with the data for this row of the database table.

The next method is getUser(), as follows:

```
protected function getUser($userID)
{
    // Set up a query to get the user object.
    $query = $this->db->getQuery(true);
    $query->select('*')
        ->from($this->db->qn('#__users'))
        ->where($this->db->qn('id') . ' = ' . (int) $userID);

    // Set the database query object to the database connection object.
    $this->db->setQuery($query);

    // Validate that the user exists.
    $user = $this->db->loadObject();
    if (empty($user))
    {
        throw new Exception('Invalid User.');
    }
    return $user;
}
```

This method is similar to the previous one. We try to read the row from the users table for this user id. If successful, we return the row as an object. If not, we throw an exception indicating that the user id was not valid.

The next method is **sendNotificationEmail()**, as follows:

```php
protected function sendNotificationEmail($email, $subject, $body)
{
    JFactory::getMailer()->sendMail(
        $this->get('mailfrom'),
        $this->get('fromname'),
        $email,
        $subject,
        $body
    );
}
```

This method sends the e-mail using the **sendMail()** method of the JMail class (`libraries/joomla/mail/mail.php`). Note that this requires that your website is configured to send e-mail. If you are working on a local machine that isn't set up to send e-mails, you can disable this method simply by commenting out all the lines, leaving an empty method. Make sure that the method is still defined. That way, you can test and run the rest of the program even if your e-mail is not set up.

The last method is **loadDatabase()**. Recall that this is called in the constructor to create a database object with the information from our configuration file. The code is as follows:

```php
    protected function loadDatabase()
    {
        // Note, this will throw an exception if there is an error creating
➥the database connection.
        $this->db = JDatabase::getInstance(
            array(
                'driver' => $this->get('dbtype'),
                'host' => $this->get('host'),
                'user' => $this->get('user'),
                'password' => $this->get('password'),
                'database' => $this->get('db'),
                'prefix' => $this->get('dbprefix'),
            )
        );
    }
} // end of class
```

Here we simply create a new **JDatabase** object using the values from our configuration file. Recall that the **get()** method of **JCli** reads values from the configuration object.

Running Our Monitor Program

To test the program, follow these steps:

1. Enter one or more subscriptions into the subscriptions table.

2. Create a menu item to show the subscriptions.

3. Log in to the front end of the site and subscribe to some subscriptions.

4. Using phpMyAdmin (or some other database tool), change the end date on one subscription in the `jos_joompro_sub_mapping` table to be in the past and change another to be less than five days in the future.

5. Make sure the `configuration.php` file has the correct information to connect to the site's database.

6. If needed, comment out the code in the `sendNotificationEmail()` method (if you don't have your test machine set up to send e-mails). Be sure to keep the empty method.

7. Open a console session and navigate to the `platform-test/src` folder. Enter the command: `php monitor.php`

The program should run and return to the system prompt. At this point, a log file should be created in your logs folder and should have entries similar to that shown here:

```
#<?php die('Forbidden.'); ?>
#Date: 2012-10-15 01:07:35 UTC
#Software: Joomla! Platform 11.2.0 Stable [ Omar ] 27-Jul-2011 00:00 GMT

#Fields: datetime     priority     category            message
2012-10-15T01:07:35+00:00    WARNING    deprecated
↪JDatabaseMySQLi::hasUTF() is deprecated.
2012-10-15T01:07:35+00:00    INFO    -    Subscription monitoring started
2012-10-15T01:07:35+00:00    INFO    -    Subscription removed for
↪user=George Washington, title=Pontiac GTO
2012-10-15T01:07:35+00:00    INFO    -    Subscription ending
↪notification sent for user=George Washington, title=Ford Mustang
2012-10-15T01:07:35+00:00    INFO    -    Subscription monitoring ended
```

Note that the first log entry is warning us that we are using a deprecated method, `JDatabaseMySQLi::hasUTF()`. We can ignore this message. The next line shows that we started the monitoring program. Then we removed one subscription and sent one notification. Then the program finished.

Test the different error conditions by entering invalid data in the tables or by making the queries fail. For example, change a user or subscription id in the subscription mapping to a number that doesn't match an existing user or subscription. Or change the table name to be an invalid table. In these cases, you should see the error messages reflected in the log.

Running CLI Programs Inside the Joomla CMS

If we want to write command-line programs that interact with the CMS, we have two options for where to locate those programs. In this example, we created an entirely separate application that uses its own version of the platform and is completely independent of the CMS programs. All we need to know about the CMS is how to connect to its database and e-mail program. The monitor application could easily be on a separate server and could be used, for example, to monitor any number of different Joomla CMS sites (just by using different configuration files).

Alternatively, we can create command-line applications inside the Joomla CMS folder structure. In version 1.7, a folder called `cli` was added to the CMS folder structure for this purpose.

We can run this example program inside an instance of the CMS simply by copying the logs folder and the three program files (`configuration.php`, `monitor.php`, and `subscriptionmonitor.php`) from the `src` folder in the platform-test project to the `cli` folder of a Joomla CMS installation. Make sure the configuration file has the desired values. Then navigate to the CMS `cli` folder and run the `monitor.php` program from the command line. It should work exactly as before.

Also, note how similar the programming techniques used in this example are to the techniques used in the previous examples in this book. Programming in the platform is very similar to programming for the CMS. Once we have the platform loaded, the classes used, database access, and other techniques are very similar to the techniques used for programming in the CMS.

Summary

In this chapter, we introduced the Joomla platform. We covered how to install the platform and how to run the example programs both for the command line and the browser. Then we examined how the programs work, including how they load the required library classes.

Finally, we created a realistic working command-line program that could be run unattended in the web server. This program monitors our subscriptions for expired subscriptions and ones about to expire. This demonstrates how the platform can allow us to create programs that interact with a Joomla website.

The platform is an exciting new project with almost unlimited potential. It is likely that a number of interesting programs will be built using the platform. Features added to the platform will also benefit the Joomla CMS.

Appendix A

Crash Course on PHP and Object-Oriented Programming

This appendix is designed as a quick-start guide for PHP and object-oriented programming. Here we try to give you the minimum you need to get started with Joomla! programming. Our focus is on short, practical explanations. There are many online tutorials and books on these subjects that you are encouraged to explore for more in-depth information about any of these topics.

PHP File Structure

PHP is an interpreted language, so the `.php` files are both the source code and the executable code. These text files can be edited with any text editor. Note that for Joomla, we use UTF-8 encoding for all text files.

PHP-Only Files

Most PHP files in Joomla only contain PHP code. These files start with an open PHP tag of `<?php` and the remainder of the file is PHP code. Note that these files normally do *not* include a closing PHP tag (`?>`). The closing tag is not needed and in fact can cause problems if there are any spaces after the closing tag. So it is preferred to omit the closing PHP tag for PHP-only files.

Files with PHP and HTML

Layout and template `index.php` files in Joomla contain a mix of PHP and other HTML elements. In these files, the PHP code is contained inside PHP tags (`<?php . . . ?>`). It is customary to use the PHP alternative syntax in mixed files, as described later in this appendix.

PHP Syntax Basics

White Space

White space (spaces, tabs, carriage returns, line feeds, and so on) is ignored by the PHP interpreter, so formatting is important only for readability. For example, the line

```
$a=$b+$c;
```

is equivalent to

```
$a = $b + $c;
```

although the second is preferred because it is more readable. Also, a single line of code can take up more than one line of text, for example:

```
$a = $b + $c
   + $d;
```

Important Characters

Every PHP statement ends with a semicolon (";"). Curly braces ("{" and "}") are used to enclose code blocks. Code blocks are used to designate the start and end of code for classes, functions (also referred to as methods), if statements, switch statements, and loops. Parentheses are used for the conditional statement for if, switch, and while statements.

Comments can be entered as any characters after "//" in a line of code. Comments beginning with "/*" and ending with "*/" can span more than one line of code. For example,

```
/* This is a comment
   And more comments
*/
// This is a comment
$a = $b + $c; // this is another comment
```

The dash plus greater than ("->") is used to invoke a class method. For example,

```
$name = $db->loadResult();
```

calls the `loadResult()` method of the object in the variable called `$db`. Double colons ("::") do the same thing for static methods. For example,

```
$user = JFactory::getUser();
```

Table A.1 shows the common uses of special characters in PHP.

Table A.1 **Special Characters in PHP**

File Name	Contents
semicolon (";")	Ends a PHP statement
curly braces ("{", "}")	Encloses code blocks (for classes, functions, if/then statements, loops, and so on)
parentheses "(", ")"	Multiple uses—enclose method arguments, logical conditions, array values, expressions, casting operator
double slashes ("//")	In-line comments—text that follows on same line is a comment.
/* and */	Block comments—all text between /* and */ are comments (can span multiple lines)
dash + greater than ("->")	Calls a function (also referred to as methods)—for example, $db->loadResult();
double colon ("::")	Calls a static method for a class—for example, JFactory::getDate();
square brackets ("[", "]")	References array values—for example, $myarray[] = $x or $x = $myarray[$y]
equals + greater than ("=>")	Connects a key-value pair in an associative array—for example, $a = array('name' => 'Fred');
exclamation point ("!")	Used to indicate not equal to—for example, if ($x != $y)
double vertical line or pipe ("||")	Logical OR operator—for example, ($a == $b || $a == $c)
single or double quotes (' or ")	Used to enclose string values. Can use either type, although double quotes have different behavior for enclosed variables
dollar sign ("$")	Used to begin all variable names—for example, $x
at sign ("@")	Used in documentation blocks for documentation variables—for example, @package, @param, @return
comma (",")	Used to separate values in method argument lists and arrays
period (".")	String concatenate operator (puts two strings together into one)
equals sign ("=")	Variable assignment operator—for example, $a = $b; assigns the value of $b to $a (which also returns the value assigned)
double or triple equals ("==" or "===")	Logical *equals* operator. Double equals means that values are equivalent. Triple equals means that values are the same *value and* the same *type*.
less than and greater than ("<", ">", "<=", ">=")	Logical less than, greater than, less than or equal, greater than or equal

(continued on next page)

Table A.1 **Special Characters in PHP** (*continued*)

File Name	Contents
question mark ("?") and single colon (":")	Used together in ternary operator—for example, `$a = ($b == $c) ? $d : $e;`
back slash ("\")	Used to escape quotes inside quotes—for example, `$a = 'It\'s cool';`
plus, minus, asterisk, slash ("+", "–", "*", "/")	Operators for add, subtract, multiply, and divide
single ampersand ("&")	Used in method signature to indicate that parameter object will be passed by reference
double ampersand ("&&")	Logical AND operator—for example, `if ($a == $b && $c == $d)`

Common Operators

Arithmetic and String Concatenate

PHP uses +,–,*,/ for addition, subtraction, multiplication, and division. Period or dot (.) is used to concatenate (join together) two strings. For example,

```
$a = 'dog';
$b = 'cat';
$c = $a . $b; //  $c is 'dogcat'
```

Double "++" means add one (`$a++;`). Plus + "=" ("+=") means increment a value by another value. Dot + "=" (".=") means concatenate. For example,

```
$a += $b; // same as $a = $a + $b
$c .= $d; // same as $c = $c . $d
```

Setting Variable Types

To set or cast a variable type, use the type inside parentheses as the operator. For example,

```
$a = (string) $b; // $a is $b converted to a string
$c = (int) $d; // $c is $d converted to an integer
```

Specific rules apply when converting values from one type to another. For example, when converting strings to integers,

```
$int = (int) 'abc'; // $int is zero
$int = (int) '123abc'; // $int is 123
```

If the first group of letters can be interpreted as an integer, that is the value used. Otherwise, the value is zero.

Logical Operators

It is important to remember that a single equals assigns a value to a variable (and returns this value), whereas a double or triple equals is a logical equals.

```
$a = $b; // assigns value of $b to $a
($a == $b) // true if $a is equivalent to $b
($a === $b) // true if $a is the same value and the same type as $b
```

Use ! to make this a not compare—for example, ($a != $b) or ($a !== $b). Use < or > for less than or greater than—for example, ($a < $b). Use <= for less than or equal and >= for greater than or equal.

Connect logical expressions with || or OR for logical or. Use && or AND for logical and. For example,

```
($a == $b || $c == $d)
($a == $b OR $c == $d)
($a == $b && $c == $d)
($a == $b AND $c == $d)
```

If Statements

If statements are the most common way to execute code conditionally. The basic syntax is as follows:

```
if ($a == $b)
{
  // do these statements if condition is true
    $c = d;
    $e = $f;
}
else
{
// otherwise do these statements
    $g = $h;
    $i = $j;
}
```

You don't need an else block. You can use elseif to add conditions to subsequent code blocks. For example,

```
if ($a == $b)
{
    $x = $y; // if condition is true
}
elseif ($c == $d)
```

```
{
    $g = $h; // only if not ($a == $b) and ($c equals $d)
}
```

You can have as many elseif blocks as you like.

Caution: Don't use single equals instead of the double equals to compare values. Single equals assigns values and returns the assigned value. For example, consider the following code:

```
$a = 'dog';
$b = 'cat';
if ($a = $b) // used "=" instead of "==" by mistake!
{
    echo "true\n"; // result is always true
    echo $a . "\n"; // $a is now 'cat'
}
```

Here we accidentally used a single equals instead of double equals. The single equals does two things: (1) assigns the value of $b to $a and (2) returns the new value of $a. So $a = $b returns cat, which evaluates to a boolean true. Therefore, the if statement is true.

We can use a single equals inside an if condition when we are executing a method and assigning the results to a variable. For example, the loadResult() method of JDatabase returns a value or a null value if the query result is empty. So we can use the return value of loadResult() inside an if condition as follows:

```
if ($link = $db->loadResult()) {// true if query returns a non-zero result
```

This code is a bit tricky. We are really doing three things here: (1) executing the loadResult() method of JDatabase, (2) saving that value to the $link variable, and (3) using that value as the condition for the if statement. We could write the equivalent code in two lines as follows:

```
$link = $db->loadResult();
if ($link) { // link is true if query returns a result
```

There is one important caution in this. If the query could return a zero as a valid result, this code will not work as expected. This is because zero will evaluate to false in the if condition. In this case, we could use the following code to fix the problem:

```
$link = $db->loadResult();
if ($link !== null) { // only false if query result is null
```

You can use the PHP ternary operator to substitute for some simple if statements, as follows:

```
$a = ($b == $c) ? $d : $e; // returns $d if true, $e otherwise
```

This assigns $a the value of $d if the condition is true and $e otherwise.

Switch Statement

The switch is a good structure if you need to execute different code blocks based on the value of one expression. The basic syntax is as follows:

```
switch ($a)
{
   case 'abc':
      $b = $c; // do these statements if $a equals 'abc'
      break;
   case 'def':
      $d = $e; // do these statements if $a = 'def'
      break;
   default:
      $f = $g; // do this if none of the above
      break;
}
```

The break statements are necessary for the first two cases. For example, if the first break statement was omitted, when $a equals 'abc', the statement $d = $e; would also be executed.

Looping Statements

Foreach Loops

Foreach loops are the simplest way to loop through an array. The code block in the loop is executed once for each element in the array. For example, if $groups is a simple array:

```
foreach ($groups as $group) // groups must be an array!
{
   echo $group; // $group contains the nth array element;
   // do more stuff as needed
}
```

In this example, if $groups is not an array, you will get a PHP Warning. It is OK if the array is empty. In that case, the loop will be skipped.

You can use foreach loops with associative arrays by specifying the variables to use for each key and each value. For example,

```
$assoc = array('name' => 'Fred', 'age' => 29);
foreach ($assoc as $key => $value) {
```

```
    echo $key . ': ' . $value . "\n"; // prints out each key/value pair
}
```

Here, $key will hold the key for each array element and $value will hold the value for each element.

For Loops

For loops allow you to perform a loop n times. For example:

```
// start at 0, add 1 to $i each time, continue until condition is not true
for( $i = 0; $i < $len; $i++)
{
    echo $i; // will be executed until $i == $len
}
```

Here we use $i as our loop counter and increment it by one using $i++. We execute the loop until the condition $i < $len is not true.

Do/While Loops

Do/while loops allow you to process a code block until a condition is no longer true. One type executes a code block first and then checks a condition to see whether to repeat it. For example,

```
do
{
    // code block is done once and then will be repeated
    // as long as while condition is true
    // code in code block must eventually made condition false!
}
while ($a != $b);
```

The second type checks the condition first, before executing the code block. For example,

```
while ($a != $b)
{
    // code block will be executed only if condition is true
    // code in code block must eventually made condition false!
}
```

In both cases, it is important to understand that executed code block *must eventually make the condition false*. Otherwise, you will get an infinite loop condition.

Continue Command

The continue command is used to skip the remainder of the loop's code block for one iteration of the loop. For example,

```
foreach ($groups in $group)
{
    if ($group = 'Public') {
        continue; // Skip 'Public' group
    }
    echo $group;
}
```

Alternative Syntax

In files containing only PHP code, all the code is normally placed in one PHP element. In layout files, however, we mix PHP elements with other HTML elements, and we will have multiple PHP elements in the file. Depending on the situation, we may wish to output HTML elements in the code blocks of if statements and loops.

In this situation, it is generally preferred to use the alternative syntax for if statements and loops. This lets us output HTML elements outside of PHP elements, so we don't need to put HTML elements in quotation marks. It also avoids having a PHP tag that contains only an open or close bracket (for example, "<?php }>"), which is very easy to miss when looking at the code.

Table A.2 shows examples of the standard and alternative syntax. In the alternative syntax, note that PHP comments must be put inside PHP elements.

Also, although white space characters are not important inside PHP elements, they are important outside these elements. For example, the following two lines of code will produce different results:

Table A.2 **Alternative Syntax Examples**

Single PHP Syntax	Alternative Syntax

```// standard syntax```
```if ($a == $b)```
```{```
```   echo 'equal';```
``` } else {```
```   echo 'not equal';```
```}```
	```<?php // alternative syntax ?>```
	```<?php if ($a == $b) : ?>```
	``` <p><?php echo 'equal'; ?></p>```
	```<?php else : ?>```
	``` <p><?php echo 'not equal'; ?></```
	```p>```
	```<?php endif; ?>```

```// standard syntax```
```foreach ($groups as $group)```
```{```
``` $a = $b;```
```}```
	```<?php // alternative foreach group```
	```?>```
	```<?php foreach ($groups as $group)```
	```: ?>```
	``` <p><?php echo $group; ?></p>```
	```<?php endforeach; ?>```

```
<p>This is a <?php echo 'test'; ?></p>
<p>This is a <?php echo 'test'; ?></p>
```

The first one has a space between a and test. The second one does not.

Variables

All PHP variables start with a dollar sign followed by a letter or underscore (for example, $myvariable or $_myvariable). You can use numbers and dashes after the letter or underscore. Variable names are case sensitive, so $myvariable and $myVariable are different. It is very easy to mistakenly reference a variable using different case. That is one reason why it is good to be consistent about naming variables (for example, using "camel casing," like $myVariableName).

Declaring variables

You don't declare variables in PHP, but you should assign them a value before you use them in an expression. Otherwise, you will get a PHP warning.

Variable Scope

In general, variables are defined—are in scope—only in the code block where they are set. For example, if a variable is set in the outermost code block of a script, it will be in scope for the rest of that script, including in contained code blocks such as if statements and loops. If a file is included using the include or require commands, variables will stay in scope in the included files. This is why variables from a view are still in scope when we use the loadTemplate() method to load layout files.

When we are inside a class method or a function, only variables local to that method or function are in scope.

Arrays

Arrays can be created with or without initial values. The following code creates an empty array:

```
$emptyArray = array();
```

This code creates an array with two values:

```
$simple = array('zero', 'one');// $simple[0] = 'zero', $simple[1] = 'one'
```

Arrays can be indexed or associative. Indexed arrays use the integers 0, 1, 2 etc. to access the elements. For example, the following code accesses the first element in the previous example (note that the first element is 0, not 1):

```
echo $simple[0]; // will print 'zero'
```

Associative arrays are stored in key-value pairs. This example creates an associative array:

```
$assoc = array('name' => 'Jim', 'age' => 29);
```

To access the values, use the following:

```
echo $assoc['name']; // prints Jim
echo $assoc['age']; // prints 29
```

To add a new element to an indexed array, use [], as follows:

```
$simple[] = 'new value'; // adds to end of the array
```

To add a new element to an associative array, add a new key, as follows:

```
$assoc['telephone'] = '123-4567';
```

Use the unset command to remove an element from an array. For example,

```
unset($assoc['age']) // removes 'age' element
```

Array elements can be any type, including objects or other arrays. For example, this code creates an indexed array where the elements are associative arrays:

```
$person1 = array('name' => 'Jim', age => 29);
$person2 = array('name' => 'Jill', age => 27);
$people = array($person1, $person2);
```

In this example, we access an element of the inner array as follows:

```
echo $people[0]['name']; // prints Jim
```

Here, $people[0] is the first associative array, so $people[0]['name'] gives the name element of the associative array.

Working with Arrays

Here are some examples of working with arrays with the count(), is_array(), and isset() commands.

```
$count = count(array(1,2,3)); // 3: the number of elements in the array
is_array($a) // returns true if $a is an array, false otherwise
isset($person1['name']) // true if element exists, false otherwise
```

See http://php.net/manual/en/ref.array.php for more information about array functions.

Strings

Strings are variables that contain characters, including text, numbers, and symbols. PHP has a number of built-in methods for working with strings. Some of these methods do not work correctly with UTF-8 character sets. The JString class (`libraries/joomla/utilities/string.php`) contains comparable methods that work correctly with UTF-8 characters. For this reason, you should use the JString methods when operating on strings that might contain UTF-8 characters.

Here are a few examples:

```
$pos = JString::strpos('abcd', 'bc'); // should be 1
$len = JString::strlen('abc'); // should be 3
$replaced = str_replace('dog', 'cat', 'I love dogs.'); // I love cats.
```

See `http://php.net/manual/en/ref.strings.php` for more information about PHP string functions and `http://api.joomla.org/Joomla-Platform/Utilities/JString.html` for more information about the JString class.

Constants and Current Directory

We can define constants in PHP using the define statement. For example,

```
define('_JEXEC', 1);
```

defines the constant _JEXEC with a value of 1. Recall that this constant is used in almost all Joomla files to make sure we are running inside a Joomla application. Once defined, constants cannot be changed. By convention, constants are defined in all upper-case letters.

PHP includes some predefined "magic" constants. One of these, __FILE__ , is equal to the full path name of the current file. PHP also includes a function called `dirname()` that returns the name of the directory for any file (in effect, the part or the full-path name before the last slash).

We can use __FILE__ and `dirname()` together to get the directory of the current file. For example, the code

```
define('JPATH_BASE', dirname(__FILE__));
```

defines the constant JPATH_BASE as the directory name of the current file.

PHP also includes methods called `file_exists()` that check whether or not a file exists in the file system. See `http://php.net/manual/en/ref.filesystem.php` for documentation for the file system commands in PHP.

Functions and Methods

Most programming code in Joomla is contained in functions. Most Joomla functions are part of classes. In some cases, functions are created stand-alone and are not part of a class.

Functions that are inside classes are often referred to as methods (to be consistent with other object-oriented programming languages). Many people use the words function and method interchangeably. Note that there is no keyword in PHP for method, only for function.

Function Structure

A function has the following structure:

```
function <function name> (<function arguments, if any>)
{ // start function code block
   <function code, if any>
} // end function code block
```

An example of a simple function is as follows:

```
public function setLastVisit($timestamp = null)
{
   // Create the user table object
   $table = $this->getTable();
   $table->load($this->id);
   return $table->setLastVisit($timestamp);
}
```

The function's access modifier is `public`, which means that it can be called from any class. It has one argument, called `$timestamp`. The argument has a default value of `null`, so this method can be called without any arguments. If no default was supplied, you would get an error if you tried to call it with no arguments.

The function has three lines of code. The last line uses the `return` command to return a value. This means that this function can be called in an assignment statement—for example,

```
$x = $user->setLastVisit($myTimestamp);
```

In this case, the value returned by the function will be saved in the variable called `$x`. The number and order of the function's arguments are called the function or method *signature*.

Function Variable Scope

Variable names inside a function only relate to that function. In the previous example, we call the `setLastVisit()` method passing the variable `$myTimestamp`. Inside the function,

`$myTimestamp` is not defined. Instead, that value is known by the name `$timestamp`. When the function is completed, the variable `$timestamp` is no longer defined.

We could, if we like, use the same variable name when we call a function. In this case, even though the name is the same, it is really two different variables with two different scopes. One is defined outside the function, the other inside.

Passing Variables by Reference

Warning

This is a potentially confusing subject. When you pass a variable to a function as an argument, the normal behavior is that the variable passed is local to the method. This means that if the method changes the value of that variable, the change is lost when the function finishes.

If you pass a variable to the function by reference, using the "&", if you change the variable in the function, the changes are visible to the code that called the function.

For example,

```php
function pluralValue($string) {
    $string .= 's';
}
function pluralReference(&$string) {
    $string .= 's';
}
$a = 'cat';
pluralValue($a);
echo $a . "\n"; // $a is still cat
pluralReference($a);
echo $a . "\n"; // $a is now cats
```

In `pluralValue()` the change we make to the local variable is lost when we return from the function. In `pluralReference()`, because we include the & in the function signature, changes to the local variable are visible to the calling code.

Including Files and File Types

In a large code base like Joomla, it is necessary to organize the code into multiple files. It is important to understand the different types of PHP files, how they are included into the running program, and what happens when they are included. Almost all Joomla files fall into one of three categories, as follows:

- Class declaration
- Function declaration
- Simple script

Class Declaration Files

In object-oriented programming, the normal way to organize files is to have one file per class. The great majority of files in the Joomla content management system (CMS) and platform do exactly that. They are class files that declare a single class. The structure for a class declaration file is as follows:

```
class <class name>
{ // start class code block
<class fields, if any>
<class methods, if any>
} // end class code block
```

Normally, there is a line like one of the following at the start of each file:

```
defined('JPATH_PLATFORM') or die; // used for Platform files
defined('_JEXEC') or die; // used for CMS files
```

These ensure that this file is being executed inside Joomla. Often this is followed by one or more include or import statements to include the required class files for this class.

When class declaration files are included using `include`, `require`, `jimport`, or `JLoader::register()`, the class and its methods are added to working memory but no programming code is executed. The only change is that the class, including its methods and fields, are now available for use by the program that included the file.

Function Declaration Files

A few Joomla files declare functions instead of classes. Examples of this are `templates/system/html/modules.php`, which provides the basic module chrome functions, and `components/com_content/router.php`, which provides the `ContentBuildRoute()` and `ContentParseRoute()` functions.

These files can only be included by the `include` or `require` commands (including `include_once` and `require_once`). They do not declare classes, so they cannot be included using the `jimport` or `JLoader::register()` methods.

Like class declaration files, function declaration files do not execute any code when they are included. They simply add the declared functions to the working memory so the calling script has them available to call.

Simple Script

Simple script files contain a series of PHP statements. Examples in Joomla include the `index.php` files for the front end, the back end, and templates. Also, layout files are simple script files.

Like function declaration files, simple script files don't contain class declarations so they can only be included using the `require` or `include` commands (again including `require_once` and `include_once`). Unlike the other file types, when simple scripts are included in the running program, their statements are executed immediately. Also, any variables that are in scope at the point where a simple script is included are still in scope inside the script.

Mixed Files

It is also possible to mix simple script statements with function or class declarations in a single file. In this case, the declared function or class is added to working memory and the statements outside the code blocks are executed immediately. These files must be included using `include` or `require` commands (including `include_once` and `require_once`).

Including Files

The following commands can be used to include other files in the currently running Joomla program:

- `include`: Includes the file. Works for any type of file. Will cause an error if the included file declares a class or function that has already been declared. No error is caused if the file to include cannot be found.

- `include_once`: Same as include except that it checks that this file has not already been included. This can be slow on some servers. For class files, use `jimport` or `JLoader::register()` if possible.

- `require`: Same as include except that it causes an error if the file cannot be found.

- `require_once`: Same as require except that it doesn't try to include a file that has already been included. Again, this can be slow on some servers, so `jimport` or `JLoader::register()` are preferred if applicable.

- `JLoader::register()`: Preferred way to load class files. Requires that you know the class name and the file name. Uses the PHP auto-loader mechanism to improve performance.

- `jimport`: Simple way to call `JLoader::register()` but requires that the file and class names follow the Joomla naming convention. This is the most common way to include Joomla platform files.

Object-Oriented Programming Basics

Joomla is designed using object-oriented programming concepts and design patterns. Here is a brief introduction to object-oriented programming.

Classes and Objects

Classes are the building blocks for programs. A class can be thought of as a template for creating objects of that type. For example, we use the `JDocumentHTML` class to create an object variable (for example, a variable called `$doc`) that is a `JDocumentHTML` object.

Classes typically have fields and methods (also called functions). We can call a method using the syntax

```
$x = $doc->getHead();
```

where **getHead()** is method name of the class. We can access a class field with similar syntax—for example,

```
$x = $doc->template;
```

where **$template** is a field of the class. Notice that we drop the **$** when we access the field.

Constructor Method

Most classes define a special method called **__construct()**. This method is called automatically when a new object of this type is created. It contains code needed to initialize an object—for example, to set default values for an object's fields.

Creating Objects

Before we can use an object, we must create it. Three techniques are used to create most objects in Joomla:

- **JFactory::get<name>()**: The **JFactory** class is used to create commonly used global objects, including **JApplication**, **JConfig**, **JDate**, **JSession**, **JLanguage**, **JDocument**, **JUser**, **JCache**, **JAcl**, **JDbo**, **JMailer**, **JFeedParser**, **JXMLParser**, JXML, **JEditor**, and **JURI**. **JFactory** should normally be used for all objects of these types. For example, the following gets the current **JApplication** object:

      ```
      $app = JFactory::getApplication();
      ```

- **getInstance()**: Many Joomla classes provide a **getInstance()** method. This method typically checks to see if an object of this type already exists. If so, it returns the already created object. If not, it returns a new object. For example,

      ```
      $client = JTable::getInstance('Client','BannersTable');
      ```

- **new**: This is used to create objects other than ones that use **JFactory** or **getInstance()**. This creates a new instance of an object by calling the object's constructor. Some class constructors have optional or required arguments. For example,

      ```
      $registry = new JRegistry();
      ```

   Note that the parentheses are optional if no arguments are passed to the constructor.

Standard Class

PHP has a class built in called a *standard class*. You can create an object of this type as follows:

```
$person = new stdClass(); // with or without the parentheses
```

The standard class has built-in methods to create fields. For example, the following code

```
$person->name = 'Bob';
$person->age = 15;
```

creates name and age fields and sets their values. We can retrieve the values the same way—for example,

```
$age = $person->age;
```

Standard classes are convenient ways to store a list of attributes for an object.

Extends and Inheritance

Inheritance is a fundamental concept of object-oriented programming. You can create a new class as a subclass (or child class) of another class using the extends keyword. For example,

```
class JDocumentHTML extends JDocument
```

This means that JDocumentHTML is a subclass of JDocument. So JDocumentHTML automatically *inherits* all fields and methods of JDocument. For example, if we wanted to create a subclass that was similar to the parent class, but only needed one new method, we would only have to write the one new method. All the other methods will be available. It is as if we copied and pasted all the parent class methods into the child class, except that we don't have to maintain two copies of the code.

For example, JSite is a subclass of JApplication and therefore inherits all the methods of JApplication. JApplication has a method called getInstance(). If we look at the code for JSite (includes/application.php), we do not see a get-Instance() method. However, we can use the getInstance() method with a JSite object. When we do, PHP knows to look for the method in the parent class.

Joomla has many examples of classes that extend other classes. Also, classes can be subclasses of subclasses. For example, JApplication is a subclass of JObject. So JSite has a parent class (JApplication) and a grandparent class (JObject). Class hierarchies can be of any depth.

Method Overriding

When we create a subclass, we can add new methods and fields. We can also change existing methods and fields. This is called overriding. All we do to override a method is to create a method in the subclass with the same name the parent class uses. When we do this, the method in the subclass must have the same access modifier (public, protected, private) and the same method signature (arguments) as the parent class method.

The keyword parent has a special meaning. When we override a method, we can use parent::<method name> to call the method from the parent class. For example,

```
parent::loadConfiguration($data);
```

This can be useful when the subclass method is similar to the parent method. In this case, we might be able to code only the differences and then call the parent's method.

Public, Protected, Private Modifiers

When we create class methods and fields, we can designate them as public, protected, or private:

- Public means they can be accessed from any other class or script.
- Protected means they can be accessed only from this class or from subclasses of this class.
- Private means they can be accessed only from this class.

Static Methods, Fields, and Variables

Static methods are called from the class itself, not from an object. For example,

```
$now = JFactory::getDate();
```

The method getDate() is a static method and is called using the class name + "::" (two colons). Static methods are declared with the static keyword. For example,

```
public static function getDate($time = 'now', $tzOffset = null)
```

A static field is a field that is declared with the static keyword and called from the class. For example,

```
public static $format = 'Y-m-d H:i:s';
```

If a static field is accessed from outside its class, the following syntax is used: <class name> + :: + <variable name including the "$">. For example,

```
$format = JDate::$format;
```

$this, self, and parent

The special variable $this is used to refer to the current object inside its class. For example,

```
$model = $this->getModel();
```

calls the `getModel()` method of the same class. And the code

```
$this->filter = $options['filter'];
```

assigns a value to the filter field of the class from within the same class.

The keyword `self` is used to call a static method or access a static field of the current class. For example,

```
$identities = self::getGroupsByUser($userId);
```

calls the static `getGroupsByUser()` method of the `JAccess` class from within that same class. And the code

```
return self::$_buffer;
```

returns the value of the static field `$_buffer` in `JDocument` from within that class.

The keyword `parent` calls a method or accesses a field in the parent class. For example,

```
parent::display();
```

calls the `display()` method of the parent class. And the code

```
return parent::$_buffer;
```

returns the value of the field `$_buffer` from the current class's parent class.

It is important to understand that parent literally means "any super class," including parent, grandparent, and so on. For example, if class A is the parent of class B and B is the parent of C, then A is the grandparent of C. Say that the field `$myfield` and method `myMethod()` are defined in class A and not in class B or C.

In this example, if we are in class C and invoke the parent method using `parent::myMethod()`, this will execute the code in class A. And if we invoke the field with `parent::$myfield`, it will pull the field from class A.

Simple Debugging

It is sometimes helpful to be able to look inside a running program and see the values of variables. As discussed in Chapter 2, you can use an integraded development environment (IDE) such as Eclipse or Netbeans with a debugger to do this. If that is more complex than you need, you can also accomplish the same thing by inserting temporary test code into your PHP files.

Viewing Defined Variables

One way to see all variables in scope at a point in the program, along with their set values, is to insert the following code at the desired point in the program:

```
var_dump(get_defined_vars());
die;
```

The `get_defined_vars()` function returns an array of all variables defined at that point in the program. The `var_dump()` function dumps one or more variables in human-readable format. The `die` command stops the program at that point so you can see the results in the browser window.

These commands together will stop the program and print out all the variables defined (in scope) at that point in the program along with their values.

Viewing the Stack Trace

Another important part of debugging is answering the question "How did we get here?" Recall from Chapter 2 that the programming "stack" shows the sequence of function calls that got us to the current point in the program (for example, `index.php` called the `dispatch()` method of JSite, which in turn called the `renderComponent()` method of JComponentHelper, and so on).

We can print the stack at any point with the following code:

```
var_dump(debug_backtrace());
die;
```

Note that the trace prints out with the current program on top and the original calling program (`index.php`) on the bottom.

Some Advanced Code Techniques

Most of the code in Joomla is understandable with the basics covered so far. A few advanced techniques are used in some places in the code base.

Using || Instead of If Statements

In a few places in Joomla, you will see something like the following:

```
$lang->load('tpl_'.$template, JPATH_BASE, null, false, false)
    ||  $lang->load('tpl_'.$template, JPATH_THEMES."/$template", null,
↪false, false)
    ||  $lang->load('tpl_'.$template, JPATH_BASE,
↪$lang->getDefault(),false, false)
    ||  $lang->load('tpl_'.$template, JPATH_THEMES."/$template",
↪$lang->getDefault(), false, false);
```

This is executing a series of $lang->load() methods separated by the logical or operator ||.

There are two keys to understanding this code: (1) $lang->load() returns true on success and (2) the or operator (||) stops processing after the first boolean true has been returned. This means that as soon as one of the load() methods succeeds, the rest of the code (after the ||) is skipped.

We could accomplish the same result with a series of if statements. However, the code would be longer and more complex.

Method Chaining

PHP now allows method chaining. This means that when a method returns an object, that object can be used to run another method. A simple example is as follows:

```
if (!JFactory::getUser()->authorise('core.admin')) {
```

Here we need to check the user's permissions, so we need a JUser object. We get that with the JFactory::getUser() method. Then we use the results of that method (a JUser object) to call the authorise() method.

We could use the following two lines instead:

```
$user = JFactory::getUser();
if (!$user->authorise('core.admin')) {
```

However, if we don't need the $user variable for anything else in this method, we can save that line of code (and have one less variable) by using method chaining.

PHP Magic Methods

PHP includes a number of "magic" methods that automatically get called at predefined points in programs. All magic method names begin with double underscore ("__"). One example is the __construct() method. This automatically is called whenever we use the new command to create a new object. For example,

```
$r = new JRegistry();
```

Another example of a magic method is the __call() method. If it is defined in a function, this method is executed any time an inaccessible method is called. An inaccessible method might be one that is not defined in the class (or its parents) or whose access modifier (for example, private or protected) does not permit it to be called.

One way the __call() method is used is to make aliases for existing methods. For example, in the JDatabase class, we have two methods called quote() and quoteName(). We would like to be able to use alternative names of q() for quote and qn() and nq() for quoteName(). This is implemented with this _call() method in JDataBase:

```
public function __call($method, $args)
{
   if (empty($args)) {
      return;
   }

   switch ($method)
   {
      case 'q':
         return $this->quote($args[0], isset($args[1]) ? $args[1] : true);
         break;
      case 'nq':
      case 'qn':
         return $this->quoteName($args[0]);
         break;
   }
}
```

This method is called any time we try to call a method that doesn't exist in the class. The name of the method is in the first argument (`$method`) and the remaining arguments for the call are in the array `$args`.

First, we check that there are arguments. Both `quote()` and `quoteName()` must have arguments, so we are not interested in any methods without arguments. So we just return and do nothing in that case.

Then we do a `switch` command on the method name. If it is `q`, we call the `quote()` method passing the first argument and `true` if there is a second argument. If the method name is 'nq' or 'qn', we call `quoteName()` passing the first argument.

In this way, we can use `q()` for `quote()` and `qn()` or `nq()` for `quoteName()`. Note that we could also provide method aliases by defining methods for these aliases and then running the "real" method inside the alias method. For example, we could define `q()` as follows:

```
public function q($text, $escape = true) {
   return $this->quote($text, $escape);
}
```

Variable Class and Method Names

Another advanced technique used in Joomla is using variables for class and method names. For example, in the `JController` `execute()` method, we see this line of code:

```
$retval = $this->$doTask();
```

The method name being executed is in the variable `$doTask`. For example, if `$doTask` is "display," then the `display()` method is called.

One important advantage of this technique is that we don't have to know in advance the names of all the methods we might want to execute. As long as the method exists, we can use any name we like.

Regular Expressions

Regular expressions are used to do advanced search or search-replace operations on strings. In Joomla, we use regular expressions in a number of places—for example, to filter for special characters, find and replace the "jdoc:include" tags in the document object, and modify internal links when using search-engine-friendly URLs.

The two most common commands in Joomla that use regular expressions are `preg_match` and `preg_replace`. As you might guess, `preg_match` finds matching patterns in a string, and `preg_replace` does a find-replace in strings.

An example of `preg_match` is as follows:

```
$result = preg_match('#\.(?:bmp|gif|jpe?g|png)$#i', $url);
```

Here we test whether the variable `$url` ends with a period followed by bmp, gif, jpe, jpeg, or png. If so, `$result` will be true. Note that we could do the same thing with a number of if statements, but it would take a lot more code.

An example of a `preg_replace` is as follows:

```
$result = (string) preg_replace('/[^A-Z_]/i', '', $source);
```

Here we filter a string called `$source` for nonletter characters. If we find anything other than a letter or underscore, we replace it with an empty space (which in effect removes it from the string). Again, this could be accomplished with different commands, but with more code.

Using regular expressions is a large, complex subject and beyond the scope of this book. Fortunately, there are a number of online resources to help you learn about them.

Appendix B

Joomla! Filter Types

Filtering data is an important aspect of creating a secure website. Data coming from untrusted sources, such as the URL or a form, should always be filtered using the most restrictive filter possible for the situation.

The `JFilterInput` class (`libraries/joomla/filter/filterinput.php`) is used to provide the built-in filtering functionality in Joomla!. Table B.1 shows the filtering types that are available.

Table B.1 **Joomla Filter Types**

Filter Type	Description
ALNUM	Casts as string type and removes all characters except A–Z, a–z, and 0–9
ARRAY	Casts as array; does not automatically filter the array elements
BASE64	Same as ALNUM except that it also allows plus ("+"), slash ("/"), equals ("=")
BOOL / BOOLEAN	Casts value as a boolean to return boolean true or false
CMD	Same as ALNUM except that it also allows dash ("-"), period ("."), and underscore ("_")
FLOAT / DOUBLE	Casts as float. If more than one float value is in the input string, only the first value is taken.
HTML	Filters HTML elements based on desired filtering method (white tag or black tag)
INT / INTEGER	Casts as a signed integer
PATH	Filters for a valid full-path file name
STRING	Same as HTML except that it first decodes the input string for any encoded values (for example, characters encoded using the PHP `htmlspecialchars` or `htmlentities` functions)
UINT	Casts as integer and takes absolute value of result to yield a positive integer
USERNAME	Casts as string; filters for a valid user name; does not allow the characters "&<>%'"
WORD	Casts as string; only allows letters and underscore ("_")

HTML Filtering

The HTML and STRING filter types both include HTML filtering. Two different types of filtering are available: white list and black list.

White list filtering allows you to define a list of allowable HTML elements and attributes and removes any elements or attributes that are not on the list. Black list filtering allows you to define a list of elements and attributes that are *not allowed* and removes these elements (leaving elements and attributes that are not on the black list).

The default filtering method in Joomla is black list. The default elements that are not allowed are

```
applet, body, bgsound, base, basefone, embed, brame, frameset, head, html,
id, iframe, ilayer, layer, link, meta, name, object, script, style, title,
xml.
```

The default black list attributes are

```
action, background, codebase, dynsrc, lowsrc.
```

Using Filtering in Joomla Applications

There are several ways to access the filtering methods in Joomla. The classes JForm, JRequest, and JInput incorporate filtering into their operation. Also, you can use JFilterInput directly.

Filtering in JForm

When we create a JForm XML file, we can add filtering to an element using the filter attribute. For example, the attribute

```
filter="integer"
```

will cause the value entered in a field to be filtered using the INTEGER method.

In addition to the filter types listed in Table B.1, JForm provides the additional filter types listed in Table B.2.

In addition to these built-in types, you can also add custom filtering for JForm fields.

Filtering in JRequest and JInput

JRequest and JInput can filter values using any of the JFilterInput types listed in Table B.1. For JRequest, you can use one of two forms. The general form uses JRequest::getVar(). The fourth argument for the getVar() method specifies the filter type and can be any of the types listed in Table A.1. For example, the following uses the ARRAY filter type:

```
$data = JRequest::getVar('jform', array(), 'post', 'array');
```

Table B.2 **JForm Additional Filter Types**

Filter Type	Description
INT_ARRAY	Filters each element of an array as an integer
RAW	Does no filtering
SAFEHTML	Same as `JFilterInput` STRING
SERVER_UTC	Converts input to a MySQL-formatted datetime based on server's time zone
TEL	Telephone number
UNSET	Unsets the value (forces to null). Used for hidden fields on forms where no value is allowed
USER_UTC	Converts input to a MySQL-formatted datetime based on user's time zone

Note that the default filter type for `getVar()` is "none," so you always want to specify a filter type when calling it. Otherwise, no filtering is done.

`JRequest` includes the following convenience methods that include filtering: `getInt()`, `getUInt()`, `getFloat()`, `getBool()`, `getWord()`, `getCmd()`, and `getString()`.

`JInput` is a new class that was added to the platform in version 11.1 to eventually replace `JRequest`. `JInput` uses a `get()` method that is similar to the `JRequest::getVar()` method. In the `JInput` `get()` method, the third argument specifies the filter type. For example, the following three commands are equivalent:

```
$x = JRequest::getVar('option', 'post', 'default', 'cmd');
$x = JRequest:: getCmd ('option', 'default');
$x = JFactory::getApplication()->input->get('option', 'default', 'cmd');
```

The `JRequest` class is deprecated in the Joomla platform as of version 12.1. As of version 2.5, `JRequest` is used in the Joomla content management system (CMS) code base in over 700 places. Eventually these will be replaced with calls to `JInput`.

Using JFilterInput Directly

It is easy to use JFilterInput directly anywhere inside a Joomla application. For example, the following code filters the body of an e-mail message using the STRING filter:

```
$message_body = JFilterInput::getInstance()->clean($message_body,
↪'string');
```

Here we use the `getInstance()` method to get a `JFilterInput` object and then run the `clean()` method to filter the desired value.

Appendix C

JHtml Methods

The folder `libraries/joomla/html` contains a number of useful methods for creating Joomla! applications. In this appendix, we briefly describe some of them. Note that these methods are all static methods. The details for using these methods are documented at the site `http://api.joomla.org/li_Joomla-Platform.html`.

Calling JHtml Methods

`JHtml` methods are designed to be convenient to use by designers and others who are not experienced PHP coders. One handy thing about these methods is that they can be automatically imported as needed. The syntax for this is simple. Consider this example:

```php
<?php echo JHTML::_( 'string.truncate', $item->introtext,
↪$params->get('introtext_limit')); ?>
```

Here we use the _() method of `JHtml` (`libraries/joomla/html/html.php`) to call the `truncate()` method of the `JHtmlString` class (`libraries/joomla/html/html/string.php`).

The first argument of the _() method is the identifier for the method to call. It can have an optional prefix before a period, followed by the method name. The prefix is the name of the class, by default in the folder `libraries/joomla/html/html`. In this case, the prefix of "string" means the class name is `JHtmlString`. The second part of the identifier is the method name—in this case, `truncate()`.

If there is no prefix, we call a method in the `JHtml` class itself. For example, this code

```php
<?php echo JHtml::_( 'link',$url, $v, array('target' => 'helpFrame'));?>
```

calls the link() method of `JHtml`.

The rest of the arguments passed to the _() method get passed through to the method being called.

Custom JHtml Classes

It is easy to add our own JHtml classes using the addIncludePath() method. For example, this code from the administrator/com_admin component

```
JHtml::addIncludePath(JPATH_COMPONENT.'/helpers/html');
```

adds the path administrator/com_admin/helpers/html to the include path. That means we can put custom JHtml classes into this folder and call them with the JHtml::_() method. When we do that, they will be loaded automatically, just like core JHtml classes.

For example, this line in the administrator/components/com_admin/views/sysinfo/tmpl/default_directory.php file

```
<?php echo JHtml::_('directory.message',$dir,$info['message']);?>
```

calls the message() method of the custom JHtmlDirectory class in the administrator/com_admin/helpers/html folder.

JHtml Class Methods

Link

This method creates an HTML anchor element. It has three arguments: (1) the URL, (2) the text for the element, and (3) an optional associative array of attributes for the element. For example,

```
$output = JHtml::_('link', JRoute::_($url), $text, $attribs);
```

Image

This method creates an HTML image (img) element. It has five arguments: (1) the file for the src attribute, (2) the alt attribute, (3) an associative array of other attributes, (4) a boolean to indicate whether the path is relative, and (5) a boolean to indicate whether to search for an override file in the template. For example,

```
$text = JHtml::_('image','system/new.png', JText::_('JNEW'), NULL, true);
```

Stylesheet

This method creates a <link rel="stylesheet" style="text/css" /> element. It has five arguments: (1) path to the CSS file, (2) array of optional attributes, (3) boolean to indicate if the path is relative to the media folder, (4) boolean to indicate whether to search for an override in the template folder, and (5) boolean to include browser-specific CSS files. For example,

```
JHtml::_('stylesheet',$component.'/administrator/categories.css', array(),
↪true);
```

Script

This method creates an HTML script element. It has five arguments: (1) path to the JavaScript file, (2) a boolean to tell whether to load the MooTools framework, (3) a boolean to indicate if the path is relative to the media folder, (4) a boolean to indicate whether to search for an override in the template folder, and (5) a boolean to include browser-specific JavaScript files. For example,

```
JHtml::_('script','media/popup-imagemanager.js', true, true);
```

Calendar

This method creates a pop-up calendar using the MooTools calendar behavior. It has five attributes: (1) current date value, (2) name of the text field, (3) id of the text field, (4) date format, and (5) optional array of attributes. For example,

```
return JHtml::_('calendar', $this->value, $this->name, $this->id, $format,
↪$attributes);
```

Date

This method displays a date with a given format and time zone. It has four arguments: (1) the date to show, (2) the format, (3) the time zone, and (4) a boolean to indicate whether to use the Gregorian calendar. For example,

```
<?php echo JHtml::_('date',$item->created, JText::_('DATE_FORMAT_LC4')); ?>
```

HTML Folder Classes

The folder `libraries/joomla/html/html` is the folder where the `JHtml::_()` method searches by default for classes and methods. Some of the most frequently used classes are discussed briefly in this section. Each of these class names begins with the letters "JHtml".

Batch

Implements the batch operations in the back-end manager screens. Includes `access()`, `item()`, and `language()` methods to create the batch operation markup for changing access levels, categories, and language. For example,

```
<?php echo JHtml::_('batch.access');?>
<?php echo JHtml::_('batch.language'); ?>
```

Behavior

Implements the various JavaScript behaviors. See Chapter 12 for more information.

Category

Returns a cached list of categories for a given extension. Used to create list boxes for categories in back-end manager screens. For example,

```
<?php echo JHtml::_('select.options', JHtml::_('category.options',
'com_banners'), 'value', 'text', $category);?>
```

Content

Has one method, `prepare()`, that fires the onContentPrepare plugin event. Used to fire this event for nonarticle content, such as contacts, custom HTML modules, and others. For example,

```
$module->content = JHtml::_('content.prepare', $module->content);
```

ContentLanguage

Has one method, `existing()`, that creates a list of existing languages. Used to create the list box for language selection. For example,

```
<?php echo JHtml::_('select.options', JHtml::_('contentlanguage.existing',
true, true), 'value', 'text', $this->state->get('filter.language'));?>
```

E-mail

Has one method, `cloak()`, that replaces an e-mail address with a link where the e-mail address is cloaked. For example,

```
$item->email_to = JHtml::_('email.cloak', $item->email_to);
```

Form

Has one method, `token()`, that displays a hidden token field to reduce the risk of cross-site request forgery security exploits. For example,

```
<?php echo JHtml::_('form.token'); ?>
```

Grid

Contains a number of methods used for creating controls for the various manager screens in the back end. Methods include the following:

- `boolean()`: Creates clickable on/off controls—for example, to enable or disable a user
- `sort()`: Creates clickable links in column headings that allow the table to be sorted by that heading
- `id()`: Creates the checkbox for items in a grid
- `order()`: Creates an icon for saving a reordered table in a manager screen

Image

Contains two methods, `admin()` and `site()`, that load either the template override image or the default image.

JGrid

Provides a number of methods used in back-end manager screens. Some methods replace methods with the same name in Grid. Methods include the following:

- `checkedOut()`: Shows a check-out icon that allows an authorized user to check an item in by clicking
- `isDefault()`: Indicates if an item is currently the default setting (for example, a language or template)
- `published()`: Shows a clickable published icon that allows an authorized user to toggle the published state of an item
- `publishedOptions()`: Shows an array of standard published state filter options

List

Provides methods for creating different select lists. Contains a method called `ordering()` that creates the options list for selecting ordering when editing an item (for example, a contact).

Select

Provides methods for creating HTML selection lists. Methods include the following:

- `genericList()`: Creates an HTML selection list
- `groupedList()`: Creates an HTML selection list for a nested array; used, for example, to show alternative layouts grouped by template
- `options()`: Creates the option tags for an HTML select list
- `radioList()`: Creates an HTML radio list

Sliders

Provides the methods for creating the slider controls used in the back end for parameters and options. Methods include the following:

- `start()`: Creates the panels and loads the slider JavaScript code
- `panel()`: Starts a new panel
- `end()`: Ends the current panel

String

Provides two methods for working with strings in layouts:

- `abridge()`: Shortens a text string showing the first and last part of the string, separated by . . . (for example, "Really Long, Long Title" becomes "Really . . . Title")
- `truncate()`: Truncates a string to a given length and closes any open HTML tags

Tabs

Provides the methods used to create tabs—for example, in the Global Configuration screen. Methods include the following:

- `start()`: Creates the panels and loads the slider JavaScript code
- `panel()`: Starts a new panel
- `end()`: Ends the current panel

Glossary

Access Modifier   In PHP, the words "public," "protected," or "private" may be used to control where class methods and fields may be accessed. Public fields and methods can be accessed from anywhere. Protected fields and classes can only be accessed from inside the current class or a parent or child of the current class. Private fields and classes can only be accessed from inside the current class. Note that private methods and fields are not inherited by child classes.

Alias   In Joomla!, a field for entities such as articles, menu items, and contacts, that are used to create search-engine-friendly URLs. Alias fields can be entered manually or created automatically based on the title of the entered item by removing characters other than lowercase letters, numbers, and dashes. For example, "The Joomla Project" creates an alias of "the-joomla-project."

Alternative Menu Item   A modified core menu item that uses an override XML file and layout file to alter its display and function.

Apache (Apache HTTP Server)   The web server program used by most Joomla websites. The "A" in LAMPP.

API   Application programming interface. The published methods for using a set of programs. In Joomla, the API refers to the public methods and fields of all the defined classes, especially ones in the Joomla platform. Because third-party programs rely on the API, it should be changed as infrequently as possible and always with advanced notice.

Associative Array   PHP array stored in key-value pairs (for example, `name => 'George'`, `title => 'President'`).

Boolean   Type of variable in PHP that can only be true or false.

Class   In object-oriented programming, the programming code that defines a class. A class defines an object type and can have fields and methods. In Joomla, each class is normally defined in its own PHP file.

Column (Database Column)   One type of data for a database table. For example, title is a column in the `#__content` table that shows the title for each article.

Component   One type of Joomla extension. Components are normally the main thing on a Joomla page. Core components include `com_content` (articles in the front end) and `com_users` (User Manager in the back end). One Joomla page normally contains only one component.

Constructor   A special (or "magic") PHP method that is called to create a new object. Invoked with the "new" command (for example, `"$reg = new JRestistry()`).

Controller   Part of the model-view-controller (MVC) design pattern used for Joomla core components. The controller executes tasks based on user commands.

cron   A Linux program used to schedule command-line (CLI) applications. Can be used in conjunction with Platform CLI applications to automatically run programs on a schedule.

CSS   Cascading style sheets. CSS is a style language used to control the appearance of web pages. This can include the layout, fonts, colors, and graphics. Normally, style commands go in separate .css files included with a template.

Data Definition Language (DDL)   SQL database query commands that create and change the structure of database tables (for example, `CREATE TABLE` or `ALTER TABLE`).

Data Manipulation Language (DDM)   SQL database query commands that work with the data inside SQL database tables (for example, `SELECT`, `UPDATE`, or `DELETE`).

Data Set   The data returned by a `SQL SELECT` query. Contains rows and columns of data.

Deprecated Method or Field   A method or field that is planned for removal from the API. Deprecating a method or field puts users of the API on notice that they should change their code so as not to use these parts of the API in future releases.

Eclipse   An open-source integrated development environment (IDE) that includes a version for working with PHP projects. Used by many Joomla developers.

Escaping Text   A method or function to replace or remove special characters so a string can be safely displayed on a web page. For example, `htmlspecialchars()` changes the "<" character to "\". This will display in a web page as "<" but will not have the special meaning of opening a tag.

Extension   In Joomla, an extension is a set of programs that provide a set of functions for the site. Extension types include components, modules, plugins, languages, and templates. Extension can also refer to third-party programs that extend the functionality of the core Joomla package (for example, programs available on the Joomla Extensions Directory at extensions.joomla.org).

FOSS   Free and open-source software. Software, like Joomla, that is available for use without charge. FOSS software typically uses a special software license, such as GPL, that requires any derivative works to also be free.

Function   A set of PHP programming code that does some work. Also known as a method (if it is inside a class). Most Joomla code is inside functions/methods.

GPL   General public license. A software license used by Joomla and many other FOSS projects. Available in different versions. Joomla uses GPL2.

Hack (Core Hack)   Changing a core Joomla file. This is permitted but not recommended because changes can be lost during updates. In most cases, Joomla can be changed to do a required task without doing core hacks.

Hit   The number of times a specific page or item is accessed (for example, an article or a banner ad). Joomla tracks hits for many item types.

HTML Hypertext markup language. The language of the web. All web pages are displayed in the browser as HTML text. The browser interprets the HTML code and formats the page accordingly.

HTML5 A new standard for web pages that eventually is expected to replace XHTML. It provides improved processing of audio and video files and is supported by most mobile devices. It is still under development but is expected to become the standard for websites in the future.

IDE Integrated development environment. A set of programs designed to make software developers more productive. For example, IDEs can auto-complete commands, detect syntax errors, debug a program, or allow you to jump to a parent class or method. Examples for PHP include Eclipse and NetBeans.

Identical Operator In PHP, triple equal signs ("==="). Tests that two values are of the same type (string, integer, etc.) and the same value.

IIS Microsoft Internet Information Services. A web server that runs on Microsoft Windows. Can be used instead of Apache HTTP Server for Joomla.

Indexed Array Array in PHP stored by numerical order, starting with 0.

INI File File with a ".ini" extension. Used in Joomla to store language files.

JavaScript Programming language that runs inside the client browser, used in many web applications. In Joomla, JavaScript is used to enhance the user interface and provide AJAX functionality.

LAMPP Acronym originally coined from "Linux Apache MySQL Perl/PHP/Python." Designates the group of programs used to run many dynamic websites. Most Joomla sites run with Apache and MySQL. All run with PHP. In addition, JavaScript is now an important part of the Joomla "stack."

Language Pack An installable language extension that provides the option to view a Joomla site in a different language. Language packs can be for the front or back end of the site.

Language Key The name for a specific piece of language-specific text in a Joomla application. In a Joomla program, language keys are used instead of literal language strings. The actual text is substituted at runtime based on the currently active language.

Language Override An optional file that allows the site administrator to override any language string in a Joomla site. Two override files are available, one for the front end and one for the administrative back end.

Layout Override Files that allow you to change the way modules or components are displayed. Override files are placed in special folders and can be used in place of the standard layout files. Unlike Template Overrides, which override layout files of the same name, Layout Overrides are additional layout files.

Magic Constants Constants in PHP with special meaning. For example, "__FILE__" is always set to the full path of the current PHP file being executed.

Magic Methods   Special methods in PHP that get called automatically. Examples include "__construct()", which gets called when a new object is created, and "__call()", which is called whenever a nonexistent method is called.

Method   Another name for a class function. Often used to refer to functions that are inside a class.

Method Chaining   Using the results of one method to directly call another method. Added to PHP in version 5.

Method Override   A method created in a subclass with the same name as a method in a parent class. If defined, this method is executed instead of the parent method. An override method must have the same method signature as the parent method. A method override can call the parent method with the key word "parent" (for example, "parent::display()").

Model   One of the three elements of the model-view-controller design pattern. The model typically includes the "business" or "domain" logic and works with the database.

Model-View-Controller (MVC)   The design pattern used to create the core components in Joomla A standard OOP design pattern that separates different logical functions into different classes to improve the maintainability of the software.

Module   A type of Joomla extension. Modules typically are small, simple, and lightweight. A single Joomla page typically contains multiple modules.

MySQL   The database used by most Joomla installations and by most dynamic websites in the world.

NetBeans   An open-source integrated development environment (IDE) that supports PHP programming.

Object Oriented Programming (OOP)   Programming technique based on using classes, objects, and methods. Joomla is based on OOP. OOP is a key advantage of working with Joomla programs.

Options (Parameters)   Options (also known as parameters) are settings that the site administrator can set for a Joomla site that can change the behavior of the site. The core extensions in Joomla offer many options that allow control over many aspects of the site without requiring any programming knowledge.

Override   See Language Override, Method Override, Alternative Menu Item, Template Override, and Layout Override.

Override, Template   See Template Override.

Override, Language   See Language Override.

Override, Menu Item   See Alternative Menu Item.

Override, Method   See Method Override.

Override, Layout   See Layout Override

PHP   The programming language that most Joomla code is written in. Also by far the most popular programming language for dynamic websites.

Plugin   A type of Joomla extension. Plugins are executed at predefined points in the Joomla programming cycle (events) to allow changes to the standard behavior.

Plugin Event   A predefined point in the Joomla execution cycle where a type of plugin is executed.

Refactoring   Revising a program or set of programs to improve its internal structure without changing its external behavior (the API). For example, reworking the internal workings of a method to improve efficiency while keeping the same method signature and functionality.

Router   In Joomla, a program that translates between a URL and an array of commands. Normally a router contains two methods, build() and parse(). The build() method takes an array of commands and returns a JURI object. The parse() method reverses this and turns a JURI object into an array of commands.

Row   A row is part of a database table. One row normally contains the information for one item, such as an article or a user.

Slug   In Joomla, a value containing the item id and alias for an item, separated by a colon (for example, "123:my-article-alias" or "234:my-category-alias"). Slugs are used to help create SEF URLs

SQL   Structured query language. The language used to create SQL queries to work with a SQL database. Includes data-definition language (DDL) and data manipulation language (DML).

Template   A Joomla extension that controls all aspects of the site's appearance. The template controls the layout of the pages, as well as the fonts, colors, and graphics.

Template Override   A template override is a layout file that is placed in a special subfolder of the template. If found, it will replace the standard layout file for that template.

Ternery Operator   In PHP, a way to assign a variable based on a true/false condition, with the syntax

```
$a = ($b == $c) ? $d : $e;
```

View (MVC)   One of the elements of the model-view-controller design pattern used for Joomla core components. The view is responsible for displaying the component in the browser.

View (Database)   In a SQL database, a saved query that can be used like a table. As of Joomla version 2.5, no views are used in the core database.

Web Server   The program that provides the communication between the browser on the client device and the server where the website files and database are stored. Joomla works with two web servers: Apache and Microsoft IIS.

XHTML   Extensible hypertext markup language. A more structured version of HTML that is based on XML. Most Joomla pages are based on XHTML.

XML   Extensible markup language. XML files are used in Joomla for installation files, options, and JForm forms.

Index

L

S